0I $4.50

THE EDUCATED AFRICAN

THE EDUCATED AFRICAN

A Country-by-Country Survey of
Educational Development in Africa

Compiled by
RUTH SLOAN ASSOCIATES

Edited by
HELEN KITCHEN

FREDERICK A. PRAEGER
Publisher • New York

BOOKS THAT MATTER

First published in the United States of America in 1962 by
Frederick A. Praeger, Inc., Publisher
64 University Place, New York 3, N. Y.

© 1962 by Frederick A. Praeger, Inc.

All rights reserved

Library of Congress Catalog Card Number: 62-13738

Manufactured in the United States of America

370.96
R974e

138955

MOUNT UNION COLLEGE
LIBRARY

Preface

THE EDUCATED AFRICAN is the second in a series of functional reference surveys on Africa to be compiled by Ruth Sloan Associates, Inc. The first, *The Press in Africa,* though published in 1956, remains a standard reference work in the field; a revision and enlargement of it into a communications survey is projected for 1964. Additional research surveys carried out for foundations and universities have included: *A Survey of Education* (1954) for the Twentieth Century Fund; *Resources and Needs for Training Facilities for Africans in British East, West and Central Africa, Liberia and Ethiopia* (1956) for the Ford Foundation; *Mission Education, Past, Present and Potential in Nigeria and Ghana* (1956) for the Ford Foundation; *The Effect of American Race Relations on the Internal and External Policies of Ghana, Nigeria and Egypt* (1954) for the Lehman Brothers, New York; and *A Preliminary Survey of Existing Resources for Training in African Languages and Linguistics* (1957) for Georgetown University.

12.1.70 pub. $4.50

The central organization of Ruth Sloan Associates is purposefully small, but twenty years of experience in and with Africa have enabled me to draw selectively into this nucleus, as necessity has arisen, qualified Africanists for any particular project. In effect, an informal roster of friends, deeply steeped in knowledge of Africa, represents the principal resource of Ruth Sloan Associates, which conceives of itself as a kind of "holding company" for African expertise. Financially and morally supported by Arthur W. Sloan, Treasurer and Vice-President of Ruth Sloan Associates, the organization owes its very existence to his sympathetic and kindly critical advice and encouragement.

Helen Kitchen, who edited *The Press in Africa,* also served as editor of the present volume. Mrs. Kitchen has been associated with Ruth Sloan Associates since its inception in January, 1954, and was the first editor of this organization's *African News,* a pioneering newsletter on Africa published in the United States from 1954 to 1957. Mrs. Kitchen is well known in the United States and abroad for her perceptive analyses of social, economic, and political developments and as editor of the excellent American monthly journal *Africa Report*. Before becoming an independent writer and editor, she served for twelve years in the State Department in Washington and in the Near East, much of the time as Special Assistant to the Chief of Research for the Near East, Africa, and South Asia. In 1957, she was given an Outstanding Service Award by the Secretary of State. Through her efforts, the disparate contributions and critiques of more than a hundred Americans, Africans, and Europeans have been blended in this volume into a meaningful over-all view of the educated African.

—Ruth C. Sloan

List of Contributors

Contributors of Working Papers

Joan Gillespie, Manfred Halpern, William Berry, Leon Carl Brown, Bahia F. Gulick, Helen Kitchen, Alphonso A. Castagno, Ruth C. Sloan, Gordon Hagberg, Betty George, Jane Campbell, William A. Payne, David M. Burns, Janet and Eduardo Mondlane, Pablo Eisenberg, Reverend Father R. Guilbeault, Raymond K. Kent, Sanford Berman, Anne Fredericks, Thomas Thorne, Reginald Bunting, Martin Kilson, Winifred Armstrong, Père Jean Le Gall, Louis C. D. Joos, Vera and Aristide Zolberg, Monique Dugue, Francette Drin, Jo Saxe, Henri M'Ballah, Victor T. Le Vine, J. P. Dannaud, Seydi Diallo, Victor Du Bois, Sally Willcox, G. Beis, Adam Clymer

Consultants, Critics, and Friendly Advisers

Mekki Abbas, Gabriel d'Arboussier, Walter Adams, Rudolph Aggrey, Aleke Banda, Reginald Barrett, Robert Baum, W. L. Bell, Reverend Father J. Paul Bordenet, William O. Brown, G. B. Cartland, Sir Andrew Cohen, Sir Christopher Cox, A. K. Chanderli, Daniel Chapman, James B. Coleman, Guy de Commines, Charles Cotter, Joan Cox, Stella Davis, Baron Dhanis, Wilton Dillon, William R. Duggan, Donald Dumont, Richard Erstein, Camara Faraban, E. Lee Fairley, Robert Fleming, Reverend Father Gordon Fournier, Melvin Fox, Eugene Friedman, Donald Y. Gilmore, J. T. Gleave, J. E. Goldthorpe, Frieda Gwilliams, Robert Hartland, John Hennings, George Houser, Harry S. Hudson, Okon Idem, Ruth and Judith Imru, John Karefa-Smart, Andrew Kamarck, Gikonyo Kiano, Lavern Kunke, William M. Lyons, Y. K. Lule, G. Mabille, Herbert Madison, Joanne MacManus, Abu Mayanja, Lucien Matte, Mr. and Mrs. Edwin S. Munger, Julius Nyerere, W. Nylander, John A. Noon, Thomas Okuma, Mai Padmore, Barrett Parker, Frederick Patterson, Frank Linder, Dorothy Porter, Dr. Emory Ross, V. P. Sassoon, Saudi Gabri Selassie, Sayyid al-Siddiq al-Mahdi, Ruth Schachter, Raymond Smyke, Efua Sutherland, Mary Tedessa, E. Trudeau, Sir Ernest Vasey, William Walker, J. B. Whitehead, William B. Wilson, Douglas Williams, M. Philippe Yace

Universities in Africa

State	Universities	Year Founded	Number of Students (1960 figures)
Algeria	University of Algiers	1879	6,027
Basutoland	University College of Pius XII	1945	170
Congo (Brazzaville)	Center of Administration and Technical Studies (to become a university shortly)	1960	350 (not all at university level)
Congo (Léopoldville)	Lovanium University	1954	485
	State University, Elisabethville	1956	141
Ethiopia	Haile Selassie I University (Addis Ababa) (incorporating University College of Arts and Sciences, est. 1950)	1961	426
Ghana	University of Ghana (formerly University College of Ghana, est. 1948)	1961	671 ('61)
	Kwame Nkrumah University of Science and Technology (formerly Kumasi College of Technology, est. 1951)	1961	800 ('61)
	University College of Cape Coast	1961	n.a.
Ivory Coast	Institut des Hautes Etudes (to become a university shortly)	1958	288 ('61)
Kenya	Royal College	1956	290
Liberia	University of Liberia	1951	750
	Cuttington College (originally founded in 1888, but closed from 1929 to 1948)	1948	136 ('59)
Libya	University of Libya	1955	728 ('61)
Malagasy	University of Madagascar (incorporating the Institute of Higher Studies, est. 1955)	1961	862 ('59)
Morocco	University of Rabat	1957	3,686
	Qarawiyin University	859	2,086
Nigeria	University College, Ibadan	1948	1,100
	University of Nigeria, Nsukka	1960	800 ('61)
	Nigerian College of Arts, Science, and Technology	1948	1,200
	Additional planned universities: Ahmadou Bello University (Northern Region); University of Lagos; University of Ife (Western Region)		
Ruanda-Urundi	University of Ruanda-Urundi	1960	30

Senegal	University of Dakar	1957	1,398 ('61)
Sierra Leone	University College of Sierra Leone (formerly Fourah Bay College, est. 1827)	1960	302
South Africa	University of Cape Town [a]	1918	4,671 European 563 non-European [b]
	University of Natal [a] (Durban and Pietermaritzburg)	1909	3,859
	Non-European Medical School of Durban (founded as branch of University of Natal)	1951	201
	University of Orange Free State [a]	1855 (univ. status, 1950)	2,031
	Potchefstroom University for Christian Higher Education [a]	1869 (univ. status, 1951)	1,781
	University of Pretoria [a]	1908 (univ. status, 1930)	7,933
	University of Stellenbosch [a]	1916	4,520
	Rhodes University [a]	1904 (univ. status, 1951)	1,453
	University of Witwatersrand [a]	1896 (univ. status, 1922)	5,180 European 269 non-European [b]
	University of South Africa (correspondence courses serving all races)	1873	7,863 European 2,064 non-European
	University College of Fort Hare (restricted to non-Europeans)	1923	360
	University College of Zululand (restricted to non-Europeans)	1959	41
	University College of the North (restricted to non-Europeans)	1959	80
	Western Cape University College for Coloureds (restricted to Coloureds and Malays)	1959	157
	Teachers Training College at Durban (restricted to Indians)	1951	n.a.
Southern Rhodesia	University College of Rhodesia and Nyasaland	1955	168 (inc. 38 Africans)
Sudan	University of Khartoum (formerly Gordon Memorial College, est. 1902)	1956	1,000
Tanganyika	University College of Tanganyika	1961	n.a.
Tunisia	University of Tunisia (incorporating the Institute of Higher Studies, est. 1945, and Zitouna University)	1960 n.a.	2,495 ('61) 881
Uganda	University College of East Africa (Makerere) (originally a secondary school, est. 1921)	1950	912 ('61)

[a] Restricted to Europeans by law since 1959.

[b] Non-European students enrolled in courses prior to 1959 and allowed to complete studies.

(Reprinted, with permission, from the November, 196[illegible], issue of *Africa Report*)

Contents

PART III: CENTRAL AFRICA

PART IV: PORTUGUESE AFRICA

PART V: SOUTHERN AFRICA

PART IX: FRENCH-SPEAKING WEST AFRICA

THE EDUCATED AFRICAN

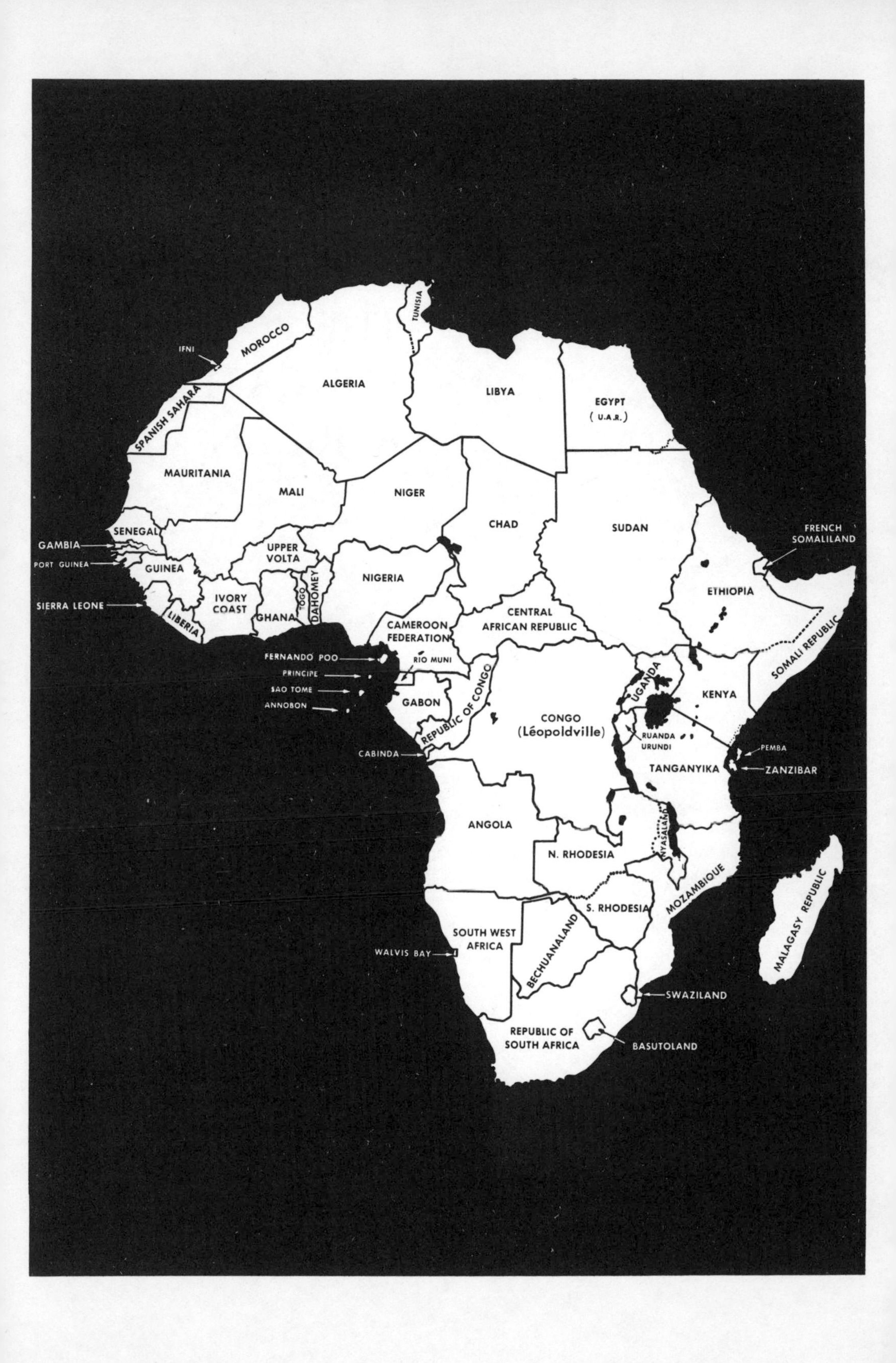

TUNISIA
IFNI
MOROCCO
ALGERIA
LIBYA
EGYPT
(U.A.R.)
SPANISH SAHARA
MAURITANIA
MALI
NIGER
CHAD
SUDAN
FRENCH
SOMALILAND
SENEGAL
GAMBIA
PORT GUINEA
GUINEA
UPPER
VOLTA
NIGERIA
ETHIOPIA
SIERRA LEONE
IVORY
COAST
GHANA
TOGO
DAHOMEY
LIBERIA
CAMEROON
FEDERATION
CENTRAL
AFRICAN REPUBLIC
SOMALI REPUBLIC
FERNANDO POO
RIO MUNI
PRINCIPE
SAO TOME
ANNOBON
GABON
REPUBLIC OF CONGO
UGANDA
KENYA
CONGO
(Léopoldville)
RUANDA
URUNDI
PEMBA
ZANZIBAR
TANGANYIKA
CABINDA
ANGOLA
NYASALAND
N. RHODESIA
MOZAMBIQUE
MALAGASY REPUBLIC
S. RHODESIA
SOUTH WEST
AFRICA
WALVIS BAY
BECHUANALAND
SWAZILAND
REPUBLIC OF
SOUTH AFRICA
BASUTOLAND

Introduction

ANYONE who writes a book about African education in the 1960's must accept the fact that events will move faster than the printing presses. Within the last three months of 1961, four new universities made their appearance in the African continent, and at least that many more are likely to be created in the first half of 1962. Under Tunisia's Ten-Year Plan, adopted in 1958, primary-school enrollment jumped from 320,362 to 408,758 in the first two years and is expected to reach nearly 850,000 by 1968; there were more than 3,000 Tunisian Moslems in higher education in 1961—three times as many as in 1956. In Sudan, where technical education was once rejected by parents and children alike, there are now 1,200 on the waiting list at the Khartoum Technical Institute. Basutoland's Pius XII University had more than 1,000 applicants in 1960, with places for only 200. In Nigeria, the government has endorsed a massive educational-development plan that could increase the number of children entering secondary school each year from 12,000 to 30,000, enlarge the roster of universities from two to five by 1970, and create facilities for a total annual university population of 10,000. In Ghana, universal free primary- and middle-school education has already been introduced, and a crash program now seeks to enlarge the flow of qualified students from the secondary level to the country's three universities. Everywhere, increasing portions of the national budget are being earmarked for educational purposes.

The public apathy and suspicion that greeted the first efforts to introduce modern education into Africa have given way to an almost mystical faith in education as the indispensable key to personal and national progress. Many economic and social factors have helped to create this new and extraordinary faith in the importance of books, but perhaps none has been more persuasive than the spectacular political accomplishments of the educated African since World War II. It was in the classroom that the African acquired the linguistic and technical competence to confront the white man as an equal—a fact that has enormous significance at every level of African society.

To survey, however briefly, the educational systems that are shaping the new leadership of nearly fifty different countries within the covers of a single book is an enormous task. It is particularly awesome in the case of Africa because the educational development of the continent mirrors its political fragmentation. Aside from the special cases posed by Liberia and Ethiopia (which suffered educationally by their lack of exposure to colonial rule), South Africa (where the political objectives of *apartheid* have been furthered by the deliberate creation of an educational system that prepares the black child for life in a subordinate society), and Somalia (where Italian influence is strong), the continent can be divided into five major educational areas: those governed, either now or in the past, by Britain, France, Belgium, Portugal, or Spain. Although experimentation is everywhere in the air, only Guinea has made drastic changes in the inherited system.

The concept of imperial trusteeship—that is, recognition that its overseas possessions might eventually revert to some sort of home rule—was present in British policy far earlier than in that of any other colonial power in Africa. The original objective of education in Britain's African territories was not, however, to train a ruling class. For, under the system of indirect rule instituted by Britain in its colonies, the local authority of traditional chiefs was carefully respected—and there was no pressure on either side to train the people in modern skills. The first schools in British Africa were mission schools with missionary objectives; as schools became increasingly secular in their curricula and objectives (though not necessarily in administration), a primary concern was to produce white-collar Africans with sufficient education to man the expanding administrative and commercial establishments of each country. Although British educational methods were used and examinations were standardized, the individual territorial administrators were accorded a large degree of autonomy in adapting the schools under their jurisdiction to local political, tribal, and economic conditions, and the vernacular was generally used at the lower levels. Despite these elements of flexibility in the British approach, British policy found itself psychologically unprepared to deal with the new kind of African who began to emerge from such schools as Ghana's Achimoto, Sudan's Gordon College, Nigeria's Kaduna, and Uganda's Makerere. Full acceptance of the political results that education had wrought came only when these new Africans, with their determination to change the whole structure of both tribal and colonial authority, had clearly become too powerful a genie to put back in the bottle. Even so, it came earlier than in the other European spheres of influence in Africa.

France's educational policies did not take firm shape until the early part of this century. In the beginning, as in the British territories, the official role consisted chiefly of providing some financial assistance to pioneering missionaries. By 1900, there were only seventy state schools in all of French West Africa, with a total enrollment of some 2,500 pupils. Beginning about 1903, however, efforts were begun to bring the schools in France's African colonies under closer central control and to establish an increasing degree of uniformity in the approach to the schooling of the African child, whether in Abidjan, Conakry, or Rabat. Although the French Government continued to grant subsidies to mission schools (and at least 40 per cent of all primary-school children in French-speaking West Africa are still educated in church schools), it was required after 1924 that all mission schools conform to a state model. This model was, in turn, patterned closely on the schools of metropolitan France—indeed, so closely that African children learned the botany of French plants rather than of African ones and the provinces of France rather than the districts of their own country. Although primary education became increasingly pervasive, the overriding objective of the new centralized system was to create a political and professional elite of high intellectual quality—and in the French image. This implicitly required the use of French as a medium of instruction from the earliest grades, the concomitant use of a high percentage of expatriate teaching staff in the schools, and the maintenance of a careful relationship between demand and supply in the higher levels of education. The resolution on education passed at the 1944 Brazzaville Conference on French colonial policy set forth these goals simply: While instruction must be directed to teaching the mass of the people how to improve their standard of living, its result must also be *aboutir à une sélection sûre et rapide des élites.*

Even as late as 1955, it was regarded as radical heresy when a Belgian professor proposed self-government for the Congo in thirty years. Under the system of paternalistic rule that was in force in Belgium's major colony until the very eve of independence, neither the elaborate educational system nor the country's political institutions were designed to produce or train personnel for leadership positions. Literacy was estimated at an impressive 40 per cent, facilities for technical education were among the best in the continent, and the Africans shared many material and social benefits of the country's was reportedly fewer than twenty, and none of these had served in economic prosperity. But the total number of university graduates positions of major responsibility in government or industry when the decision was suddenly made in Brussels in 1959 to grant the Congolese full independence in less than a year.

In the Portuguese territories schools are primarily used to indoctrinate the African population with the Portuguese language and culture. This educational objective is closely keyed to the Portuguese Government's political objectives in its African colonies, which have been to imbue the Africans within its jurisdiction with Portuguese nationalism and to insulate them against the heretical doctrines of African nationalism. There are no institutions of higher learning in the Portuguese territories, and there has been no intention to train Africans for eventual self-government.

Although the Spanish political objective in Africa—like that of Portugal—is to retain full control of its colonies indefinitely, Spanish educational policy has been adjusted to the possible. In Spanish Guinea, considerable progress has been made toward Hispanization of the heterogeneous African population. This goal is furthered by the discouragement of vernacular languages in favor of universal use of Spanish in schools and the press, and the educational program is heavily infused with Catholic theological precepts and Falangist doctrine. Advanced training and full assimilation into Spanish society is possible for a small minority, but heretical (i.e., nationalist) views are discouraged by the fact that virtually all members of the Guinean elite are dependent on the state for their status, the tenure of their jobs, and their privileges. In Spain's two desert provinces, Spanish Sahara and Ifni, the authorities have never attempted a full-scale program to turn the inhabitants into Afro-Spaniards, apparently recognizing that geographical distances and the firm Islamic faith of the thinly spread populace rendered the prospects distinctly unpromising.

While the educational systems introduced by these various European powers thus varied in many details, they were all shaped by Europeans who, as Lord Hailey expressed it in his *African Survey,* "assumed the intrinsic value of European civilization." Improvement in the lot of the African was seen in terms of making Africa more like Europe. For the most part, the African of the last century accepted unquestioningly this view that he had no cultural heritage of his own and that to be educated was to pattern himself on a European model.

In recent years, with the growth of nationalism and the scholars' rediscovery of Africa's pre-European history, there has been a strong movement of opinion in favor of the Africanization of curricula and textbooks. To give African education the roots it so badly needs without resorting to chauvinism is one of the most delicate tasks confronting political leaders and educators in every newly independent country. Professor Ayo Ogunshaye of Ibadan University in Nigeria is one of those who warns that the pendulum could swing too far in this new direction, thus creating another useless stereotype around "overidealization of the African past."

Above all, however, the basic educational problems in Africa today are financial and technical—where to find the financial resources and the qualified personnel to develop an effective system of primary, secondary, and higher education keyed to the enormity of the challenge. Even in countries with flourishing economies, hard choices must be made between education and capital development, between mass education and strengthening of secondary education, between the vital need for "bread and potatoes" technical education and the glittering prestige to be gained from opening a new university.

For the poorer countries of Africa, whose pastoral or agricultural economies operate at near-subsistence level, educational development of any kind is impossible without continuing outside financial aid. But in all countries, rich or poor, one basic question must be answered: Is the nation better served by a system of education that places major emphasis on providing a basic general education for all or by a system that concentrates its limited resources on the intensive training of selected men and women with the special professional and technical skills so desperately needed if Africa is to hasten its strides toward modernization? Expansion of primary education has already moved so fast in some countries that the corps of trained teaching staff is being diluted to a point where standards of instruction are suffering. To comply with the growing popular pressure for universal free primary education would bankrupt many African states. On the other hand, political leaders trying to create a sense of nationhood out of an amalgam of tribal societies recognize that universal education for the young is a vital tool.

A middle-ground approach receiving increasing attention everywhere is two-stream education. These two-stream schemes, such as the one now being developed in Upper Volta, are based on the assumption that all citizens should be educated, but not necessarily in the same way or at the same high per capita cost. For example, special schools and curricula are being devised for African youths with no prospect of continuing beyond the primary level and with little access to printed materials after they leave the classroom. In the past, it is now believed, too many rural Africans have spent an inordinate amount of time studying abstract material about life in alien cultures and too little in learning skills and opening the doors that would make the kind of lives they are likely to lead more rewarding both materially and spiritually.

Each of the chapters in this volume deals with five major aspects of a particular country: (1) the political, social, historical, and geographical context in which education developed, with particular attention to the economic, religious, ethnic, linguistic, and political factors that have influenced its evolution; (2) the stated educational goals of the colonial power or indigenous government and the relationship of educational policies to political objectives; (3) the nature and scope of the educational system as it developed up to independence or during the colonial period, with appropriate statistics; (4) the conceptual and practical changes that have been made or are envisaged by the new African leadership, and the pattern of post-independence expansion and priorities; (5) the university-educated elite and its size, political power, ideological orientation, and ties with the less educated elements of the population.

If there is a conclusion to be drawn from this book, it is surely that the African states face a far more complex task than most of us realize in adapting the educational systems of a colonial era to the political and social demands and economic realities of a new age. The problems are not only pedagogic, for the great dependence on external aid for educational development raises fundamental political questions as well. It is apparent that any educational advisers or teachers sent to Africa in the next few crucial years should, as Sayyid al-Nasr al-Hag Ali, Vice-Chancellor of Khartoum University, said recently, "be the best in the world, for the problems are more demanding than in advanced countries."

—HELEN KITCHEN

Part I

NORTH AFRICA

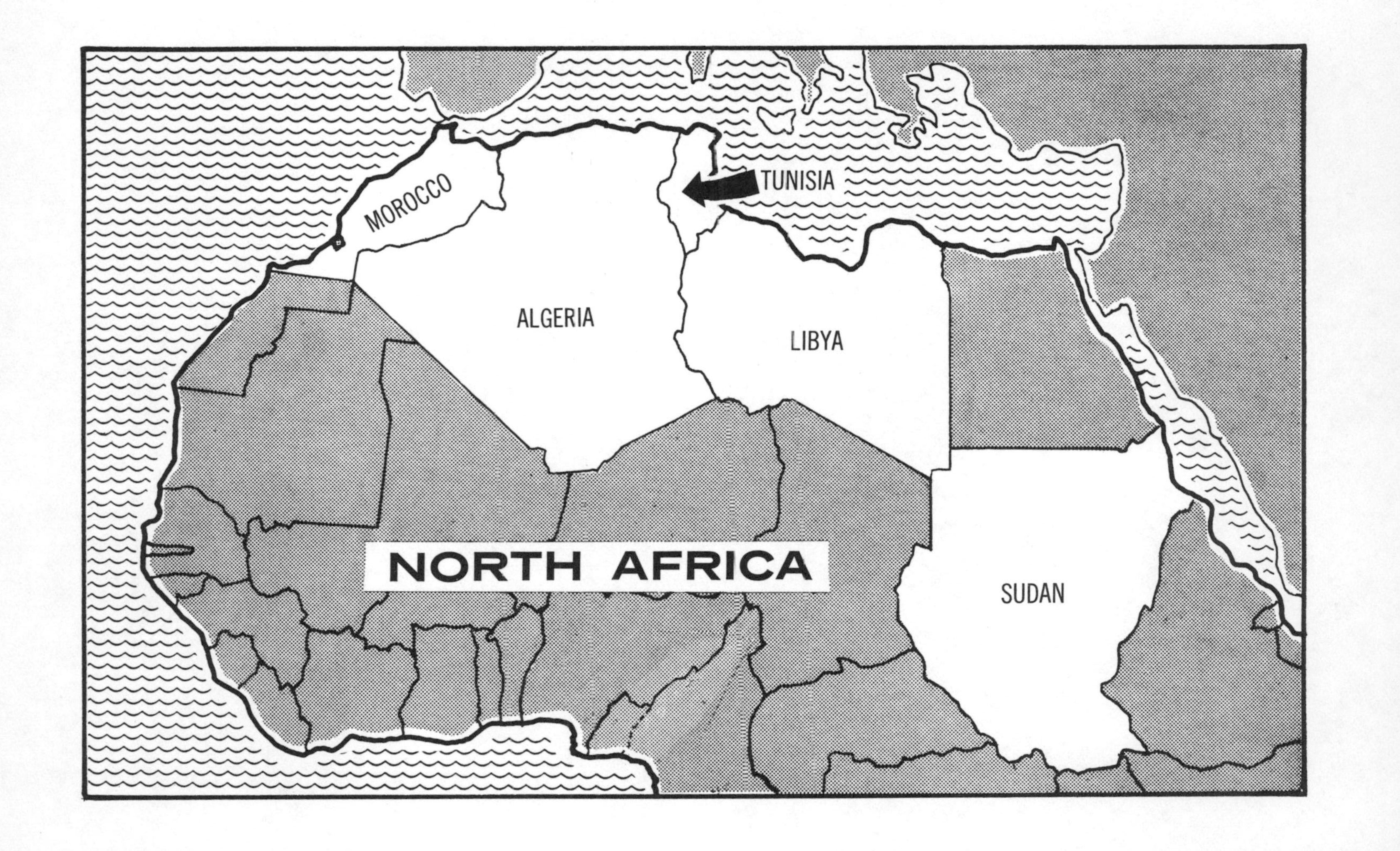
NORTH AFRICA
MOROCCO
TUNISIA
ALGERIA
LIBYA
SUDAN

1. Algeria

Capital: Algiers
Population: 10,300,000 (est.)
Area: 851,300 sq. miles
Political status: Department of France; in rebellion

THE educated Algerian Moslem,* like the educated African elsewhere on the continent, is a rare individual. He is usually literate only in French and French culture, not in his native Arabic or Berber tongue. He is in this sense a "man between two cultures," since his own language and culture have been taught to him, if at all, as "foreign" subjects. Without becoming a full-fledged Frenchman, he is increasingly a modernist, and as such the only available intellectual leader of his numerous rural illiterate compatriots.

The primary and secondary education of the educated Algerian Moslem is virtually the same as that of a French child of metropolitan France. His higher education is probably received in a French university, rather than in the nearer University of Algiers. In France, he can find greater opportunity and can escape the prejudices of the children of Algeria's European settlers. Finally, the educated Algerian Moslem is likely to be a man of the law, the liberal arts, or medicine; one reason for this is that higher education in the scientific and technical fields has been virtually closed to him. Since the beginning of the rebellion in Algeria in November, 1954, most educated Moslems have gravitated to the liberation movement.

Algeria—like Kenya, the Central African Federation, and the Republic of South Africa—is a European-settler area, and the educa-

* Both the indigenous Arab-Berber Moslem of Algeria and the European settler call themselves "Algerian"; both are, since 1946, "French"—i.e., French citizens; both are about to change their status in an independent Algeria. The terms Moslem and European are used here for cultural differentiation.

tion of its more than 1 million European *colons* and about 9 million indigenous Algerians must be viewed against this background. The vast majority—over 90 per cent—of Algerian Moslems are illiterate, while the *colons'* illiteracy rate is under 10 per cent. Only some 15 to 20 per cent of Algerian Moslem school-age children are in schools; more than 2 million such children are without facilities. Virtually all children of the *colons* are receiving the education they want. This sharp contrast occurs at every level of education, despite a rapid increase since World War II in French expenditures on Moslem education. As late as 1945, for example, the total number of Algerian Moslem pupils was about equal to that of *colon* pupils, although the Moslems at that time outnumbered the *colons* by more than eight to one.

The Trend of French Educational Policies in Algeria Since 1830

France's "civilizing mission" in Algeria was undertaken soon after the conquest of the Regency of Algiers in 1830. In theory, the policy was one of assimilation and was based on an assumption of the universal validity of French culture. The Catholic Church was intended to help but was not to predominate in achieving French goals. By giving the Algerian Moslems a wholly French education and suppressing what Arab-Islamic institutions of learning remained after the devastating war of conquest, the French hoped to create civilized Arab Frenchmen devoted to France. This civilizing mission has continuously suffered, however, from lack of sufficient funds to achieve its aims, from discrimination in favor of the *colons,* and from opposition by the *colons* themselves, who considered the education of an "inferior race" to be impossible and the education of a mass of unskilled labor decidedly dangerous. Vestiges of the traditional education and culture remained, and even the best "French" Algerian Moslems were never fully accepted into French society.

The French Army of Africa that invaded Algeria in 1830 met with stiff resistance, and it was not until some years later that French authorities were able to devote much attention to the education of the "natives." In the interim, the confiscation of revenue-producing lands endowed for the benefit of schools disrupted the traditional Islamic educational system, and the doors of several Arabic universities in Algeria were soon closed. In 1848, Algeria was officially organized into three French departments, thus giving it a unique status among France's African possessions, and a new educational system based on that of the metropole was set up.

A law of 1883 extended France's public-school system to Algeria and specified that education would henceforth be free and compulsory for those between six and fourteen years of age; however, the provision regarding compulsory attendance was never implemented and later was modified. In the schools set up under this law, children of the *colons* received the same education they would have had in France, while schools catering to young Algerian Moslems concentrated primarily on the reading and writing of French. Except for a few Franco-Moslem schools in the main cities, the Algerian Moslem children and the *colon* children were segregated until the middle of this century. The local Koranic schools continued to function. Meanwhile, the education of the largely nomadic peoples in the vast southern territories was left in the hands of French missionaries and the military.

By 1944, it was clear that reform was needed. Additional schools had to be provided for the rising number of young Moslems and the quality of the education offered them had to be improved if the nationalists were to be placated. A twenty-year plan begun in December, 1944, was to provide schools for 1 million Moslem children by 1964. The plan has fallen far short of its goals because of lags in school construction and the underestimation of the rapid rate of growth of the Algerian Moslem population, more than half of whom are under twenty years of age.

The outbreak of the Algerian rebellion in November, 1954, underscored the inadequacies of the French educational effort in Algeria. In 1958, General de Gaulle announced, as part of his Constantine Plan for the economic and social development of Algeria, that two-thirds of all school-age children would be in school in five years, and 100 per cent in eight years.

School Systems

Befitting its status as a group of French Departments, Algeria has a complete lay public-school system, ranging from nursery schools through the *collèges and lycées* to the University of Algiers. There are variations of this system, primarily for Algerian Moslems, that go as far as the secondary level. There are also state-run vocational and agricultural schools at the primary, secondary, and higher levels. Private lay primary and secondary schools exist for the European population, and Catholic and Protestant mission schools are operated throughout Algeria. Primary education is also provided for some Moslems in state-subsidized Koranic schools; and independent primary and secondary Moslem education is carried on by the Society of Reformist Ulema.* One rabbinical school is maintained in Algiers by the Federation of Jewish Communities.

The European child who lives within a reasonable distance of a town in Algeria is likely to attend a nursery school between the ages of two and six and then enter classes run by the *lycée* or *collège,* which he will attend until twenty. At the end of this primary and secondary education—an exact replica of that given in France—he may pass the two parts of the *baccalauréat* examination and go on to attend a university or, depending on his specialization, one of the *grandes écoles* (advanced professional schools) in France.

The fortunate Algerian Moslem child is more likely to attend a series of modified primary classes during the years of compulsory education (six to fourteen). These are divided into preparatory, elementary, and middle classes (ages six to eleven), followed by primary superior classes (ages eleven to fourteen). Although segregation in these primary schools was officially abolished in 1949, many schools are still largely Moslem, some largely European, and others "mixed." The curriculum in the schools resembles that in France to a large degree, and the reading and writing of French is particularly stressed. A frequent comment of Algerian Moslems has been that they learn too much about "our ancestors the Gauls," but little about their own history. In some schools, however, Algerian history and geography are taught, and there is an opportunity to learn the Arabic language. The Organic Statute of Algeria of 1947 provided that the teaching of Arabic was to be undertaken at all levels, but the Algerian Assembly did not take the requisite action to implement the law, and the introduction of Arabic has been slow.

Some complementary courses exist for the general education of the Moslem child on the secondary level. These are few and of a highly practical nature; they may lead to primary-teacher training, but not to a university. A unique and very successful experiment in the secondary education of Algerian Moslems has been the organization of Franco-Moslem *lycées* (three started in 1951, a fourth in 1954). The curriculum includes subjects from both cultures and is preparatory to

* The Society of Reformist Ulema (Association des Ulémas Musulmans d'Algérie) was founded in 1931—an expression of Algeria's participation in the Arab renaissance. The society took its inspiration from the early twentieth-century reformist doctrines of the Egyptian Sheik Mohammed Abdu. Seeking to halt the decadence of Islam, the members denounced the heretical or superfluous practices of the Moslem religious brotherhoods, the marabouts (local saints), and other mystics, and asserted the supremacy of the Koran and the Sunna (precepts taken from the conduct of the Prophet Mohammed). At the same time, they tried to incorporate many modern scientific ideas, renovate the Arabic language, purify Islam, and unite its believers.

entrance into the Institute of Higher Islamic Studies of the University of Algiers. Graduates of the Franco-Moslem *lycées* and of the Institute usually find employment as teachers of Arabic, as interpreters in the Algerian Government-General, or as Moslem legal officials.

Higher education for Europeans and the few Algerian Moslems who are able to complete successfully the requisite secondary education is available at the University of Algiers or any French university in metropolitan France. The University of Algiers, founded in 1879, ranks third in status in the French Community; it has faculties of law, medicine, pharmacy, science, and letters, and specialized institutes dealing with philosophical studies, hygiene and colonial medicine, higher Islamic studies (since 1946), Saharan research, urbanism, and the like. In 1961, the staff comprised eighty-eight full professors, fifty lecturers or teachers with doctorates, twenty-four laboratory and research directors, and sixty-one laboratory or research assistants.

Agricultural and vocational training is available on the primary, secondary, and higher levels in Algeria, but, like general education, primarily to Europeans. In the agricultural field, the facilities are particularly inadequate for a population that is over 80 per cent rural; and, despite its small number of industries, Algeria suffers from some skilled-labor shortages. Primary agricultural and vocational training is provided for young Algerian Moslems in the Rural Vocational Centers. In mid-1957, there were thirteen such centers, nine specialized sections, and fifty-five agricultural schools for all primary and secondary agricultural education. These schools provide special training in tree culture (particularly olive, fig, and cork) and livestock raising, in addition to basic agricultural techniques. Secondary agricultural education is offered at the Experimental Center in Algiers, where there is also an Agricultural Home Economics School for girls. Very few Algerian Moslems reach this secondary level; and by 1955 no Moslem had been admitted to the National School of Agriculture at Maison Carée, which offers the only advanced agricultural education in Algeria. Maison Carée's pupils are selected by the requisite French entrance examination and may obtain a degree in agricultural engineering. The school also carries on advanced agronomic research coordinated by the Algerian Committee for Agricultural Research, set up in 1944.

In addition to the training provided by the Rural Vocational Centers, vocational education in carpentry, automobile engineering, masonry, and a variety of arts and crafts is given to Moslem men and women in apprenticeship centers, complementary and evening courses, and craft centers. Schools of maritime apprenticeship are open largely to Europeans, as is the secondary vocational training in about a half-

UNIVERSITY OF ALGIERS—LIBRARY. *(Photo courtesy of French Embassy Press & Information Division.)*

dozen schools offering construction and machine-tool techniques, electrical and automobile engineering, woodworking, and the like. The *lycées* and *collèges* also offer vocational courses in their technical sections. Higher technical education is provided in the Commercial School of Algiers and the National School of Engineering, Public Works, and Building. A Higher Council of Applied Scientific Research was established in 1946. In both the agricultural and technical fields, Europeans may attend one of the *grandes écoles* in France, which are virtually inaccessible to Algerian Moslems because of educational prerequisites, age requirements, and other difficulties.

The shortage of qualified teachers, even those with only secondary-school certificates, was one of the key reasons for the failure of the 1944 plan. In 1945, there were 6,433 practicing elementary teachers in all Algeria; in 1954, 11,304. Before the outbreak of the rebellion in 1954, teachers were trained in six normal schools, with annual graduating classes far below the demand. Except for a few teachers of the Arabic language, most of the Algerian teaching force are French, the majority trained in metropolitan France and given a short orientation course before teaching in Algerian schools.

Educational facilities that fall under the direction of the Rector of the University of Algiers include the Pasteur Institute and a number of regional public-health centers for the training of medical auxiliaries, midwives, and social workers; a School for Deaf Mutes; a School of Fine Arts, where 90 per cent of the students are European; and various sports and recreational facilities, used largely by Europeans. An educational film service was started in 1947; Radio Algiers has a small number of educational broadcasts; and the government maintains several public libraries and museums.

Private education exists for European children from the nursery school through the secondary level, undertaken by lay teachers and different religious orders. There are fewer than 100 such institutions throughout Algeria; and the curriculum is generally of a lower standard than that of public schools. Protestant and Catholic missionaries also operate schools, particularly in the outlying rural districts. The general, vocational, and agricultural education provided by the White Fathers and Sisters in the remote southern territories has been particularly influential, although it has only reached several thousand young Moslems. For the most part, Jewish children attend Algeria's public or mission schools (Algeria's Jews have been citizens since 1870, except for a period under the Vichy regime, and are considered to be part of the European community), and there is one private school for the training of rabbis in Algiers.

Private education by the Moslem community for its own children is of two types: primary Koranic schools, where the young Moslem learns little more than to recite the Koran and to read and write Arabic and sometimes French, and primary schools and one secondary institution run by the Society of Reformist Ulema. The Koranic schools may receive a subsidy from the government if they fulfill certain French teaching requirements. More than 100,000 Moslem children attend these rudimentary schools.

The Society of Reformist Ulema inaugurated its first schools in 1936, in pursuance of its cultural program for an Arabic renaissance. By 1955, young Moslems attending coeducational primary schools run by the Ulema amounted to some 45,000. The curriculum included both modern and traditional Islamic subjects: Arabic, arithmetic, geometry, geography, history, science, and morals. Textbooks came from the Middle East as well as France; many of the teachers received their education at the Zitouna Moslem University in Tunis. Lessons in Arabic, Arab history, and Islam were also provided in Ulema schools for pupils already attending French schools.

On the secondary level, the Ulema established the Ben Badis Institute in 1947, named after the extraordinary Ulema leader who died in 1940. In 1954, just before the rebellion began, the Institute had about 1,100 pupils a year. In addition to the usual secondary courses, Institute pupils could read Moslem law, and lessons were provided in the French language. After two years, pupils could qualify for Zitouna University and work toward the degree of doctor of Moslem law, or continue for another two years at the Institute itself. Pupils in the Ulema schools began their daily lessons by chanting in unison: "Arabic is my language, Algeria is my country, Islam is my religion." Although the Ulema took no direct role in Algerian politics prior to the rebellion, they were frequently subject to French repressive measures on the grounds that their preaching and schools fostered Algerian nationalist tendencies.

Literacy Statistics and Their Political Significance

By 1944—after 114 years of French rule—there were only 110,686 Moslems receiving all types of education in Algeria, or 1.6 per cent of the total Moslem population at that time. Europeans receiving education amounted to 133,000, or 14.1 per cent of the European population. By 1954, the number of Moslems in primary schools had risen to 322,000—17.1 per cent of the Moslem population between the ages of six and fourteen. In the same year, 94 per cent—143,000 out of a possible 152,000 European children of primary-school age—were in schools. There were 34,468 pupils in Algerian secondary schools, of whom 6,890 (about 20 per cent) were Moslems. At the University of Algiers, there were 5,149 students in 1953–54, of whom 513 were Moslems. A number of Moslems also attended French universities. In the agricultural field, 9,422 were receiving primary training in 1954, a majority of them Moslems; 244 were receiving secondary training, of whom 51 were Moslems; and 152 were receiving higher training, all of them Europeans. This total—9,818—may be compared with the more than 2.5 million persons actively engaged in agriculture. Figures for technical and vocational education of various kinds range from 12,000 to 21,000 for 1953–54. Moslems accounted for 38 per cent of those in primary training, 23 per cent in secondary courses, and 2 per cent in higher education. Of the 165 students at the National School of Engineering, Public Works, and Building and at the Commercial School of Algiers, there were two Moslems in 1955, one in 1956. The over-all number of those receiving technical training may be compared with 650,000 to 700,000 engaged in commerce, industry, public works, and administration—a much more favorable ratio of trained persons than in the agricultural field. To summarize for the year 1955–56, which was somewhat affected by the rebellion, there were some 450,000 primary pupils in all categories in Algeria (70 per cent Moslem), 37,000 secondary pupils (20 per cent Moslem), and 7,280 Algerian-origin students in higher education in both Algeria and France (23 per cent Moslem). In that year, there was approximately one Moslem student for every 5,050 Moslems, and one European student for every 175 Europeans.

The twenty-year plan of 1944 was expected to increase the number of young Moslems in school from about 100,000 to 1 million through the construction of 20,000 new schoolrooms. But even if lack of funds, teacher shortages, and other pressures had not prevented the implementation of the plan, the increase of the Moslem population would have made it necessary—and, indeed, will—that facilities be provided for more than twice as many children in 1964. This rapid rate of growth—2.5 per cent—and the youthful character of the population will continue to cause difficulties for any government in Algeria.

The Impact of the Rebellion

The seven years of rebellion in Algeria have disrupted education both morally and materially. In July, 1956, Ahmad Tawfig, head of the Algerian delegation to the First Arab Teachers' Conference in Alexandria, Egypt, reported that, out of 800 Arab teachers in Algeria at the outset of the rebellion, 90 men and 5 women had by then been killed in the fighting, 220 men were in prison, 70 women were in "concentration camps," and 120 were serving with the National Army of Liberation. By the spring of 1956, moreover, almost one-fourth of the schools had been destroyed, damaged, or closed because of rebel activities. This destruction did not indicate a lack of respect for education on the part of the rebels, but was an inevitable by-product of a tactical plan calling for the creation of general insecurity and the denial of important facilities to the French. The French Government soon closed most Ulema schools, including the Ben Badis Institute, on the grounds of complicity with the rebellion.

The atmosphere at the University of Algiers, where Moslem students were in a minority of about one-tenth, became politically charged; and several professors either resigned or were transferred as a result of political pressures. The European student union at the university, Association Générale des Étudiants (AGE), was quick to protest against measures taken in favor of Moslems, and it later played a key role in the rightist coup of May 13, 1958.

In early 1955, Moslem students for the first time formed their own student association, the Union Générale des Étudiants Musulmans Algériens (UGEMA), to foster their interests, "to safeguard and defend the Algerian personality by striving for the recognition of Arabic as the official language of the country, for the organization of national education, for the freedom of the Moslem creed, and for the inclusion of the Algerian element in the structure of the country"—in short, to express student solidarity with the aims of the rebellion. The UGEMA called a strike in May, 1956, of the Algerian Moslem students in Algeria, France, and elsewhere. This strike was largely effective, and it continues to be so above the primary level, despite the fact that the UGEMA was ordered dissolved in 1958 and its leaders arrested. French authorities estimate that some 120,000 children were kept out of elementary schools in October, 1956, though not all for the same reason. Many secondary and university students joined the rebel forces, while others stayed home because of destruction of schools or as a result of intimidation.

By 1958, however, Algerian rebel authorities took account of the importance of education for the future of Algeria, and some students were permitted to resume their interrupted studies in European countries outside France, in the Middle East, and elsewhere. Few schools have been destroyed since 1958, and the Army of National Liberation is engaged in basic health education patterned after similar UNESCO programs in Central America. Administrative training is provided for Algerian rebel cadres by Tunisia, Morocco, and other friendly governments. The rebel-oriented Algerian trade union, the Union Générale des Travailleurs Algériens, maintains a small vocational-training center in Tunisia.

The French Government, realizing that resentment over lack of educational opportunity was a partial cause of the 1954 outbreak, has taken steps to increase the number of schools and teachers available to the Moslem population of Algeria. In this effort, the French Army, sent to fight the rebels but increasingly engaged in administrative functions of all kinds, plays an active part. Beginning in September,

1955, the army set up Special Administrative Sections (SAS) in the rural areas and Urban Administrative Sections (SAU) in the cities, manned by a carefully selected officer corps to act as liaison between the army and the Moslem population and to improve local conditions. By the beginning of 1957, the army had opened 212 schools, with 355 army teachers and 11,700 pupils. However, these schools are described by FLN sources as organs of psychological warfare rather than true schools.

In August, 1958, General de Gaulle's government of the Fifth Republic finally abrogated the unfulfilled twenty-year plan of 1944 and replaced it with a new eight-year program. Admitting that from 1949 to 1956 the average number of new classrooms built annually was only 436, it proposed in the new program the annual construction of 2,025 classrooms, along with living quarters for the teaching staff. Instead of the previous annual teacher supply of about 300 from Algerian normal schools and 350 from France, the new plan was to improve Algerian teacher-training facilities to the point where it would be possible to recruit teachers locally for 1,800 new posts per year. By 1965–66, according to the de Gaulle plan, 1.3 million children in Algeria will be receiving French elementary education. Another innovation—the Social Centers of the Basic Education Service, organized in 1955 to provide elementary "all-round social, health, and intellectual education for the less advanced populations"—were to increase in number to 700 in 1966.

On the secondary level, *lycées* and *collèges* (2,500), teachers colleges (150), and general complementary courses (2,000) were to be expanded to accommodate a total of 4,650 additional pupils per year for the next eight years; and for technical and vocational training, an additional 3,550 pupils. Thus the number of secondary *lycée* and *collège* pupils was to increase from 37,000 (1958–59) to 57,000 (1965–66); the number of other secondary pupils from 17,000 to 33,000; technical and vocational trainees from 10,500 to 35,000; and the number of teacher trainees was to be doubled. The eight-year plan recognizes that expansion of higher education in Algeria depends on the number of qualified secondary pupils and provides for such projects to be drawn up at a later date. But the reconstruction of the Faculty of Liberal Arts as well as the construction of a large Institute of Nuclear Studies, an annex to the Science Faculty of the Institute of Saharan Studies, and of a new Faculty of Medicine are already planned or in progress at the University of Algiers. The School of Engineers was expanded in the fall of 1958.

"It may be said without exaggeration that the present Ordinance [the eight-year plan] marks a decisive and historic date for the future of Algeria, from the economic as well as the social and cultural points of view." So concludes the official French pamphlet on De Gaulle's educational plan for Algeria. It seems unlikely, however, that this plan will ever be implemented, for by late 1961 most observers were agreed that both the rebels and the French Government were ready to negotiate the formation of an interim government that would lead Algeria toward early independence.

In an independent Algeria, Arabic will most certainly be introduced as the official language of the country and the schools, but French will long remain the language by which the country's leaders will talk to each other and communicate with most of the world. The only language in which all the leading figures of the FLN are fluent is French. All novels produced in Algeria's recent literary renaissance by Moslem writers—Mouloud Mammeri, Mouloud Faraoun, Mohammed Dib, among others—are written in French. These men are products of an educational system that minimized Arabic, and gave Moslems only enough knowledge to discover what opportunities they were being denied and a new tongue to speak their grievances. Those who seem most likely to hold the positions of authority in an independent regime will undoubtedly make sure that the history of Algerian and other Islamic areas is added to the curriculum. But their educational program, on the whole, is more likely to expand into technical fields than to try to recover a parochial glory.

—Based on a draft by the late JOAN GILLESPIE;
revised and updated by MANFRED HALPERN

2. *Morocco*

Capital: Rabat
Population: 11,600,000 (est.)
Area: 170,000 sq. miles
Political status: Independent monarchy

DESPITE the centuries of independence it knew prior to 1912, when the French established a protectorate that lasted until 1956, Morocco remains a country and a nation still in the process of formation. Although it came within the compass of the great Mediterranean empires from the Romans to the French, Morocco was separated—by its mountains and desert and by foreign occupation of the littoral—from the currents of change in thought, society, and technology that were flowing throughout the Mediterranean basin. Under the protectorate, a modern economy and an extensive administrative system were created, and Morocco might have appeared to have caught up. But despite the very real material gains achieved, Morocco during this period actually moved even further from being one country and one people.

During the protectorate, Morocco was administered as four separate entities. France governed the major portion; Spain ruled a narrow strip along the Mediterranean coast and a second area in the extreme south bordering on Spanish Sahara; and Tangier and a tiny hinterland were controlled by an international commission. The laws, institutions, and economy of each of these four sectors and the differing external influences to which they were oriented gave to each a separate existence and a history not shared by the others. Into them, particularly the French zone, came tens of thousands of foreigners to found and man commercial, mining, farming, and industrial establishments and administrative offices. Rural poverty, periodic crop failures, and the attractions of the new cities brought a steady migration to the cities and the growth of an urban proletariat. In the fashion typical of colonial territories, Morocco became a land of plural communities in which the indigenous society grew increasingly complex. Along with the divisions that had existed prior to the protectorate, Morocco's population developed new and fundamental economic, social, and cultural divergences under the pressures of new opportunities and experiences.

With the 1956 restoration of sovereignty to a central government whose authority extended over all the parts into which Morocco had recently been divided, steps to unify Morocco's diverse peoples became both desirable and possible. But even time may not overcome many of their differences: the religious cleavages among Moslem, Jew, and Christian; the ethnic differences among Arab, Berber, and European; the communications problems among speakers of Arabic, Chleuh, French, and Spanish. Among those who think of themselves as Moroccans, however, there are differences of experience, outlook, and preparation for participation in Morocco's present social and economic life that education can do much to overcome or reduce. It is to this task, as well as to the production of the trained personnel the country needs, that the educational system of Morocco is being oriented.

Education Under the Protectorate

The economic development that Morocco experienced during the protectorate was both a product and a cause of immigration from Europe. The growth of a European population that considered itself permanent brought immediate need for a school system identical with that in the metropole. Provision of the schools was a governmental obligation, but little or no restriction seems to have been placed on private efforts. So long as the educational system in the French zone was considered as a branch of the French educational system, there was no need to try to duplicate in Morocco the universities and technical-training institutions of France. This same system of schools also met the needs of some Moroccan students, primarily those from upper-class and politically correct families. A separate set of schools, referred to as Moslem schools, provided instruction that could culminate in the French *baccalauréat,* in a Moroccan *baccalauréat,* or in training for clerkships and junior technical jobs in private business and administrative services. In the rural areas, practical instruction in farming, hygiene, and simple construction was given. In the Jewish quarters, there were also both public elementary schools and elementary schools operated by the Universal Jewish Alliance with governmental control and assistance.

During the school year 1953–54, these schools accommodated 299,638 students, in comparison with 95,724 enrolled on November 10, 1944. In 1953–54, there were 60,872 in European (also called Franco-Moroccan) primary schools—46,204 French, 6,014 Moroccan, and 8,654 others. An additional 16,073 were enrolled in European secondary schools—12,275 French, 2,713 Moroccan, and 1,085 others. Jewish primary schools had 29,878 pupils, Moslem primary schools 187,600, and Moslem secondary schools 5,215. These figures are placed in better perspective, however, by Table 1.

Table 1
Graduates of Moroccan Secondary Schools

Year	French	Moroccan		Other	Total
		Moslem	Jewish		
1945	578	52	39	39	708
1950	959	138	110	66	1,273
1953	1,142	124	122	59	1,447

Almost without exception, those students who desired and could arrange for further education went to France. It was for French schools that their education had prepared them, and it was a French degree that had meaning in Morocco. During the school year 1951–52, 261 Moroccan Moslem students were pursuing higher studies in France, compared with approximately 160 Moroccan Jewish students and 1,430 French students from Morocco. Of the Moslem students, 66 were studying medicine and 51 law, or 45 per cent of the total. Of the Jewish students, 44 were in medicine and 11 in law, or 35 per cent of the total. Only 25 per cent of the French students were following these studies, however—242 in medicine and 116 in law.

Changes Since Independence

The educational system inherited at the end of the protectorate was considered unsatisfactory in several respects by Moroccan leaders. It did not provide for enough of Morocco's children. The various systems operating on separate principles perpetuated social and cultural differences. Many of the materials and methods did not reflect Moroccan values or points of view. There was inadequate provision for the training of personnel urgently needed at all levels of business and government, so that training and recruitment abroad were necessary.

What was desired was an educational system that provided the same kind of opportunities for Moroccans of all cultural, regional, or economic backgrounds; gave them an education firmly based on Morocco's history and traditions; expressed a Moroccan point of view; and yet was oriented toward modern life and the practical needs of Morocco. The creation of such a system required three steps: expansion, reorganization of the structure, and reform of the content and materials of instruction. Special provision for illiterates, adults, and children outside the formal school system was also considered essential in order to reduce the gap in outlook between generations, city and countryside, Arab and Berber, and government and people.

An over-all view of the structure that existed at the end of the protectorate is provided in Table 2. Between the restoration of Morocco's independence (March 2, 1956) and the date of these figures (November 10, 1957), a great expansion had already taken place. At the beginning of the last school year under the protectorate—in October, 1955—25,000 new pupils were enrolled in school. In contrast, the following year, under the Moroccan Government, 133,000 new pupils were enrolled, and in October, 1957, 166,000 new pupils were added. Secondary and technical education showed comparable increases.

Primary Education

The great increases in enrollment in 1956 and 1957 brought unprecedented demands for teachers. In 1956, some 6,400 were recruited as teachers in training after being given courses of two to three months. In 1957, 6,500 more were added. These student teachers were given as close supervision as possible and required to attend three hour-and-a-half classes each week for further training. Regional teacher-training centers had been opened at Oujda, Fez, Rabat, and Marrakech in 1955; others followed at Meknes in 1956 and at Ouarzazate, Beni Mellal, Casablanca, and Ksar-es-Souk in 1957. The normal output of these centers was 300 a year, with a nine-months course. By compressing the training, two classes could be given five months of training each year, raising the output to 600 a year.

During 1958–59, more than 800 teachers were being trained at the regional centers to take up posts in October, 1959. In the spring of 1959, 300 former students at Qarawiyin University were given an accelerated three-month training course to prepare them as teachers. In October, 1958, 2,000 students entered secondary schools on scholarships to prepare as teachers; after completing the three years of the first cycle of secondary education and obtaining the Brevet of Studies

Table 2
Moroccan School Population, November, 1957

Schools: Type	Schools: Number	Students: Moroccan: Boys	Students: Moroccan: Girls	Students: Moroccan: Total	Students: Foreign: Boys	Students: Foreign: Girls	Students: Foreign: Total	Students: Total
Moslem								
Primary	2,545	340,357	128,008	468,365	8,385	4,718	13,103	481,468
Secondary	72	19,208	3,255	22,463	498	243	741	23,204
Private	n.a.	42,130	30,220	72,350				72,350
European								
Primary	224	4,242	4,310	8,552	10,031	8,675	18,706	27,258
Secondary	14	1,016	1,138	2,154	1,953	4,415	6,368	8,522
(Private)	(46)			(742)			(9,087)	
Jewish	86	14,877	15,244		286	460		
Franco-Israelite	11			2,376			185	2,561
Universal Jewish Alliance	75			27,745			561	28,306
Islamic								
Higher	11	11,077	291	11,368				11,368
Others								
Normal	6 [a]	6	1	7	54	45	99	106
Lower technical	n.a.	4,989	3,160	8,149	847	188	1,035	9,184
Upper technical	n.a.	1,427	703	2,130	2,464	1,465	3,929	6,059
Total		*439,329*	*186,330*	*625,659*	*24,518*	*20,209*	*44,727*	*670,386*

[a] 2 European, 4 Moslem.

of the First Cycle, they were to have one year of training at a regional center and then take up teaching posts.

In 1959–60, six new primary-teacher–training schools were opened, each with a capacity of sixty students. Fifty primary teachers with the first or second part of the *baccalauréat* were recruited abroad. The number of inspectors—including local inspectors, those in charge of the teaching of Arabic, those in charge of the teaching of French, and assistant inspectors—was increased to 104 in 1960, so that no inspector was responsible for more than 200 teachers. In addition to observing and correcting the work of the teachers, the inspectors gave pedagogical lectures, held demonstration classes, and listened to and criticized test lessons prepared by the teachers.

To reduce the demand for teachers and for classrooms, many classes were placed on a half-day schedule. In 1956–57, 20 per cent of the classes were on half time, a proportion that it has been hard to reduce. To provide housing for teachers and classes, local communities all over Morocco constructed, renovated, and donated buildings. In many instances, the accommodations could only be considered temporary, but at least they satisfied an immediate demand for space. During 1958–59, out of 1,200 new classrooms added, the Moroccan Government built 500 and rural communities the other 700. Under agreements signed in 1957 allowing French and Spanish cultural missions to establish schools for French and Spanish children, 1,000 classrooms were lent to these missions, to be returned in three stages from October, 1959, to October, 1961. In 1960, it was reported that transfer of the French children still in Moroccan public schools to schools run by the French cultural mission was expected to free an additional 300 classrooms.

By January, 1960, 722,215 Moroccan children were receiving primary education. Table 3 accounts for all except 5,821, who were attending primary classes in secondary schools. Of the potential school population (ages six to fourteen), estimated to be 1.9 million at that time, 38 per cent were attending school. The aim is to continue the expansion at such a rate that by 1964 two-thirds of the children between six and fourteen will be in school.

Table 3
Moroccan Children in Primary Schools, January, 1960

Type of School	Boys	Girls	Total
Public schools	468,837	172,553	641,390
Private schools	28,567	21,061	49,628
Universal Jewish Alliance schools	12,551	12,765	25,376
Total	*509,955*	*206,379*	*716,394*

In October, 1958, the Division of Education of the First Degree was formed by a merger of the previously separate administrative services of primary Moslem education and of primary European and Jewish education. Inclusion of Moroccan private primary schools within the responsibility and authority of this division has been under study. The government has already drawn on the experiences of these schools in conversion from French to Arabic as the medium of instruction and in revising curricula to meet Moroccan desires and needs. The government has also provided some staff members for certain private schools, as well as student scholarships, teacher grants, books, food, and medicine. By the terms of the French-Moroccan Cultural Convention signed on May 30, 1957, French children in Moroccan schools were to be given an education conforming in schedules, programs, and teaching methods to that in France. The transfer of French children to French cultural mission schools is ending this requirement.

Because of the diverse school systems of the past, Moroccan school children have been subject to a confusing variety of regimes. Unification of primary education under a single administrative service has simplified the task of establishing a single system of primary education, but such fundamental steps as reviewing all texts and replacing those found unsuitable with new ones written by Moroccans, qualifying teachers to teach in Arabic rather than in French, and providing teaching materials in Arabic are still in progress.

Regarding the use of Arabic as a medium of instruction, all schools that had been part of the system previously known as Moslem primary schools were required as of October, 1958, to provide thirty hours of instruction in classical Arabic during the first year and fifteen hours each in French and classical Arabic during the remaining five years of primary school. The same requirement was to be applied to the first year in Jewish schools, with the rest of the program to come into effect progressively. In the schools that were part of the former European system, Arabic was introduced in the first year only, and solely for Moroccan children, in October, 1959.

With the opening of the 1960–61 school year, major changes in policy were announced in conjunction with the inauguration of the five-year plan (1960–64). Some 288,000 children, or 80 per cent of the seven-year-olds, entered school; it was planned to accommodate 100 per cent of the seven-year-olds by 1963. To make it possible to receive such large numbers, all classes in the first two years were placed on half time, or 15 hours a week. Each classroom and each teacher would then be able to serve 100 pupils each day. Students over fourteen or those who had already had seven years of schooling would not be continued in primary school. At the end of five years of primary school, 80 per cent would be permitted to continue to secondary school. The others would be given two years of terminal studies, including general instruction and elementary practical instruction in agriculture, handicrafts, or housekeeping. Afterward, they would return to their families or enter public or private trade schools.

In providing for the large numbers of primary students, it is intended to give equal opportunities to all parts of the country and to all social and economic classes. In the Sousse and Ouarzazate regions, where absenteeism has been especially high, the Ministry of National Education intends first to seek the cooperation of administrative authorities in trying to increase enrollment before reallocating posts unused because of a scarcity of students. The same means are to be used to encourage attendance by girls where this is necessary. Further action to equalize educational opportunities for all sectors of the population will include the integration of Jewish education in a single national system of primary education. Private Jewish schools not integrated will, however, receive subventions under the same conditions as those given to private Moslem schools. On October 1, 1960, 261 classes out of a total of 671 (including 11,000 of the total of 26,000 students) in schools of the Universal Jewish Alliance were taken in charge by the Ministry of National Education. The official regime of studies was applied to these schools, and their teaching and administrative personnel were added to the official cadres.

As a further means of unifying the educational system and making the best use of available resources, it was decided that recruitment into the traditional Islamic schools should end. It was pointed out by the Minister of National Education that the credits made available to the traditional schools for the current year amounted to 10 per cent of the Ministry's budget, whereas the students involved amounted to only 2 per cent of the total. Furthermore, to allow for the entry of twenty-year-olds into traditional schools, children of seven were being left to learn what they could in the streets. Enrollment in these schools had risen from 3,603 in 1955–56 to 24,436 in 1959–60. Taking account of the objectives of traditional education, the Ministry had decided on two steps. The first was the creation of a Faculty of Sharia for the training of higher cadres and for research in Islamic sciences. The second was the creation of specialized schools under the jurisdiction of the Ministry of Habous for the training of cadres less qualified than those the former system produced, but on a level in accord with actual needs. The teaching personnel in these schools would be provided by the Ministry of National Education.

With Arabization of the first year of primary school largely accomplished in 1958–59, it was extended to the second year in October, 1960. In 1956 only 33 per cent of the total instruction given in primary schools was in Arabic. In 1960–61, 70 per cent of the 5,400 hours of primary school (3,780) was in Arabic.

In October, 1960, 1,000 candidates entered the sixteen regional training centers to begin a year's training to become teachers, having already completed the first cycle of secondary studies. During the year, the construction of three more regional schools would increase the annual capacity to 1,500.

Out of an estimated 2 million children between six and fourteen, 800,000 were enrolled in public schools and 120,000 in private schools by October, 1960.

Secondary Education

Secondary education has undergone developments very similar to those in primary education since 1956. From November, 1956, to November, 1957, enrollment of Moroccan students increased from 13,374 to 23,204, while enrollment in European secondary schools dropped from 16,691 to 8,522. This decline in the European schools came primarily as a result of the temporary transfer of some secondary schools to the French cultural mission. Much of the expansion in Moroccan enrollment was made possible by the creation, in the outskirts of the principal cities or in the larger towns, of sixteen *collèges* offering only the first half of the secondary program. Thus, at the opening of the 1957–58 school year, the Moslem secondary-education system consisted of five provincial *lycées,* six *collèges* for boys, two *collèges* for girls, and sixteen *collèges* offering only the first cycle. In October, 1958, the European secondary schools were joined with the Moslem schools to form the Division of Education of the Second Degree. After the merger, 32,079 students were receiving secondary education in thirteen *lycées,* seventeen *collèges,* and twenty-four first-cycle *collèges.** Boarding facilities and technical-training sections were provided at some of these establishments.

The expansion of secondary education, the pressure for further expansion produced by the great increase in primary education, and

* *Lycées* located in Agadir, Azrou, Casablanca, Fez, Kenitra, Marrakech, Meknes, Oujda, Rabat, and Tetuan; *collèges* in Casablanca, al-Jadida, Fez, Khouribga, Meknes, Oujda, Rabat, Settat, Sidi-Kacem, Tangier, and Tetuan; first-cycle *collèges* in Alhucemas, Arcila, Beni Mellal, Berkane, Casablanca, Chaouen, al-Jadida, al-Ksar al-Kebir, Khemisset, Kenitra, Ksar-es-Souk, Larache, Nador, Ouezzane, Safi, Sefrou, Taroudant, Taza, Marrakech, Meknes, and Oujda.

the departure of qualified foreign teachers have made it difficult to maintain the desired quality of secondary instruction. A training institute providing a two-year course for the preparation of secondary teachers was opened in October, 1957, and the first sixty-two graduates took up posts in October, 1959. Foreign recruitment was necessary, but was barely enough to maintain the level of qualification of the staff, which in 1958–59 included 48 *professeurs agrégés* and 492 *professeurs licenciés,* together with others of lower qualifications. In the following year, official figures indicated that 28 per cent of the staff were qualified only as primary-school teachers. Teachers of scientific subjects are in especially short supply, and persons with professional qualifications, such as engineers and chemists, have been drawn upon to take science classes. Close supervision of teaching methods and various training activities for teachers have also been instituted.

The progressive introduction of a reformed system of secondary education began in 1957. This system divides the six years of secondary studies into two cycles of equal length. The first cycle consists of general education and is taken by all students. The second cycle consists of five specialized sections: Section A, classical letters (Arabic and Islamic sciences); Section B, modern letters (study of a second living foreign language and economic and social subjects); Section C, science (with emphasis on experimental sciences); Section D, science (with emphasis on mathematics); Section E, technical instruction. Secondary education terminates in the Brevet of Studies of the First Cycle, Certificate of Moroccan Secondary Studies, or the Modern *Baccalauréat.* A Center of Research and Pedagogical Action was established in 1958 to study questions arising in the introduction of the reforms, with respect to such matters as schedules, teaching methods and materials, and texts.

During 1959–60, 19,733 boys and 9,328 girls were attending general-education classes. With the addition of those in technical and professional classes administered by the Division of Education of the Second Degree, the total was 35,502, of which 77 per cent were Moroccan. To limit the demand for more classrooms and staff, the minimum number of students in each class of the first year of secondary studies was raised to forty. The actual increase in secondary education is not adequately indicated by these enrollment figures, however, for secondary schools have been a prime source of recruits for the Moroccanization of government services.

To provide for the estimated 33,000 students in secondary schools in 1960–61, it was necessary to establish a minimum of thirty-five to forty students per class in the first cycle and a twenty-student minimum in the second cycle. Teachers of some secondary subjects, such as mathematics, had to be assigned classes at several schools so that all schools would be able to offer these subjects. Ninety-five teachers for secondary education were recruited in France to fill posts in 1960–61. To reduce the necessity for recruiting foreign teachers, the Ministry of National Education began planning for a school to train holders of the *baccalauréat* (secondary- education degree) to become secondary-school teachers.

The Reformed Structure of Secondary Education

In October, 1960, coincident with the fundamental reforms announced for primary education, a complete reorganization of secondary and technical education came into effect. Three branches of secondary education were formed: one, terminating in the *baccalauréat,* offers six years of pre-university work; the second, terminating in industrial or commercial *brevets,* offers six years of preparation for middle-level commercial and industrial employment; the third, terminating in certificates of professional aptitude, offers three years of training for a wide range of industrial, commercial, and agricultural work. The six-year branches are under the Division of Education of the Second Degree, while the three-year branch is under the Division of Technical Education. Because of the great transformation, figures for students, staff, and schools are not comparable with figures for previous years, but it was estimated that 33,000 students would be enrolled in the six-year branches and some 14,000 in the three-year branch.

The six-year branches, known as the "long course," consist of two cycles of three years each, the first cycle being taken by all students and consisting of general education. At the end of the first cycle, the following specialized sections are open to students working for the *baccalauréat:* classical letters (Moroccan thought and civilization), modern letters (Arabic, French, history, geography, philosophy), experimental sciences, mathematics, science and technical studies, and economics. Students working for *brevets* choose between industrial and commercial studies. Among the 2,109 students entering the second cycle under the new system in October, 1960, the distribution was as follows: classical letters, 132; modern letters, 722; experimental sciences, 400; mathematics, 377; science and technical studies, 119; economics, 39; industrial studies, 139; commercial studies, 181.

The three-year branch, known as the "middle course," consists of five sections: general, industrial, commercial, agricultural, and social (for girls). Those students completing the section of general instruction are qualified to enter the regional teacher-training schools and will provide the major source of primary teachers. The range of occupations prepared for in the other sections includes electricians, automobile mechanics, masons, carpenters, dressmakers, hairdressers, mothers' helpers, industrial designers, and stenographer-typists. The industrial section alone offers more than sixty specializations. In 1960, 1,085 industrial certificates of professional aptitude (CAP) were granted—706 to Moroccans and 379 to other nationalities. An additional 369 commercial CAP's were granted—128 to Moroccans and 241 to other nationalities; 190 girls' CAP's were awarded—115 to Moroccans and 75 to other nationalities.

In November, 1960, an Engineering School was opened in Rabat to meet the need for works engineers *(ingénieurs d'exécution)* in the administration, the public services, and private industry. Morocco's present annual requirements are estimated at seventeen engineers for public works, eighteen for mining, and thirty in mechanics and electricity. Further expansion and Moroccanization of industry will increase these needs.

Normally, the students entering the school will be secondary-school graduates with a *baccalauréat* in mathematics. As there were not yet enough secondary-school graduates to ensure that the Engineering School would be able to produce classes of sixty-five, a preparatory school was opened in October, 1958. By competitive examination, students who have completed the first three years of secondary school can be admitted to the preparatory school, where they are given two years of mathematics and science that are intended to be equivalent to the training received by holders of the *baccalauréat*. The direct admission of holders of the Brevet of Industrial Studies to the second year of the preparatory school is under study.

In the Engineering School, a year of general science training is followed by two years of specialized training offered in three sections: public works, mining, and mechanics and electricity. The Faculty of Sciences of the University of Rabat will provide the teaching staff for the first-year courses. Until a permanent staff can be formed of those who have received training in foreign engineering schools or industries, senior technical staff members of the public services and private enterprises will teach the specialized courses and organize practical training.

The progressive use of Arabic as the language of instruction is being given a high priority throughout the long course and in the general-instruction section of the middle course. Arabization at this level will provide teachers capable of teaching primary classes in Arabic and students capable of receiving university-level instruction in Arabic. Subjects of particular national importance such as civics, history, and geography will be the first to be Arabized, leaving the natural and exact sciences to be taught in French. Instruction in Arabic will be given priority in the distribution of materials and staff.

An institute for study and research in Arabic was inaugurated in January, 1960, to work toward the solution of the problems that arise in making wider use of Arabic. Its objectives are: (1) to take a census of Arabic vocabularies and determine the number of useful words with definite meanings; (2) to attempt to unify these vocabularies, not only for Morocco but for the entire Arabic world; (3) to isolate the words for which there is no equivalent and determine their definition, in collaboration with all institutions and bodies working with Arabic; (4) to apply audio-visual means to the learning of Arabic, especially among teaching staffs that have been trained in a foreign language; (5) to develop Arabic scientific literature by the translation of texts, reference works, and popular articles. The director of the institute, Professor Lakhdar, has invented a set of printing characters with vowel signs to be used to print texts and references as well as materials for use in the campaign against illiteracy.

Higher Education

The University of Rabat was inaugurated on December 21, 1957, and consists of three faculties, a School of Applied Medicine, and a number of associated specialized institutions. At present, it prepares students for French degrees primarily, but offers an increasing number of Moroccan degrees. In October, 1960, it was announced that the scholastic year 1962–63 was the last in which the University of Rabat would prepare students for anything but Moroccan degrees.

The largest of the faculties is the Faculty of Law and Political and Economic Science. Here, students holding the *baccalauréat* may prepare for a License or Doctorate of Law in the French language—with specialization in juridical science, political science, or economics—or a License in Law in Arabic. The latter degree may also be prepared for by candidates who hold diplomas awarded at the end of the secondary level in centers of Islamic studies. Those who hold neither degree may prepare for a Diploma of Proficiency in Law or a Diploma of Moroccan Juridical and Administrative Studies. Table 4 shows the distribution of students according to degrees during the school years 1958–59 and 1959–60.

Table 4
Students Preparing for Faculty of Law Degrees

Degree	1958–59	1959–60
Law Degree in Arabic	249	359
Law Degree in French	475	560
Doctorate in Law	69	93
Diploma of Proficiency in Law	622	672
Diploma of Moroccan Juridical and Administrative Studies	62	50
Total	*1,477*	*1,734*

During 1958–59, 1,058 of the students were Moroccan, 399 French, and 20 other nationalities. For 1959–60, the respective figures were 1,367, 352, and 15. There were 163 women students in 1958–59 and 179 in 1959–60. The staff consists of eleven university professors, six university lecturers, fourteen assistant lecturers, and twenty-five teachers doing the work of lecturers.

Two centers of specialized study are attached to the Faculty of Law and Political and Economic Science. The center for the study of business administration, in Casablanca, has about 100 students and awards a diploma in business administration. There is also a center for the study of economic and social development, with about 200 students. Neither is considered an integral part of the University.

The second largest faculty is the Faculty of Arts, which provides a wide range of training, from a two-year course for Arabic interpreters to preparation for the French *licence* (i.e., master's degree). Courses leading to an arts degree in Arabic, a Moroccan *licence,* were inaugurated in 1957–58, and the Faculty of Arts also administers courses of study inherited from the former Institute of Moroccan Higher Studies, following the same syllabi as are used in France.

During the year 1959–60, 1,105 students were distributed as follows: 222 preparing for the Moroccan *licence,* 720 for the French *licence,* 74 for the Diploma in Classical Arabic, 84 for a *brevet* in Arabic, and 5 for an interpreter's diploma. Giving instruction for the French *licence* were five holders of doctor's degrees and eighteen *professeurs agrégés.* For the other courses, the staff consisted of ten holders of doctor's degrees, three *professeurs agrégés,* five holders of research diplomas, and three holders of certificates.

The percentage of Moroccan students in the Faculty of Sciences has risen steadily, going from 7 per cent at its inception to 27 per cent in 1959–60, when 225 of 842 students were Moroccan. The Faculty prepares candidates for six teaching degrees—mathematics, physics I, physics II, chemistry, natural sciences (biological sciences), and natural sciences (earth sciences)—and for a number of other Certificates of

University of Rabat—entrance to student housing.

Higher Studies, following the same syllabi as are used in France. The other certificates are awarded in: algebra, mathematics I and II, general mechanics, mathematical techniques of physics, electricity, electronics, optics, thermodynamics, organic chemistry, systematic chemistry, applied chemistry, general chemistry I and II, mineral chemistry, zoology, animal physiology, general biology, botany, general geology, historical geology, and vegetal biochemistry, microbiology, and physiology.

Two research institutions are attached to the Faculty of Sciences. The Sharifian Scientific Institute, which has seven laboratories, a museum, and a botanical garden, conducts research in zoology, entomology, flowering and flowerless plants, physical geography, geology, and paleontology. The Institute of Terrestrial Physics and Meteorology conducts research in geophysics, terrestrial magnetism, seismology, meteorology, ocean swells, and the ionosphere. It operates a seismological observatory at Berrechid, a station for registering ocean swells at Ain Diab, an ionosphere observatory at Temara, a mountain meteorology station at Ifrane, a Saharan research station at Aounet Torkoz, and about 400 meteorological posts.

The Averroes School of Applied Medicine was opened in Casablanca in November, 1959, to provide the fifth year of training in medicine. The sixth, or internship, year was already being provided in Moroccan hospitals, and the fifth year, which includes only a limited number of theoretical courses, could be added without difficulties in recruiting staff or maintaining the quality of instruction. That the level was maintained was evidenced by the fact that the entire first class of thirty students passed the examination at the end of the year, which was administered by examiners from the Faculties of Medicine of Paris, Bordeaux, and Marseilles.

Considering the cost of a full school of medicine and the limited number of students and qualified teaching personnel available, such a school is not possible now, but it is hoped to proceed toward this goal. The intent will be to give to the studies and to the diploma an explicitly Moroccan character.

Projects planned for early execution to extend the capabilities of the University include the creation of an Institute of Sociology, an Institute of Political Studies, and an Institute of African Studies. Meanwhile, the government continues to facilitate higher studies abroad (see Table 5) in specific fields for qualified Moroccans.

Table 5
Government Scholarships for Foreign Study

Country	1957–58	1958–59	1959–60
France	274	350	492
Spain	102	76	104
Egypt	110	90	66
Syria	102	91	65
Iraq	29	27	24
Switzerland	3	5	16
West Germany	15	19	15
Great Britain	7	7	9
Austria	2		3
United States	1	1	
Total	*645*	*666*	*794*

Higher Islamic Education

This section deals only with the instruction given in Qarawiyin University in Fez, Ben Youssef University in Marrakech, and the centers of Islamic studies located in Tetuan, Meknes, Oujda, Taroudant, al-Jadida, Chaouen, Nador, Alhucemas, Larache, and al-Ksar al-Kebir. The 2,439 Koranic schools at lower levels, which had 68,612 students in 1958–59 and 72,457 in 1959–60, are not included.

Strong support from the Government of Morocco made it possible for the students receiving traditional education (other than in Koranic schools) to increase from 3,603 in 1955–56 to 24,436 in 1959–60. This support has provided improved and expanded living and teaching quarters, scholarships for boarding students, food and medicine for day students, grants to teachers, and recruiting campaigns in Arab countries to provide more staff. New quarters have been found mainly in unused barracks and in buildings confiscated by the state; for example, four houses in Marrakech once owned by the late Al Glaoui Pasha now provide boarding premises for 400 students at the Ben Youssef University. Insofar as possible, classes have been moved out of mosques, and modern buildings are going up to replace the ancient dormitories. At least some of the structures at Qarawiyin University are being carefully and beautifully restored, however, and will again one day house students.

Just as modern education is being given a specifically Moroccan content and the switch to teaching in Arabic is being made as quickly as possible, so traditional education is being reformed and given a modern content. The old system included three cycles: At the end of the first three years, the first-degree certificate (or *Taour al-Aouel*) was awarded; after four years of the second cycle, a certificate of the first degree was awarded, and after six years a certificate of the second degree; the third cycle consisted of an arts section and a law section, each lasting three years and terminating in the higher diploma (or *Alimia*).

The reform of the first cycle called for its extension to five years and for the establishment of schools in rural areas to counter the tendency toward centralization in the urban centers. The decision to enroll new students only in the regular state system of primary education, which was announced by the Minister of National Education in 1960, looks to the gradual absorption of traditional education at this level into the system of modern education.

At the secondary level, an equally sweeping reform is under way. The six-year course will be divided into two phases: three years of general culture and three years of pre-specialization. The latter will be offered in three sections: a literary section preparing for the Faculty of Letters, a juridical section preparing for the Faculty of Law and the Sharia Faculty, and a scientific section preparing for the

Faculty of Science and the future Faculty of Medicine. This total reconversion of the programs and system of instruction will draw heavily on the experience of private secondary schools in the Arabization of modern disciplines. Beginning in October, 1959, a year of further training was made available to those finishing the secondary cycle in order to prepare them for work at the level of the University of Rabat. This additional year is not required for students enrolling in the Sharia Faculty. After a four-year transitional period, the additional year of training is not expected to be needed, and it is planned that a *baccalauréat* will be awarded at the successful conclusion of six years of secondary studies.

At the highest level, it is intended to create a Sharia Faculty in which Islamic subjects, the history of religion, and comparative law will be studied, and to integrate this highest level with the University of Rabat.

In this program of reform, priority is being given to the introduction of scientific subjects and foreign languages. The major problem is the provision of qualified staff. Beginning in October, 1959, training courses for primary teachers in traditional schools were offered at centers of Islamic studies in Fez, Tetuan, Meknes, and Marrakech, each accommodating about 200. At the same time, a general training and pedagogy center was opened in Rabat, with forty students. To enable modern teaching methods to be used, it is intended to reduce the average number of children per class from more than 100 to 50. Because of the serious difficulties in finding science teachers for the secondary level in the traditional schools, students at the University of Rabat are being encouraged to take up teaching careers; increased teaching salaries and the provision of a course in Arabic technical terminology are among the inducements. The latter is intended to enable Moroccan students who have received scientific training in French to teach scientific subjects in Arabic in secondary schools. These teachers, together with Moroccan teachers with degrees from schools of the Middle East, will so far as possible replace teachers recruited from other Arab countries.

Education Outside the Normal System

The expansion of the educational system that is taking place still leaves many Moroccans who have had little or no schooling and are thus shut off from better jobs, participation in a wider and more varied cultural life, or even learning better ways of performing ordinary household or farming chores. The differences in opportunities and attitudes that result from this state of affairs inevitably slow the unification of Morocco's peoples and are also unacceptable to those who are attempting to bring about a better life for all Moroccans. A wide range of activities is being undertaken to bridge this gap.

One of the largest and most immediate tasks is to provide for those children between six and fourteen who, despite the great expansion of primary education, are not yet able to go to school. Their number is estimated to be more than a million. For them, a stopgap system of education has been created that provides twenty hours of instruction a week for four years. It is not expected to be necessary beyond October, 1967. Instructors will be drawn from those who have finished primary school or the first year of secondary school. For quarters, the system will use confiscated or sequestrated buildings, barracks no longer in use, buildings given or lent for this purpose, prefabricated buildings, and those that might be built by crews formed of unemployed men. Children of eleven who have never been to school form the first group to be taken into the system. In 1961–62, children of twelve and thirteen will be added. In 1963, when all the seven-year-olds are expected to be received into the regular schools, all other children under eleven who have never attended school will be added to the special system.

At the other end of the scale is the problem of illiteracy among adults. The first great national campaign against illiteracy, which was carried out from April 16 to June 28, 1956, under the patronage of His Majesty Mohammed V, enrolled 300,000 Moroccans of all ages in the villages and countryside as well as the cities. A year later, a second campaign was held, at the end of which 20,000 certificates of literacy were awarded. By this time, a weekly publication entitled *Manar al-Maghreb* was available for the newly literate. Printed in simple classical Arabic that was fully vowelized, it provided a window on the world as well as a means of maintaining proficiency. A particular note of progress was sounded in 1958–59 when 8,000 women and girls acquired literacy through courses taken at the basic-education centers that had been organized. In 1959–60, 760 primary-school teachers volunteered to teach literacy classes as well as their regular classes, and 26,500 adults were enrolled.

In addition, a wide selection of vocational, recreational, and fundamental-education activities are carried on in both urban and rural centers. Instruction in housekeeping, hygiene, civics, care of animals, and food preparation is made available to rural women both in regular classes and in special campaigns in areas where rural centers have not been organized. Workshops in manual crafts and arts and traveling libraries, film shows, art shows, and dramatic productions are also provided.

The New Elite

The urgency with which the expansion and reform of the educational system has been undertaken reflects not only the deep thirst for education but also the need for trained cadres at all levels and the importance that Morocco's political leaders attach to the attainment of national cultural unity. In all the changes being made, the intent is clearly both to modernize and to give education a distinctively Moroccan character. In the attempt to reduce the heterogeneity of the Moroccan population, produce a more harmonious whole, and establish Morocco's place as a bridge between the European and Arab worlds, education is serving as a major instrument of national policy.

The policies being applied by those who are reshaping Morocco's educational system take full note of the country's strong roots in two cultural traditions. It is clearly intended that the students of this and coming generations shall also benefit from these two cultural traditions, although by a synthesis achieved before the material is presented to the student. That the synthesis should be made, that it should be Moroccan in nature and achievement, and that it should be offered to all Moroccans of school age are the guiding principles of the changes taking place. The aim is to mold citizens who are competent to apply modern knowledge and techniques to Morocco's problems, yet who, above all, are Moroccans sharing a common inheritance so that they may build a common future.

Given the limited base from which expansion of the educational system started and the need of other government services for qualified personnel, the provision of teaching staffs has been one of the most difficult to solve. In the eyes of most Moroccans, any deterioration in quality of instruction resulting from rapid expansion is more than balanced by the fact that hundreds of thousands of Moroccan children are now going to school, while before only a fraction of this number were doing so. Moreover, there are larger numbers of students now reaching any given level of attainment than ever before. Nor is the improvement all quantitative. To Moroccan educational planners, there are immeasurable gains from substituting texts in subjects such as civics and history that are written from a Moroccan viewpoint for texts written from a French viewpoint, and still further intangible gains from conducting classes in the national tongue.

Today's elite was formed during the long struggle to restore

Morocco's independence, and it has been shaped as much by that struggle as by the educational opportunities that were available. Their values are at once Western, Islamic, and nationalist, and the system they are creating to produce tomorrow's elite is intended to make a synthesis of these values the common heritage of Moroccans.

—WILLIAM BERRY

3. Tunisia

Capital: Tunis
Population: 3,900,000 (est.)
Area: 48,300 sq. miles
Political status: Independent republic

TUNISIA is an Arab, a Mediterranean, and perhaps only lastly an African country. While the rest of North Africa lay protected behind the barriers of mountains, sand, and an inhospitable seacoast, Tunisia's coastal plains and natural harbors were an open invitation to outside influences. For over six centuries the site of the Carthaginian Empire, Tunisia subsequently became a Roman province, was then ruled briefly by the Vandals, and was later reconquered by the Byzantine Eastern Roman Empire. However, it was the Arab conquest in the latter years of the seventh century that left the most lasting imprint. Arabic civilization came to stay, eventually imposing both the Arabic language and the Islamic religion upon the basically Berber stock.

Although Tunisia experienced the general decline of the Ottoman Empire, the country possessed certain unique qualities that held promise for the future. In the first place, Tunisia enjoyed a degree of homogeneity rare in Africa; there were no great racial, religious, or linguistic differences, and centuries of reasonably settled life along the coastal areas had already created a consistent society. There was a small ruling class of Turkish origin, but there were few great native landowners; a relatively large class of small landholders, artisans, and tradesmen existed in the towns and countryside. Also, Tunisia was a small country with easy internal communication, dominated culturally and politically by its one great urban center and capital, Tunis. (These factors making for Tunisian unity are even stronger today. Communications are much more rapid, the Bedouin—always a factor of instability—are being settled, and the small Turkish ruling class has been absorbed into Tunisian society.)

The First Reformers

The origins of the present Tunisian educational system can be traced to the latter part of the nineteenth-century doldrums, when a group of Tunisian intellectuals set in motion a reformist movement aimed at reinvigorating Tunisian society by blending into it the techniques of an expanding Western Europe. This Tunisian reformist movement, which had parallels in the Ottoman Empire and Egypt, reached its peak in the 1870's under the leadership of Khayr al-Din Pasha, a brilliant Circassian mamaluk who was the Prime Minister for the ruling Bey, Mohammed al-Ṣadiq. During this period, the reformers undertook two major efforts in the field of education: to modernize the Islamic university of Zitouna, and to establish a new secondary school that would furnish cadres for the modern state they hoped to create. It proved impossible to graft a curriculum suited to the modern age onto the traditional framework of Zitouna, but the pilot secondary school, Sadiqi College, set a whole new pattern for the education of Tunisian youth.

In attempting to reform the traditional Islamic teaching of Zitouna, the reformers ran up against strong resistance. At the base of the system of traditional education, which was the only system in existence in Tunisia at the time, was the *kuttab,* or small school usually attached to a mosque and consisting of one master teaching the Koran by rote to a handful of students. Brighter students might make their way from the *kuttab* to Zitouna University or one of its annexes for higher Islamic studies—an education preparing them, and poorly at that, only for a religious position or a spot in the Sharia (Islamic) courts. The government reforms introduced entailed regulation of the curriculum for the first time, establishment of prescribed textbooks, and the addition of optional "modern" studies such as mathematics, architecture, astronomy, and history and geography of the Arab world. As it turned out, the "modern" textbooks prescribed were over three centuries old, and the reform was decidedly superficial. As a result of the rigidity of the Zitouna authorities, the initiative passed to other hands, and the influence of traditional education in molding the present system has been slight.

Sadiqi College, on the other hand, became a pace-setter. Rather than attempting to wedge a few modern studies into the traditional system, the experimenters at Sadiqi adopted the Western pedagogical system almost in toto, though "nationalizing" it to the extent of stressing training in Arabic and Islamic studies. From the beginning, both foreign (French, Italians, and others) and Tunisian teachers were used, and only Islamic and Arabic studies were taught in Arabic. The principle of bilingual (Arabic and French) and bicultural education was continued later in the "Franco-Arab" primary schools set up under the French Protectorate after 1881, and this forms the basis of the present unified national education.

One can hardly overemphasize the influence of Sadiqi College both as a germinal idea and as a major influence on Tunisia's new political society. Situated on a hill in the old Casbah section of Tunis, where it overlooks the Presidence and the major Tunisian ministries, Sadiqi boasts President Bourguiba and eight of the eleven members of the Tunisian cabinet among its alumni. As a molder of political elites, it compares with Gordon Memorial College (now Khartoum University), the American University of Beirut, and École William Ponty in Senegal.

Education Under the French Protectorate

The establishment of the French Protectorate in 1881 temporarily checked these early attempts at modernization from within. Yet, in the long run, the seventy-five-year Protectorate period—which ended with Tunisia's independence in 1956—accelerated and ensured, partly by osmosis and partly by design, the development of a modern secular educational system for Tunisia. Although the French, until the last decade before independence, remained primarily concerned with the education of French children in Tunisia,* the mere existence of so large a European community acted as a yardstick and a spur. There were no specific restrictions against the acceptance of qualified Tunisian students into the existing French schools, but they were at a disadvantage in such schools because of cultural and language inequities. Indeed, actual participation by Tunisians in the French educational system—which was totally integrated with that of France itself—was practically nonexistent at the turn of the century and increased only slowly thereafter. However, by 1954, the year before the end of the Protectorate, roughly one student in every four in the French primary schools was a Tunisian Moslem.

Most Tunisians attending school during this period were in a special Franco-Arab system designed especially for the *indigènes*. Built upon the model of the pre-Protectorate Sadiqi College, this assimilated education was generally of good standard, though below

* There were approximately 80,000 French and 50,000 Italians in Tunisia in 1959.

Table 1
Breakdown of Students Attending French Primary Schools, 1954

Nationality	Number of students
French	29,010
Tunisian Moslem	14,525
Tunisian Jews	12,184
Italian	2,987
Other	575
Total	*59,281*

the completely French system and lacking its scope. In 1930, when most of the present political leadership was in the primary school age groups, only 35,000 Tunisian Moslems, out of a total of 476,000 eligible, were in primary school. The Moslems were especially bitter about their limited access to education in the light of virtually universal primary school attendance among the Europeans and Tunisian Jews.

The traditional Islamic system of education, which was left untouched by the French, accounted for approximately 58,000 students, but the curriculum did not prepare young people for the modern world. Moreover, as knowledge of French became increasingly necessary for advancement in any field, the completely Arabic teaching of Zitouna lost much of its attraction. A vicious circle of declining standards plus the entrance of less qualified students also affected Zitouna's position.

A partial solution to this problem was the Tunisian system of "modern Koranic schools," established by private initiative and funds at the turn of the century. Designed as modern substitutes for the *kuttab,* these schools emphasized, in addition to the usual Arabic and Islamic training, such essentials as arithmetic, history, French, and hygiene. These private schools eventually accounted for 35,000 students, or about one student for every four in the governmental Franco-Arab primary schools.

As in Algeria and Morocco, the French made a more intensive effort to increase Moslem school attendance after World War II and roughly doubled the Tunisian Moslem primary- and secondary-school attendance in the last decade of the Protectorate. Thus, figures for attendance for the final year of French control do not accurately reflect the scholastic level of attainment among Tunisians.

Education Since Independence

In March, 1956, newly independent Tunisia inherited a difficult educational challenge. Since only 26 per cent of the total primary-school–age children and 3 per cent of the total secondary-school–age children were actually in classes, it was essential to increase school attendance rapidly without sacrificing the existing high standards of education. To fulfill the Tunisian goal of female emancipation, the disparity between school attendance for girls (11 per cent) and boys (35 per cent) needed correcting. There was also an acute need to unify the disparate systems and standards of the completely French, the "Franco-Arab," the modern Koranic, and the traditional Zitouna schools. Also, there were approximately 3,300 Tunisians in local Catholic schools. There was also a strong impetus to build a bona fide university around the nucleus of the Institut des Hautes Études (established in 1945) and the country's two teacher-training schools (one for men and one for women). The total number of Tunisian Moslems pursuing university studies at the turn of independence was just over 1,000—362 in Tunisia, 500 in France, and about 200 in the Near East. (The 884 students at Zitouna are excluded from this total.)

Within the first year after independence, the Tunisian Government moved energetically to integrate both the modern Koranic schools and the Zitouna annexes into the national school system. It also scored impressive gains in school attendance, raising the total in primary school from 227,000 to 322,000 in the years between 1956 and 1958.

President Bourguiba's Ten-Year Plan

In June 1958, President Habib Bourguiba announced a Ten-Year Plan of educational reform, largely inspired by Minister of Education Mahmud Messadi. The plan embraced the following major points:

A centrally controlled curriculum for all schools, based on the Sadiqi model, was to be established. It was recognized that this would require the release of some 800 traditionally trained teachers deemed unqualified to carry out the new program.

Universal compulsory primary education was to be sought within ten years, involving an average annual increase in primary school attendance of about 50,000 per year.

To overcome the initial limitation of teachers and school facilities, students in the first two grades were to be divided into half-day shifts, and the seventh year of primary education was eliminated.

Without sacrificing the long-run aim of having all primary education in Arabic, a practical compromise was to be adopted temporarily. Education was to be in Arabic for the first two years; from the third through the sixth year, there were to be ten hours of instruction a week in Arabic and fifteen in French.

Secondary education was to be divided into a six-year preparatory program and a three-year intermediate program. The first section would follow the traditional preparatory-school pattern, though with greater emphasis on the natural sciences, and the second would be designed to give a more practical training to those who would not be going on to more advanced studies. Admittance to either type of secondary school would be based on competitive examinations. While it was accepted in principle that a terminal intermediate student who showed great promise could later transfer to the preparatory program, it was anticipated that, even at the end of the ten-year period, only one primary student in three would be able to continue in either terminal intermediate or secondary education.

A new Tunisian university was to be developed from the Institut des Hautes Études.

By its third year, Tunisia's Ten-Year Plan was clearly gaining momentum. The expansion of education at the lower levels is dramatized by the following figures shown in Table 2.

Table 2
Expansion of Tunisian Education

	1958–59 (actual)	1960–61 (planned)	1960–61 (actual)	1968–69 (planned)
Primary school	320,362	428,071	408,758	836,913
Terminal intermediate [a]	7,864	10,119	12,012	36,293
Secondary [b]	15,568	24,840	23,147	93,790
Écoles normales [c]	874		1,193	

[a] Terminal-intermediate training is replacing the former Centers for Professional Training, which were thought to be too elementary. The totals include both the new terminal-intermediate and the remaining classes of the old system.

[b] The totals exclude 3,965 students who had started their secondary education under the old Zitouna system before 1958 and who will be permitted to finish under the same system. Thus the old Zitouna secondary system will disappear completely by 1965.

[c] Projections for the *écoles normales* were not included in the ten-year reform program.

The University of Tunisia was officially established in March, 1960, and now comprises four faculties: the Faculty of Sciences; the Faculty of Letters and Human Sciences, the Faculty of Law and Political and Economic Science, and the Faculty of Islamic and Arabic studies, formerly Zitouna University.

UNIVERSITY OF TUNISIA.

A major breakthrough in higher education is not expected until after 1964, when the products of the expanded secondary-school system will reach university age. Still the record is impressive. The total of just over 1,000 Tunisian Moslems in higher education in 1956 had increased by 1960–61 to about 3,000, of whom almost half were being trained at the University of Tunisia.* A total of 1,361 Tunisians (Moslems and Jews) were pursuing their higher studies abroad on scholarships in 1960–61, as indicated in Table 3, and 100 to 400 non-scholarship Tunisians were also in foreign universities.

With the need to replace former French technicians, the government is also expanding its occupational-training program. This is financed in part by an employer tax, instituted in 1957, amounting to 1 per cent of wages paid. In the first year, this tax brought in some 215,000 dinars (about $500,000) for the Occupational Training Fund. Some training centers are already in operation, and training specialists

* The 1960–61 enrollment of 2,495 in the University of Tunisia included 1,445 Tunisian Moslems, 368 Tunisian Jews, 93 Algerians, 522 French, and 67 others.

Table 3
Tunisian Students on Scholarships Abroad

Country	Total students	Number receiving scholarships from host country	Number receiving scholarships from Tunisian Government
France	1,064	600	464
Lebanon	80		80
Iraq	61	61	
United States	55	55	
Italy	25	25	
Switzerland	24		24
West Germany	17	15	2
Belgium	15	10	5
United Arab Republic	13		13
United Kingdom	6	1	5
Netherlands	1		1
Total	*1,361*	*767*	*594*

are selected from among workers possessing a professional certificate of competency. One hundred and eighty young workers obtained scholarships in 1960 to attend courses in electricity, engineering, and industry in Belgium, France, Switzerland, and Italy. Such scholarship courses are designed to prepare them for supervisory roles. In the agricultural field, too, efforts are being made to spread knowledge and popularize modern concepts.

External Assistance

This bold program of educational reform can be achieved in its entirety only by a happy combination of heroic efforts on the part of the Tunisian Government (in financial terms: 19 per cent of the budget in 1959) plus considerable foreign aid. United States economic aid to Tunisia in the field of education has averaged $2 million to $3 million per year since the plan went into effect, totaling $7 million by early 1961. Most of this has gone for the construction and equipment of schools, especially technical secondary schools. The U.S. Government also participates in the Bourguiba School of Languages, which teaches English to a yearly average of 200 full-time and 400 part-time students.

Another major source of assistance is France, which has furnished some 1,300 French teachers for Tunisian schools and a large number of scholarships to Tunisians for study in France. By the terms of the Tunisian-French cultural agreement of 1959, the French Government not only aids Tunisia in recruiting needed personnel, but also pays approximately 40 per cent of the total salaries and allowances. In addition to the 44 French professors in Tunisian higher education, there were 1,234 French instructors in the primary and secondary schools in 1959–60, distributed as follows: 212 French teachers in secondary schools (or about one for every five Tunisian teachers); 94 French teachers in technical schools (or about one for every eight Tunisian teachers); 928 French teachers in primary schools (or about one for every seven Tunisian teachers).

In addition to the French teachers in the Tunisian national school system, there are more than 1,400 French teachers in the remaining French-operated schools in Tunisia, which continue to exist under intergovernmental agreements. These schools, too, make a contribution to Tunisia's educational needs, since they provide primary and secondary education to some 8,000 Tunisian Moslems and 6,500 Tunisian Jews, as well as to 19,600 children of French citizenship.

The New Elite

The aim of President Bourguiba and the ruling Neo-Destour Party is to make of Tunisia a modern society—intellectually, culturally, and economically. They are convinced that the solid foundation of a modern system of mass education is needed to achieve this aim. "When we attack underdevelopment in all its forms," President Bourguiba said in 1958, "we must return to the source, that is to intellectual backwardness."

Minister of Education Mahmud Messadi personifies in many ways both the educational reforms he has fathered and the "new Tunisian." Like so many others of today's ruling elite, Messadi is bilingual and bicultural (Arabic and French). A graduate of Sadiqi College, he received his university training in France and has spent much of his life in education; he also is an author of note. Conservative opponents cite Messadi as the personification of the alleged rejection by the present regime of its own past. Messadi would insist with equal vigor that the policies he and the Bourguiba Government are carrying out represent the only means of revitalizing, and thus saving, Tunisia's Arabic and Islamic heritage.

Tunisian graduates of secondary and higher education still have little trouble in finding positions commensurate with their training, and to date there has been no problem of an unemployed elite. There is also a healthy move toward the natural sciences, rare in the Arab world. Of the 200 students recently applying for government scholarships, 63 per cent expressed a preference for higher studies in the natural sciences, 20 per cent opted for law, and 17 per cent for *lettres*.

The educated Tunisian of today is inclined to be more rational and skeptical in his outlook than his father. A recent study of Tunisian youth summarized the problem, "Ask a one-armed youth how he lost his arm, and he will no longer reply: 'It is written,' but 'It was my fault, I did not pay attention.' . . . Ask a youth what he thinks about heaven, for example, and he will answer you with a smile: 'We are told that to be Moslems is the means of going to paradise. Of course we are Moslems. If paradise exists, we will go. If it does not exist, nothing has been lost.' But ask him for information on politics or sports, and he will give it to you with reasoned argument and conclusions." *

But the search for a new Tunisian identity is still far from complete and there are many signs of a society in transition. The youth's newly learned and newly accepted idea of companionate marriage, based on mutual selection through courtship, does not accord with either the traditional pattern of arranged marriages or the lower educational level of most Tunisian women. The often-read criticism in student newspapers against *embourgeoisement* indicates a youth in revolt against the old but still groping for an understanding of the new.

Still, in sum, these manifestations, rather than illustrating any major problems, seem instead to show the extent to which the educated Tunisian is thinking—for better or worse—in terms of modern concepts of state and society.

—LEON CARL BROWN

* "La Jeunesse Tunisienne," *Revue de L'Institut des Belles Lettres Arabes,* 2nd trimester, 1956.

4. Libya

Capitals: Tripoli and Benghazi
Population: 1,099,889 (1954 census)
Area: 680,000 sq. miles
Political status: Independent monarchy

THE Greeks gave the name Libya to the whole of known Africa, and the appellation remains today for the Arab kingdom that was the first nation on this continent to gain its independence after World War II. About 90 per cent of the territory is desert, and Libya claims the distinction of being the most sparsely settled nation on earth—two people per square mile. The 1954 census revealed a total population of 1,099,889, of which 738,000 were in Tripolitania province, 291,000 in Cyrenaica, and the rest scattered throughout Fezzan. The 1954 census credited Tripoli, Libya's largest city, with a population of 129,728, but the local chamber of commerce and industry claims that the figure has since risen to 180,000. Only nine Libyan towns have 5,000 or more inhabitants, and the country's border regions —adjoining Egypt, Sudan, Chad, Niger, Algeria, and Tunisia—are virtually unsettled.

In ancient times, Tripoli was known as Oea, a Phoenician capital founded around 700 B.C. Perhaps the Berbers were already on hand to meet them—more than likely in combat. The Phoenicians and Greeks were succeeded by the Romans who ruled from 146 B.C. until the middle of the fifth century A.D. The notorious Vandals made their way to North Africa in 428–29 A.D. A couple of decades later they reached Libya, which they dominated until 533 A.D., when it became a possession of the Byzantines for over 110 years. During the expansionist rule of the Caliph 'Umar al-Khattab, Cyrenaica was occupied, in 642 A.D., by the great Arab conqueror Omar ibn al-'As, and the province remained largely in Arab hands until 1517. There was a brief incursion of Normans from 1145-1160. Then the Spaniards captured and held Tripoli from 1510 to 1528; Emperor Charles V gave Tripoli and Malta to the Knights of the Order of St. John of Jerusalem (Knights of Malta) in 1528, and they held on to Tripoli until they were ousted by the Turks in 1553. The Turks remained in possession until 1911, except for the Karamanli interregnum, 1711–1835.

Italy began its conquest of Libya in 1911, and it continued until the defeat of the Axis armies in Libya in January, 1943. Between 1943 and independence in 1951, Libya was administered for the United Nations by Britain and France.

Education Before Independence

During the Turkish period, the schooling for boys was religious in character, mainly in classes attached to mosques. No public education was provided for women. Shortly after the turn of the century, in 1904, the Roman Catholic Church opened French and Italian schools for boys; nuns operated schools for girls. In these schools Italian and French were the principal languages. Arabic was in a subordinate role. An arts and crafts school, primarily for the benefit of orphans, was inaugurated at about the same time.

During the first decade of Italian rule, education suffered gross neglect. Dramatic improvements came during the regime of Governor Count Volpi in the 1920's, when spacious, high-ceilinged, well-equipped schools were built, mainly under the direction of the Roman Catholic Church. In 1935, a school of higher Islamic studies was founded. It offered a three-year junior course and a four-year senior program. The senior program had two divisions, one for training of teachers and the other for the preparation of judges, administrators, and religious officials. Admission was restricted to twelve-year-old boys who had completed the fifth year of primary school. In the same year, the curriculum of the Arab arts and crafts school was broadened to provide primary training followed by a four-year vocational course in carpentry, pottery, leatherwork, fashioning of brass, tailoring, shoemaking, and bookbinding. Also, Sidi Masri, a suburb of Tripoli, had an agricultural school.

In 1936, twenty-five Arab girls who had completed primary training in the Italian schools enrolled in a new training center for nurses, which offered three-year courses taught by physicians specializing in eye diseases, internal ailments, first aid, and midwifery. About ten girls succeeded in completing their courses, passed the examinations, and received diplomas.

Despite the ravages of war, the British administration managed to open schools in October, 1943, for boys aged six to thirteen. Instruction was in Arabic and Italian. Nine primary schools for girls were opened, but their total attendance was under 1,000. Teachers in these schools were those who had completed the fifth grade in the Italian primary school, and the curriculum consisted of the usual primary subjects, with the addition of the Koran, handwork, embroidery, and drawing.

In 1948, teacher-training centers for men and women were opened in Tripoli. The Women Teachers' Training College was founded in 1950 with a registration of twenty-seven. Parents had to be convinced before girls could be encouraged to enroll, for the college represented not only increased educational opportunity but also a new way of living. The girls were stimulated to think for themselves, to care for their clothing and for their persons, and to appreciate the value of domestic work and honest toil. In the next year, enrollment almost doubled; during the tenth year of the college's existence, enrollment had reached roughly fifteen times the initial registration. The enormous building now housing the classes of prospective women teachers in downtown Tripoli is a far cry from the college's humble beginning in five rooms.

There was an almost total disregard of Libyan cultural, linguistic, and religious interests during the period of Italian tutelage. With the advent of Fascism, the indifference to local interests that had characterized early Italian rule was replaced by hostility and contempt for the Arabs and their language.

Education in Independent Libya

The framers of the Libyan Constitution would not let their vision be dimmed by the fact that not one Libyan in ten had ever attended any school. Universal, free, compulsory education on the primary level for all the people of Libya was set forth as a national goal in the Constitution, and Articles 28, 29, and 30 called for the expansion of educational facilities. Libyan authorities point out that they have now progressed two-thirds of the way toward the constitutional aim of instruction for every child. They believe that the quantitative emphasis must now give way to greater concern for quality. Better-qualified teachers are being trained and recruited, and the goals of education are being raised. One child in three or four should go on from primary school to preparatory (junior high) school; one in seven of the initial enrollees should go on to secondary school or to a technical- or vocation-training center.

At the top of the administrative ladder is the Minister of Education, advised by a Higher Council of Education. The minister presides over the federal department responsible for dealing with the educational needs of the nation; prepares and produces textbooks and instructional materials for grades one through twelve and for the agricultural, commercial, and vocational schools; and coordinates with the Libyan National Commission for UNESCO. Nazirs head the provincial departments of education in Tripolitania, Cyrenaica, and Fezzan. The ministry and the nazirates employ specialists and a corps of inspectors to determine the efficiency of teaching and the suitability of the curricula and textbooks. UNESCO has made contributions to the educational development of Libya by (1) furnishing scholarships for Libyans to study at the Arab States Fundamental Education Center in the United Arab Republic; and (2) through providing teachers of handicrafts, fundamental education, and theoretical subjects.

In 1943, Libya had seventy-two schools with 7,280 pupils. During the first year after independence, 1952–53, there were 234 schools with an attendance of 45,000; over 93 per cent of these pupils were in primary schools. During the ensuing six years, the numbers more than doubled. In 1958–59, there were 524 schools, with 106,000 pupils; the figures for 1960–61 were 667 schools, with an attendance of 109,230 boys and 24,335 girls (a total of 133,565), and with 4,845 teachers. These figures do not include technical and vocational education.

The 1954–55 educational budget came to £1,177,000. Since then, it has almost trebled. A report on Libyan development prepared by a World Bank mission in 1960 estimated that the educational budget should grow to about £5 million (about $14 million) by 1964–65, an expenditure equaling a tenth of the present gross national product. As the report states: "There are few other countries in the world, developed or underdeveloped, in which the proportion exceeds four percent, and it appears to be more commonly in the region of two to three percent." * Currently, the percentage allocations under the educational budget are approximately as follows: salaries of teachers, 41 per cent; school buildings and equipment, 27 per cent; the University of Libya, 10 per cent; teacher-training institutions, 6 per cent; the Mohammed Ali al-Sanusi Religious Institute, 5 per cent; scholarships in foreign countries, 3 per cent; adult education, 2 per cent; and general administration, 6 per cent.

* Report of a Mission organized by the International Bank for Reconstruction and Development, *The Economic Development of Libya* (Baltimore: The Johns Hopkins Press, 1960), p. 252.

The general educational institutions in Libya begin with kindergarten and other pre-primary schools. In 1960–61, Libya had eighteen kindergartens enrolling 836 boys and 984 girls (a total of 1,820) and staffed by forty-nine female teachers. Training continues with six years (initially, it was five), of primary or elementary school. The student may then spend three years each in the preparatory (junior high) and secondary (senior high) schools, and then go on to the University of Libya, which has two constituent colleges in Benghazi and one near Tripoli. Or he may enter vocational and technical centers, which consist of two sections: the intermediate, to which primary-school graduates are admitted, and the senior, which requires completion of the preparatory school for entrance. A third alternative is the Koranic schools, which begin on the pre-primary level and continue through primary, secondary, and higher stages. Plans are being made to enrich the curriculum of the religious institutes by introducing one or more foreign languages, especially English.

Phenomenal progress has been made toward meeting the constitutional objective of universal primary schooling. In 1960–61, there were 558 primary schools attended by 97,561 boys and 22,772 girls (a total of 120,333), with a teaching staff of 3,305 men and 766 women. Many attractive new schools have been constructed. In 1959–60, 50 classrooms were renovated and rehabilitated, and 223 were built.

Notwithstanding the fact that males outnumber females in Libya —the census reported 995 females per 1,000 males in the ten- to nineteen-year-old group and only 860 females per 1,000 males under ten years of age—the school-enrollment statistics on the primary level make it unmistakably clear that equality of educational opportunity for females remains a distant goal. Boys outnumber girls in Libyan schools by more than four to one.

There is a single program of study for all primary students, urban and rural, in the three provinces. The curriculum and textbooks are now identical in both urban and rural areas, but some thought is being given to the preparation of special materials designed to foster the values of rural life in this largely agricultural country. New syllabi are being prepared with this end in view, and school gardens have been started in some localities, but these steps are only a beginning. The production of new textbooks proceeds swiftly under the auspices of the Ministry of Education. At least twenty-five new textbooks were produced in 1959–60. To be masters in their own house, Libyan scholars feel that they must write textbooks indigenous to the nation or face the alternative of being subjected to "cultural colonialism."

School furnishings are generally satisfactory. But laboratories often leave much to be desired, and the undertrained teachers are usually unable to improvise. Many schools have attractive chairs and formica-top desks. Libyans are keenly interested in such sports as soccer and basketball, but playgrounds in the villages and rural areas are inadequate. Some educators have suggested that such work as leveling and marking could be done by the students themselves as a practical lesson in the dignity of labor. The most serious deficiency seems to be in the area of libraries, which tend to be small and very limited, with few books in circulation. Many pupils are being assisted by the Ministry's feeding program, under which a variety of items—including rolls, tuna fish, cheese, dried milk, dates, and date syrup—are made available at the schools. UNICEF and CARE have collaborated in this enterprise.

Curriculum

The curriculum of the primary school consists of Arabic reading and writing, arithmetic, drawing, religion, and sports during the first three years. During the fourth, fifth, and sixth years, the foregoing subjects are continued, with the addition of history, geography, and civics. English was formerly taught in the upper elementary grades but has now been discontinued.

There are seventy-five preparatory or junior secondary schools, with an attendance in 1960–61 of 9,012 boys and 454 girls, a ratio of about twenty to one; they are taught by 456 men and 20 women. The curriculum is composed of religion, Arabic, English, mathematics, physics, history, geography, civics, drawing, and sports.

The three-year senior secondary school has a common curriculum for all students in the first year: Arabic, English, French, religion, chemistry, physics, history, geography, mathematics, Libyan society, drawing, and sports. In the second year, the students elect to follow either a literary or a scientific curriculum during the remainder of their secondary studies. In the literary section, the subjects for both the second and third years are religion, Arabic, English, French, history, geography, philosophy, sociology, physical education, and extra classes in the field of specialization. The scientific program offers religion, Arabic, English, French, mathematics, chemistry, physics, biology, physical education, and extra classes in the field of specialization.

The school term is short—from October to May—but a six-day week is followed, Friday being the "weekend." Total attendance in the sixteen senior secondary schools in 1960–61 was 1,946, consisting of 1,821 boys and 125 girls; there are 226 men and 20 women teachers.

Inordinate importance is attached to examinations in the secondary schools. The marks for all the work done during the term are assessed at only 25 per cent, while the final examination counts 75 per cent. This does not mean that a student may skip classes wholesale during the year and then get through by sitting for the final examination, for only students meeting certain attendance requirements are permitted to sit for the examination. In June, 1961, 395 sat for the final examination in the scientific section, and 311 in the literary one. Of the 706, 24 were girls—17 taking a scientific course and 7 a literary one. About half of the students were expected to pass. Those in the scientific section who receive marks of 67 per cent or higher are given scholarships to study abroad. A student who fails in three subjects must repeat the whole year's work in the subjects in which he is successful as well as in those where he falls short of the mark. If he fails in two subjects, he is permitted to study during the summer and sit for supplementary examinations in them in September. If he fails in one subject, it is disregarded, and he goes on to the next class. But if he fails in the subject for two successive years, he must repeat all the subjects studied during the second year.

Higher Education

Libyan general education attains its summit in the University of Libya. King Idris I contributed his Minar Palace in Benghazi to house the fledgling university, which was established in 1955, began operations in 1956 with the single College of Arts, Letters, and Education, and graduated its first class of thirty students in 1959. In 1960, thirty-eight students completed studies in satisfaction of the requirements for the Bachelor of Arts degree. A College (i.e., faculty) of Commerce and Economics in Benghazi was annexed to the University, and in 1957 a College of Science was opened in the suburb of Tripoli in the Sidi Masri–Miani district. The 1960–61 enrollment figures are found in Table 1.

Table 1
Student Enrollment at the University of Libya, 1960–61

College	Students
College of Arts, Letters, and Education	301
College of Commerce and Economics	311
College of Science	116
Total	*728*

Fifteen of the students attending the University of Libya in 1960–61 were from other Arab states, while the rest were Libyans. Not only is the tuition free, but subsidies are paid to the students. Students who leave their home cities to go to Tripoli or Benghazi are given free board and lodging plus a cash payment of £5 ($14) per month.

The teaching staff of the university is almost exclusively expatriate. The College of Arts, Letters, and Education has one Libyan on a staff of thirty-five; the College of Commerce and Economics has eleven teachers, all foreign; the College of Science has a staff of thirty foreigners, including assistants, demonstrators, etc. As with the secondary schools, the term is very short and is not divided into semesters. No marks are given during the term, and final grades depend on the examinations at the end of the year. Many promising Libyan students would prefer to continue their higher studies abroad, but most of the liberal-arts students and practically all the science students making less than 67 per cent in the secondary-school certificate examinations must either discontinue their schooling or attend the University of Libya.

A technological university under United Nations auspices is planned. For this Institute of Higher Technology, the U.N. Special Fund has agreed to donate $1 million to provide equipment, to pay salaries for some of the foreign teaching staff, and to grant fellowships to train Libyan counterparts. The Libyan Government has undertaken to provide about $2 million for the first five years. The Institute is expected to accept fifty to sixty students per year. Four courses extending up to five years are to be offered in civil engineering (beginning in October, 1962), electrical engineering (October, 1963), mechanical engineering (October, 1963), and food technology (October, 1964). The Libyan Government will furnish the site, buildings, and furniture, and UNESCO is to execute the program. The new institute will complement the nine existing vocational, technical, and agricultural schools with 1,043 students and a teaching corps of 137. A breakdown of teachers and students in these schools follows: There are two commercial schools, with 344 regular and 75 advanced students and 46 teachers; two technical or industrial schools, with 227 regular and 27 advanced students and 44 teachers; two agricultural schools, with 199 students and 22 teachers; one handicrafts school, with 30 students and 6 teachers; one applied engineering school, with 67 students and 9 teachers; one fundamental education center, with 74 special students and 10 teachers.

In 1960–61, 136 Libyans were studying on scholarships in European and American universities, while 68 were enrolled in universities of the neighboring United Arab Republic. Of those students in Europe

University of Libya.

and America, approximately 25 per cent were in medicine, another 25 per cent in engineering, 9 per cent (a disturbingly low percentage), in agriculture, 11 per cent in pharmacy, 7 per cent in science, 7 per cent in law, 6 per cent in dentistry, 4 per cent in literary studies, 3 per cent in commerce, and the remaining 3 per cent in miscellaneous fields. In Egypt, thirty were studying to become physicians, pharmacists and veterinarians; twenty-five were studying science, agriculture and commerce; and thirteen were enrolled in religious studies. A number of nonscholarship students are also sent abroad to study by their fathers, who tend to place greater emphasis on commerce and even less on agriculture than the foregoing figures indicate.

Foreign-Operated Schools

Foreign schools have proliferated, especially in Tripolitania. In 1960–61, there were twenty private foreign schools, with 400 teachers and 10,159 pupils. Tripoli College, an interesting Anglo-Libyan cooperative venture, opened in 1957 with 96 boys and girls and now has about 400 students; it hopes eventually to offer instruction from kindergarten through the secondary level. A Franco-Libyan school opened in Tripoli in 1956. More recently, Shell Oil opened a Dutch school. The American petroleum-exploration companies operate a school in the Nuara-Georgimpopoli district just outside Tripoli. Wheelus Air Base has schools for dependents from kindergarten through high school, and there is a British Army School, but such schools have little real bearing on Libyan education. The numerous church-oriented Italian schools exert a waning influence; in 1957, there were eighty-four of these schools, with about 9,000 pupils.

Teacher Training

There are six government-operated teacher-training centers for boys and two for girls, with a total enrollment of 2,395 and a teaching force of 176 in 1960–61. Girl students numbered 607, mostly in Tripoli, compared with 1,788 boys. The largest of the training colleges, in Tripoli, was started in October 1950. In the first four years of operation, students were admitted by examination after completion of the fifth grade in the primary school and were presented diplomas as teachers after completing four years at the college. The standard of admission was raised in 1955–56 with the institution of the requirement that entrants must first have received the certificate for finishing the sixth primary grade. The graduates of men's and women's teacher-training colleges are considered qualified to teach in the primary schools. Unfortunately, some of the better-qualified women graduates are prevented from actually becoming teachers because of their families' traditional attitudes. Even so, the training is not wasted as most of the young women are destined to become mothers. The dramatic rise in attendance by girls in the primary schools in recent years can be expected to produce a much greater demand for girls' preparatory schools and concomitantly for more Libyan teachers with better training.

As late as 1958–59, about 90 per cent of the preparatory- and secondary-school teachers were non-Libyan. It is currently estimated that there are 75 foreign teachers in the primary grades and approximately 633 in preparatory, secondary, vocational, and other training schools. The proportion of Libyan teachers will gradually increase. However, constantly expanding enrollment will for a long time absorb most of the newly qualified Libyans. Education for all remains a task of gargantuan proportions. In Fezzan, for example, the number of students has increased sevenfold in the last eight years, and there is a teaching force of 299. However, fewer than a third of these teachers (83), graduated from teachers' colleges or secondary schools; 15 are preparatory (junior high) graduates; 50 hold primary-school certificates. The rest did not finish even the primary school.

Adult Education

An early U.N. report set forth the view that it would be unrealistic to attempt to reduce the rate of illiteracy in Libya and that efforts should be accordingly confined to preventing it from spreading. Fortunately, the Libyan authorities disregarded this defeatist notion. Through the extrapolation of census statistics, it is possible to estimate illiteracy in the general population of Libya in 1954 at 91 per cent and the percentage of illiterate women at about 98 per cent. These are not precise calculations, but they are adequate for indicating the immensity of the problem.

The fact that 11,412 students are now enrolled in junior and senior high schools in Libya means that some headway has been made in the direction of cutting down this illiteracy. Perhaps two-thirds of the children aged six to twelve now attend school. The percentage figures relating to school attendance must, however, be approached with caution because of the wide age distribution. It is not unusual to find a twenty-year-old boy in the first year of secondary school.

In 1960–61, there were 131 centers for the instruction of adults on the primary level; these centers reach about 10,000 students. In Tripoli and Benghazi, secondary-school studies are taught by 142 teachers to

1,072 students who are called "evening men" (or "nighters") because of their inability to be present at the regular morning classes. These young adults are eager to learn but are often defeated by fatigue. The general standard of work and output is very low; the percentage of failures is correspondingly high. The evening classes tend to start a couple of months later than the regular ones; consequently, there is a mad scramble to "get through" the syllabus. The burden of a full course of studies on top of a full-time job is exhausting for the students. A unit arrangement, making part-time study possible, would increase prospects of success although it would give rise to administrative difficulties. The adult-education program is noteworthy for its excellent objectives, but the attendance records are not to be taken as proof of solid achievement. Its fundamental defect is that it is not tailored to meet the needs, interests, life situations, or convenience of adults. It is questionable whether the adult-education program has made a perceptible dent in Libyan illiteracy, but it has encouraged thousands of Libyans to keep on studying.

Islamic Education

In 1958–59, there were 21,946 pupils in Libyan Koranic schools, but their studies consisted largely of recitation of Koranic verses. In the same year, there were several religious institutes containing three primary sections with thirty-five teachers and 624 pupils, and three secondary sections with nineteen teachers and 273 pupils. The Muhammad Ali al-Sanusi Religious Institute had only three teachers and ten students, but it appears to be undergoing considerable expansion under capable direction.

Attitudes of the Educated

The great weight accorded to examination-determined marks tends to confuse the symbol with reality, to place grades and diplomas above learning. A bank clerk reflected an all too common attitude when he refused to attend English classes on the ground that he had already received his certificate from the secondary school. Intellectual curiosity remains a rare phenomenon—the individual search for truth and independent thinking are largely alien concepts to those accustomed to learning by rote.

The World Bank Mission questioned the overemphasis on quantity at the expense of quality, on general education rather than technical and vocational training, on education for urban rather than for country life. The Mission also expressed concern about the heavy migration from village to city among primary school graduates and the inclination to seek white-collar jobs in disdain for manual work. The Libyans in authority are aware of the educational problems they face, as attested by these remarks at the Geneva Conference on Public Education, July, 1960:

> Initially it was necessary to set admission requirements low, but with the development of educational facilities, measures are under consideration to raise the standard so that prospective teachers should have at least nine years in ordinary schooling before entering a training college. Further, programs of Rural Teacher Training are being separated from those of urban teachers and transferred wherever possible to agricultural schools and Vocational Training Centers in the three provinces. Although the course of study in rural teachers' training would follow the general three-year curriculum for other primary school teachers, special emphasis would be given to agricultural and other rural subjects. A program of in-service training augumented by summer teachers' institutes is also being organized. To maintain standards of teaching, a selected number of rural inspectors would be appointed.

—BAHIA F. GULICK

5. Sudan

Capital: Khartoum
Population: 11,650,000 (1961 est.)
Area: 967,498 sq. miles
Political status: Independent republic

FOR a country as vast and diverse as the Sudan, popular education is a complex and expensive matter. In area, it is larger than all of the NATO countries of Europe combined. Geographically, it encompasses half a dozen distinct segments, of which the most strikingly different are the sparsely populated Sahara desert of the north and west, where most of the population are nomads wandering in search of water for their camels and goats; the fertile lands adjoining the two Niles, where the country's vital cotton crop and its intellectual life flourish; and the forests and papyrus swamps of the south, inhabited by a complex of separatist, largely pagan tribal societies.

There were 10,262,536 people in the Sudan when the last census was taken, in January, 1956. Of these, over two-thirds were Arabic-speaking Moslems living in the northern and central sector. From this group—products of Sudanese intermarriage with periodic waves of Arab immigrants since 700 A.D.—comes the country's intellectual and governing elite. However, south of the 12th parallel, which is more literally the *bilad al-Sudan* ("land of the blacks"), life has only just begun to change from a centuries-old pattern, as a result of the government's intensified efforts to introduce Arabic and the Arabized culture of the north to an agglomeration of seminomadic groups whose cultures and thirty-two separate languages and about 250 dialects are allied to those of Central Africa.

Bringing the South into the Fold

Because of the threat to the Sudan's nationhood implicit in its religious, cultural, linguistic, and political heterogeneity, all Sudanese governments since independence in 1956 have given high priority to the expansion of educational opportunities and the standardization of the syllabus for all areas of the country. It is the consensus of Sudanese national planners that political unity must be protected, for the long run, by the gradual establishment of a common language, a common cultural identity, and—many believe—a common religion.

The government took a controversial step toward this end in April, 1957, when it announced its decision to nationalize the Christian mission schools operating in the three southern provinces. Under British rule, 274 Roman Catholic schools and a smaller number of Protestant missions had done virtually all of the educating in the south. Although British officials made a good case for their position that the reason for this dependence on missionary schools was lack of funds and indigenous teaching staff, Sudanese nationalists were convinced that it was also part of a nefarious "divide and rule" policy. The truth probably lies somewhere between. Two specific aspects of the mission school system hastened official action—the conviction that the missions were more concerned with conversions than with literacy, and the increasing emphasis that missionaries were placing on the institutionalization of local vernacular languages by transliterating them into Latin script. However, the official justification for the reforms introduced in 1957 was that the mission schools—in contrast to parochial and other private schools in Europe and the United States—were offering a standard of education below that provided in state schools.

Minister of Education Sayyid Ziada Arbab reported on the progress of educational plans for the southern provinces in a public address in October, 1959:

> Two years or more have elapsed since we started taking over the schools from the missionary societies. . . . Although the taking over of schools has absorbed the greater part of the time of the office in the southern provinces, some expansion has been effected. In intermediate, including technical education, the number of schools has nearly doubled. The number of elementary schools has also increased considerably and the boys of the village schools have therefore found a chance to carry on with their education. The Ministry is doing its best in girls' education and it is hoped that Meridi Girls' Intermediate School will play a leading part in this respect.

> The Office of Education still continues its efforts in two main areas, Arabicization and unification of the syllabuses. . . . Arabic is now taught in all the elementary, intermediate, and secondary schools. It has become a major subject in all the examinations. The next step is to use Arabic as a medium of instruction in more schools every year. . . . The introduction of Arabic in village schools in the very near future seems to be possible as a result of the founding of two teacher training centers at Tonj and Malakal. More than a hundred potential teachers are being trained to be able to teach in Arabic and to teach part of the national syllabus. These teachers will be offered the opportunity of teaching in the north for one year in order that they may be able to use Arabic in all forms of the schools.
>
> Our second aim is the unification of the two systems so that all the children—northern or southern—may be offered the same opportunities and so that they may have the same school atmosphere. To achieve the two aims, the Ministry has entrusted to a committee of masters, led by an expert in languages, the task of writing booklets in the different southern dialects but in the Arabic alphabet, as a first step toward the teaching of Arabic. Some of these booklets have already been written and published. We have also sent some masters to America to specialize in the science of languages, and on their return they will carry on that work.

The long-standing hostility of the southerner to his northern brother, in part a product of periodic military pacification over the years and the attitude of superiority often taken by northern administrators, is only one of several human problems involved in this enormous task of digesting the south. Officials have been particularly disturbed by the charge (articulated especially in Catholic publications) that nationalization is a form of religious persecution. The government denies this charge, pointing out that the mission churches are open, and that there is no intent to thwart the missions in their religious work. Courses in Christianity are still taught by missionaries in the government schools for children requesting it, and the only personnel change in many nationalized schools has been the addition of a government-appointed director. But the syllabus, emphasizing the historical aspects, is now provided by the government and the relationship between the missionaries and potential converts is clearly more circumscribed than in the past. The official day of rest in the south is now Friday, as in the rest of the country, rather than Sunday as heretofore. There are at present about 300,000 converted Christians (and a much smaller number of Moslems) out of a total population of more than 3 million in the southern provinces.

Changes Since Independence

Sudanese criticisms of Britain's educational policies in the Sudan were largely confined to pace and spread. Certainly there has been no significant break with British methodology since independence. In the established school system of the north, educational aims and techniques remain closely patterned on those introduced by Britain before independence. A number of British teachers are still employed in the state system, particularly as English, mathematics, and science teachers at the upper levels, and the demand for them consistently exceeds the supply. All teaching in the Sudan is now supposed to be in Arabic at the elementary level, although shortage of qualified staff has necessitated some delay in enforcing this requirement in the south. English is introduced as a compulsory subject (for ten hours per week) at the intermediate level, and is the language of instruction at the secondary and university levels. Although the primary educational objective in the first five years of independence has been consolidation and unification of the system, there has also been a concerted effort to create more schools to meet rising population needs and to ensure better-trained staff. In 1957, the government set in motion a $20 million five-year school-expansion and consolidation program, which was above and beyond the annual budgetary appropriation for routine educational costs (now running from 16 to 20 per cent of the national budget).

Of an estimated 1.6 million Sudanese children of school age, some 270,000 (or nearly 17 per cent) were officially recorded as attending school in 1960. However, this figure is somewhat misleading since a third of these are outside the state educational system in more than a thousand supervised but unaccredited subgrade village schools that give only rudimentary instruction in reading, writing, arithmetic, and (in the north) the Koran. These schools have a dual origin: the traditional *khalwa* religious schools of the Islamic north, and the Christian village schools in the southern provinces. The *khalwa* took boys and girls at the age of seven for three years of Islamic studies; they now are operated by municipal and rural councils, with subsidies up to 40 per cent of total operating costs from the central government. In the southern provinces, the village schools were run by missionary societies until 1957, when the government took them over as part of its general nationalization program. It is the present intent of the government that these village schools will be attached to municipal and rural councils as soon as these institutions develop. Most of the students attending such schools are seven to eleven years old and will not have the opportunity to go on to elementary schools. In addition to budgetary support, the government provides facilities for the training of subgrade teachers and sets minimum standards for staff. At the present time, a subgrade headmaster must have completed junior secondary (intermediate) school, after which some additional teacher training is given to him at different annual periods in selected centers. As funds and qualified teachers become available, these schools are being brought under the government school system and elevated to elementary status. This upgrading of village schools to proper elementary schools is being given priority over the opening of new elementary schools.

The accredited public curriculum begins at the age of seven and continues for twelve years through elementary, intermediate, and secondary schools. As of January, 1960, official sources noted 842 elementary, 120 intermediate, 15 secondary, and 34 religious institutes within the government system, as well as 157 nongovernment schools supervised by the Egyptian Education Mission and various Christian groups. Each of the three levels is a complete unit in itself, however, because it is recognized that only the minority will be able to continue on to the next higher level. Rote learning is perhaps overemphasized at the elementary level, and there is a pronounced Anglo-Saxon literary bias in the intermediate schools. School-leaving examinations at each of the three levels are formal, centrally controlled, and closely patterned on their British counterparts. The Sudan School Certificate for secondary-school graduates is jointly issued by the University of Cambridge Local Examinations Syndicate and the Sudan Examinations Council.

Technical Education

Students who have completed four years of elementary school are eligible to choose either academic or technical intermediate schools. When British educators first introduced the concept of technical education, there was considerable initial resistance to the *warsha,* or workshop school. But this was rapidly overcome, and the twelve technical intermediate schools in operation by 1960 had 1,413 pupils and long waiting lists. Some 2,000 persons also attend night courses at the intermediate level. The graduates of these largely self-contained schools—trained in carpentry, metal work, practical drawing, workshop technology, science, and general subjects—fill one of the most vital needs in the Sudan's developing economy, and the government's aim is to establish technical institutes in all provinces.

An intensive three-year post-intermediate course in trade is available to boys leaving the technical intermediate schools who are not academically suited to proceed to the secondary level at the Khartoum Technical Institute. These trade courses, now available at four centers (with a total enrollment in 1960 of 277), include machine-shop engineering, motor-vehicle mechanics, electrical installation, carpentry and joinery, furniture making, bricklaying, and plumbing. Three days a week are spent in the workshops and the remaining three school days are devoted to mathematics, drawing, trade, science, and technology. At the end of the three-year course, students sit for the internationally recognized Intermediate City and Guilds Certificate in their particular trade.

In addition to responsibility for the various technical intermediate schools, the Khartoum Technical Institute offers five-year courses at the secondary level to boys successfully passing the school-leaving examination at the intermediate technical level. Courses leading to an Ordinary National Certificate award (or, after a sixth and seventh year, to a Higher National Certificate) are offered in mechanical, electrical, and civil engineering, textile manufacture, and commerce. All examinations at this level are parallel with those used in the United Kingdom, and the results obtained are gained in direct competition with British students. The Higher National Certificate is considered equivalent to that of a University Pass Degree in the subjects taken. This policy of tying Sudanese technical education closely to British models is designed, according to Minister of Education Arbab, to remove all doubt as to the standards of the country's educational system at a time when "so much heavy responsibility will rest upon their shoulders in the technical development of the country."

In 1959–60, there were 351 students enrolled at Khartoum Technical Institute, working with a teaching staff of ninety-six. Here students receive a general education in English, history, geography, Arabic, and religion, as well as specialized theoretical and practical training in one of three schools: Engineering, Fine and Applied Art, or Commerce. There is also a Department of Further Education which offers evening and other part-time technical and academic studies designed to raise the standards of skill and craftsmanship of tradesmen, or to help those whose general education is incomplete. Similar night courses for employed people are held in technical schools in the provinces.

Secondary Education (Academic)

The aim of the secondary academic schools is, according to official Sudanese statements, "to meet the requirements of life in towns and to serve as a feeder to the university." By 1960, there were thirteen government secondary schools for boys and two for girls, with a total enrollment of 5,603. Of the students completing government intermediate-level schools, 31 per cent went on to secondary schools in that year. All the government secondary schools are now supervised by Sudanese headmasters, although a number of expatriate (mostly British) teachers are employed as staff.

A relatively large roster of private schools at the secondary level also helps to bolster the Sudanese educational pyramid at a point which is often weak in African countries. There were 4,980 boys and 1,319 girls (not all Sudanese, of course) in privately operated secondary schools in Sudan in 1960. Outstanding among these were the Khartoum Egyptian Secondary School, Coptic College, Comboni College, the Catholic Mission Sisters School, the Anglican Cathedral's Unity High School for Girls, the American Mission School in Khartoum North, the Ahfad Schools, and Beit al-Amana. (There were also 4,949 girls and 13,316 boys in private intermediate schools, and 4,016 boys and 3,944 girls in private elementary schools in 1960.)

Education for Girls

Efforts to introduce education for Sudanese girls met strong resistance in the early years of British rule, but the demand now far outpaces the supply of the required separate facilities and teachers. In 1924, there were only 5 elementary schools for girls; by 1945, there were nearly 100; and by 1958 there were 213 elementary schools and 22 at the intermediate level. In 1960, official figures showed 42,935 girls in government elementary schools (as compared with 116,998 boys); 3,427 in intermediate schools (as compared with 18,794 boys); and 490 in the two secondary schools for girls at Khartoum and Omdurman (as compared with 5,113 boys). There were more than 10,000 girls in private schools in 1960, but a sizable percentage of these were not Sudanese.

Girls who have completed their secondary education with suitable records may attend either the University of Khartoum, the Khartoum Branch of Cairo University, one of the two teacher-training schools for women, or the three-year Nursing College. There were fifty-two women students entered at the University of Khartoum in 1960 and thirty at the Khartoum Branch of Cairo University. In rural areas, the government's schools of midwifery have had an educational triumph in overcoming local prejudices. There are now at least 1,000 trained midwives in the country.

Another potentially important development in women's education in recent years is the creation of a corps of sixty to seventy "Women

Guides," trained teachers seconded from the Ministry of Education to work on a pilot village-improvement project under the auspices of the Community and Social Development Projects section of the Gezira Board. These women, who are graduates of Sudanese teacher-training schools, have been additionally trained (with some initial help from UNESCO) at Wad Medani to work with women in the Gezira villages in alleviating illiteracy and improving health and child care. Eventually, it is planned to extend this pilot project to other areas of the country.

Teacher Training

Training of Sudanese teachers, publication of educational texts, and the testing of teaching materials for their suitability to local Sudanese conditions and the coordination of syllabi are centered at Bakht-er-Ruda Institute, seventy miles south of Khartoum, and its two affiliated schools at Dilling and Shendi. This unique institution, which celebrated its twenty-fifth anniversary in 1959, has received widespread praise from visiting educators for its experimental work based on sound educational principles. Originally created in 1934 to train elementary school masters for rural areas, Bakht-er-Ruda now encompasses intermediate, secondary, and agricultural education as well, and is playing the key role in establishing procedures for the Sudanization of education in the south. All training of intermediate teachers is concentrated in Bakht-er-Ruda, but there are seven centers for training elementary school teachers (four for men and three for women) and three for subgrade teachers.

Religious Education

Religious (i.e., Islamic) education in Sudan is supervised by the Department of Religious Affairs. Three levels of government-operated instruction are offered (for boys only): intermediate, secondary, and higher Islamic schools. Boys who finish their elementary schooling in secular government schools can enter the four-year intermediate religious school, after which they may go on to a four-year secondary course. Higher Islamic studies are centered in one institution in Khartoum.

There were twenty-eight government-operated intermediate religious schools in 1960 with 4,316 pupils and six such secondary schools with a total of 1,289 students. Another 284 older boys were taking higher Islamic studies at the government institute in Khartoum. In addition, another 2,000 boys were attending government-subsidized private religious schools and 1,500 were in private non-subsidized religious schools.

Adult Education

In 1956, it was estimated that only 23 per cent of Sudanese males and 4 per cent of Sudanese females were literate. Adult education, which was introduced into the Sudan in 1939, is now being carried on in every province, with primary emphasis on increasing literacy. The method being used in the provincial campaigns is the American one of "each one teach one." Special teaching booklets employing the Laubach approach are used, and follow-up reading, comprising both books and a monthly magazine, is supplied to the new literates. According to official figures, some 130,000 adults have learned to read and write through this literacy campaign since World War II. A number of voluntary organizations also are active in the field of adult education.

The Gezira Scheme, which is in a sense the social laboratory of the Sudan, employs twelve full-time district education officers in the adult field as well as a superintendent of women's education. Here the emphasis is on community development, public health, and other larger issues. Gezira women study primarily cooking, sewing, and home hygiene; but the first literacy classes for women were opened in 1960.

There is still only one major public library in the Sudan, in Omdurman, but some town councils have small reading rooms and there are ten specialized reading rooms open to the public, including those of the United States Information Agency, the British Council, Sudan Railways, and the Antiquities Service.

Higher Education

Sudan's highest academic institution is the University of Khartoum, which evolved through several stages out of the old Gordon Memorial College. Gordon College, established as a primary school in 1902, was raised to secondary level in 1913, and to the post-secondary level in 1938. By 1947, the academic standard of the institution was recognized by the University of London, and in 1951 it was combined with the historic Kitchener Medical School to become a University College granting degrees jointly with London. In 1956 it was raised to full university status and qualified to grant its own degrees and diplomas in medicine, arts (Arabic, history, English, geography, philosophy), economics, science (pure and applied mathematics, physics, chemistry, botany, and zoology), agriculture, engineering, veterinary science, and law. The University of Khartoum is financed partly by the government and partly by the interest from a £1 million endowment given by the British Government in recognition of the part played in World War II by the Sudanese people.

There were 140 members of the academic staff at the University in 1960, of whom 35 were Sudanese; the remainder were expatriates from the U.K., the United Arab Republic, the United States, Lebanon, Sweden, Italy, Yugoslavia, Holland, Canada, Germany, Czechoslovakia, New Zealand, Ceylon, and India. In 1960, the Academic Secretary toured American academic institutions in an effort to fill some twenty-five vacancies. Sayyid Nasr al-Haj Ali, who became the first Sudanese Vice Chancellor and operating head in 1958, was formerly Director of Education for Sudan.

Between the 1930's and the military coup of 1958, the Sudan's one institution of higher learning was also the country's principal debating society. Here political lines were vigorously drawn and issues discussed with passion and conviction. Indeed, the first nationalist party, the Graduates' Congress, was formed around a nucleus of Gordon College graduates in 1937. When the military regime was established by *coup d'état* in 1958, political activity was officially banned from the campus, and the university became, at least superficially, a model of aseptic academic diligence. Under its placid exterior, however, the University of Khartoum remained as intensely political as before. Within a few months after the 1958 coup, the outlawed political parties were again flourishing subversively on the campus. Protest demonstrations against various government policies and decisions were occurring with increasing frequency by the academic year 1960–61. In November, 1960, for example, almost the entire student body signed a petition to the Council calling for the repeal of the rule prohibiting student participation in political affairs. Student demonstrations also marred the visit of U.A.R. President Gamal Abdel Nasser to Khartoum in the same month. Adding fuel to the government's concern about the atmosphere of growing unrest on the campus was the fact that the memorandum presented to General Ibrahim Abboud on November 29, 1960, by eighteen prominent Sudanese requesting a return to civilian rule contained the signatures of two members of the University Council. By the end of 1960, the government had concluded that the university's traditional autonomy must be curtailed.

Thus, on January 18, 1961, the Sudanese Government announced several amendments to the Khartoum University Act of 1956 * which

* The amendments were published in full in the Official Gazette dated December 31, 1960, but this publication was not actually released until January 18, 1961.

University of Khartoum. *(Photo courtesy of Sudan Government.)*

in effect placed the university under close government control. Under the amended Act, the power to appoint the principal administrative official of the University, the Vice Chancellor, has been removed from the University Council and transferred to the Chancellor. The position of Chancellor has customarily been held by the head of state, but the appointment was previously made by the University Council only as a ceremonial gesture. Now President Ibrahim Abboud will hold the position by direct appointment from the Government and the University Council will become an advisory body to him. The composition of the thirty-member University Council has also been changed to ensure a closer cooperation with the government. Under the amended Act, fifteen members of the Council—six from various government departments, eight representatives of the learned professions, and the Vice Chancellor—will be directly appointed by the Chancellor or the Government.* Moreover, all statutes written by the University Council must henceforth be reviewed and approved by the Attorney General.

The only other university-level institution in Sudan is a branch of the University of Cairo established in 1955. By 1960, it had an enrollment of 825 Sudanese men and 30 Sudanese women (out of a total student body of 1,043). There were 43 Sudanese graduates from this institution in 1960, distributed among its three faculties: Arts, Law, and Commerce.

A small percentage of Sudanese secondary graduates have always gone abroad for their university training—chiefly to Egypt and Britain—and almost all advanced work was done in Cairo or London prior to independence. In 1960, according to informal government estimates, there were some 300 Sudanese studying in the U.K., about 150 in the U.S. (of which 135 were on scholarships), 150 in Eastern Europe, 100 in Western Europe, and 100 in Cairo.

The Educated Sudanese

The records of the University of Khartoum and its antecedents (including the Kitchener Medical School) indicate that the University had produced 975 graduates by 1960. There are no records for those Sudanese who have graduated from other universities, but the number from abroad is estimated at 500, making for a probable total of 1,475 university graduates out of a total population of over 11 million.

* Under the original 1956 legislation, the government was represented by six members nominated by various government departments but even then subject to Council approval.

Although most of these university graduates join government service in areas for which they have been specifically trained, and often rise in time to the second echelon of the service, they do not predominate at the policy-making level. None of the Sudan's provincial governors, for example, is a university graduate, and fourteen out of twenty-six key department directors in the central government were not, in early 1961, men with university degrees. One reason for this, some observers suggest, is that Sudanization of the civil service occurred well before independence, and length of service rather than academic qualifications became the criterion.*

The army, which has closely dominated the government of Sudan since 1958, is accused by its civilian critics of being anti-intellectual. Few of the army officers now in controlling positions are university graduates themselves, and traditionally the Military College has drawn the second- and third-level secondary school graduates rather than the honor students. On the other hand, it is noteworthy that the revolutionary government has given high priority to the advancement of education at all levels. The number of students attending the University of Khartoum and the Khartoum Institute of Technology has virtually doubled since 1958, and the number of students going abroad to study is increasing annually. Moreover, with the rise of the army to political prominence and the progressive closing of a range of civilian avenues to professional advancement and political prominence, the military is beginning to draw better material from among Sudanese school leavers.

But the Sudanese intellectual's role remains an ambiguous one. It is perhaps significant that, in spite of the steady growth of university graduates in Sudan and an expanding economy needful of their expertise, there is more complaint than a decade ago of the smallness of their number, the "insecurity" of their position, and their "alienation from the mainstream of society."

—HELEN KITCHEN

* Dr. Mohammed Omar Beshir, "The Sudanese Intellectuals and the Changing Society," a paper delivered to the Seminar on Tradition and Change—Problems of Development, at Khartoum in January, 1961.

Part II

EAST AFRICA

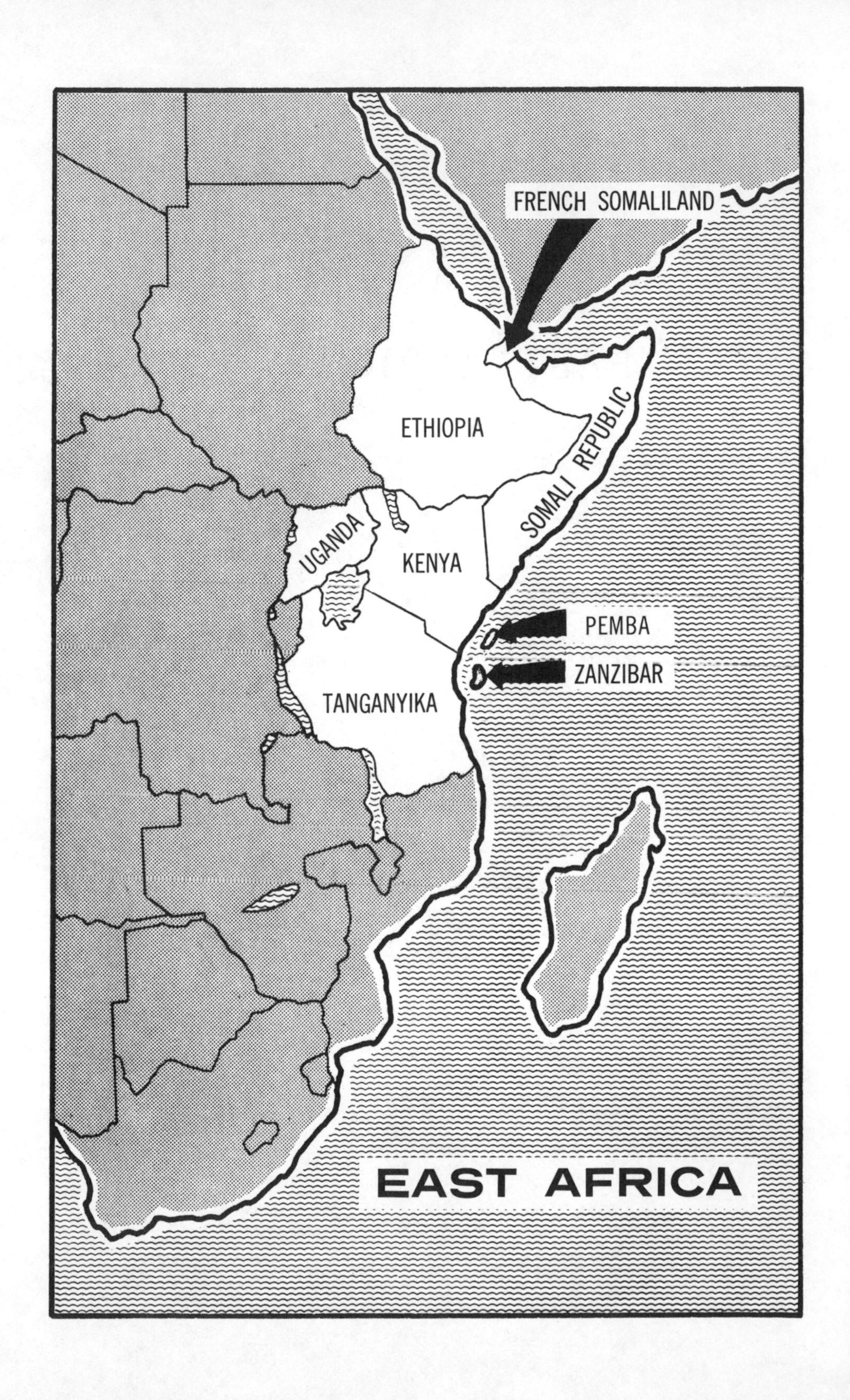

FRENCH SOMALILAND
ETHIOPIA
SOMALI REPUBLIC
UGANDA
KENYA
PEMBA
ZANZIBAR
TANGANYIKA
EAST AFRICA

6. Somali Republic

Capital: Mogadiscio
Population: 1,950,000 (est.)
Former Italian Somaliland: 1,300,000
Former British Somaliland: 650,000
Area: 246,000 sq. miles
Political status: Independent republic

On July 1, 1960, the Italian-administered U.N. Trust Territory of Somalia and the British Protectorate of Somaliland were joined in an independent Somali Republic. The legislative organs of the two territories are now united, and they have a common executive and administrative system. But the educational policies which were established by the Italian and British rulers, each reflecting a different pedagogic approach, remain essentially as they were before unification. This, in addition to the fact that the republic does not in the near future contemplate any broad change in the two educational systems, requires that separate consideration be given to each of the territories. (French Somaliland, since it has no political connection with the Somali Republic, will be treated in a separate chapter.)

The Somalis constitute one of the largest homogeneous ethnic groups in sub-Saharan Africa. They belong to the sub-Cushitic cultural complex and are, with the exception of a few individuals, Moslems who follow the Sunni sect of the Shafi'i. Although all speak the same language, there are some differences in dialect. Essentially a nomadic people, the Somalis differ from the sedentary agriculturalists who inhabit most of Africa south of the Sahara. The dynamic pattern of nomadism, with its highly developed individualism, is reflected in the traditional social system which permits no rigid form of hierarchical organization or government authority. The only form of indigenous education is found in the memorization and recitation of passages from the Koran and in oral literature, which instructs the young in the customs of the people and in the modes of behavior.*

Ex-Italian Somaliland

Italian and British Rule: 1922–50

Although Italian rule began in 1885, it was not until the Fascist period (1922–41) that effective administration was applied. The Fascist approach to education in the colony revolved around its overall conceptualization of the African as racially inferior and therefore not entitled to enter into the social, economic, and political pursuits enjoyed by Italian nationals. Nonetheless, economic development, slight as it was, and the expanded military and administrative activities needed to service the invasion of Ethiopia required some educational development. It is estimated that during the Fascist period about 7,000 Somalis received some degree of elementary education under a program implemented by the state-subsidized Catholic mission schools. Given the Somali identity with Islam and the pro-Arab policy of Italy, the missions did not seek to proselytize. Only one secular school was founded (in 1938), and this expressly for the sons of traditional leaders.

The Fascist government was anxious not to evoke or advance Somali nationalism. For this reason, the texts which were used during its administration were expunged of all references to Mazzini and Garibaldi—the two leaders of the Italian nationalist movement. Ironically, however, the core of clerks, interpreters, hospital attendants, and noncommissioned officers who received some degree of education under the Fascist regime was to constitute a large part of the elite of the Somali Youth League, the political party now governing Somalia.

The occupation of Italian Somaliland by the British (1941–50) gave a major impetus to Somali secular education. It was not that the British had an organic plan of educational development, for they did not, but rather that they were receptive to Somali demands for educational opportunities. The more liberal British approach derived from Britain's foreign policy aim at that time to secure a trusteeship over the Somalis and also from the personal inclinations of British officers

* For an ethnographical study of the Somali regions, see I. M. Lewis, *Peoples of the Horn of Africa: Somali, Afar, and Soho* (London: International African Institute, 1955).

who were sympathetic to Somali goals. By 1950, twenty-nine public elementary schools had been established, with an enrollment of about 1,600 pupils and a teaching staff of 45. In 1949, for the first time in the territory's history, a school for girls was set up. In the same year, through the initiative of a Somali chief and trader, the first Somali secondary school was established. In addition to these, the Somali Youth League organized classes in English and Arabic in some of the major towns. Political development and educational advancement were thus linked by this incipient attempt by the League to become an effective social, as well as political, organization.

The frame of reference within which the British administration operated was a narrow one since, as the "occupying" power, it was required only to establish a tentative "care and maintenance" administration. The Department of Education in the territory was harassed by a shortage of manpower and a lack of continuity. Nonetheless, by the time Italy returned as the administering authority, the Somali quest for education had sharpened, the traditional opposition to female education had weakened, and the beginnings of a teacher-training program had been laid down. The contributions of the British during this period transcend the mere establishment of a skeletal educational system. By removing the Fascist-imposed ban on indigenous political activities, the British helped to provide a means by which politically conscious Somalis could articulate their demands for the educational advancement of their nation.

The Trusteeship Period: 1950–60

It was a different Italy that returned to Somalia in April, 1950. The lower echelons of the Trusteeship Administration were comprised largely of colonial officers of the old regime, but the top executives and the educators represented a new spirit. They sought to create a nation-state by 1960, as decreed by the United Nations. The target date, as well as the provision that the Administering Power seek the "aid and advice" of the permanent U.N. watchdog in Somalia, the U.N. Advisory Council, was a unique feature of the Trusteeship Agreement. Another unusual aspect of the Agreement was that the administration was bound by "constitutional principles" to assure the establishment of "democratic political, economic, and social institutions."

Given the innumerable obstacles inherent in the social system, the economy, and in the high illiteracy rate, serious doubt was expressed by some observers that such institutions could be established—certainly, it was stated, not in ten years. The basic challenge was the economy. In the Western world, education developed to a large extent as a response to the commercial, industrial, and agrarian growth of society. But in Somalia, where the economy is less specialized, where the people are less sedentary, and where the society is less capable of change—even when compared with many other African territories—there could be little, if any, economic propulsion to educational advancement. And, in fact, something quite to the contrary was to occur in Somalia; educational progress was to become the key to economic, social, and political change.*

The general framework for the development of education was set forth in Article IV of the Italo-U.N. Trusteeship Agreement, under which the Administering Authority undertook to establish as rapidly as possible a system of public education consisting of elementary, secondary, and vocational schools. Further, Italy was required "to provide that an adequate number of qualified students from among the indigenous population receive university or professional education outside the territory."†

Implicit in the target date and in the political structure of the territory were two other requirements. First, the ideal of gradualism in education had to be sacrificed in order to meet the independence deadline. Second, the Administration had to develop an educational system that could accommodate the dual nature of the society: on the one hand, the stable population (about 400,000) of the sedentary areas, and on the other hand, the mobile nomads and seminomads (about 900,000).

UNESCO and the Administration, after 1954, established three fundamental educational centers with the aim of improving livestock-raising methods and agricultural techniques, teaching modern health measures, developing handicrafts, providing literacy courses, and inculcating concepts of community development. The projects at Dinsor and Villabruzzi deal with farmers and with seminomads, who for a portion of the year confine their activities to land cultivation. These centers have met with some limited success. However, the project at Afmedu, which was directed at the purely nomadic population, was discontinued after two years of operation at the recommendation of its UNESCO director, who found little receptiveness to the

* For a brief background of the political, social, and economic development of Somalia, see A. Castagno, "Somalia," *International Conciliation,* No. 522 (March, 1959).

† *Trusteeship Agreement for the Territory of Somaliland Under Italian Administration,* Sales No. 1951, Vol. VI, A–1 (United Nations, 1951).

program among the pastoralists and little encouragement from the government.

Several reasons for the limited success of these projects can be pointed out:

(1) Nomads and seminomads have always frowned on manual labor, and the former, in particular, are resistant to "outside interference."

(2) It is still difficult to persuade rural Somalis to think beyond traditional kinship loyalties and to embrace "community" concepts.

(3) Parents are unwilling to dispense with the services of their children, who perform important economic functions.

(4) It is difficult to develop a corps of teachers who would be willing to abandon the main centers in order to teach in the interior.

(5) The extensive range of pastoralism itself has been a major limiting factor, since the rhythm of pastoral movements is a fast one, with widely segmented nomadic groups covering considerable territory. Both the wide dispersion and the smallness of the groups has made it impractical to develop a system of mobile educational units which could follow the nomads. But were it possible to do so, the financial weight would be so staggering as to deprive the more viable sedentary areas.

Nomadism is not unique to Somalia; in other semiarid areas of the world, approximately the same problems exist. The Soviet Union is said to have mastered the problem in its nomadic areas, but data confirming its experiments are lacking. In any event, because of the problems that accompany nomadism, the majority of the Somali population have been unable to keep up with the social and cultural transition taking place in the towns and villages; thus, the dual nature of Somali life is now more distinct than it was ten years ago. Although the Somali nomad has an incipient national consciousness, he cannot be expected to participate in the civic obligations that the modern state requires. Whether the changes that are taking place in the villages and towns will gradually and eventually spread to the interior is a matter of conjecture. It is very likely that they will have some influence.

Primary and Secondary Education

It was by necessity that the Trusteeship Administration and the Somali Government concentrated their efforts in the sedentary areas and in particular in the forty-five villages, towns, and municipalities scattered over the 1,300-mile-long nation. As early as 1952, with the assistance of UNESCO, a Five-Year Education Plan was drawn up; the plan was subsequently extended two years to 1959. The philosophy of the Administration was stated thus: "It is not enough to form a restricted ruling class. We must create in the minds of the masses a consciousness of citizenship, and we must establish that cultural basis which constitutes a fundamental prerequisite to progress." *

The plan established a network of primary, secondary, and vocational schools which, it was believed, would raise the level of literacy and improve social and economic conditions. Realistically, the Administration sought to meet the needs of a territory with limited resources, and it geared its program to the future financial capabilities of the state. It was anticipated that the Somali financial structure would continue to be characterized by deficits in the public budget and in the balance of payments; the policy was to set up a system that the state could support after it became independent.

The Five-Year Plan programmed an annual intake of 22,080 pupils in the 160 elementary schools and 19,600 in adult-education classes. The following figures of enrollment give some indication of the educational accomplishments and shortcomings during the trusteeship period. These figures do not include the 500-odd pupils in schools operated by the Catholic, Sudan Interior, the Mennonite missions, and by the British Council. Nor do they include the 1,000-odd members of the national police and army who are required to take some elementary- and secondary-school courses in order to receive promotions and increments in pay.

In the primary schools, wastage has been high; that is, there has been considerable loss of pupils after the first two years of primary education. Indeed, only about 50 per cent of the pupils have gone through the full five-year program of the primary schools during the past decade. Since four years of primary schooling have been regarded by educators as the minimum requirement for attaining adequate literacy, the significance of wastage on future educational development becomes readily apparent—and education becomes very expensive when so many pupils drop out before attaining literacy.

The basic causes of wastage are easier to discern than to rectify. Many pupils lose confidence in indigenous teachers, who sometimes lack competence or are unable to secure confidence because their lineage affiliation differs from that of their pupils. There is, further, the problem of foreign teachers. Some Somalis have complained that the Italian and Egyptian instructors teach outside the mental framework and cultural background of the pupils. Another problem is

* E. Joppi, "Scuola di base," *Corriere della Somalia,* April 18, 1951.

Table 1
Students in Schools in Somalia

	1952		1959–60	
	Male	Female	Male	Female
Primary schools				
Day pupils	4,852	633	12,206	3,766
Adults	8,705	353	15,987	2,169
Private (national) [a]			1,546	188
Total primary	*13,557*	*986*	*29,739*	*6,123*
Secondary schools				
Somali lower secondary				
Mogadiscio	164	24	545	23
Mogadiscio			365	36
Galcaio			10	
Baidoa			51	1
Total lower secondary	*164*	*24*	*971*	*60*
Somali higher secondary				
Mogadiscio (public)	331		317	11
Mogadiscio (private)			380	
Total higher secondary	*331*		*697*	*11*
Vocational schools				
Industrial School	42		265	
Agricultural schools	29		57	
Maritime and Fisheries	91		66	
Commercial	158	44	39	10
Home Economics		42		43
Total vocational	*320*	*86*	*427*	*53*

[a] "National" schools are financed and operated by Egyptians. Their curricula and activities are controlled by the Somali Government.

SOURCES: Ministère des Affaires Étrangères, *Rapport du gouvernement italien à l'Assemblée générale des Nations Unies sur l'administration de la Somalie, 1954* (1955), pp. 230–33; U.N. Trusteeship Council, *Report of the United Nations Advisory Council for the Trust Territory of Somaliland under Italian Administration Covering the Period from 1 April 1959 to 31 March 1960* (T/1516), Annex IV, pp. 1–2.

that parents sometimes withdraw their children from school at an early stage. This is due to a lack of appreciation of educational goals and to the reluctance of parents to give up the economic benefits they derive from their children's assistance at home or on the farm or in the pasture. In order to bridge this rift between the two generations, "Didactic" school committees, comprised of traditional and political party leaders and parents, have been set up in each major town and village. To some extent these committees have mollified the traditional opposition to modern education, but it will take some time before the benefits of education are appreciated on a wide scale among people of the older generation.

To narrow the ideological gap between the new and the old generations, the Trustee Power also introduced a program of adult education. This program continues for three years and offers training in Italian, Arabic, arithmetic, civics, geography, and hygiene. Besides tackling the problem of illiteracy, the program has, as one of its main goals, the aim of extirpating the ignorance, superstition, and prejudice that, among the older generation, militate against change. It was apparent to the Administration that an educational system which concentrated on the new generation to the exclusion of the old would reinforce the traditionalists in their conservatism and at the same time further divorce the older generation from the new social and political institutions. The goal of an annual intake of 19,600 adult pupils set by the Five-Year Plan has fallen short by several thousand, and the record of regular attendance has been only about 60 per cent. Thus, it is obvious that there has been some, but not an overwhelming, enthusiasm among adults for the program and its aims.

In secondary education, the Administration began in 1950 with a single three-year lower secondary school; in 1953 it added a four-year upper secondary school. In 1959 two lower secondary schools were added, one at Galcaio, the crossroads of the northern nomadic and trade movements, and the other in the south at Baidoa, the center of the rain-fed agricultural region. Both levels of the secondary schools concentrate on a liberal-arts program. The curriculum for the upper secondary school has been designed to give graduates the necessary prerequisites for entering foreign universities.

Progress in secondary-school development has been below expectations. Enrollment has only been about 6 per cent of the primary-school outflow. Part of this shortcoming can be traced to the fact that up to 1959 secondary education was confined to the capital city of Mogadiscio. Boarding-school facilities were offered, but few pupils were willing to leave their families for the whole academic year. Presently, even with the establishment of the two additional schools, the enrollment remains low. Since the lower secondary school is a major source of recruitment for government and commercial clerical employees and for teacher training, and since the upper secondary school is the only source of students for the university, the bottleneck in secondary education can seriously retard future development programs. However, it is assumed that this problem eventually will be solved as activities of the new secondary schools pick up momentum.

One of the major objectives of the Administration during this period was to create a class of Somali craftsmen capable of replacing non-Somali personnel. Political independence, it was conjectured, would have little significance should there be an overdependence on foreign technicians. The Administration, with the aid of U.N. experts and the ILO, designed a system of technical education which sought to assure the talent necessary to sustain the elementary technical services of government and private enterprise. The five vocational schools established have been classified academically along with the lower secondary schools. Most of the vocational schools are of three years' duration and require the primary-school certificate for admission. During the past decade, the better students in the vocational schools have been sent to foreign countries for more intensive specialization.

In each of the technical schools, much of the first year is given over to general education, and liberal-arts subjects are offered throughout the full program. An example of this is the Agricultural College, where fourteen out of thirty-three hours per week during the first year are given to history, languages, geography, and mathematics; thirteen hours per week in the second year; and nine in the last year. UNESCO experts have criticized this as seriously depriving the students of more useful technical knowledge, and they have suggested that the liberal-arts subjects could be eliminated if students were required to have the lower secondary-school certificate for admission. Whatever alternative is selected, the stress on general education is justified by the fact that one primary need of the territory is to diffuse a sense of civic consciousness.

Professional and Higher Education

Although a main objective of the Administration was to lay down the foundation of a system of "mass education," the stress during the Trusteeship period was on professional and higher education. The Administration saw its crucial task as the creation of a "ruling elite" —that is, a corps of men who from 1960 onward would be responsible for educating the young, for administering and governing the nation, virtue of the absence of major industrial and commercial activities, and for supplying the essential technical and social services which, by could not be supplied by private enterprise and private institutions. Under the Trusteeship Agreement, the Administration was required only to provide sufficient scholarship programs abroad. It was not required to construct institutions of higher education in Somalia

Table 2
Professional Schools in Somalia

School	1954		1959–60	
	Male	Female	Male	Female
Teacher Training Institute	37		59	43
School of Islamic Studies	142		189	
School of Politics and Administration	83		88 *(1957)*	
University Institute of Somalia	19		81	

SOURCE: U.N. Trusteeship Council, *Report of the United Nations Advisory Council . . .*

itself. Various U.N. organs believed that the economic basis of the country and the financial outlay required would not warrant their establishment. Although the Administration did not agree with this position, it did not seek to be overly ambitious. The theme of caution was struck early when it noted that "we must not build skyscrapers when simple dwellings will do."

The data in Table 2 reveal the extent to which the Administration went in building the "professional" training basis of education in Somalia. The Teacher Training Institute, opened in 1953, takes students from the lower secondary schools and offers them a three-year course of training. The usual training period in other territories is two years. The School of Islamic Studies was established in 1952 and has been classified as a lower secondary school. It offers a four-year course, with the first two years devoted to general education and the last two to religious and juridical studies. The scope of the school is to provide *khadis*—that is, judges who administer the Sharia (Islamic law) in the religious courts—and to train religious leaders.

Of the four professional schools noted above, the Teacher Training Institute is perhaps the most important from the long-range point of view, for the extent to which the educational system can expand in the future depends largely on the availability of well-trained, competent, indigenous teachers. And so important is the quality of the teacher that educators have stressed that wastage can be reduced principally by improving the teaching quality.

Aside from the problem of teacher quality, there is also a serious shortage. The Administration in its Five-Year Plan anticipated an annual outflow of 100 teachers, but the number has actually been about 40. There has been a reluctance among the more talented young men to enter the teaching profession, particularly since government and private business are more attractive from the point of view of financial remuneration and prestige. Nevertheless, the development in this sector has been considerable: in 1950, there were 171 teachers, of whom 72 were Italian, 62 Somali, and 37 Arab. In 1959, the number jumped to 578 teachers, of whom 104 were Italian and 474 were Somali. Of the latter, 290 had teacher diplomas and the remainder were assistant teachers. In addition, there were 89 Egyptian teachers who staffed the "national" schools. Still, the situation is far from satisfactory. The nearly 200 foreign teachers must eventually be replaced by Somalis. The teaching staff in the secondary schools is entirely expatriate.

Of considerable importance to the political and administrative development of the territory have been the School of Politics and Administration and the University Institute of Somalia. The urgent demand made by Somali nationalists from the beginning was complete Somalization of all governmental and administrative posts. This called for a program for Somalis above the age of eighteen who already had some degree of education.

To meet these demands, the Administration created the School of Politics and Administration in 1950–51. Admission was confined to mature men who had some experience in commercial, political, or governmental operations. The three-year course of the school concentrated on public finance, history, civil and public law, and geography, with some attention to mathematics, Italian, and Arabic. The better students were sent to Italy for further study in an eighteen-month Course of Perfection designed to meet the particular needs of middle-level administrators. In 1954, the first group returned from Italy and assumed responsible positions in district and central administration. By 1958, practically all posts were Somalized. The school thus had fulfilled its particular function, and in the same year was transformed into a School of Public Finance and Commerce with an academic level of an upper secondary school.

As the next step toward meeting the U.N. requirement that "a sufficient number of qualified personnel be made available" by 1960, the Administration set up a Higher Institute of Economics and Law in 1954. The title of the Institute itself suggests that it had no intention of satisfying the needs in the fields of medicine, engineering, and the physical and natural sciences. These broad, and more complex, areas could be more appropriately accommodated by foreign institutions. It was felt, however, that some of the requirements of the nation in the field of political and social science and law could and should be handled in an institute structured at the level of the American junior college. Thus, in January, 1960, the Institute became the University Institute of Somalia.

The University Institute has a public board of trustees. Its eighteen-member teaching staff is largely comprised of lecturers drawn from the Italian advisers (mainly lawyers and jurists) and from a number of statutory professors who were formerly attached to Italian universities. Occasionally, distinguished Italian professors visit the University Institute as guest lecturers. Candidates for admission must have a diploma from the upper secondary school or the School of Politics, or a certificate from a normal or vocational school. In the latter case, the student is required to take a supplementary examination. The two-year curriculum places emphasis on law, history, economics, and political science. That the requirements for the Institute diploma are relatively demanding is indicated by the fact that although the Institute had an enrollment of 336 students from 1954 to 1960, only 58 received diplomas. Most of those who have received diplomas have been granted scholarships to Italian universities. The Institute is now linked to the University of Rome, which grants two years' credit toward a university degree to graduates of the Institute.

By offering courses during the evening, the Institute has allowed Somali public servants to remain at their posts during the critical period of transition and at the same time to pursue a two-year college program. Further, it has permitted students to conduct elementary research on problems peculiar to the Somali environment on their home ground. The Institute may be regarded, therefore, as having made a major contribution to the political—as well as to the educational—development of the nation. Several of Somalia's major political leaders, as well as a substantial portion of the administrative officers, have been trained here.

The Institute has, however, some notable deficiencies. Law, administration, and economics courses have been highly theoretical, with slight attention given to practical application. Although research has been encouraged, no provisions have been made for field work. And, for some reason or other, the Administration—although generous in its expenditures—did not provide for an adequate library. There is an almost complete void, for example, in literature on African problems. Another shortcoming is the absence of effective courses on sociology and cultural anthropology. In part, this may be traced to the Somali reluctance to deal directly with the traditional factors of the social system—a reluctance related to the vigorous denunciation of "tribalism" by the political parties. It also stems from the rejection of modern sociology and cultural anthropology by Italian academic circles. If the Institute is to become a leading African institution of higher learning, library facilities must be expanded, methods of research improved, and basic courses in sociology and cultural anthropology taught by competent teachers.

But by no means has university education and secondary and professional education been confined to local institutions. Somalia has had a rather extensive foreign scholarship program—one that began in 1952 with Italy and Egypt taking the lead in offering scholarships. In 1959–60, there were 290 students in Italy, 232 in Egypt, about 30 in the United States, 15 in the U.S.S.R., 8 in the U.K., and 4 at the United Nations in New York.* The bulk of these were in secondary and vocational schools. On the university level, about forty Somalis are expected to get their degrees from non-Italian institutions within the next few years.

As for Italian universities, fifteen Somalis graduated in 1959, and thirty-five in 1960; fifty-seven are expected to get their degrees in 1961, and sixty-eight in 1962. The majority of these will be in the fields of political science, law, economics, and the humanities. Twenty-eight are presently in the faculties of medicine, the physical and natural sciences, and engineering.

Clearly, the number of graduates will be inadequate to meet the current social and physical needs of the state. It is, however, a beginning. To fill the gap, 250 Italian doctors, technicians, jurists, and administrative experts have been retained by the Somali Government. The Italian Government and other foreign countries (particularly Egypt) have agreed to continue their scholarship programs during the next few years. But it will be several decades before the basic professional and technical requirements of the nation can be met.

Ex-British Somaliland

Ex-British Somaliland, with a population of 650,000, differs from Somalia in several respects. The percentage of persons engaged in nomadic pastoralism is higher—90 per cent, compared with 70 per cent in Somalia. Furthermore, the territory does not have the economic basis that may be found in the secondary industries and the cash crops of Somalia. But the most significant difference between the two areas is attributable to the disparate experiences they had in

* The Istititu Italiano per l'Afrique in Rome also has a scholarship program.

the decade from 1950 to 1960. The British administration was under no external compulsion to adhere to a timetable for granting independence, and its actions were not guided by the United Nations.

The early history of British Somaliland's educational growth was marked by intense traditional opposition to Western education. A Catholic mission school was opened in 1891, but was discontinued after it incurred the opposition of Somali religious leaders. The first government schools were established between 1898 and 1908, but again hostility brought about their discontinuance. Similar attempts in 1937 and 1939 proved abortive. In 1942 the government reported that there were sixteen Somalis receiving some kind of formal education. Another small group of Somali students were in Aden and the Sudan. The only source of "mass" education was provided by the Koranic schools, which gave instruction in Arabic and religion to about 10 per cent of the population. But the limitations on educational growth cannot be assigned exclusively to indigenous opposition. The British Government frankly regarded the Protectorate as one of the least important areas in the Empire and the most difficult to administer. It found nothing in the territory to merit its making any serious efforts to build an educational system. Its 1939 expenditure on education was about £500.

During World War II, the Somalis showed a marked change in their attitude toward education. The military administration was confronted with a new enthusiasm among the non-nomadic Somalis for education. They saw the Africans of the Kenyan African Rifles, who were in the territory, securing better paid positions, for which the Somalis could not qualify because of their lack of education.

The appointment in 1944 of an educator with a command of the Somali language, C. R. Bell, as Superintendent of Education was the first move in a new direction.* In a tour of the territory, Bell found that, although the desire for education was growing, the opposition continued. He faced up to this opposition by recruiting for his own staff those religious leaders who were able to overcome the objection that education "is an instrument of Christianization." The Colonial Office was persuaded by the military administration to increase its expenditures on grounds that the work of all departments was being held up because of lack of an educated Somali staff; the colonial officers had to carry out far more routine and executive duties than was usual in a colonial administration. But in his report to London, Bell emphasized that there was grave danger in educating the people

* See Bell's book *The Somali Language* (London: Longmans, Green and Co., 1953).

beyond the needs of their society and that educational expansion should be limited; otherwise the administration "would have on its hands an unemployed class of semi-educated men." * The administration concluded that eight elementary schools and one intermediate school could meet the needs of the country.

After the war, the government began to expand its educational program, but the basic philosophy of 1953 remained essentially unchanged. The Education Department's 1953 *Annual Report* noted: "Quite apart from the very strict limitations imposed by financial considerations on the rate and extent of the expansion of educational facilities, it is not intended at present to attempt to provide formal education on a very wide scale nor to make an attempt at mass literacy." However, the government did move. By 1955, there were nineteen boys' elementary schools with an enrollment of 1,107, a girls' elementary school with 64 pupils, three male intermediate schools with 368 pupils, two trade and vocational schools with 87 enrolled, and a secondary school with 47 pupils.

When the Somalis in Somalia were given their own government in the spring of 1956, the British Government hinted that British Somaliland, too, would eventually have self-government. A year later, a Three-Year Educational Plan, along the lines recommended by the educational adviser to the Colonial Office, Sir Christopher Cox, got under way. The plan provided for an expansion of educational facilities on all levels and for an adult-education program. The sum of £340,000 was appropriated for this purpose—the largest sum of money ever voted in the Protectorate for education. Even so, the plan was denounced as totally inadequate by the Somali representation in the Legislative Council. Acrimonious debates on the rate of growth persisted from 1957 to 1960 with the Somalis insisting that the government, as evidenced by the limited expenditures, clearly had no intention to Somalize the civil service and hence did not seek to secure its stated objective of self-government for Somaliland. Comparisons were made with the rapid increase in educational activities in Somalia. The government rebutted with the view that the work of the Italians was "superficial."

The government admitted that there were only thirty Somalis in the 350-odd senior positions, most of which were occupied by British and Indian employees, but it was unable to move forward with Somalization because there were no qualified Somalis to fill the senior or clerical posts. This was in 1958. To the Somalis, it seemed that the

* T. R. Holland, *Education in British Somaliland* (unpublished manuscript, Hargeisa, 1949).

Administration was arguing in a circle. One Somali spokesman noted: "It is over 70 years since the British have administered this country. If we compare the number of Somalis educated or trained by the Government to the number of years the Government has been ruling this country, the answer will be one in every year." *

Colonial officers admitted that the Somalis were right, that they were caught in an embarrassing position. The demand for education, which paralleled the cry for independence, had far outstripped the educational facilities. In its triennial report (published in 1958), the Education Department commented: "That the need for rapid expansion is urgent cannot be disputed and it is now clear that the very slow rate of progress between the years 1943 and 1956 has resulted in an acute shortage of boys and girls with the necessary basic qualifications."

The main problem was the "very serious bottleneck" between elementary and intermediate schools. The Somalis complained that 60 per cent of the graduates of elementary schools were being denied further education because of the insufficient number of intermediate schools.† The government agreed, and added that there would not be enough Somalis to take over control of the administrative positions until 1968.

The realities of the educational system could not, however, offset the realities of growing nationalism. The momentum of change in Somalia and the movement for self-government in Somaliland forced Britain to alter its policy drastically. The Foreign Office announced in February, 1959, that Somaliland would receive its independence by December, 1960. As a result, the educational development program was widened on all fronts, and there were increased grants from the Colonial Development and Welfare Fund. By May, 1960, all district administration posts and some top-level positions in the police and central government were Somalized. On June 26, Somaliland was granted its independence, and on July 1 it joined with its southern neighbor to form the Somali Republic. Clearly, the more rapid political and educational development in Somalia—whatever the compromises with European standards—had placed the Italian-trained Somalis at an advantage in the new government.

But the Somalis in Somaliland were at least given a wider basis for future educational development than anyone could have predicted

* Legislative Council *Minutes,* First and Second Sessions, 1958.

† Memorial presented to W. L. Gorrell Barnes, Head of African Department, Colonial Office by National United Front on April 7, 1956 (mimeographed, Hargeisa).

in 1957. In 1960, there were 2,020 pupils enrolled in thirty-eight male elementary schools; 1,039 in the twelve male intermediate schools; 319 in three girls' elementary schools; 70 in two secondary schools; and about 100 in the vocational and trade schools. In 1960, there were 45 trained and 85 untrained teachers,* compared with a total of 21 trained and 65 untrained teachers in 1955. In 1955, there were approximately 30 Somalis on scholarship in Britain and her colonies; in 1960 the number was about 150.† By 1962, some 40 of these will have returned with university degrees, 50 with professional qualifications of diploma or degree status, and the remainder with lower technical qualifications. There are, in addition, about 100 Somalis from Somaliland in Egyptian institutions (mostly in the secondary schools). As a result of the accelerated program introduced in 1959, it is now predicted that by 1962—not 1968—there will be sufficient Somalis to fill all senior administrative and technical posts. Britain agreed to undertake the financial costs of the scholarship program through 1961.

138955

Although the political system has changed, the educational structure is exactly as the British left it. Discussions with regard to integrating the educational systems of the two Somali regions have taken place, but it is unlikely that any significant changes will be made in the near future. It is even possible that the Republic will eventually formalize the educational system along the British model, for the Somali attitude toward the English language and toward the British educational system is very favorable. Here we can only outline some of the main features of that system as it exists in Somaliland and draw some contrasts with the system in Somalia.

We have already noted that one main distinction between the two Somali areas is the higher degree of nomadism in Somaliland. In Somalia the Italian administration did not pursue an effective policy of nomad education. First, concentrating on the nomadic side would have detracted financially and otherwise from the educational drive in the towns and villages. Second, the government nourished the hope that it would, through its agricultural and well-digging programs, succeed in reducing the amount of nomadism. The British similarly concentrated on the towns, but they assumed that the pattern of nomadism could not be changed. For this reason, they seemed more

* Interpolated from various issues of the Somaliland *News* and *The Somaliland Protectorate* by the U.K. Reference Division (No. R 4558; May, 1960).

† In 1960 there were 2,145 students in the U.K. from East Africa. See British Information Services, Reference Division, *University Education in the UK Dependencies* (I.D. 1317, April, 1959) and *Education in the UK Dependencies* (I.D. 1193, May, 1959).

intent than the Italians in constructing a scheme of nomadic education. The scheme started on an experimental basis in 1955. A number of teachers of Koranic schools working with the nomadic tribes were offered a special six-month course consisting of arithmetic, Arabic, soil preservation, hygiene, and livestock improvement. Up to 1960, twenty teachers had received such training and returned to their tribes to teach. Although we have no statistical indications of the success of the program, reports from tribal leaders and district commissioners suggest that the work of these teachers has been "satisfactory."

As far as primary education is concerned, Britain departed from the Italian approach in several ways. Italy never required Arabic as a prerequisite, nor did it insist that pupils go through a two-year program of approved Koranic schools before admission to elementary schools, as is the case in Somaliland. The elementary school in Somaliland is of three years' duration and has a more direct focus on vocational subjects than the primary school in Somalia. Up to 1959, both male and female elementary schools were unable to accept more than a small portion of the youth seeking admission. At the end of the elementary courses, boys may take an examination for admission to the intermediate schools or to the trade schools. The intermediate schools offer a four-year program with a stress on the liberal arts. At the end of intermediate school, pupils may enter either the two-year courses at the Vocational Training Center (for clerks and teachers) or, if they can pass the rather strict selective tests, they may be admitted to the secondary school.

Owing to the more restricted educational opportunities in Somaliland, wastage has not been so high as it has been in Somalia at the elementary and intermediate levels. As far as the educational standards are concerned, visiting educators agree that they are high. Students from intermediate schools who have gone to neighboring territories (Aden, the Sudan, and Kenya) have been placed in a class higher than local pupils with the same number of years in school.

The first secondary school (with a four-year program) was opened in 1953, and the second in 1959. There have been several persistent problems. For example, it has been difficult to recruit competent teachers of Arabic and science. But the most important deficiency has been the slow pace at which the schools have turned out boys with sufficient basic education to proceed to courses of higher professional, academic, and technical studies. There has been the additional difficulty of getting institutions in the United Kingdom to accept boys for admission for study up to the Advanced Level of the General Certificate of Education. An obvious impediment to creating an educated governing group exists when the outflow from secondary schools is so small.

The secondary schools in Somaliland have been judged as ranking with the best in African territories. Despite the severe shortage of staff, equipment, and accommodations, the Somali students have been outstanding on the General Certificate Examinations. In 1959, the average percentage of passes obtained by the Somali candidates was 5.3, compared with 2.5 by U.K. candidates and 3.6 by candidates from Aden College. The British Government officials have frequently noted that the high level of academic attainment in both elementary and secondary schools has been due in large part to the initiative and personal accomplishments of Somali school principals. But it is also a result of the high demands made by colonial educators who felt that the educational system should be highly competitive. They strongly pressed the position that, since there were limited funds, the choice rested between producing a limited number of soundly educated students and turning out a much larger number of half-educated ones. The former alternative was chosen, but it is not known whether currently the same attitude prevails—given the need to placate increased demands for educational opportunities.

In the field of adult education, the Education Department did not get a program under way until 1957, when funds for this purpose were made available for the first time. The subjects of instruction are limited to arithmetic, Arabic, and English. The response has been encouraging—more than 1,000 adults registered in 1959; but, as in the case of the other institutions, there were not enough teachers to fill the demand. Only when the present strain on teachers is relieved can a more extensive adult program be implemented.

Technical education and training in Somaliland is provided at three levels, two of which are in the territory and the other overseas: (1) a three-year post-intermediate trades school, (2) a two-year post-intermediate clerical training course, and (3) courses overseas up to Intermediate City and Guilds Standard. The Trades School was opened in 1952 and is integrated with the Public Works Department. The school prepares the students to meet the requirements of the Intermediate City and Guilds Examination and afterwards to fulfill a two-year apprenticeship with the Public Works Department. Until recently, pupils could enter the Trades School after the elementary course. It was found, however, that pupils needed at least an intermediate education to be successful at the trades.

The training of elementary teachers is conducted at a single Teacher Training Center where the normal course is of two years' duration. Candidates for teaching intermediate and secondary schools are sent to the Sudan or the United Kingdom. There are about thirty teachers in training at the Center. In 1956, a voluntary course was organized for teachers in private Koranic schools in the towns; the aim was to improve the quality of teaching and provide a high standard of entrance to the government elementary schools. The number of untrained teachers has been twice that of trained teachers —a result of the rapid expansion in educational facilities. The observations we have made on the teachers in Somalia would seem to apply equally to teachers in Somaliland.

There is no institution of higher education in Somaliland. Graduates of the secondary schools may enter the University Institute in Mogadiscio, but they are under a serious handicap there because Italian is the sole language of instruction.

Contrasts Between Somalia and Somaliland

In one important respect, the British approach to education was superior to the Italian. The Protectorate Government from the outset tried to place some responsibility for maintaining the educational system on the Somalis themselves. In Somalia, "self-help" was encouraged during the interval of the British military occupation, but these attempts were abandoned by the succeeding Italian administration, which was anxious to meet the criticisms of some Trusteeship Council members that it was going too slowly. The Italian propensity to undertake tasks which Somalis might themselves have undertaken with time was also influenced by the target date. Furthermore, the centralized features of the educational system in Italy did not endow the Italian educators with the experience needed to develop local initiative in Somalia.

In Somaliland, small fees were charged for all levels of education. This tended to weed out those who were incapable or who were uncertain about their long-range educational goals. In Somalia, the administration bore the full costs of education. The sense of individual financial responsibility in Somaliland was accompanied by a program that encouraged the establishment of Local Authority elementary schools—as distinguished from the government elementary schools, which were completely maintained by the administration. More than half the elementary pupils were enrolled in the Local Authority schools. This sharing of responsibility had the effect of intensifying the interest of local councils in educational matters to a degree unattained in Somalia. The low rate of wastage and shortfall in Somaliland may be traced partly to fee-charging and local government accountability.

As to the quality of education on the lower levels, it can be said that the British were more demanding in their requirements. But it is too early to draw conclusions on the relative merits of the "quality versus quantity" debate. From the Western point of view, quality is of higher value, but it is conceivable that at this stage of development in the republic, quantity is a more crucially needed item in attaining the objectives of building a modern nation-state.

Modern education in Africa has sought to reduce illiteracy, develop broader concepts of political relationships, overcome social isolation and prejudice, and reduce poverty and illness. But above all, it has sought to build a responsible governing class. That so much depended on this was recognized in a U.N. report which noted: "The future of the African society . . . depends essentially on the formation of a ruling class with responsibility. The lack of this class can prevent the realization of effective progressive measures." *

In sum, the problem of new African states is to produce an effective leadership that will be sensitive to and responsive to the cultural and economic needs of the people. In this sphere of action, the Italian approach seems to have been superior to the British. A lot of original thought went into its planning; the Course of Perfection, the School of Politics, and the University Institute, with their stress on administration, law, history, and economics, were all departures from the standard forms in other territories. The various stages of political growth seemed almost naturally to fall into logical sequence: Graduates of the School took Courses of Perfection; they then filled middle-level administrative positions. After several years of "understudy" or of education at the Institute, they moved up to higher posts. By the time of the March, 1959, elections, some Somalis had returned from their university training and ran for election. When independence came in July, 1960, five of the cabinet posts, including that of the premiership, were held by Somalis (two were "British" Somalis) who had had university training.

It seems now that the British requirement that top administrative positions be held by university graduates was unreasonable. The administration had neither a Course of Perfection nor an "understudy" scheme. This had the effect of depriving Somalis of opportu-

* United Nations, *Études speciales sur la situation de l'enseignement dans les territoires non autonomes* (1954), p. 76.

nities to gain practical experience when it was most important for them to gain it. In any event, the drive of nationalism forced the British administration to abandon its requirements and to Somalize rapidly during 1959 and 1960. It is further questionable whether its educational demands were suitable for the needs of the country. For example, the district commissioner's primary task is to maintain tranquillity among competitive nomadic groups and to introduce modern methods of health, agriculture, and education. Highly intelligent Somalis in Somalia with Institute training have proved capable of performing the functions required by district administration. Parenthetically, one of the most capable and articulate men in the republic, the Commandant of the police, has had little formal education.

Perhaps one of the objectives of the Italian administration in spreading education—although thinly—over as large an area as possible was to diffuse the thought patterns of nationalism and the modern concept of the nation-state. In Guinea, Sekou Touré has mobilized the people in concerted nationalist aims. In Ghana, Dr. Kwame Nkrumah was able to lead his people to the "political kingdom." But in Somalia, where the social system militates against charismatic leadership, where traditional political relationships are of a quasi-acephalous nature, and where territorial concepts are absent among the nomads, the administering authority had to be a positive factor in building nationalism. "Quantitative" education was one of its major instruments.

Characteristics of the Educated Somali

Although the educated Somali is not sure what it is in his history that he wants to preserve, he does feel a sense of pride in what he regards as the genuinely democratic features of indigenous life. He cherishes the image foreign observers have held of the Somali—that "each is his own Sultan" and that he is "the Irishman of Africa." Being educated has not made him lose his distrust of strong political leaders; * he is not likely to tolerate the monolithism either of an emperor, as in Ethiopia, or of dictatorial rule. Modern education has given the Somali an insight that enables him to articulate these indigenous attributes in broader—national—terms.

* Muhammad ibn 'Abd Allah Hassan, the "mad Mullah," led a twenty-year *jihad* against the foreign rulers. One reason educated Somalis have not fully accepted him as their "national hero" is that his rule was tyrannical.

There are, however, things that many educated Somalis feel they must change. Collective responsibility for individual criminal acts must go; jurisprudence must be individualized. Tribalism, the "scourge of Somalia," must be extirpated from national life because it is enervating to the body politic. Wherever inequality exists, it must be eliminated. Hence, women have been given the privilege of voting (in Somalia, not Somaliland) * and the right to education. The educated Somali wants to secularize the state, but he does not want to trample on the religious codes of behavior and worship.† He is dedicated to abolishing those customary laws that seem to him to run counter to Western standards of justice. And he wants to inculcate new concepts of labor, government, economics, and social reform.

The Somali who has received his university education in America and Great Britain is prone to be more impatient with the status quo than is the Italian-educated Somali. He is inclined to be more critical, and he is infected with the Anglo-American attitudes of "success" and the need for change. As a consequence, he tends to be more divorced from the realities of the nation's limitations. The Somali student in Italy found quite a different value system; wherever he traveled he came in contact with the external signs of "veneration of the past." He sensed the Italian attachment to history. Despite the strong hold which romanticism exerts on Italian academic circles (note the rejection of sociology and pragmatism), the Italian-educated Somali tends to be conservative about the goals that can be accomplished.

In any case, the extent to which the ruling elite can alter indigenous customs and ideas does not depend on the degree of exposure to Western education so much as it does on the changes that can be wrought in the country's economic structure. Nomadism, and the severe competition among the tribes for water and pasturage that nomadism perpetuates, demands from the Somali a strong identification with the kinship group. The system engenders a host of divisive factors that militate against change and particularly against modern concepts of nationalism. The psychological hold of kinship loyalties and particularism is strong even among the intelligentsia, and this is often reflected in current political, economic, and social affairs. What

* A new electoral law has not been drafted in the republic. Women had the privilege of voting in Somalia's 1959 election; but this privilege has not yet been established in the ex-Protectorate, which is more conservative.

† The power of the *khadis* over criminal jurisdiction was eliminated. At the same time, the Somalia Legislative Assembly passed a rigid "Moral Law." This was vetoed by the Italian Administrator on recommendation of the U.N. Advisory Council.

modern education has done is to give the Somali a set of universal values that permits him to think beyond the particular needs of the kinship group—at least to a degree sufficient to enable him to run a modern state. It also gives the political leader and the administrator a sense of balance between the needs of the old and the new. But in order to maintain that balance the elite may have to use more originality and develop a more critical spirit in dealing with the problems the new state faces.

Perhaps the greatest impediment to advancement in all political and social aspects of Somali life is the crucial problem of the absence of a written national language. That many African states should find it difficult to establish their own written languages is understandable, since most, if not all, of them are comprised of different language groups. This is not the case in Somalia, where, with the exception of some differences in dialect, there is linguistic homogeneity. But despite the repeated pleas of various organs of the United Nations since 1951, Somali political leaders have been unable to agree on the script to be employed—Osmania, modified Arabic, or Roman.*

Somali children have to learn English or Italian and, very often, Arabic. This subtracts from the time which could be allocated to other subjects. The linguistic gymnastics prove discouraging, and many pupils who cannot cope with foreign languages drop out of school. Some Somalis oppose the Osmania script because "it comes from the Darod clan family." The modified Arabic is suspect because it seems to corrupt the language of the Koran. The Roman script seems to carry a taint of Christianity. To complicate matters further, a number of conservative religious leaders insist that Arabic alone must be the official written language.

The majority of Somali students have agitated for either the Roman or Osmania script. They insist, along with a number of political leaders, that the government must act soon, no matter what the

* The Osmania (Ismaaniyeh) script was invented by a Somali, Isman Yusuf, in 1923. Its serious disadvantage is that it would require special typewriters and print. The modified Arabic script was developed by a Somali student at the School of Oriental and African Studies. It requires a modification of Arabic typewriters and printed type to produce literature. The Roman script was devised by English, Italian, and Somali authorities. It is regarded as the most "practical" of the three alternatives. There is another script, the Gadabursi, but it has little popularity. For the literature dealing with the Somali language, see B. W. Andrzejewski and M. H. I. Galaal, *Hikmad Soomaali* (London: Oxford University Press, 1956); Bell, *The Somali Language;* J. W. C. Kirk, *A Grammar of the Somali Language* (1905); I. M. Lewis, "The Gadabursi Somali Script," *Bulletin of the School of Oriental and African Studies,* Vol. XXI (1958); M. Maino, *La Lingua Somala Strumento d'Insegnamente Professionale* (1953); and L. Reinisch, *Die Somali Sprache* (3 vols.; Vienna: Alfred Holder, 1900–1903).

political repercussions. Since all newspapers, periodicals, and books are written in Arabic, or one of the European languages, they are not truly mass media of communication. Therefore, the lack of a written language is regarded as a seriously limiting factor for the educational development of the nation.

—ALPHONSO A. CASTAGNO

7. French Somaliland

Capital: Djibouti
Population: 67,000 (est.)
Area: 8,494 sq. miles
Political status: French Overseas Territory

In the 1958 referendum on the French Constitution, French Somaliland voted against republic status, electing instead to remain in the Community as an Overseas Territory. The area differs from the Somali Republic in that it has a higher degree of ethnic heterogeneity: the population of 67,000 is roughly broken down into 30,000 Somalis, 28,000 Dankali, 6,000 Arabs, and 3,000 French. The importance of the territory lies in its port of Djibouti, regarded by France as highly strategic, and the Djibouti–Addis Ababa railroad. Beyond Djibouti, the area is a grim waterless land, devoid of almost any vegetation. In the political realm, some major advances were made in 1957 when the *loi cadre* was applied and the powers of the Territorial Assembly and Council were expanded.

The educational system in French Somaliland was established by a decree of April 12, 1913, which provided that "education is free to all children regardless of origin or religion." But the first school, the Djibouti public primary school, was not opened until 1923. This was followed by the establishment of schools in Tadjoura (1932) and in Dikhil (1940). There was one Catholic mission school. Figures for the pre–World War II period are lacking, but we can infer that the total number of pupils in any one year did not exceed 500. The number of schools and students in 1947, as recorded by the United Nations, is seen in Table 1.

On appearance, the U.N. figures, in Table 1, if they are correct,*

* In another, more definitive report, the figure given for the number of pupils in 1947 is 555. See République Française, *Côte Française des Somalis, 1956* (1958), p. 114.

Table 1
Number of Schools and Students, 1947

Type of School	Number of Schools	Enrollment
French Government	5	463
Mission	2	204
French Islamic	1	150
Koranic	13	482
Jewish	1	20
Brahmin	1	14
Vocational training	1	57
Total	*24*	*1,390*

reflect a more vigorous educational growth in the earlier stages in French Somaliland than in Somalia or ex-British Somaliland. Although it is not possible to secure an accurate breakdown of racial composition, we can assume that the number of Somalis and Dankali in the enrollment did not exceed 600.

The main opposition to educational growth came not from the administration, but from traditionalists. Parents were either indifferent to or opposed to education. But the rise of the nationalist movement in the Horn of Africa also had an effect on French Somaliland and by 1949 the Somali club, Jeunes Issas, organized an extensive campaign to persuade parents to send their children to school. This campaign, plus the rise of political parties, universal suffrage, and the new directions of French colonial policy, permitted educational expansion. From 1952 to 1956, the school system expanded beyond the elementary level to include secondary, technical, and vocational education. The number of schools and pupils in December, 1956, is shown in Table 2.

Statistics for 1959 (2,498 pupils) suggest that student enrollment has not increased significantly. Nonetheless, the proportion of pupils to school-age population (26 per cent in 1958) is substantially higher in French Somaliland than in either region of the Somali Republic (8 per cent for Somalia, 2 per cent for Somaliland). This may be due to the concentration of population in Djibouti (estimated population, 30,000).

The School System

The school system in the territory follows closely that of other French and ex-French African territories. Primary education includes a six-year program, with the first year devoted to French and the remainder essentially to the liberal arts. An attempt has been made to adapt the French system to local needs; throughout the six-year

Table 2
Number of Schools and Students, December, 1956

	Public	Private
First Degree (primary schools)		
Number of institutions	**12**	**3**
Number of pupils		
Male	**1,079**	**396**
Female	**111**	**304**
Total Pupils	***1,190***	***700***
Second Degree (secondary schools)		
Number of institutions	**1**	**2**
Number of pupils		
Male	**69**	**42**
Female	**8**	**34**
Total pupils	***77***	***76***
Technical Instruction		
Number of institutions	**1**	**2**
Number of pupils per section		
Woodwork	**8**	**16**
Mechanic	**11**	
Navigation	**21**	
Commerce	**12**	**13**
Printing and binding		
Male	**52**	**24**
Female		**35**
Total pupils	***104***	***88***

curriculum, attention is given to hygiene and the simple crafts. Pupils who pass the Certificate of Primary Studies (CEP) are entitled to four years of secondary education (*premier cycle du second degré*), the completion of which brings the diploma of the *brevet d'études du premier cycle* (BEPC). The examinations are identical to those given in France. The casualty rate of candidates for both the CEP and the BEPC has been high. Beyond the *lycée,* which is primarily for French children, there is no institution of higher learning in the territory. Since the number of pupils who enter the *sixième* are few (22 in 1957), it is doubtful that French Somaliland can hope to match the scholarship programs that were designed by Britain and Italy for the other Somali areas. In July, 1959, there were four Somalis in France —one studying law and the others medicine. A considerable number also are said to be studying in Egypt.

Prior to 1954 there was little systematic organization of technical or vocational education. In that year, a navigation "section" of three years' duration was established, and this was followed in 1956 by a commercial "section" with a two-year course. Commercial pupils who complete their work for the *certificat d'aptitude professionnelle* (CAP) do not have access to the higher *brevet d'études commerciales* (BEC), a diploma found in most former French African territories. Sections for mechanics, domestic science, and woodwork offer two to three years of training; these students are entitled to the *certificat d'études industrielles*. Work toward the next degree, the *brevet d'études industrielles* (BEI), is not offered. Accelerated training courses (*formation professionnelle rapide*) of the type offered in other French territories have not been introduced—at least not up to 1960. Nonetheless, the percentage of pupils in the existing technical and commercial courses is high; in 1957 the percentage for all French territories was 27.5 per cent—for French Somaliland, it was 31.5 per cent.*

Teaching has essentially been a monopoly of the French and Arab population. A teacher-training program was established only recently. It is limited to preparing students to be assistant teachers *(instituteurs-adjoints)*. There are now approximately sixty primary-school teachers and fifteen instructors in technical and commercial education.

Little investment has been made by the administration in the fields of adult and nomadic education. In 1958–59, a two-year nomadic school was established at Yoboki, center of the nomadic zone. Courses for adults, instituted to combat illiteracy, were formalized in 1955. No statistics are available upon which to base an evaluation of the adult and nomadic programs.

Comparisons with Somalia

Despite the relatively high percentage of the school-age population which attends schools, educational development in French Somaliland is behind that in the Somali Republic in the post-primary level. It would seem that the rather high degree of commercial and industrial activities connected with the port and the Djibouti–Addis Ababa railway would have brought more Somalis and Dankali into the technical and commercial schools than has been the case. About 7,700 persons are employed in the administration, public works, commerce, transportation, industries, and banks. Of these, 700 are

* M. Salgues de Genies, *"Formation professionnelle dans les Territoires d'Outre-mer," Civilisations,* VIII, No. 2 (1958), 248. See this article (pp. 231–52) for a rather comprehensive description of technical and professional training in the French Overseas Territories.

Europeans who presumably hold the important technical and administrative positions, while the 7,000 Africans fill the lower levels of the working force.

In the political evolution of the three Somali territories, it can be said that France was ahead of Britain up to 1958, for Somalis and Dankali dominated the executive and legislative branches of government in 1957. But no attempts were made to Africanize the administration, and the administration did little to create an intellectual and ruling elite by developing higher education. Former Prime Minister Mahamud Harbi pleaded in 1956 for a "French cultural formation of a young Somali elite," pointing out that there was only one *bachelier* out of a population of 67,000. He warned that unless the administration adopted a scholarship program for Somalis and Dankali, "the best elements would be attracted by Egypt . . . and Arab influence will supplant French influence in this territory." *

Because Djibouti is regarded as a major French naval base and because France is linked to Ethiopia in opposing a Pan-Somali political movement in the Horn of Africa, the administration probably could go no faster than it did. In 1959, however, it realized that it must accelerate if it intended to buffer the impact of independence in Somaliland and Somalia. In November, 1959, the Governor announced that there would be a program of replacing expatriate staff members with local Somalis. He noted that there was a "grave shortage of trained local men." There were only thirteen non-Europeans in the senior service, of whom ten were assistant teachers. The 152 non-Europeans in local services were mostly orderlies, chauffeurs, and hospital dressers. In the spring of 1960, the government suggested that it would finally tackle the problem of Africanizing the administration without waiting for the return of the few students being trained in France.

The Outlook

Lucien Paye, President of the University of Dakar, pointed to the tremendous efforts which had been made by the French Government in African education, but he was careful to add that "however substantial and rapid these increases may be, they are as yet insufficient."† It is obvious that in French Somaliland much more can be done, particularly on the technical and post-secondary school levels. Students do not have to be sent to France, for French-speaking institutions of

* *Le Réveil de Djibouti,* March 3, 1956.

† French Cultural Services (New York), *Education in France,* No. 9 (March, 1960), p. 2. See the whole issue for a review of the French approach to education in Africa.

higher learning exist in Senegal, Malagasy, and North Africa. Admittedly, the local administration faces an obstacle to educational development in the official policy of the Quai d'Orsay, which is opposed to the Pan-Somali nationalist movement. Since higher education only intensifies (or further rationalizes) nationalism among Africans, it would seem prudent from the point of view of French policy not to encourage it. But if France does not provide opportunities for its Somalis and Dankali, those students who have a strong drive for education and political leadership will find that other countries do provide the educational opportunities they are seeking.

—Alphonso A. Castagno

8. Ethiopia

Capital: Addis Ababa
Population: 21,000,000 (est.)
Area: 400,000 sq. miles
Political status: Independent monarchy

EDUCATION of the Ethiopian was for several centuries the sole responsibility of the Coptic Church, whose purpose was to teach him enough Geez to read the Scriptures and understand the religious teaching. Similarly, Roman Catholic and Protestant missionaries—mostly French—who came to the country in the middle of the nineteenth century helped expand educational facilities for religious reasons. As elsewhere in Africa, these missionaries found the language problem serious; Amharic, the official language, is one of some fifty languages and dialects spoken in Ethiopia.

Lay education was begun in 1906 when Menelik II set up the first public primary school in Addis Ababa, staffed mostly with Egyptian and Syrian Copts. Even in this early period, a certain select few were sent abroad each year to study. From 1917 to 1935, Emperor Haile Selassie (first as Prince Regent and later as Emperor) carried on an active program for educational expansion. During the Italian occupation from 1935 to 1941, however, most pre-Italian educational facilities were suppressed as a matter of policy. By an Italian decree of 1937, no non-Italian missionaries could conduct schools. Of approximately 180 missionaries in Ethiopia in 1935, only 8 remained in 1942; moreover, most of the 125 Ethiopians who had been educated abroad prior to 1935 were reportedly decimated by the Italians at one time. At the close of the occupation, the governmental system of education had to be completely rebuilt. There was almost a total educational vacuum.

Since 1941, Emperor Haile Selassie has generally reserved the portfolio of the Ministry of Education for himself, and the Vice Minister of Education has acted as the principal officer of the Ministry. In 1960, a Minister of State for Education was appointed. As early as 1944, the Emperor announced his intention to aim for universal elementary and secondary education—and to make both available to all youth on a tuition-free basis as soon as possible. The development of Ethiopian education since the liberation has been greatly aided by the technical-assistance programs of the various international organizations and friendly governments. Today there is at least one secondary school in each of the provinces, and there are more than ten in Addis Ababa. The country's twelve provinces and the federated territory of Eritrea have been grouped into two administrative units, each of which works under a provincial educational officer responsible to the National Ministry of Education. The Act of 1950 federating Eritrea with Ethiopia under the sovereignty of the Ethiopian crown guarantees the individual citizen's right to education and ostensibly reserves local jurisdiction in education matters to the Eritrean Government, though in practice Eritrean autonomy is decidedly limited.

At first, emphasis was placed on getting higher education for as many young Ethiopians as possible in order to train them for government, and the bulk of the federal educational allocations went into the creation of secondary schools and the export of their graduates to universities and colleges in Europe, Canada, and the United States. Because of this intensive emphasis on secondary schools, too little attention has been devoted to developing Ethiopia's primary and intermediate schools. The first national budget after the restoration (1942) allotted 12 per cent of the total budget for education; this was increased to 20 per cent by 1954–55. Appropriations for education increased from 9 million dollars to 24 million dollars (in U.S. dollars, from $3.69 million to $9.84 million) * in the period 1949–50 to 1959–60. It is reported that 1 million dollars was turned back to the treasury in 1958–59 because of the administration's inability to use it.

The school population in 1958–59 was estimated at 4 million out of a total population of perhaps 21 million; there were 125,211 boys and 32,794 girls enrolled in state-directed elementary schools. Under the current scheme of organization, there are eight years of elementary and four years of secondary schooling. Consideration is being given, however, to the introduction of a revised pattern, in which six years of elementary schooling will be followed by five years of secondary schooling (two years junior, three years senior). This is already being tried experimentally in certain selected schools.

The Ethiopian-Eritrean school system in 1959–60 included 4,834

* An Ethiopian dollar is equivalent to about .41 in U.S. currency.

local teachers and 552 foreigners of twenty-two nationalities. The quality of the teaching, in general, is still not very high, and there is very little uniformity of curricula due to differences in background of the foreign teachers employed. In the primary schools many of the teachers have not completed the eighth grade, and it is said that less than half have any special preparation for teaching. In 1959–60, 50 per cent of the elementary teachers had less than four years of elementary education.

In addition to the government system, the various missionary groups have long operated schools in Ethiopia. Direct assistance is now being provided to the mission schools by the Ethiopian Treasury, but in return they are increasingly being required to reorganize their programs to correspond more and more closely with those of the state schools.

The language of instruction in the state elementary schools of the Empire is in the national language (Amharic) for the first four grades, but thereafter teaching is in both Amharic and English. Since the restoration, English has replaced French as the second official language, and the official government gazette is now published in both Amharic and English. French is now taught as a subject in the secondary schools. As more materials are produced, it is intended that Amharic should be used at progressively higher levels in the system. In fact, a new program proposed in 1960 calls for instruction in the new six-year elementary schools mainly in Amharic, with English taught as a subject.

Financing of elementary education in the provinces has largely been left to the responsibility of the provincial governments, which collect a land tax for this purpose. There has been no recent industrial survey, however, and the division of the land is not well defined; hence, this tax is quite inadequate. Moreover, traditional opposition to increased taxation has handicapped expansion. In Addis Ababa, where no land tax is levied, school funds are supplied by the national treasury. The national treasury also provides all funds for secondary and for higher education throughout the country. There is no charge for tuition, and students are given free use of textbooks. At the secondary level, stipends are paid to needy day students and to all students obliged to leave home to attend schools. Some of the boarding schools for boys are now being converted to day schools (with allowances given for living expenses where necessary); however, boarding schools for girls are being maintained.

Secondary Schools

Admission to secondary schools is ostensibly open to any student of sixteen years or younger who has satisfactorily completed elementary schooling, is recommended by the director of his elementary school, and has attained a prescribed grade in the national eighth-grade general examination. This latter examination includes papers in Amharic, English, science, social studies, and arithmetic, as well as intelligence and special-abilities tests; it is given each year by the Examinations Department of the Ministry of Education. Preference is given to candidates with a high level of attainment in English and mathematics, though tribal and regional considerations sometimes also enter into the selections. At the end of the school year 1959–60, 6,078 students took the examination, and 2,749 of these were placed in secondary schools. The student taking the examination is asked to indicate in order of preference his choice of a secondary school.

The secondary schools now available offer academic, theological, agricultural, commercial, health, technical and vocational, police and service, and teacher-education programs. There are also special schools and programs offered by different ministries and departments, including Police, Civil Aviation, Telecommunications, and Public Health. Only the academic and agricultural secondary schools are intended to prepare students for admission to college; opportunities for college training are also open to outstanding students of other schools, but their programs are not specifically directed to this end. Secondary education may lead to general or specific courses at the college level or to entrance upon careers requiring professional, commercial, or technical skills and qualifications. Secondary enrollment in 1959–60 included 2,730 males and 548 females in special types of secondary schools and 4,875 males and 398 females in the regular academic secondary schools.

At the completion of the twelfth grade, students are eligible to sit for the Ethiopian School Leaving Certificate and the London General Certificate of Education Examinations. To be eligible to receive an Ethiopian School Leaving Certificate, students are required to pass in Amharic, English, mathematics, and any two other subjects.

Secondary Technical Training

A technical school was established in Addis Ababa in 1942 to train competent technicians for various fields of industrial training; in 1960, there were 450 students enrolled for the four-year program. All students must have completed eight years of elementary schooling, and entry is competitive. The school curriculum includes a good basic education in Amharic, English, mathematics, general science, mechanical drawing, practical mechanics, shop management, morals, and physical training, together with a sound shop training in a specialized skill, such as auto mechanics, cabinetmaking, drafting, electronics, forging and welding, foundry machine shop, radio and electronics, sheet metal, or surveying. The better graduates may go to the College of Engineering or the Building School. Approximately three-fourths of the teaching staff is Ethiopian.

Teacher Training

Teaching and school administration on the secondary and college levels has remained almost completely in the hands of foreign personnel (except for the teachers of Amharic). The 306 foreign teachers in 1954 included 122 Indians, 63 Canadians, 35 British, 34 Americans, 15 Egyptians, and 37 others from eleven different countries. In 1960, the 452 foreign teachers included 220 Indians, 23 Canadians, 11 Americans, 11 French, 8 Swedes, 7 Germans, 6 Armenians, 5 Israelis, 4 Norwegians, 3 Greeks, 3 Finns, 3 Lebanese, 3 Swiss, 2 Iranians, 2 Italians, 2 Sudanese, 1 Iraqi, 1 Syrian, 1 Yugoslav, and 136 of unknown origin. Since the postwar restoration, the Ethiopian Government has followed a deliberate policy of recruiting teachers from as many nations abroad as possible in order to ensure against the educational system becoming primarily French, Italian or British, for example, and thus obscuring the traditional Ethiopian culture. Despite a token acceptance of the basic curriculum and the establishment of standard school-leaving examinations, this system (or lack of it) has led to administrative confusion and lack of uniform standards of accomplishment.

The first teacher-training school was established at Addis Ababa in 1943–44. Foreign experts were hired to train teachers and to assist in raising the standards of the school to those of a teacher-training college. The enrollment gradually increased from 20 in 1943 to 120 in 1952, when the school was transferred to Harar. The Harar Teacher Training School prepares students in academic and professional subjects so that they may become teachers of grades one through eight and also take the Ethiopian School Leaving Certificate. The program covers a period of four years and includes the usual academic instruction in Amharic, English, mathematics, science, and social studies, together with additional courses in psychology, teaching methods, principles of education, student teaching, and visual aids. Practice teaching is done in neighboring government schools and at a model school attached to the training school. The school is open to both boys and girls, with preference being given to older, more mature students and to persons who have had one or more years of practical teaching experience. In 1959–60, applicants were required to have completed the ninth grade of secondary school, but it was subsequently decided to continue to provide places for recruits from the eighth grade. All applicants are required to present health certificates. The school provides free housing, food, clothing, textbooks, stationery, essential medical and dental care, and travel expenses for the long vacation. There are no fees or deposits.

A four-year teacher-training program is offered at the Haile Selassie I Day School in Addis Ababa, in addition to in-service courses for directors and inspectors. The four-year program enables students to take the examinations for the Ethiopian School Leaving Certificate and the London University General Certificate of Education as well as to become teachers. The course of study includes the regular academic secondary school subjects plus psychology, teaching methods, history of education, statistics, and practice teaching. All applicants must have passed the eighth-grade general examination. Both girls and boys are accepted, some preference being given to girls. Graduates are assigned as teachers to schools throughout the Empire. Outstanding graduates of the four-year program are eligible for admission to the University College of Addis Ababa and other colleges in Ethiopia.

In addition to the above teacher-training facilities, there are four others of importance:

(1) The Debre Birhan Community Education Teacher Training School, which was established by the Ministry of Education in collaboration with the United States Technical Assistance Program, trains teachers for the village schools. Although experienced teachers who have completed the sixth or seventh grade of elementary education may be accepted, all student applicants must have completed the eighth grade.

(2) The Arts and Crafts Teacher Training School in Addis Ababa offers four-year courses for candidates between the ages of sixteen and twenty-one who have successfully completed the eighth-grade general examination and agree to teach in government schools for at least three years following completion of their studies.

(3) The Eritrean Teacher Training School in Asmara offers a two-year program for mature candidates who have completed the eighth grade or better. The course of study is open to both men and women between the ages of seventeen and twenty-two who pass aptitude and physical entrance examinations and agree to serve the Eritrean Gov-

ernment as teachers for at least two years following graduation.

(4) A special teacher-training program for girls, similar to the four-year course at the Haile Selassie I Day School and additional to the regular four-year academic program, is taught at the Empress Menen Girls' School in Addis Ababa. At the end of four years, students earn a one-year Teachers' Training Certificate and are also eligible to sit for the Ethiopian School Leaving Certificate and the London University General Certificate of Education. Candidates for admission must be between twelve and sixteen years of age and must have passed the eighth-grade general examination. Students from Addis Ababa are day scholars; girls from the provinces are admitted as boarders. Textbooks are issued free of charge, the stationery fee is 6 dollars ($2.46) a year, and, in addition, students are required to pay 10 dollars ($4.10) for a school uniform. Travel expenses for the long vacation are paid by the Ministry of Education. Graduates are eligible to continue their education at college level or to enter office work or teaching.

A high turnover rate has long existed among teachers in Ethiopia. During 1953, it was reported that seventy teachers withdrew from the profession; 22 per cent of these were among the better teachers, and they cited inadequate salary as the reason for resignation. In September, 1953, a long-term planning committee was established to study the teacher supply problems, the key to any serious expansion of Ethiopian education. The committee recommended additional teacher-training schools, the expansion of the University College's program for teacher training, the development of in-service study courses to upgrade teachers, and the introduction of realistic certificate requirements for teaching at the different levels. In 1955, a teacher-training branch was established at the University College of Addis Ababa (now part of Haile Selassie I University), and many of the other recommendations have since been carried out. Salaries for Ethiopian teachers still remain pitifully low, and it appears that insufficient incentives are offered for additional training or for outstanding service records. Also, as in other parts of Africa, it is still very difficult to persuade a trained Ethiopian teacher to accept a position in the remote rural areas.

Education for Women

Education for women was long neglected in Ethiopia, but a vigorous women's educational program was introduced in 1957. Three centers in the Addis Ababa area are now in operation, and extension into the provinces is planned. The program at these centers includes home economics, child care, and cottage industries; instruction is in

Amharic. Home economics has been established as a regular subject for girls. Plans are also under way for setting up a Home Economics Teacher Training Section at the secondary level in cooperation with UNICEF and FAO; such a section was opened experimentally in 1959 at the Empress Menen School. It is now claimed that 38,371 girls are in attendance in government primary schools, 398 in academic secondary schools, 916 in special secondary schools, and 49 in universities and colleges. This compares with 2,535 enrolled in 1946.

Special Schools

Other special schools in Ethiopia include the Police Cadet School; three military cadet schools for training officers of the Imperial Navy, the Army, and the Air Force; the Empress Menen's handicraft school; a civil-aviation school that trains pilots and provides courses in the nonflying aspects of the aviation industry; a theological school; a school for the blind; an art school; a music school; a social-work diploma course; and schools in public health, telecommunications, and handicrafts. The Gondar Medical School in Bagemdir Province provides intensive training in public health under a joint Ethiopian and U.S. Technical Assistance program. Through this program, Ethiopians are receiving training in audio-visual aids, curriculum planning, library service, and in the translation of English texts into Amharic for use in the lower grades.

Higher Education

On December 18, 1961, academicians and government officials from many countries were invited to Addis Ababa for the formal Founders' Day of the new Haile Selassie I University. This institution, which is being created by the Ethiopian Government in cooperation with the United States Administration for International Development, incorporates the University College of Addis Ababa, the Alem Maya College of Agricultural and Mechanical Arts, the Institute of Public Administration, the Theological College at Addis Ababa, the Imperial College of Engineers, and several other existing institutions. The Emperor has given a palace and extensive grounds for the project, and several new faculties are planned. An Institute of African Studies will be established in 1962 under the direction of a professor from the University of Chicago. The acting President and permanent Vice President of the new university is Harold W. Bentley, formerly of the University of Utah.

The most important component of the new university is, of course,

Haile Selassie I University—Faculty of Arts Building.

the University College of Addis Ababa. Under decree of Emperor Haile Selassie I, the University College was founded on March 20, 1950. Lectures began on December 11, 1950, with a largely expatriate faculty, and the institution was formally inaugurated by the Emperor on February 27, 1951. In May, 1951, an approach was made to the British Inter-University Council for Higher Education with a view to having the University College recognized by English universities. This attempt failed, reportedly due to the lack of sufficient instructors with advanced degrees, the inadequacy of the physical equipment, and the theological emphasis of the curriculum. In July, 1955, the Emperor granted the University a Civil Charter making it an independent and fully autonomous institution under the control of a Board of Governors of six high-ranking government officials. This autonomy is, of course, largely theoretical in so highly centralized a monarchy as that of Ethiopia. The Emperor instructed the Board to adapt the University's training to the needs of Ethiopia and to provide the youth of the country with a sound academic background in the arts and sciences to prepare them for further study abroad or at the Haile Selassie I University later to be established.

The University College's administration has been in the hands of a College Council, comprising the President, the dean of each faculty and school, the Dean of Students, and one elected member from the staff of each faculty. From its inception, the college has been under the direction of a French-Canadian Jesuit, Dr. Lucien Matte. The catalogue of the University College for 1959–60 listed a faculty of sixty-five and an administrative staff of thirty-one, composed of British, Ethiopian, French, Canadian, American, Greek, Polish, Armenian, Yugoslav, and Czech educators. Fifteen of the faculty were Ethiopian and fifty, non-Ethiopian; twenty-nine held Ph.D.'s, twenty-eight master's degrees, and six bachelor's degrees.

Situated in Addis Ababa, the original one-building institution of 1950 had grown by 1961 into a network of laboratories, dormitories, and classrooms. The library, established in 1960, had 30,000 volumes, including a special collection of works in Amharic and another one of books on Ethiopia. The University College also had a radio transmitter of 500 watts, a geophysical laboratory, and excellent chemistry and physics laboratories.

The language of instruction at the University College has been English. For admission, the student had to have an Ethiopian School Leaving Certificate (or its equivalent) and must have passed, in addition to Amharic, at least four subjects of the London University General Certificate, ordinary level. Ethiopian citizens paid no fees.

In the year 1953–54, there were approximately 130 students

registered at the University College for the first three years. (The fourth year was added in 1954.) In August, 1954, the Emperor presented degrees to thirteen successful candidates of the faculties of Arts and Sciences. At the graduation ceremony, the University College President pointed out that there were 440 students in the faculties of Arts, Science, and Law, the Extension Department, and the Berhane Zaria Neo Institute (the adult-education division). In 1958–59, there were 346 students; in 1959–60, there were 426 students. In 1960, forty-seven students received degrees, and eighteen received diplomas. The Extension Department was opened in 1954 and offered courses for adults, especially for employees of the various ministries and of the State Bank of Ethiopia. However, the Department of Engineering was closed in 1960, and the law school was discontinued.

The Alem Maya College of Agricultural and Mechanical Arts was established in 1952 under an agreement between the Imperial Ethiopian Government and the U.S. Government for a cooperative educational program. It was set up as an independent agency of the Imperial Government to "develop and carry out a national program of agricultural education, agricultural research, and agricultural extension among the farmers in Ethiopia" and was dedicated by the Emperor on January 16, 1958. It is located on Lake Haramaya, in Harar Province, and has some 100 acres of farmland, a modern dormitory for 180 boys, and administration and classroom buildings. Any graduate of a secondary school in Ethiopia may be considered for entrance into the first-year college course. The courses lead to the Bachelor of Science in general agriculture. Students are granted scholarships by the Ethiopian Government and receive free instruction, food, room, clothing, minor medical expenses, books, and some transportation costs. The library has more than 3,000 books, 1,200 bulletins, and 450 journals. The faculty is made up of Ethiopians and Americans, mainly graduates of the University of Oklahoma and Iowa State College. In 1958, there were 95 Ethiopian students enrolled; by 1961, it was expected that the enrollment would reach 350.

The Imperial Ethiopian Academy was set up in Addis Ababa to preserve the Amharic language. The Academy will compile and publish a dictionary of the Amharic language, in addition to various bulletins, monographs, and books, and it is to determine Amharic equivalents for scientific and technical terms used in research, education, industry, and commerce. An official system of transliteration into and from the Amharic and Latin alphabets is also being prepared.

Ethiopian Students Abroad

In the period 1951–59, 1,323 Ethiopian students were sent abroad for education to twenty-seven different countries (mainly to Europe, America, and the Near East). The 822 abroad in 1960 were studying in the following major fields: agriculture, 39; education, 63; secondary education, 135; elementary education, 24; engineering, 162; fine arts, 13; humanities, 46; medical science, 97; military science, 7; natural sciences, 3; social sciences, 103; and unclassified, 130. Table 1 provides a breakdown by country.

Table 1
Ethiopian Students Abroad, 1960

Country	Number of Students
U.S.A. and Canada	207
United Arab Republic	117
Germany	105
Italy	86
Lebanon	80
United Kingdom	57
France	37
Israel	31
India	31
Greece	12
Sweden	12
Yugoslavia	9
Mexico	6
Japan	6
Austria	5
Czechoslovakia	5
Denmark	4
Sudan	2
Finland	2
Netherlands	1
Norway	1
Jordan	1
Tanganyika	1
Ghana	1
Haiti	1
Australia	1
Portugal	1
Total	*822*

The Emperor's Scholarship Program for Visiting African Students

In November, 1958, the Emperor offered 200 scholarships in Ethiopian colleges for African students. In most instances, these were for four-year programs leading to bachelor's degrees. Fifty scholarships per year were to be granted for four years. Tuition fees, board and room, pocket money, and textbooks are included in the scholarships. Students who do well are to receive grants every year until they complete their degree course. The first forty students accepted came from the following African countries: Egypt, 4; Ghana, 5; Kenya, 12; Liberia, 1; Nigeria, 3; the Sudan, 2; Tanganyika, 10; Uganda, 2; and Zanzibar, 1. The scholarships were offered at the College of Engineering of Addis Ababa, the Faculty of Science of the University College, the Faculty of Arts of the University College, the Alem Maya College of Agriculture and Mechanical Arts, the Public Health College of Gondar, and the Ethio-Swedish Building Institute. In his speech of welcome, the Emperor stated:

> We hope that during your period of study here you will be enabled to observe our people at first hand and to come to know that you are of their same African blood. We shall not fail to send Ethiopian students to schools in other parts of Africa so that the program of cultural and educational exchanges which we have initiated will extend yet more widely. We rely heavily upon and pursue tenaciously our program of education. We believe that education is the hope which shall assure the progress of our people and it is our wish to secure the spread of education among all African peoples as much as among our own subjects.

The Outlook

The educational accomplishments of the Ethiopian Government in the twenty years since the restoration have been considerable, even though the Emperor's stated goal of universal free primary and secondary education is still far from achievement. The educated Ethiopian today is still a member of a limited elite group. Although the ruling Amharas, who represent only a relatively small percentage of the total Ethiopian population, predominate in this elite group, the educated class includes persons from various parts of the Empire, from both rural areas and cities, females as well as males. There are holders of bachelor's, master's, and doctor's degrees from universities and colleges in Western Europe, America, the Near East, South Asia, Australia, Czechoslovakia, and Yugoslavia. These students have been exposed to social philosophies and political theories that conflict with the traditions of the monarchic Ethiopian society, where rank and status play such an important part. To what extent the abortive 1961 *coup d'état* against Emperor Haile Selassie indicated social and political unrest among the educated elite is difficult to say. Informed observers believe that Ethiopia's future holds drastic political changes, although these may not come until after the death of Haile Selassie.

Table 2
Summary of Schools, Teachers, and Enrollments, 1959–60

Schools	Number of schools	Teachers	Enrollment	
			Male	Female
Government	643	4,834	140,429	39,734
Mission	150	773	14,553	5,376
Private	75	550	9,910	4,880
Community [a]	41	136	4,276	819
Church [a]	60	180	3,931	458
Total	*969*	*6,473*	*173,099*	*51,267*

[a] Partial report.

There are probably no more than 1,000 college graduates in a population variously estimated at 11 million to 21 million, yet some graduate engineers are finding difficulty in obtaining suitable positions. The new emphasis on technical training in the Ethiopian Government's educational program has been undertaken with such energy that it has outpaced the planned industrialization it was created to serve. There is a vast and growing disproportion between the number of students leaving the technical schools and the availability of suitable employment in which their training can be utilized.

Political factors also contribute to the underutilization of educated Ethiopian youth. As in many countries of Africa, the figures on higher education are not always an accurate indicator of the educated citizenry's availability for public service. A considerable number of Ethiopians educated abroad do not return home. Other young university graduates, disenchanted with the anachronism of life in an absolute monarchy in twentieth-century Africa, sit bitterly on the sidelines.

—Ruth C. Sloan

9. Kenya

Capital: Nairobi
Population: 6,550,700 (est.)
Area: 224,960 sq. miles
Political status: British colony and protectorate

ALTHOUGH Kenya's 224,960 square miles reach from the Indian Ocean inland to Lake Victoria, and its climate ranges from tropical heat to the snow and ice of Mount Kenya, a large portion of the country is located on a plateau with a temperate climate.

The economy of the country is mainly agricultural, and a great part of the revenue is derived from exportable agricultural produce. Kenya's African population lives for the most part in rural areas, although there is an increasing drift to towns. The Asian population is engaged mostly in trade and technical and public services. The Europeans, predominantly British, form an important farming community, although they are also engaged in the civil service or in commerce and industry.

The building of a railroad some sixty years ago had a significant bearing on the pattern of education that has evolved in Kenya. When the British started the line from Mombasa just before the turn of the century, their primary purpose was to establish a link with Uganda. However, there were two by-products that led to the racial streams of education now existing in the colony. One was the opening up of the fertile White Highlands to European settlement; the other was the introduction of Asian semiskilled labor in the construction of the railroad.

Kenya's population now comprises an estimated 6,270,100 Africans, 174,300 Asians, 67,700 Europeans, and 38,600 Arabs. Under British rule, there have been corresponding systems of education at the primary and secondary levels, with each of the four communities having its own facilities, its own standards, and its own fees. Higher education is multiracial, and for the last six years there has been one multiracial primary school, the Hospital Hill School in Nairobi. In 1960, a start was also made in multiracial education at the secondary level, but on a limited scale.

The government urges that Kenya's educational deficiencies be viewed against a background of rapidly developing social services whose costs threaten to outstrip the country's revenues. It also points out that some of the reserves which were being built up to meet future costs were necessarily dissipated in suppressing the Mau Mau revolt in 1952. African leaders, while recognizing these factors, feel that much can be done for African education within present means. They claim that a disproportionate amount of the educational budget has been spent on European education and do not accept the view that the larger tax load of Europeans should exempt them from responsibility for development of the country's total human resources. African education has become a key political issue, and one on which both of the major African political parties vying for predominance—the Kenya African National Union, headed by Jomo Kenyatta, Tom Mboya, and James Gichuru, and the Kenya African Democratic Union, led by Ronald Ngala and Masinde Muliro—are of much the same mind.

European Education

There is compulsory education for all European children from the ages of seven to fifteen. Primary education runs for seven years and is followed by four years of secondary school. The Cambridge Overseas School Certificate examination is taken at this point. A two-year course then leads to the Higher School Certificate, which in turn leads to university training. More than 11,000 European children attend Kenya schools. Of these, about 3,000 are receiving secondary education. The government operates eighteen primary schools, with an enrollment of around 6,000; an additional 2,500 children attend private primary schools. There are separate secondary schools for boys and girls, with some students coming from Uganda and Zanzibar. In 1961, the fees were £30 per term for board, £5 for primary tuition, and £11 for secondary tuition, but increases appeared imminent.

Asian Education

Education is compulsory between the ages of seven and fifteen only for Asian children in the main towns (Nairobi, Mombasa, and

Kisumu). However, throughout Kenya the enrollment of Asian boys is nearly 100 per cent, and the enrollment of girls is slowly approaching that figure. In 1958, there were more than 47,000 Asian students enrolled in government schools and in private institutions receiving government aid. Tuition fees are 33 shillings per term for primary school, and 87 shillings per term for secondary school. Asians have the same period of training as the Europeans, seven years primary followed by four years secondary, but school facilities are considerably more limited than those for Europeans. Double sessions are frequently resorted to, and the Kenya Asian Preliminary Examination, which governs whether or not one can continue in a grammar-type secondary school, has become the object of intense competition.

Considerable dissatisfaction over Asian education led to a government investigation recently, and the resulting recommendations have been incorporated to a large extent in the 1960–63 development plans, which call for the construction of more Asian schools.

Arab Education

There is no compulsory education for Arabs, and all the primary schools set aside for them are day schools. In Mombasa, the main center of Arab education, there are two primary schools and a secondary school for boys, as well as the Mombasa Institute of Moslem Education. This latter institution, built from government funds and private contributions, provides technical training for Moslems of all races in Kenya, Uganda, Tanganyika, Zanzibar, and Somaliland. The education of Arab girls has presented some difficulties, but progress is being made in Mombasa. Arab girls, as a rule, attend Asian schools at the secondary level. In 1958, there were more than 2,700 Arab students in school. Fees are 18 shillings per term for secondary school and from 2 to 12 shillings per term for primary, with 100 shillings charged for board.

African Education

Unlike the programs for the other racial groups, education for Africans is divided into three four-year courses—primary, intermediate, and secondary. Education is not compulsory for the Africans, but the government contends that practically all African students who are able to pay the fees can at least attend primary school if they wish. It is the government's aim to provide eight years of education for every African child, and a pilot scheme to achieve this for children residing in Nairobi has been termed a success. Fees for African students are 20 shillings per year for primary education, 45 shillings for intermediate tuition, with 100 shillings for board where it applies, and a 250-shilling fee for secondary education (including board).

Early Development of African Education

The present zeal for education among Africans is in marked contrast to early indifference and in some cases outright hostility toward schooling. From 1895 to 1911, missions carried almost the entire burden of African education, and there are numerous instances on record of African reluctance. One of the early American missions, for instance, reported that pupils had gone on strike because they were not being paid enough for attending school. The interest in education for girls was even more negative, and in some cases there was a rather vigorous opposition to attempts to enroll females.

The Kenya Government entered the African educational field with the establishment of the Education Department in 1911. Thereafter, it subsidized approved mission schools on an increasingly large scale, and also started to build up its own system. In 1913, the government opened a school at Machakos that offered technical subjects and teacher training. In the same year, the budget for African education was £1,850, and the entire staff of the Education Department comprised a director, a clerk, and an office boy. In 1918, a system of school inspection was introduced, and in 1926 the first secondary school for Africans was established.

Reforms Since 1950

The Beecher Report, written in 1949 by a committee chaired by the Bishop of Mombasa, emphasized teacher training and devised a plan with target figures to be achieved in a ten-year period (1950–60). Its recommendations were later supported by the Binns Commission of educational experts, which examined the whole question of East African education in 1951–52.

In response to the Beecher Committee recommendations, the government reorganized the system of African education in the three stages described above. These culminated in the School Certificate examination which determined whether a pupil could be selected for training at Makerere College in Uganda or at the Royal Technical College in Kenya. Primary and intermediate schools came under the responsibility of local education boards, with the use of funds provided partly by the central government and partly by local authorities. Secondary schools remained the responsibility of the central government.

The main recommended target was that, by 1961, every child who wished to enter primary school should be able to do so. It was further planned that upon completion of the first four years of primary school, which aimed to achieve literacy in the local vernacular, about 25 per cent of the children were to be selected for training in intermediate courses. Instruction was to be in English at this stage, and the curriculum was designed to prepare children for further training in skilled employment, as well as for secondary education. At the end of this second four-year period, the Kenya African Preliminary Examination was to be administered. The results would determine which pupils would be selected for secondary schools and which for technical or vocational training. The quota of pupils to proceed from the intermediate to the secondary stage was 10 per cent. This program has been carried out, and government statistics show that all its targets have been essentially attained.

The Present System: Primary and Secondary Education

The 1959 attendance of 397,929 African boys at the primary schools was estimated to represent about 97 per cent of the total available. In the case of girls, the 181,261 who attended primary schools represented about 45 per cent of the total available. The government also reported that in 1959 more than 28 per cent of the children completing the primary course went on to intermediate schools. In some areas, it was expected that this percentage would increase to 50 per cent. The Ministry of Education holds that all African children can get eight years of education without a break in Nairobi and predicts that, in a few years, this will also be true of Mombasa.

According to Ministry statistics at the beginning of 1960, about 13 per cent of the children completing the intermediate course went on to the four years of secondary education. School Certificate results in Kenya African schools in 1959 showed that, out of 746 candidates, 605 boys passed, while 49 out of 53 girl candidates passed, making a total of 654 successful candidates out of 799.

Of those students who took the School Certificate examination in 1959 (including 96 private students), there were 750 successful candidates, as follows:

First-division passes	150
Second-division passes	355
Third-division passes	245

The following figures, furnished by the Ministry of Education, indicate the opportunities for further training that were made available for 742 of these students:

Preliminary courses, Makerere College (Uganda)	98
Preliminary courses, Royal Technical College (Kenya)	61
Overseas scholarships	20
Teacher training	315
Railway-training school	20
Medical-training school	68
Commercial course, Kabete	20
Commerce and other government departments	140

Tables 1, 2, and 3 provide an over-all statistical view of African enrollment and teacher strength in Kenya schools in 1960, as well as the distribution by classes.

Table 1
African Enrollment in Primary Schools, 1960

	Standard 1	Standard 2	Standard 3	Standard 4	Total
Classes	4,761	4,600	4,254	4,061	17,676
Pupils	171,656	153,138	145,782	147,555	618,131

Teachers	
Trained	8,703
Untrained	3,437
Total	*12,140*

Table 2
African Enrollment in Intermediate Schools, 1960

	Standard 5	Standard 6	Standard 7	Standard 8	Total
Classes	935	781	632	481	2,829
Pupils	37,745	29,606	23,230	17,153	107,734

Teachers	
School Certificate, trained	345
Trained graduates	32
Secondary school and training	1,213
Intermediate school and training	1,920
Untrained	504
Total	*4,014*

Table 3
African Enrollment in Secondary Schools, 1960

	Form 1	Form 2	Form 3	Form 4	Total
Classes	60	56	45	39	200
Pupils	1,712	1,545	1,177	975	5,409

Teachers	
Trained graduates	141
School Certificate, trained	101
Untrained graduates	46
Total	*288*

Technical Training

At the six technical and trade schools for Africans, the total 1959 enrollment was 1,228, composed mostly of boarders. Students entering these schools are usually those who have completed eight years of academic education, but are judged to be more suited for trade and technical training than for further academic work. Examinations are set by the city and guilds of London Institute, and those who pass them have no difficulty in getting useful jobs. A good example of the practical application of these skills is the fact that most of the African secondary schools in Kenya have been built by teams trained at these trade schools. Table 4 shows the variety of courses given in these schools and the numbers enrolled.

Table 4
Trade and Technical Schools, 1960

Courses	Number of Students
Carpenters	372
Masons	368
Painters-decorators	59
Plumbers	51
Electrical wiremen	22
Fitters and turners	27
Farm and general mechanics	46
Shoemakers and leatherworkers	19
Tailors	58
Sheet-metal workers	49
Clerical trainees, secondary technical	149
Total	*1,220*

Close cooperation is also practiced with private employers in an effort to provide the type of tradesmen needed. For example, the government recently collaborated with oil distributing companies in establishing a special training scheme for pump mechanics, making use of equipment supplied by the companies.

While not under the jurisdiction of the Ministry of Education, the in-service training provided by the former Jeanes School for government employees used to help meet some of the country's educational needs.

Teacher Training

Teachers for primary schools usually have received eight years of education and two additional years of training at one of forty teacher-training "colleges" in Kenya. Such a large number of colleges is admittedly uneconomic, but their existence can be attributed to denominational and vernacular-language considerations. The intention is to consolidate this type of training (T.3) into twenty-five colleges. The capital expenditure needed to effect such a consolidation is estimated at £500,000, but there would be no increase in recurrent costs.

The expansion of intermediate schools depends largely upon the training of teachers (KT.1) who have passed the School Certificate examination (twelve years of education) and received two years of professional training. A minimum of two KT.1 teachers in each intermediate school is believed essential. This training, however, is not attracting as many candidates as needed. In 1960, for instance, only 183 of the planned quota of 240 were actually recruited.

The teacher for the secondary schools or teacher-training colleges receives two years of professional training after taking the Higher School Certificate course (but not necessarily passing the exam). The course for this category (T.1) is now given at Makerere College in Uganda. In 1963, it will be removed to a training college in Kenya. Makerere will continue to give the one-year postgraduate teaching course, which, however, has also proved not too popular. In 1960, only four Kenya Africans were taking the course, but it is hoped that this number can be increased in the future.

Higher Education

Higher education in East Africa is both interracial and interterritorial. The four governments of Kenya, Tanganyika, Uganda, and Zanzibar contribute to the operational costs of the University College of East Africa (Makerere) in Uganda * and to the Royal

* *See also* p. 174.

College in Nairobi (formerely the Royal Technical College). They likewise send an allotted number of students to each institution. Students who are qualified but cannot afford the fees are assisted by their governments.

The Royal Technical College in Nairobi (now redesignated the Royal College in accordance with plans to make it a university college) took in its first class of students from all four territories in April, 1956. Courses in architecture, domestic science, applied art, commercial subjects, surveying, and engineering are offered, in addition to intermediate courses in arts and sciences.

In 1960, there were 169 places for Kenyan African students at the two colleges, although eight places were not filled. Tables 5 and 6 show the distribution of students at both colleges in 1959.

Table 5
Students at Makerere College (Uganda), 1959

Nationality	African	Asian	Arab	Others	Total
Uganda	285	16		3	304
Kenya	323	30	1	1	355
Tanganyika	183	14	1	2	200
Zanzibar	2	9	4		15
Northern Rhodesia	2				2
Nyasaland	2				2
Total	*797*	*69*	*6*	*6*	*878* [a]

[a] There were also two students from the U.K. and one from the U.S., making a total of 881.

Table 6
Students at Royal College (Kenya), 1959

Nationality	African	Asian	Others	Total
Uganda	55	25		80
Kenya	72	92	11	175
Tanganyika	6	21		27
Zanzibar	2	5	1	8
Total	*135*	*143*	*12*	*290*

A Working Party on Higher Education in East Africa, under the chairmanship of Dr. J. F. Lockwood, Vice Chancellor of the University of London, visited East Africa in 1958. Its report, published in 1959, recommended that the Royal Technical College be reorganized as a university college in which both academic and professional courses would have equal standing within faculties of arts, science, engineering, and special professional studies. This recommendation has been accepted, and steps are being taken to implement it. The name of

ROYAL COLLEGE, AT NAIROBI.

the College has been changed to the Royal College, and it will become the second interterritorial university college in East Africa, giving examinations leading to degrees of the projected University of East Africa and of London University.

The capital cost of Royal College has, up to now, exceeded £1 million, with the British Government and the East African governments contributing the largest share. Sizable contributions, however, have come from the Gandhi Memorial Academy Society and from the U.S. International Cooperation Administration (now the Administration for International Development). The latter provided close to $500,000 for the construction of an American Engineering Wing and the purchase of equipment for it.

The Working Party also recommended the establishment of a University of East Africa within the next five years and the formation of a university college in Tanganyika that would be open to students of all four territories.

Higher Education Overseas

Kenya students receiving higher education overseas for the year 1959 totaled 1,731. They were distributed as follows: in the United Kingdom, 94 Africans, 668 Asians, 18 Arabs, and 238 Europeans; in India and Pakistan, 415 Asians and 70 Africans; in other Commonwealth countries, 20 Europeans; elsewhere (mostly the United States), 182 Africans, 17 Asians, and 9 Europeans.

Most of the Europeans and Asians were private students. The majority of the Africans and Arabs received government or other scholarships or loans. Of the 150 Kenya students receiving bursaries from the Kenya Government for higher education overseas, there were 29 Africans, 62 Asians, six Arabs, and 53 Europeans.

Table 7
Scholarships for Overseas Study Awarded to Kenyans by Outside Sources, 1959

Source of scholarship	Number of scholarships
Commonwealth postgraduate courses	7
Commonwealth teacher scholarships	16
India and Pakistan	79
Ethiopia	20
Italy	4
U.S.A.	22
Rattansi Trust	51
Other commercial and private trusts	15
Total	*214*

In 1961, there were considerably more than 700 Kenyan students in the United States and about 70 in Canada.

The Airlift

The most dramatic effort to build up Kenya's reservoir of educated Africans through study abroad has been the Kenya Airlift—a project conceived by Tom Mboya in 1959 to fly young Africans to the United States for study at both the high school and university levels. An airlift of 81 students was arranged in 1959 by the newly created African-American Students Foundation, and it was followed in 1960 by a much larger airlift of 289 students drawn from all of East Africa. In both cases, funds for meeting the cost of the air transportation were raised in the United States, but a considerable portion of the supplementary costs was raised in Kenya. While many of the airlift students applied for and received scholarship assistance from American sources, such assistance was usually insufficient to meet their total costs. One of the instruments created to help the students raise the necessary funds locally was the Kenya Educational Fund, comprised of educators, professional and commercial leaders, and political leaders from both of the main African parties.

In reply to criticism that the selection of students for the airlift was haphazard and inefficient, Mboya pointed out that the African-American Students Foundation merely sponsored the airlifts and that the students themselves applied directly to the American institutions; thus selection of students was by the American colleges on the basis of credentials and correspondence. To the charge that tribal favoritism had been shown in the selection of students, Mboya replied that the tribal distribution among airlift students had been the same proportionately as among African students receiving bursaries to the U.K. and among those admitted to Makerere College. Finally, in reply to the government's charges that the airlift was cutting into the supply of students for local technical-training and teacher-training facilities, Mboya argued that this pointed up the urgent need for a crash program in secondary education to help meet the country's need for educated personnel.

The Kenya airlift, while a controversial subject, was a significant reflection of the intense desire of the African for education at almost any cost and his willingness to make extreme efforts to attain it. It also served to awaken educators and government officials to the need for a sharply increased educational exchange effort—an awakening that led to the African Scholarship Program of American Universities and the 1961 program of the Council for Educational Cooperation with Africa.

Future Development

In all developmental planning, the major problem is that of achieving balance. The most serious bottlenecks in Kenya, as in many other African countries, are in secondary education and teacher training The Kenya Government has set its sights on increasing the number of intermediate schools until every child who enters Standard 1 is assured of eight years of schooling. One-third of the cost of these schools (after the school-fee revenues have been deducted) is now being met by the African local-government authorities, and two-thirds by the central government. The rate of growth is now so fast that the central government may not be able to meet its two-thirds share of the cost on an indefinite basis. Expansion depends to a large extent upon the ability of the local authorities to raise their share of the cost. Rather than looking for external aid, however, the government believes that the methods of financing the schools should be re-examined and, if necessary, the pace of expansion slowed to permit a period of consolidation.

All children who reach the top class of intermediate schools take the Kenya African Preliminary Examination to determine whether they go on to secondary school or receive some other type of training. It continues to be government policy that 10 per cent of all those leaving intermediate school should go on to secondary school. While the figure is being exceeded at present, the development of intermediate schools, the high cost of setting up and running secondary schools, and the shortage of teachers are some of the considerations that might make it impossible for the government, given present resources, to maintain this selection rate after 1962.

Tables 8, 9, and 10 illustrate this problem and show the planned development for African secondary schools in Kenya.

Table 8
Additional Classes Required to Accommodate 10 Per Cent of Intermediate-School Leavers

Year of entry	10 per cent of intermediate-school leavers	Form 1 places available	Number of places short	Additional Classes required
1961	1,670	2,160		
1962	2,230	2,430		
1963	2,810	2,700	110	4
1964	3,370	3,000	370	13
1965	4,200	3,300	900	30

Table 9
Planned Development of Secondary Schools

Year of entry	Number of new Form 1 classes	Intake into new classes	Total Form 1 intake	Total intake as percentage of intermediate-school leavers
1961	17	510	2,160	12.9
1962	9	270	2,430	10.9
1963	9	270	2,700	9.6

Table 10
Projected Output from Secondary Schools

1960	1961	1962	1963	1964	1965
1,100	1,260	1,500	1,590	1,950	2,160

Up to 1960, the first two years of study at Makerere College and Royal Technical College were devoted to Higher School Certificate work, studies that in Britain would be carried out in the Sixth Form of the secondary schools. Both to save costs and to expand university training capacity, a new policy was applied in 1961 whereby Higher School Certificate classes were started in selected secondary schools. From now on, Makerere will recruit its students only on the basis of Higher School Certificate results. Royal College will continue some recruitment at the School Certificate level, but eventually will also switch over to the new policy. During the period 1960–63, it is planned to spend £181,000 on the capital costs of ten such classes, with a recurrent expenditure over the three years of £270,500. This expansion in the secondary-school system will require 295 graduates and 154 nongraduates to staff the schools adequately. If the development continues at the rate planned up to 1963, the staff required in 1965 will be 402 graduates and 192 nongraduates.

This presents a major problem, for an increase of this magnitude in the teaching staff over a period of five years cannot possibly be met from the present anticipated supply of African graduates. The bulk of the required increase in graduate teaching staff will have to be met by expatriate teachers. (An imaginative step being taken to help solve this problem, the "Teachers for East Africa," is described below.)

The anticipated flow of students passing the Higher School Certificate examination during 1961–65 is shown in Table 11.

Reference has already been made to the Working Party on Higher Education in East Africa and its recommendations for a University of East Africa, with university colleges in Uganda, Kenya, and Tanganyika. The three East African governments and Zanzibar have accepted the recommendations of this body.

Table 11
Anticipated Entry to Degree Studies

Year of entry	Students available with pass in Higher School Certificate			Estimate of students going overseas [a]	Degree places required	Degree places available
	African	Asian	Total			
1961		60	60	35	25	25
1962		67	67	37	30	30
1963	120	75	195	50	145	145
1964	150	100	250	65	185	185
1965	150	115	265	75	190	190

[a] Mainly Asians proceeding overseas at own expense.

In the field of technical education, expansion of courses for electricians, painters, decorators, and plumbers at trade schools where these subjects are not offered at present is planned for 1961–62. A new trade and technical school will be built in Rift Valley Province, and the first annual intake of forty-five students was scheduled for the beginning of 1962. Perhaps the most significant development in technical education was the establishment in 1961 of the Kenya Polytechnic in Nairobi to provide training for grades of skill above artisan but below professional level. Apprenticeship courses will also be given. The school eventually will accommodate residential as well as day students, although planned enrollment for 1961 was announced as 150 day students and 500 evening students. Present plans call for a later expansion to permit an enrollment of 500 day students and 2,000 for evening classes.

Outside Assistance

The foregoing development plans represent the maximum effort that the Kenya Government can make during the 1960–63 period with available resources. Among these resources has been included probable aid to Kenya from the Colonial Development and Welfare Fund, as well as from AID. Development of the sort anticipated would not be possible without such assistance. Even so, this help will be devoted to capital costs, and the problem of meeting the recurrent costs of the expanded educational system will put a great strain on the country's resources.

The Ford Foundation has given grants to special projects such as the research center established by the Ministry of Education to develop new methods of teaching English to Asian students. Another forthcoming project supported by the Ford Foundation is the sending of specially experienced American science teachers to Kagumo to help develop improved science-teaching methods.

Strathmore College was recently established in Nairobi by a Catholic organization, the Opus Dei society. This college will give Sixth Form training on an interracial basis, but it is expected that most of the students will be African.

Missions of all denominations continue to play an important part in the total educational scheme through the many government-aided schools. A new rural day secondary school established by the African Friends Society at Kaimosi, with the help of AID, is a good example of experimental expansion in this field.

The College of Citizenship, originally sponsored by the Capricorn Society but later receiving wider support, is an example of educational experiment at the adult level.

One of the sources of assistance that was not anticipated in the budget preparations of the Kenya Government but was later negotiated after initial discussion at the Princeton Conference on Education in East Africa (December, 1960) is the project now known as Teachers for East Africa. This is a cooperative arrangement among the Administration for International Development, Columbia University Teachers College, and the governments of East Africa whereby 150 graduates will be made available for teaching positions in the four territories of East Africa after various stages of training. Under plans that were just beginning to be implemented at this writing, American graduates were being recruited in three groups: (1) holders of a bachelor's degree with no teacher training and no teaching experience, (2) graduates with a degree and some teacher training or certification, and (3) graduates with teacher training and some teaching experience.

The group without any teacher training or experience will receive nine months of training in education at Makerere College and then will be assigned to secondary teaching posts in the various territories as needed. The second group will attend a summer session at Teachers College, and then proceed to London for a few months training in the British system of education, and finally go to Makerere College in Uganda for a brief period of area orientation before its members receive assignments. The third group will receive a brief orientation at Teachers College and some further orientation at Makerere College before its members are assigned to secondary schools in the three territories. The American graduates will be joined by a small number of graduates from the United Kingdom who will in general follow the same procedure. This project is a unique cooperative effort and will be watched with great interest, not only by the ministries of education and governments of the four territories, but by other African countries and by educators in Great Britain and the United States.

Politics and Education

The sharp differences of opinion between African leaders and the Kenya Government regarding both the nature and the pace of development suggest that some radical reassessments of Kenya's educational system are around the corner. Constitutional changes introduced in 1960 resulted in an African majority in the Legislative Council and an African leader of government, and British policy is now directed toward independence under majority rule.

As elsewhere in Africa, the overriding need of Kenya in the years ahead will be for proper development of its human resources. While the country approaches independence with an impressive roster of articulate, seasoned, and well-educated leaders, their number is perilously small to man a complex governmental machine and a growing economy.

The Ashby Commission's report for Nigeria has established a valuable prototype of careful projection of the manpower needs of a developing country over a period of years. Tom Mboya's call for the adoption of a ten-year plan for education in Kenya, made in a speech before the Legislative Council on February 25, 1958, may well be reiterated with the added support of a useful precedent. Certainly there can be no doubt that African education will have high priority in the development of Kenya as the needs for trained manpower come into sharper focus.

—GORDON HAGBERG

10. Tanganyika

Capital: Dar es Salaam
Population: 9,237,000 (est.)
Area: 362,688 sq. miles
Political status: Independent dominion in the British Commonwealth

On December 9, 1961, the British-administered U.N. Trust Territory of Tanganyika became the first of the territories of the multiracial belt extending southward from Kenya to the Republic of South Africa to achieve independence under predominantly African control. Although Tanganyika's resources are modest and largely undeveloped and its contact with the West has been of relatively short duration, a combination of special factors has made it a pace-setter for the other colonies.

First, Tanganyika—though properly termed a multiracial country—has no white-settler "problem" comparable to that of Kenya. Of its estimated 9,237,000 people, more than 98 per cent are Africans. The great majority of the 125,000 non-Africans are Indians, Pakistanis, and Arabs; only about 20,000 are Europeans, and, of these, perhaps only 3,000 are permanent residents. Secondly, Tanganyika's political evolution has been shaped in the image of Julius Nyerere, one of the most able leaders who has emerged on the African scene. Nyerere, whose Tanganyika African National Union won a sweeping victory in the 1958–59 elections and again in 1960, has blended the talents, loyalties, and enthusiasms of members of all racial groups in Tanganyika without losing his character (and credibility) as a legitimate African nationalist.

Language has also played a significant role in forging Tanganyika's political homogeneity. Although the Africans belong to some 120 different tribal groups varying in size, social structure, language, religion, and social development, the official *lingua franca,* Swahili, is understood by some Africans in all parts of the territory, and the country has, generally speaking, been spared the tribal dissension and separatist movements centered on large traditional kingdoms that have hindered political unification elsewhere in Africa. Finally, Tanganyika's status as a trust territory drew United Nations attention, resulting in increased pressures for progressive political changes as well as practical assistance toward this end.

A Slow Start

Despite its relatively stable political situation, Tanganyika cannot be numbered among the better-developed countries of Africa. History and geography are largely responsible. First brought under Western control by the Germans in 1884–85, it remained for several decades part of German East Africa. It did not come under British administration (under mandate of the League of Nations) until after World War I, and then uncertainty as to its future status, the effects of the depression, and finally World War II adversely affected its economic development. (As *The Economist* cogently put it, "The Germans opened it up in truly surgical fashion in the 1890's and the British then let it stagnate in tropical silence between the wars.") * Although a more forceful program of development was launched after World War II, Tanganyika remains a predominantly agricultural country dependent largely on the production of cash crops—sisal, coffee, cotton, oil seeds, and nuts—for export and on staple foodstuffs for local consumption. The average per capita income is less than $60 a year.

The three major communities—African, Asian, and European—differ widely in language, educational level, productivity, and standard of living. A very high percentage of African adults are illiterate. The majority are subsistence farmers, smaller numbers are engaged in cash-crop production, and only about 5 per cent are in paid employment. Average productivity among them, reflected in earning power and standard of living, has been much lower than among the non-African communities. According to estimates made a few years ago, the per capita African contribution was £8, as compared with £400 among Europeans and Asians. Generally speaking, economic and social stratification has been along racial lines.

In the last year before Tanganyika became independent, an extensive reappraisal of its educational system was undertaken. Two major goals have been set by Nyerere and the governing Tanganyika African National Union: the integration of the racial systems of

* *The Economist* (London), April 5, 1958.

education and a rapid increase in the facilities required to train Africans for responsible positions in the territory. It is intended that a single integrated system of education serving all races in Tanganyika should be established in 1962, and that the output of African secondary school graduates should be rapidly increased. The magnitude of the changes proposed can be measured only against the educational structure of the past.

Primary and Secondary Education Prior to Self-Government

In Tanganyika, as in other multiracial countries in Africa, the law has required that separate primary and secondary schools be provided for the children of the different racial groups. Four separate systems have been maintained in Tanganyika to serve four different communities: (1) Africans (including, for educational purposes, Arabs), (2) Indians, (3) Europeans, and (4) "other non-natives (including Goan)." Some of the schools within these systems have enrolled children of different communities, but, generally speaking, interracial education has not been extensive at this level. However, in accordance with what has evidently been the policy throughout East Africa of introducing integrated education gradually from the top downward, Tanganyika's Technical Institute at Dar es Salaam has been open to students of all races since instruction began there a few years ago.

Linguistic diversity has frequently been cited as a major reason for segregation at the primary level, on the grounds that the child should be taught first in the language in which he can most readily assimilate knowledge. Thus, Swahili has been used as the first language of instruction in all African primary schools; in the schools for the other communities, the primary grades have been taught in the first language of the group mainly concerned. The government took the view that a practical basis for interracial education did not exist until the secondary level, where English is the language of instruction for all students, and that even here it should not be forced at the risk of interracial disharmony. It was necessary, the government said, to provide appropriate education for the children of expatriates who were assisting in the development of the territory.

The primary-secondary program has been structured differently in the African and non-African systems. In the African system, there have been three four-year cycles—primary, middle, and secondary. In the other systems, a six-year primary course has been followed by a five- or six-year secondary course. At the primary level, there have been variations in the curriculum as well as in the language of instruction. All the secondary courses have led to the Cambridge Overseas School Certificate, and the further two-year course leading to the Cambridge Overseas Higher School Certificate has been offered in some schools in the European, Indian, and African systems.

The African system that existed at the end of the 1950's was largely a postwar creation. Since the system of the German period had been almost completely disrupted by World War I, practically a new start had to be made by the incoming British administration. Progress was limited, however, by both the depression and World War II. It was only in 1947 that the first large-scale program was undertaken, with the immediate objective of achieving "the educational advancement of the more backward sections of the territory's population." This Ten-Year Plan (1947–56), partially revised in 1950, was followed by a second plan that was originally drawn up for the five-year period 1957–61 but was later extended, for financial reasons, to cover seven years.

At the time of independence, two different categories of African schools came under the supervision of the Department of Education. The first included the fully recognized schools, formerly called registered schools, which had attained the standards desired by the government and thus constituted what was regarded as the African education system. Some of them, including secondary schools, teacher-training centers, trade schools, and primary schools in urban areas, were managed by the central government. Others, primary and middle schools in rural areas, were native-authority institutions. Still others—more than 60 per cent of the schools providing the first eight years of schooling, and more than half of the secondary schools and teacher-training institutions—were operated by voluntary agencies, generally Christian missions. Most of the voluntary-agency schools are aided financially by the government and are known as assisted or aided schools; grants-in-aid paid to them from central-government and native-authority funds probably cover a major portion of their educational expenditures. There were also unaided or private schools. All of these fully recognized (or Part 1) schools, regardless of management, had attained certain common standards, including trained staff. They followed the same syllabi and prepared students for the same examinations.

The second major category included the subgrade or "bush" schools; these employed untrained teachers, who were required only to have completed Standard 8, and provided secular instruction approximately equivalent to the first two years of the primary course. Most of these "bush" schools, which have grown up in response to popular pressure for more education, have been operated by Christian bodies, but some of them were started by the TANU Party and then turned over to parents' associations. Legislation enacted in 1954 provided for the first time for the registration of these substandard schools in Part II of the register of schools; they were thus brought under departmental supervision, and their legality was established. They have not been financially aided by government, however, and are regarded as a temporary expedient.

The stated aim of the Ten-Year Plan, which went into effect in 1947, was to expand the system at all levels so as: (1) to ensure that the greatest possible number of children might become literate in the shortest possible time; and (2) to enable increasing numbers to enjoy secondary and higher education in order that they might play an effective part in the development of the territory. The first objective, widespread literacy, was granted first priority. It was considered that the minimum schooling required to impart literacy was a four-year primary course and that suitable follow-up literature would have to be provided if permanent literacy was to be secured on this basis. Major emphasis was placed on the expansion of a system of four-year primary schools, and these became the foundation of the system. It was expected that most of those completing the four-year course—that is, those educated in their own communities and literate in Swahili—would remain in their home areas and live more useful lives there. Only a minority would proceed for further schooling.

The original Ten-Year Plan provided that three levels of education should succeed the four-year village school course: a two-year district primary school course given in district schools, a two-year pre-secondary course, and a four-year senior secondary course. The revised plan of 1950 proposed the development of the district schools into four-year middle schools. It was considered that students completing the six-year primary course were little better prepared for employment than those completing the four-year course, that they were "likely to become unemployed, unemployable, and unsettled," and that a properly devised eight-year course would turn out students "far more capable of earning their own living." Later, it was decided that pre-secondary standards should be abolished and that entrance to secondary school should follow the completion of middle school. By 1959, all but twenty district schools had been replaced, and all pre-secondary standards had disappeared.

At the end of the second cycle, as at the completion of the first, only the majority were expected to remain in their own communities. a minority were to be selected for further education or training, and Each cycle had a dual function—to prepare those who would proceed to the next stage, and to complete the schooling of the great majority.

It was proposed that "each of the three stages . . . should be properly rounded off as the end of a certain cycle of education."

Moreover, each of the stages, while carefully integrated with the others, was to be "inspired by a practical and lively approach related to the environment from which the pupils were drawn and in which they were likely to spend their future lives." This attempt to relate education to African conditions and the lives the great majority of the African students might be expected to live has been a prominent feature of the African school system in Tanganyika. It may be one of the outstanding experiments of its kind on the continent—though, as will be noted later, it has had a mixed reception from Africans.

The Ten-Year Plan called for enrollment in maintained and aided primary schools, by 1956, of 36 per cent of all children in the four-year primary-school age-group, compared with 15.5 per cent in 1947. One in five children completing the primary course was to proceed to the middle course, and about 10 per cent of those completing the middle course were to proceed to the secondary course. With the 1956 target for primary-school enrollment achieved, the subsequent Five-Year Plan provided for a slower rate of expansion at this level and stressed improvement of the quality of existing primary schools and the further expansion of the middle and secondary facilities. It was expected that, at the completion of the plan, 45 per cent of the children in the primary age-group would be enrolled, that 30 per cent of the boys and 16 per cent of the girls completing primary school would enter middle school, and that enrollment in the first year of the secondary course would be almost one-fifth of that in the last year of the middle course. New institutions to provide vocational and technical training were also provided under the plans, and an expanded program of teacher training was developed.

It was the policy of the government to distribute primary- and middle-school facilities fairly evenly among all of the African people of the territory. Under the Ten-Year Plan, assistance was to be provided to each province for the schooling of 30 per cent of its children of the primary age-group. The remaining provision for 6 per cent of the age-group was to be allocated separately for areas in which "special development is considered desirable." The amount of assistance toward middle-school education was to be derived from the primary-age statistics on the basis that one child in five completing primary school should proceed to middle school.

Despite the more recent emphasis on middle- and secondary-school expansion, the wide base of primary education previously constructed remains a striking feature of the Tanganyika system. By the end of 1959, there were 375,000 children enrolled in almost 2,700 primary schools. There were places in these schools for more than half the estimated number of children in the primary-school age-group—which the government estimates at approximately 10 per cent of the total African population. Many of these places were empty, however, and about 42 per cent of children of school age were actually in school. The Department of Education, suggesting reasons for the unfilled places, has noted that "the very rapid development in school building . . . would seem to have over-reached itself in some areas," that there is "a certain amount of resistance in some backward areas to a tightening up of the collection of the primary school fee," and that "some parents would prefer to send their children to a 'bush school' run by teachers of their own religious denomination rather than to a primary school run by another denomination or by a local authority." Individual Africans have expressed the view that many parents do not feel that it is worth while to send their children to school for a four-year course only; others note that too many of the schools have been placed in more backward areas where the interest in and ability to pay for education are not as high as in more developed sections.

A wider gap than intended remains between the last standard of the primary course (Standard 4) and the first standard of the middle course (Standard 5). In recent years, fewer than one-fifth of the children completing primary school have gone on to middle schools. At the end of 1959, almost 40,000 children—about 4 per cent of the estimated number of children in the middle-school age-group—were enrolled in schools providing the middle course. The percentage of children of primary- and middle-school age attending school probably does not vary much from province to province. Wide variations have, however, been noted among different districts or tribal areas within a province.

Approximately one-fourth of those completing an eight-year course have proceeded to secondary schools in recent years. Another comparatively small group go on to the training courses available at this stage. Some enter the two-year Grade II teacher-training course to prepare themselves for primary-school teaching. Others (boys only) may enter the two large trade schools, each accommodating 600 pupils, which have been built under the education development plans. They may take one of several three-year courses of training there in trades associated with the building and engineering industries and, after a further two years of training on the job, may qualify for a certificate of apprenticeship. The great majority of middle-school leavers, however, do not receive any further schooling.

In 1959, the total enrollment in African secondary schools was about 4,000. This is less than half of 1 per cent of the estimated number of children in the secondary-school age-group. More than three-fourths of these students were in the first two years. Of those who have entered secondary school in recent years, the majority have not proceeded to School Certificate level. A good proportion of the African secondary schools—twelve of the total of twenty-eight in early 1960—have provided only a two-year course. In a recent year, only one-third of the students completing Standard 10 proceeded to Standard 11.

At this stage, as at the end of Standard 12, students could enter a two-year Grade I teacher-training program designed primarily for middle-school teachers; courses at the Technical Institute, which offers subprofessional technical and commercial training at the secondary and post-secondary level; or one of the many training programs operated by departments of the Tanganyika Government or the East Africa High Commission. Considerable numbers are enrolled in such courses, and the proportion of students who complete Standard 10 and do not continue for any further training is smaller than at the lower levels.

In 1959, enrollment in Standard 12, the final year of the four-year secondary course, reached 318, exceeding for the first time the target set for 1956 (230), and 245 students passed the Cambridge Overseas School Certificate examination. About 180 candidates took this examination in 1960.

The further two-year course leading to the Higher School Certificate was first offered in four African secondary schools in 1959. Some ninety students were to take the examination at the end of 1960. Courses at this level, required for admission to degree courses at Makerere College in Uganda, had previously been available for Africans only at the interterritorial institutions of higher education.

As in many African territories, the education of girls has lagged behind that of the boys. Fewer girls than boys are sent to school, and the ratio of girls to boys becomes progressively smaller at each succeeding step of the educational ladder. Special attention has been given to this matter, and considerable improvement is evident. However, even as late as 1959, girls accounted for about one-third of the primary-school enrollment, about 17 per cent of the middle-school enrollment, and about 10 per cent of the secondary-school enrollment. Only twenty-three girls were in Standard 12, and very few have proceeded beyond this stage.

When African children enter primary school, between the ages of six and ten, they are first taught enough Swahili to enable them to begin reading, and Swahili remains the language of instruction throughout the primary course and part of the middle course. It is then replaced by English. The use of the *lingua franca* as the first language of instruction in all African primary schools is a feature that distinguishes the Tanganyika system from those of many English-speaking African countries where more than one local language is used for this purpose. Moreover, Swahili is taught as a subject until School Certificate level. The extensive use of a single local language in the educational system has undoubtedly facilitated the development of a powerful and cohesive nationalist organization. From one end of the country to another, the TANU cry of *Uhuru*—freedom—has been shouted in Swahili.

The basic subjects in the primary course are language (that is, reading, writing, language, and composition), arithmetic, an introduction to geography, nature study, hygiene and citizenship, and English, but the last two are taught only in Standards 3 and 4. The suggested timetables also provide for handwork (with which gardening can alternate according to the seasons), for religious instruction in all schools, and for physical education and singing in some schools. The Ten-Year Plan did not provide for the teaching of English in primary schools, and during this period few primary-school teachers knew enough of the language to be able to teach it. It was just introduced in 1957, and this addition to the curriculum has, in effect, changed the nature of the primary-school course. A double-session system, under which the individual child attends school for part of the day, is in effect in all Standards 1 and 2 and in some Standards 3 and 4. Single sessions for Standards 3 and 4 have been progressively introduced under the Five-Year Plan. Most of the teachers are Grade II teachers who have completed eight years of schooling and a two-year training course.

The provisional syllabus for middle schools, issued in 1952, states that the middle course was "designed to be complete in itself so that those who pass through it, whether they proceed further or not, will have received an education which will assist them to follow in a more intelligent and capable manner whatever pursuits they take up and, generally, to play a more useful part in the development of the locality to which they belong." The "form and bias of the course at any particular school" was to be "related to the needs and reflect the life of the area in which the school is situated." The bias was to be of a practical nature. There was to be a "practical approach to learning, the practical and theoretical parts of the training being closely integrated." The course was also to provide character training and moral and religious instruction.

The curriculum includes arithmetic and practical geometry; English; Swahili; general knowledge, comprising geography, history, civics, and current affairs; general science, including health science, biology, and agricultural science in boys' schools, and health science in girls' schools; agriculture and animal husbandry, where applicable; handicraft in boys' schools or homecraft in girls' schools; and religious instruction. Different schedules were suggested for the different types of schools. For rural boys' schools—the majority of the middle schools —it was proposed that almost as much time be spent on farmwork and handicraft as on the basic subjects in the curriculum. Middle-school education is provided mainly by Grade I teachers, who have completed at least Standard 10 and two years of training, and by Grade II teachers.

All the primary schools are day schools and are, as a rule, coeducational. Some of the middle schools are of this type, but the majority are boarding schools for girls or boys, as are all the African secondary schools.

The four-year secondary course leads to the external examination for the Cambridge Overseas School Certificate, and the curriculum is largely determined by the requirements of this examination. In accordance with the syllabus for secondary schools issued in 1955, all students take the following subjects throughout the four years: English, mathematics, science (biology, physics, chemistry) or domestic science and needlework, history and civics, geography, and Swahili. Provision is also made for religious instruction, art or handwork, and current affairs. In the history and geography courses, there is a considerable emphasis on Africa. Greek and Latin are not taught. English is the language of instruction except in the teaching of Swahili as a subject and, when instruction in English cannot be arranged, for religious instruction.

The Five-Year Plan suggested that technical and/or commercial subjects be included in the curriculum in a number of schools, thus providing a wider range of subjects for selection by students. Such courses have not yet been introduced in the secondary schools, and the program there may be described as of the academic type. But different types of courses are to be established in separate institutions. A secondary technical course was to be introduced at the Technical Institute in 1961, and a secondary commercial course in 1962.

Higher Education

Higher education has been provided on an interterritorial basis in British East Africa, and a specific number of places have customarily been reserved for Tanganyikans at the University College of East Africa (Makerere) in Uganda and at the Royal Technical College in Kenya. In 1961, however, a third interterritorial university college—

to be known as the University College of Tanganyika—officially opened its doors to a few students in temporary quarters in Dar es Salaam. It is envisaged that all three of these institutions of higher learning will become integral parts of an over-all University of East Africa to serve the combined needs of the projected political federation of the three East African territories after their independence. By 1966, it is hoped that the Tanganyika institution's law faculty—the first in East Africa—will be able to accommodate 500 to 600 students. In addition to law, the university college will offer courses in arts and sciences. Development of a research program in African studies and an extension department will also be given high priority.

Figures prepared in mid-1959 indicated that at that time only seventy Tanganyikan Africans held university degrees, while another forty-four held diplomas. During the academic year 1959–60, however, about 430 Africans were studying outside the territory. Of these, 180 were at Makerere in Uganda, 6 were at the Royal Technical College in Nairobi, and about 250 were known to be taking courses (though not all at the post-secondary level) outside East Africa. About half of this latter group were in the United Kingdom and Ireland, about 16 per cent in the United States, about 14 per cent in other African countries, and about 12 per cent in India and Pakistan.

Comparatively few Tanganyikan African graduates have entered secondary-school teaching, and this has been a particular source of concern. In 1959, only 15 of 116 graduate teachers in the country's African secondary schools were Africans, and only 29 Tanganyikan Africans were pursuing higher teacher-training programs, then available only outside Tanganyika, and preparing for this career. There were only four Tanganyikan Africans in the postgraduate Diploma in Education course at Makerere.

Plans for the Future

The racial systems of education and the limited opportunities available for secondary and higher education have been the most obvious and predictable sources of African criticism. There has, in addition, been considerable dissatisfaction with the three-cycle system introduced in 1950. Africans have protested that the four-year primary course—which is all that the majority of children entering school have received—provides a neither-here-nor-there education and have indicated that they preferred the older six-year course. In many areas of the country, Africans are said to have pressed for an extension of the length of the course, in preference to an increase in the number of places available for children of school-entering age.

In addition, they have expressed dissatisfaction with the content of education at the middle level. An objective at this level has been to relate the education provided for African children to the local environment and the life that most of them may be expected to live. This approach has occasionally won the plaudits of visiting educators, but it has not been popular among Africans. They have maintained that the time spent on agricultural and practical work in the middle schools has left the students inadequately prepared for further education or training. There seems to be a general feeling now that this three-level system should be abolished and replaced by a two-level system of primary and secondary schools.

Occasionally, Africans in more developed areas, referring to the policy of fairly uniform educational development throughout the country, have complained that they have been held back while unappreciated facilities have been provided in more backward areas. There have also been objections to the government's policy of charging primary-school fees to cover the cost of materials. The government had taken the position that, until universal primary education was achieved, the parents of the children profiting from schooling should contribute to the recurrent cost. Under popular pressure, however, fees have now been abolished in a few districts and the cost of the equipment met from native-authority funds.

Moreover, the system of the past has not provided the number of trained Africans the country needs; therefore, in both public and private sectors, Tanganyika relies heavily on expatriate personnel. In mid-1960, of more than 4,000 senior posts in the civil service, which generally require a post-secondary qualification, only 506 were filled by local people, of which 380 were Africans. The first step must obviously be an expansion of secondary-school facilities.

Many of these criticisms are met in plans now in hand for the future reorganization and development of the educational structure: (1) the plan for racial integration, (2) the proposed Three-Year Development Plan, and (3) the projected establishment of an institution of higher education in the territory. The integration plan, which began to take shape with the appointment of a Committee on the Integration of Education shortly after the 1958 elections, is designed to remove all purely racial barriers to educational opportunity. A government White Paper approved in December, 1960, set forth the principles for the new system to be introduced in 1962. A pupil of any race will be eligible for admission to any school provided he has the necessary aptitude for the language of instruction. For an initial three-year period, however, priority in admission to a primary school will be given to the community for whom the school was originally established, and the language of instruction in the school must be acceptable to the community concerned. It has been recognized that different languages of instruction must be retained at the primary level for the foreseeable future and that integration at this level will be gradual. The primary course will be eight years in length, and the secondary course will consist of a four-year course leading to the School Certificate, followed by a two-year course leading to the Higher School Certificate. Local responsibility for primary education will increase. Subsidies for nongovernment schools will depend upon their acceptance of the principles of integration.

The Three-Year Plan for the development of the educational structure prepared by the Ministry of Education represents a new approach to the expansion of education in Tanganyika. In contrast to the previous plan, which provided for fairly even expansion at all levels throughout the territory, it is now proposed that a high proportion of central-government funds available for educational expansion be devoted to secondary-school expansion and to the reorganization required for integration in urban areas. Local authorities would be largely responsible for providing the resources for further development at the primary level in rural areas. Moreover, the emphasis in expansion at the primary level would be on extension of the length of the primary course rather than on an increase in the number of places available for children of school-entering age. The latter figure is already comparatively high.

Three of the priority projects within the proposed Three-Year Plan relate to secondary-school expansion and the introduction of the 8–4 system. The first, designed solely to produce a much larger output from the African secondary schools, provides for a considerable expansion at the levels of Standard 11 and 12, so that the existing break after Standard 10 will disappear and all who enter the program will have an opportunity to reach School Certificate level. There will be additional Higher School Certificate courses and a steady increase at the Standard 9 level. It is intended to increase the number of African School Certificate candidates from 479 in 1960 to 2,275 in 1964, and the number of African Higher School Certificate candidates from 90 in 1960 to 300 in 1964.

A second project provides for the lengthening of the primary-school course in urban areas to eight years and also, as the secondary course in non-African urban secondary schools is reduced from six to four years, for the addition of enrollment in selected secondary schools. It is expected that eventually the number of School Certificate candidates in urban areas will increase by 1,100 and the number of Higher School Certificate candidates by more than 200.

To carry its over-all program forward, Tanganyika will need external financial assistance to meet both capital and recurrent costs. Even if financing is assured, the proposed secondary-school expansion cannot be achieved unless the additional teaching staff required is available. Since few Africans are entering or preparing for secondary-school teaching, recruitment from abroad will be essential. It was in response to this need for secondary-school teachers in Tanganyika and the other countries of East Africa that the U.S. International Cooperation Administration (now AID) arranged to send 155 American teachers to the region beginning in 1961.

Adult education is also a priority concern of the new African government. In March, 1961, Nyerere announced that the Social and Community Development Department and other organizations would join forces in establishing a top-level committee to direct a nationwide literacy campaign. In a radio broadcast to the nation, Nyerere urged Tanganyikans of all ages over fourteen to sign up for classes that would be held in schoolhouses after school hours, and in community centers, church halls, under the shade of trees, and during lunch-hour periods in canteens and bars. Initially, these classes will concentrate on reading and writing in English and Swahili, though later it is planned to include arithmetic and lessons on community development and agriculture. A call was issued for 4,000 volunteer teachers from Tanganyika's literate population to man the schools; each volunteer will attend a three-month course on "How to Teach Adults." Tuition for the adult-education classes will be free and all students will be supplied with necessary books and pencils. This new campaign complements earlier, more modest efforts in adult education, as well as the Kivukoni College, established in 1960 under the aegis of TANU and its trade-union affiliate and patterned after Ruskin College, Oxford.

What about the spirit behind education in the new Tanganyika? Julius Nyerere, who became Prime Minister of his country at the age of forty and remains its most influential political figure despite his retirement from that office, was concerned with Tanganyika's educational system long before he became a politician. One of twenty-six children of Chief Nyerere Burito of the largely animist Zanaki tribe, he did not leave his home village to attend school until he was twenty years old. By 1952, however, he had become a devout Roman Catholic, earned an M.A. degree from Edinburgh University, and was a schoolteacher at a Catholic school near Dar es Salaam. It was in 1955, or so the story goes, that his headmaster called him in for a fatherly chat to urge him to continue his natural vocation as a teacher and "leave politics to others."

Acknowledging his elevation to Chief Minister barely five years later, Nyerere set the tone for his party's educational program—and his administration—in an address to a mass meeting in Dar es Salaam on September 4, 1960:

> I know that the people of this country have already earned the admiration of millions of other people abroad through the way in which the struggle for freedom has been conducted. Militant nationalism has been combined with a smile and good humor. Temptation to violence and lawlessness as a means to independence has been resisted. The people of Tanganyika became fervent nationalists without becoming racialists. Colonialism was hated but the hatred did not spread to the people who represented colonialism. Bad laws were resented but there was no resort to lawlessness in order to remove them. This is maturity.
>
> I know this maturity has a firm foundation in our character as a people. It was the character of our people which made inevitable our achievement of responsible government and which again renders inevitable the achievement of our complete independence. It is that same character which ensures our success in the struggle against ignorance, poverty, disease and fear—a struggle in which I am proud and privileged to lead you.

11. Uganda

Capital: Entebbe
Population: 6,536,616 (est.)
Area: 93,981 sq. miles
Political status: British protectorate

By a number of objective criteria, Uganda might well have been among the first rather than the last territories of Africa to become independent. European settlement was never encouraged after the country became a British Protectorate in 1894, acquisition of freehold rights to land was forbidden to non-Africans, and British policy has for some time favored the development of the territory into a self-governing state primarily African in character.* In addition, Uganda has a basically stable agricultural economy, considerable potential for development, and a larger group of university-educated Africans than either neighboring Kenya or Tanganyika. The relatively slow pace of Uganda's political evolution is primarily the result of the lack of a national party or leader capable of transcending the country's deep religious, tribal, and regional cleavages and of establishing national consensus on basic political questions.

Although internal self-government was established under an African Prime Minister in 1961 and full independence has been tentatively scheduled for October, 1962, the Uganda political scene remains uncrystallized. The traditional leadership of Buganda, the country's

* The 1959 population was estimated at 6,536,616, of whom 69,000 were Asians or Arabs, and 10,866 European. About 1,200 of the Europeans were missionaries. Non-Africans are said to control by concession only 500 square miles of Uganda, and this area is largely devoted to the production of tea, sugar, and coffee. The rest of the country's arable land is cultivated by African peasants, who are the mainstay of the country's largely agricultural economy. Eighty per cent of the population are occupationally engaged on the land, most of these persons being settled folk, with the exception of the Karamonjong cattle-grazers of the Northern Province of Ankole.

largest, wealthiest, and most advanced provincial kingdom, has now withdrawn its threat of secession and has agreed in principle that the province should remain an integral part of Uganda after independence. This agreement hinges, however, on the condition that Buganda's internal autonomy on certain key matters is guaranteed in the constitution. New agreements are also to be negotiated with Uganda's three other kingdoms—Ankole, Bunyoro, and Toro—to devise safeguards for their traditional status.

Meanwhile, disunity also persisted through 1961 among the modern nationalists favoring a unitary state. As a result of elections held in March, 1961, the Catholic-based Democratic Party, which won forty-three of eighty-two seats, formed a government under Prime Minister Benedicto Kiwanuka. However, the party that gained the majority of the popular vote was the Uganda People's Congress, led by A. M. Obote. Besides these two major groupings, there are a number of smaller and often ephemeral parties. A rumored tactical alliance between the Uganda People's Congress and the leaders of Buganda could bring the UPC to power before independence—although such an unlikely coalition would probably be an unstable one. One way or another, Buganda is bound to play a significant role in the future of Uganda, since it occupies a quarter of the total area of the country, is located almost directly in its geographical center, and, among its 1,880,765 residents, contains Uganda's largest reservoir of educated leadership.

The Growth of Education

Explorers first discovered Uganda—a country of great natural beauty, favorable climate, and highly fertile soil, located some 500 miles inland from the Indian Ocean—in 1862. When Stanley arrived in 1874, he was much impressed with the reigning King of Buganda, Mutesa I, and wrote a letter to the Church Missionary Society urging it to send missionaries to the country. Protestants came first, followed shortly by the Catholic White Fathers; by 1890, their respective efforts had resulted in the creation of six schools with 454 students enrolled.

The first over-all educational survey of Uganda was made in 1925 by the American Phelps-Stoke Foundation. It reported that school enrollment had grown from 454 in 1890 to 157,000; of this total, 18,000 were in central schools and the balance in "little-out-schools." No more than 500 of these students were in standards above the fourth, however, and the entire educational system remained involved in a tug-of-war among rival religious groups. The bloody religious wars fought among externally supported Ugandan factions in the nineteenth century left serious cleavages, which more than a half-century has not erased. Even today, there are areas where three schools supported by different religious groups exist, although one school would suffice. Indeed, there are still relatively few nondenominational schools in the country, and even political parties tend to have denominational characteristics. Educational development varies considerably from one area to another: The Baganda and some of the Bunyoro people are, because of greater wealth and British favoritism over the years, the most advanced, while the nomadic low-income Karamonjong people of the Northern Province have the lowest literacy rate.

Although the great majority of Uganda's schools are managed by voluntary agencies (mostly missionaries) supported by government grants-in-aid, there are some private schools and a growing number of secular government schools, particularly at the secondary and technical levels. In the past, all Uganda schools have placed great emphasis on those academic subjects essential to Cambridge examination success. However, new primary and junior secondary syllabi, revised in the light of local experience and criticism, have been in use in training colleges for the last few years.

The school system, which is adhered to by both government and government-aided schools, comprises a six-year primary course, a two-year junior secondary course, and a four-year senior secondary course. Entrance to the senior secondary schools is by examination given at the end of the second year of the junior secondary course. For those who do not obtain entry into the senior secondary schools, there are opportunities in technical and trade schools, teacher-training schools, and some departmental training courses. In 1960, it was proposed that alternative secondary courses of shorter duration and with less academic content be set up. In 1959, sixth forms for Higher School Certificate work (i.e., university entry) were opened at three secondary schools, and henceforth no new entrants will be accepted for pre-university preparatory courses at Makerere, Uganda's university college. Makerere has been relieved of this function in order to increase its output of university graduates without materially increasing the size of the college.

The immediate aim of Uganda's educational planners, as stated in a 1960 report on the status of education in the territory, is to ensure a minimum of four years of schooling within walking distance of the home for every child who wishes to go to school. The ultimate aim is to provide a basic education of eight years for all children. In the more densely populated areas, the first goal is now in sight.

The age of entry into the primary schools continues to fall, and the problem of teaching mature young men and women in primary schools is disappearing. Primary-school fees range from £1 to £1.5 per year. Secondary fees are higher, especially in the senior schools, which are generally boarding establishments; here the average fee is £27 per year. However, bursaries are available from local education authorities, commercial firms, and private individuals for qualified candidates unable to pay the fees. According to the Department of Education's annual report for 1960, few children "with capacity to profit" are barred by financial reasons from entrance to a secondary education.

Primary schools are financed from Protectorate Government funds, local-government funds, voluntary-agency contributions, and local-community effort. All senior secondary schools (including the Kampala Technical Institute), training colleges, and technical schools have their own boards of governors and receive direct grants-in-aid from central funds.

Years of Rapid Educational Expansion

The broad and imaginative eight-year program of educational expansion initiated in 1952 was based on a report by a committee of specialists appointed by Governor Sir Andrew Cohen and headed by Professor Bernard de Bunsen of Makerere College. These recommendations were refined in subsequent years on the basis of a government memorandum on the report (1953), plans drawn up by the Central Advisory Council on Education and local educational authorities, and departmental plans drawn up in detail within the broad framework of government policy.

In 1953, the Uganda Legislative Council voted to spend more than £11 million from the Cotton Price Stabilization Fund on African welfare and development during the period 1953–61. Much of this sum was to be spent for African education—for example, £415,000 for agricultu.al education, including £225,000 for the creation of two farm institutes, £141,000 for eight agricultural institutes, £100,000 for the agricultural faculty at Makerere, £86,000 for a local government center, and £7,600 for the Forestry School.

Early in 1955, the Legislative Council approved a five-year (1955–60) capital-development plan involving the expenditure of about £30 million, of which specific amounts were earmarked for continued development of education to help prepare the people to play a full part in public life and economic progress.

By 1959, the Education Department could report that the eight-year program formulated in the De Bunsen report had been substantially completed in six years. The over-all expenditure on education in 1958 in Uganda was £4.25 million, as against £1.65 million in 1952. In 1959–60, £4,972,713 was spent on education out of an annual budget of £26,082,012—or approximately 19 per cent. The estimate of educational expenditure for 1960–61 was £5,242,997 out of a total budget of £27,775,240, again approximately 19 per cent.

The number of boys in grant-aided primary schools increased by 66 per cent between December, 1952, and December 1959, and the enrollment of girls increased by 11 per cent; the number of boys in government and grant-aided secondary schools increased by 6,000 (or 67 per cent), and the girls by 2,000 (or 100 per cent). In 1952, 285 government and grant-aided school candidates, including 9 girls, sat for the Cambridge Overseas Certificate examination; 181 boys and 5 girls passed. In 1959, there were 659 candidates, including 50 girls; 501 boys and 48 girls passed.

Effects of the Economic Recession

Since 1958, the pace has been considerably slackened because of the lack of finances. Of the funds for the 1952–58 expansion, 30 per cent came from thc cotton and coffee marketing boards, but the resources of these boards have been drastically reduced in recent years as a result of declining world prices for Uganda's two principal exports. Reduced revenues from income, export and import, and excise taxes have also had ramifications for Uganda's education planners. In addition, there has been some flight of capital from the Asian community because of uneasiness over the political outlook following the 1959 boycott of Asian businesses organized by the Uganda National Movement. Also, few European businessmen are inclined to expand their businesses at this time.

The Department of Education's Annual Report for 1959 dealt bluntly with the effect of the recession on development plans.

> Development of this order (1952–58) was facilitated by a period of financial buoyancy during which revenue was expanding rapidly and by the existence of the African Development Fund. Neither of these factors now holds good. The heavy recurrent costs previously met from these funds are now a charge on the general revenue at a time when it has ceased to expand; in addition, the capital element of the fund is exhausted . . . it is now necessary to redeploy resources, both financial and human, in order to concentrate effort on providing only the more urgently needed facilities and on making available to teachers the advice and assistance to enable them to reach and maintain the high professional standards so vital to the realization of the country's demands.

The Primary Plan for 1960–63, prepared by the Ministry of Education on the basis of revised estimates of the country's financial prospects, emphasized that the development of primary education was essentially a local function, and that the purpose of a central plan was simply: (1) to set forth the policy objectives, (2) to indicate the interrelationship of the twin problems of improvement and expansion, (3) to define the extent and direction of the central government's financial contribution, and (4) to indicate the anticipated annual output of new teachers. It emphasized the necessity of attaining a Protectorate-wide parity of primary places by bringing the lagging districts up to the present over-all average level of one place for every two children.

In January, 1960, it was estimated that about 40 per cent of Uganda's school-age population were enrolled (1 out of every 2 in primary school, 7 out of every 1,000 in secondary school, and 5 out of every 10,000 in the sixth form). Areas falling below the Protectorate average—usually because of poverty or nomadism—were found to be the districts of Karamonjong (11.17 per cent), Kigezi (25.4 per cent), Ankole (27 per cent), and Busoga (37.4 per cent). The alarming degree of wastage found within Uganda's schools, both of pupils and places, prompted an application in 1960 for a foundation grant to carry out a country-wide survey on this problem. In 1959, for example, 159,837 places in primary schools throughout the country were reported unused.

The consolidated plan for educational expansion during years 1959–63 calls for an increase of only 34,720 primary places. In the light of Uganda's continuing financial crisis, the government has stated that it feels impelled to make a deliberate choice between expansion at the secondary level and consolidation at the primary level. Taking into account the tremendous expansion of primary education in the 1950's and the extent to which peaceful transition to independence depends upon educated leadership, educational planners opted to concentrate on secondary schooling. The public clamor for universal free compulsory education continues, however, and the government has drawn up a "notional plan" designed to acquaint those "who so light-heartedly campaign for universal education with the hard facts that lie behind the catch-phrase." The conclusions reached by the "notional plan" were:

At the present time, educational expenditures represent about 15 per cent of Uganda's budget and primary education about 7 per cent. Assuming that the proportion remains constant through the years, the projected expansion would entail a budget of £78 million in 1971, not far short of four times the present size. Again, assuming that taxation would continue to bear constant relationship to the present national income, the projected expansion would require a compound rate of increase of 12 per cent in the national income, and this does not appear likely, at least for the present. Finally, the average tax burden would have to rise from 51 shillings in 1959 to 229 shillings in 1971, a four-fold increase, at a time when crop prices are falling, and when far more moderate increases in personal taxes have already been bitterly resented in certain areas of the Protectorate.

The Report concluded that "eight years of education was the maximum which the majority of Uganda children could ever hope to obtain" and that, during the period 1960–63, "the great majority of Uganda children can aspire to no more than six years." The conclusion drawn from this harsh reality was that it was vital that the syllabi of the primary schools be attuned to the life that the children would have to live when they left school. Consequently, a new syllabus that pays particular attention to gardening, nature study, and hygiene has been compiled and issued, and a request has been made to the U.S. Administration for International Development for experts in the field of simple agricultural education to train African teachers. Supporting this change in emphasis in the curriculum, Minister of Education Y. K. Lule stated in 1960 that there were only about 300,000 paid jobs in all of Uganda, of which over two-thirds were in manual labor and did not require literacy; there were only 50,000 white-collar employees. Although much progress has been made in Africanization, a recent manpower survey of Uganda noted that only 99 of the top 879 administrative jobs in the government were held by Africans; of the 889 jobs for technicians, only 75 were filled by Africans.

In 1960, only 22 per cent of the children finishing primary school (266 out of 1,187) were able to obtain entry into junior secondary classes (although 40 per cent of those in the Kampala municipality were able to enter). The number of government and grant-aided junior secondary schools in 1958 was 154, with an enrollment of 11,722 boys and 2,579 girls; in 1959, there were 173 such schools, with an enrollment of 13,659 boys and 3,189 girls. Table 1 shows the progress between 1950 and 1959.

Out of a hundred students enrolled in the first year of primary school, fewer than fifty can expect to complete six years.

Deficiencies at the Senior Secondary Level

Of the children in the senior secondary age-group (estimated at 484,000), only 0.7 per cent were registered in senior secondary schools

Table 1
Enrollment in Uganda Schools, 1950–59

	School Enrollment		Number in age group	Percentage of age group in school
	1950	1959	1959	1959
Primary schools	159,200	337,578	993,000	34.0
Junior secondary	4,368	16,848	271,000	6.2
Senior secondary	688	3,412	484,000	0.70
Sixth form			232,000	0.05
University education			500,000	0.046

in 1960. There were 782 African boys and 78 African girls who obtained the Cambridge Senior Certificate in that year, and 49 boys and 4 girls who received the Higher School Certificate. On the other hand, there were 318 Asian boys and 210 Asian girls who received the Cambridge Senior Certificate, and 13 Asian boys who received the Higher School Certificate. For a population of over 6.5 million, these numbers are very small.

Planning for the improvement and development of senior secondary education in Uganda has been essentially a function of the central government. The senior secondary schools, regardless of their location, are expected to serve the whole Protectorate and to draw their staffs and students from all districts and all tribes. All senior secondary schools are boarding schools, and none is coeducational. They are frequently located outside the towns and resemble small American colleges in appearance. Generally, there are several small dormitories, two or three classroom buildings, an assembly hall, a handicrafts shop, a dining hall, some faculty homes, playing fields, and a chapel or church. Senior secondary education is still highly selective, and the curriculum is generally academic in character, designed primarily to prepare the students for the Cambridge examinations. English is used as the medium of instruction, although Swahili is generally taught as a subject. In addition to English, the subjects usually include mathematics, science, history, and geography, as well as some art, music, religion, handiwork, and physical education.

The 1960–63 educational plan sets the following objectives for senior secondary education:

(1) To provide senior secondary education for about 4 per cent of the local population in the fourteen to eighteen age-group—assuming that this will be the percentage of children likely to have the necessary ability to study at this level, and that the number graduating will meet the needs of the country for boys and girls educated to the School Certificate level.

(2) To build up existing schools to their most economical level of efficiency.

(3) To establish new schools where it is clearly more expedient to do this than to expand existing schools.

(4) To approve the establishment and development of new unaided schools where the need exists and the minimum requirements of staff, buildings, and equipment are satisfied.

In June, 1960, there were 3,728 senior secondary places (1 for every 26 children completing primary six), of which 3,578 were grant-aided. The teacher-pupil ratio was one to sixteen. These figures do not include seminaries.

It is the government's intention that all pupils holding a Grade I Cambridge School Certificate or its equivalent, as well as about 20 per cent of those obtaining a Grade II Certificate, will be able to complete the two years of study for the Cambridge Higher Certificate or its equivalent. Special provision is to be made for girls in this category. In 1960, there were 90 places available for entry; 150 places have been planned for 1961–63, and 185 for 1964.

Integration

In certain respects, educational facilities for Asian and European children still differ from those available for Africans. Up until 1956, all education in Uganda was organized on a religious and racial basis —African, European, Asian, and Goan. Teaching for Africans was in the vernacular in the primary stage and in English at the junior secondary level and above. The government has long been committed in principle to a policy of eventual integration, but had insisted that language difficulties made segregation necessary. However, an experiment in integration was tried in 1956, in a primary school in Entebbe set up for the children of African ministers who had come from various parts of the country to serve in the central government, and whose children did not speak the vernacular used as the language of instruction of the capital city. Rather than attempting to teach them still another vernacular, it was decided to use English as the medium of instruction and the same curriculum as that of the European schools. Information regarding the school spread, and other African parents were soon providing their children with private instruction in English in order to bring them to the required English-usage level for entry into the school. Today, European schools throughout Uganda admit African and Asian children whose command of English has been certified as adequate after testing by a special board and who have the money to pay their tuition (although some scholarships are offered).

Integration is also being practiced in some Asian and African schools that are being used as experimental centers for the use of English as the medium of instruction from the first grade. Since 1958, the government has embarked on a policy of integration for all existing government secondary schools; it is encouraging non-governmental schools to admit pupils of all races on a gradual basis, and has decreed that all new secondary schools are to be open to all races, with entry based on competitive examinations. Most of the secondary schools in operation prior to 1957 now admit some pupils —usually about 5 per cent of the total enrollment—from races other than those for which the schools were originally intended.

While integration has gone fairly smoothly in secondary schools, progress has been slower in the primary schools because of the diversity of languages, religions, and backgrounds. The first new interracial secondary school opened in January, 1960, and courses up to the Cambridge Certificate level are now being offered there.

Technical Education

Provision for technical education on a substantial scale is a comparatively recent development (1953). In addition to the Kampala Technical Institute, there are now twelve technical schools: five central-government schools (with 756 boys enrolled), one managed by the government of Buganda Province, and six operated by voluntary agencies. In addition, there are seventy-nine rural trade schools, of which fifty-five receive grants toward the cost of staff salaries and sixteen have obtained sizable capital grants. For girls, there are twenty post-primary homecraft centers, to some of which a third year of vocational training has been added. During 1959, responsibility for seven farm schools (with a total enrollment of 2,260 boys and 503 girls) managed by the local education authorities was transferred from the Ministry of Natural Resources to the Education Department. In addition, 790 students were being trained in apprenticeship courses.

The Kampala Technical Institute started in 1921 as the Uganda Technical College. This was a rather grandiose title for what was then a small technical school catering to the building, motor-vehicle, and tailoring trades. In 1953, in accordance with a general plan for development of technical education, the school was moved to Kyambogo and united with several other small centers to establish the School of Building and Civil Engineering; the Mulijibhai Madhvani

School of Commerce and Art; and the School of Mechanical, Electrical, and Automobile Engineering. Separate sections were also established for science and mathematics, technical-teacher training, and women's studies. In 1959, with a staff of sixty-seven (not all fully qualified), the Institute had an enrollment of 400 full-time students and more than 1,000 part-time students, including both men and women, attending eighty-three different courses—an all-time high for Uganda.

Gradually, a pyramidal structure of technical education has developed in Uganda, with a broad base of training facilities for craftsmen, a smaller layer of training facilities for junior supervisors and more advanced technicians, and an apex comprising the schools for engineers, architects, and other professionals. The Kampala Institute was given the responsibility of taking care of the midsection of the pyramid. Because it was thought to be uneconomical to train separately the few top-ranking technicians needed in each of the three territories, the Royal Technical College in Nairobi, Kenya, has taken over the training of candidates for the top of the pyramid for all of East Africa. Uganda student enrollment at the Royal Technical College in 1959 included fifty-five Africans and twenty-five Asians.

Actually, Uganda's technical-education program is running ahead of the country's needs: of the output of 235 graduates from technical schools in 1959, only 88 could be immediately placed in apprenticeships. Candidates for a few trades and crafts are being overproduced. Except for the Institute, the caliber of many of the technical and trade schools is not high, and some of the schools have far too few students.

Teacher Training

The primary-teacher–training schools have been geared to produce 1,000 primary teachers a year. In fact, this is too many, for with the slower pace of school expansion since 1958, some 500 to 600 would be sufficient. The average primary-school teacher has only six years of primary education, plus four years of further academic and teacher-training classes. The average junior secondary teacher has a Cambridge School Certificate, plus two years of professional training. A good solution to current overexpansion would be retirement of the older, less qualified teachers and their replacement with younger qualified persons. This has been done in some schools, but any dismissal evokes a storm of protest. In the period 1961–65, only 948 teachers will be eligible for retirement on pensions—that is, at fifty-five years of age. This same problem of overproduction has occurred in the training of development teachers; 700 have been produced annually, although funds did not exist to pay their salaries. Their intake has now been temporarily cut to 200.

In 1959, 126 men and 14 women were awarded certificates from the five junior-secondary-teacher–training colleges. These colleges provide a two-year course for students who have passed the Cambridge Overseas School Certificate examination; in addition, a one-year course for outstanding primary teachers is available, from which forty-six men and three women were upgraded to junior-secondary status in 1961.

The overproduction cited above does not apply to secondary-school teachers. It is, in fact, a matter of major concern to the government that, of the 256 established teaching posts in the senior secondary schools in 1959, 171 were filled by expatriates. Of fifty African teachers, only twenty-two had a graduate degree or its equivalent; all principals were expatriates. The average African senior-secondary teacher has been trained at Makerere University College (where average output has been three yearly). Frequently, Africans who have trained as secondary-school teachers take employment in other fields offering greater prestige, better salaries, special allowances, and better living conditions.

In order to encourage local graduates to enter the teaching profession, the government has established scholarships for the postgraduate Education Diploma course of the Institute of Education at Makerere College. These scholarships, six of which were awarded in 1960, cover the full cost of the courses and also provide some spending money.

The primary-school teachers were taught in thirty-two colleges by a staff of 270; of this total staff, 118 instructors and all the principals were expatriates. Ten of these colleges were run by the Anglican Church, eighteen by the Roman Catholic Church, and one by the Moslems; three were nondenominational.

Teacher-training–school output for the period 1957–60 is shown in Table 2.

Table 2
Teacher-Training-School Output, 1957–60

	Primary			Junior secondary			Senior secondary
	Men	Women	Total	Men	Women	Total	
1957	614	243	857	73	24	97	Average: 15 per year
1958	673	257	930	141	34	175	
1959	656	339	995	130	52	182	
1960	307	169	476	160	50	210	

In 1960–61, a joint Anglo-American plan was initiated for recruiting U.S. teachers for East African secondary schools; preparation for this assignment was to include study at Makerere for one to three years. Uganda was also likely to benefit from a UNESCO plan to recruit overseas teaching personnel at the same cost as salaries of local African teachers, with the difference to be met by UNESCO.

Training of Administrators

A training center at Nsamizi has been set up by the government at a cost of £1 million to speed the Africanization of government administrative posts. In 1959, there were sixty-eight courses offered, with 1,084 students enrolled. The original target reportedly was to have a quarter of the senior administrative positions in the government Africanized by 1963, but the pace of Africanization is being speeded up, since independence is now scheduled for 1962. In September, 1960, it was said that half the staff of the Ministry of Social Development were Africans, but that the degree of Africanization varied from ministry to ministry, depending upon the number of trained Africans in specific fields. In the fall of 1960, the female teaching staff of the Nsamizi center was reportedly all African, but there was only one African among the male teachers.

In 1961, Uganda's first law school was opened at the Nsamizi training center. Twenty-eight persons from various parts of the country, many of them drawn from existing native judiciaries, began a one-year course designed to develop a nucleus of better-trained judges and magistrates.

Women's Education

The women of Uganda have traditionally had much greater freedom than those in many other parts of Africa, and they have long played an important social and economical role. Even when illiterate, they have exercised considerable influence on the daily life of their community. In 1956, it was reported that there were 3,000 to 4,000 employed women, out of a total of 250,000 employed persons. Figures for 1952 gave the number employed in manufacturing as 350; in agriculture and forestry, 1,100; and in medical, health, and educational sciences, 1,176. Women were employed in the East African tobacco factories at Jinja for the first time in 1950. A few educated women work as teachers, nurses, and nursemaids for European and Asian children.

In the matter of education, however, African women have lagged far behind the men. The first formal education for girls was initiated by the Christian Missionary Society in 1895; by 1903, it was reported that 7,800 were enrolled in primary schools. In 1905, a boarding school for the daughters of chiefs and important persons in the community was opened at Gayaza. The success of this experiment encouraged the CMS to open other boarding schools in six other places. By 1928, there were 77,362 girls enrolled in schools, mostly in subgrade schools unsubsidized by the government. In 1936, there were 81,265 (but only 4,121 in recognized primary schools)—that is, 17 per cent of the total number of pupils enrolled. By 1952, the proportion of girls had increased to 20 per cent.

As late as 1947, there were only three secondary schools for girls, although a few girls were attending coeducational secondary schools. The first girls (three) sat for Cambridge School Certificates (that is, university entry) in 1941, but there were no more girl applicants until 1944. In 1951, thirteen girls took the examination. Makerere first admitted women in 1945.

The De Bunsen Committee's 1952 report recommended the extension and strengthening of the existing senior secondary schools for girls, the establishment of a junior secondary boarding school for each mission in every district, the increase of post-primary homecraft centers, provision for boarding facilities for girls in classes five and six, increased training facilities for African women teacher candidates, and upgrading of courses to meet the immediate need for primary and junior secondary teachers.

The report of the Minister of Education for January, 1960, showed that, despite rising budgetary difficulties, marked progress had been made in expanding education for women at all levels in the period 1953–59. There were 142,558 females in primary schools in December, 1959; 3,535 in junior secondary schools; 379 in senior secondary schools; 1,270 in teacher training; 23 at Kampala Technical Institute; and 68 in Makerere University College.

The results of the junior secondary examination in 1959 showed that 84 girls and 222 boys had passed. Of 659 candidates (50 girls and 609 boys) for the Cambridge Senior Certificate, 48 girls and 501 boys passed. Forty-nine boys and four girls received the Cambridge Higher Certificate.

Table 3 shows the progressive increase in the number of women at Makerere College between 1950 and 1961.

The first African woman in Uganda's Legislative Council was appointed in 1955; the first African woman doctor was qualified in December, 1958.

Table 3
Students at Makerere College, 1950–61

Year	Female	Male
1950	8	249
1953	13	314
1958	58	765
1960-61	68	912

Higher Education

Two institutions of higher education serve the four countries of East Africa today: Uganda's University College of East Africa (better known as Makerere) and the Royal College in Nairobi, Kenya. A joint-government decision was made in 1960 to work toward the establishment of a University of East Africa by 1966.* This proposal dovetails with the political federation of the East African territories envisaged by Tanganyika's Julius Nyerere and the principal nationalist leaders of Kenya and Uganda. It would ensure the coherence of university education in East Africa and provide an institution that ultimately could award its own degrees. How this University of East Africa will be financed and organized is still undecided, but the Tanganyika component was officially opened in 1961. It is now hoped that the over-all university can be established by 1963.

Located at Kampala, on a site of some 350 acres, Uganda's Makerere was founded in 1921 as a government-operated trade and technical secondary school. On August 1, 1922, the title of the school was changed to Makerere College, certain medical courses from Mengo Hospital Medical School were incorporated, and other faculties were added. In 1937, Makerere became an autonomous institution of learning for all of East Africa; its board was composed of representatives of each of the territories, as well as of the academic staff. Each of the four East African governments took a share of the responsibility for financing the school. In 1938, Makerere's status became comparable to that of a junior college. Eleven years later, it was rechristened the University College of East Africa under the same special relationship with the University of London enjoyed by other university colleges in English-speaking Africa. Examinations for the London degrees of B.A. and B.Sc. were held for the first time in December, 1953.

By 1949, Makerere had faculties of arts, science, medicine, agriculture, and veterinary science. There were 27 full-time and 5 part-time staff members and 222 students (213 men and 9 women), mostly African. The Faculty of Education was separated from the

* *See* pp. 154–55 for a further discussion of the proposed university.

University College of East Africa, at Kampala.

college in that year and established as a separate teachers' college. A 1949 grant of £1 million from the British Government's Colonial Development and Welfare Fund was used to undertake the first phase of an extensive building program aimed at creating facilities for an ultimate enrollment of 2,000 students. Buildings completed by 1960 included: four halls of residence for men and one for women; several staff residences; buildings for arts, medicine and veterinary science, and education; the Williamson Physics Laboratory; and laboratories for chemistry, botany, and zoology. Most of the cost of this building program has been met from British Government funds (£1,666,576) and from East African governments (£435,106). An additional £1 million is to be provided by the British Government for further capital development up to 1964.

Although major emphasis has been on improving teaching staff and facilities, there has also been an increase in the provision for research in all departments of the college. Makerere's East African Institute of Social Research is wholly devoted to research, for example, and its work extends throughout East Africa.

From the beginning, Makerere's charter stated that the college was to be open to all students of all races, but in 1950–51 registration was temporarily restricted to Africans in order to give as many Africans as possible an opportunity for higher education. This restriction was removed in 1952, but few Europeans and Asians have registered since that time. Of 912 students registered in 1960–61 (a four-fold increase since 1949), 812 were Africans, 6 Arabs, 83 Asians, and 11 Europeans. Almost two-thirds of the students were registered in the arts and sciences. Of Makerere's African students, about 38 per cent were from Kenya in 1960–61, 26 per cent from Tanganyika, 33 per cent from Uganda, and 2 per cent from Zanzibar.

The academic staff of 170 members, mostly recruited from British universities, included 23 Africans, at least three of whom held degrees from American universities. A new educational-development plan for 1961–66 envisages an increase of 1,200 students at Makerere, leading to a total of 2,100 in 1966. This expansion is designed to accommodate the increasing number of students graduating from secondary schools. The recurrent expenditures for 1960–61 were estimated at £645,000, as contrasted with £170,022 in 1949.

The Nature of Uganda's Educated Elite

In a study of 1,697 of Uganda's elite (former Makerere students, but not necessarily all graduates) prepared in 1958 by Professor J. E. Goldthorpe and Margaret MacPherson of the Sociology Department of Makerere,* it was found that the proportion of Baganda people in the enrollment of Makerere had dropped from 100 per cent in 1922 to about 50 per cent and that attendance by members of other Uganda tribes had risen correspondingly. Nevertheless, the largest numbers of educated Africans in Uganda are found among the Baganda; 671 out of the register of 1,697 names of "educated Africans" appear to be from Buganda. In the other Uganda provinces, educated Africans were said to be "not only fewer in numbers but also relatively younger and less mature and experienced."

By far the predominant occupation among former Makerere students was found to be teaching. According to information available to the college in late 1957, no fewer than 542 of its former students either were teaching at the time or had been teaching previously. Agriculture claimed the next largest number, with 103 working in governmental agricultural service and 27 as farmers. Among other occupations, 117 were working as medical practitioners, 72 as businessmen, 62 as administrators, and 79 as clerks, cashiers, etc.

Sixty-five chiefs, including the Kabaka of Buganda, the Kyabazinga of Busoga, the Rwot Adwong of Acholi, the Mukama of Ukerewe, the Ntemi of Usukuma, and the Chief of the Hehe tribe were listed as former Makerere students, as were sixteen county, divisional, or location chiefs, thirty-nine sub-county chiefs, and four parish chiefs and village headmen. The prime ministers of Ankole, Toro, and Bunyoro provinces also attended Makerere, as did two of the six ministers in the Buganda provincial government, three secretaries-general of African district councils, and two ministers of the Protectorate government.

In contrast to the gravitation toward law in some other parts of Africa, there were only seven lawyers in the group studied. There were also eight clergymen, three architects, and five independent journalists. Fifty-two men and women were working in community development and in cooperative societies, and fifty-three engineers on the register indicated training at Makerere before transfer to the engineering school at Kampala Technical Institute. Forty-four former Makerere students were working in the government veterinary service and fifteen were police officers.

The major employers of former Makerere students were the central governments of Uganda, Kenya, Tanganyika, and Zanzibar, which together employed 719 in 1958; another 162 worked for local governments. The Christian missions employed 273, of whom 260 were teachers. Smaller numbers were employed by business firms (96) or

* Goldthorpe and MacPherson, "Makerere College and Its Old Students," *Zaire,* Vol. XII, No. 4 (1958).

worked on their own (102). Many of the self-employed were small traders, but the number included fifteen doctors in private medical practice, five lawyers, three newspaper editors, seven building contractors, and seven headmaster-proprietors of independent schools. Nine worked for African cooperative societies. Makerere College itself employed five of its former students as lecturers, and others as librarians and on its laboratory staff. Ten former students had been teachers in the secondary-school section, when the Faculty of Education was still part of Makerere.

Professor Goldthorpe's survey indicated that 371 of those on the register of 1,697 had gone beyond East Africa for further education after leaving Makerere—a strikingly high percentage. Interviews indicated that study abroad had come to be regarded as an indispensable part of the education of the fully educated man. While the urge for overseas education undoubtedly was due in part to considerations of social prestige, there were also definite tangible benefits to be gained, especially in fields not yet offered locally.

By far the largest number to go abroad for study thus far have gone to the U.K., but smaller numbers have gone to South Africa, the United States, Canada, the West Indies, West Africa, Cairo, and Beirut. In the fall of 1960, the Minister of Education stated that there were about 1,100 students overseas, 1,000 of whom were in England (367 Africans, the balance Asians and Europeans). Table 4 shows the fields of study of the 367 Africans studying in England.

Table 4
Fields of Study of African Ugandans in England, 1960

Field of study	Number of students
Nursing	64
General education	55
Academic degrees	41
Engineering	38
Medicine	37
Education	32
Accounting and secretarial studies	20
Agriculture	18
Law	16
Administration	8
Miscellaneous diplomas	8
Semi-technical	6
Veterinary science	5
Building	4
Surveying	4
Architecture	3
Bookbinding	3
Forestry	2
Boat building	1
Cotton technology	1
Estate management	1
Total	*367*

Sixty-four Africans were said to be in India in 1960–61, four in Pakistan, and possibly two dozen in Communist-bloc countries (including twenty-two in Moscow and one at the University of Peking). In May, 1961, there were forty-eight Ugandan students in the United States studying in thirty-five institutions in twenty states. Six were also registered in Canada.

The Outlook

For many years, Uganda was looked upon as the Gold Coast of East Africa. Despite its present economic woes and its continuing failure to develop a cohesive nationalist movement, the outlook for the long run remains promising. An educated group is being imaginatively trained and progressively employed by a protecting power sympathetic to the Africanization of the country, and education for citizenship is increasingly widespread and practical. Uganda's Africans are critical of the pace of Africanization, but there appear to be few who take serious issue with the substance, methodology, or intent of present educational policies.

—Ruth C. Sloan

12. *Zanzibar*

Capital: Zanzibar
Population: 290,300 (est.)
Area: 1,020 sq. miles
Political status: British protectorate

Zanzibar and its sister island, Pemba, lie roughly twenty-four miles off the coast of Tanganyika; together they are no larger than Rhode Island, and their population in 1960 was less than 300,000.* In the nineteenth century, however, Zanzibar was the wealthiest and most important port of East Africa, and its Sultan ruled vast domains stretching up to the Persian Gulf and reaching deep into eastern Africa. The Sultan personally, and the island's Arab minority as a class, controlled the great wealth of Zanzibar—that is, the clove plantations and the slave trade. The Indians acted as middlemen for these enterprises. The Africans were the laborers and the merchandise.

Zanzibar's golden age faded at the end of the last century; its death knell was sounded by the abolition of the slave trade, the imperialist scramble for Africa, and the island's transformation into a British protectorate in 1890. Placed under the Colonial Office in 1914, Zanzibar continued to be an Arab state, modified only by the fact of ultimate control by a British Resident. Since 1914, Zanzibar's economy has been tied to the clove plantations, which produce over 80 per cent of the Protectorate's revenue. With the decline in the world clove market during the past few years, Zanzibar has fallen into serious financial straits. This economic recession has had important ramifications for education, rendering it increasingly difficult to maintain the existing system and postponing planned expansion.

Meanwhile, however, the public demand for education in Zanzibar is growing steadily, encouraged by the new nationalist political

* The estimated 1960 population included 50,000 Arabs, 220,000 Africans, 20,000 Indians, and 300 Europeans.

parties that have arisen in recent years. Although politics in Zanzibar reflect the traditional economic and social alignments on the island—the Arabs in one camp, the Indians in another, and the Africans in still another—all elements are aligned in pressing the demand for a rapid increase in educational facilities.

Constitutional reforms introduced in 1960 resulted in an elected majority on the Legislative Council in 1961 and the establishment of "responsible self-government" under a Zanzibari Chief Minister. The government is based on a fragile coalition between the Arab-dominated Zanzibar Nationalist Party and the small Zanzibar and Pemba People's Party, with the African-dominated Afro-Shirazi Party in opposition. The elections were marked by grave outbreaks of violence between the island's two major racial groups, a development likely to slow the transition to independence.

Policy vs. Reality

The over-all policy aim of the British Government in the field of education in its East African territories has been to provide primary education for all children and secondary education for about 20 per cent. There is, however, a wide divergence between policy and reality in Zanzibar because the declining economy has sharply restricted the availability of needed funds. Primary education for all Zanzibar children would mean 65,000 students in Standards 1 through 8. In fact, there were 17,602 (11,427 boys and 6,175 girls) in primary school in 1958—or less than one out of three children of primary-school age. There are approximately 28,000 children in Zanzibar of secondary-school age. If 20 per cent of these were in school, there would be 5,600 students; as of November, 1958, there were only 871 in secondary schools.

Even the more modest aims of the government for the period ending in 1960—primary education for all girls and boys in the urban areas, and for half the boys and as many girls as possible in the rural areas—have proved unattainable. The 1959 report by the Committee on Education admitted that this goal would not be reached, specifically citing the economic and financial depression of 1959 as the principal reason for the lag. Indeed, the Committee observed, the government would have difficulty maintaining the status quo unless urgent steps were taken to diversify Zanzibar's crops, expand its economy, and/or obtain foreign assistance.

In addition to its intrinsic inadequacies, the limited public education system in Zanzibar perpetuates inequalities between children who live in urban areas and those in rural areas, between boys and girls, and among the different racial groups. The literacy rate in urban communities is 5 to 10 per cent higher than in the rural areas. The rural areas of Pemba suffer most: in 1959, only 14 per cent of the eligible boys in rural Pemba were attending primary school. Girls' education receives far less attention than does boys', as Table 1 shows.

Table 1
Sex of Students in Zanzibar Schools, 1958

Type of School	Boys	Girls
Primary	11,427	6,175
Secondary	613	258
Technical	129	61
Teacher training	117	54
Total	*12,286*	*6,548*

The fact that Moslem girls are married very young presents a serious deterrent to the continuation of their education. Furthermore, the insistence that girls above Standard 3 or 4 must be educated apart from boys is a great drawback when classrooms and teachers are limited. However, during the period 1955–58, the over-all increase in girls' enrollment in schools was 47 per cent; this is largely attributed to the determination of the girls themselves and their mothers (and even their fathers) and the very gradual withdrawal from the practice of purdah.

There is serious imbalance in the educational opportunities for the different races in Zanzibar, with the African majority in the least advantageous position. In Standards I through 4, African children are in the overwhelming majority; but their numbers decline sharply in Standards 6 through 8, and there are very few Africans who reach the secondary level. In 1957, for example, there were only fifty-four African boys enrolled in the government secondary school for boys—approximately 19 per cent of the total enrollment. In the same year, ten African girls were enrolled in the government secondary school for girls, approximately 6 per cent of the total enrollment. In 1957, two out of nine African candidates passed the Cambridge Higher School Certificate examination. In comparison, 95 out of 164 candidates of all races passed the examination. Two major reasons cited for the lag in education of Zanzibar's Africans are that the African population has traditionally been in a poorer economic and social position than the Arabs and Indians, and that the home environment of the African child is often not conducive to serious interest in studies. The government reports a marked apathy toward education in many African parents, which causes truancy and dropouts among their children. Probably more important, there are few African children who can pay the fees necessary to board at the upper-level primary and secondary schools. (All of Zanzibar's six secondary schools are in or just outside Zanzibar Town.)

Since the more prosperous families in Zanzibar society often educate their children outside the government system, the balance in educational opportunities is even more distorted than official figures suggest. The Indian community has long run schools for its young; these are classified as voluntary-agency schools and are aided by government funds. The wealthier Arabs often send their children overseas or employ tutors. For example, the children of Sheikh Ali Muhsin, the leader of the Zanzibar Nationalist Party, were educated for a time in the United Arab Republic. No separate facilities are provided for European children in Zanzibar, and most of them over seven are sent either to the mainland or to England for schooling.

The Present System

Moslems represent 99 per cent of the people in Zanzibar, and Koranic schools have been in existence since Islam was first introduced there in the tenth century. Before the beginning of the twentieth century, secular education on the island consisted solely of mission schools (whose principal purpose was to care for freed slave children) and the schools established by the Indian community for its children. Government education began in 1905 with the foundation of a Department of Education, but there was very little progress in the field of public education until after World War I. Table 2 compares the numbers of schools and students in Zanzibar from 1920 to 1958.

Table 2
Schools and Students in Zanzibar, 1920–58

Year	Primary schools	Attendance
1920	27	2,151
1945	47	7,535
1958	77	17,602
Year	**Secondary schools**	**Attendance**
1925	n.a.	83
1945	n.a.	195
1958	6	871

Today, all schools in Zanzibar that teach secular subjects (except for a few primary schools) are either government schools or receive government grants-in-aid. There is no compulsory education. All schools receiving government support are open to any child, subject only to certain language limitations. Most primary schools employ Swahili (the official language) as the medium of instruction. Certain schools run by the different racial communities use Arabic, Gujerati, or English. English is taught from the earliest grades, and all upper standards are taught exclusively in English. Primary education through Standard 6 is free. Small fees are charged for the higher grades; however, these are often remitted if a student cannot afford to pay.

Almost every school child's education begins (and not infrequently ends) with the Koranic schools. These are self-supporting, and each of them forms as much a part of the life of its particular village as does the mosque. In 1958, there were an estimated 11,000 Koranic schools, with an estimated total enrollment of 19,200 (11,000 boys and 8,200 girls). Children enter Koranic schools at about the age of five and stay for one or more years.

Primary schools cover Standard 1 to Standard 8. At the end of the primary-school course, pupils sit for a common examination that is the main means of selecting those students who will continue into one of the government or government-aided secondary schools. However, out of every ten children who finish Standard 8, only one is able to go on to secondary school.

As in many other African countries, the most serious educational bottleneck is at the secondary level. There are only five regular secondary schools (three for boys and two for girls) although a Moslem Academy (not government-aided) started in 1952 offers post-primary instruction in Arabic and Islam. All five regular secondary schools (i.e., those for Standards 9 through 12) follow a four-year course leading to the Cambridge Higher School Certificate. These schools account for only 4.1 per cent of the total student enrollment in the Zanzibar school system; primary schools account for 93.5 per cent, technical schools for 1.2 per cent, and teacher-training colleges for 1.2 per cent.

Table 3 gives an indication of the scarcity of secondary-school space available to students who finish the final year of primary school.

Higher Education

There is no university training available in Zanzibar. Students must go either to the University College of East Africa (Makerere) in Uganda or to the Royal College in Nairobi, or they must seek places in foreign universities. At present, the Zanzibar Government pays an annual block grant of £5,000 to Makerere College and £3,000

Table 3
Number of Students Completing Primary School and Those Admitted to Secondary School

Year	Number who took primary-school leaving examination	Number admitted to secondary school the following fall
1952	304	152
1953	330	153
1954	528	172
1955	697	227
1956	783	232
1957	1,093	210
1958	1,070	213

to the Royal College in Nairobi, in addition to the normal tuition and residential fees paid by or in behalf of Zanzibar students. Under this arrangement, each year five new Zanzibar students are accepted at Makerere College and three new students at the Royal College.

In 1959, official statistics indicated that there were 15 Zanzibari students of all races at Makerere, 8 at Royal College, 156 in the United Kingdom, 20 in India and Pakistan, 20 at the Mombasa Institute of Moslem Education in Kenya, 3 in Iraq, 2 at the University of Khartoum in the Sudan, and 1 in the United States. There were also about 100 students in Egypt, but they were distributed among the primary, secondary, and university levels. More recently, at least twenty students are believed to have gone to Communist China on scholarships arranged by the Zanzibar Nationalist Party.

Most of the students who study abroad receive some government assistance in the form of scholarships. These students are chosen by a selection committee on the basis of the results of their Cambridge Higher School Certificate examinations. The percentage of Africans receiving such scholarships is extremely low, although no specific racial breakdown is available.

Teacher Training and Special Education

In November, 1958, there were 610 teachers in primary schools, 57 in secondary schools, 10 in the five technical schools, and 24 in the two teacher-training colleges. Many of these were foreigners, since there are still not nearly enough Zanzibaris to fill the required posts. Recruitment from overseas is becoming more, rather than less, difficult as Zanzibar approaches self-government, especially in regard to qualified women teachers. The turnover is very high, for only a few non-Zanzibari women teachers renew their contracts after one year; the Standard 12 government secondary school for girls had nine different teachers of English in 1957. The problem of turnover is not confined to foreigners, as administrative jobs in the government are luring many of the better-trained Zanzibari teachers away from the classroom, especially from the secondary schools.

The only post-secondary education available in Zanzibar is that provided by two teacher-training schools, which take the students two years beyond secondary-school level; one of these institutes is for men (117 students in 1958) and the other for women (54 students in 1958). Far too many teachers in the primary schools have not had such training, however—or much education of any kind, for that matter. The drag on student attainment caused by inadequately trained primary teachers will become more acute with the planned change from a six-year to a four-year primary course.

In addition to the teacher-training schools, there is a Domestic Science School, as well as a few small schools that specialize in vocational instruction.

Adult-education, technical-training, and vocational evening classes are organized on a modest scale by voluntary organizations and often conducted by government teachers in Zanzibar Town. Plans for extension-type courses that would reach rural and urban communities in both Pemba and Zanzibar are under consideration, but at present no money is available for such a project.

The Outlook

Zanzibar's greatest needs, as it advances toward self-government and eventual independence, is for capable and experienced political leaders. The Arab-dominated Zanzibar Nationalist Party, under the leadership of Ali Muhsin, has a considerable reservoir of educated people to call upon; but the African-dominated Afro-Shirazi Party, led by Abeid Karume (who has had little formal education), would be hard pressed to find enough adequately educated supporters even to fill cabinet posts. Because of the overwhelming preponderance of African voters, it seems likely that the Afro-Shirazi Party eventually will become politically dominant; it is especially urgent, therefore, that the government move rapidly to correct the racial imbalance in Zanzibar education and that it give priority attention to the rapid training of an African elite in skills comparable to those found in the Arab and Indian communities. Moreover, even taking into account the fact that Zanzibar is, and probably will remain, a basically agricultural and rural economy, there is general agreement that provision must be made for the education of its populace to some of the new responsibilities of life in the twentieth century. This would seem to require readjustments in the curriculum for those unlikely to go beyond primary level.

Financial considerations remain the principal deterrent. All government funds for education are derived from territorial revenue. In 1947, the government spent £80,000 on education; in 1953, £205,500; and in 1957, £372,800. In the year ending December 31, 1959, the Department of Education spent £347,284, of which £46,672 was in special nonrecurrent expenditures; and voluntary agencies spent £58,173. Simply to keep up the existing educational services, with no development of them, the government will have to provide funds amounting to £460,000 in 1962; £486,000 in 1963; £507,000 in 1964; and £530,000 in 1965. To finance proposed new programs in the period 1960–65—including the development of existing primary schools and the establishment of new primary schools, housing for teachers, coeducational primary-teacher training colleges, and a secondary school in Pemba—would require an additional £643,080. Of this total, Zanzibar hopes to receive £276,500 from the U.S. AID Special Fund for Tropical Africa and £157,700 in other American aid.

In the long run, however, Zanzibar must increase its own revenues in order to sustain and expand its educational system. As a 1959 Committee on Education pointed out, this would require a diversification of the economy to cease the nearly total dependence on one crop—cloves. There are, as far as is known, no significant natural resources on Zanzibar; but there is the potential for an impressive tourist trade, given a good modern hotel, a peaceful political transition, and suitable publicity. In short, Zanzibar is a country where educational reform (and, indirectly, prospects for long-term political and social stability) is crucially dependent on economic rebirth.

—JANE CAMPBELL

Part III

CENTRAL AFRICA

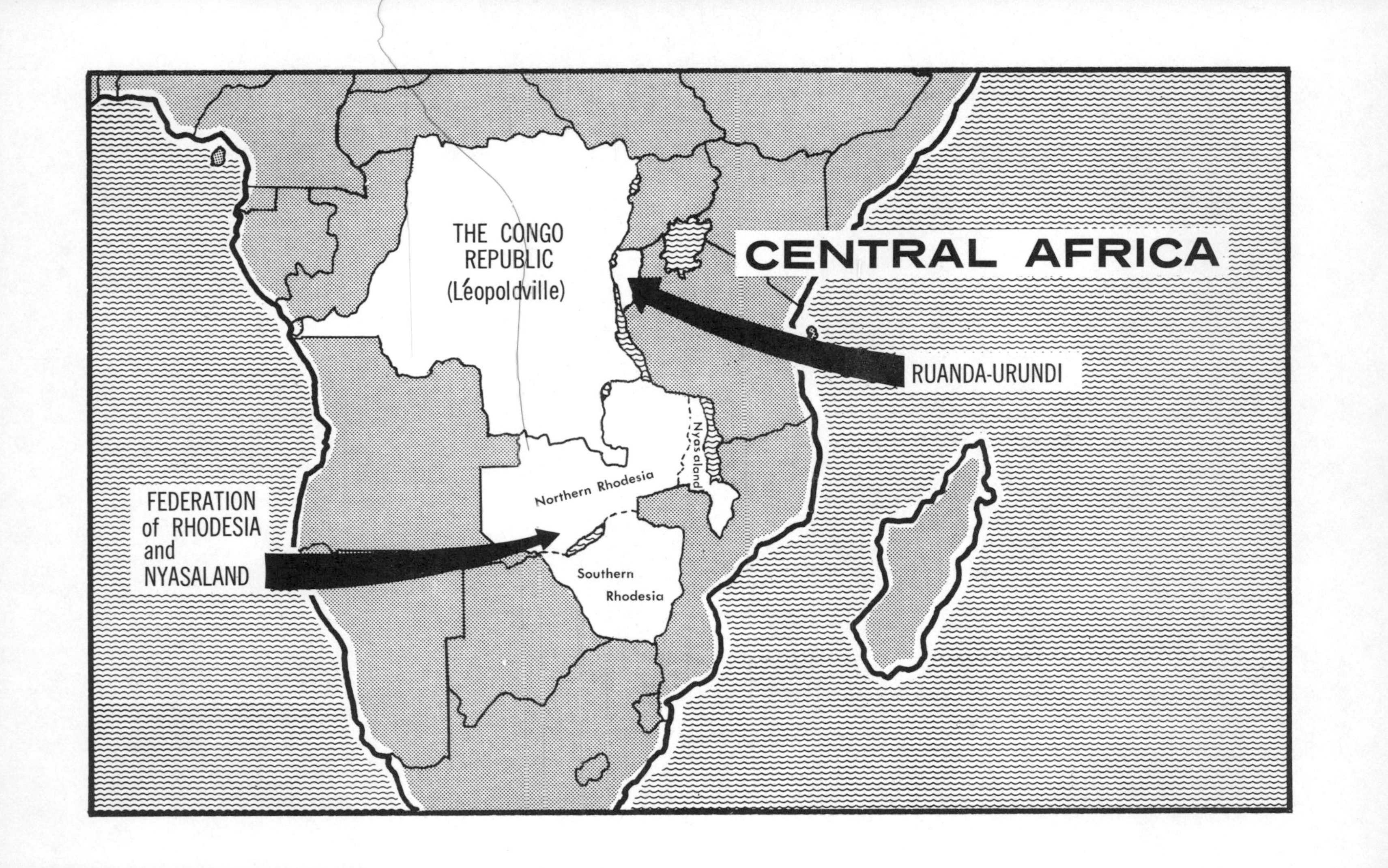
CENTRAL AFRICA
THE CONGO REPUBLIC (Léopoldville)
RUANDA-URUNDI
Nyasaland
Northern Rhodesia
Southern Rhodesia
FEDERATION of RHODESIA and NYASALAND

13. The Congo Republic (Léopoldville)

Capital: Léopoldville
Population: 13,652,857 (est.)
Area: 905,378 sq. miles
Political status: Independent republic

THE opening of the first school in the Congo took place in 1892, when the country was the Congo Free State, with Leopold II, King of the Belgians, as monarch. The educational policies for the Congo, as developed by the Belgians between 1892 and the new era that began with the 1959 negotiations for independence, reflected a concept of colonization sharply different from that of the other major European powers in Africa. Whereas Britain and France focused, in their educational systems, on cultivating a small, well-educated African elite capable of sharing almost from the beginning—and one day assuming—the responsibilities of administration and government, Belgium set its sights on building a social pyramid from the bottom to the top. The stated objective was to lift the Congolese masses to a fuller economic and social life, and thus give the population as a whole a personal stake in a productive and prosperous nation.

However, the progressively "fuller life" was to be within the African's native milieu. The Congolese were not to be turned into pseudo-Europeans. There was to be no African participation whatsoever in the political process until the pyramid had been firmly established. Pending the development of a stable bourgeoisie to serve as the base, creation of the apex of the pyramid—university-trained professional men capable of leadership roles in society—was to be given low priority. The time when Africans of the Congo would be able to act politically was placed vaguely somewhere in the future.

In Congolese schools, the Belgians placed the primary emphasis on a utilitarian education that would equip the child for a productive role in society and provide him with a solid religious faith.

The *Manual for Congo Personnel of the Territorial Administration,* first published in 1920, urged European administrators "to promote the moral and material evolution of the native population." It set forth a pattern:

> We should avoid one error in particular. The advancement of primitive peoples to a higher and better level is possible only if, instead of importing our ready-made concepts, principles, and institutions, we patiently strive to develop native civilization on its own grounds, according to its customs, its deepest trends, and in its own language. We should not attempt to form Europeanized natives but to train Africans, better equipped for life, possessing greater skill, and instructed in the knowledge that suits their mentality and their environment.

Thirty-three years later, Pierre Rychmans, who had served as Governor General of the Congo from 1934 to 1947, explained Belgium's educational policy in strikingly similar terms. The aim, he said, was to lead the Congolese toward "a measure of civilization and progress" rather than to form a small group of ersatz European elite "who would not be likely to have an interest in the welfare of the masses of Africans."

In an address delivered in 1954, André Dequae, Belgian Minister for the Colonies, pointed with pride to the differences between Belgium's concept of colonial education and that of Britain and France:

> Civilization cannot be limited to a few individuals or even to a thousand, for its purpose is to raise the whole people to a higher level. I do not think that the method which some countries have applied has had very favorable results. We have seen that those natives who have been shown Europe and given a very advanced education did not always return to their homelands in a spirit favorable to civilization and to the mother country in particular. They have gone back as *blasés,* estranged from their own people or turned against those who opened the door to civilization for them. In our view, civilization founded on a solid basis in their own environment offers greater guarantees.

Within the framework imposed by these policies, Belgium made remarkable strides in educating the Congolese people in over a half-century of rule. The rate of literacy—estimated at 40 to 60 per cent —is one of the highest in Africa, and no other country in the sub-Sahara can boast that between 50 and 75 per cent of its school-age African children have actually been in schools in any given year since 1950. When the Congo Free State became a Belgian colony in

1908, there were fewer than 100,000 pupils registered in Congo schools. By 1950, there were 921,386 pupils (50 per cent of the school-age population), and by 1958 there were 1,482,785 (excluding those in kindergarten). Between 1950 and 1959, the Belgian investment in education in the Congo and the Belgian trust territory of Ruanda-Urundi totaled $42 million annually—$36 million for Africans and $6 million for Europeans.

Table 1
School Evolution in the Congo [a]

Type of education	Number of students		
	1938	1950	1958
Primary education	725,000	904,000	1,413,603
Domestic science	343	4,233	14,038
Teacher training	1,954	4,819	17,552
Vocational and technical education (including higher institutes)	1,641	4,335	19,643
Secondary education (including high school, junior college)	660	4,004	17,949

[a] Excludes kindergarten figures.

SOURCE: Belgian official statistics.

The flaw in these impressive statistics lies in their relation to the revolutionary political changes that have taken place in the Congo since 1958, irreparably upsetting Belgium's long-term timetable. Once it became clear that the effort to keep the Congolese people from the tides of nationalism sweeping Africa had failed, Belgium moved quickly to adjust its educational and other policies. But it was too late. When the Congolese attained independence in June, 1960, their experience with political processes had been painfully brief, and they had no reserve of educated Africans with experience at the higher levels of administration.

Of the 1,482,536 children enrolled in the Belgian Congo schools in 1958, about 87 per cent were in primary schools; 43 per cent of these were in the first grade, and only 3.5 per cent (about 60,000) had reached the sixth grade. At the secondary level, there were about 300 schools with a total enrollment of 13,583. However, only 2,000 students were taking an academic course at the senior high-school level. The majority of the secondary schools were trade or technical-training schools. Fewer than 0.1 per cent of the children entering primary school were graduating from either academic or technical high schools by the time the Congo became independent in 1960.

The new multiracial Lovanium University, near Léopoldville, graduated its first Africans—seven of them—in 1958, but the new State University at Elisabethville had not yet produced its first graduates by independence. Although 136 able "medical assistants" had completed training by independence, the first Congolese M.D. was not graduated from Lovanium University until 1961, and no Congolese had been educated as a lawyer during the entire period of Belgian rule. Higher education abroad also was discouraged before 1959, although a few Congolese had received foreign degrees by independence. Figures on the number of Congolese university graduates by 1960 vary sharply, but even the official Belgian figure does not exceed thirty-one.*

Although the majority of teachers at the primary and elementary levels were Congolese, the country's secondary schools had only eighty-four African teachers—all at the junior-high level. One reason for this was that the Congolese school system required that teachers in senior secondary schools have a university degree with some post-graduate training. When the great push came in 1959 to move Congolese civil servants up the ladder more rapidly and train them for the monumental task ahead, the government had to comb the junior public services to find 500 Africans for promotion to middle positions. Relatively few of the 500 had a secondary education.

On the other hand, Belgium took justifiable pride in the scope and excellence of the system of technical education developed in the Congo. As early as 1907, at Léopoldville and at Stanleyville, the government created training schools as annexes to its workshops. But the major progress in this field was made after 1948, when mission establishments, the government, and private industry combined forces to develop a national program for the creation of a reservoir of technical and professional staff and artisans for the Congo's developing economy. In 1957, there were 460 students enrolled in six secondary-level schools for the training of agricultural assistants, 1,308 Congolese in twenty agricultural training schools, 192 in three horticultural schools, 44 in a fishing school, and 33 in veterinary schools. In the same year, 13,980 Congolese were in special schools for the training of transport workers, and thousands of others were studying, at various levels, carpentry, masonry, mechanics, iron crafts, welding, clothing manufacture, and other similar subjects. At the secondary level, many Congolese were in training as medical assistants, junior administrators, or school assistants.

* This figure does not include 417 Congolese Catholic priests, who had completed seminary training.

The School System as Established by Belgium

During the Belgian rule in the Congo, some 95 per cent of the Congolese children attending school went to mission schools. Under the terms of the Concordat of 1906 between Leopold II and the Vatican, Catholic missions were made the principal vehicle of African education in the Congo and were given a liberal government subsidy. Lesser subsidies were later allotted to certain Protestant missions, but Catholicism remained the quasi-official religion of the country. As late as 1957, the government's subsidies to missions totaled more than $23,493,000 per year.

When the Liberal Party came to power in Belgium in 1952, the Minister for the Congo and Ruanda-Urundi, Auguste Buisseret created a heated controversy when he announced his intention of introducing secular government schools. The influential Léopoldville newspaper *Courrier d'Afrique* published letters from leading Catholic organizations, African associations, and scores of individuals castigating the new Minister and insisting that African children in the Congo must continue to receive their education through religious channels. But the Association of Former Pupils of Protestant Missions and certain segments of the press—notably the other major Léopoldville daily, *L'Avenir Colonial Belge*—supported the policy of secularization. The new schools proposed by the Ministry included primary, normal, and technical schools in all important centers, as well as a state university in Elisabethville. The first government schools opened in 1955, but by the time the country had become independent only 25 of the 300-odd secondary schools were state schools. The first students to complete their course in a state high school were graduated in 1961. But, as of 1960, the majority of Congolese children still received their education in mission schools, of which over 80 per cent were Roman Catholic.

Administratively, the schools were classified in four groups, according to the financial support they received from the government:

(1) Schools operated by the Roman Catholic Church under government supervision. The government owned the buildings and equipment and paid the teachers' salaries. The teachers were mostly laymen, but were hired and supervised by the Church.

(2) Schools operated by Catholic and Protestant church missions. The government provided subsidies of about 70 per cent of costs to the Catholic schools and something less than 50 per cent to the Protestant schools.

(3) State schools owned and operated by the government.

(4) Nonsubsidized schools owned and operated by church missions, largely for the purpose of training priests and ministers. This category also included a few schools operated by private companies.

The first two categories comprised the great majority of schools in the Congo.

All Congolese schools, both religious and secular, have employed the same curriculum for the first two years of primary education. After that, education was channeled in two directions, depending on the natural capacity of each child as determined by a selective screening process. Those Congolese children who did not seem to have the capacity for a classical type of secondary education and those who were considered too old to gain advantages from a secondary education were directed into three-year schools classified as second-degree *ordinaire*. In urban centers, the children who entered these schools were trained, according to aptitude, in the trades or mechanical work; in the rural areas, they studied agriculture, animal husbandry, or allied subjects. Children who were likely to benefit from secondary education and those who seemed suited for technical courses entered the four-year primary *sélection,* which aimed at preparing students for academic secondary school and possibly higher education.

Secondary education was provided in two kinds of schools: technical (or "modern") schools, which complemented the education received in the *primaire ordinaire,* and academic (or "classical") institutions, which complemented the *primaire sélection*. Instruction in the secondary *ordinaire* prepared the Congolese student for a specific place in society. Enrollment was carefully calculated in relation to the number of expected job opportunities for graduates. In well-equipped and well-staffed schools and workshops, students at this level learned to become furniture makers, masons, motor mechanics, lathe workers, workshop supervisors, plant foremen, or, if they showed special aptitude, medical assistants or dispensers.

The "classical" secondary schools, far fewer in number, offered languages, literature, history, and other liberal-arts subjects, but they also usually prepared students for a special kind of work—as administrative or commercial clerks, teachers, or clergymen. On the basis of highly selective examinations, a few students were given the kind of foundation in the humanities, arts, and sciences required as preparation for university study. The vast majority of the secondary schools terminated at the ninth or tenth grade, however. Only 67 out of some 300 secondary schools existing at independence offered courses as far as the twelfth grade.

Alongside this basic school system (known as the *régime congolais),* a second curriculum (called the *régime metropolitain)* was developed for the children of Europeans who lived in the Congo. Its higher academic standards were geared to meet the school and university entrance requirements of Belgium. From 1948 until 1955, Congolese students admitted to a full six-year secondary course were largely confined to schools offering the *régime congolais* curriculum. With the establishment of state schools with *régime metropolitain* standards in 1955, the *régime congolais* secondary schools were spurred to modify their curricula in order to meet the new competition. In 1958, reforms were begun in the junior high schools *(écoles moyennes)* to bring all of them up to the same standard, but this has been a slow process on the whole, and the educational system in the Congo in 1960 was still characterized by a dual academic standard. Forty-two of the sixty-seven full senior high schools in the Congo used the *régime congolais* standards at the time of independence. Although the students in such schools receive a diploma, they must take a special entrance examination for admittance to the freshman class at Lovanium University. In order to pass this examination, an extra year of preparation is usually needed by the students, and such a course is given at the university. Students receiving their diplomas from metropolitan standard high schools are automatically qualified to enter Lovanium, as well as any Belgian university. Expansion of secondary education of all types has become, since 1959, a priority matter in all educational planning in the Congo.

More teachers are also needed. At the primary level, there were approximately 40,000 teachers and assistant teachers in 1960, most of them Congolese; by the time of independence, many of the primary-school principals in rural areas were also Congolese. The quality of primary-level education varies considerably from one school to another, and is further impaired by a teacher shortage in the upper primary grades. Training schools for teachers for grades one and two had an enrollment of 13,174 in 1959, for example, while the total enrollment for the same year in teacher-training courses for grades three to six was 566 students. At the secondary levels and at university levels, all teachers were European, with the exception of eighty-four Congolese teachers at the junior high-school level. There was a shortage of some 1,800 teachers at the secondary level when the schools opened for the 1960–61 year.

The Problem of Language

When the question of language of instruction first received official consideration, in 1922, the Commission of Education recommended that "native idioms" should be the principal instruments of education among Congolese Africans. Consequently, until 1959—when the changed political outlook impelled the government to introduce French as the language of instruction at the primary level—all teaching during the first two years of primary school was in local vernaculars—i.e., either one of the five main languages of Lingala, Bapende, Kikongo, Swahili, and Tshiluba, or an important local dialect such as Zande, Kirundi, or Kinyaruanan. The teaching of French as a subject started in the *primaire sélection* schools. African students moving on to secondary and higher education had to have acquired enough linguistic skill to follow the technical courses, which have always been taught exclusively in French at the upper levels. English and Flemish have also been taught in the secondary schools, although not to all students. Both secondary and higher institutions include intensive courses in the Bantu culture and languages.

Although many plausible reasons have been given for the emphasis on indigenous languages, there seems little doubt that this policy supported the Belgian Government's general intention to insulate the Congolese from disturbing outside influences. Since missionaries were virtually the only translators into the local vernaculars, they had a very close control of the reading materials available to Africans. Another factor limiting the use of French was the cultural prejudice against the language entertained by some of the Flemish missionaries. Certain tribally based Congolese nationalist groups supported the colonial government's policy on languages because of their desire to preserve particular tribal languages and literature. On the whole, however, there has been increasing African pressure in recent years for more extensive teaching of French, so that the full range of European knowledge would be more accessible to students.

Interracial Education: A New Development

The maintenance of two separate educational systems for European and Congolese children continued as a matter of policy from 1920 until the mid-1950's, when the government decided that the general advance of the country had proceeded to a point where it was feasible to take the risk of Europeanizing some of the best-qualified African students. As the standards of several of the schools for Africans had reached those of the European schools, it was decided in 1952 that some of the Congolese pupils emerging from these schools might be able to proceed with their education in schools heretofore reserved exclusively for European children. Only Africans "who possessed the necessary capacity"—i.e., were considered able to compete successfully with European children of the same age—were allowed to make the transfer.

While the principle of interracial education in the Congo had been recognized by the government in 1952 as part of its plan to arrange "the proper way to facilitate the coexistence of the two groups of inhabitants of the Congo," no Africans were actually admitted until 1954. Access to the European schools was initially restricted to those who fulfilled very strict intellectual and moral conditions and were suitable from the point of view of family standing. In Léopoldville, for example, only sixteen out of forty candidates were accepted in the first year. To obtain admission, the children had to provide parental guarantees that they would be brought up in conformity with Western precepts of behavior. Their father had to have only one wife, neither parent could have been in prison, the father's job had to be sufficiently stable to ensure that the child would be able to complete the full course of study, and the prospective pupil could not be older than the average age of the children in the class he wished to join.

To be admitted to an integrated kindergarten, the child was required to have an elementary knowledge of French. To enter higher grades in the primary school, he had to pass a written examination on his studies of the previous year. Admission to the classical section was to be determined by the same rules applied to European children. The standards for selection were made most severe, and it was stated that it was necessary that they be so "in order to compensate those parents who try to raise themselves and their children toward a European civilization."

In 1957, the Belgian Congo Government took additional steps regarding admission of the African children into schools organized for the Europeans. Hitherto, admissions had depended in part on the economic and social standing of the candidates' parents or guardians; but now a scholarship plan was developed. Directors of schools were instructed to apply the same standards to all candidates for admission, without regard to their color. Once admitted, the African child was to be governed by the same rules regarding moral or health contamination of co-pupils that applied to the expulsion or removal of European children. Directors and teachers were instructed to take particular care to develop joint activities for the European and Congolese children so that the schools would generate the atmosphere of mutual comprehension that would become the solid base on which the interracial society of the Belgian Congo would grow.

In 1959, the Belgian Parliament enacted legislation (introduced by the Minister for the Belgian Congo) establishing that the secondary and higher education certificates awarded in all approved schools in the Belgian Congo and Ruanda-Urundi were to be regarded thenceforth as equivalent to and interchangeable with those obtainable in Belgium. This legislation was designed to ensure that Congolese students would receive a standard of education comparable to that accorded European students, both in the Congo and in the metropole.

Education for Women

As in most of Africa, education for women has lagged far behind that for men in the Congo. The official reason given for this has been that Congolese parents who were willing to have their boys educated were not equally willing that their daughters go to school. Also, many girls were put to work in the fields as apprentices to their mothers.

Of the total Congolese school population of nearly 1.5 million at the end of 1958, only some 246,000 were girls. However, 233,746 of these were attending primary schools, as compared with 36,916 in 1946 and 6,377 in 1938. Teacher-training institutions had 2,367 women enrolled in 1938, 3,494 in 1948, and 11,549 in 1958. Vocational training for women is fairly recent; only 242 women were enrolled in such training in 1958. Also, there were only 242 women enrolled in Congolese secondary schools in 1958; a few others had been sent to Belgium for secondary schooling. On the other hand, 359 Congolese girls were reported to be receiving medical training in 1958—308 as midwives' assistants, 46 as midwives, and 5 as hospital nurses. The recent increase in school attendance by women has been attributed partially to the desire of the educated Congolese to have educated wives.

Boarding schools for Congolese young ladies have recently been established, mainly in the provinces of Léopoldville and Katanga. Secular and religious monitors teach in schools and in the social centers, and some have taken specialized courses in home economics and pedagogy in Belgium. A Congolese woman is a member of the Community Council in Léopoldville; others are speakers for African programs on the Congo radio. Some are typists and filing clerks, and others work in factories and stores and as children's nurses in European homes. But none had yet graduated from high school in 1960.

New Universities to Build the Apex of the Pyramid

With the 1954 opening of the University of Lovanium, a private Catholic institution attached to the University of Louvain in Belgium and heavily subsidized by the government, the Belgians finally began the task of building an apex for their Congolese educational pyramid. A second institution of higher learning, the Belgian Congo and Ruanda-Urundi State University, was created by decree on October 26, 1955, under the sponsorship of four Belgian universities.

Lovanium's 675-acre campus is located at Kimuenza, eight miles outside Léopoldville. The State University is located in temporary quarters at Elisabethville, in the heart of the rich Katanga mining area, but a plot of 1,250 acres has been selected on the site of the former Elisabethville airfield for a permanent campus. The initial cost of creating these two universities was high. The outlay between 1945 and 1959 was equivalent to about $8 million for Lovanium and about $3 million for Elisabethville. This, of course, was just the beginning, for it has been estimated that each professor costs the equivalent of $10,000 a year (including salary, lodging, and allowances) and that each student costs approximately $1,000. Both Lovanium and the State University were established as multiracial institutions, although, in practice, the percentage of Africans has been much higher at the former than at the latter.

In January, 1954, thirty students were entered in a university preparatory course at Lovanium, and ten months later eleven Congolese and three Europeans began their first year of university-level work, studying in the fields of natural and applied sciences, administration, education, and agronomy under a staff of thirteen professors. Admission standards are strict, for, in general, the same principles have been applied as those that exist in Belgian universities. Students seeking entrance must possess a recognized certificate proving that they have completed their secondary education and are capable of going on to higher studies. Access to the faculty of engineering is dependent upon a special entrance examination. Since these strict rules handicap some Congolese who may have completed six years of secondary education and appear to be intellectually equipped, but who lack certain academic or cultural requisites, a pre-university section is maintained to fill the gap. The pre-university year at Lovanium places major emphasis, for obvious reasons, on providing

Lovanium University, at Léopoldville—study room. *(Photo courtesy of Belgian Government Information Center.)*

the transitional student with a general cultural background—that is, a broad introduction to literature and fine arts; a course in general biology, with some discussion of the concepts of physics and chemistry; general mathematics; and considerable emphasis on modern languages.

Tuition, examination fees, and other college expenses at Lovanium are high, but a system of scholarships was developed so that qualified Africans need not be barred on economic grounds. Students whose parents' incomes are below about $3,000, for example, may receive a scholarship of about $400 and a small loan on trust. The amount of the scholarship and the loans diminishes in relation to the size of the parents' income. When the income exceeds about $3,600, no financial help is given. At the opening of the academic year, each student automatically receives free transportation from his home town or village; return fare at the end of the academic year is also paid, regardless of success or failure in courses.

The enrollment at Lovanium has steadily increased: For the academic year 1955–56, there were 77 Africans and 10 Europeans; in 1956–57, 119 Africans and 50 Europeans; and in 1958–59, 248 Africans and 117 Europeans. Despite the political chaos in the months following independence and the uneasiness among Lovanium's largely Belgian staff, the enrollment in June, 1961, was 350, of which 25 were Belgian and the balance African. The aim, according to Lovanium's rector, Monseigneur Gillon, is to have 750 students by 1962 and 2,000 by 1965.

Of the 251 students enrolled for the academic year 1957–58, 60 were in the pre-university general course and 14 in the pre-university scientific course; 54 were in the Faculty of Political Science; 25 in the Institute of Pedagogy; 23 in the Institute of Science; 23 in medicine; 19 in the Polytechnic Faculty; 13 in the Faculty of Philosophy and Letters (including the Congo's first 9 law students); 13 in the Institute of Agronomy; and 7 in the Faculty of Theology. The faculty at that time consisted of 72 European professors.

The first degrees were granted from Lovanium in 1958 to seven Africans and four Europeans. For the time being, these degrees are awarded on the authority of the parent institution, Louvain University in Belgium, but it is assumed that eventually Lovanium will be authorized to grant its own degrees and diplomas.

The State University at Elisabethville began its first academic year in 1956–57 with 10 Africans and 94 Europeans registered; in 1957–58, enrollment had risen to 17 Africans and 124 Europeans, with 10 additional Africans registered at an affiliated Agricultural Institute established in Astrida, Ruanda, in 1958. Like Lovanium, the State University has also found it necessary to establish a pre-university institute to prepare certain African students for a full university load. This institute was originally set up at Usumbura, Ruanda-Urundi, but has now been transferred to Elisabethville.

The State University was set up under indirect ministerial control, with policy-making centered in a Board of Trustees sitting in Brussels and in an Administrative Commission resident in Elisabethville. To ensure the equivalence of its diplomas with those awarded in Belgian universities, it necessarily follows Belgian curricula. However, in order to adapt itself also to specific African needs, the State University includes in its program courses that deepen the students' knowledge of the African environment—for example, general linguistics with special reference to African languages, African literature, African history, an introduction to tribal law of the Belgian Congo and Ruanda-Urundi, African art, the Congo economy, and physical and social anthropology in the African context. The teaching staff, by the university's second academic year, consisted of three principals and about fifty full- and part-time professors and lecturers. Post-independence data for the student body and staff are not available, but the university is reportedly operating with expanded enrollment.

Professors and other personnel in the Congo universities have, in general, been required to possess the same qualifications as those in comparable faculties in Belgian universities. To be appointed as a lecturer, the candidate is legally required to have a doctor's, chemist's, or civil engineer's degree, although there are some exceptions in practice. Financial and staff limitations rendered it impossible, of course, to create at the outset every faculty envisaged for the future. but by now the range of studies available to an African in the Congo is impressive. These include political science, administration, social studies, law, medicine, veterinary science, biology, pharmacy, agricultural science, geography, physics, mathematics, civil engineering, teacher training, applied psychology, and physical education. Examinations are held before examining boards that include a professor from each of the Belgian universities. As a result of the general satisfaction of these examiners with the competence of those earning diplomas in 1959, a measure was passed later that year recognizing the full interchangeability of degrees from the Belgian Congo and Ruanda-Urundi with Belgian universities. This meant that Congolese university graduates who wished to go to Belgium for graduate work could be guaranteed equality of opportunity.

The task of filling the Congo's leadership and professional vacuum has now fallen largely on these two fledgling universities. They are impressive institutions by any standards and, given time and seasoning, appear to be capable of providing a top layer of experts competitive with any in Africa. But really effective education is a slow process, and it will be at least a decade before the trickle of Congolese graduates from Lovanium, the State University, and universities abroad can be expected to affect the course of events. In the interim, both universities' high academic standards will be under mounting pressure as expanding secondary education swells the influx of students to the institutions of higher learning and the needs of the government and public life become increasingly more urgent.

Post-Independence Crash Programs

Although the new Congolese Government and the United Nations advisers in the Congo have given special priority to the placement at home and abroad of as many university students as possible, they have also been working at two other acute educational problems: (1) the inadequacy of existing secondary schools to absorb the qualified products of the primary system and feed the universities, and (2) the serious teacher shortage. There were only twenty Congolese in training to become secondary-school teachers a year after independence.

UNESCO undertook an emergency program in 1960–61 to recruit 500 French-speaking teachers for the Congo's secondary schools, teacher-training colleges, and technical schools to replace Belgian teachers who had left. In addition, UNESCO sought some fifty-four specialists to work with the central government's Ministry of Education and provincial ministries in re-establishing and developing the school system to meet the Congo's new needs. The cost of this operation, which is being carried out within the framework of the U.N. civilian operation in the Congo, is estimated at $4.15 million. By June, 1961, however, UNESCO had recruited only sixty-six teachers for secondary schools and fifteen experts in the administration of education from eleven different countries. Its task was complicated by the fact that Belgians were specifically excluded by U.N. directive and that France discouraged its citizens from participating in the U.N. Congo operation. Meanwhile, of course, the situation has been eased somewhat by the return of many Belgian teachers to their posts.

In April, 1961, a unique effort to accelerate the training of Congolese for higher-level jobs was announced in New York by its co-sponsors, the U.S. National Council of Churches, the Agricultural Technical Assistance Foundation of Los Angeles, and the Congo Protestant Council. This is the Congo Polytechnic Institute, which intends to operate twenty-two different centers of post-secondary training in medicine, agriculture, home economics, political science, public administration, and technical subjects. The total cost of the project, which has the blessings of the United Nations and the Congolese Government, is estimated at $28.5 million. It was envisaged that members of the American Peace Corps would eventually help bolster the staff.

Scholarship aid for both secondary and university training abroad also came from a wide range of sources to help fill the Congo's critical leadership vacuum. By early 1961, there were some 400 to 500 Congolese studying in Belgium, 300 of whom (including several African women) were on Belgian scholarships; and 90 in the United States, 35 of them privately sponsored and 55 on ICA grants. Three hundred additional U.S. scholarships have been promised. An estimated fifty students were reported to be in Soviet-bloc countries as of March, 1961. Two medical doctors have now been graduated from Lovanium; seven Congolese have completed the first year of medicine in universities in Europe on World Health Organization fellowships; and fifty-eight Belgian-trained "medical assistants" are being given accelerated training in France to enable them to qualify as medical doctors as quickly as possible. WHO has also provided additional professors for Lovanium, so that more students can be trained at home. The Food and Agricultural Organization is helping to restore training facilities for agricultural assistants, veterinarians, mechanics, village workers, and nutritionists to full operating capacity.

—RUTH C. SLOAN

14. Ruanda-Urundi

Capital: Usumbura
Population: 4,500,000 (est.)
Area: 20,915 sq. miles
Political status: Belgium-administered U.N. trust territory

RUANDA-URUNDI, Belgium's Switzerland-sized Central African trust territory, is moving toward a dubious future. A poor, landlocked area with the highest population density in sub-Saharan Africa (214 persons per square mile), it is also beset by unresolved tribal-political cleavages. Yet, under United Nations pressure, independence from Belgian rule is now set for 1962.

Although successive occupying powers and the U.N. have regarded Ruanda-Urundi as a single unit, it is, in fact, two separate entities. Before the advent of European rule, its two autonomously ruled kingdoms were constantly at war with each other. Political leaders from Ruanda and Urundi demanded separate independence during the U.N. debate on the area's future in early 1962.

Early Developments

Because of the physical isolation imposed by its central location and its forbidding terrain, Ruanda-Urundi was controlled by Europeans only after the Conference of Berlin awarded it to Germany in 1885. In 1884, Count G. A. von Gotzen had crossed Ruanda from east to west, met Ruanda's reigning Mwami, and set up a system of semi-direct rule through the indigenous feudal kings. The territories remained under German rule until 1916, when the Belgians, seeking a labor reservoir for their understaffed mines in Katanga, moved in from the neighboring Congo to take over the territory. Belgian control was sanctioned by the League of Nations in 1923, and Ruanda-

Urundi became a mandate of the League. In 1946, its status was changed to that of a U.N. trust territory.

Culturally speaking, the peoples of Ruanda-Urundi belong to the Nilo-Hamitic cattle-complex of East Africa and not to the Bantu agricultural complex of the Congo Basin, to which the territory has been recently grafted. Both semi-feudal kingdoms comprise three distinct cultural groupings or castes—the Batutsi, the Bahutu, and the Batwa. Until recently, the rulers of both sections of Ruanda-Urundi were the Batutsi, a Nilo-Hamitic people comprising about 14 per cent of the population; they supposedly came from the Galla country in Ethiopia over 400 years ago, and some anthropologists believe that they are descendants of the early Egyptian Pharaohs. In any case, they came to the area as a warrior class and became the rulers of the indigenous Bahutu majority. As lords of the land, the Batutsis believe in their innate superiority and abstain from manual labor and menial work. The Bahutu are a Bantu, agricultural people who have traditionally served as serfs of the aristocratic Batutsi. They comprise about 85 per cent of the population of the territory and ruled the land in the period before the coming of the Batutsi. Below them in the social pyramid are the Batwa, a pygmoid, hunting people indigenous to the area. Because of the dearth of hunting grounds, they have become wandering jobbers. The Batwa now constitute barely 1 per cent of the total population and are the dregs of Ruanda-Urundi society.

Political Prospects

Almost all the social and political revolutions that Africa is undergoing in the twentieth century can be found in microcosm in Ruanda-Urundi. The overthrow of the Batutsi aristocracy by the Bahutu majority, begun in 1957, is leading, for better or for worse, to a democratization of the society. The spontaneity of this development is in considerable doubt, however, since Belgium has openly shifted its support to the Bahutu and is thus playing a significant role in the internal power shift that is going on. Meanwhile, Ruanda-Urundi is being propelled toward political independence by pressures both within and outside its borders—especially by events in the Congo, by the inclination of the U.N. to speed the transfer of power to indigenous peoples in all its trust territories, and by the Batutsi-Bahutu struggle for power. The territory is also being drawn into the movement for larger African groupings. On economic criteria alone, its potential for survival as an independent state is very slim, and there is some talk of federating one or both of its component kingdoms with neighboring Tanganyika; an alternative possibility is that Ruanda might join Uganda and Urundi might federate with Tanganyika. In any case, the East African Federation envisaged by Julius Nyerere, Tom Mboya, and other leaders is seen as one day embracing Ruanda-Urundi. There is apparently little sentiment in favor of federation of either of the kingdoms with the Congo since the latter's independence. Despite different educational systems and different elite languages, Ruanda-Urundi is drawn to English-speaking Uganda and Tanganyika by long-standing cultural affinities that transcend the period of European rule.

In U.N.-supervised elections held in September, 1961, the voters of Ruanda officially abolished the Batutsi monarchy of Mwami Kigeri IV, already overthrown by a *coup d'état* in January, 1961, and gave thirty-five of the forty-four seats in the Ruanda Legislative Assembly to the Bahutu-led PARMEHUTU Party. Meanwhile, voters in Urundi gave fifty-eight out of sixty-four Legislative Assembly seats to the Batutsi-led UPRONA Party, which advocates early independence and the retention of the monarchy. A common front of twelve Bahutu parties took only six seats.

The Present System of Education

As in the Congo, the educational system developed by Belgium for Ruanda-Urundi has sought to adjust the African to life in a modern economy without uprooting him from his tribe or creating an educated political group. Although the Batutsi have been accorded more educational opportunities than have other parts of the population, the school system has not attempted to exploit the historical intellectual focus of the Batutsi, whose esoteric folklore, poetry, and speech patterns are a matter of record. The level of literacy is high by African standards, but there were no university graduates until the late 1950's. The language of instruction at the lower primary level is in the vernacular (Kinyarwanda or Kirundi) in rural areas and in Swahili in the urban areas; French, the elite language, is a second language in the European centers.

Role of the Missions

Education in Ruanda-Urundi, as in the Congo, has largely been a function of the Catholic Church through its missions and state-supported mission schools. Until the latter half of the 1950's, those few in the territory educated beyond the elementary level were trained for the priesthood. Secular schools are of recent vintage and have been inspired largely by the U.N. A modest program of adult education to combat illiteracy is carried on by mission schools, and evening classes for workers are sponsored by mining companies.

Developments Since 1951

In the 1951 U.N. Mission report, it was stated that about 400,000 of the territory's school-age population were in some type of school; however, 75 per cent of this total were enrolled in a Ruanda-Urundi peculiarity, the chapel or rudimentary reading schools (*écoles de simple lecture*) operated by Catholic and Protestant missions without government supervision or financial aid.

By 1955, in the third year of a Ten-Year Plan begun in 1952, 191 million of the 210 million francs allocated for education under the plan had been budgeted. In that year, the U.N. Mission prodded the Belgians for more secondary and vocational education and for a longer period of schooling for those already enrolled; the Ten-Year Plan allocation for education was subsequently increased by 80 per cent to 380 million francs. Indeed, education has comprised an increasingly large percentage of the Ruanda-Urundi budget every year since the territory came under U.N. supervision. In 1946, it claimed 5.3 per cent; in 1950, 9.6 per cent; in 1953, 16 per cent; in 1956, 16.9 per cent; in 1957, 20 per cent; in 1958, 21.8 per cent; and in 1960, 25 per cent.

By 1953, there were 200,000 pupils in approved primary schools; however, 146,000 of them were in the first and second years of school; 50,000 in the third, fourth, and fifth years; and only 4,000 in the sixth and subsequent years. Most of the expansion was thus in the lowest rungs of the system, and many of these schools ran only two-year courses. In 1957, there were 241,389 Ruanda-Urundians in school, as indicated by Table 1.

In 1959, the number of pupils in primary school was 247,133. This seeming slowdown in the rate of growth was caused by the shift on the part of the Belgian administration to the development of other educational sectors. The budget, strained at this point, could not stand continued developments in all sectors of education at the same time, and the United Nations was pressing for more attention to the post-primary student.

Secondary Education

The number of secondary schools in the territory rose from one to nine between 1950 and 1956. Notable among the new secondary

Table 1
The School System of Ruanda-Urundi, 1956–57

Type of school	Number of schools or sections	Number of pupils
State Schools		
Kindergartens and primary schools	17	2,912
Schools for male and female teachers	1	61
Teacher-training schools	1	36
Secondary schools	2	365
Preparatory school to higher education	1	10
Special schools	4	401
Subsidized Mission Schools		
Kindergartens and primary schools	2,686	234,010
Schools of pedagogic training	8	391
Schools for male and female teachers	15	1,515
Secondary schools	2	219
Special schools	29	1,469
Total	*2,766*	*241,389*

SOURCE: Belgian official statistics.

schools were the Athénée Royal, a nondenominational state school for 126 boys and 31 girls at Usumbura;* Lycée Stella Matutina, a Catholic girls school at Usumbura; and others at Nyanza, Kibeta, Nyakibanda, and Birambo. In 1957, there were fifty students in Belgium receiving secondary-school education. However, only 1 per cent (4,300) of the 430,000 Ruanda-Urundians in the age group from thirteen to nineteen were receiving post-primary schooling at that time.

In January, 1960, what has been described as Africa's most elaborate secondary school, the Collège du Saint-Esprit, was opened in Usumbura. It is run by the Jesuits for 380 pupils, including 51 European and Asian day students and 329 African boarders. Two-thirds of the Africans were Batutsi. By 1960, additional secondary *collèges, lycées,* and *athénées* also existed in Kigali, Kitega, and Kisenyi.

Vocational and Technical Education

In 1950, vocational education was obtainable at the Vocational School in Usumbura and at five manual-training shops there. Other types of technical training and specialized instruction were available at the Astrida school and at the School for Auxiliary Administrative Staff at Nyanza. There was also the Rubana Agricultural School.

By 1956, there were more than 1,800 pupils in the various voca-

* In this group were 72 Europeans, 74 Africans, 9 Asians, and 2 mulattoes.

tional schools throughout the territory. Two vocational schools (at Usumbura and Kigali) were then training 650 students as carpenters, mechanics, masons, and tailors. In the interior, there were fourteen trade schools operated by the various missions with around 500 students. A nine-month post-secondary School of Administration in Astrida had thirty students enrolled in 1960.

Teacher Training

Two types of schools were created by the Belgian administration to prepare staff for Ruanda-Urundi schools: (1) two-year teacher-trainee centers to prepare teachers with a requisite education of five years of primary school to teach in lower primary schools, nurseries, and kindergartens; and (2) three-year teacher-training schools (with an optional fourth year) designed to prepare candidates with a minimum background of six years of primary school to teach in primary schools. The "optional" fourth year is mandatory for those chosen to teach in the "selected" upper primary school.

The 1951 U.N. Visiting Mission observed that the teacher-training program was inadequate and that the standards for both African and European missionary teachers were too low. By 1954, the low-standard trainee centers were beginning to disappear, and more actual teacher-training schools were beginning to appear.

In 1956, there were more than 2,000 pupils in the various training schools and centers, but these schools lacked both the necessary facilities and qualified instructors.

Education of Women

Although women of the Batutsi aristocracy played an important role in traditional society, education for girls has not been emphasized in the school system set up by Belgium in the territory.

The 1951 U.N. Visiting Mission reported that the education program of the Belgian administration made no provision for "selected" upper primary schools for girls. After the basic five-year primary course, the girls might take one more optional year and then go on to teacher-training schools or intermediate domestic-science schools. The first Ten-Year Plan did not call for the creation of any secondary schools for girls.

In 1954, there were still no secondary schools for girls, although there were now three-year, post-primary domestic-science schools. The authorities said the people did not want women educated, but many educated Africans rejected this view, and the Bami (pl. of

Mwami) of both Ruanda and Urundi requested more educational facilities for girls in that year.

In 1956, there were only 4 girls in European-syllabus primary schools, although 61,595 were studying under the African syllabus. There were 7 girls receiving European-syllabus secondary-school education in that year and none in African-syllabus secondary education. Meanwhile, 569 girls were in teacher-training centers and 653 in vocational and domestic-science schools. By 1957, however, there were three girls' secondary schools; the Athénée Royal, for example, had 31 girls registered in that year. As of early 1961, there were still no college graduates among the women of Ruanda-Urundi.

University Education

In 1951, there was one Ruanda-Urundian studying at the University Institute of Overseas Territories at Antwerp. There were no Ruanda-Urundi Africans in other European universities, and no one was expected to qualify for entry before 1954–55, when the territory's first secondary-school graduates would complete their studies. The U.N. did not share the Belgian fear that higher education abroad would be too disturbing to the African and urged haste toward this end. In 1955, a few Ruanda-Urundian seminary graduates, with government assistance, went to the University Center of Kimuenza near Léopoldville in the Congo.

In 1956, the official University of the Belgian Congo and Ruanda-Urundi opened its doors at Elisabethville. This was a great disappointment to many Ruanda-Urundians, for an alternate plan had been to create a university center at Astrida offering courses in medicine, veterinary science, agriculture, pedagogy, and administrative and commercial studies. There were twelve students from Ruanda-Urundi enrolled at Elisabethville in the academic year 1956–57 and twenty students from the territory at the new Lovanium University in Léopoldville.

Twenty African students from Ruanda-Urundi were in universities in Belgium by 1957. Although Belgium had usually discouraged students in its colonial territories from going to countries other than Belgium or the Congo for schooling, four students from Ruanda-Urundi were at the University Institute of the Vatican in 1956, two at al-Azhar University in Egypt, and one at Oxford University in England.

Of the forty-one Ruanda-Urundians at Lovanium University in 1958–59, thirty-seven were Batutsi. There were eight in theology, eight in political and social sciences, four in medicine, three in chemistry, three in agronomy, two in law, two in commercial sciences, two in teaching, two in geology and mineralogy, two in biology, two in applied sciences, one in economics, one in psychology, and one in administration. Of the ten from the territory studying in Elisabethville (at the State University) in the same year, four were in agronomy, three in commercial sciences, one in law, one in administrative or social sciences, and one in education.

By 1960, there were two institutions of higher education in Usumbura: the official University of Ruanda-Urundi, which opened on October 20, 1960, with sixteen professors, thirty pupils, and two departments (agronomy and applied science); and a smaller Catholic institution.

In January, 1961, there were 156 Africans from Ruanda-Urundi studying in Belgium and the Congo, and the territory's first African doctor was about to complete his studies in Paris.

—William A. Payne

15. *Federation of Rhodesia and Nyasaland*

Capital: Salisbury, Southern Rhodesia

Northern Rhodesia
Capital: Lusaka
Population: 2,300,000 (including 73,000 Europeans)
Area: 287,640 sq. miles
Political status: British protectorate within the Federation of Rhodesia and Nyasaland

Southern Rhodesia
Capital: Salisbury
Population: 3,070,000 (including 215,000 Europeans)
Area: 150,333 sq. miles
Political status: Self-governing British colony within the Federation of Rhodesia and Nyasaland

Nyasaland
Capital: Zomba
Population: 2,830,000
Area: 45,365 sq. miles
Political status: British protectorate within the Federation of Rhodesia and Nyasaland

THE Federation of Rhodesia and Nyasaland came into being in 1953 when the self-governing British colony of Southern Rhodesia and the British protectorates of Northern Rhodesia and Nyasaland were united. It is a vast country—larger than the United Kingdom, France, Germany, and Holland combined, or, in U.S. terms, as big as Texas, California, and New York. The two Rhodesias form a savannah plateau, most of it over 3,000 feet high, cut by deep tropical valleys; the pleasant climate provided an attraction for European immigrants. Nyasaland, smaller than either of the two Rhodesias and not as well endowed with natural sources of wealth, is a green hilly country on the shores of Lake Nyasa.

The European settlement of Southern Rhodesia began when the Pioneer Column, under the auspices of the British South Africa Company, trekked north from the Transvaal to raise the British flag over Fort Salisbury in 1890. The company operated as the *de facto* government for thirty years, parceling out land and making "laws." The BSA Company police force established order, permitting the whole country to be opened to settlement. European immigrants came in increasing numbers just before and after World War I, and by 1923 the white population of Southern Rhodesia had grown so large and was so well organized that the colony was able to demand and get self-government. The Crown, however, reserved certain rights over legislation affecting Africans.

Compared with Southern Rhodesia, there have never been many European settlers in Northern Rhodesia, and there are even fewer permanent European residents in Nyasaland. Partly inspired by the antislavery efforts of Livingstone, chiefs in Nyasaland and the Paramount Chief of the Lozi, one of the largest tribes in Northern Rhodesia, concluded treaties with Queen Victoria; by 1900, the two northern territories were under the protection of the British Crown.

The Rhodesias, although not agriculturally rich, have enjoyed progress and prosperity because of their great mineral wealth, especially in the copper mines of Northern Rhodesia. But agriculture, chiefly at the subsistence level, still engages the great majority of the population. Nyasaland is the poorest of the three territories; aside from small exports of tea and tobacco, its major asset is its manpower. Africans from Nyasaland form a large part of the labor force for Northern and Southern Rhodesian industry, and their annual remittances to their families in Nyasaland form a sizable proportion of that country's revenues.

The total population of the three federated countries is more than 8 million, comprising 7,760,000 Africans, more than 300,000 Europeans, and 35,000 Asians and Coloureds. In Southern Rhodesia, the ratio of Africans to Europeans is 12 to 1; in Northern Rhodesia, 30 to 1; and in Nyasaland, 300 to 1. Since the establishment of the Federation in 1953, the federal government has been responsible for the education of Europeans, Asians, and Coloureds, and for the higher education of all races. African education is a responsibility of each of the territorial governments and must therefore be discussed separately for each.

Southern Rhodesia has been dominated from the beginning by its white-settler minority. The Matabele Rebellion of the early 1890's was crushed by settlers and the BSA Company police, and since then it has been considered a conquered country. Racial antagonism has been intense in recent years. While the necessity of providing some education for Africans was recognized from the start, a significant number of Europeans have felt that Africans were more useful "unspoiled." Many feared that if Africans were educated, they would compete with European labor. Some white extremists argued that Africans were uneducable. In whatever form, racial prejudice has slowed the pace of African education.

In Northern Rhodesia and Nyasaland, the white population has always been small, and government control remained in the hands of the British Colonial Office. But this has not been of noticeable benefit to African education in the northern territories. While the British Government envisaged gradual Africanization of these governments, the march of events in the territories has been much faster than anticipated. It has only been in the last few years that one could perceive a real sense of urgency in regard to African education.

Creating an adequate educational system in a vast country of 8 million people is an immense undertaking. Inevitably, any discussion of progress made must emphasize the work still to be done. It is well to point out that European settlement is less than seventy years old and that, in a rapidly developing country, there are a great many demands upon available financial resources, all of which compete with education for a share of the tax income. African education got off to a slow start, but has made rapid progress since World War II; under the pressure of African nationalism, the indications are that even greater efforts will be made and that the pace of development will be increased.

In the early years, Christian missions bore the entire burden of African education. The first mission was opened in Southern Rhodesia in 1859 by Robert Moffat and a group of the London Missionary Society. They were followed eventually by nearly thirty other sects. The educational efforts of the six leading denominations in Southern Rhodesia in 1950 are shown in Table 1.

Table 1
Leading Denominational Schools in Southern Rhodesia, 1950

Denomination	Number of schools	Number of pupils
Dutch Reformed	428	39,946
Roman Catholic	399	35,667
Wesleyan Methodist	249	31,171
Church of England	228	25,814
American Methodist	179	20,462
Salvation Army	139	14,621

The primary interest of missions was, of course, converting "heathens" to the Christian faith. Emphasis was often on quantity of pupils rather than quality of education. But the missions laid the foundation for African education throughout the Rhodesias and Nyasaland, and even today all but 6 per cent of the Africans in school in Southern Rhodesia attend mission schools. However, few of these African schools offer more than five years of schooling (through Standard 3).

The missions worked singlehandedly until 1899, when the first education ordinance was enacted in Southern Rhodesia, providing government financial assistance to missions and setting up minimum requirements for schools receiving aid. Thus some uniformity was imposed on existing schools. By 1947, when the government assumed responsibility for the payment of salaries of all approved teachers, the annual government contribution nearly equaled the annual contribution of the combined missions. In Northern Rhodesia, mission schools began receiving public funds in 1925, when the administration passed from the BSA Company to the Colonial Office.

African education has posed serious problems for both government and missions: a constant shortage of money and teachers, a multiplicity of African languages often intermingled in the same area, the difficulty of long-range educational planning in a new country where census figures were unreliable, and the fluctuation in African demand for education. Thirty years ago, it was sometimes difficult to get African children into school because parents were reluctant to lose their labor on the farms. Nathan Shamuyarira, Editor-in-Chief of African Newspapers, Ltd., recounts that his father, a teacher at the Waddilove Mission (S.R.), often offered sweets to the village children to entice them into the classroom. Sometimes he even "rounded them up" on his bicycle. Today, however, African parents and children alike view education as their greatest goal. In the reserves, most of the school buildings are built and paid for by the parents themselves. Families often make enormous sacrifices to save enough money for school fees.

Southern Rhodesia

R. M. Cleveland, Southern Rhodesian Minister of Local Government and Native Education, said in August, 1960, that 80 per cent of Southern Rhodesia's school-age children were actually at school. This figure, often cited, was probably arrived at by including all children who had begun primary school. Unfortunately, many drop out after a few months (as can be seen in Table 2). In any event, Southern Rhodesia has the best record of the three territories in the field of African education. The bulk of the school population is in the lower primary grades. The educational pyramid is very steep indeed.

Table 2
Enrollment in African Schools at the Beginning of 1958

Primary Education

	Sub-Standard		Standard					
	A	B	1	2	3	4	5	6
Boys	67,356	56,769	43,050	31,874	25,990	12,058	8,801	6,597
Girls	56,792	46,206	34,250	21,616	15,949	6,256	4,305	2,961
Total	*124,148*	*102,975*	*77,300*	*53,490*	*41,939*	*18,314*	*13,106*	*9,558*

Secondary Education

	Standard					
	7	8	9	10	11	12
Boys	2,119	1,821	858	327	20	11
Girls	891	641	96	52	6	2
Total	*3,010*	*2,462*	*954*	*379*	*26*	*13*

As the grade level rises, there are fewer schools and fewer qualified teachers available. Most African schools do not yet offer facilities beyond Standard 3, and many of the children who finish Standard 3 are unable to find places in the next grade. Age limits for the different grade levels have been imposed in an attempt to eliminate wide age ranges within grades: to enter junior primary school, a child must be past six and not yet eight; he must be under fourteen years of age to enter senior primary. Thus, if a child finishes Standard 3 at the age of thirteen and cannot find a place in Standard 4 the following year, he will be too old to try again the next year. Age limits help standardize the classes, but they also mean that many pupils are denied further education.

The real bottleneck occurs at the secondary level. Southern Rhodesia has two full government secondary schools. One, Fletcher High School near Gwelo, was opened in 1957. Goromanzi was opened in 1946 and now accepts about ninety new students each year. It is the only school in Southern Rhodesia that offers Standard 11, preparatory to university work. There are fifteen mission or privately operated secondary schools giving the general secondary course, most of them offering courses up through Standard 8. In 1958, a little over 1 per cent of all students were in secondary schools or their equivalent.

In Southern Rhodesia, as throughout the Federation, the secondary-school bottleneck has produced a surplus of Standard 6 school leavers. At this level of education, Africans often consider themselves too well educated for manual labor, yet they are unqualified for skilled jobs. J. B. Mwemba, Assistant Headmaster of Munali School in Northern Rhodesia and President of the Northern Rhodesian African Teachers' Association, says that in the 1930's a Standard 6 man was rare and could be assured of getting a white-collar job. But the situation is quite different now, and those completing Standard 6 are beginning to realize that they are not sufficiently prepared for skilled jobs. The following "letter to the editor" in the April, 1960, issue of *Parade* magazine illustrates the frustration of this group:

> After I had passed Standard 6, I spent the whole year at home because I could not get a place anywhere to further my education. At the beginning of this year I went to look for work but failed to get it again, from January until now. If I had known that my education would be useless, I would have told my father not to waste his money in educating me from the beginning to Standard 6.
>
> *(signed)* Frustrated

Dr. Walter Adams, Principal of the University College of Rhodesia and Nyasaland, said in Bulawayo on June 14, 1960, that a drive should be made to expand secondary education rapidly and to improve its quality. In his view, this deserved top priority in a consideration of the educational and national needs now that the university had been established. He also stressed the great need for training at post-secondary level, pointing out that the university would be able to take only 10 to 15 per cent of high-school graduates and that the rest must be given further vocational training for the good of the country as a whole.

The chief problem at the secondary level is a shortage of qualified teachers. Until there are more qualified teachers, secondary schools cannot be staffed; and until there are more graduates of secondary schools, there will be insufficient candidates for teacher-training colleges.

During the two decades between 1930 and 1950, teacher training in Central Africa advanced slowly. The numbers graduated in Southern Rhodesia were: 99 in 1935, 148 in 1940, 216 in 1945, and 334 in 1950. At the same time, losses were discouragingly high. In 1949, 299 African teachers were given certificates, while 222 teachers left teaching—mostly for better-paying jobs in business and industry. Between 1951 and 1954, the number of Africans teaching in local schools increased almost 100 per cent. Authorities anticipated that 5,000 teachers would be graduated from the colony's twenty-seven training schools between 1957 and 1961. In 1959, nearly 6,000 of the approximately 11,200 African teachers in Southern Rhodesian schools had teaching certificates, and of the remainder only some 500 had literacy qualifications below Standard 6. (The minimum qualification for untrained teachers was raised to Standard 6 in 1951.) There were also 465 qualified European teachers in Native Education.

Efforts are being made to cut losses in trained personnel by improving the status of the African teacher: with better pay and standards, the right to vote in territorial elections, and exemption from pass laws. Students who are unable to get into a secondary school often go into teacher training as the only way to continue their education. Then, when a more lucrative job comes along, they leave the teaching profession. Teacher wastage could perhaps be reduced by maintaining a balance between secondary schools and teacher-training colleges.

In 1956, the Southern Rhodesia Government introduced a five-year plan for African education. The objectives of the plan were:

(1) To provide five years of education for children up to fourteen years of age in the rural areas.

(2) To add annually in the rural areas thirty schools providing up to Standard 6 education, with the cost to be borne by government and/or native councils and missions on a pound-for-pound basis.

(3) To provide eight years of schooling in urban areas for children, provided they were not over fourteen years of age when they reached Standard 6.

(4) To have 420,000 children enrolled at school, 6,300 fully trained teachers, and an additional 3,600 uncertified teachers by the fiscal year 1960–61.

The enrollment objective was fulfilled in less than three years, and it was expected that the teacher objective would be met by the end of 1961.

A number of mission trade schools in Southern Rhodesia give rudimentary training in building and carpentry. But their graduates have been described by a senior government official as "mere handy-men." Two government schools, at Domboshawa and Mzingwane, provide thorough grounding in agriculture, building, and carpentry, as well as regular junior secondary-school education.

A new African technical college (built at a cost of £160,000) near Luveve Township, Bulawayo, opened in January, 1960, with forty-three students. Five-year courses meeting international standards are given in bricklaying, carpentry and woodwork, plastering, painting and decorating, plumbing, electrical installation, metalwork, and motor mechanics. The college is staffed by nine Europeans, of whom the principal and two teachers are university graduates. No Africans at present have the teacher training required, but, when the five-year course is completed, the best of the graduates will be selected to join the staff.

Until very recently, Africans have not been apprenticed by European journeymen. However, apprenticeship training in the engineering trades has recently been opened to Africans, provided they have the same educational qualifications as European apprentices.

Northern Rhodesia

The Colonial Office Report of 1958 states the government policy on education in Northern Rhodesia:

> It is the government's long-term policy to provide a full primary course of eight years for all children and it is estimated that already about 90 per cent of the lower primary age group (8 to 11 years of age) in the rural areas are at school. In the towns, however, the figure for children of this age group is less than 50 per cent. After the age of 11 or 12, only 50 per cent of the children are able to carry on with the upper primary course. Until more money becomes available for the building of schools and more teachers with secondary education qualifications can be trained, no rapid progress can be expected and the practical prospects of providing full primary education for all children therefore remains fairly remote.

The problem is most severe in the urban areas. The industrial boom in the Copperbelt created a large urban African population in Northern Rhodesia. By 1948, education was compulsory, but the pressure on the schools became so great that compulsory education had to be suspended in 1951 because space was available for only half the children of school age. Since then, the problem has worsened. In 1958, the Copperbelt, with an African population of 700,000, had no African secondary school, and only about twenty children from that area could be absorbed into secondary schools elsewhere.

On March 15, 1960, the copper-mining companies administered by the Rhodesian Selection Trust and the Anglo-American Corporation announced that they "propose to make available £1.3 million toward the cost of additional facilities for African education in the Copperbelt." By arrangement with the Northern Rhodesia Government, this sum will be devoted to the capital cost of providing "six years of primary education for those African children on the Copperbelt reaching the age of eight for whom no places would otherwise be available." This donation will make possible six years of compulsory lower primary education in the Copperbelt, and two out of every five children will be able to go on to upper primary and secondary schools. A new secondary school is to be built in each of the four main mining centers, and an existing secondary school at Ndola will be raised to senior secondary standard, training pupils to Standard 11. A teacher-training college is also to be built.

In 1958, Munali Government School in Lusaka was the only secondary school in Northern Rhodesia offering a complete matriculation course (Standard 11) to the Senior Cambridge Certificate level. Munali is a boys' boarding school, accommodating 400 pupils. Northern Rhodesia does not yet offer college preparatory work for girls, so the territory uses Southern Rhodesian facilities. In 1958, three girls from Northern Rhodesia were enrolled in the Sixth Form (Standard 11) at Goromonzi. Until recently, there was some reluctance on the part of African men to have their daughters educated. Today, however, education for women is not only accepted but demanded.

More than 500 teachers are graduated annually from fifteen teacher-training schools. Ninety-two per cent of the teaching staff in Northern Rhodesian schools is trained—the best record in British Africa. Some

Table 3
African Schools in Northern Rhodesia, 1958

	Lower primary	Upper primary	Secondary	Teacher training	Technical
Government schools	1	1	1	2	2
Local authority	378	134	5	1	11
Aided schools (other)	1,020	218	9	12	25
Unaided schools	33	10	2		
Total	*1,432*	*363*	*17*	*15*	*38*

twenty graduates of secondary schools go annually to the University College of East Africa in Uganda, to the United Kingdom, or to the Jeanes Training College at Chalimbana, Northern Rhodesia, for advanced teacher training.

In 1959, the British Government offered £250,000 annually for five years to provide scholarships for students of Commonwealth countries to attend teacher-training colleges in the United Kingdom. In 1960, nine African teachers from Northern Rhodesia were among the first to receive these awards.

At the end of 1958, there were thirty-two Northern Rhodesian Africans taking advanced courses outside the territory with the aid of scholarships from the federal and territorial governments, the British

Council, and the Beit Trust. Eleven were in the United Kingdom, and the others were in Africa, including five at the University College of Rhodesia and Nyasaland.

Nyasaland

The government educational plan for Nyasaland for the 1957–61 period included the following points:

(1) *Primary education.* In 1956, the proportion of the population between six and eighteen years of age enrolled in school was 41 per cent. It was proposed to increase this to 57 per cent at the end of 1961 by expanding schools and by building twenty-one new schools. This would require 230 new teachers and an increase in annual expenditure for primary education from £403,000 to £614,000 (a 52 per cent increase). Further attempts to limit the age range of pupils in each class were called for.

(2) *Secondary education.* The number of junior secondary schools was to be increased from eight to twelve, increasing the annual intake from 240 to 360. Existing senior secondary schools were to be expanded and a new school opened in order to increase the annual intake at this stage from 120 to 270. Annual expenditures on secondary education were to be increased from £59,000 to £163,000 (176 per cent) by 1961.

(3) *Teacher training.* Approximately 1,200 new teachers would be required to implement the plan. A new training college was to be opened, and two existing ones rebuilt. The expenditure was to be increased from £68,100 to £95,000 (40 per cent) in 1961.

(4) *Education of girls.* Places available for girls were to be raised from the over-all ratio of one girl to five boys to the over-all ratio of one to three by enlarging existing secondary schools for girls and coeducational schools.

Nyasaland's educational problems are much the same as those of the other two territories, but the situation is aggravated by poverty and the urgent need for educated Africans to take over in preparation for early independence. An African elected majority now exists in the Legislative Council as the result of constitutional changes introduced in 1960 and implemented in 1961, and further political evolution is only a matter of time. Nyasaland Africans have been violently opposed to federation from the beginning. Despite the possible economic advantages that might result from association with the two more prosperous territories, Nyasaland Africans feared that the Federation would be politically dominated by the powerful European minority of Southern Rhodesia. Dr. Hastings Banda, leader of the dominant Malawi Congress Party in Nyasaland (which swept twenty-two of twenty-eight elected Legislative Council seats in general elections held in 1961), waged his election campaign on a pledge of independence for Nyasaland outside the Federation.

Real progress in Africanizing the middle and upper echelons of the civil service has been made only since 1960. The Nyasaland Government, which will have to rely heavily on imported teachers for some years to come, recently launched an energetic campaign to recruit British teachers for its expanding secondary schools.

Table 4
Number of African Pupils in Schools

	1956		1957		1958	
Type of School	Boys	Girls	Boys	Girls	Boys	Girls
Primary	163,896	95,283	168,050	95,341	172,276	97,317
Secondary	835	44	827	92	1,035	164
Vocational	261	43	340	136	444	483
Teacher training	619	135	711	182	735	211

Of the 270,882 pupils receiving education in Nyasaland as of October, 1958, less than 0.5 per cent were in secondary schools. The first high school in Nyasaland was built in 1941. Standard 11 classes are now offered at Dedza Secondary School, and Nyasaland students are no longer obliged to do college preparatory work at secondary schools in Southern and Northern Rhodesia. The government secondary schools at Blantyre and Zomba also offer the full course leading to the Cambridge Certificate; they had a total enrollment of 310 in 1957. Eight junior secondary schools have been built since 1950, offering the first years of secondary education to another 452 students. The number of candidates for the government Standard 6 examination rose from 123 in 1953 to 3,914 in 1958. In the same period, candidates for the Standard 8 examination increased from 123 to 360. The government has recently built another secondary school at Mzuzu.

The government teacher-training college at Blantyre is planned as the coordinating institution for other Nyasaland teacher-training colleges. In 1958, the number of teachers increased by 944—of whom 305 were certificated. In that year, about half the teachers were formally qualified: 3,309 had certificates, and 3,053 did not (although 1,871 of the latter had some training). Ten Nyasaland African teachers received grants in 1960 under the Commonwealth teacher-training program.

The Government Trade School at Soche offers building and mechanical training. The present two-year course will be combined with a further three years of apprenticeship. The school will eventually produce seventy-five trained graduates a year.

The Economist (April 29, 1961) reported that Nyasaland had only thirty-three citizens with degrees or professional qualifications at the end of 1960; forty-three other Africans were in degree courses and twenty-nine in diploma courses abroad. On the basis of the present rate of development, it is expected that four trained graduates will be produced in 1969, and twelve in 1971. With no increase in the rate, there would be about 120 trained graduates and professional men available ten years from now. At present, 580 posts in the civil service and teaching require degree or professional qualifications. In the 1959–60 academic year, six Nyasas were studying at universities in the United States.

Major Problems

None of the three territories has ever had "enough money" for African education. Although the Federation is a country of more than 8 million people, its tax base is only several hundred thousand. The average per capita income of Africans in the Federation is equivalent to about $45 per year, less than 5 per cent of the European average.

Every European child in the Federation has a chance to get a high-school education; the schools and the teachers are there for him. But an African child has had less than one chance in a hundred of getting a high-school education; there is not "enough money" to provide the schools and teachers. Europeans point out that they contribute fifteen times as much tax revenue per capita as do Africans. R. M. Cleveland stated that the £3,267,000 appropriated for African education in Southern Rhodesia for the fiscal year 1960–61 represented about three and a half times the amount paid in various forms of taxation by Africans in the colony in the year 1958–59. On the other hand, as Thomas M. Franck, in his book *Race and Nationalism,* comments:

> Such reasoning ignores the generally accepted purpose of taxation, which is to redistribute wealth according to need, and not merely to pay it back in services to each donor in proportion to his contribution. It also ignores the realities of an economy in which the base of revenue-producing citizens can only be widened by increasing and more equitably distributing educational benefits.

The importance to the European community of bringing the African rapidly to the fore as a taxable-income earner is apparent when one extrapolates present rates of increase of the two communities. If 70,000 European taxpayers cannot provide for the educational needs of 7,000,000 Africans, how will 120,000 provide for 14,000,000? The longer substantial sacrifices on the part of the European community are put off, the greater the sacrifices will have to be. The sooner the African masses are educated to the point where they are capable of earning a taxable income, the sooner the European will be relieved of the burden of paying for African education.

Between 11 and 14 per cent of the annual expenditure of each of the three territories is devoted to African education. This is a high percentage by world standards.

Another problem common to the three territories has been the language of instruction in the schools. English is the official language throughout, but educational authorities believe that literacy in the mother tongue is essential to the study of English as a second language. Thus, the general policy is that the mother tongue should be the language of instruction up to about Standard 4, at which time English should be introduced as the language of instruction. By Standard 6, instruction should be entirely in English. Oral English is introduced in the first or second year of school as a second language, with reading and writing beginning in Standard 1.

The problem is that each of the three territories is a patchwork of different tribes speaking different languages and dialects. Often several tribes are intermingled in the same area. School administrators have had to determine which language should be the language of instruction in each area or primary school, and have then had to find teachers and texts for that language. Even if an African child is literate in his own language, there is seldom much reading material available in that language after he leaves school. Where several African languages are spoken in one area, a single vernacular must be chosen. But educational authorities have recommended that the culture of the other language groups be taught in teacher-training schools and passed on verbally in the traditional manner to the children whose language has not been chosen. The principle is that, if the language is lost, the culture is in danger of being lost, too. If Africans are to make a contribution to world culture, they must know and respect their own cultural inheritance, and this inheritance is irrevocably tied to language.

The language of instruction involves numerous problems of both theory and practice. The majority of children do not receive more than four years of schooling; since it generally requires four years to achieve permanent literacy in a language, is it wise to spend time on teaching English to these children? Frequently, no qualified English teacher is available in reserve schools. At the Standard 6 level, the competence in English of both teachers and students is often so weak that students cannot understand what is being taught. These problems can be solved only by general improvement—more qualified teachers and fewer drop-outs. In Kenya, an experiment was tried of giving one year of intensive English at the beginning of secondary school. This solid foundation in English enabled the students to progress in the other subjects at a much faster rate in subsequent years, and the disproportionate amount of time spent on English in the first year was judged worth while.

Higher Education

The University College of Rhodesia and Nyasaland, in Salisbury, was incorporated in 1955 by Royal Charter as an affiliate of the University of London. It is independent of any government, although Britain gave an initial grant of £1.4 million, and the government of the Federation committed £150,000 annually for five years. The Queen Mother is the president of the college, which offers courses in science, general arts, and agriculture leading to degrees of the University of London.

The first classes at the University College began in March, 1957, with 71 full-time students, of whom 8 were Africans. By 1960, there were 38 Africans in a student body of 168. The University College announced its first graduates in January, 1960; these included three Africans. The number of African students will presumably increase as more African secondary schools offer Form 6 work, although authorities hope to maintain the institution's present multiracial character. The Malawi Congress Party of Nyasaland discourages Nyasas from attending the University College on the grounds that it is used to publicize and institutionalize the Federation. Dr. Banda's dream is to establish a Nyasaland university—the University of Malawi—on the site of the Scottish mission school in Livingstone.

The federal government has announced plans to build, equip, and staff a teaching hospital (with about 350 beds) adjacent to the University College. While the government has accepted responsibility for the teaching hospital, the question of the medical school remains. The University of Birmingham has offered to sponsor the school, and a number of donations have been offered. The hospital will cost £1 million, with annual recurring costs of about £235,000.

UNIVERSITY COLLEGE OF RHODESIA AND NYASALAND, AT SALISBURY—DINING HALL OF MANFRED HODSON (RESIDENCE HALL FOR MEN). *(Photo courtesy of Linforth & Robinson.)*

Attitudes Toward Education

Africans in all three territories pursue education with passionate intensity. They view it as a right, not a privilege. Education is seen as the open sesame to European power and prestige. A diploma is revered and often has a significance far beyond academic achievement. Many Africans who have reached a certain stage of education have a positive aversion to physical labor. For example, the luxurious, multiracial Ridgeway Hotel in Lusaka wanted to train a cadre of African hoteliers. They hired students from Munali secondary school and started them from the bottom up. But not many Africans with secondary schooling were interested in training that included manual labor, and the scheme has been abandoned. Similarly, the copper mines have difficulty finding educated Africans for responsible, well-paid positions, if the job involves dirtying one's hands. As a result, many Standard 6 graduates continue to seek work as white-collar clerks, often with little success.

Administrators have tried to maintain British standards in the schools. But many African children, especially in the reserves, do not reach the level of academic achievement of European children of the same age or class. Primary schools are often crowded, teachers poorly qualified, and reading material limited in many of the vernaculars. Standards in the government secondary schools are generally on a par with European schools, however, and results of the final examinations for the Cambridge Certificate at Goromanzi school compare very favorably with those of European secondary schools.

Educated Africans in the Rhodesias and Nyasaland feel that they are often denied the opportunity to use their abilities to the fullest. While they readily find employment, usually as teachers or with the government, they believe they are not regarded as equals by their European colleagues, and as a result they lack self-confidence. Africans are often paid less for doing the same work as Europeans. An African secondary school graduate who becomes a teacher may find that he is paid so little that he cannot qualify for the full voter's roll. In some areas, however, wage scales of Africans and Europeans doing the same jobs are being brought into line.

African governments in Northern Rhodesia and Nyasaland may find that the demands of the African population will make universal primary education a political necessity. At the current stage of economic development of the two northern territories, this could mean a curtailment of secondary education. Since one of the first goals of an African government would be Africanization of the civil service, there will be an acute shortage of secondary and university graduates to fill these jobs. A more prudent course would be to maintain a rapid expansion of secondary-school facilities, even if it means delaying universal primary education. Imported teachers will undoubtedly be required for some years to come.

The long-range future of mission schools is uncertain. In the 72nd Session of the Nyasaland Legislative Council, H. B. Chipembere, a leading African politician, called for a policy of progressive take-over of education from the missions. He said: "I think it is a sign of failure that a state should depend on certain voluntary agencies in educating the people that it rules."

One thing is certain. African governments will face the same basic problem that the European governments have faced—wise allocation of limited resources to a variety of pressing educational needs.

Political Attitudes of the Elite

Are there differences among the leadership cadres that have emerged in each of the three territories? It has been said that most Southern Rhodesian Africans were, at least until recently, more "moderate" than Northern Rhodesians and Nyasas. One might conclude that this stemmed from the fact that a good number of Southern Rhodesians were educated in South Africa, particularly at Fort Hare, while Nyasas and Northern Rhodesians more often went to Makerere, the United Kingdom, and India. But a more accurate conclusion would probably be that differences arose not from different educational backgrounds so much as from different political contexts. Educated Africans in all three territories are politically minded, and the goals of all are more or less the same. It is the means advocated that have varied. The government of Southern Rhodesia is controlled by the white minority. To Southern Rhodesian Africans, "partnership," at the time it was conceived, sounded like the most they could hope for. In Northern Rhodesia and Nyasaland, African leaders have never accepted the Federation. Why should they tie themselves to a borrowed white-settler problem when the alternative could be independent African governments? By 1960, African views in Southern Rhodesia had hardened noticeably, and the earlier stereotype of a placid Southern Rhodesian elite was quite outdated.

Part IV

PORTUGUESE AFRICA

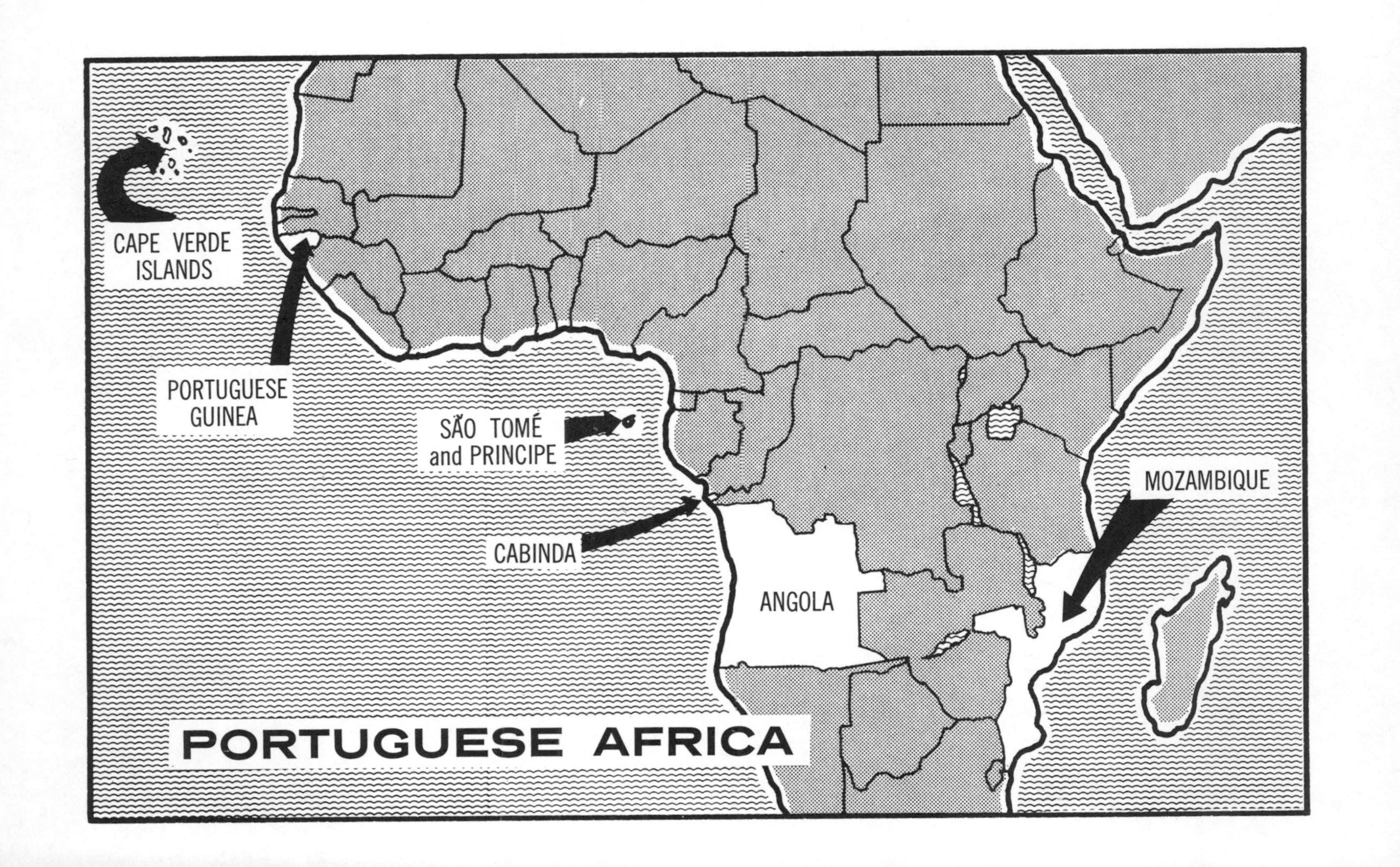
CAPE VERDE ISLANDS
PORTUGUESE GUINEA
SÃO TOMÉ and PRINCIPE
CABINDA
ANGOLA
MOZAMBIQUE
PORTUGUESE AFRICA

16. Portuguese Africa

Mozambique
Capital: Lourenço Marques
Population: 6,310,000 (est., including 65,798 Europeans)
Area: 297,731 sq. miles
Political status: Portuguese overseas province

Angola
Capital: Luanda
Population: 4,500,000 (est., including 80,000 Europeans)
Area: 481,350 sq. miles
Political status: Portuguese overseas province

Portuguese Guinea
Capital: Bissau
Population: 565,000 (est.)
Area: 13,944 sq. miles
Political status: Portuguese overseas province

Cape Verde Islands
Capital: Praia
Population: 147,326 (1952 est.)
Area: 2,000 sq. miles
Political status: Portuguese overseas province

São Tomé and Principe
Capital: São Tomé
Population: 60,159 (1954 est.)
Area: 372 sq. miles
Political status: Portuguese overseas province

For the African child growing up in Angola or Mozambique—or in the other, smaller Portuguese provinces in Africa—the prospect of education beyond the rudimentary level has so far been remote. According to 1958 UNESCO statistics, the illiteracy rate among Angola Africans was 97 per cent. In Mozambique, fewer than 300,000 African children (out of a total school-age African population in the territory of about 900,000) were enrolled in some kind of school during 1957; less than 1 per cent of these were above the third-grade level.* Intermediate and higher education have been available only to whites, Asians, and children of those few thousand Africans who have so completely absorbed the Portuguese language and culture as to become officially regarded as first-class citizens (*assimilados* in Mozambique and *civilizados* in Angola), on a basis of equality with white Portuguese.

Precisely how the new political reforms announced by Portuguese Overseas Minister Adriano Moreira on August 28, 1961, will affect the system of education now existing in Portugal's African provinces is not yet clear. These reforms would abolish the legal distinction between those Africans who have "assimilated" Portuguese civilization and the great majority of tribal Africans. All will henceforth share the same constitutional rights, Dr. Moreira said, "with no distinction of race, religion, or culture." However, the vote will generally be limited—as in metropolitan Portugal—to persons who can read and write Portuguese or who can pay 200 escudos (about $7.00) per year in taxes. In some local elections, however, all heads of families will vote. In the same announcement, Dr. Moreira also noted plans to increase white settlement of both Angola and Mozambique, and expressed a particular hope that many of the soldiers engaged in suppressing the Angola rebellion would decide to remain in the territory as settlers.

The Philosophy of Education

At all levels, the schools for Africans are primarily agencies for the spread of the Portuguese language and culture. The educational policies followed in Africa reflect the Portuguese Government's unique concept of its colonial responsibility—to work toward integration of the Africans within its jurisdiction into Portuguese culture and society, rather than toward the goal of preparing them for eventual self-government. Broadly, the Portuguese ideal has been that carefully controlled education will in time create an African populace that speaks only Portuguese, embraces Catholicism, and is as intensely Portuguese nationalist as citizens of the metropole. If all Africans in these territories become Portuguese nationalists, *ipso facto,* there is no threat of African nationalism. But only 30,089† Africans in Angola and 4,349 in Mozambique had reached the

* These statistics must be seen, however, in relation to Portugal's own educational problems. According to 1958 UNESCO figures, the rate of illiteracy in Portugal was 44 per cent. Similarly, more than 50 per cent of Angola's Europeans are illiterate.

† Including families of Africans and mulattoes (called *mistos*).

legally recognized state of complete assimilation into Portuguese culture by 1950.

In implementing these policy objectives, the Portuguese Government has decreed that only one language—Portuguese—is to be taught in schools under its jurisdiction in Africa. African languages are used chiefly as a means of facilitating the teaching of Portuguese, but even this is rare. Whatever the long-range prospects for this approach, the intermediate situation has been the creation of a class of people that looks down upon its own traditional languages, but is not sufficiently educated to be able to use Portuguese effectively.

On the assumption that political unity is founded upon a moral unity, the Portuguese have attached great importance to religion in African education. Although the constitution of Portugal specifies no preference among religious faiths, 98 per cent of the populace of metropolitan Portugal are Roman Catholic, and Portuguese law and practice in recent years have largely restored the pre-Republican unity between Church and state.* On the assumption that creation of a spiritual link between the motherland and overseas territories is vital to the establishment of the desired political oneness, the Salazar regime encourages the diffusion of Catholicism in Africa and has virtually turned over the elementary education of Africans to government-subsidized Roman Catholic mission schools.

School Systems

There are two categories of school systems in the Portuguese territories of East and West Africa: (1) the Roman Catholic mission schools, whose primary function is to educate Africans through the primary level; and (2) the more sophisticated government school system, catering to whites, Asians, and *assimilados*. The schools for Africans are organized as follows:

* Portugal was officially secularized after the overthrow of the monarchy in 1910, but the separation of Church and state was never entirely effective. By 1919, subsidies had been restored to Catholic educational institutions. In 1926, when the present authoritarian regime took control after a decade of violence and instability, the special role of the Church in the civilizing of Africa was given legal status. By the Colonial Act of 1930, Catholic missions were accorded a privileged position as against all other religious groups on the grounds that Catholicism represents the national faith of Portugal and is therefore the logical "instrument of civilization and national influence." The Missionary Agreement of 1940, supplemented by the Missionary Statute of 1941, restored all property confiscated by earlier regimes and emphasized the national character of the Catholic missions. A 1941 decree prohibits the granting of subsidies to other than Portuguese Roman Catholic missions.

Ensino de adaptacao (or *ensino missionario*)—This program is officially the responsibility of the Roman Catholic missions, although some Protestant missions also are permitted to operate modest schools. The school years are: *Iniciacao* (kindergarten), *Primeira Classe* (first grade), and *Segunda Classe* (second grade).

Ensino primário—This program is for students who have passed the *ensino de adaptacao.* It comprises: *Terceira Classe* (third grade), *Quarta Classe* (fourth grade), and *Admissao* (preparation for admission to the *liceu* program).

The schools for Europeans, *assimilados,* and others are organized along the following lines:

Ensino Primário (primary education)—A five-year program; the last year is prescribed for entrance to the high-school program.

Ensino Liceal—Including the *Primeiro Ciclo* (two years), the *Segundo Ciclo* (three years), and the *Terceiro Ciclo* (two years). The third cycle is designed for those preparing for entrance into a Portuguese university.

Prior to 1940, all school curricula for African schools were established by the Department of Education and Instruction in the territory; examinations were conducted by the state, and certificates were awarded solely by the Director of Education. From 1940 to 1960, the Catholic Church officially took charge of preparation of the curriculum, and the examination questions and tests were conducted and certificates awarded to students on Church authority. Preparation of the curriculum is now in the hands of the Ministry of Education in Lisbon, in line with the 1960 reorganization of the African colonies into provinces of Portugal, and inspectors from the territorial office of the Director of Public Instruction pay periodic visits to the mission schools. It is clearly understood, however, that no government inspector may visit a Catholic school without the permission and cooperation of the proper religious authorities. For all practical purposes, the office of the Cardinal Archbishop of Lourenço Marques is the central point of educational authority in Mozambique, while the office of the Archbishop of Luanda directs African schools in Angola and São Tomé. In all schools for Africans in Angola, Mozambique, and Portuguese Guinea, the curriculum is uniform except for a few local variations.

The *ensino de adaptacao* program, the equivalent of kindergarten and the first two grades in most other African territories, is designed to introduce African children to the Portuguese language and the beginnings of the three R's. Since the teaching is done in Portuguese, many African children are unable to pass the *adaptacao* examinations (normally given after three years of instruction) until they are twelve to fourteen years of age.

The *ensino primário* program—that is, the third and fourth years—covers materials similar to those used for Portuguese children at the same level. Content analysis of the textbooks used indicates that the entire focus is on Portuguese culture; African history and culture are totally ignored. Emphasis is on the Portuguese language; the geography of Portuguese territories; the history of metropolitan Portugal, including Portuguese discoveries and conquests; Christian morals; handicrafts; and agriculture.

Beyond the fourth year, there is a class where students are theoretically prepared for either high school or industrial or technical schools. However, very few mission schools actually have this fifth-year program, so the opportunity for an African child to gain the necessary certification to permit him to enter secondary school has been almost nil, unless he moved to the city to attend a private school qualified to prepare him to take the admission exams for the secondary program.

Although over 98 per cent of the white Portuguese living in the African territories are Catholics, the government has retained control of the schools catering to the educational needs of whites, Asians, and *assimilados*. Children from these groups may attend either state-owned or privately owned schools, but curricula and examinations are, in both cases, supervised by the state. These state schools for Europeans are under the administrative direction of the Ministry of National Education in Lisbon. Within the Ministry, education in Portuguese Africa and Asia is supervised by the Department of Overseas Education. There is a Division of Education for Portuguese East Africa, another for West Africa, and one for Guinea and the islands, each headed by a territorial director. Each director is assisted by two inspectors, one for primary schools and the other for school health.

Education is compulsory for all European children who reside within three kilometers (almost two miles) of a school and are between seven and twelve years of age. Although the prescribed age of entry into primary school is seven, children may be admitted one year earlier. The curriculum of these state schools is the same as that of all Portuguese schools at the same level in metropolitan Portugal, except for some minor adjustments to local geographic, climatic, and social conditions.

A considerable number of European and Asian children, and a very few Africans, attend private schools supervised by the government. These schools—all Catholic in orientation, since Protestant schools are generally forbidden to receive Europeans—do not discriminate against Africans, but only a few Africans can afford to send their children to tuition schools. The average tuition is the equivalent of about $17.50 a month, and most of the African students are necessarily boarders, which raises the cost to a prohibitive level for middle-class African parents.

The Protestant Role

The over-all character of the private schools in Portuguese Africa has undergone considerable change in recent years, with the number of Protestant institutions dwindling sharply and the number of parochial schools rising proportionately. Although there is no specific legislation covering private schools catering to whites and assimilated Africans, government policies have increasingly favored Catholic institutions, especially in Mozambique. In 1940, when the Missionary Agreement turning over African education to the Church was signed, there were eighty Swiss mission schools in the southern region of Mozambique. These have gradually been reduced to eleven. Usually, the sequence has been a report that the school buildings were not in accordance with the requirements of the Department of Health, followed by a "temporary closure" to correct the shortcomings. During the period of suspension, a Catholic mission sets up a bush school a few miles away. When the Swiss mission, having brought its facilities up to standard, applies for reopening, the application is rejected on the ground that it is illegal to have more than one school within five kilometers (about three miles). The few Protestant schools still in operation in 1961 regarded their days as numbered. In most private missionary schools, the government urges that instructors be Portuguese nationals.

Protestant missions have been in a much more favorable position in Angola than in Mozambique because government authorities there have accepted them as one of the means of "Europeanizing" the Africans. However, there has been a marked increase in anti-Protestantism since the rebellion began in Angola in early 1961, and local Portuguese vigilante groups have reportedly killed several Methodist African ministers because of a belief, encouraged by the controlled press, that the Protestant missions were centers of subversion against the regime.

Teacher Training

The same dual standards that apply to the educational process in the Portuguese territories are carried over to the training of teachers for African and European schools. When the Catholic missions took over education of unassimilated Africans in the 1940's, the training of teachers for these African schools also became a function of the Church. The government normal school in Mozambique, which was closed down after the Missionary Agreement of 1940, reopened in 1945 as a Catholic rather than a government institution. Prior to that time, African teacher candidates needed only to complete the fourth grade to be eligible for admission to the training school, but now membership in the Catholic Church is also a prerequisite. Teacher candidates for the African rudimentary schools are drawn largely from nonassimilated Africans, though *assimilados* may also apply in Angola.

In 1960, there were four of these teacher-training schools in Mozambique operated by the Church and subsidized by the government; total enrollment was 341 male students, with some 65 graduates per year. In Angola, there is one such school for training teachers for the beginning *adaptacao* program; the 1954 enrollment was 121 males, with a graduating class of 89.

Staff for the government-operated primary and secondary schools for the "civilized" population of Angola, Mozambique, and other Portuguese areas come from metropolitan Portugal. There is one registered normal school in Angola legally entitled to prepare teachers for the private "civilized" schools. During the year 1954–55 (the last year for which statistical data is available), this school at Sa'da Bandeira had only thirteen students registered.* However, it is possible for an individual who has completed the first cycle of high school to obtain a teacher's certificate qualifying him to teach in the lower grades in the private "civilized" schools.

Schools in Relation to Population

In 1955, according to official reports, there were 2,311 educational establishments in Mozambique, including government, Catholic, Protestant, and private schools. Of these, 2,041 were rudimentary schools, with a total enrollment of 242,412; they consisted of 2,000 Catholic mission schools for Africans, 12 government schools, 27

* *Anuario estatistico da Provincia de Angola,* 1954 (Luanda, 1956), pp. 158–85.

Protestant mission schools, and 2 other private schools. Most of the schools at this level are really bush schools with poorly trained personnel and inadequate equipment. There were, in the same year, 190 elementary and transitional schools with 17,663 students. Ninety-four of these were government schools for Europeans, Asians, and *assimilados;* sixty-seven were Roman Catholic schools, chiefly concerned with education of Africans; two were Protestant schools for Africans; and there were twenty-seven other private institutions catering primarily to whites, Asians, and *assimilados.* In effect, the approximately 6 million Africans in Mozambique are served by 69 schools at the third- and fourth-grade level, while less than 100,000 Europeans and other minorities are served by 121 schools at this level. For the Africans, moreover, this level is—except in a few rare cases—the highest they can expect to go. Of the 240,000 African children in schools, two-thirds were male.

In Angola, the total number of pupils (all probably Africans) in the beginning *ensino de adaptacao* schools was officially reported in 1956 as 49,144, of whom 38,849 were in Catholic schools and 10,295 in Protestant schools.* The Angola statistics are of little value for comparison with those for Mozambique, however, since they appear to exclude many bush schools that are obviously included in the Mozambique figure. Lord Hailey† reported that the total enrollment of Protestant schools in Angola was said to be over 79,000. Since this compared with an official total of 10,295, it could be assumed that the bush schools accounted for the very large discrepancy.

In Portuguese Guinea, a territory of 14,000 square miles located between independent Guinea and Senegal, there were ninety-nine rudimentary schools and twenty-three primary schools in 1955; while enrollment figures are not available for that year, unofficial statistics for 1954 indicate that 4,075 European and African children were in rudimentary schools, 2,700 in primary schools, 150 in secondary schools, and 160 in four vocational training schools. These were not all Africans, of course, but the racial breakdown is not available. In an address in Lisbon in January, 1961, the Governor of Portuguese Guinea, Commander Peixoto Correia, said of education in his domain:

> There are no separatist ideas afoot in Portuguese Guinea, and there is not the slightest vestige of racial discrimination. . . . With regard to education, one of our main preoccupations has been to make it available to every inhabitant of Portuguese Guinea. Already there exists a high school, also an industrial and commercial school, and, in

* *Ibid.*, 1956, p. 73.

† Hailey, *An African Survey* (rev. ed.; London and New York: Oxford University Press, 1956), p. 1215.

> addition, a school for agricultural apprentices. There are courses in nursing; workshops for the training of artisans; a postal, telephone, and telegraph school; night courses for office workers; about 170 primary schools in the charge of a considerable number of African teachers, and to which farms are annexed for the purpose of staging agricultural demonstrations. We also have twenty night courses for primary education of adults in the interior of the country, and a large number of scholarships for attendance at higher-education courses.

Although the Governor went on to describe Portuguese Guinea as a stable province that enjoys "complete integration with the Portuguese Community and has successfully resisted the influence of all infiltration and propaganda," there were other signs that political stability might be short-lived. A congress of three revolutionary nationalist groups was held in Dakar, July 12–14, 1961, to form a united front against Portuguese rule. At that time, Ibrahim Diallo, leader of the largest of the three groups—the Movement for the Liberation of Guinea and the Cape Verde Islands—declared that "armed action will definitely begin before the end of the year."

The islands of São Tomé and Principe, in the Gulf of Guinea, about 125 miles off the coast of Africa, have been governed as a Portuguese province since 1522. Out of a total population of 60,159 (including 1,152 Europeans), primary-school enrollment in 1954 included 12 whites, 432 Africans, and 69 children of mixed parentage. There were 13 whites, 23 assimilated Africans, and 7 children of mixed parentage in secondary schools.

In the Cape Verde Islands, according to official reports, there were 5,884 pupils of all races in primary schools and 520 in secondary schools in 1952 out of a total population of 147,326 (3,034 whites, 101,725 mixed, 42,475 Africans and *assimilados,* and 93 of other origins).

Technical and Secondary Education

Technical and academic secondary education in the Portuguese territories have so far been reserved largely for non-Africans. In 1955, there were six high schools in Mozambique, five of them operated by private organizations. Of the 955 students registered in these high schools, there were 858 Europeans, 7 Chinese, 16 Indians and Pakistanis, 14 Goans, 47 mulattoes, and 13 Africans. In the same year, there were 887 students enrolled in commercial schools in Mozambique, of whom 513 were Europeans, 21 Chinese, 46 Indians and Pakistanis, 109 Goans, 140 mulattoes, and 58 Africans. The 457 students in Mozambique industrial schools included 232 Europeans,

17 Chinese, 33 Indians and Pakistanis, 49 Goans, 90 mulattoes, and 36 Africans. In other words, a total of 107 Africans were attending school at the technical or academic secondary level in Mozambique in a given year.

In Angola, there are twenty-four high schools, of which three are state-controlled and twenty-one privately owned. In 1953–54, the total number of high-school students in the territory was 2,578, of whom 2,023 were Europeans, 462 mulattoes, 91 Africans, and 2 *assimilados*. Students enrolled in Angolan technical schools (both commercial and industrial) in 1953–54 totaled 1,463, including 880 Europeans, 223 mulattoes, and 50 Africans. Thus, at that time, 141 Africans out of Angola's total African population of 4.5 million were attending technical or academic secondary schools.

Higher Education

There are no institutions of higher learning for either Africans or Europeans in Portuguese Africa. Some Europeans and Africans receive their university training in metropolitan Portugal, however. By 1961, there were at least three Angolan doctors, two lawyers, two engineers, and several dentists—all now employed by the government. There are said to be a few Mozambique Africans with university degrees, one of them a Ph.D. from an American university. Several university-educated Angolans are leaders of the rebel group based in Conakry. Some 300,000 Angolans had filtered across the border to the Congo by mid-1961, and many of the 60,000 in Léopoldville were receiving education at various levels there.

Theory vs. Practice

The gap between the Portuguese theory of education in its overseas territories and its actual practice has been a very wide one. Some 500 years of Portuguese colonial rule in Angola and Mozambique have resulted, not in the creation of millions of full-fledged black Portuguese citizens, but in the evolution of barely 36,000 *assimilados* out of a total population in the two territories of over 10 million. Universal education, even at the beginning *adaptacao* level, is still a long way off. Schooling beyond the fourth grade is reserved for a few hundred Africans a year. Moreover, the continuing encouragement of large-scale migration of Portuguese settlers to Angola and Mozambique raises new questions regarding the ultimate intent of Portuguese policy.

Despite the oft-repeated official claim that there is no discrimination along racial lines in the Portuguese territories, the fact is that most African education is both separate from and decidedly inferior to that available to non-Africans in Angola and Mozambique. The official rationalization for the maintenance of a completely separate system of schools for Africans is that the purpose of these schools is to introduce African children to Portuguese culture and language and that the approach required would be too elementary for children born into that culture. This argument would have more validity if the same measuring stick were applied to children of other non-European cultures as well; but the Asians in Mozambique, most of whom share the Africans' unfamiliarity with Portuguese language and culture and usually are not Christians, are eligible for entry into government and private schools catering to Europeans. On the other hand, it is quite true that fully assimilated Africans who have already become citizens of Portugal by official act have been accepted with a minimum of color bias in Portuguese schools, although their role in Portuguese society has remained ambiguous.

However sincere may have been the original intent of Portuguese educational policy, practice in recent years has clearly been directed toward keeping the lid on African education. This is accomplished by isolating Africans within Portuguese jurisdiction from the mainstream of African thought and education, discouraging the use of indigenous languages by prohibiting them even at the primary level of education, and educating Africans to a minimal level in a highly controlled, Portuguese-oriented educational environment.

—Janet and Eduardo Mondlane

Part V

SOUTHERN AFRICA

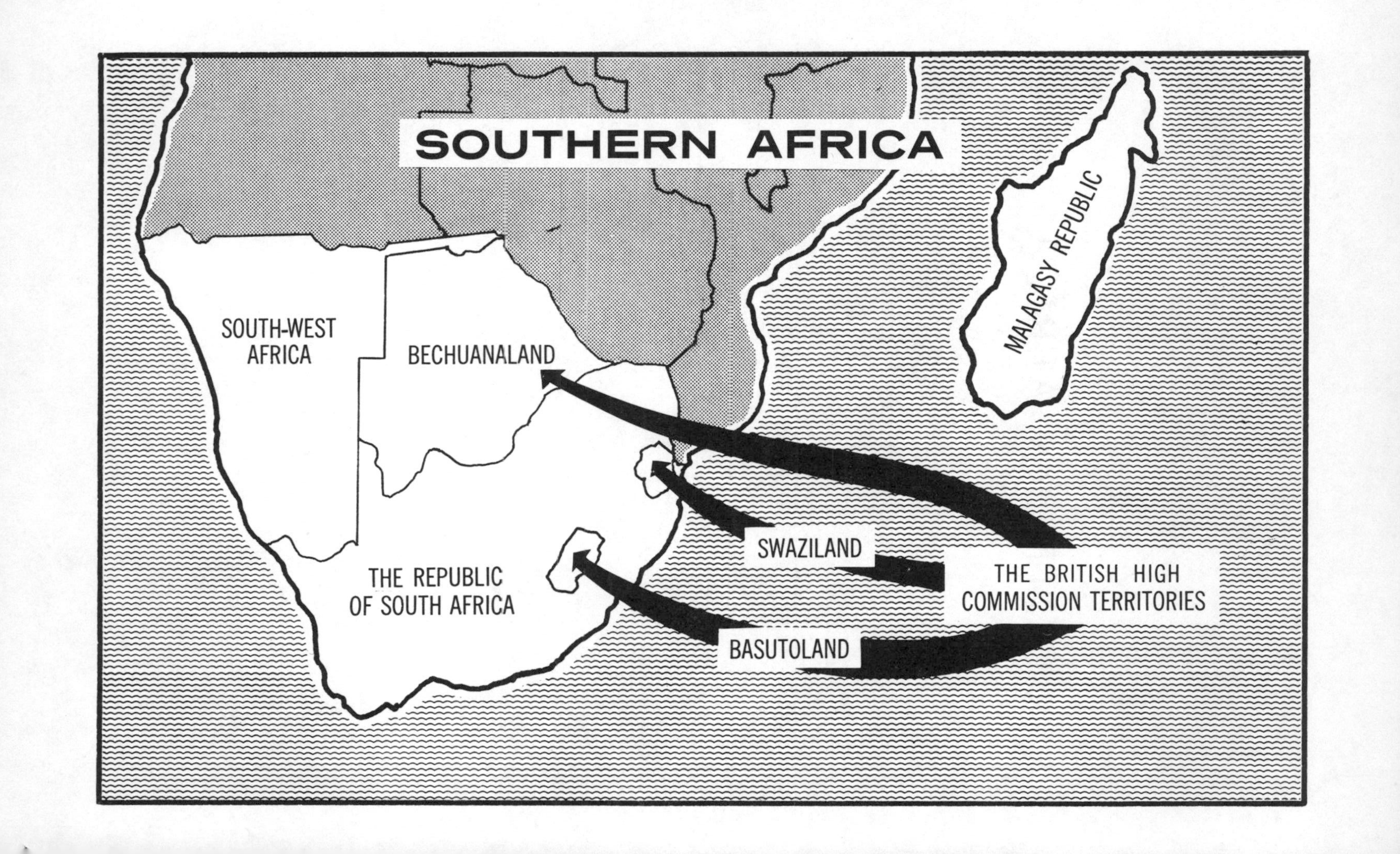
SOUTHERN AFRICA
MALAGASY REPUBLIC
SOUTH-WEST AFRICA
BECHUANALAND
THE REPUBLIC OF SOUTH AFRICA
SWAZILAND
BASUTOLAND
THE BRITISH HIGH COMMISSION TERRITORIES

17. Malagasy Republic (Madagascar)

Capital: Tananarive
Population: 5,191,085 (1959)
Area: 227,900 sq. miles
Political status: Independent republic

If the clock of history were to bring back the year 1836, Parisians and Londoners might encounter several sophisticated Malagasy sent on a diplomatic mission by the Merina Prime Minister Rainihary. In Paris, they called on the government of Louis Philippe. In London, they discussed in impeccable English with Lord Palmerston the possibility of an Anglo-Malagasy treaty of commerce.

The educated Malagasy predated the colonial period and is closely associated with two institutions, the Christian mission and the Merina state. By 1836, nearly 10,000 Malagasy could read and write, the first Malagasy-English and English-Malagasy dictionary was in circulation, and some forty schools were being attended by more than 3,000 students, including several hundred girls.

The island of Madagascar has for centuries been the melting pot of diverse ethnic groups, cultures, and influences. The two pervasive ethnic types are African Negro and Indo-Melanesian. While the two are integrated to the extent that racial animosities have not been an issue of significance, traditional elites among the coastal populations have tended to be African; those among the high-plateau population, Indo-Melanesian. Similarly, the coastal populations have been exposed to Islamic influences, while those on the high plateau reflect the influence of Christian missions. The Antemoro of the southeastern coast used ink and paper of their own manufacture to write the sixteenth-century *Sora-bé* manuscripts. The calligraphy of the *Sora-bé* is Arabic, but the language is a Malagasy (Malgache) dialect. In the background of missionary activity in the high-plateau regions there were discernible patterns of Anglo-French rivalry, with Great Britain supporting the Protestants, and France the Catholics.

Of the three most notable attempts in the eighteenth and nineteenth centuries to establish a state that would transcend the purely tribal and regional limits, only one succeeded. Expanding slowly from the high-plateau region around Tananarive, the present-day capital of the Malagasy Republic, the Merina, by 1861, had extended their rule over two-thirds of Madagascar, an area almost as large as France. The Merina state collapsed thirty-five years later, leaving behind an efficient administrative system adapted to direct and indirect rule, one that the colonial administration found to be invaluable. The Merina state also bequeathed five major pieces of social legislation, codified into 572 articles, some of which are still operative. Finally, it gave rise to an elite with a sense of history and power—an elite that the succeeding colonial administrations alternately sought to weaken, reorient, and replace.

From 1866 onward, the first generation of Malagasy intellectuals began to contribute to periodicals such as *Teny Soa* and *Mpanolotsaina,* published by the London Missionary Society, *Isankeritaona,* published by the Quakers, *Resaka* and *Feon'ny Marina,* published by the Catholics, as well as to the weekly newspaper *Lakroa* and the daily *Isan'andro.* In 1886, the first medical academy was founded in Tananarive. It had a five-year curriculum and was attended by forty-eight students. Dozens of Merina were sent to Europe to study medicine. This was also a period in which the Malagasy language as it is written today was perfected by European and Malagasy scholarship channeled through the missions. Two important works were written in Malgache by Father Callet and by a minister of the Merina Government, Rainandriamampandry. The first, *Tantaran'ny Adriana eto Imerina,* remains one of the most extensive histories of the Merina kings and is being currently translated into French. The second, *Tantara sy fombandrazana,* was the first major work by a Malagasy scholar on the history and customs of his people. An observatory was established in Tananarive by a missionary-astronomer, and the first accurate maps of Madagascar were prepared by Father Roblet and Alfred Grandidier. Alfred Grandidier and his son Guillaume are the most illustrious scholars to have written on Madagascar, contributing more than three dozen volumes on virtually every aspect of the island. These volumes are as yet unmatched in scope, depth, and detail.

Role of the Missions Before French Annexation

Partial statistics indicate that when France annexed Madagascar in 1896, there were 164,000 Malagasy children attending primary schools run by the missions (137,000 in Protestant schools and 27,000 in Catholic schools). Much of the education among the Merina and elsewhere in Madagascar hardly deserved the name, however, for it was little more than acquisition of a certain amount of literacy, in return for which the pupil accepted a certain degree of religious teaching.

For the purposes of appraisal, the distribution of schools and their social role are more important. The Merina accounted for roughly one-fifth of the total Malagasy population, and yet most of the missions' educational facilities were within a hundred-square-mile area around Tananarive. The Society for the Propagation of the Gospel (SPG) had established a few schools among the Antanakarana of northern Madagascar in 1864, but a substantial part of its personnel transferred to Tananarive in 1874. A small Lutheran Mission from the United States worked among the Antanosy and Antandroy on the southeastern coast and later among the Mahafaly and Vezo on the southwest coast. The Norwegian Lutheran Mission (NLM) established several schools in the neighborhood of Fianarantsoa in 1866, and later in southern Madagascar as well. Catholics had schools in Majunga, Tuléar, Tamatave, and Nossy-Bé. Aside from the Merina and the Betsileo, however, the total number of Malagasy receiving more than the rudiments of education did not exceed 3,000.

Among the Merina, the missions did not seek to alter the social and economic stratification; they merely adapted to it. Except for those Merina selected to become instructors and evangelists, the best private tutoring as well as secondary and intermediate education available through the missions went to the *andriana* and the *hova,* two social groups almost exclusively under Protestant influence.

Protestantism became the official creed of the Merina state in 1869, and only four of the 142 highest officials in the government in 1894 were Catholics. Consequently, the student body in Catholic schools consisted primarily of *andevo* and peasant children, the lower socio-economic strata. Without an awareness of these differences in the quality of education, the social and economic status of the students, and the patterns of development and competition, the substance of the more recent history of Madagascar cannot be fully understood.

Educational Aims of French Policy

The educational aims of the first colonial administrations were clearly stated in Article 5 of the initial ordinance of April 16, 1899: "To make the young Malagasy faithful and obedient subjects of France [and] to offer an education the character of which would be industrial, agricultural, and commercial, so as to insure that the settlers and various public services of the colony can meet their personnel requirements."

The theoretical implications of this statement were obvious. In the private sector, Madagascar and its development would be geared to a colonial economy dominated by the settler, the mining corporations, and the commercial establishments. The duty of the public administration was therefore dual in nature: to devise a system of education that would turn out a certain number of youngsters possessing training and skills in demand, and to insure and insulate the educational system against any kind of influence that could challenge, or even question, the French presence in Madagascar. The central idea of education was a kind of assimilation without equality, which was to be attained by means of vocational, not academic training. Aside from minor modifications in 1916 and 1933, this theoretical framework did not change until after World War II, more specifically until the educational-reform ordinance of November, 1951.

Two types of schools —*écoles officielles* and *écoles privées*—were established in 1899. The public schools were subdivided into three categories: primary rural schools, regional schools, and superior schools.

The primary schools taught reading, arithmetic, the metric system, outlines of history and geography, gardening for boys, and embroidering for girls. All instruction was in Malgache; the French language was taught as a subject. Geography texts were confined to France and Madagascar, and history instruction was designed to inculcate the children with the idea that the French presence in Madagascar was synonymous with progress. Classes in drawing and hygiene were added in 1903, as were regulations allotting a certain amount of hours per subject per week.

The most gifted products of the primary rural schools were selected to attend the regional schools (one per district or province). Each regional school had an experimental farm (*terrain de culture*) and a workshop *(atelier d'apprentissage)*. While most of the primary-school instructors (90 to 95 per cent) were Malagasy, all principals of regional schools were French.

There were, lastly, four superior schools, which drew their student body from graduates of regional schools and from private schools that conformed to the same standards applicable to public schools. An *école normale* in Tananarive offered courses leading to certificates for school teachers (*instituteurs*), commercial and administrative employees (*employés de commerce et diverses administrations*), and specialists in applied agriculture and skilled workers (foremen, mechanics, etc.). The *école normale* was buttressed by an *école professionelle* and an *école d'agriculture*. Another superior school, *l'École François-de-Mahy*, was located in Fianarantsoa.

In theory, private schools could be established either by independent instructors with acceptable qualifications or by the missions. In practice, however, all private schools were run by the missions. The ordinance of 1899 had codified the separation of Church and State and, although mission schools were partly subsidized by the administration, they were recognized as valid *écoles privées* (or *écoles libres*) only if their instruction conformed broadly to the secular curriculums offered in public schools and if their staffs held schoolteacher certificates or had equivalent qualifications. This meant that the missions had to overhaul their schools in order to be able to compete with the administration. Although the missions, continuing their own teacher-training programs and theological seminaries, experienced a heavy loss of students at first, they rapidly adapted to the new requirements and subsequently recorded a continuous gain.* The public schools, however, increased at an even faster rate.

Table 1
Public and Private Schools, 1894–1931

	Number of schools		Number of students	
Year	Public	Private	Public	Private
1894	—	?	—	164,000
1904	329	183	25,882	18,615
1905	351	212	26,902	20,635
1906	376	311	28,966	25,685
1907	408	315	32,408	24,935
1908	451	356	34,377	27,200
1909	490	369	40,458	28,515
1910	517	390	46,822	30,959
1931	959	481	110,928	65,596

* The missions continued to offer rudimentary education outside the acceptable private school. In 1906, some 27,000 pupils were reported "outside" the system. Subsequent writers have mentioned figures ranging from 20,000–30,000, but no statistics are available.

If the theory of education and its purpose was relatively simple and straightforward under French colonial rule, the social, economic, and political realities were not. Instead of representing France, the local administration became an entity unto itself, concerned with its own growth and welfare and altering or amending its outlook only when a governor proved to be stronger than the machine, which was rarely the case. The pendulum can thus be said to have swung from a fluid and decentralized situation at the turn of the century to a highly centralized system at the outbreak of World War II. General J. S. Gallieni, the first Governor of Madagascar (1896–1905), was a humanist, a disciple of Spencer, and a personal friend of Alfred Grandidier, who believed in evolution and Franco-Malagasy cooperation. Although anticlerical in his feelings, Gallieni allowed the missions to participate both inside and outside the restricted educational system. (In fact, all of the leading figures within the Malagasy nationalist movement from 1910 to 1960 received their primary and secondary education in missionary schools.) It was Gallieni who established the Académie Malgache (1902), the only institution of high scholastic standards until the late 1940's. Another feature of the Gallieni administration was the deliberate effort to minimize the strong differences between the Merina and the rest of the Malagasy by opening as many *écoles officielles,* both primary and regional, as possible on the coasts.

Governor Victor Augagneur (1905–10), on the other hand, immediately set out to establish a centralized administration, increasing both the number and the power of civilian personnel in Tananarive. Running into financial problems, Augagneur abolished several secondary schools outside Tananarive, thus maximizing again the old and painful differences between the capital and the hinterland. All superior schools were merged into the single École le Myre de Vilers in the capital. Both Augagneur and his successor, Albert Picquié (1910–14), being fully aware that a student movement was growing around the Union Chrétienne de Jeunes Gens (an equivalent of the YMCA), sought to weaken missionary efforts in the realm of education. Since the theological seminaries and the missions' teacher-training institutions could not be touched by the administration (under the ordinances of 1899 and 1904), the Augagneur and Picquié regimes did not really prevent the formation of a nationalist-oriented student elite. But the use of educational standards as a weapon against the missions caused thousands of children—especially in rural areas—to be deprived of all educational opportunities.

The stresses and strains of World War I, which did not bypass Madagascar, brought the student movement into the open in 1916.

Some 300 students, organized into cells (*sakelika*), formed a secret society, Vy Vato, seeking to overthrow the administration. Considering the odds, the society's aim could only be regarded as a puerile student plot. The administration did not see Vy Vato that way, however, and the retaliation was swift and severe. Thirty-six students were condemned to forced labor ranging from fifteen years to life. Altogether, 247 students were placed in *résidence fixe,* many in the least hospitable parts of Madagascar. Five years later, however, all of the students were set free. As a French historian remarked dryly:

> Unjustified in the light of the acts themselves, this repression can only be explained by an atmosphere of passions heightened by wartime circumstances. It also left its traces. The level of general education available in superior schools was lowered and all future gatherings subjected to [specific] authorization. As for those sentenced, their sentiments toward French authorities were certainly not improved. These facts should have opened the eyes of the government [to the fact] that a Malagasy [public] opinion was in existence and that there was need for political guidance. The government did absolutely nothing.*

The return of Malagasy war veterans—of whom some 30,000 saw combat in Europe—and the amnesty for former Vy Vato members led to the re-emergence of nationalist activity in the 1920's. By any standard of measurement, the movement was "moderate," for its principal demand was for French citizenship (based on the Law of Annexation of 1896) for all Malagasy. Because of the Malagasy contributions to the war effort and the fairly moderate attitude of Governor Marcel Olivier (1924–29), the administration at first tended to look the other way in regard to the budding nationalist movement led by a mission-trained Betsileo schoolteacher, Jean Ralaimongo. The tendency to associate movements seeking to alter the *status quo* with Communism is not a novelty in colonial history and it was not long before Ralaimongo's associations during and after his military service in France (from which he returned as a Free Mason, not as a Communist) led the administration to assume incorrectly that the movement was Communist-dominated. Following a demonstration in Tananarive at the end of 1929, nationalist aspirations were thwarted once more, this time by Governor Léon Cayla (1930–39).

The aim of public education—to provide enough well-trained Malagasy for the development of a colonial economy—did not anticipate the limitations of the educational system itself, just as the goal of assimilation without equality could not foresee its own intrinsic weakness. Those who managed to graduate from *écoles supérieures*

* Hubert Deschamps, *Histoire de Madagascar* (Paris, 1960), p. 261.

almost inevitably ended in the lower and middle ranks of the administration. Since primary education was not compulsory, the rate of attrition in rural primary schools was often considerable. Moreover, most graduates of rural primary as well as of regional schools returned to the village agriculture, i.e., the noncolonial sector of the economy. Meanwhile, the colonial economy itself developed at a slow rate. Madagascar was far from France and it was not easy to recruit potential settlers.* The basic assumption that public education would meet the personnel requirements of the European enterprise neglected a very simple problem—how to force a school graduate to work for the *colon*. Also, the 1920's were a period of agricultural prosperity, and a Malagasy farmer in 1924 or 1926 could make more money by selling crops he himself had raised in a few weeks than by working for a whole year as a wage earner for the *colon*. Commercial establishments found that many of the Malagasy who came to work for them as clerks, accountants, foremen, and skilled laborers did not have an adequate command of French.

In part, these applicants' language deficiencies were the product of a power struggle between those in authority who advocated the exclusive use of French in schools and those who were equally adamant in favor of Malgache because they feared that too many "subversive ideas" would filter down through the French language. Neither emerged victorious from the battle until 1952, but it left in its wake an irrational compromise: Malgache prevailed in primary education, and French in the secondary schools. The outcome was that all too often the "educated" could not speak, read, or write either language well.

In 1931, there were 959 public schools in Madagascar, with a total of 110,928 students. As can be seen from the breakdown given in Table 2, 94 per cent of public-school facilities and 98 per cent of the student body were in the realm of primary education.

There were also 244 Catholic and 237 Protestant private schools, with a total of 65,596 students. The École Flacourt, a special private school with 348 students, was attended by sons of notables. Among the primary schools were also those renamed *écoles de type européen*. Their students were drawn from three categories, legally defined according to the *Code de l'Indigénat* as Europeans, Malagasy with French citizenship, and those enjoying special status (*statut personnel*),

* The true *colon* (settler-farmer) in Madagascar never exceeded one-sixth of the total European population. Most of the French were engaged in commerce and administration. The 1958–59 figure—68,430—is the highest European population total ever attained.

Table 2
Schools and Students, 1931

Type of school	Number of schools	Number of students
Primary (1st degree)	877	107,200
Primary (2nd degree)	19	1,899
Regional (midwifery)	15	
Regional (ateliers)	34	510
Special schools	1	348
Industrial sections	7	149
Schools of industry	1	87
Schools of agriculture	3	130
Schools of medicine	1	201
Superior schools	1	404
Total	*959*	*110,928*

which meant any one so designated by the administration for a variety of reasons.

With this over-all total of 176,524 students enrolled in 1931, the ratio of total school-age population to those actually attending school (*taux de scolarisation*) in Madagascar was considerably greater than that of other French colonial territories—about 32 per cent. However, the old differences persisted. The number of school-age Merina actually enrolled was nearly 55 per cent; of Betsileo and Sihanaka, 45 per cent; of Sakalava, Betsimisaraka, Antaifasy, and Antanakarana, 20 per cent; and of the other ten main population groups, 6 per cent or less. Equally important, the administrative consolidation of superior schools between 1905 and 1910 made it extremely difficult for non-Merina students to reach the upper level of secondary education in Madagascar and, hence, to enter the public services. Under French rule, the educational system leveled some of the inequalities existing among the Merina themselves, but did not open up the administration to other Malagasy. As a result of the economic difficulties in the 1930's, and because of the strong centralism of Cayla's administration, only ninety new rural primary schools, fourteen *ateliers,* and one commercial section were established for all of Madagascar between 1931 and 1939. Statistics for 1940 show 130,082 students in public schools, or an increase of only 19,154 since 1931 (assuming the same rate of attrition for both 1931 and 1940).

The greatest increase took place in the *écoles de type européen,* attended in 1940 by some 5,000 students. Although part of the primary-education system, this type of school was of a far higher caliber than its more wide-spread counterpart, the *école de type local.* Metropolitan standards, French teachers, exclusive use of French language, and better general facilities made the difference. While approximately one-third of the student body in the European-type primary schools consisted of Malagasy, few of them were non-Merina.

Toward the end of the 1930's, signs of a more relaxed trend in Franco-Malagasy relations were in evidence. Labor battalions (*service de la main-d'oeuvre des travaux d'intérêt général*) were abolished, requirements for acquisition of French citizenship lowered, and Madagascar became one of the first overseas territories to have a labor code and be granted the right to form labor unions. Resuming their activities, the Malagasy who had taken part in the nationalist movement of the 1920's were joined by a new generation. Their favored vehicle for expression was poetry, and much of it carried the message that youth wished to become progressively more French while remaining essentially Malagasy. Translated into political terms, this intellectual message warned that assimilation without equality would not survive and that, at the same time, assimilation with equality did not mean that Malagasy culture would be submerged by French, but rather that there would be a synthesis of the two. In 1939, the first Malagasy delegate was seated on the Conseil Supérieur des Colonies as a result of the first election held in the island under French rule, but the number of voters was limited to about 14,000. These winds of change, it should be pointed out, blew not from Tananarive but from Paris, and they were not strong enough to permeate the domain of education or seriously to alter the attitudes of the local administration.

Postwar Changes in the Theory of Malagasy Education

The French Government's so-called Brazzaville reforms of 1944 and the first *Loi Lamine Gueye* altered the legal and political structure of Madagascar and, with it, the theory of education. Being *citoyen au même titre que les nationaux français de la métropole,* i.e., enjoying the same rights as the Metropolitan French, meant that the Malagasy were to be represented in the French National Assembly and in the Advisory Assembly of the French Union, as well as in their own provincial assemblies and in the Malagasy National Assembly in Tananarive. As French citizens, they had the right to equal opportunities in an educational system required by law to adhere to Metropolitan standards. Between 1946 and 1958, the Investment Fund for Economic and Social Development (FIDES) was to appropriate more than $270 million toward the over-all objective. In essence, all of these measures were implemented by 1958 (when Madagascar became an autonomous republic within the Community)—but not without difficulty and opposition from local French officials.

The struggle between Malagasy nationalists and a local French administrative Establishment unwilling to accept the spirit of the Brazzaville reforms led to an intense, if regionally limited, revolt in 1947. The traumatic effect of the revolt forced Paris to get the upper hand over the Establishment by sending to Tananarive a series of governors who could not be "captured" and by initiating reforms such as the Education Reform Ordinance of 1951 and a new labor code in 1952.

The fundamental aim of the pilot educational reforms carried out in 1952 was to integrate the multiplicity of scholastic standards in Madagascar and to bring the new system as close as possible to that existing in Metropolitan France. In the *écoles de type métropolitain,* criteria for admission were no longer legal but linguistic. Regardless of his background, the more proficient an applicant was in French the more likely he was to be admitted. Ninety-five per cent of the student body in five metropolitan-type primary schools opened in Tananarive in October 1952 was Malagasy. In the *écoles de type local,* there was also a renewed emphasis on French at all three levels: preparatory, elementary, and middle. At each successive stage, French-language instruction received greater emphasis, until Malgache became one of the subjects rather than the language of instruction. By the middle level, most of the teachers were French. Both in the metropolitan and local types of primary school, new and better textbooks were introduced and subject courses expanded in scope.

At the end of 1952, there were five secondary schools in Madagascar with a total enrollment of 2,378: the Lycée Gallieni (boys) in Tananarive, the Lycée Jules-Ferry (girls) in Tananarive, the Collège Moderne et Technique (co-ed) in Tananarive, the Cours Complementaire (co-ed) in Tamatave, and the Cours Complementaire (co-ed) in Diego-Suarez. The holders of the baccalaureate (*titulaires de baccalauréat*) increased, from 144 in 1954, to 524 in 1958. There were five *lycées* and eighteen *collèges classiques et modernes* in 1958. In the field of technical education, three levels were introduced in 1952: rural, provincial, and national. The first, consisting of *ateliers de district,* was given the specific task of training village artisans. The *centres d'apprentissage,* which operated on the provincial level, provided specialized training in skills most needed in each of the six provinces. On the national level, the *école industrielle et collège technique* prepared students for positions in teaching, management, commerce, printing, and other professions or trades. Technical-education facilities in existence at the beginning of 1959 are shown in Table 3.

Partly as a result of vast outlays of money and the reorganization of the educational system, the *taux de scolarisation* rose from 32 per cent in 1946 (the same percentage as in 1931) to 46 per cent in 1958, and almost 50 per cent at the end of 1959. While the percentage was highest in the Tananarive Province (74 per cent) and lowest in Tuléar (22 per cent), considerable effort in the 1950's went into improving educational opportunities in hitherto-neglected areas of the island. From 1946 on, both the quality of education and the number of students increased.

Table 3
Technical-Education Facilities, 1959

Type of school	Number of schools
Technical colleges	3
Professional training centers	15
Applied-arts *ateliers*	1
Home-economics schools	5
School workshops	94
Teacher-Training sections	1
Commercial and printing sections (adults only)	2
Total	*121*

Table 4
Number of Students, 1946–47 to 1958–59

	1946–47		1950–51		1958–59	
Level	Public	Private	Public	Private	Public	Private
Primary (male)	74,299	39,658	104,308	44,933	139,623	72,426
Primary (female)	47,324	31,527	63,937	32,077	98,032	58,813
Secondary (male)	375	299	426	399	4,479	7,778
Secondary (female)	228	274	283	268	2,576	4,283
Technical (male)	1,419	265	2,649	501	4,440	557
Technical (female)	471	59	503	274	514	663
Higher (male)	49		217		734	
Higher (female)	6		42		128	
Total	*124,171*	*72,082*	*172,365*	*78,452*	*250,526*	*144,520*

Table 5
Growth of Education, 1938–39 to 1958–59

	Number of students		Number of schools		Number of classes	
Academic year	Public	Private	Public	Private	Public	Private
1938–39	123,505	70,500	990	706	1,200	n.a.
1946–47	124,171	72,028	1,078	702	1,367	1,187
1950–51	172,365	78,452	1,235	n.a.	1,938	n.a.
1956–57	190,231	98,223	1,349	802	2,244	n.a.
1958–59	250,526	144,520	1,594	1,043	3,188	2,553

Education for Women

A higher percentage of Malagasy females are in school than in any other French-speaking area in Africa, as indicated by Tables 6 and 7.

Table 6
Female Students in Countries of French-speaking Africa, 1957

Country	Females (percentage of total student population)
Madagascar	41.8
Gabon	33.1
Senegal	30.0
Upper Volta	28.2
Dahomey	27.7
Congo (Brazzaville)	27.7
Niger	27.5
Ivory Coast	23.4
Mali	22.5
Central African Republic	16.5
Chad	10.5
Mauritania	7.8

Table 7
Female Students in Areas of French-speaking Africa, 1946 and 1957

	1946		1957	
Area	Total number of students	Females (percentage of total)	Total number of students	Females (percentage of total)
Madagascar	196,199	40	345,451	42
French Cameroons	114,722	14	278,889	27
French West Africa	107,470	19	379,186	24
French Togo	17,230	18	67,950	23
French Equatorial Africa	34,150	9	175,956	22

Recent Developments in Higher Education

Following the war, attempts were made to enhance the intellectual endeavor in the island not only through the Académie Malgache (which, by 1946, had about 300 Malagasy and European members and had published more than 100 volumes of scientific works), but also through institutions such as the Cercle d'activité littéraire et artistique and the Alliance Française. Between 1947 and 1949, law courses leading to the L.L.B. degree were introduced along with science courses leading to certification in physics, chemistry, and biology (PCB), mathematics, physics, and chemistry (MPC), and physics,

UNIVERSITY OF MADAGASCAR, AT BEFELATANANA—SCHOOL OF MEDICINE. *(Photo courtesy of French Embassy Press & Information Division.)*

chemistry, and the natural sciences (SPCN). Still later, a certificate in liberal arts *(certificat des études littéraires générales)* was added. Each discipline had its own examination center affiliated with the Université d'Aix-Marseille. Each year, the appropriate faculties sent a professorial board to preside over the examinations in Madagascar.

Another important institution established during the same period was the Institute of Scientific Research of Madagascar (IRSM), with departments in pedology and soil sciences, hydrology, geography, geophysics, botany, animal biology, and human sciences. Soil studies were carried out both to reduce soil deterioration and to pinpoint areas best suited for development. Hydrological stations were set up along major rivers to report on the daily water volume and level for the purposes of irrigation, electrification, and flood control. The department of geography has made some important discoveries on the changing nature of the southwest coast and the effect of these changes on port facilities. Geophysical researchers have worked on gravimetric maps, which provide information for oil prospecting and the location of mineral deposits. Because of the importance of aviation in Madagascar (there are over 400 airfields on the island), the geophysical section has provided a yearly magnetic-deviation map. Botanists of the IRSM have made extensive analyses of herb species to determine nutritive values for livestock. The animal-biology section discovered that the anopheles mosquito in certain areas had become immune to ordinary antimalaria insecticides. Over the past thirteen years, the IRSM, in an important study (*Faune de Madagascar*), has catalogued some 3,000 animal species hitherto unknown. The human-sciences department has collected Malagasy folklore and has carried out economic and social studies supplementing the work of other IRSM departments. (For example, the department of pedology and soil sciences has sought to develop cotton in the Bas-Mangoky area, while the social scientists tried to find out how acceptable the cotton industry would be to the Masikoro people who inhabit the Mangoky delta.) The IRSM has also an oceanographic section at Nosy-Bé, which studies currents, water temperature, and salinity to help navigation and the fishing industry. The Oceanographic Station at Nosy-Bé has often taken part in international oceanographic studies.

In 1955, a Center for Advanced Studies (Institut des Hautes Études) was established in Tananarive. Its schools of law, sciences and liberal arts have brought together the separate courses introduced in the late 1940's and granted the appropriate degrees. In 1958–59, an expansion of the science and liberal arts curricula took place in the *écoles supérieures*. New courses leading to degrees equivalent to B.S. and B.A. in geology, mathematics, natural and soil sciences, geography, French literature, and modern and medieval history were introduced. A Department of Malagasy Jurisprudence was added in 1959. Those graduating from the four-year Law School could study for an additional year in order to become magistrates. The School of Medicine and Pharmacy does not as yet grant degrees, having facilities for premedical training only. Two recent additions to the Center are the École Pratique des Hautes Études and a Department of International Affairs. The former is devoted exclusively to Malagasy affairs, with particular stress on research and publication. In a sense, it represents the growing interest of the Malagasy in their own past and present. The Center for Advanced Studies had 862 students in the 1958–59 academic year. In November, 1961, it was formally renamed the University of Madagascar.

Another notable group of educational institutions consisted of *grandes écoles,* or higher professional schools (shown in Table 8).

The number of Malagasy students with full scholarships studying in France increased from 127 in 1952, to 270 in 1957–58, to 458 in 1960–61, as indicated in the breakdown in Table 9.

Table 8
Higher Professional Schools

School	Number of students
School of Medicine and Pharmacy at Befelatanana	180
State School for Midwifery	40
State School for Male and Female Nurses	40
School of Agriculture	45
School of Forestry	15
School of Animal Husbandry	15
School for Advisers in Farming	26
National Administration School	n.a.

Table 9
Malagasy Students with Full Scholarships Studying in France

Academic year	Engineering degree candidates	M.D. candidates	Others
1957–58	19	78	173
1958–59	26	94	241
1959–60	24	111	308
1960–61	32	113	313

The 1960–61 figure of 458 does not include Malagasy students studying in France on partial scholarships or without any scholarships at all. No statistics are available for these categories. According to unofficial estimates, between 100 and 200 Malagasy students were in the Soviet Union and the satellite countries in 1960–61. No Malagasy students are to be found in the United States, and those who in the past wished to major in subjects such as American literature or history have had to study in France.

Adult Education

In 1959–60, an adult literacy campaign was carried out in 150 centers throughout Madagascar. The results have been encouraging: Of the 3,500 adults (age-group 16–60) enrolled, more than 75 per cent learned to read after thirty-four lessons.

Approximately 400,000–500,000 people in Madagascar listen daily to Radio Tananarive on 60,000–70,000 receivers; several million Malagasy annually see motion pictures in mobile units and in thirty permanent theaters. Educational films, introduced in 1938, are fairly well developed. The Educational Film Office of Madagascar has a library of 1,300 16-mm reels, which are loaned out to film clubs. The Library of the Office of Documentation, in existence since 1919, owns more than 70,000 volumes and 200,000 documents. The number of readers for this library increased from 46,000 in 1953 to more than 60,000 in 1960. Teachers and students at various levels of public education make use of institutional libraries, which, in 1959, stocked more than 20,000 volumes. No library information is available for private and religious organizations.

For the literate, there is a wide selection of small newspapers as well—eleven dailies and eight weeklies in the Malgache language, two daily news bulletins and four weeklies in French, and twenty-one other periodicals.

Franco-Malagasy Cooperation Since Independence

The Malagasy Republic has been independent since June 26, 1960; Franco-Malagasy relations have never been better, and the government of President Philibert Tsiranana has indicated that it plans no radical changes in the educational system inherited from France.

While the Malagasy Republic has, by and large, one of the most advanced educational systems in Africa south of the Sahara, there are recognized gaps to be filled—in numbers as well as in quality of teachers and skilled workers, including at the middle level in commerce, industry, agriculture, and administration. In addition, the educational system finds itself under mounting pressures from a population that, increasing at the rate of 200,000 a year, places new premiums on education.

In 1960, the government allotted 843,773,000 francs (CFA) * to the field of public education and another 25 million to private secondary education. In addition, France granted an additional 114.3 million francs (CFA) to both private and public education in Madagascar during the same year. "Malgachization" is now in progress, but it is being carried out without undue hurry, on the basis of qualifications, not political patronage. In public schools, the Malgachization of the teaching staff (estimated at 82 per cent Malagasy staff members in the 1957–58 academic year) is chiefly affecting secondary and primary schools, but to some extent technical schools also. In higher

* In 1960, $1.00 = 247 francs (CFA).

education, the Malagasy government has asked recently for more professors from France and has stated that if France cannot meet the demand, other French-speaking countries, such as Switzerland and Belgium, will be approached.

Educational expenditures at both the federal and provincial levels are, as a matter of deliberate policy, in inverse proportion to the ratio of school-age children now in school in each of the six provinces. As a result, old differences are beginning to lose political significance and new and more complex sets of relationships are evolving.

—RAYMOND K. KENT

18. Republic of South Africa

Capital:	Cape Town (parliamentary)
	Pretoria (administrative)
Population:	14,673,000 (est., including
	9,751,000 Africans,
	1,800,000 Dutch-descended Afrikaners,
	1,200,000 Europeans of English descent,
	1,406,000 Coloureds, and
	450,000 Asiatics)
Area:	472,685 sq. miles
Political status:	Independent republic

EDUCATION in South Africa not only reflects the nation's racial pattern and problems but serves directly to enforce and promote the existing social system. As the Interdepartmental Committee on Native Education of 1935–36 noted, "The education of the White Child prepares him for life in a dominant society and the education of the Black Child for life in a subordinate society." Since 1948, under the Nationalist Party's apartheid policy to achieve the physical, cultural, and psychological separation of the races while maintaining European economic and political domination, the education of the non-European population has become an increasingly more significant means of perpetuating the South African way of life. For this reason, the government in its program for African development is giving top priority to the reformation of the educational system.

At the heart of this education policy is the desire to condition non-Europeans to an acceptance of apartheid and to wean them away from the concept of a shared or mixed society. The statements of Prime Minister Hendrik Verwoerd have left little doubt about the government's determination to shape education into the pattern of over-all state planning. For example:

> Racial relations cannot improve if the wrong type of education is given to Natives. They cannot improve if the result of Native education is the creation of a frustrated people who, as a result of the education they received, have expectations in life which circumstances in South Africa do not allow to be fulfilled immediately, when it creates people who are trained for professions not open to them, when there are people who have received a form of cultural training which strengthens their desire for the white collar occupations to such an extent that there are more such people than openings available. Therefore, good racial relations are spoilt when the correct education is not given. Above all, good racial relations cannot exist when the education is given under the control of people who create wrong expectations on the part of the Native himself. . . . It is therefore necessary that Native education should be controlled in such a way that it should be in accord with the policy of the State.*

While the school system is organized along Western administrative lines, it is increasingly using tribal tradition as a basis of education and aims to train Africans for integration into their own, not European, society. Toward this end, the government has increased its control over all facets of the educational system and is trying to establish a state monopoly of schooling. It thus hopes to prevent the continued growth of the already sizable cadre of Europeanized Africans, who pose the main threat to continued rule by the dominant European minority.

The Bantu Education Act of 1953

Prior to the passage of the Bantu Education Act in 1953, African education in South Africa was largely limited to church and missionary enterprise, although many of the mission schools received various forms of government financial aid. By 1950, the number of African schools developed in this way had risen to 5,213, and total enrollment to 746,324, approximately 40 per cent of African children of school going age. In 1951, 84.5 per cent of all educational institutions were church schools.

There were both African and European critics of the education provided in the mission schools, and, by the late 1940's, the need for reform was pressed by conservative and liberal groups alike—although for different reasons. Many Europeans believed that the curriculum was too "bookish" and expressed concern that the mission schools were developing Africans whose views would not be in line with

* Dr. H. F. Verwoerd, House of Assembly Debates, *Hansard,* Vol. 83, Col. 3576.

South African tradition and thought. Africans, for their part, urged secularization and centralization of the system and noted the wide gulf between the schools and the African community. Concern was general about such matters as low enrollment, the shortage of teachers, administrative disorder, and the uneven standards of education. The Malan Government consequently appointed a commission of inquiry under the chairmanship of Dr. W. W. M. Eiselen to report on the whole complex of African education in South Africa.

The resulting Eiselen Commission Report, which has become one of the blueprints of the Nationalist Government, embodied principles that were for the most part in agreement with apartheid philosophy. The assumption that the Bantu people constitute an independent race with its own history, culture, and personality led to the Commission's conclusions that satisfactory Bantu development could take place only within a Bantu social framework and that Bantu education would therefore have to have its own individual character. The report suggested that traditional tribal culture was fully capable of satisfying Bantu aspirations and of meeting the needs of the modern world. In emphasizing the social and communal purpose of education at the expense of the training of individuals, it pointed to the Bantu tribal reserve areas as the fertile ground in which fruits of Bantu culture could be nurtured.* The Africans of South Africa emerged in the report as a people with inborn social and cultural characteristics that acculturation could not modify.

To make Bantu education an integral part of Bantu socio-economic development, the Commission recommended its complete administrative reorganization under the Department of Native Affairs (now renamed the Department of Bantu Administration and Development), the ultimate but gradual transfer of schools from church to government jurisdiction, the revision of curricula to meet the postulated needs of the Bantu, and the formulation of an extensive development plan.

* The Bantu reserves, comprising about 13 per cent of South Africa's total land area and serving as the home of approximately 43 per cent of the total African population, are still impoverished. The following passage from a publication of the Economic and Social Planning Council, although written over ten years ago, still presents an accurate picture of general conditions in the reserves: "There is no doubt that under existing conditions the Native reserves are not used to their best advantage. They are generally backward areas, and the whole atmosphere in them is one of stagnation, of poverty of people and resources. There has been little if any attempt to integrate them into the national economy; they have been largely ignored and neglected. Isolated experiments have indicated what some of the possibilities of large-scale development are, but such experiments are relatively insignificant in relation to the problem as a whole."

The Commission's principles and recommendations were incorporated in the Bantu Education Act of 1953 and in the subsequent administrative reorganization of the school system. The Act, which provoked heated criticism from opposition parties and nearly all articulate African groups, is a skeletal measure concerned only with administrative matters. It leaves the details of educational development entirely to the discretion of the administrators. Indeed, African anxiety about the reform of the schools has stemmed more from this administrative leeway and from the spirit in which the Act has been implemented than from the Act's specific provisions.

The Act authorized the establishment of Bantu Community Schools served by local school committees and boards and run by Africans themselves under the guidance of government officials. Eventually, such schools will replace all private institutions. By 1959, 483 school boards and 4,102 school committees, on which more than 40,000 Africans sit, had been created. Although the schools have thus been brought closer to the community and Bantu sub-inspectors and supervisors have been appointed, policy-making and administrative control have been kept safely in European hands.

The Act also repealed the Native Education Finance Act of 1945, which, in providing for funds for African education from general revenue, made such education in principle the financial liability of the entire South African community. The Exchequer and Audit Amendment Act, passed in 1955, provides that funds for Bantu education be drawn from a special account into which a fixed sum of £6.5 million from general revenue plus four-fifths of the general Bantu tax are to be paid annually. Additional sums needed for the extension or improvement of education are, by implication, to come directly from African sources, through either increases in taxation or the efforts of individual communities. In view of the depressed state of the African economy, the measure in effect sets well-defined limits to educational expansion. However, some officials of the Department of Bantu Education believe that the government will not be able to hold to this position and will have to write off existing loans and contribute from general revenue.

Through the withdrawal of state subsidies, administrative harassment, and, on occasion, intimidation, the government has since 1952 forced many church groups to shut down their schools or sell them to the government. However, at least 554 unaided registered schools—the overwhelming majority of them Roman Catholic—were still operating in 1959. All such private schools are required to conform to the established social pattern of South Africa and are subject to close supervision.

The Bantu Public School System Today

By focusing so much attention on education as a cornerstone of apartheid, the Nationalists have given the education of Africans an urgency and momentum that it previously lacked. Between 1953 and 1961, enrollment grew from 858,079 to 1,518,063, and by 1959 approximately 55 per cent of school-age African children were in schools. The introduction of double sessions has enabled an additional 200,000 children to enter the lower primary grades. The number of teachers rose from 17,678 to more than 26,000 during the period 1950–58. The education budget, which for the fiscal year 1950–51 was £5,762,907, grew to £9,400,000 for the fiscal year 1959–60. Despite these advances, educational development is still hampered by the large size of classes, the stress on examinations and rote learning, and the high rate of early withdrawals from school. A large proportion of the seemingly significant increase in annual educational expenditure during the past ten years has been consumed by the rising prices of materials and higher teachers' salaries, not by expansion.

The administration is giving primary emphasis in the over-all education scheme to the four-year, self-contained lower primary course, through which it hopes all African children will soon pass. It is in these four grades that enrollment increases have been most spectacular. Enrollment falls off sharply at the secondary level: African students in secondary classes in 1949 amounted to 2.6 per cent of total African enrollment, and by the middle of 1957 this percentage had climbed to only 3.5 per cent, representing 36,189 pupils. The comparatively slow growth of secondary education has produced African charges that the government—primarily with political objectives in mind—is sacrificing the training of more highly educated and capable Africans in favor of diluted education for the masses.

Since assuming control of all teacher training in 1956, the government has not only reorganized and expanded facilities but utilized the training colleges as an instrument to encourage regional isolation. An increasing number of training institutions are limiting their enrollment to members of a particular language group, and an official regulation specifies that student trainees must receive their training in colleges located in the area in which they plan to teach. As the remaining European teachers are withdrawn from the Bantu educational system, African teachers will be increasingly cut off from contacts and influences outside their immediate environment and ethnic group.

Vocational and agricultural education has been slow to develop because of the cost of such training, the limited opportunities available to African tradesmen, and a continuing African preference for the more academic disciplines. Husbandry and agriculture are taught at several schools in Bantu areas, and the government reported in 1961 that there were some 2,000 Africans receiving institutional training in forty-six different centers in such trades as building, leatherwork, and tailoring. Nurses-training and domestic-science courses are open to women. Short courses for chiefs and headmen and four schools for their sons provide training in leadership and the operation of tribal government.

The syllabi introduced into the schools have in general been well received, but, as the Institute of Race Relations was careful to emphasize, they will stand or fall by the teachers' attitudes and the quality of instruction. It appears to be largely for this reason that the government has increased its direct controls over the teaching profession.

By the end of 1960, the Bantu languages were to be used as the medium of instruction through standard six and then gradually extended to the secondary-school system and eventually to the university colleges. The growing stress given to the vernacular on all educational levels is meeting with strong opposition from many Africans, who feel that their mother tongues cannot meet modern educational needs. It may also succeed in isolating the educated African from the mainstream of Western education and thought.

Higher Education

Until 1959, higher education for nonwhites in South Africa was mainly under control of the English language universities. Many nonwhites were enrolled in the University of South Africa, an exceptionally good correspondence college, and in the universities of Cape Town, Witwatersrand, Rhodes, and Natal. In 1958, for example, there were approximately 1,800 Africans enrolled in universities, more than half of them in part-time studies at the University of South Africa.

Each of these schools had selected its own pattern of instruction for nonwhites. Cape Town and Witwatersrand admitted non-Europeans to classes with Europeans, while withholding some social privileges. Natal admitted them to its Non-European Medical School and to segregated classes at its Durban branch. Rhodes supervised the Fort Hare University College, overseeing its standards and examinations.

Fort Hare was well on the way to becoming a university in its own right.

In 1959, after six years of debate, the Nationalist Government passed what are known as the university apartheid measures: the Extension of University Education Bill and the University College of Fort Hare Transfer Bill. These acts barred all non-Europeans who were not registered by January 1, 1959, from entering any of the "white" institutions, except for the medical school at Natal and the correspondence courses of the University of South Africa. They also empowered the government to take over Fort Hare and to establish entirely new institutions of higher learning for the specific use of non-Europeans.

The measures were attacked as infringements on university autonomy, and the question was raised as to whether the new government-controlled institutions could gain acceptance as reputable academic institutions. The government ignored the objections in an all-night sitting of Parliament for the second reading, then closed debate on the remaining stages of the bills. Throughout the all-night debate, students of Cape Town stood outside Parliament carrying a torch symbolic of academic freedom.

The first Bantu colleges officially opened their doors in March, 1960. Their rectors have rigid control over all student activities, while the Deputy Minister for Bantu Education has similar control over the faculty. Fort Hare, located in Ciskei but scheduled for eventual relocation in Umtata in the heart of the Transkei, is to become the Xhosa college; the University College of Zululand, at Ngoya, is for Zulus; and the University College of the North, at Turfloop, is for the Sotho, Tsonga, and Venda Africans. At Belleville, there is the Western Cape University College for Coloureds, and an Indian college opened in Durban in January, 1961.

A South African journalist has described the motive behind this facet of apartheid: "Afrikaners are persuaded that they are being as fair as they can possibly be in the historical situation of South Africa. They wish for everybody what they wish for themselves—to live in large but closed family circles and suffer no foreign interference. Only, for the time being, the Afrikaners must have absolute control of the process of forming the circles for everybody." *

Staffing these institutions, called "tribal colleges" by the opposition press, has been a hard task for a variety of academic and political reasons. Many on the Fort Hare faculty resigned in protest against the

* Anthony Delius, "Separate But Equal on the Veld," *The Reporter,* December 24, 1959.

University College of the North, at Turfloop—Administration Building.

new policy, while others were not rehired when the government took over the college. Although some of the directors and staff are able and dedicated educators, there are not enough qualified applicants to fill existing positions. Retired civil servants have occasionally been hired to fill in as professors.

Students at the non-European universities can take degrees in arts, education, natural science, and theology, and diplomas in education, social work, trading, and commerce. The colleges are being equipped with libraries and laboratories, and the government says that more research laboratories will be added as the need arises. The total fees for tuition, lodging, board, and other items amounts to £90 a year for a degree course, £55 for the education diploma, and £60 for other diplomas.

The present annual intake of the Non-European Medical School at Natal University is reported to be about forty students. A number of full and partial bursaries and scholarships are available from government and private sources. Bantu medical training will continue at this center until such time as the necessary facilities are available at the Bantu university colleges.*

The long-range plans for these universities are unclear, but the government wants them to become cultural focuses for the tribes they serve. Above all, it does not want them teaching the egalitarian ideas disseminated at the formerly "open" universities of Cape Town and Witwatersrand. On the technical side, however, the government is sincerely trying to make them showpieces. For example, the Natal medical school probably offers better medical training than is available to Africans anywhere else south of the Sahara, and the Western Cape University College for Coloureds has the most modern scientific equipment. All of the physical plants are impressive. Even so, the government's plan to use the Bantu languages as mediums for instruction at the university level raises grave doubts as to their academic standing. These languages, as African leaders recognize, are not suited to many academic disciplines. Even the Afrikaans universities lean heavily on English in some fields, and the technical vocabulary of Afrikaans is vastly superior to that of, for example, Xhosa or Zulu.

Approximately 1,800 Africans were enrolled in universities in 1960 (see Table 1)—about the same as in 1958. More than half of these students were engaged in part-time studies at the University of South Africa—an institution that conducts its teaching solely by correspondence, although it has external examiners.

* *Progress of the Bantu Peoples Toward Nationhood,* No. 2, Union of South Africa Information Bureau, 1961.

Table 1
Nonwhite University Enrollment, 1959–60

Schools	Number of students
University College of Fort Hare (1960)	
Bantu	245
Indian	66
Coloured	49
Total	*360*
Note: Non-Bantu students were allowed to complete the courses for which they had enrolled prior to the new legislation.	
University College of the North (Turfloop) (1960)	
Bantu	80
University College of Zululand (1960)	
Bantu	41
Non-European Medical School, Durban (1960)	
Bantu	108
Other non-Europeans	93
Total	*201*
Witwatersrand University (1960)	
Bantu	52
Asiatic	188
Coloured	29
Total	*269*
Cape Town University (1960)	
Bantu	27
Asiatic	140
Coloured	396
Total	*563*
Western Cape University College for Coloureds (1960)	
Coloured	143
Malay	14
Total	*157*
University of South Africa (1959)	
Bantu	1,252
Asiatic	601
Coloured	211
Total	*2,064*

Note: 115 of the Bantu were from Southern Rhodesia; 24 from Northern Rhodesia; 7 from East Africa; 89 from Bechuanaland, Basutoland, and Swaziland; and 4 from other parts of Africa. The extramural Bantu students from South-West Africa are included in the figures for South Africa. Six of the Asiatics were from outside South Africa, as were 2 of the Coloureds.

SOURCE: South African Information Service.

Adult Education

Adult education for Africans has progressed little in the last fifteen years. The drop in illiteracy to 65 per cent during this period was almost entirely the effect of formal school training. Existing adult-education facilities are, with few exceptions, restricted to urban areas and are, on the whole, still unsatisfactory. State subsidies to night schools and continuation classes have been considerably reduced during the past years. The government—for theoretical, economic, and political reasons—tends to give adult education a low priority in its education planning.

The Outlook

Bantu education presents a two-sided picture. On the one hand, it is clearly expanding at a rapid rate. On the other, the restrictions on the African's intellectual horizons are being progressively narrowed. The Nationalists, by introducing indoctrination into the school system, have given African education a new dimension that they hope will help perpetuate separate development of the races. The present system of Bantu education is too new to have yet produced significant and lasting results in terms of the African mentality—and the employment of 25,000 African teachers in the system will probably continue to limit the effect of government reforms.

Africans have by no means been united in their reaction to Bantu education. Many, particularly in the Bantu reserves, have given it their approval. A considerable number have accepted it because of its immediate advantages without giving much thought to its implications. Educated Africans in general, however, appear to be unalterably opposed to the narrowing of intellectual horizons implicit in education for apartheid. Government controls (as well as the attractions of security and status) have reduced most of the teaching profession to acquiescence, but the atmosphere is one of suspicion and tension not conducive to either teaching or learning.

On the whole, the leaders of the small African educated elite in South Africa have so far been a conservative force, particularly if measured against standards of African political behavior elsewhere on the continent. Chief Albert Luthuli, who won the 1960 Nobel Peace Prize, and Professor Z. K. Matthews are not unrepresentative of this older generation. But a new and more militant generation, clearly in the making, is unlikely to be as amenable to compromise.

While the ethnic-centered Bantu university colleges may foster the localism and conservatism desired by the administration, they are likely also to intensify the frustrations of African students. By extending apartheid to the "open" universities, the Nationalists have closed a potentially valuable forum for interracial contact. It is doubtful whether segregation and isolation can temper growing African demands for contact with the outside world.

—Pablo Eisenberg

19. The High Commission Territories

Basutoland

Capital: Maseru
Population: 800,000 (est.)
Area: 11,716 sq. miles
Political status: British High Commission Territory

Bechuanaland

Capital: Lobatsi (temporary)
Population: 350,000 (est.)
Area: 225,000 sq. miles
Political status: British High Commission Territory

Swaziland

Capital: Mbabane
Population: 255,000 (est.)
Area: 6,470 sq. miles
Political status: British High Commission Territory

THE three High Commission territories of Bechuanaland, Basutoland, and Swaziland have been associated in one form or another with Britain since the late nineteenth century: Basutoland since 1868, Swaziland since 1884, and Bechuanaland since 1885. When the National Convention of the four South African colonies met in 1908–9 to form the Union, it was assumed by many—both in South Africa and in the United Kingdom—that these territories would also become part of the Union. However, the vigorous protests of the local tribal authorities against incorporation in the new South African state were supported by many voices in London, and they were finally left under British protection. Nevertheless, the Union of South Africa Act contained a section setting out the conditions under which the three territories might one day be incorporated—if and when the governments of the Union and the United Kingdom should agree, and if certain specified conditions were met pertaining to land and other rights for the indigenous population. Although the Nationalist Party and important sections of the South African press have brought up the question of incorporation from time to time, the South African Government has not made any formal demand in recent years. Indeed, Prime Minister Verwoerd indicated in 1961 that it was no longer feasible to consider the integration of these territories because their internal policies were now so divergent from those of the Union.

Since 1909, all three territories have been administered directly by Great Britain through a High Commissioner resident in the Union, with the assistance of resident commissioners located in each territory. With the departure of South Africa from the Commonwealth in 1961, it was generally assumed that responsibility for U.K. relations with South Africa would be transferred from the Commonwealth Relations Office to the Foreign Office and that control of High Commission affairs would be moved to the Colonial Office. Consideration was also being given to changing the existing framework of administration and separating completely the diplomatic and gubernatorial functions exercised by the High Commissioner, though an alternative proposal would allow the ambassador (i.e., former High Commissioner) to serve as both diplomatic representative in South Africa and governor of the three territories. Under the latter plan, day-to-day administration would be in the hands of the resident commissioners, who would be given enhanced status somewhat comparable to that of minor colonial governors. A debate in Parliament on May 24, 1961, made one point quite clear—that Britain will continue to be responsible for the territories and will not countenance their incorporation into South Africa as long as present policies remain in force there.

In all three communities, the British have from the first used the familiar system of "indirect rule"—that is, employing the machinery of traditional local African institutions to carry out the executive and judicial functions of government for the African segment of the population. While power rested with the Resident Commissioner, the paramount chiefs in Swaziland and Basutoland and the senior chiefs in Bechuanaland served as heads of the administrative and judicial institutions carrying out governmental policy as it applies to Africans. The 1959 constitution for Basutoland and the May, 1961, constitutional recommendations for Bechuanaland are steps in the direction of more democratic rule, and constitutional changes for Swaziland were also under discussion in 1961. Such political changes are more workable in Basutoland, where no Europeans may acquire land or settle permanently, and in Bechuanaland, where only certain limited areas are set aside for European settlement, than in Swaziland, where approximately 35 per cent of the land is owned by the 2 per cent of the population made up of Europeans.

In addition to internal sources of revenue, all three territories receive substantial grants-in-aid from the U.K. and a specified proportion of South Africa's customs revenue under an agreement reached before World War I. In Basutoland, this allotment amounts to about 40 per cent of the territory's total income (exclusive of income from the Colonial Development and Welfare Fund); in Bechuanaland, it is about 30 per cent; and in Swaziland, about 15 per cent.* If the South African Government were to recalculate the distribution of these revenues in accordance with 1961 realities, the loss to the territories would be substantial.

Another important outside source of support for the economies of the three territories is the money brought home by laborers who work in South African mines or industries. South Africa's withdrawal from the Commonwealth raises questions about the future status of these laborers, who have heretofore been judged as nonforeign Africans and given free access to available jobs. To lose such identity would impose serious economic hardships on them, especially in Basutoland.

Basutoland

Basutoland is only slightly larger than the state of Maryland and is entirely surrounded by and economically dependent on the Republic of South Africa. Yet, under the new constitution introduced in 1960, it is making rapid strides toward internal self-government, and there is now even hesitant talk of independence.

The principal unifying factor among the country's various political leaders—who range from militant radical Pan-Africanists to still powerful traditional chiefs—is opposition to incorporation into the Republic of South Africa. Britain has consistently supported this position, and elections were held under the new constitution in early 1960 to establish an eighty-seat national legislative assembly (half of whose members are Africans indirectly chosen by popularly elected district councils) to share governing responsibility with the British Resident Commissioner and the traditional leader of the Basuto people, the Paramount Chief.

The Basutoland Congress Party, a modern political party whose

* *The Times* (London), April 27, 1961.

leaders echo the more radical African nationalism of Guinea's Sekou Touré, won a surprisingly heavy victory. Congress leaders acknowledge the crucial importance to the territory's meager economy of the wages brought back from South Africa by thousands of Basuto, who go there to work in the mines, and they know that independence from Britain would gravely jeopardize their independence from South Africa. Yet, in practice, it is increasingly frustrating to accept the limitations imposed by these hard realities. Since the 1960 disturbances following the Sharpesville incident, Basutoland has become a gathering point for nationalist exiles from South Africa, and this "oasis of freedom in a sea of apartheid"—as the liberal South African weekly *Contact* put it—is likely to play an increasingly important role in the political evolution of southern Africa.

Within Basutoland, some 150,000 out of 160,000 families have holdings of land, including the families of men working in the Republic of South Africa. Of the total area of 11,716 square miles, only about 1,500 are cultivatable because most of the country is hilly; much of the remainder, however, is grassland suitable for grazing. Since there are neither industries nor any known mineral wealth in the country, the value of the few agricultural exports—wool, mohair, wheat, sorghum, and cattle—seldom equals required imports. About 40 per cent of the territory's revenue comes from its share of the Republic of South Africa's Custom and Excise Tax, still paid under the terms of the Customs Agreement of 1910, although direct taxation yielded 25.3 per cent of the 1960 revenue. An important factor in the economy is the money sent to relatives in Basutoland by those persons who go to work in the mines, industries, and farms of South Africa. (Of the total population of some 800,000, including 2,000 Europeans, it is estimated that 130,000 of Basutoland's male citizens reside outside the territory most of the time.) Since 1946, the Colonial Development and Welfare Fund has spent over £1.4 million to finance agricultural development schemes in the territory.

The Development of Education

Although Basutoland's economic resources remain appallingly minimal, its human resources are being usefully shaped into an economic asset by one of the more pervasive educational systems in Africa, topped by the only remaining multiracial university in southern Africa. The fact that Basutoland enjoys both ethnic and linguistic unity has greatly facilitated educational growth: Almost all the people are Basuto, and the *lingua franca* is Sesotho.

Education in Basutoland remains largely in the hands of three missions—the Paris Evangelical, the Roman Catholic, and the English Church. The only two government schools in the territory are the trades school and the coeducational Basutoland High School, both at Maseru, although a few nondenominational schools are run by local committees. To the extent of its resources, the Basutoland Government assists all schools in the system with grants-in-aid, spending on education about a sixth of its total expenditure of £2 million.

Primary education is free but not compulsory. By 1959, there were more than 1,000 primary schools in the territory with more than 128,000 pupils. Nine hundred of the primary schools provide the first six years of education only, but 100 go through to the eighth year—the completion of the primary stage. Approximately half of the population in the five to nineteen age-group are in school at any one time, but perhaps 95 per cent of the children go to school at some time. While nearly all girls between ten and sixteen are at school, half the boys do not attend, usually because they are tending cattle. The government estimates that nearly all the female population will soon be functionally literate in English or Sesotho, but only half the male population. Relatively few students of either sex go beyond Standard 4, and even fewer obtain any secondary training. Only about 1,600 were enrolled in secondary schools in 1960.

Although the first complete high school was not opened until 1939, there are now twenty schools, in various stages of development, offering secondary facilities. Four offer the full five-year course up to matriculation, and the rest are to develop into three-year schools (up to Junior Certificate level). Four of the fifteen junior secondary schools are privately financed, but the rest are grant-aided by the government—though only enough to offer the barest minimum facilities.

Because Basutoland is a mountainous country of scattered villages and hamlets, boarding accommodation is essential, yet only a few schools are so equipped owing to lack of funds and the heavy cost of building in the mountains. Much of the equipment has to be transported by pack animals, and the mountain climate is so rigorous that strong weatherproof buildings are necessary to withstand the severe cold during the winter. Aerial reconnaissance in 1959 showed huts and schools buried up to the roof in the heaviest snowfall for many years.

Educational criteria are not uniform, and a recent survey of Basuto education observed that "too many of those who take the examinations for primary, junior, and senior certificates fail to pass." A major reason for this poor showing is the shortage of qualified teachers. Although there are seven teacher-training centers, the requirements for entrance are low (only primary or junior certificates are required for admission, depending on the type of training desired), and the centers lack fully trained staff. Also, better salaries and opportunities elsewhere lead to a steady drain of the better teachers from Basutoland to other areas of Africa. Nevertheless, it is a significant accomplishment that 95 per cent of the teachers in Basutoland primary and secondary schools are Africans.

Higher Education

The University College of Pius XII, the only accredited institution in southern Africa offering equal academic facilities for all races, is located in Basutoland. Established in 1945 by the Catholic Church, Pius XII has a staff embracing fourteen different nationalities. Its courses in the humanities, science, commerce, and education are under the supervision of the University of South Africa, which fixes the standards of instruction and examination and endorses its B.A. and B.S. degrees. Extracurricular courses are given during the year (especially during the holidays) in economic development, agriculture, and political leadership. The multiracial student body of 170 in 1960 included a few Asians and whites and a number of non-Basuto Africans from Kenya, Uganda, the Federation of Rhodesia and Nyasaland, and South Africa. There were more than 1,000 applicants in 1960, and the college administration hopes soon to add additional residences so as to accommodate a total of 800 students and to improve its staff and standards.

Table 1 shows the numbers of Basuto who, in 1959, were studying at universities outside Basutoland with government bursaries or financial assistance.

Table 1
Basuto Studying Abroad with Government Assistance, 1959

Country	Number of students	
	Male	Female
United Kingdom	13	1
South Africa [a]	7	2
Federation of Rhodesia and Nyasaland	3	
United States	2	1
India	3	

[a] Students completing studies undertaken before the ban on enrollment of Africans from outside South Africa.

Technical Education

Technical and vocational education is provided mainly in two trades schools, and the total annual output is about thirty-five. Courses are offered in masonry and brickwork, carpentry and joinery, cabinetmaking, leatherwork, tailoring, motor mechanics, and commercial subjects. Commercial training is now being offered in one of the secondary schools at post–Junior Certificate level. However, consideration is being given to the establishment of a five-year secondary school with a strong technical bias as soon as funds are available.

The Agricultural School operated by the Department of Agriculture in conjunction with its research program trains agricultural demonstrators; however, its capacity would need to be trebled to meet the requirements of a projected enlargement of Basutoland's agricultural-extension and soil-conservation program. Another valuable contribution in the area of adult agricultural and cooperative training is being made by the privately operated Machobane agricultural school, where hundreds of adults are undergoing training in agriculture, cooperative organization, and civics. This endeavor, in turn, complements a program of community-development training now underway at the University College.

Until recently, there has been no opportunity for Basuto to obtain commercial training at the secondary level, with the result that there are few Basuto in clerical and bookkeeping positions in the European trading establishments.

Bechuanaland

Bechuanaland is only the northern part of a larger British protectorate originally established in 1885.* Even so, present-day Bechuanaland is much larger than the other two High Commission territories—225,000 square miles sandwiched between South-West Africa on the west and Southern Rhodesia on the east. The western two-thirds of the territory lies largely within the Kalahari Desert, and thus the main centers of population and the only railway and major road are concentrated in the better-watered eastern border region. The 1960 population, estimated at about 350,000, comprises eight

* The southern part of the original protectorate was detached in 1885 to become the Crown Colony of British Bechuanaland, and was finally incorporated in Cape Colony in 1895; it is now part of the Republic of South Africa.

main African tribal groups plus some 3,000 Europeans, 700 Eurafricans, and 250 Asians. The literacy rate is estimated at about 20 per cent.

Separate advisory councils of eight Europeans and thirty-nine Africans once advised the British Resident Commissioner, but since 1950 a Joint Advisory Council composed of both African and European representatives has been carrying on this function. A new constitution introduced by Britain in May, 1961, carries the country one stage toward self-government; it provides for a new legislature comprising ten officials, ten elected Europeans, ten elected Africans, and one elected Asian.

Apart from government officials, missionaries, and traders living in the larger villages, the European population is composed mainly of farmers, railway employees, and employees of two companies that recruit labor for the mines in South Africa. About 5 per cent of the male Africans work in South Africa, but the most important occupation in Bechuanaland is cattle-raising. However, owing to the general shortage of water in much of the territory and deterioriation of pastures under poor management, this is a declining industry, and will continue to be so unless the country gets additional badly needed geological, hydrological, and agricultural research and extension services. Bechuanaland depends upon its allotted share of South African customs and excise taxes and on British grants-in-aid to take up the slack in its ordinary budget, and on Colonial Development and Welfare assistance for general development.

Development of Education

Prior to 1955, educational facilities for Africans consisted of: (1) about 150 primary schools, mostly operated by tribal authorities, offering four- six- and eight-year courses, with an enrollment in 1955 of 20,475; (2) 2 secondary and 2 junior secondary schools with an enrollment in 1955 of 242; (3) a small missionary Homecraft Center for girls; and (4) some Public Works and Veterinary Department training for prospective employees. By 1959, enrollment had increased to 32,406 (13,166 male and 19,240 female) in 179 primary schools, and to 431 in 5 secondary and junior secondary schools.

By 1960, an estimated 56 per cent of some 60,000 children of primary-school age were attending schools. Except for the Homecrafts Center in Mochudi, all schools are coeducational. The number of students completing more than the four-year primary course continues, as before, to be little more than one-sixth of the total enrollment.

The breakdown of enrollment in African schools from 1946 to 1959 is given in Table 2.

Table 2
Enrollment in African Schools in Bechuanaland, 1946–59

Year	Primary education		Secondary education	
	Male	Female	Male	Female
1946	8,045	13,129	28	29
1947	6,413	10,921	42	15
1948	6,218	10,128	*total:* 34	
1949	6,509	10,921	51	28
1950	5,866	10,204	100	46
1951	6,341	11,122	92	67
1952	6,344	11,398	87	55
1953	6,757	11,427	92	60
1954	7,439	12,475	111	58
1955	7,764	12,711	153	89
1956	9,312	14,813	202	123
1957	11,219	17,294	197	138
1958	12,548	17,376	243	142
1959	13,166	19,240	245	186

SOURCE: 1959 *Annual Report.*

Vocational and Technical Training

Until recently, technical training was practically nonexistent in Bechuanaland. A few students were able to enter the trade schools in Basutoland, Swaziland, and South Africa, but none of these arrangements was wholly satisfactory, and South Africa is now closed to students from Bechuanaland.

Systematic vocational training has been introduced at the Lobatsi Teacher Training College, opened in 1956; at the Ramathlabama Veterinary Research Station, which gives a six-month course of training for cattle guards and veterinary assistants; at the Public Works Department workshops in Gaberones, where men are given a kind of apprenticeship training for jobs as repair mechanics, builders, and carpenters; and at St. Joseph's College, one of two secondary boarding schools that have recently instituted a commercial course. Somewhat less systematic training for telephone-exchange repairmen is provided by the Posts and Telegraphs Department.

Plans for 1960–61 included construction of the first section of a Trades School to be operated in conjunction with the Public Works Department workshops and training program in Gaberones. It was also planned to add another year to the commercial course at St.

Joseph's. Long-term plans call for a course in agriculture at Moeng College, the other secondary boarding school.

Teaching Staff

As in the other two High Commission territories—indeed, as in the rest of Africa—improvement in the standard of education is retarded by the shortage of qualified teachers and by the limited facilities for teacher training. Classroom accommodations are also inadequate. Basing its estimates on forty students to each teacher, the government cited a shortage of 477 classrooms in 1959 and an immediate need for an additional seventy-four teachers.

In 1959, sixty-four male and forty-two female students were enrolled at the Teacher Training College at Lobatsi; twenty-eight qualified as teachers in that year (nineteen for primary lower schools, and nine for primary higher schools). The program here is well conceived, but present output is barely sufficient to provide for new appointments and normal withdrawals; thus, little progress has been made in replacing the larger number of untrained and unqualified teachers.

Higher Education

During 1959, six Bechuanaland students were studying at the University College of Pius XII in Basutoland. One student completed requirements for a science degree at the University College of Fort Hare in South Africa in that year, and two others were awarded bursaries—one to study law in London and one to study medicine in Dublin.

Swaziland

The Swazi proudly recall one of the oldest national traditions among the Bantu people of southern Africa. White settlers and prospectors first entered the domain of the ruling Swazi Paramount Chief, King Mbandzeni, in about 1878, and in 1888 he granted the Europeans in the country a charter of self-government and the right to control their own affairs, subject to his veto. This plan did not satisfy the Europeans, however, and a joint commission subsequently sent by the British and Transvaal governments to study the situation proposed that the King and Council of the Swazi nation turn over control of European affairs to the commission. Since 1890, therefore, there have existed in this small country two more or less parallel systems of government—one primarily for the Europeans and one for the control of native affairs. The present King (or Paramount Chief), Sobhuza II, CBE, has ruled his people since 1921.

In this early period, the Swazi King and various chiefs gave one land concession after another until, as noted in the 1907–8 *Annual Report*:

> Practically the whole area of the country was covered two, three, or even four deep by concessions of all sizes for different purposes, and for greatly varying periods. In but very few cases were even the boundaries defined; many of the areas had been sub-divided and sold several times, and seldom were the boundaries of the super-imposed areas even co-terminous. In addition to this, concessions were granted for all lands and minerals previously unallotted or which, having been allotted might lapse or become forfeited. Finally, it must be remembered that over these three or four strata of conflicting interests, boundaries and periods, there had to be preserved the natural rights of the natives to live, move, cultivate, graze and hunt.*

In 1904, the government established a commission to investigate the problem of land concessions. Under the subsequent Concession Proclamation of 1907, one-third of the land and grazing concessions was expropriated for the exclusive use and occupation of the Swazi people, who were required to move from the remaining two-thirds of the land area unless they made agreement with the concessionaires to remain. Since 1907, considerable portions of the remaining two-thirds of Swaziland have been purchased by the Swazi nation or by individual Swazis. The government, with the help of the Colonial Development and Welfare Fund, has also purchased land to resettle squatters who remained on European-owned land. Of the some 4,280,000 acres in Swaziland, about 2,251,000 are now available for Swazi use, but plots are scattered in different areas. The validity of the Concession Proclamation was challenged in 1922, but it was upheld. Many of the Swazis continue to feel aggrieved, however, and the British Government has recently proposed new measures to adjust land inequities.

At the close of the Boer War in 1902, an order-in-council was issued transferring control of Swaziland from the Transvaal, under whose jurisdiction it had come in 1884, to the British High Commission. Under this arrangement, as revised in 1944, the Paramount Chief is regarded as a constitutional monarch bound by the advice of a National Council and invested with power to issue to the Swazi Africans (but no other residents of the territory) legally enforceable

* Cited in *Economic Survey, 1960,* Her Majesty's Stationery Office, p. 419.

orders on a wide variety of subjects. The National Council traditionally consisted of the heads of every Swazi household of good standing, but today it is confined in practice to the chiefs and a number of the senior commoners.

On the European side, there is a European Advisory Council consisting today of ten members elected by British subjects over twenty-one years of age who fulfill certain residential requirements and other qualifications. The operating link between the two systems of internal government is a standing committee that meets weekly. A Eurafrican association is also consulted by the government regularly.

A new political element that has recently arisen in the territory is the Swaziland Progressive Party, an African nationalist movement seeking a nonracial democracy in the near future and a specific timetable for progress toward independence. While the Progressive Party is not yet a formidable force in terms of numbers, the point of view it represents is likely to appeal to growing numbers of the younger and more educated Swazis. Discussions begun in 1961 under British aegis over a new constitution for Swaziland had not progressed very far by the end of that year because of the wide differences among the three viewpoints represented by the powerful Swaziland traditional authorities, the modern nationalists of the Progressive Party, and the Europeans.

The population of Swaziland in 1959 comprised an estimated 244,700 Swazis, 8,700 Europeans, and 1,600 Eurafricans.* Some 8,000 adult African males are estimated to be across the border in South Africa at any given time working in mines and on farms. From 1946 to 1956, the European population increased by 84.9 per cent as against an increase of only 16.9 per cent in the previous decade. Over 60 per cent of the European population were born in South Africa, 20 per cent in Swaziland, and 8 per cent in the United Kingdom.†

Economic Conditions

Swaziland's 6,470 square miles are divided into four distinct geographical and climatic regions ranging in elevation from 500 to 6,000 feet. Only in the lowest region along the border of Mozambique is there any substantial area of flat fertile ground, but the Highveld is suitable for forestry, and grazing and dryland farming are widespread. At present, asbestos is the most important export, but large deposits of high-grade iron ore have been discovered in the northwestern part of the country near Mbabane. Also, a new pulp industry was expected

* 1959 *Annual Report,* p. 7.
† *Ibid,* p. 10.

to produce 100,000 tons of wood pulp in 1961, and a sugar mill is producing 60,000 tons of sugar annually. Agricultural experimentation will soon add citrus and other new cash crops to the cotton, tobacco, rice, and vegetables already produced. Exports amounted to some £4 million in 1957–58, half of which came from asbestos. The largest single source of government revenue is the income tax, followed by Swaziland's allotted share of South Africa's customs and excise taxes. Some money from the Colonial Development and Welfare Fund has been made available for development programs, and it is estimated that such grants will amount to £2 million in the 1960–64 period.

The 1960 *Economic Survey* of the protectorates observed: "Swaziland has apparently greater economic potentiality than either Bechuanaland or Basutoland. The task of government here is not so much to search for economic possibilities and initiate development where they can be found, as to create and help create conditions under which its known resources can be exploited to the best advantage of the territory."

The Development of Education

Education for all races in Swaziland is administered by the government through an Education Department staffed with a director and a deputy director, four educational officers, six African supervisors of schools, plus a clerical staff. Three separate divisions are set up for each of the three population groups, with different systems of education for each. School enrollment of Africans in 1956 and 1959 is shown in Table 3.

Table 3
Enrollment of Africans in Swazi Schools, 1956 and 1959

Type of school	Enrollment 1956	Enrollment 1959	Increase (percentage)
Sub-standards	13,999	14,505	3.5
Standards 1 to 4	8,635	13,264	53.6
Standards 5 to 6	1,718	2,643	53.8
Total primary enrollment	*24,352*	*30,412*	*25*
Secondary classes	480	805	68
Grand total	*24,832*	*31,217*	*25.7*

The funds expended for all schools in 1957, 1958, and 1959 are shown in Table 4.

Table 4
Funds Expended for Swazi Schools, 1957–59

Purpose of expenditure	1957	1958	1959
African education			
Recurrent	£106,329	£118,293	£135,589
Capital	26,762	27,799	25,122
European education			
Recurrent	50,535	58,650	66,813
Capital	17,150	22,460	25,542
Eurafrican education			
Recurrent	5,600	7,173	9,014
Capital	1,420	500	
Total	*£207,796*	*£234,875*	*£262,080*

Although African enrollment has trebled in the past ten years, fewer than half the Swazi children of school age have been in school at any one time. Many fail to go beyond Standard 2 level and consequently never receive any instruction in English (which starts at Standard 3). Of those who do continue, about half drop out before they reach Standard 6, and they probably do not achieve a high degree of literacy. About 85 per cent of the Eurafrican school-age population is enrolled, and about 98 per cent of the European. Compulsory attendance applies only to European children.

Most schools are operated by one or another of nineteen church missions that receive government grants-in-aid toward teachers' salaries, books, equipment, and buildings. The encouragement of voluntary effort is an important feature of the territory's educational policy, and the missions are well represented on the district and territorial advisory boards.

The syllabus for all schools is prescribed by the Education Department, and an external examination is set at the end of Standard 6. The primary course extends over eight years (two sub-standards and Standards 1 and 2). The full course is offered at the higher primary schools, while lower primary schools offer a six-year course to Standard 4. In 1959, there were 200 African primary schools, of which 55 offered the full eight-year course.

The full secondary course extends over five years, culminating in a matriculation examination supplied by the University of South Africa. Three high schools offer the full course, while four junior secondary schools conduct classes to the Junior Certificate level (two years below matriculation), their pupils being prepared for the Junior Certificate examination of the University of South Africa. At seven other schools, junior secondary departments are being established.

At the end of 1959, as Table 3 indicates, there were 805 pupils in secondary classes.

Technical Education

Technical and vocational training is provided at the Mbabane Trades School, where boys are taught building, carpentry, and motor mechanics (all four-year courses); at two small lower primary teacher-training centers; at one housecraft training center; at the Ainsworth Dickson Nursing Training School (accredited to a large mission hospital at Bremersdorp) and at the Mdutshane Agricultural Training Center conducted by the Department of Land Utilization. The 1960 *Economic Survey* pointed out, however, that there is a need for many more Swazi students to receive secondary training with a technical bias and to go on to take technical post-matriculation courses and university degrees.

Adult Education

In the field of adult education, the Education Department conducts a mobile film and library service that operates in various parts of the country. Adult education among women is carried on through women's clubs, where simple courses in dressmaking, needlework, and cooking are taught. Literacy classes are also conducted for prisoners in jails.

Teacher Training

In 1958, 833 teachers were employed in African schools—767 in primary schools, 50 in secondary schools, and 16 in vocational and technical schools. The over-all teacher-pupil ratio was reported to be thirty-five to one.

Teacher-training facilities in the territory are inadequate at all levels, however, and more than half the teachers in the primary schools in 1955 were reportedly untrained. The current output of fifty primary school teachers per year is twenty short of the estimated seventy needed to meet increasing enrollment. It has been necessary to recruit large numbers each year from South Africa, but this is proving increasingly difficult because of the higher salaries offered there. The 1960–64 Development Plan calls for the establishment of a teacher-training center to graduate an additional sixty-four teachers a year. The aim is to replace all unqualified teachers within a decade.

There is no center in Swaziland for training of secondary-school teachers. Since secondary enrollment is expected to rise from 655 in 1958 to 2,300 in 1965, the only current hope for improvement is that the University College of Pius XII in Basutoland will be able to admit additional teachers for training. But funds must be supplied for this.

Higher Education

There are no universities in Swaziland, nor, in view of the size of the territory and its small population, is it likely that any can be financed in the foreseeable future. In the 1959 *Annual Report,* it was reported that eight Swazi students were reading for degrees at Pius XII; one had begun a medical course in South Africa and two were enrolled at the Goromonzi High School in Southern Rhodesia with a view to entering the University College of Rhodesia and Nyasaland in Salisbury. In addition, four Swazi students were studying in the United Kingdom.

20. South-West Africa

Capital: Windhoek
Population: 554,000 (est.)
Area: 318,000 sq. miles
Political status: Administered by South Africa under a League of Nations Mandate, which the administering power has thus far refused to convert to a U.N. trusteeship arrangement

South Africa governs the adjoining former German territory of South-West Africa under a League of Nations mandate that called upon the administering power to treat it "as an integral portion of the Union of South Africa," promoting "to the utmost the material and moral well-being and the social progress of the inhabitants." With an advisory opinion of the World Court as support, the United Nations contends that it has inherited the supervisory function of the League's Permanent Mandates Commission, and it has repeatedly asked South Africa to place the territory under Trusteeship. In October, 1961, the U.N. General Assembly's special investigating committee on South-West Africa charged "the unfitness of the Government of South Africa to further administer the territory" and urged "the immediate institution of a United Nations presence in South-West Africa." Meanwhile, a formal case filed in the World Court in 1960 by Liberia and Ethiopia asks for a binding judgment on whether South Africa has violated the mandate.

This controversial territory is a vast and thinly populated land of 318,000 square miles. Its estimated population of 554,000 in 1960 comprised 464,000 Africans, 69,000 Europeans, and 21,000 people of mixed blood (officially called Coloureds). The largest of the several African tribal groups in South-West Africa is the Ovambo, concentrated in the far north, but the smaller Herero tribe (estimated at

50,000) is the most urbanized and politically active.* The central Police Zone—so called because it is directly governed by whites, whereas the north remains an almost exclusively African preserve—is divided into a complex of Native reserves, towns, and European areas.

The Europeans are concentrated for the most part in the central area. Of the territory's 69,000 Europeans, 22,000 are said to have been born in South-West Africa and about 18,700 in South Africa proper. A reported 45,437 are South African citizens, and just over 33,000 are classified as Afrikaans-speaking. There is also a German community of approximately 20,000. The Europeans, in general, have no strong convictions against eventual incorporation into South Africa. However, occasional complaints are heard that South-West Africa is administered too much as though it were a colony of South Africa, and a small liberal opposition party, the National Union, was formed in 1960. The official languages are Afrikaans and English, although German is also widely used. The over-all rate of literacy among the non-Europeans is estimated to be 20 per cent, but this includes literacy in local languages.

In 1949, the South African Government added six white representatives of South-West to its House of Assembly and two more to the Senate (one to be appointed because of his special knowledge of nonwhites in South-West Africa). Economically, too, the governing Nationalist Party has increasingly dealt with South-West as an integral part of South Africa itself, with the result that separate economic statistics on the territory are no longer available. Through these and other gestures, the South African Government has made it clear that it does not recognize United Nations jurisdiction over South-West.

While the territory is one of the world's prime sources of karakul furs and apparently exports sufficient quantities of diamonds and other minerals to assure a favorable balance of trade, its importance to South Africa is not primarily economic but as a political buffer zone. To allow the United Nations to set up an independent African state at the very door of South Africa would profoundly limit the chances of containing African nationalist pressures within South Africa itself.

The government freely admits that apartheid policies are applied in the territory as stringently as in South Africa itself. In May, 1956, Dr. Vedder, the Senator appointed to represent nonwhite interests in

* Some 11,000 of the Hereros live in exile in Bechuanaland, where the Chief and some of his people fled during the period that South-West was under harsh German rule; the two sections of the tribe have maintained connections and have worked together in seeking assistance from the United Nations.

the Union Senate, spoke with pride of the progress made toward separate development of the races in South-West:

> In South-West Africa, the foundations of apartheid were laid fifty years ago. . . . The German Government started this. The mixing of Europeans and non-Europeans has since 1918 been prohibited by law. . . . In South-West Africa, we have the only country in the world where apartheid has been exercised in an increasing degree for fifty years.

Educational Policies

Since the educational policies of South-West Africa are based on apartheid, separate schools are required for the three racial groups. General control and supervision of education are vested in the territory's Administrator, but the actual maintenance and operation of the schools are delegated to a Director of Education.

Education for non-Europeans is not compulsory, and most of the educational facilities available to them are provided by Christian missions, many of them subsidized by the government. The total number of non-Europeans (Africans and Coloured) enrolled in schools in 1959 was reported to be 36,717, and the total government expenditures for these two segments of the population for that year was £251,295, including assistance to missions. In the same year, £1,027,892 was spent on the separate educational system for the territory's 15,523 Europeans in primary and secondary schools. All the African pupils in the northern territories outside the Police Zone were in primary classes (Standard 3 or below) in 1958; in the Police Zone, only 367 out of 9,969 were above Standard 3, and no Africans or Coloureds were above Standard 9. Of the 9,969 Africans in school in the Police Zone, all but 1,085 were in mission schools; outside the Police Zone, all African education was in the hands of missions. There were 238 African students in the government's teacher-training school at Augustineum in Okahandja, and 212 were at the Roman Catholic teacher-training schools at Doebra.

Higher Education

While there are no higher educational facilities available in South-West Africa, students from the territory have until recently theoretically had access to those of South Africa. As of January 1, 1960, when new legislation went into effect forbidding entry of non-Europeans into any of South Africa's European universities, South-West Africans are allowed access only to the medical school for non-Europeans at the University of Natal, to correspondence courses of the University of South Africa,* and to the one Bantu university in South Africa open to non-Europeans from outside its immediate vicinity, the University College of Fort Hare. The admission of Africans from South-West Africa to two other Bantu university colleges requires in each case individual permission from the Minister of Bantu Education. As of 1961, there were only two known African university graduates from South-West, both in exile.

The government has in the past refused or withdrawn passports from non-Europeans from South-West Africa who have been granted scholarships to study at the University of Oslo, at Oxford University, and at the University College of Ghana.

Commission of Enquiry into Non-European Education

In May, 1958, a Commission of Enquiry was appointed to investigate and report to the South African Government on several aspects of non-European education in South-West. The Commission's voluminous report was sent by South Africa to the United Nations in November, 1959. In essence, it recommended that a system of Native education modeled on the one existing in South Africa be extended to South-West—but suggested that Coloured education be on a par with European. It also recommended that consideration be given to the transfer of supervision of Native education in the territory to the Department of Bantu Education in the Union. Various church and mission societies that had in the past provided most of the educational facilities for the non-Europeans would be asked to transfer control of their schools to the territorial Administrator. In the event that this transfer was not made voluntarily, it was proposed that the church and mission schools should forfeit any government financial aid and be required to apply for registration as private schools—but subject to governmental syllabi and official inspection.

In justifying a separate and special system of education for the Africans similar to that in South Africa itself, the Commission suggested that education, in order to be effective, must be geared to the needs of a particular group resident in a particular area and in a particular stage of development. The Commission recommended that Native education aim, for the time being, only at putting at least 80 per cent of the African children of school age through Standard 2 of the lower primary school, noting that 70 to 80 per cent of these pupils would probably not proceed beyond this level. The aim of these lower primary courses should be to enable the masses to read and

* Acceptance requires the written consent of the Minister of Bantu Education, however.

write their local vernacular and to make useful elementary calculations. For economic reasons, some knowledge of Afrikaans and English was recommended.

It was suggested that religion, health, hygiene, handicrafts, nature study, and other subjects, based on South African syllabi, should be introduced. Teachers for the primary level, it was recommended, should have eleven years of schooling (previously reduced to ten years in view of the teacher shortage). Only one higher primary school should be established for the area outside the Police Zone; within the Police Zone, at least one higher primary school should be established for each of seventeen Native reserves. Junior secondary schools were also to be provided for the Police Zone, but the Commission recommended that the establishment of senior secondary school up to matriculation standard could be postponed since existing training schools could take the few pupils who would qualify for the upper grades. It recommended additional teacher-training facilities and vocational training schools, however. With regard to adult education, it proposed that the system of adult Bantu education used in South Africa should be extended into South-West Africa and that suitable reading matter be provided for adults, especially for those who lived in compounds at industrial centers.

In 1960, the Administrator for South-West Africa informed the South African Legislative Assembly that the report of the Commission of Enquiry into non-European education in South-West Africa had been considered and that implementing legislation would be introduced shortly.

Another report on education in the territory, of quite different tenor, was received by the United Nations Committee on South-West Africa in 1960 from the South-West African People's Organization (SWAPO), one of two major African nationalist organizations in South-West.* Reporting that Bantu education had already been introduced into two schools in the territory and was soon to be introduced into all African schools in South-West Africa, the petitioners warned that Bantu education's object was "to teach African children from childhood that they were inferior to Europeans" and stated that all Africans in South-West Africa were opposed to its imposition. Another petition from African critics of the regime in South-West stated that Bantu education, with its emphasis on vernacular languages, had been introduced in order to prevent people from reading books and newspapers through which they might be informed of the world situation.

* SWAPO claims a membership of 50,000. Another nationalist group is the South-West Africa National Union (SWANU), with an estimated 8,000 followers.

On the basis of South Africa's official reports and petitioners' information, the United Nations Committee concluded in its 1960 report:

> Proposals have been made to introduce into the Territory a special type of education for "Native" children based on the system of Bantu education established in the Union of South Africa. At the same time, the Natives in the Territory have been deprived of practically all opportunities for higher education on a level equal to that of Europeans. Beyond some minor teaching and menial positions at the lowest levels, their training and education seem directed merely to preparing the "Natives" as a source of cheap labor for the benefit of the "Europeans."
>
> Lastly, the Committee considers that as far as the "Native" and "Coloured" population of the territory are concerned, the basic ills of administration stem directly or indirectly from the rigid enforcement of the policy of apartheid based on the concept of White supremacy over all other races. Unless and until this basic policy is changed, there can be no hope for the maintenance of a peaceful and orderly administration of the Mandated territory.

Part VI

SPANISH AFRICA

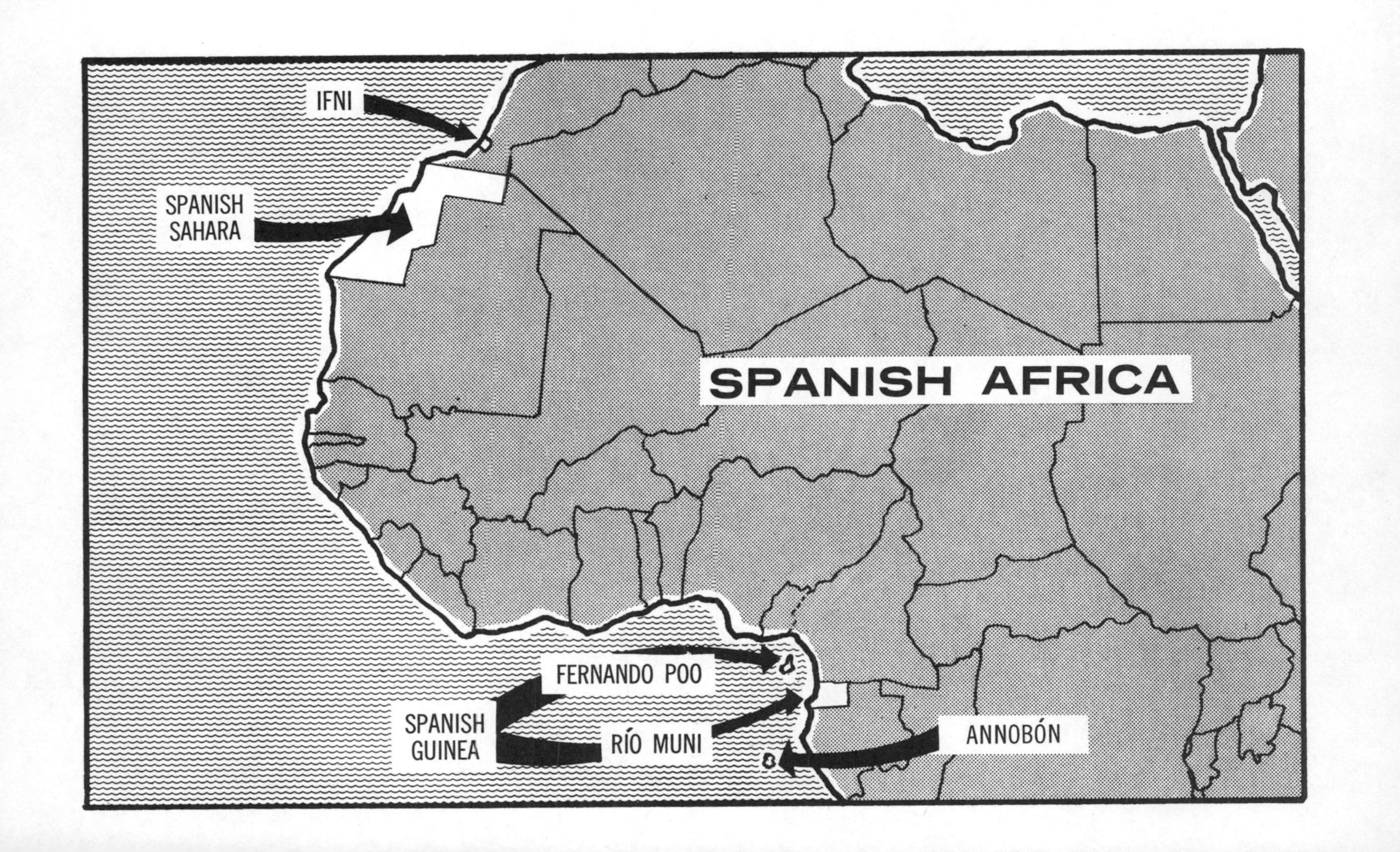
SPANISH AFRICA
IFNI
SPANISH SAHARA
FERNANDO POO
SPANISH GUINEA
RÍO MUNI
ANNOBÓN

21. Spanish Africa

Spanish Guinea
Capital: Santa Isabel de Fernando Poo
Population: 216,600 (est.)
Area: 10,852 sq. miles
Political status: Two Spanish provinces (Río Muni and Fernando Poo, jointly administered)

Spanish Sahara
Capital: El-Aaiún
Population: 20,000 (est.)
Area: 105,448 sq. miles
Political status: Spanish province

Ifni
Capital: Sidi Ifni
Population: 46,000 (est.)
Area: 741 sq. miles
Political status: Spanish province

Spanish Guinea

Spanish Guinea is one of the smallest territories in Africa, but its educational pattern is among the most complex, and its total school enrollment—10 per cent of the African population—compares very favorably with those in other parts of the continent.

The territory consists of two provinces: Río Muni, the rectangular mainland enclave, and Fernando Poo, a cacao-growing island in the Bight of Biafra. Attached to Río Muni are Corisco, Elobey Grande, and Elobey Chico, small islands located near the mouth of the Muni estuary. The isle of Annobón, slightly below the equator, is administratively assigned to Fernando Poo, which since 1778 has been the territory's social, commercial, and political center. A Governor-General administers the area under authority from the Dirección General de Plazas y Provincias Africanas in Madrid. All major legislation and appointments emanate from Spain.

Despite its small size and meager population, Spanish Guinea contains at least nine indigenous ethnic groups speaking more than fifteen languages and dialects. The most prominent are the 150,000 Pamúes (or Fang) on the mainland and the nearly 21,000 Bubis on Fernando Poo. There is also a sizable complement of immigrant African laborers, mainly Nigerians; about 4,000 Europeans of five or six nationalities; a group of 800 Moslem Hausas; and a relatively cosmopolitan, prosperous, and somewhat Anglophilic community of mixed Sierra Leonean, Kru, Gambian, and Cuban descent—the Fernandinos—localized in Santa Isabel on Fernando Poo. This highly variegated demography; the area's hot, humid climate; exuberant vegetation; the current politico-religious atmosphere and financial state of the metropole; and the peculiar history of variously Dutch, Portuguese, English, French, and German hegemony over portions of the territory have combined to give education in Spanish Guinea a distinctive character.

Complete Spanish authority over the region is of relatively recent date. The first colonizing expeditions dispatched in the late eighteenth century failed, and, because of subsequent political turmoil in Spain, the area suffered neglect for long periods during the nineteenth and early twentieth centuries. Consequently, English Baptist and Primitive Methodist missionaries enjoyed practically exclusive sway over education on Fernando Poo for several decades, American Presbyterians once dominated the Corisco Bay islands and adjoining mainland, and French clerics evangelized freely at Bata on the continental coast through 1918. The long-contested borders of Río Muni were officially established only in 1900, and the region was not thoroughly explored, much less settled, until the 1920's. State schools established at Evinayong and Niefang in 1928 and 1929 were the very first outposts of public education in the continental interior.

Objectives of Spanish Educational Policies

Secular-clerical friction transplanted from the peninsula, local maladministration, irregularity of teaching funds, and lack of personnel made anarchic and ineffective what there was of Spanish pedagogy during the first 145 years of the colony's formal existence. Catholic mission schools, which were chiefly responsible for Spanish education in the colony's infancy, claimed 17,413 enrollments for the period from 1884 to 1926, an average of about 400 students per year. These schools, confined to Fernando Poo, the Gulf islands, and the mainland coast, supplied little more than rudimentary instruction, largely pietistic and linguistic in character, to small, already Westernized segments of the African population. Not until the 1923 Primo de Rivera regime was education in Guinea revitalized, purged of foreign elements, and extended into the more populous and still "uncivilized" hinterland.

Only one British Protestant missionary and two American fraternal workers remain in the territory today. France and Germany no longer plan, as they once did, to divide the colony between themselves; and Spanish occupation of the mainland is at last complete. But official anxiety is nevertheless fixed upon consolidating and ensuring Spanish suzerainty over the whole area, an obsession reflected educationally in emphasis upon Spanish-language instruction and the inculcation of Hispanic culture. Special concern derives from the proximity of two newly independent African nations to Río Muni and the current international trend of anticolonialism, including the direct attacks upon continuing Spanish-Portuguese dominion in Africa.

The Spanish are making a more determined effort than ever to fortify culturally their holdings on the Bight of Biafra, to erase lingering vestiges of non-Hispanic influence such as Fa d'Ambu, an Afro-Portuguese dialect spoken on Annobón, and pidgin English, which is widely diffused on Fernando Poo and along the continental littoral; in sum, to transform the heterogeneous African populace into a unified body of black Spaniards firmly loyal to Generalissimo Franco, impregnable to schismatic notions of *negritude* or autonomy, and harboring no affection toward other powers.

Simply put, the fundamental aims of Spanish education in Guinea are:

(1) To replace all other tongues with Castilian, thus effecting a linguistic unity amid what has been considerable diversity. Vernacular idioms are accordingly employed as a pedagogic necessity only until fluency in Spanish is achieved. No newspapers, magazines, or books are any longer issued in African languages.

(2) To implant religious, moral, and patriotic values consistent with metropolitan orthodoxy. This objective, partially enunciated as early as 1907 in the statutory enjoinder to "etch in their hearts the holy fear of God," results in an educational program infused with Catholic theological precepts and Falangist political doctrine, the latter a compound of authoritarian and syndicalist principles with a generous admixture of mystic nationalism. Even school names manifest a definite political and religious orientation: for instance, José Antonio (founder of the Falange), Calvo Sotelo (Rightist Deputy assassinated in 1936), General Mola (Nationalist war hero), and Cardenal Cisneros (sixteenth-century prelate responsible for Spanish expansion into North Africa).

(3) To equip the average African with technical and agricultural

skills that will make him a more productive component of the Guinea economy. For reasons of climate and prestige, Europeans do not perform much manual labor. Exploitation of the territory's potentially valuable land, forest, and mineral resources thus depends wholly on African manpower.

For only a small minority of Africans is advanced training and full assimilation anticipated. This handpicked elite is intended to perform a variety of sub-administrative and quasi-professional tasks. Its members are mainly dependent on the state for their preparation, job placement, tenure, and privileges. There is a real apprehension among Spanish policy-makers that unlimited access to higher education, widespread instruction in liberal arts, and undue exposure to "abstract theories" would make ordinary labor less attractive to the African and might produce an unmanageable class of discontents and frustrated intellectuals susceptible to heretical or divisive ideas.

The School System

Although the educational system is grossly bifurcated into official and private spheres, substantive differences are not pronounced, since all instruction must conform to the same legal requirements.

Official or public education for Africans is cast into six segments. The first is "elementary" training conducted exclusively by African teaching auxiliaries in 106 schools. These schools, attended by children from six to twelve years of age, concentrate on language, religion, arithmetic, physical hygiene, "patriotism," and manual or domestic arts. Since only a fraction of Africans proceed beyond this level, it is here that a major effort is made to divest them of "pagan" beliefs and "immoral" habits, by placing particular emphasis on such Christian dicta as monogamous marriage, the virtue of labor, and modesty in dress. In 1960, the reported elementary enrollment was 18,185. This phase of education is compulsory and free, but many mainland zones still lack school facilities, and teacher shortages have sometimes compelled half-day sessions (three hours for boys, two for girls). Moreover, the prescribed school year, extending from February 16 to December 15, is actually shortened on the mainland because heavy rains during February and March prohibit attendance. Some children must travel 6 miles or more to school across difficult terrain.

The second, or "primary," phase, for youths twelve to fourteen years old, is conducted in thirteen centers operated either by European instructors or Africans who possess a teaching certificate from a Spanish normal school. The curriculum combines practical instruction with "cultural and moral formation," including units on Spanish geography and history. In 1958, there were nineteen European and two African instructors at this level; 1960 enrollment was 932.

Santo Tomas de Aquino, established at Santa Isabel in 1941, represents the third step in African education. This high school offers a two- to four-year course of study for selected students of fifteen years of age who have successfully completed both elementary and primary schooling. Its object is to prepare African auxiliaries for various administrative agencies and to produce qualified assistants for local commercial enterprises. There are three curricula: a four-year course for teachers, a three-year course for technical-administrative personnel, and a two-year course of mercantile training. Distribution of students among the three curricular sections is based upon expected personnel needs. Sectional quotas are assigned by the Governor-General in consultation with the Director of Education and other department chiefs. All entering students, however, undergo an initial four-term cycle of general instruction in mathematics, music, religion, physical education, geography, history, and language. Introductory courses are taught by European instructors attached to the Education Service; subsequent specialized training is administered by European technicians from various official agencies. The total faculty numbers nearly twenty. Student costs, including tuition, clothing, and meals, are borne by the state; the entire student body is housed in an adjoining dormitory during the ten-month school year. In the period 1946–53, 129 Africans received diplomas. Average enrollment is 100; approximately 27 per cent of the students are girls.

The fourth segment of African instruction is an alternate program of vocational secondary education. Carpentry, mechanics, shoemaking, tailoring, and other polytechnic courses are offered to elementary-school graduates at the Centro Laboral La Salle in Bata and an Escuela de Artes y Oficius in Santa Isabel. There are also two specialized schools of agriculture and puericulture. The former, attended by twenty Africans in 1960, is managed by an agronomic engineer. The latter, created in 1945, trains Africans for duty in infant-hygiene dispensaries; operated by the Sanitary Service, it is the only state school not under the authority of the Directorate of Education.

European children receive both primary and secondary education at government schools in Santa Isabel and Bata, the first created in 1929, the second in 1943. These centers, staffed wholly by European teachers, recorded a 1958 enrollment of nearly 200 pupils. Unlike most African schools, classes are not segregated by sex. Curricular matter is identical to what is taught in Spain for the same age level.

The fifth phase for Africans, adult education, is designed "to contribute to the expansion of [Hispanic] language and customs among adults who have not undergone elementary education." Six-month classes are conducted once a year by European instructors and African auxiliaries in seventeen towns. The program, servicing some 300 Africans, includes women's homemaking courses at Santa Isabel, Bata, and San Carlos (on Fernando Poo). Specialist training at civilian institutes in the Canary Islands or on the peninsula is another recent innovation in adult education.

The sixth and highest stage, inaugurated in 1942, is centered in the Patronato de Enseñanza Media Cardenal Cisneros, a general secondary school in Santa Isabel. Here only, at the pinnacle of the education system, are classes racially integrated. The men's and women's sections of the school are allied, respectively, with the Ramiro de Maeztu and Isabel la Católica institutes in Spain. The 1957–58 faculty consisted of twelve European instructors, including three licentiates and two priests; from 1949 to 1958, there was a total of seventy-seven graduates. The school, offering first- and second-degree baccalaureates (*bachilleratos*) in science and in philosophy and letters, as well as lesser certificates, is part of a new building complex that embraces the Public Library, Government Archives, and Museum.

Mission Schools

Private education in Spanish Guinea is wholly parochial. Eighty-seven instructors maintain twenty-one primary schools throughout the territory; 1960 enrollment was reported as 2,019. There is a college-level seminary, El Pilar, at Banapá on Fernando Poo, with a usual enrollment of thirty. Courses are offered in philosophy and theology by members of the Missionary Sons of the Immaculate Heart of Mary, an order that has dominated Catholic pedagogy in Guinea since 1855. A Catholic sisterhood operates a novitiate for oblates at Basilé on Fernando Poo. Another, Hermanas de Jesús-María, through a program known as Sigsa, provides hygienic and homemaking instruction to African girls about to be married canonically. All Catholic parochial schools, except for 100 catechetical stations, are state-supported, receiving about 6.5 per cent of the public expenditure on education.

Four African ministers and fifty catechists service the estimated 5,000 Presbyterians in Río Muni, but there are no formal Presbyterian schools. Neither are there separate scholastic centers for Moslem children. The only recognized non-Spanish, non-Catholic institution is the British Chaplaincy School operated since 1945 by a Protestant minister in Santa Isabel and subsidized by the Nigerian Government. The student body consists almost entirely of Nigerian children, the sons and daughters of migrant workers. At least five hours per week of Spanish-language instruction are required, and the school is subject to inspection by Spanish authorities.

Role of the Directorate of Education

The Directorate of Education, with headquarters in Santa Isabel, supervises all educational activity and circulates a monthly information bulletin among teachers. The agency is headed by a director-inspector, who is assisted by a sub-inspector. Both are invariably Europeans. Standardized terminal examinations at the elementary and primary levels are administered by the Directorate every year in late December. The state provides textbooks whose use is mandatory in all Guinea schools. According to the Education Code, texts must exhibit "purity and Hispanism in concepts and ideas, as well as simple, adapted language."

Sports, especially interscholastic soccer and basketball competitions, are encouraged at every level, public and private, as a means to promote social fusion and physical development. In 1947, the first Colonial Olympiad, a territory-wide athletic contest in which 100 Europeans and 70 Africans participated, was held.

The free public library serves as an adjunct to the educational system. It maintains nearly 8,000 volumes at the central building in Santa Isabel, operates a 2,500-volume branch at Bata, and conducts an extension service by mail and book cart. Average yearly circulation has exceeded 14,000, but the readership has been overwhelmingly European. While official statistics do not indicate either the extent or degree of African literacy, it may be assumed from the low percentage of Africans educated beyond the elementary level, the small editions of local Spanish-language periodicals, the complete absence of vernacular publishing, and the comparatively few African users of the public library that active literacy is not widespread.

Higher Education

There are two extraterritorial sources of education. One is Dager Seminary in Cameroon, where from two to five Guinea Africans pursue five-year courses leading to ordination as Presbyterian ministers. The second and far more important external source is Spain itself. As many as ten Africans a year have received state scholarships to study in Spanish colleges or normal schools. In 1961, thirty-five

Guineans entered Spanish military academies. The scions of wealthy Fernandino families traditionally attend a metropolitan university at private expense. Wilwardo Jones Niger, Fernandino Mayor of Santa Isabel and member of the Spanish Cortes, studied at Bilbao; his seven children are currently enrolled in peninsular schools. Recent formation of an Association of Guinea Students at the University of Barcelona and the establishment of a residence hall for Guineans attending the university in Madrid attest to the appreciable influx of African scholars on the peninsula.

Aside from the handful of Dager seminarians, one Presbyterian pastor who received a degree from Lincoln Seminary in the United States, and an occasional priest sent to Italy or the Canary Islands for further training, no Africans are known to have been permitted to study outside either Spain or Guinea. How many university-educated Africans ultimately return to Guinea is not known precisely, but there is evidence that a number remain indefinitely in Spain.

What Kind of an Educated Elite?

The Spanish claim is that Guinea's school network is proportionately the best developed in West Central Africa. Over two-thirds of the school-age population on Fernando Poo and nearly one-half in Río Muni receive at least six years of fundamental training; in 1948, the combined public and parochial school enrollment was 60 per cent greater than ten years earlier; the 1960 total of 119 public schools represents a monumental increase over the 1 school that operated erratically from 1875 to 1902 and a 100 per cent rise over the 59 existing as late as 1934. Moreover, these figures do not include public technical-education facilities or any private schools. These are spectacular quantitative achievements, given Spain's economic malaise and the short time devoted to serious expansion of Guinea education. Moreover, creation of the Escuela de Estudios Superiores and admission of Africans to the general secondary level have greatly liberalized the school structure and constitute at least partial abandonment of Negro inferiority as an underlying assumption of pedagogic policy. Heriberto Ramón Alvarez García, a recent and highly articulate Director of Education, has vigorously maintained that Africans are educable beyond merely mechanistic and imitative planes. But a contrary opinion—that the African is mentally deficient, infantile, and incapable of intellectual achievement—has been no less insistently expounded by such eminent personalities as A. Yglesias de la Riva, formerly Judge of the Bata district; Dr. Vicente Beato Gonzalez and

Dr. Ramón Villarino Ulloa, who conducted intelligence tests among Guinea Africans; Ricardo Ibarrola, an anthropologist; and former Governor-General Juan María Bonelli y Rubio.

Although rapid numerical growth and a more liberal concept of the African are distinguishable trends in Guinea pedagogy, there remains a broad gap between education in the metropolitan and sub-Saharan provinces. For instance, a much larger percentage of students receive secondary training in Spain than in Guinea; the peninsular teaching corps is on the whole better educated; proportionally more girls are admitted to secondary schools on the peninsula; there is no pre-primary schooling in Guinea, although it has existed for several years in the metropole; most Guinea public schools outside the three or four largest towns are understaffed and therefore unable to offer simultaneous graded instruction. Such a metropolitan innovation as the appointment of school psychologists apparently has not been effected in Guinea. Apart from the Banapá seminary, no center for higher instruction exists in the twin African provinces, so that university education is a luxury permitted only to the rich and to the few fortunates selected for state scholarships.

Qualitatively, all indications are that the Guinea school system has done just what its planners hoped. It has produced more than a dozen priests; more than fifty nuns; a soccer star on the Atlético de Madrid; a novelist who eulogizes his Spanish mentors in Castilian; numerous auxiliaries in education, public works, customs, and sanitary services; three African deputies in the Spanish Cortes; an abundance of photographers, clerks, domestic servants, radiotelegraphers, police, and craftsmen; a growing corps of farmers, plantation workers, and lumbermen; an African bullfighter; and a Doctor of Law at the University of Madrid who in 1960 co-founded the Friends of Black Africa, a Catholic lay group. But—if Spanish sources can be entirely trusted in this sensitive area—it has not spawned a single political agitator, nationalist, Communist, disaffected intellectual, or similar malcontent. It might also be added that the system has produced no African leadership in the uppermost ranks of government and commerce (the Cortes posts and Santa Isabel mayoralty are largely honorific), no group of independent African professionals (the 1950 census lists only three African professionals outside government service), no vernacular literature, and no genuine mass literacy. Nor has it allowed the African populace an alternative to wholesale obliteration of their traditional culture and impending estrangement from the rest of the continent.

Spanish Sahara

The educational system in Spain's two desert provinces is radically different from that in Guinea. Since they are sparsely populated by virile, seminomadic peoples of Islamic culture, there is little possibility for the kind of wholesale Hispanization undertaken among Guinea's larger, ethnically fragmented, and far less mobile population.

In the Spanish Sahara, with a population of about 20,000 (although some estimates go as high as 60,000), there are only eight primary schools, staffed by ten teachers. Localized in the two urban centers of El Aaiún and Villa Cisneros, the schools reported a total 1958 matriculation of only 357 students, more than half of whom were Europeans. In addition, some 100 men registered for adult-education classes, at which average daily attendance was only about 35.

Since Europeans constitute a small fraction of the whole populace, it is evident that they receive a hugely disproportionate share of public education. The negligible role of native Saharans in the school program is underscored by the fact that there is only one Saharan-born instructor within the teaching corps; out of 800 library patrons recorded for 1958, fewer than 50 were persons indigenous to the province.

It seems just to conclude that education in the Spanish Sahara is addressed almost entirely to the minority European contingent and that the impact of Hispanic pedagogy upon the Africans of the Sahara has been extremely slight.

Ifni

Because of its unique geographical character as a tiny enclave of 46,000 persons, including nearly 5,000 Europeans, Ifni possesses a more highly diversified educational program than its sister province and educates a greater percentage of the indigenous youth. Nevertheless, there is still a marked disproportion between European and Ifneño enrollment. Moreover, school facilities among the 36,000 rural Berbers are notably inferior to those in Sidi Ifni, the port-capital.

Ifni's pedagogic structure is tridimensional: primary, secondary, and adult. Two racially integrated primary schools, one for boys and the other for girls, operate in Sidi Ifni; rural elementary schools are located at Tiugsa, Tiliuin, and Telata. Only the urban schools offer graded instruction. Statistics for early 1961 show 22 primary-school teachers and 1,561 students.

Secondary education, as in Spanish Guinea, may be either academic or vocational. Academic education is provided by the Centro de Enseñanza Media General Díaz de Villegas, a handsome edifice in Sidi Ifni with nine instructors and a 1961 student body of 227. Since the school is affiliated with the Instituto Nacional de Enseñanza Media at Las Palmas in the Canary Islands, Centro students are annually examined by visiting professors from both the Las Palmas institute and the University of La Laguna.

Manual-arts training is given at the Escuela de Artes y Oficios, founded in 1955, where there are 13 teachers and 123 pupils.

A breakdown of secondary enrollment into nationalities reveals that academic or pre-collegiate instruction is received almost exclusively by Europeans, while Europeans and Ifneños secure polytechnic training at a ratio of about three to two. Clearly, very few Ifneños obtain any secondary-school education, and no more than a handful would qualify for university work.

Approximately 120 males attend adult-education courses. The Islamic influence in both Ifni and the Spanish Sahara evidently discourages female participation, whereas in Guinea men and women alike have engaged in adult studies.

A unique feature of Ifnian pedagogy is the employment of seven Koranic scholars to instruct youths in Arabic and the Islamic faith. This is accomplished at special class sessions during which European and indigenous children are separated. Otherwise, both groups are subjected to the same curriculum.

Free lunches are furnished to all students, needy pupils receive winter clothing, and candidates unable to afford residence costs sometimes obtain state grants. The emphasis for local youths, however, is upon vocational training "in order to liberate the working class from perpetual privation, which robs it of any will to improve itself and denies the province those technicians necessary to the development of its various activities." A new polytechnic school will soon be built to accentuate this goal.

As in the neighboring Spanish Sahara, there is little evidence of Hispanization among Ifni's indigenous community. European library users outnumber Africans by three to one, and there are 220 Islamic mosques but only 4 Catholic chapels.

At a recent academic convocation in Ifni, Secretary-General José Yanguas Miravete declared:

> This fraternity between Christians and Moslems, civilians and soldiers, religious and lay persons, offers to a world rent by racial discrimination and politico-religious persecution a vivid example of what can be achieved by a country that loves peace and seeks it by means of liberty and respect for human rights.

While somewhat overstated, this tolerant formula is surely required for Spanish survival amid a tradition-conscious, well-knit people who have strong ties with nearby nations and would resist any attempt to recast their way of life into an alien mold. Hence the provision of non-Catholic religious training in public schools, classes in a tongue other than Castilian, and a reluctance to compel school attendance in rural districts.

—Sanford Berman

Part VII

ENGLISH-SPEAKING WEST AFRICA

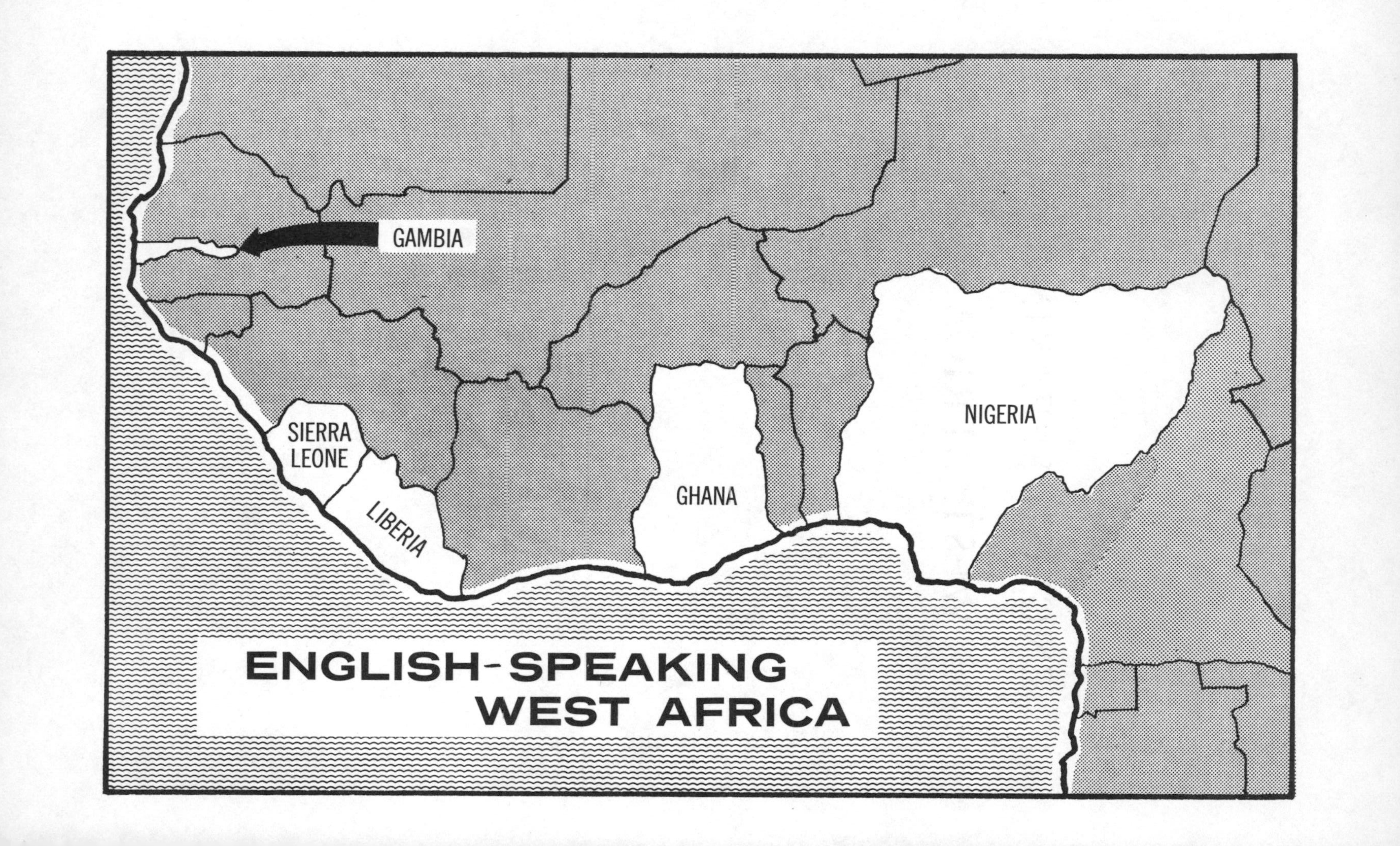
GAMBIA
SIERRA LEONE
LIBERIA
GHANA
NIGERIA
ENGLISH-SPEAKING WEST AFRICA

22. Gambia

Capital: Bathurst
Population: 279,600 (est.)
Area: 4,011 sq. miles
Political status: British colony and protectorate

GAMBIA, Britain's only remaining colonial possession in West Africa, is a long finger of land bordered on its three landward sides by Senegal. It consists of a Colony at the mouth of the Gambia River on the Atlantic coast, which has been under British authority since 1783, and a narrow Protectorate strip extending 300 miles upstream along either side of the Gambia River. The great majority of the population resides in the Protectorate and is composed of Moslem peasant farmers of the Mandingo, Wolof, Jola, Serahuli, and Fula tribes. Their livelihood depends upon peanuts, the one cash crop of Gambia. Indeed, the peanut harvest and its price on the world market are the controlling factors of Gambian economics, politics, and development.

The achievement of independence by neighboring Senegal and other West African territories has awakened Gambia from its long political quiescence, and major constitutional changes introduced by the Governor in 1960 reflect the new political interests of the populace. The franchise, which formerly was limited to the adult population of the Colony, was extended to the adult population of the Protectorate as well; the legislature was enlarged to thirty-four, including seven members from the Colony and twelve members from the Protectorate directly elected by the people. Under an agreement reached at a constitutional conference in London in July, 1961, Gambia will have internal self-government in 1962 and full independence in 1963. Although Gambia is a logical candidate for federation with Senegal, an interministerial conference on future Gambian-Senegal relations held in Dakar in June, 1961, decided against early steps toward union of the two countries. However, representatives of the two governments favored coordination of transport facilities, telecommunications, and economic planning.

Early History of Education

The popular demand for increased educational facilities has been incorporated into the platforms of all contending Gambian political parties. Although government expenditure on education has increased steadily in recent years—from 5.2 per cent of the total budget in 1947 to 9.1 per cent in 1958—the country's total revenue is less than £2 million, and development has inevitably fallen short of expectations.

For over 120 years after Gambia first came in contact with Europe, all schools in the Colony and Protectorate were established and operated by the Methodist, Roman Catholic, or Anglican missions. While the government often aided these schools financially, it did not assume direct responsibility for Gambian education until after World War II. The Wesleyan Methodist Mission opened a primary school in Bathurst, the chief town of the Colony, in 1821. Twenty years later, there were three Methodist primary schools operating with a total enrollment of 268 children. By 1860, Roman Catholic and Anglican missions had also opened their own schools. With the increase in the number of schools in the Colony and the establishment of small mission schools in the Protectorate after the turn of the century, the government finally created an independent Education Department in 1930 to supervise over-all educational policy and systematize the granting of aid, but the first full-time education officer was not appointed until 1937. The first Board of Education (established by ordinance in 1937) consisted of a representative from each of the mission societies and three other members—including one woman and one African.

The Education Ordinance of 1947 decisively put the major responsibility for education into the government's hands for the first time. The Board of Education was enlarged to include a member of the Legislative Council, three Gambians representing the Moslem community and the Protectorate, a representative of the Gambia Teachers' Association, and two women to represent female education. An officer from the medical service, the senior agricultural officer, the senior commissioner, and the senior education officer were ex-officio members. The government, backstopped by this new Board of Education, took over direct control of the finances and operation of the primary mission schools. The ordinance stipulated that the government should eventually assume full responsibility for secondary schools as well, although it assured the continuation of the religious observances practiced in the individual Protestant, Catholic, and Moslem schools.

The total number of children in school in Gambia when these changes took place in 1947 was 2,788. There were five primary schools, three "infants' schools," and four mission secondary schools in the Colony; the Protectorate had nine small village primary schools, four of them run by missions, and the Armitage boarding school—then a primary school for the sons and relatives of chiefs—with an enrollment of 136 boys. As a consequence of this unequal distribution of facilities, 60 per cent of the school-age children in the Colony were enrolled in school, as compared with perhaps 0.5 per cent of the school-age children in the Protectorate. The population of the Colony is some 29,000, while the Protectorate has almost ten times that number.

That the capital city of Bathurst and the rest of the Colony have always had educational facilities greatly superior to those in the Protectorate is due in large part to historical and geographical factors. Trade with the British, Portuguese, and French had been carried on in Gambia since the days of Queen Elizabeth I, and the Africans of the river estuary were logically the first to be influenced by white men's ways and the first to be subject to British authority. The Island of St. Mary, on which Bathurst is situated at the mouth of the Gambia River, and some coastal land on the southern bank were the sites of the first permanent British merchant settlements in 1816 and comprised the original Colony. The various inland districts along the river banks were only gradually brought under British administration by agreements and treaties with the different chiefs, and it was not until 1902 that the Protectorate territory was finally defined and placed under a regularized jurisdiction. Bathurst and the Colony, then, have had the advantage of a head start in education of almost 100 years.

Educational Facilities in the Colony

By 1957, after ten years of direct government control of the educational system, there were four infants' schools and eleven primary schools in the Colony, with a total enrollment of 4,585. The children enter the infants' schools at the age of five and, after three years, progress to the primary schools for a four-year course. For the 70 per cent of the Colony primary pupils who are not accepted into one of the four mission secondary schools, there is a senior primary course of three additional years. The government also maintains a Domestic Science Center for senior primary girls and an Arts and Crafts Center for senior primary boys. All instruction in Bathurst is in the English language.

The Methodist and Roman Catholic missions each maintain a boys' and a girls' secondary school in Bathurst. These follow courses leading to the West African School Certificate; their total enrollment in 1957 was 747 pupils; in December, 1957, 38 pupils took the West African School Certificate examination. The secondary schools send their science students to an independent School of Science in Bathurst, where, at present, only biology is taught to school-certificate level. The Science Center also offers courses to the junior staff of the Medical Department. The salaries of the secondary-school staffs are now reimbursed to the missions by the government, and about twenty government scholarships are awarded each year at the secondary level to particularly able pupils.

In 1958, the government opened a modern secondary school for 480 pupils at Bathurst. The curriculum is of a more practical and vocational bent than the mission secondary schools, and is designed to further the education of the children from the senior grades of the primary schools who do not gain admission to the more academic mission schools. A new nondenominational, coeducational high school designed to accommodate more than 400 pupils is under construction in Bathurst. Nearly 300 pupils are already enrolled and are following courses in temporary buildings.

The government also maintains a technical school in Bathurst that offers courses in carpentry, masonry, motor fitting, and electrical trades to a maximum enrollment of thirty pupils for a period of five years; a government clerical school trains forty students a year in shorthand, typing, English, arithmetic, and bookkeeping. About forty trainees are enrolled in apprenticeship schemes for training mechanics and marine workers over a five-year period at the Marine Department and at the Public Works Department.

Despite the increasing advantages offered to pupils in Bathurst and the Colony, educational facilities remain inadequate to keep pace with the growing public demand. Three new schools have been built by the government in the last ten years, but there is a continuing problem of shortage of buildings and an acute shortage of trained staff. In 1960, for example, the new motor-fitting workshop of the technical school was closed for lack of a qualified instructor, and the clerical school was also closed for the same reason. Many classes are meeting in afternoon sessions, and teachers cannot be trained fast enough locally to meet the steadily increasing Bathurst enrollment, which now exceeds 400 a year. The number of pupils enrolled at both the primary and secondary levels is double that of 1951.

The Situation in the Protectorate

The low enrollment figures for the Protectorate reflect in part the basic conservatism of this predominantly rural and Moslem area. The chiefs' distrust of infidel institutions of learning and city temptations has also kept many able boys from Bathurst. The official statistics do not take account of the large numbers of boys in the Protectorate who attend Koranic schools outside the accredited system.

Administratively, the Protectorate is comprised of four main divisions along the Gambia River; these are subdivided into thirty-five districts, each of which is governed by a Native Authority under a chief. The average population of a chief's district is about 8,000 persons, and the chief is responsible for local taxation, the expansion of agriculture, rural development, and the management of the district school. Matters concerning the Protectorate as a whole are considered at an annual chiefs' conference.

In the Protectorate, the present policy is for the district authorities to bear the costs of building and maintaining the village schools, while the salaries of qualified teachers are paid by the government. When the government assumed control of primary education in Gambia in 1947, there were five village schools run by Native Authorities; today there are thirty village schools in the Protectorate, of which twenty-two are owned by the districts. The Roman Catholic mission operates six village schools, the Anglican mission one, and one is operated jointly by the Methodist mission and a district authority. All these schools are primary schools, and they vary in size from 19 to 188 pupils. Several of the smaller schools teach in the vernacular, but there are no vernacular textbooks available. The total enrollment of the Protectorate village schools in 1957 was 1,444 pupils; this was probably well over double the number of children enrolled ten years before. Even so, a scant 2 per cent of school-age Protectorate children are in schools, and more than half of these are in the first two years of primary school.

The government drive to open more village schools in the Protectorate did not meet with an unqualified welcome at first. Community appreciation of a non-Moslem education varied greatly from village to village, and a number of the new schools were initially located where there was very little demand for them; in fact, one school had to close for lack of pupils.

The Protectorate attitude is beginning to change, however, and the chiefs themselves are now making increasing demands for educational improvements at their annual conferences. They are dissatisfied with the Protectorate's four-year primary schools, which do not accept pupils until they are eight years old and stop short of the preparation required for entry into a secondary school in Bathurst. The chiefs are pressing for more post-primary facilities in their own region, since the only post-primary courses available in the Protectorate are at the secondary boarding school in Armitage, which takes only eighty-two pupils. Even the Armitage school only recently dropped its primary courses to become a modern secondary school.

Education for Women

Perhaps the most significant change in educational concepts in Gambia has been the slow acceptance of education for girls. At their 1959 annual conference, the Protectorate chiefs asked specifically for more women teachers to encourage the enrollment of girls in the village schools. Although there were only about 190 girls in school in the Protectorate at this time, the chiefs also asked for the establishment of a girls' post-primary school. In the more sophisticated Colony, there are more girls in schools: Government statistics indicate that, out of a total of 4,585 children in primary school in 1957, 1,842 were girls; at the secondary level, 219 pupils out of a total Colony enrollment of 747 were girls; by 1959, there were 241 girls in secondary schools.

The interest in technical and vocational training for women is also growing—not only in the fields of teaching and nursing, but also in clerical work, nutrition, laundry work, dressmaking, and other trades. The new high school in Bathurst is coeducational, but the more conservative Protectorate is unlikely to accept so revolutionary a step for some time to come.

The Teacher Shortage

One of the greatest deterrents to plans for the expansion and improvement of education in Gambia is the acute shortage of qualified teachers. Yundum College, located in the Colony about seventeen miles from Bathurst, is the only teacher-training school in the territory. It was started in 1949 with an enrollment of thirty students. By 1957, there were fifty-seven students—both men and women—enrolled at Yundum, but ten of these were working teachers who were returning for further training. Yundum has extended its original two-year course to three years, and it also offers refresher courses to teachers during vacations. The Yundum curriculum emphasizes the teaching of English, handwriting, art, the use of textbooks, and subjects of a rural or local interest. The minimum entrance requirement is completion of Standard 7, but all applicants are also examined and interviewed. Before the establishment of Yundum, students were sent on government scholarships to teacher-training institutes in other British West African territories: to Freetown in Sierra Leone, or to Achimota or Kumasi in the former Gold Coast. Since 1954, the government has been sending a few experienced primary teachers to England for a year's further training, and some outstanding students have also been sent to England to attend the Ministry of Education's two- and three-year courses.

Statistics for 1957 indicate that there were 61 primary teachers and 6 secondary teachers in the Protectorate. In the Colony, there were 149 primary teachers and 31 secondary teachers. Enrollment of boys and girls in the teacher-training college has been fairly well balanced: In 1953, there were 14 boys and 12 girls at Yundum, and in 1957 there were 29 boys and 21 girls. At the primary level, there is an equal number of women and men teachers, but there are twice as many men teachers as women teachers at the secondary level. Despite an increasing entry of women into the teaching field, and a slow but steady increase of pupils enrolled at Yundum, the recruitment of suitable candidates remains a difficult task, and Yundum, even operating at its maximum capacity of thirty new enrollments a year, cannot turn out qualified teachers in sufficient numbers to meet the ever increasing demand. As a result, a high proportion of primary teachers are uncertified, and the quality of instruction is uneven.

Political and Economic Factors

With the extension of the franchise to the more populous Protectorate, a shift in the balance of power in nascent Gambian politics is likely. The leaders of the Protectorate are becoming increasingly and competitively aware of the political implications of the gap between the education available to their young people and that available to children in the Colony. As recently as 1954, over 76 per cent of the funds spent on education was used in the Colony.

A number of studies of the educational problems of Gambia have been made in the past decade. In the 1957 comprehensive survey of education in the British West African territories prepared by Dr. G. B. Jeffrey, Director of the Institute of Education of London University, it was noted that Gambia's major educational problems were shared by other British colonies in West Africa: a shortage of staff, a conservative and less developed hinterland, and a curriculum too much divorced from the daily life of the children. Observing that "the supply of teachers lies at the very heart of the educational problems of the West Coast," Dr. Jeffrey warned that political pressures could lead to the collapse of all educational standards.

In the same year, a report dealing specifically with Gambian education was prepared by T. Baldwin of the Colonial Office, and its recommendations have become the basis of all subsequent educational planning for the territory. The Baldwin Report called for an extension in length and scope of the teacher-training course, increased use of vernacular teaching in the Protectorate primary schools, establishment of nondenominational secondary schools, a 25 per cent increase in secondary education, the development of a curriculum more closely related to the agricultural environment of the children, the provision of a four-year primary course for all Protectorate boys and for one-third of the Protectorate girls, and a sharp increase in the proportion of educational funds spent in the Protectorate.

Funds, or rather the lack of them, remain a crucial factor in the outlook for Gambian education. The records of 1863 show that the government contributed £150 to the educational efforts of the missions in the Colony. In 1958, over £124,000 was spent by the government in support of education, and an additional £55,000 was recorded as capital expenditure on education. The estimated cost of carrying out the recommendations of the Baldwin Report is £164,000 per year in recurrent expenses, as well as an initial capital expenditure of £163,000. In addition, district authorities of the Protectorate will have to raise £180,000 for expenditures on buildings and equipment.

These are very considerable sums for a modest one-crop economy such as Gambia's, especially in view of the fact that the peanut price has been so low since 1958 that there has been some difficulty in meeting even the salaries of the new ministerial posts established by the 1960 constitution. Gambia is now basing its hopes on the development of rice as an additional export crop and the improvement of agriculture in general. This is a long-term process, and it can probably be expected that the full realization of the modest educational scheme drafted on the basis of the Baldwin Report will be a long-term process as well, unless sizable assistance comes from abroad.

—ANNE FREDERICKS

23. Ghana

Capital: Accra
Population: 6,690,730 (1960 census)
Area: 92,000 sq. miles
Political status: Independent republic

GHANA (known as the Gold Coast until it became independent in March, 1957) has a long educational tradition. European traders and missionary groups appear to have established schools in the coastal settlements even in the seventeenth century, but little is known of their work. Educational activity was begun by the Society for the Propagation of the Gospel in the eighteenth century, but its work was interrupted. Education was carried on, beginning in the first half of the nineteenth century, under the auspices of other missionary groups, most notably the English Methodists, the Basel Mission Society, and the Bremen (or North German) Mission Society. Still further activity followed the re-entry into the Gold Coast of the Roman Catholic Church (1880) and the Church of England (1906), both of which had unsuccessfully attempted to establish permanent missions earlier in the country's history.

British official interest in education was necessarily limited until Great Britain formally annexed the Gold Coast in 1874. The first education ordinance was drawn up in 1882; it provided for a greater degree of uniformity than had hitherto existed in the management of mission schools, established a system of government financial assistance, and provided for inspection of schools to ensure compliance with government standards.

The mission schools were understandably oriented toward religious education, but they did not neglect secular instruction. As Great Britain's commercial and political interests in the Gold Coast grew, education became increasingly secular in its objectives (though not in its administration). The new aim was to provide qualified Africans with a modicum of modern skills, in order to fit them for subordinate and routine tasks—for example, as clerks and bookkeepers—in the British administration and commercial establishments.

The idea of imperial trusteeship—recognition that the colonies might eventually revert to some sort of home rule—was present in British policy far earlier than in that of any other colonial power in Africa. British educational policy, nonetheless, did not seek to educate an African ruling class. There was already a ruling class in existence—the chiefs, on whom the British relied in accordance with the doctrine of indirect rule. And, all things considered, the efficacy of the chief rested on not bringing him too far, or at least too rapidly, into the modern world. However, once education was introduced into a colonial territory, the process could not be stopped or contained. Even early in the period of British rule, there were talented Africans who became truly educated and who appeared to be equally at home in both worlds—the Western one and that of their indigenous culture. In the Gold Coast, this group first emerged in the coastal settlements, in the old towns like Cape Coast and later Accra. It was a very small group and tended to be upper-class and aristocratic—that is, to have ties of kinship to the ruling chiefs. In choice of occupations, this educated group tended toward commerce and the liberal professions, especially law, since all but the lowest posts in the administration were closed to its members.

This first circle of educated Africans developed political interests and, organizing itself as the Aborigines Rights Protection Society (ARPS), successfully contested the Crown-lands issue at the turn of the century. The upper-class educated Africans whose political views were represented by the ARPS entered politics as the spokesmen of the chiefs, yet they could hardly have been unaware of the gap between them and the traditional rulers for whom they spoke. They must have known, too, that traditionalism, at least in any "pure" form, was a lost cause and that it was they and not the chiefs who were enlisted on the side of the future. There was no clear-cut split, however, and it may be that many of those involved had little or no awareness of the gap or of its consequences.

These educated Africans gradually came to harbor distinct political ambitions of their own—to supplant the chiefs in substance if not in form, to become the main reliance of the colonial administration, and perhaps eventually to win some degree of home rule within the British Empire. Their hopes received a sharp setback in the 1920's and 1930's, when the British, by reinforcing the institutions of indirect rule, reaffirmed the role of the chiefs in the administration of the Gold Coast. These developments emphasized the estrangement between the small educated African elite and the chiefs, and marked the beginning of the educated group's dissatisfaction with the colonial regime. In time, this was to have important political consequences.

Nationalism and Education

Some time in the 1920's, another and more important transformation was beginning in Gold Coast society. A non–upper-class educated and semieducated group began to take form; it was composed mostly of young men with primary- and sometimes middle-school education who had gotten far enough into the modern world to have a sense of their inadequate preparation for it and of the opportunities that were beyond their grasp. These were the young men who became schoolteachers and clerks; drifted into the cities and formed tribal unions for mutual support and to spur progress back home; or stayed, often unwillingly, in the villages, forming debating societies and "improvement unions" and in general making their chiefs and elders unhappy. They felt alienated from the traditional order, which they regarded as backward and as circumscribing the role of the educated. It was this new group, with its new vexations and attitudes, which first began to think of a future for their country radically different from its past. As the ideas of the modern world filtered into the Gold Coast, they were put together in new combinations and sequences that pointed to far more than a mere expulsion of the colonial rulers. The mystique of African nationalism began to take shape, and it became increasingly concerned with a total reconstruction of African society.

The young were by no means the only major group or interest represented in the nationalist movement that developed after World War II, but they were one of its mainstays from the beginning. In the early phases of postwar political activity, the younger elements still accepted the leadership of the old upper-class political elite. It was the older generation of leaders that organized the United Gold Coast Convention (UGCC), the first political party claiming to speak for the entire country, and brought Kwame Nkrumah back from London to the Gold Coast in 1947 as secretary and political organizer of the UGCC. Once Nkrumah was back, however, it did not take him long to discover that the old-line leaders of the UGCC were too conservative for him and for the situation then existing in the Gold

Coast. By addressing himself to the young, he built up a personal following, shattered the UGCC from within, and established his own Convention People's Party (CPP), which almost immediately monopolized the nationalist movement.

The Role of the CPP

The founding of the CPP marked the end of the old tribally oriented elite as a major force in Ghana's politics. The leaders of the old elite continued to operate for a while through the UGCC, and later joined forces with the traditionalists in the Ashanti-led National Liberation Movement (NLM), which organized a bloc of regional parties opposed to the CPP. When the CPP government, after independence, made it unlawful for a party to bear either a regional or a religious name, the NLM and its allies coalesced into the United Party (UP), which continues to be the only opposition party in the Ghana Parliament. None of these opposition movements has proved really successful, however, and, for all practical purposes, the old elite has been eliminated as an effective force in Ghana's politics.

The split between the CPP and the old educated elite is paralleled by another (and, at least for the present, less serious) rift between the CPP and the modern technical and administrative elite. While the latter group perhaps overlaps to some extent the old elite, it is by and large a distinct group, more or less parallel with the higher levels of the civil service, which in Ghana is proportionally far more important and extensive than in most Western countries. The rift is essentially that between the technician and the leader, between the bureaucrat (used here in a neutral sense) and the politician. It is a phenomenon that is by no means confined to Ghana, and it is not so much a clash over objectives as over approach and methods. In Ghana and elsewhere, the technician and administrator tend to think in terms of what is feasible, the politician in terms of what is necessary. Ideally, the union of these opposing attitudes is likely to produce the best results, but the opportunities for friction in the process are innumerable. In Ghana, where the governing Convention People's Party is closely interlocked with the state apparatus at all levels, these points of friction are particularly numerous. While it would be misleading to exaggerate their effect, they are nonetheless likely to exist for a long time to come and to confirm the country's political leaders in their suspicion of a professional educated class that is not closely linked with the party.

Thus, the accusation that the CPP is "anti-intellectual" is not really accurate. It is antipathetic only to an *independent* educated class, which it tends to regard (1) as a privileged order incompatible with an egalitarian society (an emotional reaction from the colonial period), and (2) as an anomaly or worse in a state in which the party views itself as a comprehensive national movement enveloping all phases of the national life and commanding the loyalty of all groups.

Certainly there is no question of the party's—and the people's—enthusiasm for education. Indeed, Ghanaian nationalism was in part a revolt for education, and the impressive progress that has been made in this field testifies both to the genuineness of the popular demand and to the government's determination to meet it. The credit for progress in educational development should properly be shared by the present government and its colonial predecessor. Under British rule, a ten-year plan for educational development was introduced in 1946. Beginning in 1951, at the start of the transition to independence, African political leaders shared power and responsibility and made substantial contributions to the formulation of the Accelerated Development Plan for education. Between 1951 and 1959, Ghana spent over £17 million on education—almost 15 per cent of its total development expenditure during this period and second only to its expenditure on communications. Between 1950 and 1959, enrollment in all educational institutions increased from 281,000 to 663,000; attendance in primary, middle, and secondary schools was considerably more than doubled; enrollment in trade and technical schools increased almost fivefold, and in teacher-training colleges considerably more than twofold. Ghana has acquired three institutions of higher learning since 1948—the University of Ghana (at Legon, near Accra), the Kwame Nkrumah University of Science and Technology at Kumasi, and the University College of Cape Coast. At the other end of the spectrum, mass-education campaigns have brought literacy to thousands of adults outside the scope of the regular school system.

The Second Development Plan (1959–64)

Under the Second Development Plan (1959–64), projected capital investment in education will be £27.8 million—11.4 per cent of the anticipated total expenditure under the plan and second only to the outlays for communications and health and water. During the first phase of the plan, £14 million will be spent on education; as a correspondent for the London weekly *West Africa* has pointed out, this represents 1 per cent of Ghana's gross national product. (By way of comparison, the annual capital investment in education in Great Britain is 0.05 per cent of the GNP.)

Despite the need to show progress on all fronts, the government has been able to allocate its resources in such a way as to ensure an integrated development of the school system. Primary and middle schools were emphasized under the earlier educational plans, and enough progress has been made to warrant an emphasis on secondary education under the current plan.

Beginning in the fall of 1961, primary education (which was already free) was made compulsory, and middle-school education was made both free and compulsory. The achievement of universal education at these levels is not to be expected immediately. The supply of teachers is one major obstacle. Another is the difficulty that many local authorities will have in meeting their own heavy financial responsibilities under the new arrangements. Indicative of this latter problem is the need for more than 1,000 new schools during the 1961–62 school year and the introduction of the two-shift system in some areas where the local authorities have not yet been able to provide enough classrooms. The gap that must be bridged is an impressive one. A total of 638,151 pupils were enrolled in primary and middle schools in 1959, but it has been estimated that there are as many as 2 million school-age children.

The goals for secondary education are statistically more modest, but the problems that must be overcome are more difficult. The objective is to raise secondary-school intake to 10 per cent of the potentially eligible candidates, compared with the present 4 to 6 per cent. This goal does not adequately convey the extent of the emphasis on secondary education, since a considerable effort is simultaneously being made to develop the Sixth Form in the secondary schools in order to provide adequately prepared students for the universities in Ghana and overseas. The bottleneck in secondary-school development is teaching staff, for which no adequate supply of university graduates is yet in sight.

Major Problems

For the foreseeable future, Ghana must also cope with a number of special problems of school coverage that are not altogether amenable to solution by planned capital investment. On a geographic basis, the northern part of the country continues to lag in educational development. In spite of continuing special attention to northern needs, the popular responsiveness to education in this area is still unsatisfactory. In addition, irrespective of region and at all levels of the school system throughout Ghana, there is a heavy attrition, or wastage, of pupils from class to class. Finally, school enrollment of women is considerably below their proportion in the school-age population. Female pupils accounted for 32 per cent of the total enrollment in all educational institutions in 1959; in primary schools, they accounted for 34 per cent of the enrollment; in middle schools, for 27 per cent; and in secondary schools, for 18 per cent.

Quality is much more difficult to measure and to plan than investment and intake, and it is difficult to frame clear-cut judgments that will apply to broad sectors of Ghana's educational system. In undertaking forced draft development of a nationwide school system, it is only rarely that quantity and quality can be simultaneously improved. At some point, one has to take precedence over the other. In Ghana, for example, the government has deliberately chosen to expand primary education through the wholesale recruitment of pupil-teachers with only a middle-school education. No other choice seems to have been practical under the circumstances. A beginning has to be made somewhere, and the alternative would be to delay the development of the system until enough teachers could be trained—10,000 in the case of the Accelerated Development Plan begun in 1951, and perhaps 20,000 under the present compulsory-education scheme.

The decision to expand at the expense of immediate quality has not by any means meant an abandonment of standards, and one of the most interesting and promising developments has been the emphasis that is being placed on quality through the improvement of teacher training. There are, in addition, a number of built-in checks in the educational system that serve to promote standards at all levels: the use of entrance examinations for middle and secondary schools, the work of the West African Examinations Council in providing an independent examination for middle- and secondary-school leavers, and the high qualifications required for admission to the University of Ghana. Over the next several years, the focus of the effort to achieve quality is likely to be in the middle schools, in view of their responsibility to prepare pupils for the secondary schools, and in the secondary schools themselves, which must prepare students for the universities. In both cases, progress will depend to a considerable extent on the availability of qualified teaching staff. Finally, the decision to introduce free and compulsory primary- and middle-school education in 1961 creates an eventual need for as many as 20,000 additional teachers at these levels. Here again, one of the basic problems of educational policy is to ensure that, insofar as possible, educational standards remain intact despite expansion.

The School System: How It Operates

The central government is responsible for education, its control originally having been established by ordinance during the colonial period. The Ministry of Education (a portfolio combined from time to time with other ministries) is the main government agency in the educational field. It determines educational policy, sets and enforces curricular and teaching standards, and administers grants to approved schools. The Ministry's executive agents in the field are the regional and district education officers, who supervise the schools in the administrative regions and districts into which the country is divided.

There are strong decentralizing trends simultaneously at work in the day-to-day operations of the school system. Practically all schools are managed by local authorities (local or urban councils), missionary groups, or private organizations or individuals. Out of a total of 5,246 educational institutions at all levels in 1959, only 14 were directly managed by the government, most of them teacher-training colleges or technical schools. All government primary and middle schools were transferred to local authorities in 1956, and the government's policy has been to place increasing responsibility on them for educational development. Capital expenditure on primary and middle schools, for example, is now a local matter, except in the northern region. Many local authorities, however, face serious financial problems in the educational field.

Schools other than those run directly by the central government are divided into two categories: approved schools, which receive financial aid from central or local government; and private schools, which receive no aid. According to 1959 statistics, there were 4,608 approved schools and 621 private schools.

The missions continue to play a major role in education, and many of the local-authority primary and middle schools are run under contract by missionary organizations. Approved mission schools are subject to government requirements and inspection, and they share in government financial aid. Of the 4,546 approved primary and middle schools in 1959, only 1,345 were directly managed by local authorities. The remainder were operated by missionary organizations, either in their own right or under contract with local authorities. A number of churches are engaged in educational work, of which the most important are the Roman Catholic, the Presbyterian, the Methodist, and the Anglican.

Primary Schools

The primary schools offer a six-year course for students of approximately six to twelve years of age. (The projected reorganization of the primary-education structure calls for a seven-year course with entry at age five.) Primary education is free for all in the regular age-group, but parents must provide textbooks and uniforms. Most primary schools are coeducational. Efforts are made—especially in the rural areas—to relate the primary syllabus to environment and to conserve the indigenous culture. In addition to reading, writing, and arithmetic, the curriculum includes handwork (crafts), gardening, games and physical education, civics, history, geography, singing, storytelling, drumming, and dancing.

The language of instruction poses certain complications in the primary schools. The first language of most children is usually one of the many indigenous vernaculars. These languages are likely to be used for some time to come, since they are the common tongues, and the government has encouraged the development of literacy in them through the mass-education program and the work of the Vernacular Literature Bureau. At the same time, English is the language of "modern life" in Ghana—of government, business, and post-primary education—and it is essential for the student to develop proficiency in it.

English is taught as a subject beginning in Class 1 and is the language of instruction beginning with Class 2. The local vernacular is also taught in the primary grades. The objective is to achieve literacy in both the vernacular and English by the end of primary school. In the towns of southern Ghana, which are undergoing such rapid growth, the problem is complicated by the influx of children from other areas who are unfamiliar with the local languages.

Under the development plans for education in the 1950's, the government placed major emphasis on the primary and middle schools, and substantial progress had been made before the end of the decade. In 1950, the total number of primary schools was 2,393; in 1959, there were 3,713. The growth of primary-school enrollment over the same period was even greater. Between 1950 and 1959, the number of pupils more than doubled, rising from 211,994 to 483,425.

A breakdown of primary-school enrollment in 1959, by sex and region, is given in Table 1.

Table 1
Primary-School Enrollment in Ghana, 1959

Region	Male	Female	Total
Western	71,622	34,697	106,319
Eastern	89,162	57,151	146,313
Volta	47,806	28,196	76,002
Ashanti	87,354	40,568	127,922
Northern	20,379	6,490	26,869
Total	*316,323*	*167,102*	*483,425*

It is not easy to tell to what extent the quality of primary education has been affected by the expansion program. A widely used index to this has been the extent to which pupil-teachers have been used in the primary schools. Of the 15,546 primary teachers (in approved and private schools) in 1959, 8,570 (55 per cent) were pupil-teachers. Although it seems unlikely that an expansion of the magnitude noted above could be achieved without some sacrifice of standards, there have been certain developments toward improved quality over the past decade. The most important of these have probably been the sharp decline in the number of private primary schools and the concomitant rise in the number of approved schools. In 1950, there were 1,081 approved primary schools and 1,312 private primary schools. In 1959, the comparable figures were 3,428 and 285. Many private schools became approved schools under the educational development program and, while retaining their nongovernmental management, became eligible for government financial aid. At the same time, they also became subject to government supervision over curriculum and instruction; as a result, the quality of many of them has probably been improved.

A serious problem at the primary level is the attrition from class to class (shown in Table 2, which follows one year's intake of pupils through the full primary course in approved schools).

Table 2
Intake by Class of Primary Pupils in Approved Schools

Class	Year	Pupils
1	1954	105,789
2	1955	75,190
3	1956	70,365
4	1957	66,563
5	1958	60,376
6	1959	57,455

A major cause of attrition would appear to be the temptation—particularly strong in rural areas, where most of the population live—to put children to work at an early age. The problem exists throughout Ghana, but is probably less serious in the coastal and central regions, which have a fairly long history of educational activity, than in the northern part of the country.

Middle Schools

Pupils who successfully complete the primary course and desire further schooling go on to the middle schools. The proportion of those who continue is reasonably high. In 1957, registration in Form 1 (middle school) was equal to more than 75 per cent of Class 6 registration (in primary school) during the preceding year; in 1958, it was slightly under 70 per cent; and in 1959, 76 per cent. Since the comparable figure was more than 80 per cent in 1953, the statistics appear to indicate that the proportion of primary-school graduates absorbed by the middle schools has declined slightly over the past decade. This presumably results from the inability to expand middle schools as rapidly as primary schools, although another factor is almost certainly the lag in popular acceptance of what constitutes a minimum education. Parents who accept the obligation to send their children through six years of primary school may balk at the four additional years of middle school; the boys and girls themselves may feel that the opportunity to go to work is more attractive or at least more pressing. This pattern is likely to change, however, now that middle-school education is free and compulsory.

The middle school consists of a four-year course, designated as Forms 1, 2, 3, and 4. Pupils are twelve to fifteen years of age. Most schools give their own entrance examinations, although some use is made of district-wide examinations. Fees were formerly charged in the middle schools, ranging between 24 shillings and 60 shillings per year; books and uniforms were provided by the parents.

English is the language of instruction in the middle schools, but the study of local vernaculars is continued. The curriculum includes the usual academic subjects: English, arithmetic, civics, history, geography, and nature study. In addition, an effort is being made to expand vocational courses at this level as part of the regular curriculum: agriculture, crafts (such as woodworking), and for girls, housecraft and needlework. Finally, the middle schools offer instruction in arts and in subjects related to village life and culture: drawing and painting, singing, games and physical exercises, and hygiene.

The expansion of the middle schools has now reached a level where the government has felt justified in introducing free and compulsory attendance. For reasons mentioned above, however, it is not altogether certain that all eligible applicants can be accommodated immediately.

The number of middle schools increased from 511 in 1950 to 1,394 in 1959. In one respect, the middle schools provide an exception to the general pattern of Ghana's educational growth: The number of private middle schools increased from none in 1950 to 276 in 1959. The increase in private middle schools has contributed little in the way of quality, however; of the total private middle-school teaching staff of 504 in 1958, only 4.2 per cent met the Ministry of Education's standards for trained teachers. But in the approved middle schools, the maintenance of standards has been encouraging. In 1958, for example, over 78 per cent of the staff were trained teachers. A useful index to the quality of the middle schools is the Middle School Leaving Certificate examination, given to pupils at the end of Form 4 by the West African Examinations Council. The percentage of successful pupils for three recent years is shown in Table 3.

Between 1950 and 1959, middle-school enrollment increased by more than 250 per cent—from 59,960 to 154,726 pupils. Table 4 shows middle-school enrollment in 1959, by sex and region.

Attrition in the middle schools is less serious than at the primary level. A comparison between the 1955 Form 1 and the 1958 Form 4

Table 3
Successful Candidates for Middle-School Leaving Certificate

Year	Candidates	Passed	Percentage Passed
1955	22,180	12,343	55.6
1956	24,701	15,656	63.4
1957	24,389	14,567	59.7

Table 4
Middle-School Enrollment, 1959

Region	Male	Female	Total
Western	24,794	8,445	33,239
Eastern	33,667	15,456	49,123
Volta	18,510	6,755	25,265
Ashanti	31,917	9,724	41,641
Northern	4,426	1,032	5,458
Total	*113,314*	*41,412*	*154,726*

indicates that slightly more than 76 per cent survived the middle-school course. Wastage was therefore about 24 per cent. (The comparable wastage figure for the primary schools is about 50 per cent.) Although some of this is accounted for by pupils who enter secondary schools directly from Forms 2 and 3, it is believed that by far the greatest part of the decline in enrollment over the four-year course stems from lack of interest, academic failure, and financial hardship.

The middle schools are now in transition to a new role in the educational system. At present, they are a link between primary school and education at the secondary level. From middle school, the pupil who wishes to continue his education may enter a secondary school, a secondary technical school, a government trade school, or a teacher-training college. This may be done directly from Form 2 or 3, however, provided the pupil meets the entrance requirements of the institution of his choice. The government's policy is to encourage this, so that it will eventually be possible and even customary for students to enter secondary school directly from the primary grades. When this becomes the normal practice, middle school will no longer be a link between primary and secondary school, but one of the alternatives that could be chosen by those students who, for one reason or another, did not plan to go beyond the middle school. Additional emphasis will be placed on vocational instruction in the middle schools.

The future of the middle school may also be closely bound up with the social problem posed by the middle-school leaver who does not go on to a higher level of training. The middle-school leaver is educated to a level roughly equivalent to the American ninth or tenth grade. He has often acquired just enough education to give him a view of the world beyond the village or small town, ambitions that usually cannot be realized on the basis of a middle-school education alone, and a distaste for manual labor and rural life. The opportunity to live in a city is one of the great rewards and prospects of an education in an underdeveloped country (and in more advanced ones as well). The middle-school leaver in Ghana tends to set out for one of the larger towns to make his way in the world in a white-collar occupation. The resulting problem cuts two ways. The towns, especially along the coast, are overcrowded as it is, and the continuing influx of migrants who will work in lower-paid jobs merely intensifies the problems of overcrowding and sanitation. If the middle-school leaver gets a white-collar job, it is likely to be a low-paid one. Even so, there are not enough clerkships to go around, and the less lucky middle-school leaver is likely to wind up as a casually employed manual laborer. The problem is also serious for the rural areas, since the influx of middle-school leavers into the towns drains the countryside of an element it needs—young men who will provide community leadership and improve rural living standards and agricultural practices.

The problem is not simply one of social welfare. There are political undertones as well to a situation in which the partly educated crowd into the cities and are unable to find employment of a sort which, rightly or wrongly, they consider due them. One approach to a solution has been the formation of the Builders' Brigades, which are roughly comparable to the U.S. Civilian Conservation Corps of the 1930's. The members, who live under semimilitary discipline, are employed on public projects and schooled in various trades. It remains to be seen whether the Brigades can provide a satisfactory solution to the middle-school–leaver problem, or whether they will prove to be only a stopgap measure. A more promising approach may be the further adaptation of the middle-school curriculum to vocational (including agricultural) instruction.

Secondary Schools

Beyond middle school, the Ghanaian student has several educational alternatives open to him. He may go on to a regular secondary school (a "grammar school" in the British sense), a technical or vocational school, or a teacher-training college. The proportion of those who continue is still fairly small. In 1959, enrollment in all secondary-level institutions, including trade and technical schools and teacher-training colleges, was only 16 per cent of the middle-school registration.

The course in the regular secondary (grammar) school is five to seven years, and the age of the students ranges from thirteen to nineteen years. The curriculum is both literary and scientific, and the language of instruction is English. There are coeducational secondary schools as well as schools for boys or girls only. Admission is by a common entrance examination, and at the end of the course students sit for the Cambridge School Certificate examination. All secondary schools charge tuition and, in the case of the resident schools, board; but scholarships are available to help defray these charges.

The number of students in secondary schools * more than doubled

* For statistical purposes, the term "secondary schools" in this paragraph and the next includes both secondary grammar schools and Ghana's single secondary technical school.

between 1950 and 1959, increasing from 6,162 to 15,317. During the same period, the number of schools increased by thirteen, from fifty-six in 1950 to sixty-nine in 1959. Of these sixty-nine schools, thirty-six were approved schools run by missionary or other private groups, two were government-run (the secondary school at Tamale in the northern region, and the secondary technical school at Takoradi), and one was an autonomous institution, the famous Achimota School. The remaining thirty were private schools.

Secondary education is the main concern of the educational phase of the current development plan, and the £7 million allocated for expansion of secondary schools accounts for one-fourth of anticipated capital expenditure on education under the plan. The first objective is to increase secondary-school capacity to accommodate approximately 10 per cent of the potentially eligible candidates in each region (the present capacity is 4 to 6 per cent). In absolute figures, the annual intake is to be increased from slightly more than 2,000 to about 6,000 in 1964. In terms of schools, this will require the expansion of fifteen existing institutions (and the rehousing of two others) and the construction of thirty-four new ones. A second objective of the plan is to increase the number of sixth forms—the final layer of the secondary schools and an almost indispensable preparation for university work. Here, the goal is to increase Form 6 admissions from 350 (the 1959 figure) to about 1,300. Since Form 6 is a two-year course (and wastage appears to be slight), total enrollment at this level would rise from 700 to 2,600. The attainment of even these modest goals, however, is jeopardized by the shortage of teachers. To date, the quality of secondary-school staff has remained high—over 40 per cent had university degrees or their equivalent in 1958. More widespread use of teachers without degrees is one possible solution, but recruitment would have to be highly selective, since the work of the secondary schools is subject to automatic review through the certificate and university entrance examinations. In any event, it is questionable whether teachers without degrees could undertake sixth-form work. Recruitment of University of Ghana graduates is difficult because of the better-paying opportunities in other lines of work. The one bright spot in teacher recruitment is the increasing responsiveness of Great Britain and other senior Commonwealth countries to the educational needs of the newer members. At the 1959 Commonwealth Education Conference, both Britain and Canada agreed to make additional teachers available to other Commonwealth countries, and it is possible that this may ultimately help to ease the problem of secondary-school expansion in Ghana.

Technical Education

In Ghana, as in all African countries, the need for technical and vocational education is particularly pressing. The problem is not only to produce engineers and other advanced technicians, but also to train craftsmen in the innumerable skills and trades required in a modern economy—electricians, carpenters, masons, mechanics, and others. Although continuing efforts are being made to integrate vocational subjects into the primary- and middle-school curricula, the main emphasis in trade and technical education is at the post–middle-school level.

The Government Secondary Technical School (Takoradi) offers four- and five-year courses leading to industrial employment or to technical training at a university or an equivalent institution. Programs are offered in engineering, construction, and handicrafts. Entrance is by the common secondary-school entrance examination, and the students are about thirteen to eighteen years of age. The first class was graduated in 1957.

Government junior institutes (formerly known as trade schools) provide four- and five-year courses in building and masonry, carpentry, and mechanical trades. There are four such institutes, and they had a total enrollment of 567 in 1959. Students are normally sixteen to nineteen years of age.

Four government technical institutes are intended to provide a full range of technical and vocational training courses in many forms—full-time, part-time, and evening courses, and special programs for apprentices. In addition to the usual trade and technical courses, some of the institutes provide instruction in commercial and domestic-science subjects. The institutes, located at Accra, Takoradi, Tarkwa, and Kumasi, had a total enrollment of 1,500 students for the 1958–59 sessions.

In addition to the government junior and technical institutes, there were thirty private technical schools in 1959 with about 1,800 students. Many (if not most) of these are believed to be commercial schools. Finally, a wide range of technical and vocational training is carried on by government departments and agencies and by large foreign firms operating in Ghana.

Perhaps the major defect in the system of trade and technical education is the lack of well-defined forecasts of the need for various types of technicians and tradesmen. The Second Development Plan gives no guidance on this subject; its provision of £1.5 million for technical education (aside from an additional £1.8 million for the

University of Science and Technology at Kumasi) is related to a reorganization of vocational education. Under the new plan, courses in both the junior and technical institutes will be recast so as to make a sharper distinction between preparation of artisans and of technicians. It is also proposed to establish a National Apprenticeship Scheme that will be closely integrated with the work of the institutes. The plan calls for eight new junior institutes and two more technical institutes.

Teachers and Teacher Training

In 1959, total staff in all educational institutions from primary through university level was 22,082. Of these, 9,537 (43 per cent) were carried in official statistics as "unqualified" and consisted of so-called pupil-teachers who had completed middle school but taken no further training. Pupil-teachers are found exclusively in the primary and (to a much less extent) the middle schools. It had been anticipated that their number would henceforth decline steadily, but this can no longer be expected in view of the decision to introduce free and compulsory primary- and middle-school education in 1961. Since an additional 20,000 teachers will be required, continuing reliance on pupil-teachers will presumably be necessary.

The percentage of trained teachers in primary and middle schools in 1959 is shown in Table 5.

Table 5
Percentage of Trained Teachers, 1959

Type of school	Primary schools	Middle schools
Approved	43.3	79.9
Private	1.4	1.8

Of a total educational staff of 22,082 at all levels, only 834 had a university degree or equivalent. All of these taught beyond the middle-school level.

The category of "trained teachers" in Ghanaian educational statistics is restricted to teachers holding "A" and "B" certificates. It excludes not only the large group of pupil-teachers but also a much smaller group of teachers who hold various special certificates and whose qualifications are not always clear from the official statistics. Certificate "A" qualifies teachers for both primary and middle schools —in some circumstances for the junior forms of secondary schools, and, in the case of experienced teachers, for the faculty of teacher-training colleges. Certificate "A" is awarded on successful completion of a four-year post-middle or two-year post-secondary (or post–Certificate "B") course in a teacher-training college. Certificate "B," awarded on successful completion of a two-year post-middle course at a teacher-training college, qualifies holders for primary-school teaching only. It has been common for teachers to begin as pupil-teachers and to enter the Certificate "B" course later, and it was the introduction of this system on a wide scale that helped make possible the growth of primary education over the past decade.

Expansion of teacher training has been a major aspect of the Ghanaian educational development program. The number of teacher-training colleges (government and approved) rose from nineteen in 1950 to thirty in 1956, and has remained at that figure since then. Four new colleges are to be set up under the Second Development Plan. Enrollment increased from 1,777 in 1950 to 4,274 in 1959. Of the teachers who were training in 1959, 1,476 were in the Certificate "A" course and 2,798 in the Certificate "B" course. In addition, intensive courses are conducted for pupil-teachers during their period of service (before they move on to the Certificate "B" course), and there are refresher courses for regular teachers.

Higher Education

Under a reorganization of higher education introduced in 1961, Ghana has three university-level institutions: the University of Ghana at Legon (near Accra), founded in 1948 as the University College of the Gold Coast and later known as the University College of Ghana; the Kwame Nkrumah University of Science and Technology at Kumasi, founded in 1951 as the Kumasi College of Technology; and the newly established University College of Cape Coast (1961). Both the former University College and Kumasi College of Technology were established by ordinances as autonomous institutions and were self-governing in practice, although they depended heavily on government financial assistance and included government representatives on their governing boards. Under the new reorganization plan, it would appear that the government will henceforth play a more active —and even decisive—role in the determination of academic policy and in the management of the universities. Each of the three institutions of higher learning is a separate body that awards its own degrees and diplomas. A National Council of Higher Education and Research is being established by the government, however, for the general direction and coordination of higher education. Since Ghana's

University of Ghana, at Legon—Commonwealth Hall.

universities are just beginning to operate within the new framework, it is too early to judge the effects of these changes. The following discussion necessarily focuses on developments predating the reorganization.

The University of Ghana has been organized into academic departments grouped in faculties as follows: Faculty of Arts (classics, English, phonetics, French studies, philosophy, and divinity); Faculty of Social Studies (archaeology, history, economics, geography, sociology, and the Institute and School of Education); Faculty of Physical Sciences (mathematics, physics, chemistry, and geology); Faculty of Biological Sciences (botany and zoology); and Faculty of Agriculture. In addition, adult-education and extension courses are provided through the Institute of Extra-Mural Studies.

The University of Ghana had an enrollment of 671 students in 1961 and hopes to have 2,000 students in residence by 1966. In the 1958–59 academic year, there were 519 students (488 men and 31 women). The official statistical breakdown of the student body for that year according to field of study (Table 6) does not correspond exactly with the organization by faculty.

Table 6
Fields of Study of Students at the University of Ghana, 1958–59

Field of study	Number of students
Arts	181
Economics and sociology	112
Science	105
Agriculture	38
Divinity	23
Institute of Education	60

In 1958–59, the University of Ghana (known as the University College then) had a full-time staff of 143, and therefore an extraordinarily high teacher-student ratio. From its founding through 1959, 439 students received degrees, and about 300 students received various special certificates. A total of 166 candidates were presented for final degree examinations in 1961, of whom 148 were successful.

Admission to the university has been from the sixth forms of secondary schools by entrance examination; there will presumably be no change in this practice under the new system. The high entrance qualifications and standard of performance have been a continuing incentive to the secondary schools to keep up and improve their own standards; the importance attached to the development of sixth forms is a case in point. Until 1961, the university's own standards were guaranteed through affiliation with the University of London, which had substantial supervisory powers and in whose name degrees were awarded. This special relationship has now been terminated.

The University of Ghana has consistently sought to develop itself as an institution that would be adapted to Ghanaian needs and yet would preserve the quality of the British university. The pursuit of excellence as thus defined was the source of most of its problems, since the conditions required and the nature of the goal itself are not easy to justify to a developing country, where other needs seem more urgent. A particular difficulty was the reliance on an inherited tradition as the criterion, since this exposed the university—rightly or wrongly—to the reproach that it was not, in fact, responsive to the requirements of the time. For one thing, the costs of the University of Ghana were heavy in terms of capital investment, recurrent expenditure, and cost per student. These expenses were particularly criticized in terms of the university's impressive physical plant and its rather small number of students. In point of fact, the university operated considerably below the capacity of its physical facilities—there were vacant places for several hundred students—and probably somewhat below the capacity of its teaching staff, although the decision to maintain a high staff-student ratio was deliberate. The administration, however, insisted that entrants must meet its standards and not vice versa, and, in terms of the future interests of Ghana, it is hard not to sympathize with this approach.

Finally, and perhaps most serious—and apart from questions of educational policy and performance—the university came to be regarded by some Ghanaian leaders as hostile to the ruling Convention People's Party and the government. President Nkrumah himself publicly voiced these suspicions in a strong speech in 1959. The true position was never easy to assess from the outside, especially the question of whether there was, in fact, any strong sympathy for the CPP's opponents among staff and students. A number of observers have commented on the absence of deep political interests and enthusiasms among the students, a point that has been particularly striking because of the sharp contrast with so many other underdeveloped countries. Actually, the major source of tension was probably the university's own efforts to maintain its autonomy as an academic community. Its independent atmosphere encouraged a freely critical attitude that was not always appreciated by working politicians and administrators and intensified their suspicion that the country's leading institution of higher education was not committed to their goals for Ghanaian development. The current reorganization of university education is, needless to say, a direct reflection of this dissatisfaction.

The Kwame Nkrumah University of Science and Technology has offered a fairly wide range of programs in technical subjects, all of them on a post-secondary level, but most of them leading to special diplomas and professional certificates rather than degrees. Its aim has been to train highly specialized technicians somewhat rapidly, rather than to turn out specialists with a broad general background. In addition to a degree course in engineering, the university has offered programs in surveying, architecture and building, estate management, accountancy, secretaryship and administration, pharmacy, agriculture, physical education, domestic science, music, and arts and crafts. In 1959, there was an enrollment of 615 (600 men and 15 women) and a full-time staff of 81; in 1961, there were 800 students.

In addition to the Ghanaians studying in the three national institutions of higher learning, there were 523 enrolled in universities or law schools in the U.K. in 1961–62 (plus 2,370 others in "practical training" and 100 in nursing schools there); about 240 in the U.S. and Canada; 300 in West and East Germany; about 20 in Yugoslavia; 200 in the Soviet Union; and about 50 in technical training in Czechoslovakia.

24. Liberia

Capital: Monrovia
Population: 1,000,000–2,000,000 (est.)
Area: 42,990 sq. miles
Political status: Independent republic

LIBERIA and Sierra Leone alone among the West African countries have found their political, economic, and social development deeply influenced by a sizable Negro-settler group from America and England. The first of numerous parties of Negro settlers from the United States set sail for Africa in 1820, under the aegis of the American Colonization Society, to found the country of Liberia. At least 18,858 of these American colonists, aided by expenditures of over $2 million by the Society, reached Liberian shores before the Civil War. The 10,000 to 12,000 descendants of these original Americo-Liberians live for the most part along the coastal areas of the country and continue to dominate the social and political life in the capital city of Monrovia. Indigenous tribal peoples make up the remainder of Liberia's population, which, in the absence of a census, has been estimated at anywhere from 750,000 to 2.5 million.

By comparison with most African colonial territories, Liberian development has lagged. Although ties with the United States have remained unbroken (if often somewhat tenuous) from the time of the first settlements, little economic development was undertaken until the Firestone Plantations were established in the 1920's. The development of an adequate system of schools was delayed even longer, with the result that the country's educational deficiencies are now acting as a brake on further economic growth. While members of the Americo-Liberian ruling class measured their superiority over the tribal people of the hinterland in terms of "modernity" versus the indigenous inhabitants' "primitiveness," they were not very education-minded until recently. Education was at times more formal than substantial, and there has often been a tendency to concentrate on appearances rather than content. In fact, among upper-class Liberians the range of occupations requiring formal preparation was limited. Success in agriculture depended, or so it was thought, on other factors; the law was read in a practicing attorney's office rather than studied in a law school; and the ministry did not demand arduous theological studies. The second career for most Americo-Liberians—and one that often began simultaneously with their first occupation—was politics, and it generally required even less formal preparation than the others, political advancement in the Liberian context hinging on elements that were for the most part already determined by heredity and character. Furthermore, the Americo-Liberians operated more or less as a colonial ruling class, but without (until quite recently) making any regular provision for the schooling of the tribal people who were under their tutelage.

Major Problems of Liberian Education

Liberia thus labors under several handicaps. The ruling group—by comparison with its counterparts in the West African countries that were under British and French rule—has had a limited educational background itself and, therefore, has not been very critical in its approach to education. Furthermore, as many Liberians are quick to point out, the country has had no experience of colonialism. Whatever else this may have meant, it prevented the Liberians from developing a university of good quality, alert school inspectors, and an educational service trained in modern pedagogical techniques. Finally, Liberia's rulers have had to overcome a peculiar inertia that has permeated many aspects of Liberian life. The country's first "century of survival" in a sea of colonialism evoked justifiable pride among Liberians, but it also caused them to look almost wholly inward. Having adopted themselves as a standard and measure, Liberians found it difficult to judge either the true state of African affairs or their own backwardness in relation to many of the colonial territories. The tremendous velocity of West African political movements in the 1950's probably surprised Liberians more than anyone else. As their contacts with other West African territories have multiplied, and as they have probed into political developments there, they have been almost equally surprised to find a much higher degree of development in these territories than they had imagined. The virtual shock that has followed the recognition of these facts has spurred Liberia to accelerate the momentum of its development—and especially in the field of education.

Like all African countries, Liberia faces difficult choices in allocating its limited resources because of the multiplicity of demands arising from the sudden upsurge of development in all fields and the telescoping of a process of growth that has taken decades—in some cases, centuries—in Western countries. Even within the field of education, there is a convergence of competing demands. The Liberian Government is now under steadily mounting pressures to provide the widest possible education for the greatest number of people. Primary education is still badly retarded and yet obviously is the key to all other stages in the educational process. At the same time, the development of this (or any other) level of the school system will touch off chain reactions in two directions. As each stage is developed, there will be accumulating pressures to expand the next higher level, so as to broaden opportunities still further; simultaneously, each level is likely to demand improvement in the quality of preparation at the lower levels.

Education in Liberia in the nineteenth century was almost entirely in the hands of missionary groups and cost the government little or nothing. Even as late as 1946, it was estimated that 80 per cent of the country's formal education was still in the hands of missionaries, and their role continues to be extremely significant. Missionary organizations in Liberia are required by law to operate schools, although most now receive government subsidies. The government's Department of Public Instruction was established in 1900; compulsory education was provided by law in 1912; a general education code was promulgated in 1937 and amended in 1942 and 1944. As a result of these acts, Liberia had a fairly advanced educational system on paper, copied mainly after American educational patterns.

Unfortunately, however, the Liberian Government has never had the financial or technical resources to enforce its educational legislation. At late as 1920, the total sum appropriated for education was $2,000 (only $1,116.56 of which was actually spent); and in 1946, only $154,212.30 (12 per cent of the annual budget) was appropriated, in addition to $200,000 spent by missions. When one considers these facts, it becomes clear why less than 3 per cent of the children of school age were receiving any formal education in 1946. Even today, it is estimated that some 70 per cent of the Liberian people are illiterate by Western standards. Until the last decade, the only education received by the indigenous children in the hinterland was that given in the local bush schools of the Poro and the Sande, the secret societies that initiate boys and girls into the rites of manhood and womanhood and teach the fundamentals of traditional social, religious, economic, and political life. In the inland Moslem areas, there were also Koranic schools where Arabic was taught and where the pupils mastered the elements of the Islamic religion and learned to recite the Koran.

The percentage of the annual budget expended by Liberia on education today is actually higher than that in some of its wealthier neighbors, but its over-all income—and consequently its educational expenditures in absolute figures—is considerably lower. For the year 1958–59, Liberia allotted $2,278,710 ($278,710 more than in the preceding year), or 15 per cent of its budget, for education. In addition, it has been estimated that in recent years there have been additional educational expenditures of about $2 million annually from the following sources: (1) government expenditures for school construction; (2) assistance from the U. S. International Cooperation Administration and UNESCO; and (3) expenditures of missions and private groups. By comparison, Ghana's Minister of Education, Kofi Baako, proposed the sum of $18,754,008 for the year 1959–60. From these figures, it can be seen that the amount allotted for education in Ghana is very close to the figure for Liberia's annual budget for all governmental services combined. It must, of course, be kept in mind that Ghana's population is approximately three times that of Liberia and that its revenues have long been much greater. The pace of advance is largely set by revenue, and Liberia is only beginning to reach a point where it can support an adequate system of education. Now that Liberian mines are producing iron ore in ever expanding quantities, revenues may reach as high as $100 million a year by 1970, as compared with $1 million just before World War II.

In his fourth inaugural address in January, 1960, President William V. S. Tubman announced that local towns and communities would be requested to provide material and manual help in the construction of educational and health facilities; he also proposed that an Educational and Health Fund be created to collect financial contributions from individual Liberians. This fund would be subscribed to on a voluntary basis by civil servants, but supported as a matter of public and party * policy by all persons holding political appointments or elected by popular vote. Persons subscribing to this fund would receive bonds every quarter; such bonds would mature ten years from the date of their issuance, and income from them would be exempt from taxation. A fixed proportion of the Educational and Health Fund would be invested in the capital of the Development Bank to facilitate the retirement of the bonds as they became due.

Another major educational problem of Liberia arises from the

* The True Whig Party has been the governing party in Liberia since the 1870's.

simple lack of reliable statistics on the population as a whole, on vital rates, on the school-age population, and on various aspects of the educational system. A national census has been planned, but has not yet been carried out, although several pilot enumerations have been made in coastal towns. Until reliable statistics are available, Liberian educational planning will be seriously handicapped, and most of the statistics used in discussions of the educational system—including the present one—must be regarded as estimates only.

The School Population

One informed writer on Liberia's educational problems has calculated the conventional school-age population at about 20 per cent of the total number of inhabitants. Calculated on the basis of the "round figure" often used for the Liberian population (1 million), the school-age population would be 200,000. In any event, the size of the school-age population is only a partial index to the scale of Liberia's educational needs since, as in any developing country, adult education is an important aspect of the total educational picture.

A recent estimate of the total number of students in the regular school system is shown in Table 1.

Table 1
Estimated Enrollment in Liberian Schools

Types of schools	Number of pupils
Elementary	
Government schools	35,000
Missionary and company schools	20,000
Total	*55,000*
Secondary	
Government schools	1,000
Missionary and private schools	1,500
Total	*2,500*
Grand total	*57,500*

On the basis of these figures, 29 per cent of the estimated school-age population are under instruction. The total number of students at all levels in 1944 was 12,000, and in 1953 it was 33,000. According to the *Liberian Year Book 1956,* the total number of elementary students by that year was 40,353. No comprehensive breakdown of students by sex is available, and impressions of the extent to which girls are being educated vary widely. Of two recent on-the-scene observers, one reported that girls make up 25 per cent of secondary-school enrollment (which would be one of the highest percentages for all Africa); the second noted that girls were "extremely few in number" in primary and secondary schools.

A report prepared by the U.S. Embassy at Monrovia for the Department of Commerce gave statistics for 1958 on the number of schools; these are shown in Table 2.

Table 2
Schools in Liberia, 1958

Type of school	Elementary	Secondary	Total
Government	356	10	366
Mission	134	13	147
Company and other	67	1	68
Total	*557*	*24*	*581*

In 1944, there were 268 elementary and secondary schools of all types; in 1952, there were 446.

Structure of the Educational System

Structurally, the Liberian educational system is similar to that formerly used in the United States, with eight years of primary instruction and four of high school. However, plans are now being formulated to reorganize the system to a six-year elementary course, three years of junior high school, and three years of senior high school. (In addition, there are about 1,300 children in government kindergarten schools in the coastal counties.) In theory, primary education has been compulsory since 1912. Until 1944, tuition was charged in all schools. Since then, primary education has been free where available, but fees are charged in secondary schools. Despite the unquestioned gains made in recent years, there continues to be a heavy attrition of primary students. A study prepared in the early 1950's reported that for every ten students who began the primary course, eight dropped out before the end of the third year. A more recent field study commented on the large number of over-age students found in all primary grades, especially at the fourth grade and beyond, where "boys" are often sixteen to twenty-five years of age. Most primary schools are in session for only half a day.

At the secondary level, the "quantitative problem"—that of providing adequate coverage—is obviously linked to the development of primary schools. Liberian high schools cannot improve until the primary-school system consistently produces suitably qualified entrants. In turn, the secondary schools have an obligation, still not being met, to provide the institutions of higher education in Liberia, and the overseas universities that Liberians attend, with students capable of undertaking college-level work. At the same time, secondary schools in Liberia, as in almost every other African country, have an important role to fulfill in and of themselves. For some years to come, the "middle elite" of clerks, accountants, managers of small enterprises, lower-level officials, and teachers will be an elite of high-school graduates. The results of secondary education, therefore, are likely to be felt not in the universities alone but in Liberian society at large.

Standards have varied widely from school to school. In recognition of this weakness, the government revised its elementary-school curriculum in 1960 and announced that a national examination would henceforth be given at the end of the sixth and ninth grades in an effort to point up weak schools and bring them up to standard. The Department of Public Instruction hoped to have new curriculum guides ready for the senior high schools shortly and to administer national school-leaving examinations for all twelfth graders by the end of the 1961 school year. Following the British pattern, these objective national examinations will be drafted by an outside board of educators and marked by outside examiners.

A long-range plan for accrediting the Liberian schools is being worked out by the National Evaluation Board. The purpose of this accreditation as indicated by the Board is fourfold. It is intended: (1) to help the schools of the country improve in those characteristics under their control; (2) to give the Department of Public Instruction firsthand information of what schools are doing and the problems with which they are faced; (3) to compare the management, operation, accomplishment, and self-help initiative of schools, so as to encourage local communities to take interest in the operation and support of the schools in their areas; and (4) to establish an objective means of appraising the accomplishments of schools.

In evaluating the schools, such factors as curriculum or course offerings, physical plant, extracurricular activities, qualification of the staff, teacher-pupil ratio, library facilities, and academic growth as measured by the annual national examination will be taken into consideration. It is proposed that the evaluation will be made once every five years, thus giving schools an opportunity to improve before the next evaluation period.

The government's educational plans reportedly call for the enrollment of 180,000 students—90 per cent of the estimated current school-age population of 200,000—in the coming decade. In his 1960 inaugural address, President Tubman promised that "a low-cost but durable elementary school building will be designed and constructed in cooperation with local labor in every major town or village in the country."

The expansion of secondary education will probably also require a wider introduction of the boarding-school system, since it is highly unlikely that each village will be able to support a high school for the foreseeable future. The lack of dormitories in government-supported high schools often prevents primary graduates from nearby towns from attending, since jobs and lodging are often difficult to obtain.

The Teacher Shortage

In September, 1959, Liberia had 1,798 elementary-school teachers and 217 high-school teachers, the vast majority of whom had not finished secondary school. If the government succeeds in its goal of enrolling 180,000 students at all levels of the educational system by the end of the coming decade, an estimated 10,000 additional elementary teachers, 300 secondary teachers, and 500 college and university teachers will be required at the present teacher-pupil ratio. To close this gap in ten years would require the training of more than 1,000 teachers per year; at the present time, the combined annual output of all existing teacher-training schools is fewer than fifty, and some of these do not go into teaching after they have completed their training. The Liberian Government is proposing an upward revision of salary scales and retirement allotments in order to attract more graduates. But the problem is not simply one of increasing quantity. While adequate standards are provided by law for the licensing of teachers, a sufficient number of qualified candidates has never been available, with the net result that temporary or provisional certificates have had to be issued to unqualified candidates, who have then been recertified from year to year. In April, 1961, the magazine *West Africa* estimated that approximately 70 per cent of Liberia's teachers were untrained. In 1960, acting on the report of a special committee of educators, the Department of Public Instruction announced plans for the establishment of a Certification Board to set up minimum standards for teachers at each level of education and pass on candidates' qualifications.

The first of a series of village teacher-training and educational centers programmed by the government to meet these needs is being established on a thousand-acre campus in the Zorzor district of

Western Province. Here it is hoped to train fifty elementary teachers per year in a two-year program for eighth-grade graduates. In his 1960 inaugural speech, President Tubman proposed, through multilateral or bilateral arrangements, to invite a corps of teacher-training specialists to Liberia to organize three additional rural teacher-training centers. Until these teacher-training schools have graduated additional rural teachers—for it is here that the need for expansion is greatest—President Tubman proposes that contract teachers be brought to Liberia to staff at least some of the rural schools.

A program to improve educational standards by compulsory "in-service" training for teachers has also been inaugurated. The first "vacation school" for teachers was organized in 1952 under the joint U.S.-Liberian cooperative program; it offered courses in languages, arts, social studies, elementary arithmetic, science and nature study, physical education, and school administration and supervision. Emphasis was placed on good classroom teaching and the introduction of simple instructional materials related to the needs of the students. Similar but smaller vacation schools have since been set up in various parts of Liberia, and evening courses for teachers have been organized during the school year. Tests are given to all teachers in these schools, and cumulative records on each teacher attending the sessions have been set up.

School libraries, facilities, and equipment are all far from adequate, and a recent observer has noted that proper maintenance of school properties is often neglected. Only about 20 per cent of the children in school are reported to have textbooks. It has been proposed to develop, with the aid of U.S. technicians, textbooks related to the Liberian environment that can be reproduced by offset printing in sufficient quantity to meet the needs of expanded educational programs and at a price that the students can afford to pay.

Education and National Unification

On a geographical basis, a considerable proportion of the educational effort must be directed toward the rural areas of Liberia, and especially the interior tribal areas commonly referred to as the "hinterland." President Tubman, in his sixteen years of office, has gone far toward reversing the policy of reserving education for the elite, the Americo-Liberians, and has developed extensive plans for spreading education into this hinterland. Prior to his first inauguration in 1944, most of Liberia's educational effort was devoted to this small elite group and to the 40,000 or 50,000 more or less Westernized Liberians of tribal ancestry also living along the coast. Under what might be described as "the old regime," the country was both class-conscious and tribe-conscious. Most people thought of themselves as Vais, Krus, or Mandingos first and as Liberians second, if at all. At the First National Executive Council meeting in 1954, Tubman set his goals in blunt language: "We must now destroy all ideologies that tend to divide us. Americo-Liberianism must be forgotten, and all of us must register a new era of justice, equality, fair dealing, and equal opportunities for everyone from every part of the country, regardless of tribe, clan, section, element, creed, or economic status."

In the implementation of this policy, the tribal people have been enfranchised and given representation in the legislature; qualified individuals of tribal descent have been promoted to high posts in the government, of whom one of the most conspicuous is the present Secretary of Public Instruction, Nathaniel Massaquoi.

Thus, education is an important aspect of the sought-for national unification and integration of the tribal peoples, with the broad objective being to introduce a sense of Liberian national consciousness and new ways of life without abruptly breaking with indigenous patterns and traditions. In building new schools, the government is making an effort to locate them in the rural villages where more than 95 per cent of the population live, rather than bringing the village youths to the city, where they are all too frequently educated out of their village environment. The national-unification policy envisages an educational program in its broadest sense: community development stimulated and sustained by the transfer of "know-how" from teachers and technicians to villagers. By educating youth in the village schools and at the same time carrying on an extensive mass education and literacy program for the adults (a joint program of the Liberian Government and UNESCO, inaugurated in 1953), the government hopes to educate the entire community. As an outgrowth of the national literacy campaign inaugurated in 1950, a Bureau of Fundamental Education was set up in 1957 and today operates the National Fundamental Education Center (at Klay, near Monrovia) and more than 150 literacy classes throughout the country. Since 1954, the Center has trained 170 rural workers, both men and women, and although the number is small in comparison with the need, observers agree that they have done solid work in the rural areas.

Technical Education

Closely related to community or mass education—which supplements literacy courses with practical instruction in subjects closely related to village life—is the development of vocational and technical education. In a sense, vocational education is central to the entire Liberian educational program, since its objective is to make modern knowledge and skills accessible and thus to accelerate economic and social development. For example, foreign companies operating in Liberia have stressed the fundamental importance of literacy to the teaching of all technical skills, and a visiting U.S. expert who conducted a survey of Liberian vocational education has emphasized that the extension and improvement of primary education is basic to all vocational instruction.

Vocational and technical instruction in Liberia is offered under a number of auspices and programs, but in almost every case U.S. advice and assistance are closely involved. The potential keystone of Liberian technical education is the Booker T. Washington Institute (BWI) at Kakata, founded in 1929 under the auspices of several American missionary and philanthropic organizations and transferred to the control of the Liberian Government in 1953. BWI is presently a coeducational technical school, from the eighth through the twelfth grade, offering courses in agriculture, various industrial arts, business, and home economics. It still fulfills its original purpose of training craftsmen, but the opportunities for the craftsman and the framework within which he operates have altered vastly in the three decades since its founding. Thus, BWI is in transition toward a still undefined role at the center of Liberian vocational and technical education. For some time, it has technically been the School of Agricultural and Mechanical Arts of the University of Liberia, and there has been some tendency to regard it as the future engineering school of the university. There has also been another tendency, reflecting in part the thinking of outside advisers, to adopt a more flexible approach to the future development of BWI and to encourage its growth along the lines of the American land-grant college. This would leave ample scope for the development of an engineering faculty and, at the same time, permit the college to develop other equally important programs of instruction and service. A report prepared in 1959 by Frederick D. Patterson, President of the Phelps-Stokes Fund (one of the joint founders of BWI), recommended that: (1) BWI be officially designated as the agricultural and mechanical institution for the Republic of Liberia, and that the agricultural education program be centered there; (2) a research and extension program be developed at BWI comparable to similar programs in U.S. land-grant institutions; and (3) BWI offer instruction in agricultural and mechanical arts at any level that may be required. In his 1960 address, President Tubman announced that he had requested a survey team of specialists to develop a master plan for the development of BWI as the National Center of Vocational Education.

Among other vocational-education programs in Liberia, the most important perhaps are those being carried out under the auspices, or with the aid and guidance of, the U.S. technical-assistance program. In addition to the assistance given to Liberian schools under this program, there are Liberians working under the direct instruction of U.S. technicians (as many as 600 students at a time, under some 55 technicians) or being trained in the U.S. or in third countries where training facilities are better suited to Liberian needs. Also, Cuttington College has an important agricultural program, and the University of Liberia offers instruction in such fields as forestry, home economics, and business subjects in addition to its regular arts programs. With a few notable exceptions (such as the Episcopal Mission School at Cape Mount), there appears to be little trade or technical training in the primary and secondary schools. Finally, U.S. and other foreign firms operating in Liberia, through formal instruction and on-the-job training, are making important contributions to the small but growing pool of skilled workers and technicians.

Higher Education

Higher education in Liberia is still in a fairly rudimentary stage of development, and the country is more dependent on overseas higher education than, say, Ghana or Nigeria. Again, the deficiencies of Liberian higher education can be explained to a considerable extent by the peculiar and isolated circumstances of Liberian history. In the French colonial territories, where the policy of assimilation long prevailed, an African intellectual elite was encouraged and sponsored, so long as it was Gallicized and stayed clear of heterodox political notions. In the British territories, the university colleges were backed by ample resources and, through the system of affiliation with British institutions, had to conform to strict standards. In Liberia, by contrast, there was no intellectual tradition, domestic or imperial, and hence no encouragement of a highly educated group; moreover, neither the government nor the missions had the resources to create a modern university.

Over the last decade, the former indifference to higher education has been replaced by an intense effort to make up for lost time. While progress has been somewhat random, there have been real gains. Currently, the most important need (other than the ever-present ones of money and trained personnel) would appear to be for a sound plan

University of Liberia—students in the library. *(Photo by Eric Schwab, courtesy of UNESCO.)*

of higher educational development with realistic goals, which would avoid showcase projects in favor of solid if unspectacular growth.

The country's leading institution of higher education, the University of Liberia (located on a thirty-two–acre campus in Monrovia), was chartered in 1951 and is still in its formative stage. The university is a nonsectarian, coeducational, and government-supported institution of 750 students, although it has been reported that only 300 of these are at college level. Three existing institutions were merged to form the university:

(1) Liberia College (the university's School of Liberal and Fine Arts), organized in 1862, which combined both high school (in the so-called "preparatory department") and college instruction.

(2) College of West Africa (redesignated the William V. S. Tubman School of Teacher Training), a teacher-training college dating from 1838, which offered secondary instruction and two years of normal training.

(3) Booker T. Washington Institute (now the School of Agricultural and Mechanical Arts).

Since the university's foundation, a number of other schools and special divisions have been added. Some of these do not offer college-level courses, and others now may be inactive. They include: Louis Arthur Grimes School of Law and Government, the university's law school; the School of Forestry; the Mary Ann Cheeseman School of Home Economics and Applied Science, which offers courses in home-making, sewing, etc.; the Thomas J. R. Faulkner School of Engineering and Applied Science, which gives a pre-engineering course; the Benjamin J. K. Anderson School of Commerce and Business Administration, which trains secretaries, clerks, and bookkeepers; and the School of Music. Only the William V. S. Tubman School of Teacher Training, the School of Liberal and Fine Arts, the Louis Arthur Grimes School, and the School of Forestry award degrees. One branch of the university, the People's College of Mass Education is an extension school for adult and general education, offering courses on several levels, including the secondary. There is also a Laboratory High School, attached to the School of Teacher Training, which serves as a demonstration school. To help fill the gap in technical personnel, it has been proposed to establish at the university an institute of technical studies that would train chemists, physicists, and other scientists and advanced technologists. The proposed institute would also conduct research in the pure sciences.

The university's first two presidents were Americans; the third, and present incumbent, is a Liberian, Rocheforte Weeks. Many members of the faculty are graduates of U.S. universities. UNESCO has supplied a considerable number of visiting lecturers since 1952; the science department is headed by a professor from the U.K.'s Durham University; and the School of Forestry is entirely staffed by Germans. President Tubman has given special attention in recent years to the university, and is particularly concerned with raising its academic standards. The U.S. Administration for International Development has granted $1 million toward strengthening the institution's plant and faculty, and the university's charter is to be revised so that legislators and politicians will no longer comprise the majority of the Board of Trustees.

Cuttington College, operated under the joint auspices of the Episcopal and Methodist churches, is located at Suakoko, near Gbarnga. It was founded in 1888, closed its doors in 1929, reopened in 1948, and graduated its first class after reopening in 1952. Its stated aims are "to provide a basically Christian education and to play its part in the preparation of Liberian youth for the new age." The college has a Liberal Arts School, a School of Theology, and an excellent agricultural program. Most of its students enter the teaching field. Students preparing for the ministry must either take two years of study in the Liberal Arts School or show satisfactory evidence that they have completed the equivalent elsewhere. Most members of the staff are American.

In 1958, the principal of Cuttington stated that it was prepared to handle about 200 students, but that there were only about 100 in residence. In May, 1959, it had an enrollment of 136 (130 undergraduates and 6 candidates for the Bachelor of Divinity Degree). Under the government's offer of fifty scholarships to students from other African countries, Cuttington had two students from Sierra Leone, one from Ghana, three from Nigeria, and twelve from Tanganyika. There were also three American students in 1960.

Our Lady of Fatima College, a small Roman Catholic institution in Harper, is a teacher-training college with an enrollment of thirty-two students.

Liberia also has a liberal policy of awarding full scholarships and grants-in-aid for education overseas. In return for a four-year scholarship, students have generally been required to promise to serve the government in a professional capacity for four years after their return to Liberia. Currently, more than 200 Liberian students are registered in American colleges and universities, and there are others studying in Canada, Great Britain, and Europe. For many years, this program lacked proper supervision, but since 1959 it has benefited considerably from the assignment of a Cultural Attaché to the Liberian Embassy at Washington.

Plans for Future Development

Any survey of Liberian education, by indicating the heavy handicaps inherited from the past and the numerous sectors in which rapid and substantial advance is imperative, necessarily emphasizes the discouraging aspects of the problem. As in many underdeveloped areas, however, the very magnitude of the educational requirements carries with it a positive aspect—the encouragement of imaginative experiments in education. While the educational innovations introduced in Liberia are by no means unique, the country offers a particularly wide range of them, especially in the field of international educational cooperation. Technical-assistance programs—by the U.S. Government, international agencies, missionary and philanthropic organizations, and foreign private firms—are offering any number of approaches to educational development. To catalogue only a few endeavors in the foreign assistance field, there are support and guidance of Liberian institutions by U.S. foundations and religious bodies; foreign teachers working side by side with Liberians in the schools; on-the-job training; overseas training for Liberians; the *servicio* concept (developed by U.S. technical assistance in Latin America), in which technicians work in government agencies as both technicians and instructors; and the contract arrangement under which Prairie View State College (part of the Texas A&M system) renders support to BWI. Mass-education and community-development schemes are adapting modern educational techniques to the delicate task of preserving the village community intact while gradually easing it into the modern world. The proposed integration of vocational education and economic development through the establishment of BWI as a land-grant type of college with research and extension responsibilities is another notable experiment.

Perhaps the most important development in Liberian education, however, is the new spirit of honest inquiry that the government has adopted since 1959 in examining the deficiencies of the nation's school system and in reassessing the preconceptions on which it has been based. President Tubman's 1960 address set a fresh wind blowing, and Secretary of Public Instruction Massaquoi has pursued the self-analysis in a series of blunt public speeches. Far-reaching changes are clearly in the making—not only in developing the size of the school system, but also in raising the standards of education from primary through university level.

—RUTH C. SLOAN

25. Nigeria

Capital: Lagos
Population: 35,000,000 (est.)
Area: 356,669 sq. miles
Political status: Independent dominion of the British Commonwealth

MORE than half—over 19 million—of Nigeria's estimated 35 million people live in the predominantly Moslem Northern Region; the Eastern Region has more than 8 million; the Western Region about 7 million; and about 360,000 more live in the federal capital of Lagos. The total non-African population in the entire country is only about 30,000, of which about one-third are British. By mid-1961, Africanization of the senior posts in the civil service had reached 64 per cent, and it was anticipated that only 400 expatriates would be serving the government on pensionable terms by 1962.

Of the numerous tribes and tribal groups, each with its own language, the largest is the Hausa, and in the north this is the principal language. In numerical order, the following then predominate: Ibo (east), Yoruba (west), Fulani and Kanuri (north), Ibibio (east), Tiv (north), Edo (west), Nupe (north), and Ijaw (east and west). English is the official language, however, and it is the language of instruction in all post-primary schools throughout the federation. Although their vocabulary is often limited, all children who complete the full primary course are able to read and write English.

Education has progressed much more rapidly in the south than in the Moslem north, mainly because the missions, which were the pioneer schools in Nigeria, were restricted to the pagan sectors of the country. For many years, the only children who received any education in the north were those who attended the Koranic schools, where they recited together portions of the Koran in Arabic, a language they could not understand. Britain annexed the settlement of Lagos as a colony in 1861, but did not enter the north until 1900, when the Protectorate of Northern Nigeria was established. Governor General Sir Frederick Lugard's pledge that the government would not allow any interference with the religion of the people naturally curtailed mission influence, and it was not until 1910 that the Education Department of the Northern Provinces came into being.

The situation immediately after World War I was summed up in these words by the Governor, Sir Hugh Clifford:

> In the northern provinces there has been until recently a certain tendency to regard education of the local population with some uneasiness and suspicion, as a process likely to exert a disintegrating and demoralizing effect upon the characters of those who are subjected to it; and where this feeling has been overcome, a further tendency is observable to regard education too exclusively as a handmaid to administration. . . . After two decades of British occupation, the northern provinces have not yet produced a single native . . . who is sufficiently educated to enable him to fill the most minor clerical post in the office of any government department. . . . The African staff of these offices throughout the northern provinces are therefore manned by men from the Gold Coast, Sierra Leone, and from the southern provinces of Nigeria. . . . Education in the north has been practically confined to the vernacular and to Arabic, has been allowed to become the almost exclusive perquisite of the children of the local ruling classes, and has for its main object the equipment of these children with just sufficient knowledge of reading, writing, and arithmetic to enable them in after life to fill posts in one or another of the various Native administrations. . . .
>
> In the southern provinces the position is very different. The lack of properly trained teachers is here even more acutely felt; but this does not prevent the sprouting up in every direction of a mushroom growth of "hedge" schools in the majority of which young men who are incapable of grappling with the mysteries of the Fourth Standard profess to impart "education" to large groups of boys.
>
> The position then is that there is throughout the southern provinces an abundance of schools but very little genuine education; that the children themselves are curiously eager to attend school, but are much less willing to remain there long enough to acquire any real knowledge; and that too many of them, no matter how imperfectly educated they may be, thereafter regard themselves as superior to agricultural pursuits

and prefer to pick up a precarious and demoralizing living by writing more or less unintelligible letters for persons whose ignorance is even deeper than their own.

The curricula in use . . . [must] be revised on more practical and useful lines. . . . Far too little attention is paid to the coordination of hand and eye . . . and literary acquirements are apparently regarded as the be-all and end-all of education.

It has never been the practice in British possessions in the tropics for the local government to claim the right to exercise any control or supervision over scholastic enterprises that do not voluntarily submit to these things for a grant-in-aid, the amount of which is annually determined by the degree of efficiency attained by each school, as revealed by the periodic reports of government inspectors. Having regard, however, to the extraordinary eruption of hedge schools and the evils which are therefore resulting . . . it may become necessary for the Government of Nigeria to reconsider its attitude in this matter. It will be recognized, however, that action in any such direction is, and will continue to be, exceedingly difficult until government is itself in a position to meet what is unquestionably a genuine and widespread demand for education, which the hedge schools are making-believe in some measure to satisfy.

Although the Governor, in this address to the Nigerian Council, concerned himself with the limitations and failures of the situation as he saw it in 1920 and did not mention the excellent work being done by mission centers, his summation is significant because it reveals the educational climate in which the majority of Nigerians with sons and daughters now between the ages of twenty and thirty-five were brought up. What a vast difference there is between the outlook of these two Nigerian generations! A Nigerian father and son would give widely different answers if asked to describe in their own terms "the educated African."

The missions had already established themselves in the field of education in the south long before the turn of the century, and it was soon after the establishment of the Protectorate of Southern Nigeria in 1900 that the first inspector of schools was appointed. The need for more effective governmental control foreseen by Sir Hugh Clifford was recognized by the new Education Code of 1926 for Southern Nigeria. Teachers were registered thereafter, and a school could not be opened unless the Director and Board of Education were satisfied that it would be properly staffed and conducted. The functions and duties of supervisors or mission inspectors were defined, minimum salary rates in assisted schools were laid down, and the grant-in-aid system was revised.

By 1929, there was an average attendance of nearly 60,000 pupils at the schools with which the government had a connection, while 81,000 were in unassisted schools. There were two government-operated and seventeen government-assisted secondary schools. The reluctance of parents to educate their daughters was already being gradually overcome, especially in the Yoruba areas, and about one-sixth of the school population were girls. There were 90 male students in four government teacher-training colleges, and 375 male and 41 female teachers were being trained in voluntary-agency (mission) institutions in the south. In the same year, there were 116 schools conducted by the government in the north, with the financial help of the Native administrations. The average annual attendance was just over 3,500 pupils in 95 elementary schools, 8 crafts schools, 12 primary (middle) schools, and 1 secondary school. By this time, the missions had 152 schools, of which only 5 were assisted. Some 30,000 Koranic schools had over 381,000 pupils.

Whereas the average attendance in the non-Koranic primary schools of Nigeria was 146,598 in 1929, the enrollment in 1950 was 970,768. The secondary-school population over the same period had grown from 634 to 28,430. In 1929, there were 506 teachers in training; by 1950, there were 6,000.

It was not until 1948 that the University College at Ibadan came into being, with 210 students in residence during its first year. This does not mean that there were no university graduates in Nigeria before that date, for several hundred received the final stages of their education at Fourah Bay College in Sierra Leone, or in Britain, Ghana, and the United States. Many obtained degrees by studying privately at home.

In 1925, a committee was appointed by the Secretary of State for the Colonies to "assist him in advancing the progress of education" in British tropical Africa. The ultimate goal implicit in the creation of this committee was self-government for the peoples of the territories concerned. The committee put forth thirteen broad principles in its "Memorandum on Education Policy in British Tropical Africa"; they can be summarized as follows:

1. Although educational policy will be centrally controlled, the government should cooperate with and encourage other educational agencies.

2. Education should be adapted to the mentality, aptitudes, occupations, and traditions of the various peoples, conserving as far as possible all sound and healthy elements in the fabric of African social

life and adapting them where necessary to changed circumstances and progressive ideas in the interests of natural growth and evolution.

3. Every effort should be made "to improve what is sound in indigenous tradition" in the important fields of religion and character training.

4. The crucial field of education should be made attractive to the best British personnel available.

5. Grants should be given to voluntary agency schools that satisfy the requirements.

6. The content and method of teaching in all subjects should be adapted to the conditions of Africa.

7. The rapid training of African men and women teachers is essential so that they will be "adequate in numbers, in qualifications, and in character."

8. Village schools should be improved by the use of specially trained visiting teachers.

9. Thorough inspection and supervision of schools should be enforced.

10. Technical industrial training should be given through an apprenticeship training in government workshops.

11. Additional vocational training should be given in and through government departments.

12. Particular attention should be paid to the education of women and girls.

13. An educational system should include "infant" (i.e., for children five to eight years old) and primary education; secondary education of all types; technical and vocational schools, some of which develop to university level in such subjects as teacher education, medicine, and agriculture; adult education.

These principles had as their ultimate target a goal that was only reached on October 1, 1960—the launching of Nigeria as an independent state. As T. O. S. Benson, Nigeria's Minister of Information, said in London in July, 1960:

> We have no fear that the trouble which has overwhelmed our neighbors in the Congo will be repeated in our country. As far back as fifty years ago, you in Britain were helping our people to come to your country for training in law, medicine, administration, science, and technology. The whole framework of democratic government has been firmly built. Britain recognized long ago that if you are going to hand over power, you must ensure that those receiving it understand their responsibilities and are trained to assume them.

The System During the Colonial Period

As in other British colonial dependencies, formal education in Nigeria was regulated at all stages by formal examinations. Sometimes these were given internally by the Department, sometimes externally by such bodies as the Cambridge University Examinations Syndicate or the University of London. Children about to leave the primary school took what was called the Standard Six examination—now called the Primary School Leaving Examination in some areas and the First School Leaving Certificate in others. In the early days of British rule, when very few children passed beyond the primary stage, the certificate awarded to those who passed the examination not only was outward and visible evidence of educational achievement, but also became a passport to the lower levels of white-collar employment and of escape from manual and agricultural pursuits.

If the child happened to be among the favored few who secured admission to one of the country's leading secondary schools, such as King's College, the next goal was "to pass my Cantab." The anxiety of the children who reached the short-list and interview stage had to be seen to bc believed. Despite the increase in the number of secondary schools over the years, there are still thousands of children competing for fewer than 100 places in each of these schools.

"To pass my Cantab." The tragedy of education in Nigeria is that it is still confused in the greater majority of minds with certificates. Although the West African Examinations Council has now taken over the business of running the grammar school's external examinations, and as a result the successful candidates are awarded a West African School Certificate (grades 1, 2, or 3), even now the goal is the *certificate*.

It is not difficult to see the reason for this. The Standard Six certificate was for many years the passport to a job. The Cambridge School Certificate gradually usurped its position, to be used by both government and commerce for exactly the same purpose. Now "my Cantab" is gradually giving way to such post-school certificate qualifications as the Cambridge Higher School Certificate and the General Certificate of Education, both still based on the English pattern. These are now the higher badges of prestige and potential economic betterment. In fact, it is easier today for a boy or girl with one of these qualifications to get a free university education than it is for a primary-school child to get a place in a trade center, technical institute, or grammar school—since an array of university scholarships is available annually to those formally qualified.

At the higher levels, the possession of a university degree is the mark of prestige and the key to a remunerative career. In a country where the supply of educated manpower is well below what is needed (except perhaps in certain arts subjects), the student with a degree has no difficulty in finding employment at about £700 per year to start; he is apt to have a car advance and a traveling allowance thrown in if he is a government employee. Certain commercial firms pay much higher starting salaries, especially for graduates in mathematics or science. Even so, it is difficult to persuade young men to accept employment with good career prospects early in life if they have an opportunity to pursue the golden fleece of higher studies.

Although progress is now noticeable in adjusting the educational system to the African milieu, the traditional external exam syllabus and the conservatism of the Africans themselves about changes in the educational pattern long delayed adaptation to the particular environment of Nigeria. For many years, any teacher who attempted to teach new subjects or aspects of traditional subjects that were not laid down in the School Certificate syllabus was likely to face immediate protests from the students themselves. Their eyes and minds were set on the certificate because it was synonymous with education. The press and the public have encouraged this attitude; the "best" school is the one with the highest percentage of successes in the annual examination. The next generally applied criterion is the school's performances in interschool sporting events.

Perhaps the most moving illustration of this point is to be found in Robert Wellesley Cole's *Kossoh Town Boy*.* This is the boyhood story of a Sierra Leonean surgeon, but the following passage could relate truthfully to a whole generation of West African children who are now adults:

> And so life at school continued smoothly, when suddenly a dispute arose in Freetown, starting as a rumour which in a few days swept the city like a forest fire. The dispute was simply this. Should the pupils of West Africa be allowed to sit for overseas examinations, set by bodies in the United Kingdom, or would they not be better off with local examinations framed to suit the "realities of local conditions"?
>
> Our Government Education Department proposed that the Cambridge and Oxford Senior Local Examinations should be discontinued, on the grounds that they dealt with matters foreign to African children and threw too great a strain on their minds. . . .
>
> It is difficult to appreciate now the depth of feeling which this proposal roused in the community. . . . In the end the government

* London and New York: Cambridge University Press, 1961.

issued an ultimatum. "We will see what happens at this year's Cambridge Local Examination and the matter will be reviewed after that. But in the light of previous years, unless there are definite signs to the contrary, local West African examinations will be introduced," they said. . . .

The results were not expected before the end of the following March or the beginning of April. As the time drew near, expectation mounted. The sword of Damocles hung over our heads. Bitterness increased. What was going to happen if the Government proceeded with this threat to take away from us this precious Cambridge Local Examination? It was generally realized that a local African examination, however difficult or high its standard, could never receive the same recognition in the outside world as a British one. We were a subject people, and our only chance of survival lay in maintaining these contacts with Cambridge and with Oxford, London, and Durham.

And then one Saturday morning, Father came home, and even I could tell that he had great news. Usually he was a very reticent man who kept his emotions under control. But this day, as he mounted the last few steps up the farm, he shouted for me; and as I came towards him wondering what was the matter, he told us the news.

I had passed. The Grammar School had done very well. All the boys entered by the school had passed, two with honours. Freddie Noah had a third class honours and I first class honours, the first ever in our history. Freetown was agog that week-end. We were saved.

This, then, is the picture of secondary education in West Africa when the author—the first African to be elected as a Fellow of the Royal College of Surgeons in England—was a boy of fifteen. It reveals the conservative attitude of West Africans themselves toward the idea of a change in the pattern and content of education at that time and some of the reasons for it. This attitude has undergone changes in the present generation, but the West African is still anxious to obtain qualifications which are universally acceptable.

The Present System

During 1959–60, a total of 2,944,330 school-age Nigerians were in school—1,929,857 males and 1,064,473 females. These figures may seem low for a country of 36 million, but they are by no means depressing in the African context. The government of the Eastern Region is now spending 48 per cent of its income on education, the Western Region 45 per cent, and the Northern Region 27 per cent. There are few countries in the world that can match these figures or the confidence in education as an investment revealed by them.

Almost 95 per cent of those in school in Nigeria are in primary schools (2,840,014). Since the 1954 transfer of policy responsibility to federal and regional ministers (all Nigerians elected democratically by their fellow Nigerians), the policy of free universal primary education has been introduced, first in the west and now over the whole of the south. A pilot scheme in Kano in the north may well herald extension of this rule to that area as well.

Several different approaches to primary education have been undertaken since 1954. The eight-year course, which was universal until then, is now used only in the federal territory. The Eastern Region has recently changed to a seven-year course; the Western Region has a six-year course; and the Northern Region has a four-year junior primary plus a three-year senior primary, which, unlike elsewhere in the federation, is not universal.

The content is similar in all regions, and major attention is paid to the three R's. The medium of instruction in the earliest years is usually the vernacular, but there is an increasing tendency to concentrate on English, and children must reach a satisfactory standard in English to pass the Primary School Leaving Examination. An eminent Nigerian educator, E. E. Esua, General Secretary of the Nigerian Union of Teachers and local representative of the World Confederation of the Teaching Profession, has referred to English as "the common language of the Commonwealth." Political leaders also realize its importance in a country where hundreds of different vernaculars are spoken, and present policy is to encourage by every possible means the use and improvement of the standard of English, both spoken and written, in Nigeria. Public libraries, unfortunately, are still few and far between.

Among other subjects generally found in the primary-school curriculum are handwriting, "religious knowledge," arithmetic, health, physical education, nature study and gardening, singing, history, geography, and handwork. In some areas, civics is included at the primary level, and various aspects of domestic science and simple general science are also taught. Each regional government provides an approved syllabus that is followed by all primary schools in the area concerned. Appended to the syllabus for each subject is a list of recommended textbooks. There is a reasonable choice, and, as far as is known, no regional ministry demands the exclusive use of any one book. The primary-school syllabus in all subjects is now keyed to the Nigerian background, and nearly all the textbooks are specially written for use in West Africa. The recommended list of books is revised from time to time by committees of professional men and women. Except in the north, these committees have been predominantly Nigerian for some years.

Secondary Education

At the post-primary level, children in the Western Region compete for places in grammar schools, trade centers, a technical institute, or secondary modern schools. These last schools are peculiar to the Western Region and provide a fee-paying three-year course that follows—for those who gain admission—the six-year primary course. In the secondary modern schools, the following subjects are taught: English, history, geography, rural science, domestic science, Yoruba, civics, art and craft, elementary mathematics, elementary commerce and bookkeeping, nature study and biology, woodwork, and light metalwork. The course is in many ways an extension of the primary course, and there are no graduate teachers in these schools.

Elsewhere, the pattern is similar, with some local variations. After the primary school, the children take a competitive entrance examination (to be changed as soon as improved selection tests can be devised) for the secondary (or grammar) schools. A smaller number take the entrance tests for the trade centers and technical institutes.

The secondary schools normally provide a five-year (or sometimes six-year) course leading to the West African School Certificate, the recognized equivalent of the old Cambridge School Certificate. There is, of course, a prescribed syllabus for this examination that can be taken in a wide variety of subjects. Principals of schools are free to devise their own courses leading up to the certificate and to choose their own textbooks. Guidance is given by professional experts in the respective ministries on request. English is the language of instruction throughout; in addition, some students take Latin, French, or one of the dominant vernaculars. All grammar schools provide courses in mathematics, history, geography, physical education, and "religious knowledge"; many offer a general science course; and a few provide separate courses in chemistry, biology, and physics in the last two or three years. Some girls' schools take domestic science up to West African School Certificate standard, and a number take art to the same level. Among subjects not taken for examination purposes, but gradually gaining popularity, are civics and citizenship and music.

About twenty-three of these secondary schools now provide, like the English grammar and "public" schools, a two-year post-school certificate course leading to the Higher School Certificate. Until this course was introduced at King's College, Lagos, less than ten years ago, it was impossible for anyone attending school there to obtain the minimum admission qualifications for a British university. Naturally enough, Nigerians are anxious for the extension of these facilities, and the expansion recommended some years ago by some British officials has now received the blessing of the Commission on Post-School Certificate and Higher Education.

Of the schools providing this two-year course, fewer than half have the staff or facilities yet to offer all the science subjects required. Three years ago, therefore, an Emergency Science School was set up in Lagos. Today, more than 500 students are taking mathematics and science subjects there at the advanced level of the London General Certificate of Education, which is academically equivalent to the "principal level" of Higher School Certificate. Most of those who leave obtain the qualifications necessary for university admission. Similar courses have been provided for some years for about one-third of the students at the three branches of the Nigerian College of Arts, Science, and Technology.

Teacher Training

Textbooks and teachers' guidebooks are today vastly superior to those in use a decade ago. They are written for specific use in Nigeria, and the authors, with very few exceptions, are educators who have spent years working in the country. Increasingly, Nigerians themselves are writing these textbooks, and the curriculum is being geared to Nigeria's needs and interests.

The most serious crisis is in the quality and quantity of teaching staff, and until this problem is solved, there can be no real progress in Nigerian education. Although the school population has risen astronomically in recent years—from 970,800 to 2,840,014 in primary schools in a decade—the teacher population is not keeping pace with the student growth. Over 70 per cent of Nigeria's teachers are untrained and lacking in certificates. More and better teacher-training colleges are part of the answer.* There are 319 small training colleges scattered throughout Nigeria, with an enrollment of some 27,000 students. But these training centers themselves suffer from a very severe shortage of qualified staff.

Teacher training in Nigeria is conducted at several levels. The first is a two-year course for elementary teachers at elementary (Grade

* The Ford Foundation announced in 1961 a contribution of $300,000 to the Nigerian Federal Government to help in the establishment of a model advanced training college in Lagos. Similar colleges are contemplated for each region.

3) teacher-training centers. Recruitment to these colleges is from candidates who have completed a full primary education and who have subsequently taught for two years as probationary teachers or attended a preliminary training center for one year. The second teacher-training level is higher elementary (Grade 2), also a two-year course. Recruitment is from holders of West African School Certificates or from Grade 3 teachers who have completed a minimum of two years of teacher training after qualifying for their Grade 3 certificate. There is also a straight four-year course for pupils with the entry qualifications for Grade 3 colleges.

A Grade 2 teacher is trained to teach up to the eighth year of a full primary school or in secondary modern schools in the Western Region. Owing to shortage of qualified staff, they are presently also employed as tutors in training colleges and as teachers in secondary grammar schools; in these institutions, they are completely out of their depth.

The third level is the Teachers' Senior (Grade 1) Certificate. Those eligible for the award of this certificate are qualified Grade 2 teachers who have taught for a minimum of five years (three years in the Western Region) and have passed two subjects at advanced level in the GCE examination. The candidates must also have satisfied the Regional Inspectorate in a practical teaching test.

Grade 2 teachers may qualify for a Grade 1 certificate in rural science or enter a three-year course for specialists in physical education. There are rural education centers in Ibadan, Umuahia, Bauchi, and Minna. The Nigerian College of Arts, Science, and Technology offers two certificate courses in teacher training: Teacher Training and Supervision (for which the entrance requirement is a Grade 2 certificate plus teaching experience), and Teachers Certificate for Secondary Schools. Entrance requirement for this course is the West African School Certificate. The third year of the course is devoted entirely to professional training. Normally, there is an annual output of fifteen to twenty teachers from each course. In 1958, there were 853 Grade 1 teachers in Nigeria.

Since nearly three-quarters of the primary teachers are inadequate in English themselves, it is hardly surprising that their pupils are at a serious disadvantage on this score. Thousands of very able Nigerian children are barred from advanced education because of their insufficient knowledge of English.

Another problem is the salaries of the teachers. Better prospects exist outside the profession, and the Nigerian teacher, whose family ties and obligations are more demanding than teachers in many other parts of the world, often succumbs to more remunerative employment. At present, the tendency in Nigeria is to place greater emphasis on fine buildings than on what is taught in the schools or on teacher training and incentives.

Technical Education

In the 1959–60 academic year, there were 1,587 Nigerian students at technical colleges in Britain taking general subjects as well as scientific and technical studies. There were an additional 8,000 pupils in Nigerian technical and vocational institutions at the secondary or higher level; most of the staff in these schools are expatriates, however, who are increasingly difficult to obtain and retain.

The Yaba Trade Center, near Lagos, is an outstanding example of Nigeria's technical-education program, so far limited to fewer than ten centers in the country as a whole. A three-year course is offered at the Yaba Center to boys who have completed their primary-school education and have passed the leaving examination. They are given initial aptitude tests devised by the principal at Yaba, and then take up courses designed to prepare them to become blacksmiths, bricklayers, cabinet-makers, carpenters, electricians, fitter-machinists, instrument machinists, motor mechanics, painters, plumbers, sheet-metal workers, or wood machinists. About 560 are normally in attendance at Yaba, and the courses and student population are similar in the other centers. Two-year on-the-job training in industry follows the course.

The Yaba Technical Institute offers four-year technical and commercial courses that include general education at GCE or West African School Certificate level. It also confers a post-school certificate in mechanical and electrical engineering, building construction, architecture, and printing. There are part-time day classes in art, printing, secretarial accountancy, and senior stenography; evening classes are conducted at the senior level in mechanical engineering, building construction, electrical installation, carpentry and joinery, commercial accounting, shorthand and typing, monotype keyboard, and bookbinding. Many of the courses lead to the examinations of the City and Guilds of London Institute. Shell-BP has recently given £500,000 to the federal government for the training of Nigerians from all parts of Nigeria in the intermediate grades at the Yaba Technical Institute.

In October, 1961, the new Ibadan Technical College opened with full-time courses in civil, mechanical, and electrical engineering. The college, built at a cost of about £318,000, offers courses framed to meet the standards and scope of the Ordinary National Certificate as now incorporated in the Ordinary Certificate of the City and Guilds of London Institute. Training in commercial subjects is also available to prepare students for careers in business administration and management. An Advisory Board insures cooperation with the Ministry of Education, public corporations, industry, and government departments in adjusting curriculum to the country's manpower needs.

The three regional branches of Nigeria's College of Arts, Science, and Technology, founded in 1952, are financed by the federal government. Of 1,123 students in the regional branches at Zaria, Ibadan, and Enugu, 394 are taking intermediate studies, predominantly in science. Engineering, education, pharmacy, fine arts, architecture, local government, government and administration, estate management, land surveying, stenography, and accounting are typical offerings. Most of the courses are recognized by the appropriate professional bodies in the United Kingdom. According to present plans, these institutions will eventually be absorbed into regional universities.

Agricultural Education

Although three out of every four Nigerians work on the land, agricultural and veterinary schools are still not popular with Nigerian students. Moreover, the majority of the graduates of these schools do not end up as farmers because the lot of a Nigerian farmer is not an appealing one and the trained agriculturist often finds a better-paying job only indirectly related to farming. Many "modern farmers" trained by dedicated staffs in the country's several post-primary agricultural training centers end up as teachers of rural science, as staff members in leper settlements, as overseers on large plantations, or in some other job offering status and income above that of a dirt farmer.

Approximately twelve young Nigerians are now receiving university degrees in agriculture annually at University College in Ibadan. The Veterinary Research Institute in Vom turns out thirty-five nondegree veterinary assistants and twelve laboratory technicians each year; the Agricultural Research Institute in Samaru graduates thirty-five nondegree agricultural assistants annually; the Moor Plantation School in Ibadan has an annual output of twenty-five agricultural superintendents and seventy-five agricultural assistants; the Umudike School in the Eastern Region turns out sixteen agricultural assistants each year; and the Forestry School in Ibadan produces about sixteen.

Higher Education

In 1948, a commission appointed by Britain to study higher education in West Africa concluded that "the need for highly trained Africans is too great to be met in any other way than by training them in their own country." As a result, University College was established in the Western Region at Ibadan in 1948.

University College degrees are awarded "in special relationship" with London University, which means that London grants the degrees and has full rights to determine examination schemes and to assess the candidates. There are five faculties at Ibadan: Arts, Science, Agriculture, Medicine, and Engineering. There were 1,136 resident students at the university in 1960–61, of which 1,057 were men and 79 women. The Nigerians among those enrolled included 537 from the Western Region, 452 from the Eastern Region, 95 from the Northern Region, and 9 from Lagos. Forty-two students were in the Institute of Education, which was established at the University College in 1956 to promote research in West African education and to train teachers and work with local training colleges. The engineering courses are actually given (for 144 students in 1960–61) at the Zaria College of Arts, Science, and Technology.

There is also an Extra-Mural Studies Department at Ibadan supported jointly by the federal government, the three regional governments, and the University College. With a full-time staff of ten and additional help on a part-time basis, it is attempting to provide instruction through tutorials and refresher courses to those who wish to improve their qualifications in various fields. In 1959–60, 153 classes were provided: 52 in the English language and literature, 37 in political science, 31 in economics, 13 in history, 11 in geography, 7 in French, 1 in German, and 1 in Yoruba. In all, more than 3,000 students were enrolled, and over half of these attended two-thirds of the classes. As the magazine *West Africa* noted, "This is a remarkable achievement by any standards, since the average class runs for twenty weeks." A typical class, in Warri, studying the "growth of the Nigerian economy," comprised three policemen, ten clerks, five teachers, one typist, one cashier, one transport manager, one bookseller, and one trader.

The federal government has now approved plans for the expansion of Ibadan. These include increased student accommodation at the university site and the introduction of new courses in Arabic, European modern languages, and geology. The announced policy of the

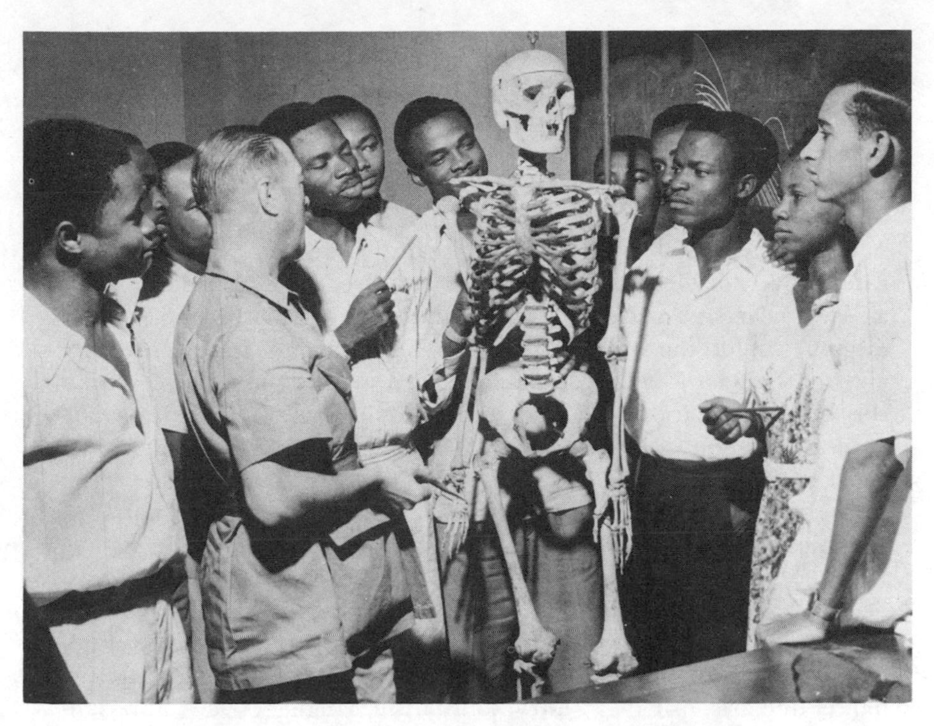

UNIVERSITY COLLEGE, AT IBADAN—MEDICAL STUDENTS.

TEACHERS TRAINING COLLEGE, AT ENUGU.

University College is to achieve academic independence. Dr. Kenneth Dike, a historian and scholar and the first African to be appointed principal of Ibadan, is seeking a charter for full university status by October, 1962, thus obtaining for Ibadan the right to establish its own syllabus and to confer its own degrees.

In October, 1960, the long-time dream of Nigeria's American-educated Governor General, Dr. Nnamdi Azikiwe, came to fruition when a new University of Nigeria was founded at Nsukka in the Eastern Region, under the joint sponsorship of Michigan State University and the Eastern Region Marketing Board, with some assistance from the U.S. International Cooperation Administration. Based on the plan of American land-grant colleges and initially headed by an American principal, Nsukka seeks to be "not only cultural, according to the classical concept of universities, but . . . also . . . vocational in its objective and Nigerian in its content."

Three hundred students were enrolled in three faculties—Arts, Science, and Engineering—for the first academic year, 1960–61. In 1961–62, enrollment was 800. Colleges or institutes of agriculture, architecture, commerce, domestic science, dramatics, education, finance, fine arts, fishery, forestry, journalism, languages, law, librarianship, medical-laboratory technology, pharmacy, physical education, music, secretarial studies, surveying, theology, and veterinary science are planned for the future. One of Nsukka's pressing problems is to improve its teacher-student ratio, for in 1960 there were only 15 faculty members for the 300 students. Like its sister university at Ibadan, Nsukka is coeducational. Although the University of Nigeria will grant its own degrees, the authorities of London University have given "assurance of cooperation if the University of Nigeria intends to negotiate special arrangements with that university."

Three other universities are likely within the next few years. The federal government has set 1962 as the target date for establishment of a new University of Lagos, which will initially offer law as well as economics and commercial subjects. The Western Regional Government intends to establish a new regional university, to be called the University of Ife, for which it will use only regional funds; a provisional council was set up in June, 1961. A provisional council has also been formed for the projected new university in the north, which reportedly will be called Ahmado Bello University. It will incorporate the Zaria College of Arts, Science, and Technology, the Ahmado Bello College at Kano, and several other existing institutions in the north.

In addition to the 1,100 students at the University College in

Ibadan, a similar number at the three branches of the Nigerian Colleges of Technology, and about 800 at the recently opened University of Nigeria, there are also several thousand Nigerians studying privately or on scholarships in Britain. Approximately 500 are in the United States, and a lesser number are at the University College of Ghana and Sierra Leone's Fourah Bay University. Some are in universities in Western Europe, and a few have found their way into Eastern Europe. Opportunities for Soviet-bloc scholarships will no doubt increase, as admission standards are low and other requirements appear to be adjusted to attract.

Special Education for Citizenship

The Man O' War Training Center, which was formerly operated by the Nigerian Government at Victoria, Southern Cameroons, was moved to Barakinladi in Northern Nigeria after the Cameroons became part of the new Federal Republic of Cameroon in 1961. The Training Center resembles the Outward Bound schools of Britain. It offers a noncredit course emphasizing citizenship and leadership training. Those who have attended have been drawn from all parts of Nigeria and the Cameroons and from all walks of life—government officials, students, teachers, clerks, business and commercial employees, police, and local-authority personnel. Applications have also come increasingly from Sierra Leone and Ghana as its reputation has grown. The intensive courses teach the skills of molding a nation—how to work together, to endure hardships, to conquer fear, to develop initiative, leadership, and responsibility. The staff is entirely expatriate.

Adult literacy centers are also being introduced at an increasing rate in various sections of Nigeria.

Political Attitudes of the Educated Nigerian

One of the results of an education that is closely geared to the requirements of external examinations has been that most of those who have experienced it have been conditioned to memorize rather than to think. The implications of this for life in a democratic community are obvious. One far-seeing Nigerian official, S. O. Awokoya, had this danger in mind when he introduced the teaching of civics and citizenship into the approved syllabus at the primary level in Western Nigeria during his tenure as Regional Minister of Education. For the first time in West Africa, a conscious attempt was made to train children to understand and practice the duties of active democratic citizenship. This idea has spread to other schools, both primary and secondary, during the last six years. It is by no means universal, but more and more youngsters are being taught the differences between the active and the passive citizen, why rates and taxes must be paid, how elections should be conducted, why the printed word is not necessarily the truth, how bribery and corruption can undermine a nation, the nature of religious tolerance, and the fallacy of racial prejudice.

Another disturbing feature of newly independent Nigeria is that the well-educated Nigerian tends to keep clear of politics. Some intellectuals do compete at the polls, and there are some very well-educated Nigerian ministers; but they are greatly outnumbered in the political arena by individuals who have not had a university education. It can be said that the members of the educated elite, a somewhat self-satisfied minority disinclined to risk their hard-earned academic reputation before the uncertain will of the untutored electorate, are the principal critics of the political drama but not yet the actors.

An article by a young Nigerian in the *West African Pilot* of November 25, 1960, points up the dramatic change that has taken place in the outlook of the young African of the new generation toward education. Femi Okunnu, educated at King's College, Lagos, in the 1950's and subsequently in England, is outspokenly critical of the period when the content of education followed very closely the English pattern, and argues that education "must be a conscious manifestation of the values and standards, history, and culture of the particular society." In his view, this does not preclude "borrowing from other communities in order to enrich what is ours," but he pleads for "Nigerianization of the curriculum," particularly in history. He endorses the view that "we must maintain a proper balance between the humanities and the sciences" and recommends a work-while-you-study program as a means of helping the student to appreciate the dignity of labor. Finally, "we must educate for citizenship" to develop a sense of "give" rather than "take" among those who have had educational opportunities not yet available to thousands of their fellow countrymen.

The key to the translation of these or other educational theories rests, of course, not merely with the policy-makers but also with the teachers. In every country in the world, it is the teachers who make the schools what they are. At the moment, those in the teaching profession who are prepared to work to bring about reforms are still few. Very few Nigerian teachers regularly read professional journals, and not more than twenty actually submit articles for inclusion in these journals, judging from the records kept by the editors of the *West African Journal of Education* and *The Nigerian Teacher* over the last two years. Only seven Nigerian educators submitted written evidence to the Ashby Commission on Post-School Certificate and Higher Education during 1959–60. Thus, the time has not yet arrived when the Nigerian members of the teaching profession are themselves concerned about educating public opinion on educational matters in their country.

Perhaps a final quotation will illustrate the gradual change of outlook concerning the content of education. It is taken from *Awo,* the autobiography of Chief Obafemi Awolowo.* He is speaking about the English principal of a missionary teacher-training college he attended:

> The Principal of the College in my time, the Rev. E. H. Nightingale, B.D., suffered a good deal of unjustified criticism. Essentially his view was that we should be proud of anything that was indigenous to us; our language, our culture and our style of dress. The official language in the classrooms and in the dining room was English. But in the College compound you could speak any language you liked so long as you were understood. It was believed that Mr. Nightingale fostered these policies in order to slow down our progress in the Western sense. I shared this view then, but I now think that he was a great pioneer. Practically all his critics are today doing precisely what he preached many years ago.

Outlook for the Future

A bold new approach to the problems of Nigerian education was sketched out in the 1960 report of the high-level international Commission on Post-School Certificate and Higher Education, appointed by the Federal Minister of Education in Nigeria in April, 1959. Under the chairmanship of Sir Eric Ashby, the Commission, composed of three Nigerian, three British, and three American educators, recommended a "massive, unconventional, and expensive" set of proposals that "will be practicable only if Nigerian education seeks outside aid and if the Nigerian people themselves are prepared to accord education first priority and to make sacrifices for it."†

The Commission's frame of reference was a projection of the

* London and New York: Cambridge University Press, 1960; p. 64.

† *Investment in Education, The Report of the Commission on Post-School Certificate and Higher Education in Nigeria* (London: St. Clements Press, 1960).

nation of Nigeria into the year 1980: a large country of some 50 million people, engaged in industrial and agricultural pursuits, and "a voice to be listened to in the Christian and Moslem worlds." The flow of high-level manpower that Nigeria will need over the next twenty years was the determining factor in the Commission's recommended alteration and expansion of the existing educational system.

In order to increase from 12,000 to 30,000 the number of children who can proceed beyond the primary level each year, it concluded, 600 additional secondary schools must be built and staffed. Indeed, the Commission calculated that it will be necessary to recruit enough teachers to man 7,000 classrooms for the next ten years. To give momentum while Nigeria expands and improves its own teacher-training facilities, the Commission recommends that a corps of expatriate teachers be imported on short-term contracts and that a group of Nigerians be sent overseas for teacher training.

At the university level, the Commission states that Nigeria's prime need is for four strong universities with a student population of well over 10,000 by the late 1970's. In addition to the universities at Ibadan and Nsukka, a new university at Lagos was proposed. The Lagos university would be linked primarily with business and commerce and would offer night classes and correspondence courses leading to a degree. The Commission endorsed the proposal to establish, as the fourth university, an institution of higher learning in the Northern Region, which, as has been indicated earlier, has had only a very limited exposure to the European educational system. The Commission also emphasized the tremendous importance of agriculture to Nigeria, pointing out that "seventeen shillings out of every pound earned from Nigerian exports come from agricultural products." The report calls for a large program of agricultural research and extension work, and courses in agriculture from the primary level upward.

In its Sessional Paper No. 3 for 1961, the Nigerian Government's Council of Ministers accepted the Ashby Report in principle and agreed that, with some amendments, its recommendations should serve as the basis for developments over the next decade. The amendments proposed do not question the principles of the Commission's extraordinary recommendation; indeed, they imply even greater capital and recurrent expenditures—and higher taxes. The sessional paper reaffirms the role of the English language in Nigerian education, noting that it will be "a vital instrument of communication" for many years, which dialectal differences "must not be allowed adversely to affect."

Where the Ashby Commission Report was cautious concerning the expansion of education in the Moslem north, the Nigerian Government's sessional paper "warmly welcomes" the introduction of universal primary education there and is "resolved to assist the Northern Regional Government" in placing half of its children of primary-school age in the classroom by 1970. In the area of secondary education, the government would establish federally supported national high schools as one step toward breaking down tribal and regional parochialism. Sixth-form work, which involves post–school-certificate studies, will be expanded with federal aid to permit 10,000 students to prepare for direct entry to universities by taking the Higher School Certificate examination. The revised target for the annual output of technicians is double the 2,500 suggested by the Ashby Report, and further expansion of facilities for agricultural, veterinary, and vocational education is also recommended.

In higher education, too, the government would like to go even further and faster than the Commission proposed. The target of 7,500 students enrolled in Nigerian universities by 1970 has been raised to 10,000 by that date. Besides the new university proposed by the Ashby Commission for the Northern Region and the projected university at Lagos (which the government now hopes to establish by 1962), the sessional paper endorses (as the Ashby Commission specifically did not) the proposal for a fifth university, at Ife, to be located in and financed by the Western Region.

Special emphasis will be given to the addition of faculties of agriculture in all regional universities, and "there must be" facilities for African studies at each as well. The government intends that existing branches of the Nigerian College of Technology should merge with regional universities in the north, in the east at Nsukka, and in the west. Although Nigerian universities will be autonomous, "national in outlook," and "enjoy academic freedom," the range of studies is "a matter on which the Inter-Regional Manpower Board and Universities Commission will exercise their influence."

If the program envisaged by the Ashby Commission could be described as massive, the revised objectives of the Nigerian Government must be categorized as colossal. The sessional paper contemplates an educational effort that can only be achieved with enormous effort and with outside injections of assistance to a degree never previously contemplated. The over-all cost of the Ashby Commission's plan for Nigeria's future educational system is estimated at between £12.5 million and £20 million by 1970, with an additional £20 million for the establishment of new universities.* The revisions proposed

* The British Government announced in July, 1961, a grant of £5 million ($14 million) toward the development of higher education in Nigeria.

by the government's sessional paper would raise the total of both of these figures significantly. For example, the burden for capital and recurrent expenditures on education below the higher level could reach £142 million by 1970. Moreover, this estimate of costs does not take into account a possible decline in the purchasing power of money, and may thus prove conservative.

—Reginald Bunting

26. Sierra Leone*

Capital: Freetown
Population: 2,500,000 (est.)
Area: 27,924 sq. miles
Political status: Independent dominion of the British Commonwealth

WESTERN education was instituted in Sierra Leone in 1787 (though Islamic education penetrated some Sierra Leonean tribes at a much earlier period) as a consequence of the activity of British philanthropic and missionary bodies. The first schools were established in a small area on the coast—what became, in 1808, the Colony of Sierra Leone (the adjoining hinterland became the Protectorate of Sierra Leone in 1896). The Colony was purchased by these British bodies for the settlement of manumitted slaves recruited from the streets of London, from North America (especially Nova Scotia), and, at a later period, from the West Indies. These repatriated slaves eventually became a community in themselves, separate and distinct from the indigenous tribes, and adopted the name Creole as their ethnic label.

As the British missions had intended, the Creoles monopolized the education that they provided, and they held this predominance well into the twentieth century. Thus, of the 300 pupils enrolled in mission schools in 1792, nearly all were Creoles. Similarly, in 1948, the Creole community (population 30,000) absorbed most of the 54 per cent share of government educational expenditure that the Colony claimed—as against 29 per cent for the Protectorate (population 2.25 million). Among the 55 per cent of school-age children in Colony schools, the majority were Creoles; in the same year, only 4 per cent of school-age children in the Protectorate were in schools. In 1827, the founding

* The material in this chapter was gathered in Sierra Leone with the aid of a research fellowship from the Ford Foundation.

of Fourah Bay College by the Church Missionary Society further enhanced the position of the Creoles; by the 1920's, some 548 students had graduated from the college, and many of them had gone to take a university degree in Britain. As early as 1854, a Creole was admitted to the British bar, and seven others were admitted between 1878 and 1890. By the mid-1920's, missionary education had provided Sierra Leone with 20 African senior civil servants (one of whom was an Assistant Colonial Secretary), a large number of clergymen, several journalists, 504 teachers, 700 clerks in private concerns, and 12 doctors. In this early period, Sierra Leone's educational progress compared favorably with that of Ghana (then the Gold Coast), where, by the mid-1920's, Western education had produced 60 lawyers, 14 doctors, 5 journalists, 66 clergymen, and 458 teachers.*

Through their positions in the professions, the church, and the colonial civil service, the Creoles were able to perpetuate their disproportionate share of education provided by missions and government until well into the twentieth century. For instance, their influence with the Church Missionary Society, which governed Fourah Bay College, was such that no Protectorate (that is, indigenous) Africans were enrolled until the 1920's; it was not until after World War II that the Protectorate obtained parity with the Colony at the college. The Creole educational and social predominance in the modern sector of society carried over into the political sphere. When Protectorate Africans finally entered modern politics in the postwar period, their overriding aim was to reduce their long-standing educational disadvantage vis-à-vis the Creoles. To this end, a few educated Protectorate Africans organized the Sierra Leone People's Party (SLPP)—whose leader and co-founder, Sir Milton Margai, was the first Protectorate African educated at Fourah Bay College. During its eleven years of political supremacy, the SLPP has made tremendous strides toward its goal.

Education During the Colonial Period

During the colonial period, education was not, for the most part, a systematic program; rather, it was as varied as the missionary bodies who were largely responsible for it. Before World War II, the main method of educational unification was through a system of government assistance to mission schools which provided that such schools meet certain teaching standards, building requirements, etc., before

* *Handbook of Sierra Leone* (London, 1925); *The Gold Coast Handbook* (London, 1928).

government assistance would be granted. In the postwar period, however, greater government control was extended over education, and a more coherent system began to appear.

At the primary level, the unified educational system that began to take shape in the postwar years consisted, in 1955, of some 421 schools. Although only 4 of these schools were directly administered by the colonial government and 34 by local government bodies (mainly district councils, but also Native authorities), 94 per cent of all primary schools received government assistance, which included partial, and in some cases full, payment of teachers' salaries. Some 25 per cent of primary schools were located in the Colony, where only 10 per cent of the population resided (as against 75 per cent in the Protectorate). Furthermore, within the Protectorate, the majority of primary schools were in the southern provinces and were therefore accessible mainly to the Mende tribe, the largest tribal group in Sierra Leone (about 800,000).

As for secondary schools, there were twenty-two in 1955, with an enrollment of 5,247 pupils; all but two were government-assisted schools, and six were wholly operated by the government. The Colony area, and within the Colony the Creole community, claimed a disproportionate share of secondary schools, twenty of them being located there and only two in the Protectorate. Moreover, the two Protectorate secondary schools were in the southern provinces, which meant that, along with the primary schools, they contributed to the Mende educational superiority over other indigenous tribes. All told, the primary and secondary-school enrollment in 1955 was 54,181, a figure that represented about 10 per cent of the school-age children. It should be noted, finally, that there were, in 1955, six teacher-training institutions, enrolling 498 students; two technical and vocational schools, enrolling 474 students; and one college, which enrolled 245 students (205 males, 40 females).

The course of study in the postwar colonial educational system was generally of a low caliber and was biased toward liberal arts to the neglect of vocational training in industrial and agricultural skills. At the primary level, the course of study covered a six-year period, being divided into Class 1 and Class 2—which were entered at the age of five to seven years—and Standards 1–4, with a few schools offering Standards 5–7. For most primary schools, Standard 4 was the point of entry into secondary school—upon the successful completion of the Common Entrance Examination—while in a few instances Standards 5, 6, and 7 were the level of entry into secondary school. Those entering secondary school from the latter standards proceeded with secondary training proper (that is, Forms 1 and/or 2) and were expected to be the ones who eventually embarked upon higher education; whereas those entering from Standard 4—constituting the majority of primary-school leavers—were required to spend one to two years taking preparatory courses in junior secondary schools. This requirement was a function of the generally poor standard of most primary schools and, as a consequence, very few of those pupils who entered secondary school in this manner ever proceeded to higher education.

The secondary course of study covered seven years and was divided into Forms 1–6, with Form 6 comprising two parts (B and A), lasting two years. Upon the completion of any of the six forms in secondary school, there were several levels of teacher, technical, and higher (that is, degree and professional diploma) training open to students. Those completing Forms 1–3 (as well as those completing Standards 6 and 7 in primary school but not proceeding to secondary school) could enter the two technical schools for vocational training in industrial and agricultural skills and the teacher-training schools to obtain the Teachers' Elementary Certificate (TEC) for primary teaching; those completing Forms 4–5 could enter the teacher-training schools for the Teachers' Certificate (TC) and the Teachers' Advanced Certificate (TAC) for secondary teaching; and those completing Forms 5–6 (B and A) could enter Fourah Bay College or overseas colleges for degree courses and professional diplomas, but first had to pass either the West African School Certificate (if they were Form 5 leavers), the Final Certificate (if they were Form 6B leavers), or the High School Certificate (if they were Form 6A leavers).

Although the formal structure of the foregoing system appeared adequate in relation to the British model upon which it was based, the substance of the system left much to be desired. The school facilities were generally poor and at times constituted a threat to the health and well-being of pupils. As the official *Report on the Development of Education in Sierra Leone* put it in 1948: "There is no wholly satisfactory [secondary] school building. In the few cases where the buildings were definitely erected for school purposes, surprisingly little attention was paid to ventilation and light. Many rooms are of an awkward and uneconomic shape, and doors have been placed in the wrong position. In one case the rented building used for a school is thoroughly bad." The quality and supply of schoolteachers was also inadequate to the task. As recently as a decade ago, most teachers were untrained, and in 1955, 42 per cent of the primary and 32 per cent of secondary teachers were untrained. Among the reasons for this situation were the relative lack of teacher-training institutions and the low requirements for admission, for, as noted above, one could enter teacher training upon completion of the upper-primary standards. Furthermore, teaching was not an attractive enough occupation—in terms of income, conditions of service, etc.—to compete with the professions, private industry, and the civil service for the better-educated people. As of 1955, teacher-training schools enrolled 498 students, only 20 per cent of whom were women. This relatively low proportion of women in teaching was related to another problem that plagued the whole colonial educational system —namely, the high rate of wastage in the primary and secondary schools, especially among female pupils. Thus, figures for 1954 show that there were 2,600 boys and 800 girls in Standard 1; 1,700 boys and 250 girls in Standard 4; and 1,050 boys and 150 girls in Standard 5. At the secondary level, the rate of wastage in 1954 was 75 per cent.

Another limitation of the colonial educational system was the lack of emphasis in school curricula on science and technical training, although Sierra Leone was overwhelmingly agricultural and could expand its economy only if persons trained in the technology of modern agriculture—as well as in certain industrial skills, since iron and diamond mining were major contributors to government revenue —were available. In 1948, there was "a widespread fear in the farming community that education . . . tends to discourage the children from remaining on the land when they grow up . . . [and farmers, therefore, regard] the schools with some degree of suspicion." * Furthermore, figures for 1955 show that only two of the secondary schools had science teaching at Sixth Form level, there were only two secondary schools whose main orientation was vocational (they enrolled only 8 per cent of secondary pupils), and at the post-secondary level Fourah Bay College offered only preliminary courses in science.

Post-Colonial Education

Although Sierra Leone's actual post-colonial period did not commence until April 27, 1961—the date of its independence—Prime Minister Sir Milton Margai and the governing Sierra Leone People's Party had exercised a large measure of internal self-government since 1957, and one can therefore date the end of the colonial control over education at this time. Since 1957, there has been a significant advance in both the quality and extent of the educational system in

* Report on the Development of Education in Sierra Leone (1948), p. 4.

Table 1
Enrollment in Primary and Secondary Schools, 1959

Type of School	Primary enrollment				Secondary enrollment			
	Number	Male	Female	Total	Number	Male	Female	Total
Government	2	339	140	479	8	1,479	71	1,550
Local government	53	6,402	2,736	9,138	—	—	—	—
Aided schools	468	39,814	20,998	60,812	18	2,801	1,707	4,508
Unaided schools	27	2,445	1,607	4,052	2	441	309	750
Total	*550*	*49,000*	*25,481*	*74,481*	*28*	*4,721*	*2,087*	*6,808*

Sierra Leone as indicated by the 1959 data shown in Table 1. By 1959, there were some 578 schools (as against 443 in 1955), of which 550 were primary schools (as against 421 in 1955) and 28 secondary schools (as against 22 in 1955). An even greater advance occurred in school enrollment during the post-colonial period—there being 81,289 pupils in 1959 (as against 54,181 in 1955), 74,481 of whom were in primary schools (as against 48,934 in 1955) and 6,808 in secondary schools (as against 5,247 in 1955). Equally striking, and of basic political significance, was the relative increase in the educational position of the Protectorate as against the Colony. Whereas in 1952 there were 16,345 pupils in primary schools in the Colony and 22,521 in the Protectorate, the Colony enrollment in 1959 had increased to 21,334; primary-school enrollment in the Protectorate had more than doubled—to 49,095.* And at the secondary level, data for 1958 show that of twelve new schools planned for completion by the early 1960's, ten will be in the Protectorate. Completion of this plan will give the Protectorate fifteen secondary schools, as against twenty-five for the Colony. The post-colonial period has also seen an expansion of teacher-training facilities: by 1959, there were six training institutions for teachers, enrolling 615 students; both the physical plant and enrollment of Fourah Bay College also advanced during this period.

Concomitant with the quantitative advance of the educational system in the post-colonial period has been an extension of government control and direction of the system. Indeed, the quantitative advance was a direct function of this extension—as indicated, for instance, in the increase of government-assisted primary schools from 396 in 1955 to 523 in 1959. Prior to 1958, the central colonial government attempted to expand educational facilities through a policy

* *Annual Report of the Education Department, 1952,* pp. 20–22; *Education Statistics, 1959,* p. 9.

that required major capital and financial contribution on the part of local government bodies. For instance, it was provided that the more developed local authorities (such as Bo District Council, Kenema District Council, and Freetown City Council) should contribute 40 per cent of teachers' salaries, taking the form of a refund by local authorities to the central government. This arrangement proved unworkable, however, for a variety of reasons, among which was the inefficient and uneconomic structure of local government units and the system of local finance—a situation that party politics has helped to perpetuate.

Accordingly, the government abolished the requirement for local contributions to teachers' salaries in January, 1959, and assumed full responsibility for them. It also assumed responsibility for 75 per cent of all capital grants toward expansion of primary schools, leaving to local authorities, as their share of the cost of primary education, responsibility for all expenditures on consumable equipment and maintenance of school buildings. Nevertheless, missions have continued to play a major role in the educational system. A recent White Paper on education noted that the government "fully appreciates that more than half the existing primary school accommodation in Freetown is already provided by the Churches . . . but desires the further cooperation of the missions in the effort to provide for . . . an additional 20 classrooms to absorb some 600 children." *

Sierra Leone's educational system has also been restructured since 1957. The levels of primary education were renamed "classes" instead of "standards," and the former eight-year course consisting of two classes and six standards was replaced by a seven-year course, at the end of which the Common Entrance Examination is taken. Automatic promotion from one standard to the next was abolished in 1958, and henceforth the decision of ability to proceed was to be taken by head teachers on the basis of formal examinations and other criteria. As a general rule, it was stipulated that a child who began primary classes at five years of age and had not completed them at the age of fourteen would be required to leave. This rule has not been actively applied, however, partly because the government added a proviso to it stating that "regulations based on age will not . . . be rigidly applied at this stage of the country's educational development."

Changes in the structure of the secondary schools went somewhat beyond those made at the primary level. Steps were taken to reduce the high rate of wastage in upper forms that prevailed during the

* *White Paper on Educational Development* (1958), p. 4.

colonial era (a 75 per cent rate in 1954). Whereas in 1955 the proportion of pupils in Form 4 was 27 per cent of Form 1 and those in Form 5 were 18 per cent of Form 1, by 1959 the proportion of pupils in Form 4 was nearly 50 per cent of those in Form 1 and pupils in Form 5 were 30 per cent of Form 1. This reduction was attained partly by restricting pupils in the grammar secondary schools from entering teacher-training institutions until completion of Form 4, whereas earlier they could embark upon teacher training from Forms 1–4. The structure of the secondary system has also been radically altered to handle more adequately the different aptitudes among pupils for academic or literary education as against technical education. Thus, three types of secondary schools have been provided during the post-colonial period: the grammar school, the technical-commercial-domestic school, and the secondary modern school.

In 1959, eleven of the twenty-eight secondary schools were grammar schools, the only one of the three types to provide six forms. The technical-commercial-domestic school provided just enough academic content to allow a few students to attain the School Certificate, but was primarily instituted, in the words of a government report, "to meet the needs of boys and girls with a practical turn of mind . . . [and] give a general education related to one or another of the main branches of industry (including agriculture) or commerce." By 1959, one such secondary school had been established in association with the Freetown Technical Institute, and others are projected as the pace of industrial and agricultural development requires. The third category, the secondary modern school, also provided technical training, but did not offer enough academic education to allow its students to seek the School Certificate. Generally, the pupils were recruited from those in the senior primary courses (classes 6 and 7) who had failed admission to grammar or technical schools. Some were also recruited from the junior secondary schools. There are now two secondary modern schools, others are projected, and the government intends eventually to develop a sort of "amalgamated" secondary school that would offer, under one roof, grammar, technical, and modern subjects.

The supply and caliber of teachers is another area in which progress has been made during the post-colonial period. As a result of the government's expansion of the number and output of teacher-training institutions, the supply of teachers grew rapidly between 1955 and 1959—from 1,851 to 2,521. If the 1958 proposals to build 155 new schools and 1,000 new classrooms by 1963 are to be achieved, however, at least 2,000 teachers have to be trained, which means an annual output of about 460. The decline in the wastage of pupils in primary and secondary schools, which has been particularly striking among female pupils since 1955, will favorably affect the supply of teachers, and the general restructuring of the educational system during the post-colonial period will undoubtedly improve the caliber of teachers. Whereas, in 1955, 42 per cent of the primary and 32 per cent of the secondary teachers were untrained, these percentages had dropped to 38 per cent for primary and 26 per cent for secondary teachers by 1959. And while 88 per cent of the secondary teachers in 1955 could claim some secondary education, the proportion increased to 98 per cent by 1959.

Higher Education

Like the rest of the educational system, higher education has registered important gains during the post-colonial period. These gains have centered around Fourah Bay College, which became the University College of Sierra Leone in 1960. At that time, its principalship passed from the hands of an able Englishman, J. J. Grant, to those of a brilliant African, Dr. Davidson Nicol.* As has been the case with the development of the whole educational system in Sierra Leone, the progressive evolution of the University College has been a direct function of greater government responsibility for its finances, which at present is nearly complete, except for capital-construction grants from the Colonial Development and Welfare Fund in the amount of £50,025.†

The SLPP has played a crucial role in the expansion of the college's student body, for its scholarship scheme brought about a marked increase in student enrollment—from 245 in 1955 to 328 in 1959 (the 1960 enrollment was 302). The government's scholarship scheme has also enabled Sierra Leonean students to obtain, for the first time, parity (or near-parity) in numbers with Nigerian students at the college. Ever since the college's founding more than a century ago, admission has been open to all West Africans (particularly British West Africans), and Nigerians and Ghanaians have normally predominated in the composition of the student body—with the ironic

* Dr. Nicol received his B.A., First Class Honors, Natural Sciences Tripos, at Cambridge University in 1946; an M.A. and M.B. at the same institutions in 1951; and an M.D. and Ph.D. at the University of London, 1956–58. He was the first African to be a don at Cambridge (Christ College), where he held the Beit Memorial Research Fellowship in 1954 and the Benn Levy University Studentship in 1955, and was Fellow and Supervisor of Studies in Natural Science and Medicine, Christ College, in 1957–58.

† *Development Estimates, 1960–61* (Freetown, 1960), p. 24.

Table 2
Analysis of Student Body of University College, 1960

Faculty	Students by nationality			Students by sex		Total
	Nigerian	Sierra Leonean	Gambian	Male	Female	
Arts general degree	41	73	2	91	25	116
Education	5	7	–	8	4	12
Economic studies	53	32	2	85	2	87
Science general degree	52	25	–	75	2	77
Applied science	–	7	–	7	–	7
Theology	–	3	–	3	–	3
Total	*151*	*147*	*4*	*269*	*33*	*302*

SOURCE: *Memo from Principal's Office* (November 16, 1960).

result that Sierra Leone, a much poorer country than either Nigeria or Ghana, has subsidized an important part of its neighbors' higher education.* By 1959, however, government policy had altered this situation to the point where Sierra Leonean students had a slight majority (179 Sierra Leoneans and 149 foreign Africans, mainly Nigerians), and the 1960 composition of the student body (shown in Table 2) was 147 Sierra Leoneans, 151 Nigerians, and 4 Gambians. Furthermore, government finance has helped to increase the number of students pursuing higher education overseas, mainly in Britain. Thus, between 1943 and 1949, only 87 government scholars were sent overseas; in 1949, there were 49 such students; and in 1958, the number of overseas government scholars stood at 179.† Moreover, these full government scholarships, combined with government aid to private students, have augmented the total number of overseas students from fewer than 400 in 1950 to 1,010 in 1958.

Both the quality and scope of higher education at the University College have improved markedly over the colonial period, when British missionaries—often poorly trained for college teaching—dominated the faculty, and when the arts, particularly theology, dominated the curriculum. Again, government assistance has facilitated this change, with the intent of bringing Sierra Leone's higher education more adequately in line with the needs of a developing nation. "My idea of the purpose of the College," wrote Dr. Nicol recently, "is for it to train men to fill positions of service and leader-

* Cf. K. A. Jones-Quartey, "Sierra Leone's Role in the Development of Ghana," *Sierra Leone Studies* (June, 1958).

† *Report to the Committee Set Up to Consider the Appointment of Africans to the Senior Service of Government (1949)*, pp. 5–6; *Annual Report of the Education Department* (1958), p. 18.

ship in Sierra Leone in all walks of life, in the government, in commerce and industry, in the Church, in education and in local government." * In 1960, the faculty of seventy-seven university-trained members† were divided among six areas of study: applied science, science, economic studies, education, arts, and theology. Moreover, through the administration of scholarship aid to students—nearly all Sierra Leoneans at the University College receive aid—the government has influenced their concentration in science and economic studies (including public administration) rather than the arts. Thus, as shown in Table 2, 56 per cent of the students were enrolled in science and economics in 1960, and 43 per cent of the Sierra Leonean students were so enrolled. Similarly, of the 179 overseas government scholars in 1958, 72 per cent were pursuing science subjects (fifty-nine in engineering, twenty-four in science, thirty-three in medicine, four in architecture, three in agriculture.)‡

Future advancement of the quality and scope of higher education at the University College will undoubtedly depend, in large measure, upon the government's capacity to finance it, and this in turn must depend upon economic growth and expansion in the country generally. Under the imaginative direction of Dr. Nicol, however, the University College is already seeking means of supplementing government sources. The university's approaches to foundations in the United States and to African and expatriate firms in Sierra Leone for funds had already netted some £60,000 by mid-1961.

The Outlook

Among the several trends worth noting by way of conclusion, the expansion of government control over education during the post-colonial period is of prime significance. Without the stimulus provided by the SLPP government (which was first elected in 1951, but did not obtain real internal control over education until 1957), there would not have been the rapid quantitative and qualitative advances in the educational system of the past five years. Yet, much remains to be done before Sierra Leone's education is adequate to the needs of a developing country, for literacy is still little more than 5 per cent if English is used as a criterion and 10 per cent in terms of vernacular

* Davidson Nicol, *Comments on the University College of Sierra Leone* (mimeographed; Freetown, November 11, 1960), p. 2.

† Of these seventy-seven faculty members, forty-eight were from Britain, and nineteen were Sierra Leoneans; the remainder came from Egypt, Ceylon, India, Holland, Germany, Ghana, and New Zealand.

‡ *Annual Report of the Education Department, 1958,* p. 18.

languages. Prime Minister Margai's government is fully aware of this and has recently elevated the proportion of government expenditure used for education from one of the smallest budgetary items in the early 1950's to 16 per cent. In 1959–60, it was second only to security (police and military) expenditures, which were about 20 per cent.*

Politically, the SLPP's emphasis upon educational advancement is central to its *raison d'être,* for from the beginning its leaders have seen education as a major tool in breaking down Creole superiority. Education was what enabled the small Creole community to secure its dominant position and what Protectorate Africans needed if they were to overthrow it. The SLPP has now virtually won its educational as well as social and political struggle against the Creole community, although, ironically, both the older generation of educated Protectorate Africans who lead the party (the median age of SLPP leaders is fifty-three) and the educated postwar generation now mirror many of the attitudes of the Creoles against whom their politics have been directed. Thus, such Creole traits as Anglophilia, political conservatism, Christianity (especially among the educated Mende†), preference for European dress, and disrespect for the masses have been adopted by the Protectorate educated elite. There are several reasons for this development. First, it was educated Creoles who, through their positions in the colonial civil service, mission schools, and churches, acted as a medium of acculturation in Sierra Leone's hinterland. The SLPP's political conservatism and aristocratic views, on the other hand, are partly a function of the social origin of the Protectorate educated elite, for many of them are related to traditional rulers. The first medical doctors among the Mende and Temne (the two largest tribal groups) were nephews of chiefs (Sir Milton Margai and Dr. John Karefa-Smart), as were the first two lawyers among these tribes (Albert Margai and I. B. Kamara).

One probable consequence of the political and social conservatism characteristic of both the Protectorate and Creole educated element is that this elite, whose members also constitute the political elite of the country, is not likely to be very receptive to demands of an increasingly self-conscious peasant and laboring mass for a greater share of political power or the benefits of economic development.

* *Sierra Leone Government Estimates, 1959–60,* pp. 21–24, 34–36.

† For instance, most of the Mende in the Cabinet are Christian: Sir Milton Margai, Prime Minister; Albert Margai, Minister of Natural Resources; A. J. Demby, Minister of Lands and Mines; Doyle Sumner, Minister of Communication; and R. B. S. Koker, Minister without Portfolio.

This trend toward solidification of the elite is demonstrated by the merger, just before independence, of the governing SLPP with the opposition People's National Party and the United Progressive Party, leaving no political parties outside the governing group except the small All People's Congress.

—Martin Kilson

Part VIII

FRENCH-SPEAKING EQUATORIAL AFRICA

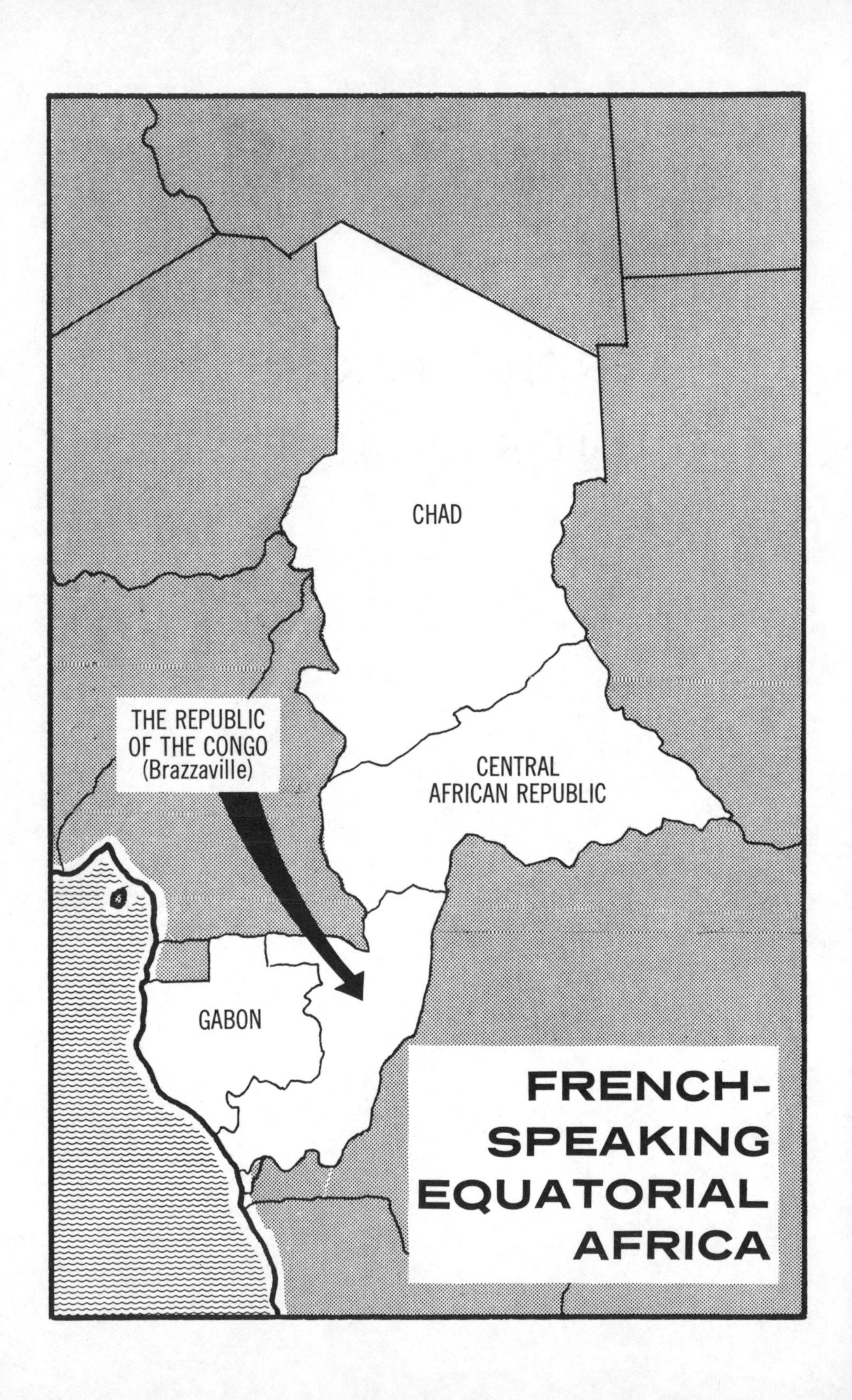
CHAD
THE REPUBLIC
OF THE CONGO
(Brazzaville)
CENTRAL
AFRICAN REPUBLIC
GABON
FRENCH-
SPEAKING
EQUATORIAL
AFRICA

27. General Trends in French-Speaking Equatorial Africa

THE territory formerly known as French Equatorial Africa (A.E.F.) comprises four countries: the Congo Republic (formerly known as Moyen Congo), Chad, Gabon, and the Central African Republic (formerly known as Oubangui-Chari). Formerly administered by France as a federation, it is one of the most economically underdeveloped and culturally diverse areas of the African continent. Together, the four nations are nearly one-third the size of the United States, and they embrace a wide range of climatic, topographical, and tribal variations; yet, their total population is only a little over 5 million, including fewer than 30,000 Europeans. Although each of the states became independent in 1960, their ties to France and to each other remain close.

French educational aims and policies were similar in the four territories, although the resulting levels of education vary considerably from one to another, with Gabon and Congo attaining the highest level. Nevertheless, the similarity of purpose, organization, and administration would seem to justify an initial examination of A.E.F. as a whole; subsequent chapters will deal with the differences and specific internal considerations.

Mission Education

The first schools in French Equatorial Africa were founded by Catholic missionaries at Libreville, Gabon, in 1845. The Protestant mission schools, first American and then French, spread at the end of the nineteenth century to lower Gabon and Moyen Congo (Middle Congo). They were and continue to be important, but have never been as numerous or as sympathetically regarded by the French administration as the Catholic ones. Neither group seriously attempted to install itself in the Central African Republic or Chad until well into the twentieth century; and the majority of the mission schools are still centered in Gabon and Congo.

France acquired Moyen Congo under the 1885 Berlin Treaty agreement, which divided much of Africa among several European powers. Treaties of friendship were subsequently concluded between the French and the chiefs of Gabon and Congo. The Central African Republic and Chad were acquired later, partly through military force. A central administration was not established over all four territories until after 1910.

Except for a few provisos requiring that teaching be in the French language, and that organizations supporting schools be legally incorporated in France and guarantee "an absolute preponderance of French influence in a French country," the missions were left relatively free to organize education as they wished until after World War II. The only concession to use of the vernacular language was in religious instruction.

A 1925 regulation required mission schools to follow the same curriculum as state schools if they wanted to qualify for official recognition and official subsidy. Even with the growth of government schools after World War II, subsidies continued to be provided to both Catholic and Protestant missions. Although the basic pay and privileges of mission-school teachers were established in 1950 at a rate considerably less than those of the public-school teachers, these have been more or less equalized by special subsidies. Mission schools have continued to grow in number and size in all territories: 112,047, or 43 per cent of the students receiving primary education in Equatorial Africa, were attending mission schools in 1960.

As government education programs have increased, the proportion of money allocated to mission schools has decreased. Although more than half the children attending schools in Gabon in 1960 were in mission schools, for example, the government allocated to mission schools less than 30 per cent of its total education budget. Chad, which has a larger Moslem population than the other states, allotted less than 5 per cent of its education funds for mission support. On the whole, however, the relationship among the French administration, the territorial governments, and the missions in the education field has been one of cooperation.

Postwar Aims

The Brazzaville Conference, organized in 1944 on the initiative of the Governor-General of A.E.F., Félix Éboué, a Negro from French Guiana, provided the impetus and laid out the plans for the subsequent political, economic, and educational development of French Equatorial and West Africa. Over-all educational aims were promulgated for the first time. These included: (1) to reach and penetrate the masses, and teach them a better way of life (i.e., the civilizing mission); (2) to select and train an elite—those capable of forming higher social or economic groups—to man the lower-level administrative posts in the government; (3) to form at least one class in each village with fifty children of school age; (4) to stress equally the education of girls and that of boys; (5) to teach in French; (6) to adapt the primary-school curriculum to local needs; (7) to maintain free education, open to all regardless of race, creed, or sex; (8) to work toward universal compulsory primary education; (9) to develop a network of secondary and technical schools in each territory, equal in every respect to those in France; and (10) to provide opportunities for higher study in France by qualified Africans.

France's Investment Fund for Economic and Social Development of the Overseas Territories—known as FIDES until 1959, when it was reorganized and renamed the Fund for Aid and Cooperation (FAC)—allocated several million dollars to implement these resolutions in its first four-year development plan, 1947–51. Most of this was earmarked for secondary education, which had been largely ignored in A.E.F. until after World War II. In its second and third development plans, FIDES has also assisted education in Equatorial Africa, both public and private.

As late as 1939, French Equatorial Africa was allocating little more than 1 per cent of its budget to education. This rose to 4.2 per cent in 1946 and to 5.4 per cent in 1954, and has averaged not less than 12 per cent since 1955. Financial responsibility for the primary schools was transferred to the individual territories in 1947. Congo has assigned the largest proportion of its budget for education (up to 26 per cent), and Chad the smallest (12.5 per cent in 1960). The total spent in 1960 for education in Equatorial Africa, including FIDES and other grants (but not including scholarships for study in France), was about $9 million. The European Fund for Development (part of EEC) has contributed another $1 million for professional, commercial, and rural primary education, to be used during the next several years. UNESCO, in 1960, provided $10,000 for technical education. In addition, the French Government pays all or part of the salaries of a number of the French secondary- and technical-school teachers. In general, recurrent costs of education are paid from the budgets of each state, while nonrecurrent costs have been paid partly by the government and partly by outside grants and loans (FIDES, FAC).

The Aims of French Educational Policy

One apparently overriding aim, probably both conscious and unconscious, of France in Africa has been the integration of the African into French culture and the establishment of French institutions, values, and culture in Africa. This did not necessarily imply a disrespect for African traditions, but rather reflected the unfaltering conviction of most Frenchmen that French culture is superior to all others.

The efforts to inculcate French traditions into the educational system were indicated in the guarantee required by the missions to further French influence; in the requirement that school standards and curricula parallel those of metropolitan France; and in the continuing insistence that priority be given to French teachers. It was also stoutly maintained that the exclusive use of the French language from the beginning of school was the only practical method of teaching, even if students had more difficulty studying in French and therefore took longer than their European counterparts to complete their courses. Several reasons were given: (1) There are too many tribal languages, few of which are written or contain abstract or technical vocabulary suitable for academic subjects. (2) It would be difficult and expensive to train staff and print books in a large variety of vernacular languages. (3) Facility in French would enable qualified students to continue working in specialized fields, to seek employment in a wider range of jobs, and to communicate with many more people than would be possible with any vernacular language.

This policy of integration, which went so far as to place Africans in the French National Assemblies, was radically different from other colonial patterns in Africa. Nowhere else were Africans included in the institutions of the colonial country and, moreover, encouraged to discuss problems other than those related to their own areas.

Administration

Before World War II, there were only fifty European instructors in French Equatorial Africa, mostly in administration. A.E.F. was divided into educational districts (called *secteurs scolaires),* each headed by a director charged with touring a district, often dispersed over hundreds of kilometers, to supervise the usually poorly trained African monitors teaching in the rural areas. This system was organized in the mid-1930's in an effort to raise the level of rural-school teachers, who, in the words of the then Governor-General, had "shown themselves unable to teach almost anything." Emphasis was placed on vocational, agricultural, and manual training. This was resented by many Africans, who felt that a lack of attention to secondary education and the creation of a primary curriculum different from that of France would hold back African advancement. Evidence that the educational system was inadequate to meet local demands is seen in the initiative of villagers in Congo and Gabon who built schools and raised money to pay monitors because the government had not provided them.

After the war, Governor-General Éboué set up educational advisory boards at both federal and territorial levels, and endeavored to strengthen the General Inspectorate of Education of A.E.F. by appointing territorial inspectors, who were usually teachers in the secondary schools. This system, based on the *secteur scolaire* organized before the war, was intrinsically inefficient and diverted a number of the few well-trained teachers into administrative work. It was only when additional teaching staff were recruited from Europe—with difficulty and at considerable cost—that the inspectorate became a specialized branch of the education service and European teachers could return to their teaching.

The establishment, in 1946 and 1947, of elected territorial and federal assemblies, with power over budget allocation, resulted in frequently vigorous examination and criticism of existing educational policies and programs.

Each country has had its own ministry of education for more than a decade and had developed its own policy and budget for education long before actual independence. In each of the countries, there is an inspector of education who heads the administrative machinery of education. Informal coordination takes place among the territories, however, and their autonomous educational systems are similar in that all continue to follow the French system and prepare for French exams. The bilateral agreements signed by France and each of the four countries at the time of independence provide for joint French-African decisions on higher education and a maintenance of French standards if French teachers are to be recruited.

Primary Education

To obtain a certificate of primary studies, a student must complete six years of schooling and pass a final standardized examination; this does not automatically admit him to secondary school, however, since he must pass a separate entry examination. The first two years of primary education are often referred to as preparatory, the second two as elementary, and the last two as upper. Schooling is free; attendance is not compulsory (except in those few areas where there are nearly enough schools to accommodate all the children). The drop-out rate is high. In part, this is because there are simply not enough schools that go beyond the first two or three years. Even as late as 1958, the average number of grades per school was less than three. Thus, only a few thousand of the many who begin primary school actually complete the six-year course. Present development plans emphasize expanding existing schools to include the higher primary grades, rather than building more schools.

Primary education has expanded rapidly in all territories since the end of World War II. At the beginning of the war, there were approximately 25,000 children in primary school, more than two-thirds of whom attended mission schools.* By 1951, the number had risen to 93,462. By 1960, there were 265,000 students in the primary schools of the four territories. Roughly 28 per cent of school-age children in Equatorial Africa are now believed to be in school. This percentage varies greatly from country to country, however; in Congo, some 65 per cent of school-age children have been in school, while in Chad the percentage is only about 11 per cent. But this is a decided improvement over the figure of 3 per cent for 1939.

The increase in school attendance is due not only to an increase in supply of schools, but also to an ever increasing demand for education. When schools were first introduced, there was often either apathy or resistance to attending. But when the commercial value of education became apparent—the fact that a man could earn more if educated—the demand for schools grew. Nowadays it is not unusual

* An official 1954 report evaluating educational accomplishments in French overseas territories cited a number of factors that had limited school attendance. These included the dispersed population, great distances, lack of transportation and communication, the inaccessability of some areas for long periods because of weather conditions, lack of resources and personnel, and the conservative traditions of the people. Also, the French in some cases deliberately limited the number who could receive more advanced education, on the basis that only those who could be employed should be educated.

to see young boys at night seated under public lampposts, studying their lessons.

Education for Girls

Education for girls was initially resisted as inconsistent with tradition and as having no useful purpose. However, from a total of 3,700 girls in school in 1939 (almost all in mission schools), female enrollment rose by 1958 to more than 45,000 girls in primary schools, or approximately 23 per cent of the total primary-school population. Over-all, girls now account for close to a quarter of school enrollment, but the proportion varies considerably, from Gabon, where roughly a third of the students in primary school are girls, to Chad, where Moslem conservatism keeps the proportion to about 10 per cent.

Teacher Training

The vast majority of teachers in the primary schools are Africans. In theory, primary-school teachers must have either the *certificat d'aptitude pédagogique* (CAP), a diploma awarded for a one-year professional teacher-training course following the completion of the full seven years of secondary education, or the assistant teacher's certificate (BEPC), received upon completion of a four-year secondary course following primary school. But actually, the majority of primary-school teachers in Equatorial Africa have neither the CAP nor the BEPC. They are monitors—students who attended secondary school, but did not reach the point of taking even the first examination. As of 1957, for example, only about 7 per cent of the teachers in Gabon and Chad had attained the qualifications of instructor (holder of CAP). Of 4,575 teachers in the primary schools in 1960, probably not more than 25 to 30 per cent were trained beyond the stage of monitor.

The problem is not one of numbers, for the profession of teaching is a respected one, and there is no shortage of candidates. Rather, it is one of training. In 1958, there were twenty-four teacher-training schools in A.E.F., attended by 1,623 students. This was not enough to fill even existing openings, and so teachers without diplomas have continued to be used. Moreover, classes are often very large: It is not unusual in some areas for a teacher to have a class of seventy-five or more students, and even to have a double shift, teaching one class in the morning, another for the afternoon. Books and teaching materials are very sparse.

Because education in these countries had few roots in the local culture or economy and was oriented toward the values of the West, the African exposed to it was often out of step or even in conflict with the ideas of his elders. One result was often a flight to the cities to look for white-collar jobs. Attempts to adapt these schools to African realities have been resisted by African teachers as well as leaders, however, for this has been interpreted as lowering the standard. Nevertheless, the primary-school syllabus now includes manual work for boys and domestic science for girls, and the rural schools give special emphasis to agriculture, particularly during the first four years. Since students so often lack any mechanical background, which the child in industrialized countries gets from the cradle up, these courses are important. But teachers remain frequently contemptuous of this nonacademic activity.

Secondary Education

Secondary education began in A.E.F. only after World War II. The secondary-school course is divided into: the long cycle (seven years), terminating with a standardized (French) examination, which, if passed, earns the *baccalauréat* degree; and the short cycle (four years), with an elementary certificate or certificates of the first cycle (BE or BPC) or assistant teacher's certificate (BEPC). The standards and curricula follow the metropolitan pattern. Teacher-training schools are usually included as part of secondary education. Self-sufficient, post-primary *cours complémentaires,* which correspond to the level of the short cycle, were added in 1959. These courses, designed for students who are not going on to senior secondary academic schools, are often attached to primary or other schools and frequently include teacher-training sections.

Secondary-school teachers must be university graduates. Thus, at present, most teachers in such schools are French. In 1960, there were 7,827 secondary-school students in all four territories, 20 per cent of whom were in mission schools; this compared with 1,201 in 1951. Similarly, the number of schools increased from thirteen in 1951 to sixty in 1960. Few of the students reach *baccalauréat,* however. In 1951, only 10 passed the full *baccalauréat,* while 24 passed the short cycle. By 1957, 274 passed the short cycle (representing 36 per cent of those who tried), but only 39 the full *baccalauréat.* It is from these 274 that assistant teachers and others for general employment are selected, while those taking the full seven-year course may go on to higher education.

Tuition in secondary schools is free. Indeed, boarding fees, clothing, and even pocket money for students coming from outlying districts are supplied out of public funds. In 1955, 1,154 students were receiving scholarships for secondary schools. Secondary scholarships to France were discouraged after 1949, in an effort to build up local institutions. However, there were still 62 students on scholarship in secondary schools in France in 1960, of whom 15 were girls. This percentage is higher than in Equatorial Africa itself, where less than 20 per cent of students in secondary schools are girls.

Technical and Vocational Education

Despite the increasing need for Africans with technical skills, the prestige of manual or technical work remains low, and relatively few enter technical schools as a first choice. In 1960, only 3,278 students were enrolled in the technical schools in Equatorial Africa, as compared with 2,068 in 1957.

There is one technical college in Brazzaville, with 450 students who are admitted by examination after primary school to a four-year course, leading to an industrial or commercial diploma or, after further specialization, to a professional diploma for accountants, secretaries, or intermediate foremen or technicians. Only three diplomas were awarded in 1957.

Three-year post-primary courses are given in specialized apprenticeship centers in mechanics, carpentry, domestic science, commercial subjects, etc.; those who finish the courses (which only a minority do —fifty-five in 1957) receive a certificate of professional aptitude. In 1958, there were nine such centers in Equatorial Africa.

Vocational courses of varying length are also offered: for example, handicraft classes for boys, which are attached to certain primary schools and teach the handling of simple tools; domestic-science courses; and agricultural training schools, of which there is at least one in each of the four countries, and which offer a completely practical two-year course for agricultural monitors who subsequently may join the Agricultural Service to do field-level work. Excluding the agricultural courses, there were 40 vocational centers in 1958. Also, some government departments periodically run nine-month rapid trade-training centers for men to provide special training for whatever particular skills are then needed. As is true throughout all areas of education, the shortage of qualified teachers seriously hampers the operation of the technical training schools.

In an effort to encourage technical and vocational education, the European Development Fund of the EEC has given $134,000 for the commercial section at the professional school in Libreville, Gabon, and for the extension of the professional school in Chad. UNESCO provided $10,000 for a technical-education project for 1960.

Literacy courses for adults are given in French in a number of cities. The over-all rate of literacy * is estimated at 5 to 10 per cent, although it is considerably higher in some areas and among people under thirty-five.

Higher Education

Since secondary education was not organized until 1945, it is only in the last few years that Equatorial African candidates for higher education have begun to appear in substantial numbers. To enter universities in France (and with very few exceptions, all the university students have gone to France), one must have successfully completed his *baccalauréat*. In 1955, there were only six bachelors of art in the four countries.

In 1957–58, there were 34 students from Equatorial Africa on government scholarship in French universities; by 1960–61, this number had risen to 188, of whom 5 were women. In addition, there are 138 scholarship students studying to be technicians (electricity, agriculture, commerce, etc.) and 24 scholarship students preparing for professions not requiring a degree (midwives, printers, journalists, etc.). There are, no doubt, still other students on private scholarship. One of the problems at present in France is the growing number of private African students who come without sufficient qualifications or funds for higher studies. Some of these students go to private schools of varying quality. Others turn to correspondence courses that have been organized for this market, too often by opportunists who care little for standards.

Until recently, Equatorial African students at universities in France have not been as active politically as their counterparts from French West Africa. They have had their own student associations and have taken less part in the reputedly more radical African students' organization, the Federation of Students of French Black Africa (FEANF). In the 1960's, however, Equatorial African students are taking a more active role and developing more assertive positions on political issues.

One of the bilateral agreements signed by Congo and France at the time of Congo's independence stipulated that the two governments would cooperate in all ways to facilitate the functioning of the existing Center of Administrative and Technical Studies at Brazza-

* It must be noted that literacy figures in the four Equatorial African countries measure literacy in French; in most English-speaking African areas, on the other hand, literacy is measured in vernacular languages as well as in English.

ville and its transformation into a full-fledged university designed to serve the four Equatorial African countries. Originally intended to represent the four Equatorial African republics, the governing board now includes representatives of only Chad, Congo, and Central African Republic, as well as France. In 1960, there were approximately 350 students enrolled in the center's three programs: university-level instruction in law and preparatory work in letters and science; specialized administrative training; and technical training for those already employed. By 1965, the center hopes to be a fully operating university with 700 students.

Present Relations with France

Congo, Gabon, Central African Republic, and Chad are all members of the French Community. All employ a high proportion of French personnel and money in their economic and educational programs. All use French administrative and educational systems as a matter of course. All use French as the *lingua franca*. All have signed bilateral accords with France providing for various cooperative arrangements concerning the conduct of their foreign and financial affairs, defense, technical aid, intellectual cooperation, and participation in the EEC and the French Community. Almost without exception, their university students have been educated in France. It would seem likely that, for some time to come, their closest links will be with France.

The constitutions of October 4, 1958, and the two decrees implementing the *loi-cadre* of 1956 gave overseas members of the Community the right to administer primary, secondary, and technical education. But higher education was to be the common concern of France and the members of the Community. This necessitated the maintenance of French as the medium of instruction and the standardization or coordination of the syllabi of classes preparing for the examinations for entrance to institutions of higher education. The agreement also provided for recruitment of teaching personnel in France, for the training in France of locally recruited personnel, and for the equivalence of local and metropolitan examinations.

A number of these provisions were subsequently written into the bilateral accords signed at the time of independence in 1960. These accords include the following points relevant to education:

(1) Periodic conferences will be called of the chiefs of state (of members of the French Community) and of ministers and experts to discuss important problems of common concern.

(2) Each country agrees to search, with France, for a "harmony

of position and action" on all important decisions concerning foreign affairs. They are obliged to deliberate together before all international conferences in which both parties are interested.

(3) France will give all possible aid in the form of equipment, experts, technicians, and financial advice, with amounts and methods to be determined by special convention.

(4) France will make a special effort to help in the field of education and agrees to put at the disposition of the signatory countries qualified personnel in research, teaching, cultural affairs, youth counseling, and sports. The signatory country agrees to give priority to France in seeking expatriate teaching staff. A cultural commission consisting of a representative of France and of each signatory, is to be constituted to apply this agreement.

(5) France agrees to help with the establishment of a university at Brazzaville.

(6) The signatories agree to coordinate professional educational standards and salaries.

It is probable that these countries will eventually want additional aid, besides that provided by France, in developing their educational systems. They will presumably welcome a limited number of scholarship opportunities for university and specialized training in other countries—although, like other French-speaking countries in Africa, they will face problems of degree equivalences because France and the United States have not yet reached agreements on recognition of degrees. Shortages of foreign currencies limit the prospect that these countries will send students to countries outside the franc zone from their own resources.

The ministers of education of most of the French-speaking African countries met in Paris in February, 1961, to discuss problems of common concern. The major problem raised was the necessity (and the difficulty) of recruiting additional technical-assistance personnel to staff the expanding education and economic programs. Other proposals included a meeting each year in France between young African schoolmasters and French teachers leaving for Africa; the need for more flexible conditions of access to the French professional schools; the need for additional teacher-training schools to develop more and better teachers; the desirability of creating at the University of Brazzaville a program to train teachers of the *cours complémentaires;* the advantages of working out a pooling arrangement to enable the French-speaking African countries to share specialists and thus achieve Africanization more quickly and economically; the desirability of placing more stress on physical education in the school programs; and the desirability of adapting teaching materials and curricula to African conditions, with particular reference to the natural sciences, history, geography, and French. (The Chad representative pointed out, for example, that it should not be a precondition of graduation for every Chad primary-school student to be able to name every one of the ninety provinces in France.) Each state was urged to appoint a commission charged with preparing the first plan for curriculum adjustment, to be sent to the Office of Cooperation in Paris. That office will then establish a general commission comprised of specialists from each of the states to put definite programs into operation.

The Outlook

The four French-speaking Equatorial African countries face educational problems similar to those of other African countries, but will probably have to bear them longer than some of their neighbors. Education above the primary level has existed for only fifteen years, and university education for even a shorter time. Yet, the need is enormous for qualified personnel in technical, administrative, and commercial positions to staff the government, the schools, and the development projects. The resources to pay for outside help are exceedingly limited. But the countries cannot develop at the rate that internal political pressures demand without such help. The schools cannot expand without teachers—yet the teacher-training schools are producing only half of what is necessary to fill the available posts. The obvious compromise of lowering standards has been rejected in principle. The lack of African technicians will continue at least as long as prestige and salaries are higher for the administrative and professional positions—yet the need for technicians is an expanding one.

One way or another, these problems will be met, if not solved. How and when they are met may well be decisive in determining the political futures of these countries.

—This chapter and the succeeding four chapters on the individual countries of French-speaking Equatorial Africa were prepared by WINIFRED ARMSTRONG in cooperation with PÈRE JEAN LE GALL.

28. *Central African Republic*

Capital: Bangui
Population: 1,180,000 (est.)
Area: 238,000 sq. miles
Political status: Independent republic

THE Central African Republic, known as Oubangui-Chari until 1958, is a large, landlocked country with only one major town—the important river port of Bangui. Its principal exports are coffee, cotton, and diamonds, but it is also a major trading center of Equatorial Africa because of its relatively well-developed road system and a network of navigable rivers.

French explorers arrived in Oubangui-Chari somewhat later than in its southern neighbors, and military forces were required to subdue dissidence directed initially at the exploitative policies of the concessionary companies. The French did not establish an administration until after 1910, and the country's inland location postponed the arrival of missionaries until somewhat later and limited their numbers.

For all these reasons, and also because of the reluctance of the Oubangui territorial assembly to subsidize mission schools, education is behind that of the Congo and Gabon. To complicate the situation further, the territorial education service and the territorial assembly were for considerable periods at sword's points, resulting in the exodus on at least two occasions of a number of French teachers. These internal issues have now been resolved, and steady progress has been made in the last few years in building up the schools of the nation. But, owing to the late start, only 9.5 per cent of children of school age were enrolled in school in 1951; by 1960, the proportion had reached 27.3 per cent.

Primary Education

In 1960, there were 64,600 children in all the schools of the Central African Republic, as compared with 11,000 in 1949 and 20,000 in 1951. Of the 61,428 primary-school students in 1960, 37.8 per cent attended mission schools; over 90 per cent of these were Catholic. The pupil-teacher ratio in the mission schools was 57 to 1; in the public schools, it was 65 to 1.

When Barthelemy Boganda, a former priest, became the country's leading political personality in the early 1950's, the allocations to mission education were greatly increased, and attendance at mission schools also rose. Despite these subsidies, the Catholic mission was in such financial difficulties by 1958 that it had to pose the choice to its African staff of resigning or accepting big salary cuts. The Africans refused to choose, and struck, insisting that the government rectify the situation. When the Minister of Education attempted to hold out, public opinion became so aroused that he was forced to raise the mission subsidy by more than a third, to almost $350,000 in 1959. By the end of 1959, the government was paying 80 per cent of the cost of operating the mission schools.

The troubles between the territorial education service and the territorial assembly started shortly after World War II when a new head of the education service was sent out from Paris to replace an acting territorial inspector. Despite the territorial assembly's approval of the dismissal of the acting inspector, he was upheld by the local French administration, and three newly arrived professors from France departed abruptly in the resulting skirmish. At the time (1949), George Darlan, then president of the assembly, remarked bitterly: "Oubangui has twice the population of Moyen Congo and three times that of Gabon, and its children are not even half as well educated as the children of those territories. Under such conditions, it would be hypocritical of me to offer my congratulations to our education service, which obviously needs a complete reorganization."

In 1956, Boganda again took the local education service to task for the poor quality of instruction in the territory, and asked for a "profound reform" of the inspectorate. Again, there was an exodus of a number of European teachers—bringing the total loss to about fifty, which represented a substantial proportion of the country's secondary and administrative staffs. The Central African Republic was not the only territory in which such differences took place, but here they obviously retarded educational progress.

The proportion of girls in the schools in the Central African Republic increased from 12.9 per cent in 1951 to 16.5 per cent in 1958. Of the 1,591 students taking their primary-school examinations in 1957, 874 (or 55 per cent) passed. Of the 1,553 taking the secondary entrance exam, 381 (or 24 per cent) passed.

A four-year plan was drawn up in 1958 to encourage girls' schooling and to raise the over-all school attendance rate to 40 per cent by 1962. One problem that has plagued the educational authorities has been the absenteeism of students in the rural areas, reportedly because of rain during the rainy season and the need to pick cotton or hunt or fish when it is dry.

Secondary Education

In 1960, 1,560 students attended the seven public and eight private secondary schools, an increase of about 500 students since 1958. One-third of secondary-level students now go to private schools, a slightly higher proportion than in 1958. Almost all the students in mission secondary schools in 1958 were Catholic. Of those in secondary schools in 1958, 13 per cent were girls, of which only a minority of 16 per cent attended Catholic schools. Of the 17 students taking the *baccalauréat* exam in 1957, 6 passed. In the same year, 55 out of 100 succeeded in achieving their BE or BEPC diplomas.

Virtually the whole secondary system has been financed by the FIDES and FAC; emphasis has been placed on technical centers and teacher-training schools.

Vocational and Technical Education

In 1960, there were 1,412 students in the twenty-two technical or vocational schools in the Central African Republic (of which only one, with one class of 20 students, is private). This is a considerable increase over the 1958 figure of 436.

In November, 1959, a school for girls, constructed with FIDES funds, was opened. Three sections were offered: lingerie embroidery, sewing, and social work. At the time of opening, there were ninety students in five classes, about equally divided between Europeans and Africans.

Of the twelve students taking the proficiency exam in 1957, only three passed. At this time, however, there were far fewer students in the vocational schools; it might be assumed that a considerably larger number are now taking and passing this exam.

In addition to the regular vocational courses, the Inspection de

Travail gives a nine-month accelerated course to approximately forty-five students a year. The subjects taught depend on the particular needs in the private and public sectors (such as mines, public works, etc.).

Higher Education

There were twenty students on scholarship in French universities in 1960–61: five in science, five in law, and the rest in diverse courses. Another twenty-seven, also on scholarship, were studying technical, subprofessional, and secondary courses. In 1957–58, there were only four students on scholarship in French universities, and sixteen taking technical and other courses.

The Central African Republic is a signatory to the accord that will establish a new university at Brazzaville as the center of higher learning for Chad, Congo, and the Central African Republic. While there has been some discussion of developing institutions of higher learning in each of the Equatorial countries, the Central African Republic has neither the money, the staff, nor the students to initiate its own university at this time.

Future Plans

During the 1950's, expenditures on education rose from 10 to 12 per cent of the annual national budget. In 1956, the education budget totaled $1,360,000. In 1960, it was $1,932,000—about 18 per cent of the total budget. Much of this was provided by the FAC.

At the annual regional meeting of the ministers of education in 1960, the Central African Republic emphasized that its major need was to find and train more teachers. It particularly suggested the following: (1) intensification of the recruitment campaign for teachers; (2) organization by stages of an improved primary-school inspectors corps by allowing experienced instructors who have not had the chance to obtain their *baccalauréat* or *brevet supérieur* to put themselves up for candidacy for the CAIP; (3) asking the Teachers' College for Higher Education at St. Cloud in France to take on a specialist to open a program for these instructors; and (4) requesting two places at St. Cloud for immediate additional training, prior to the organization of the full program suggested above.

29. Chad

Capital: Fort Lamy
Population: 2,730,000
Area: 513,600 sq. miles
Political status: Independent republic

THE largest of the former A.E.F. territories (almost twice the size of France) is the Republic of Chad. It is also the most populous (2,730,000, including 5,000 Europeans), the least prosperous currently and prospectively, and perhaps the most divided by internal tribal and political rivalries.

Close to half, if not more, of Chad's people are Moslem, the majority of whom live in the northern and eastern parts of the country, which borders on Moslem Libya and Sudan. Animal husbandry is the primary economic activity, and most of the people are nomadic—because of the generally rough terrain and a hot, dry climate. Trade is limited, not only by the scale of production, but also by a lack (so great as to be almost an absence) of internal means of communication. Chad is a country of immense distances, yet the nearest port is nearly 1,500 miles away, few of the rivers are navigable for more than a few months a year, and there are less than 14,000 miles of inadequate internal roads and trails. Most of its trade is by air or through the port of Bangui, Central African Republic, hundreds of miles to the south. Without French subsidies, its export products—chiefly cotton and livestock products—would be unable to compete in world markets because of these exorbitant transport costs.

Major Educational Problems

These economic and geographic factors have profoundly affected educational development. Nomadic peoples rarely make good students: They do not stay long enough in one place to benefit from schooling, and the children must often forgo school to tend the animals. Because of its inaccessibility and because it was the last Equatorial African country to be settled and organized administratively by the French,* Chad had no missionaries until well into the twentieth century, and those who came—initially American Protestants—went mainly to the animist southern areas, where their welcome was more assured than in the Moslem north. The federal government in Brazzaville, occupied with other problems and disinterested in a territory so remote and unproductive of revenue, tended to leave Chad to fend for itself.

The first school in Chad was not established until 1920, and by 1930 there were no more than ten schools, attended by 425 pupils. Since 1945, however, Chad has made considerable progress in its educational growth.

Primary Education

By 1950, 4,000 boys and 467 girls were receiving primary schooling in Chad. By 1958, there were 32,610 students in 154 primary schools; by 1960, the total had reached 53,973 students in 225 schools. In 1960, 11 per cent of school-age children were in school—an important increase over the 1951 rate of 1.7 per cent and the 1957 rate of 5.4 per cent. However, there is a wide discrepancy between the proportion of the school-age population enrolled in schools in the south (where it is probably close to 25 per cent) and in the north (where it is not more than 5 per cent). One special problem in the north is that, as a result of antagonisms between Negroes and Moslems lingering over from the days when Chad was a center of the slave trade, many northerners resent having their children taught in school by Africans, whom they regard as their former slaves. Furthermore, the Moslems have long had their own system of Islamic education and are often deeply suspicious of Christian missionary educational efforts.

Students in mission schools represented 13 per cent of the total school enrollment in 1960. This was a decrease from the 18 per cent in mission schools in 1958. The teacher-pupil ratio in the private schools was approximately sixty-eight to one; in the public schools, it was fifty-six to one.

Girls made up 10.5 per cent of the 1958 primary-school population. This is almost precisely the same proportion as in 1950, although the

* Chad was under French military control from the turn of the century, but an effective civil administration was not established until after World War I.

total number of girls in primary school has increased seven and a half times. Almost one-third of the girls in primary school attend private schools.

For reasons not yet clear, a notably higher proportion of students in Chad pass their school-leaving examinations than in any of the other Equatorial territories. In 1955, 533 took the primary-school certificate exam, and 288 passed (54 per cent). Two years later, there were 492 passes (62 per cent) out of 792 taking the exam. By 1958–59, 1,733 took the exam, and 980 passed (57 per cent). These scores average 10 to 20 per cent higher than those in the other territories. Of the 283 taking the secondary entrance exam, 173 (58 per cent) passed. In none of the other territories of former French Equatorial Africa was the proportion of those passing above 30 per cent.

In southern Chad, the major drawbacks to the extension of primary education are lack of funds and teachers; in northern Chad, it is the lack of students. In 1952, Chad spent 1.3 per cent of its budget on education, but the educational allocation had risen to 11 per cent of the total annual budget by 1957 and to 12.5 per cent in 1960. The amount spent on education in 1960 was approximately $2 million—including all recurrent and nonrecurrent expenditures and FAC-budgeted contributions. FIDES contributed $4.6 million to Chad's educational development plans between 1955 and 1958. But the sum allocated for building primary schools was proportionately less than for any other territory, despite the fact that construction costs are higher in Chad.

Some additional assistance has recently been provided for primary schools in Chad, through a grant of $912,000 by the European Development Fund, to be used for the reconstruction of village "bush" schools. At present, many of the schools in the northern part of Chad are poorly built and offer only two classes, while the majority of schools in the towns in southern Chad give six classes and are better equipped.

Recognizing the need to educate parents as well as (or in order to) educate the children, the Chad Government has been giving increasing attention to enlisting the cooperation of Moslem parents in the north. Under a program drawn up in 1957: (1) the pressure of example was to be applied by persuading local chiefs to send their children to schools; (2) free lunches and some boarding facilities were to be provided; (3) separate classes were to be organized for girls wherever possible; and (4) a corps of bilingual French-Arabic teachers were to be trained. Experiments in teaching in French and Arabic, undertaken in a local area in 1958, were reportedly successful. At the present time, Chad could not begin to finance or staff primary schools for all its children, but the intent is clearly to expand facilities to the limit of its resources.

Secondary Education

In the three secondary schools existing in Chad in 1960, there were 834 students, taught by a staff of sixty-three. In 1958, there were 485 students in the secondary schools, of which 61 (or 12 per cent) were girls. All the secondary schools are public; there are no secondary mission schools. In addition to the regular secondary courses, two *cours complémentaires* were started in October, 1959.

In 1957, thirty-eight of the sixty-one who sat for the four-year post-primary exam received their BE (general) or BEPC (assistant teacher's) diploma. Of the twenty-five who took their *baccalauréat* exam, only six passed. There has been a steady and substantial increase in the numbers of persons taking (and passing) these exams.

The Collège Franco-Arabe at Abéché, which has not been included in the figures cited above, deserves special mention. The proposal was first made in 1945 to establish in Chad a center of Islamic learning, partly to offset the attraction of Cairo and Khartoum and the increasing political influence that the students trained in these cities were coming to have in Chad. It was not until 1951 that a decision was made to form such a college at the secondary level, offering both French and Arabic courses. A course identical to that of the French secondary schools was organized side by side with one in Arabic similar to those available in Egyptian schools of higher Islamic learning. The teachers of Arabic and religious subjects were given lessons in French history and language and pedagogical instruction. Most of the students take the French course while simultaneously studying Arabic. By 1958, there were 800 students studying at the Abéché college, most of whom go into local administration after completion of their studies.

Vocational and Technical Education

There were nine technical schools in Chad in 1960, teaching 353 students. This is an increase since 1958 from six schools, with 217 students. Of the 6 students taking their apprenticeship exams in 1957, none passed. An expansion of vocational education is emphasized in Chad's future educational plans.

Higher Education

In 1960–61, there were 19 students on scholarship in French universities, and 85 other students on scholarship in France taking technical, agricultural, sub-professional, and secondary courses. In 1957–58, there were 8 Chad scholarship students at French universities, and 16 in other courses. In addition, there were an estimated 100 students in Egypt and Sudan, some at the Koranic University of al-Azhar in Cairo. Students returning from Cairo and Khartoum often have difficulty finding jobs, however, for their French is usually inadequate and some of their degrees are not recognized by the Chad Government.

Chad is a signatory to the agreement setting up the new university at Brazzaville, and is represented on its administering council.

Future Plans

Chad's four-year development plan emphasizes the building of primary schools, the extension of women's education, and the opening of apprenticeship courses in the principal centers to hasten the training of African artisans.

The European Development Fund has given grants totaling more than $3 million, earmarked for construction of boarding schools in Islamic areas, reconstruction of permanent schools to replace temporary ones presently in use in the rural areas, creation of a professional center in the capital city of Fort Lamy, and development of a literacy teaching center for rural areas.

30. Republic of the Congo (Brazzaville)

Capital: Brazzaville
Population: 760,000 (est.)
Area: 132,046 sq. miles
Political status: Independent republic

THE Republic of the Congo, known as Moyen Congo until it became a republic in 1958, was part of the territory carved up in 1885 among the several European signatories to the Treaty of Berlin. It became independent in 1960, but has remained within the French Community and closely affiliated with France.

Congo is small (about the size of Colorado), geographically diverse, and has a population of approximately 750,000 Africans and 10,000 Europeans. Almost one-fifth of this population—a very large proportion in an African country—live in the main cities, Brazzaville, the former federal capital of French Equatorial Africa, and Pointe-Noire, the principal seaport of the equatorial region. Because of these concentrations of population, the accessibility to many regions by railroad and river boat, the relatively early entry of missionaries into education, and the large number of resident Europeans wanting education for their children, the percentage of Congolese school-age children actually in school is one of the highest in Africa—about 65 per cent.

The Congo exports modest quantities of timber, palm oil, peanuts, lead, and tobacco; it enjoys economic benefits from its transportation facilities (the seaport at Pointe-Noire, the river port at Brazzaville, and the only railway in the equatorial region), but it does not have a favorable balance of trade or the resources for much development. This vicious circle of "no development without education, no money for education without development" has been modified somewhat by limited injections of capital from France plus increasing internal pressure for education, and a slowly ascending spiral of both social and educational development has begun building up. Even so, the Congo—with a small annual budget of just under $16 million (somewhat more with the FAC and other grants included), an over-all literacy rate of 10 per cent (much higher among those under thirty-five years of age), and a wide discrepancy between the income and education of the rural 80 per cent and the urban 20 per cent—will almost certainly have to continue to depend on France for substantial economic subsidies.

Organization and Financing of Education

Formal education is largely the responsibility of the Ministry of National Education, although certain aspects are under the surveillance of the Ministry of Youth and Sports, and vocational education is controlled by the technical ministries.

The Congo has, in recent years, put approximately one-fourth of its total budget into education. In 1954, 25 per cent was allocated for education; in 1958, 26.2 per cent; in 1960, although the over-all budget was increased, the proportion dropped to less than 20 per cent. Four-fifths of the education budget in 1960 was spent for public education, and one-fifth for private. Since some investment credits are reserved for education, and many foreign professors teaching in schools are paid through a technical-cooperation budget, the total spent for education is somewhat higher than the stated budget allocation. Figures for the percentage of the budget spent include both recurrent and nonrecurrent items. Grants have provided a substantial portion of the Congo's education budget: from 1953 to 1960, FIDES (subsequently FAC) contributed approximately $3.25 million for education in the Congo.

Primary Education

Primary schools were begun in the Congo by both Protestant and Catholic missionaries late in the nineteenth century. Even today, more than half of the Congo's primary schools belong to the missions, and approximately 55 per cent of the primary students attend mission schools. In 1958, 81 per cent of the students in private primary schools were reported to be Catholic.

Although the mission schools in the Congo have an appallingly high (sixty-two to one) pupil-teacher ratio, it is considerably lower than that in the public schools (seventy-four to one). Teachers' salaries in the mission schools are scaled lower than in the public system, but a prolonged political battle and a strike threat by the mission teachers in 1958 resulted in the allocation of government subsidies to supplement their salaries. Although Congo's President Fulbert Youlou was trained as a priest, feeling against the mission schools on the part of some politicians is so strong that these subsidies were earmarked specifically for the teachers' salaries rather than to the missions generally for their use. In some years, the educational budget of the Congo has allocated five times as much to public as to private education, despite the fact that more than half the Congo's children are in mission schools. In discussing a $23,000 increase in the budget of 1960–61, the Congo Government indicated that part of this increase was to be used to integrate public and private teaching personnel.

Primary-school facilities and attendance have mounted rapidly in the Congo, rising from 10,250 in 1945 to 57,000 in 1955, to 99,339 in 1960, and to 115,331 in 1961. The 1960 percentage of school-age children in school—65 per cent—compares very favorably with the past rates of 10.8 per cent in 1945, 46 per cent in 1951, and 58 per cent in 1955. In Brazzaville, the number of children of school age in school is sufficiently high (about 90 per cent) that it may soon be possible to make primary education compulsory there. In the northern part of the Congo, it is considerably lower.

To a degree, however, the high percentage of children in school is illusory. For although it is true that a large proportion of children start primary school, the majority do not finish. More than half the primary schools have three classes or less; thus many children do not or cannot complete the education they start. Furthermore, a substantial proportion of those who take the final primary-school examinations do not pass; in 1957, of the 2,692 primary-school students who took the examination, 980 (36.4 per cent) passed. The number of passes has increased somewhat along with the rise in the total school attendance, however.

Education for Girls

Nearly 30 per cent of the primary-school students are girls. The proportion is expected to increase considerably over the next decade, partly because education for girls is being accepted more and more by the Africans, and partly because the past dearth of locally trained instructors for women is only beginning to be overcome; the first graduating class of women instructors completed their normal-school course in Congo in 1959.

Secondary Education

There were 4,361 students in attendance at the fifteen secondary schools of the Congo in 1961, as compared with 933 in 1951, 1,563 in 1957, and 3,363 in 1960.

Relatively few of the students in secondary schools reach the *baccalauréat,* although each year the figure increases. In 1957, only 29 students (some French, some African) out of 99 passed their *baccalauréat* examination. In the same year, 112 students (28 per cent of those trying) succeeded in the examination for the four-year course for the general BE certificate or the BEPC. In 1960, this number was reported to have risen to 192.

In 1961, 1,496 students, or slightly more than one-third of the total students in secondary education, attended mission schools. In 1958, 9 out of 10 of the students in private secondary schools were Catholic. It would appear that, contrary to a frequent assumption, girls do not attend mission schools in larger proportion than public schools. The proportion of girls in the Congo's Catholic secondary schools in 1958 was less than 21 per cent, whereas for the secondary-school population as a whole it was 24 per cent; the proportion of girls in Catholic schools to all girls in secondary schools was less than 28 per cent. The pupil-teacher ratio in the secondary schools was twenty-one to one.

The Congo Government is eager to advance secondary education as quickly as possible through the expansion of the junior *cours complémentaires* (and the training of teachers for them) and the enlargement of existing secondary schools. It has appealed to the Fund for Aid and Cooperation for additional funds to carry out these reforms.

Technical Education

In 1958, there was a total of 1,284 students in one technical college in Brazzaville (open to students from all of Equatorial Africa and supported by the four territories) and in four apprenticeship and twenty handicraft centers. In 1961, 1,610 students were taking these courses in thirty-two establishments offering technical courses, including 428 in the technical college. Of the over-all 1961 total, 257 were girls taking domestic science. In 1957, 40 students of the Congo (out of 55 in all of Equatorial Africa) received the certificate for successfully completing the three-year course at the apprenticeship centers. Only 3 students (all Congolese) received diplomas from the technical college.

The preponderance of Congolese students in the technical college, as well as in other federally supported schools located in the Congo, raises a sensitive political point. In view of these statistics, complaints have been aired in the territorial and federal assemblies concerning the proportion of financial support that should be given by the other three territories. This dissatisfaction about giving support for federal projects located in Brazzaville—with too little apparent benefit accruing to anyone but the Congolese—has been even more strongly voiced with regard to other development projects.

Higher Education

For the academic year 1957–58, eleven students from the Congo were on scholarships in French universities. Doubtless, some of these were European. There were fifty-nine others on scholarships in technical, sub-professional, and secondary courses. However, by 1960–61, the number in higher education had risen to seventy-five. Of these, seven were in medicine, six in engineering, nineteen in science, and nine in law. In addition, there were 67 students on scholarships in France preparing for various technical (agriculture, aeronaùtics, electricity, etc.) and sub-professional vocations.

The Center of Higher Administrative and Technical Studies in Brazzaville is scheduled to become a university in the early 1960's. This university will adhere to French standards. However, its managing board will include representatives of France, Congo, the Central African Republic, and Chad. A bilateral agreement broadly setting forth the terms was signed between France and Congo on the day of Congo's independence in August, 1960.

In 1961, there were 350 students from the several countries at the Center for Higher Administrative and Technical Studies, the majority concerned with courses relating only to the Center, and not necessarily to the proposed university. Advanced instruction of the university type is offered in law, letters, and science, but only in law can a student at present carry his studies through to completion. Additional courses of study are to be added rapidly, however, and by 1965 the university expects to have 700 students. FAC is financing a five-year plan to help build laboratories, faculty housing, and the schools of science and medicine.

A teachers' college to train teachers for the secondary schools is to be established and eventually incorporated into the proposed university. Aided by grants from the U.N. Special Fund and FEDOM (the EEC's Fund for Economic Development Overseas), students will initially be recruited competitively from among those holding the BEPC, and will take a four-year literary or scientific course.

Future Plans

In discussing some of the educational accomplishments and plans of the Congo Government in a speech late in 1960, the Minister of National Education set the following goals:

(1) The percentage of school-age children in school should increase from the present 65 per cent to 80–85 per cent (125,000 students) in three years. To this end, 300 new classes (10,000 places) should be started in 1961, and 200 new classes in the succeeding two years.

(2) Secondary schools must be enlarged: in Brazzaville to 1,500 capacity, in Pointe-Noire to 1,200 capacity. In three years, the total in secondary schools should increase to 5,000.

(3) Technical education must be encouraged through the opening of new apprenticeship sections, the creation of a housekeeping school in Brazzaville, and the extension of the technical college, perhaps even to giving a technical *baccalauréat*.

(4) Increasing the standard of the teaching personnel is most important, and one step in this direction is the dispatch of seven assistant primary inspectors to France to be trained as full inspectors. Also, twenty-seven teachers have been sent to the institute in Brazzaville for training to become professors in the new *cours complémentaires*.

(5) FAC must be persuaded to assist with grants for the construction needs of schools for the Congo.

In a subsequent speech, the Minister summarized the recommendations of the Congo Education Council. These included a call for new and more flexible rules concerning the age of entry into school; reorganization of the hygiene program; reform of the curricula to include a better preparation in history, geography, and local institutions; greater emphasis on physical education; and the creation of a committee to draft a new statute for private education.

The ten-year education program of Congo drafted in 1960 establishes broad objectives: universal primary education by 1970, 600 diplomas to be given in that year for the short cycle of secondary school, 400 students to be in attendance in senior secondary schools, and a tripled population in the technical secondary schools. The major drawback to the accomplishment of these most desirable plans is lack of money; all the proposals assume extensive outside financial and technical aid. Further, they assume an availability of trained teachers that Congolese facilities are unlikely to be able to produce and whose availability from abroad is also dubious.

While these plans may thus be too grandiose for total achievement, they reflect an attitude toward education which suggests that the Congo will continue to build constructively on an already impressive record of achievement.

31. Gabon

Capital: Libreville
Population: 421,000 (est.)
Area: 102,317 sq. miles
Political status: Independent republic

THE Republic of Gabon, independent since 1960, is the richest and least populous of the four Equatorial African countries. With impressive timber, petroleum, manganese resources, a favorable balance of trade since 1958 (the only one of the four countries that can claim this), a balanced budget, and an almost static population of 421,000 (averaging only 3.1 persons per square mile), Gabon has become increasingly chary of schemes calling for pooling of its resources with those of its poorer neighbors. Thus, Gabon remains a member of the French Community, has signed bilateral accords with France, and sells three-fourths of its exports to its associates in the European Common Market, but has been lukewarm toward moves for political union in Equatorial Africa. It has also declined to serve on the Council of Administration of the projected new university at Brazzaville.

Gabon's location on the seacoast facilitated the early arrival of missionaries. The first schools were established at Libreville by Catholic missionaries in the first half of the nineteenth century, and the Protestants came somewhat later. France and Gabon signed their first treaty in 1839. Approximately two out of five Gabonese are Christian, a higher proportion than in any of the other three countries of the area. Partly for this reason, Gabon has a relatively high over-all rate of school-age children in school (59.3 per cent), although the people in the rural areas have a much lower standard of both education and income than in the urban areas. A five-year development plan introduced in 1960 seeks to narrow this gap.

Primary Education

Gabon's present primary-school population of 47,743 is more than double that of 1951; the percentage of school-age children in school has climbed from 27.3 per cent in 1951, to 50.2 per cent in 1958, to 59.3 per cent in 1961. More than half (52 per cent) of the students attend the 223 mission schools, 85 per cent of which are Catholic.

Girls' education is considerably more advanced in Gabon than in its sister Equatorial countries. The proportion of girls enrolled in schools has been increasing steadily for the past ten years, and at least one-third of the primary students are now female. The familiar thesis that parents prefer their daughters to attend mission schools is not demonstrated in Gabon primary schools, however, for the ratio of girls to boys in the Catholic schools, and the ratio of girls in mission as compared to public schools, are almost exactly the same as for the total population. The pupil-teacher ratio is not yet satisfactory—an average of forty-three to one in the private schools and thirty-seven to one in the public—but this is far better than in the neighboring Congo Republic.

Of the 1,463 students who took the final national primary-school examination in 1957, 644 (42.9 per cent) passed; in the same year, 120 students (43 per cent of those who tried) passed the entrance examination to secondary school. The proportion of successful students from mission and public schools was almost equal. In 1960, there were 2,200 candidates for the primary-school certificate exam. More important, 1,000 students were admitted to secondary school—almost five times as many as three years earlier.

The relationship between the government and mission schools has generally been smooth and cooperative. Both moral and financial support seem to have been freely given to the missions. As part of the goal of universal primary education by 1970, it is planned that half of the projected 140 new primary classes to be started each year will be in mission schools. Even in the public schools, religious instruction is available when requested in writing by parents. A local religious leader is enlisted to teach these public-school religious classes, which must, however, be outside the regular course assignment and time and may in no case take on characteristics of ritual ceremony.

Secondary Education

A total of 2,070 students attended Gabon's eleven public and six private secondary schools in 1960. Unlike the primary schools, where the rate of growth of mission and public schools has been about equal, the public secondary schools have expanded more rapidly than those organized by missions. For example, 45 per cent of the 1,025 secondary students attended private schools in 1958, whereas the proportion had decreased to 35 per cent by 1960. Partly as a result of the opening in late 1959 of twelve *cours complémentaires,* the secondary-school population has more than doubled in the past two years.

Of the 55 students who took their *baccalauréat* exams in 1957, 19 passed. (Among these, it must be noted, were almost certainly a few European students, especially since the only school at that time where one might continue as far as the *baccalauréat* was in the capital city of Libreville, where most of the country's 8,500 Europeans live.) Of the 194 who attempted the four-year post-primary exam to receive a general or assistant teacher's diploma, 69 passed. In 1960, the number passing the four-year course had risen to 90; by 1962, it is estimated that this will increase to 200.

During the next ten years, the Gabon Government hopes to expand its secondary facilities to enable most students to attend in their own regions and to triple the number of those in the *baccalauréat* course. Secondary education has received heavy emphasis from FIDES (and FAC) grants over the past ten years: from 1950 to 1958, two-thirds of the $2.5 million in FIDES grants to Gabon education was used for secondary education.

Teacher Training

As in other parts of Africa, one of the factors most likely to hold up the advance of education both quantitatively and qualitatively is the lack of qualified teachers. Gabon, having had a higher proportion of students over a longer period of time than some of its neighbors, is relatively better off. (There are, for example, more primary-school teachers in Gabon than in Chad, which has over five times the population of Gabon.) But Gabon's plans for educational expansion outstrip the country's probable capacity to produce teachers, even with augmented teacher-training courses. For some time to come, the majority of post-primary teachers are likely to come from France, and the majority of primary teachers (African) will have qualified only as monitors.

Technical Education

In 1960, there were only 138 students in two technical schools in Gabon. Given the desire of Gabon to industrialize its promising economy further, and the already serious shortage of skilled and technical workers, the apparent short-changing of technical education may limit economic development.

Some encouragement may be taken from the twenty scholarship students pursuing technical courses in the universities in France in 1960–61 and from the $45,000 contribution of the Economic Development Fund of the EEC for the development of a commercial section at the professional school at Libreville. Moreover, the government has stated its intention to encourage further activity in this field in the future.

Higher Education

In 1957–58, there were eleven students from Gabon on government scholarships in French universities. Another sixty-five scholarship students were taking technical, pre-professional, or secondary courses. By 1960–61, the number of scholarship students in universities in France had risen to seventy-four, with forty-one others in the technical and other courses. Among the university students, there were nineteen in science, nine in law, and six in engineering.

Future Plans

A major section of the current five-year plan is devoted to educational advancement and reforms. Rural education, which at present lags far behind that in the more urban, populated areas, is to be given special attention. Gabon has devoted an average of approximately 20 per cent of its budget to education over the past several years, and will increase the sums spent on education as the total national budget expands.

The government hopes to open 140 new classes each year, with the objective of achieving 100 per cent enrollment at the primary level by 1970. Every effort will be made to replace primary schools built of temporary material with more permanent local materials. The number of secondary classes is to be doubled, the number of *baccalauréat* students tripled.

Given the favorable economic position of Gabon, its head start in education, and its apparent governmental stability under what is now virtually a one-party regime, these educational goals seem reasonable ones.

Part IX

FRENCH-SPEAKING WEST AFRICA

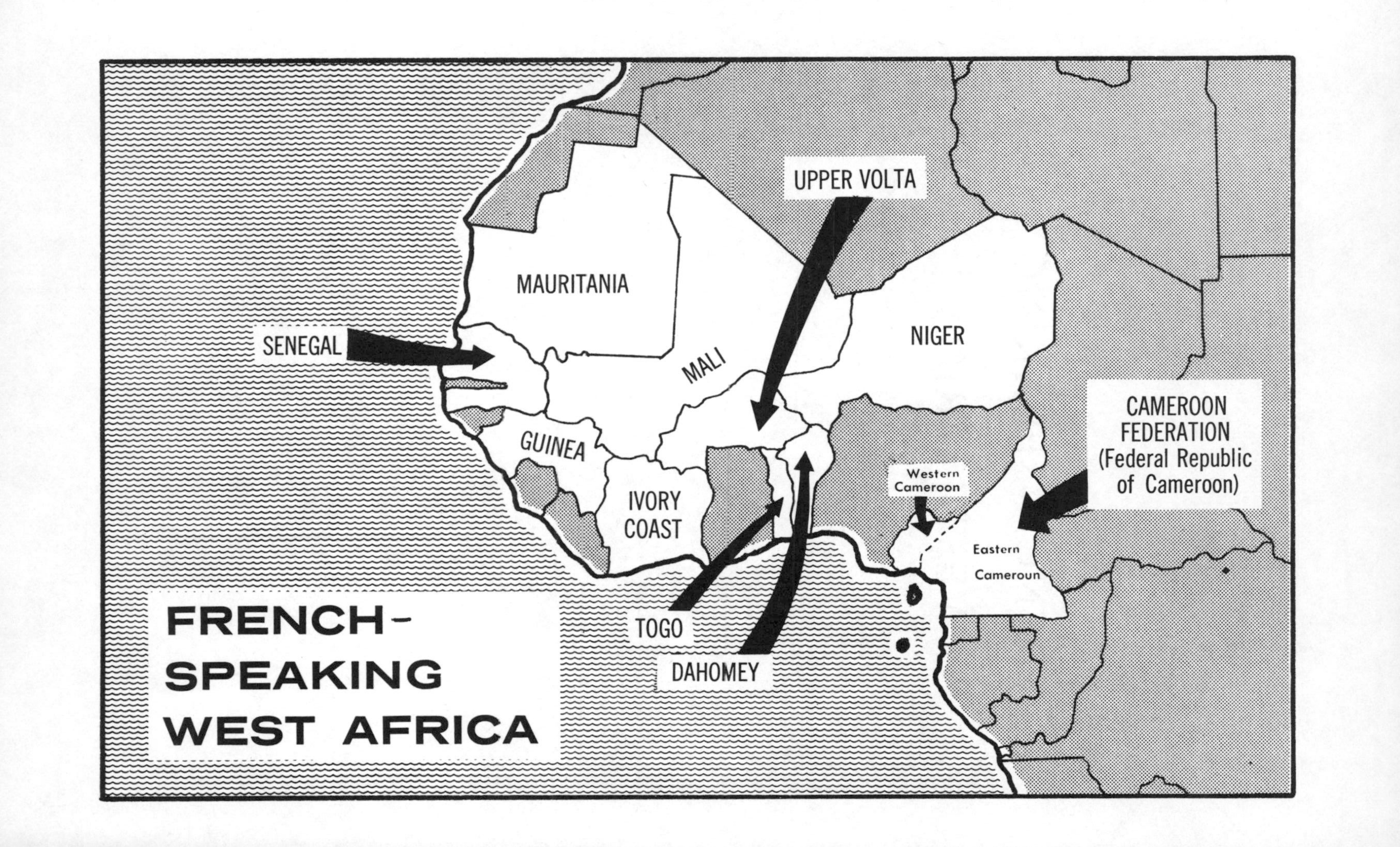
FRENCH-
SPEAKING
WEST AFRICA
MAURITANIA
SENEGAL
MALI
UPPER VOLTA
NIGER
GUINEA
IVORY
COAST
TOGO
DAHOMEY
Western
Cameroon
Eastern
Cameroun
CAMEROON
FEDERATION
(Federal Republic
of Cameroon)

32. General Trends in French-Speaking West Africa

UNTIL 1956, when the *loi-cadre* transferred the responsibility for primary-school education in French-administered West Africa to the African governments of the individual territories, education in these countries had been an exclusively French responsibility. Thus, most of the educated adults now politically dominant in Senegal, Mali, Dahomey, Mauritania, the Ivory Coast, Upper Volta, Togo, and Niger are products of a school system as French as that of the metropole. French education has had marked centralistic tendencies since the Revolution in 1789, and thus there was little or no attempt to adapt methods or curricula to individual territories in West Africa; the exposure remained virtually identical for all educated Africans, whatever the regional or local cultural or linguistic variations.

Historically, the task of educating the people of French West Africa was begun in the initial days of the French conquest in the early part of the nineteenth century. From that period until 1903, the few educational facilities introduced into the area were almost entirely those of Catholic missionaries. Impeded by topographical obstacles that severely handicapped access to certain regions and by the limited funds and personnel that the metropolitan government could spare for colonial development, the official role in education developed in a piecemeal, desultory manner. Up until World War I, annual enrollment had never passed 2.35 per cent of the total school-age population. Only in Senegal, where French settlement was oldest and most concentrated, and Catholic orders particularly active, did there occur a steady but slow growth of educational facilities.

It was not merely a question of building and staffing new schools. Before this could be undertaken, roads had to be surveyed and built in the hinterland to allow the establishment of at least minimum communication among the various territories as well as to bring vast segments of the population out of isolation; some measure of administrative control had to be introduced and organization brought to the economy. Given the extraordinary prevalence of sickness and disease, health and sanitation measures had to be introduced and enforced. The financial outlays required to meet these basic needs were given top priority, with the result that relatively little was left over for schools. These early financial difficulties were followed by the economic depression of the 1930's and subsequently by the outbreak of World War II in 1939, both of which seriously arrested educational development throughout Africa. To the persistent physical and financial obstacles were added the psychological problems of selling Western, secular education—particularly difficult in the Moslem areas. The West African populace, scratching a precarious living from the soil, was initially highly suspicious of the schools of the white man because they could see little relation to their own immediate needs.

The first general educational plan for the area was drawn up in 1903. It formed the framework within which education developed in French West (and Equatorial) Africa until the Brazzaville Conference in 1944, when education policy in the overseas territories was rewritten in light of the numerous political, social, and economic changes set into motion as a result of World War II.

In its essentials, the Brazzaville Plan called for the establishment in the overseas territories of an educational system modeled closely after that existing in metropolitan France. France, engaged in a *mission civilisatrice,* believed its ultimate obligation was to spread its language and its culture to the overseas peoples and, through a policy of assimilation, to create in its African colonies not just educated Africans, but educated French Africans. Reflecting the traditional separation of church and state prevalent in the metropole since 1903, as well as the liberal foundations on which French instruction was based, African education was to be free, nonreligious, and obligatory. Because of the vastness of the area, the sparseness of the population, the lack of communications, and the inordinate cultural and linguistic diversity of its peoples, none of these tenets was ever fully implemented—but the goal was explicit.

A Director General of Education resident in Dakar was responsible for the regulation of the educational system for the entire Federation, including the establishment of all rules and regulations concerning pedagogy, the recruitment of teaching personnel, the determination of educational programs, and the nature and content of examinations. At the territorial level, the Director General for the Federation was assisted by lower-echelon officials bearing the title of *inspecteurs d'academies,* who functioned as the principal educational administrators in their respective territories.

The Mission Influence

Although the mission role was reduced in the last five years before independence, about 40 per cent of all primary-school children are still taught in church-operated schools, and there are a number of mission "colleges" (secondary schools) as well. All the pupils must now pass set examinations before a state jury that judges the individual candidate whatever school he comes from. All mission schools necessarily adhere strictly to the curriculum laid down for state schools because it increases the chances of success of their pupils. Religion is taught as a supplementary course, although of course the ideological background percolates into such nonreligious courses as history, biology, and other sciences.

Mission schools in West Africa have enjoyed state subsidies since their early beginnings, even in the period between 1905 and 1920 when militant anticlericalism was predominant in French government circles and religious schools in the metropole were under heavy attack. This state help was maintained primarily because the administration conceived of a French missionary as a sort of colonial agent without pay. It was taken for granted that he would combine Christian teachings with a national propaganda which, in the end, would presumably serve the interests of the anticlerical state. The attitude toward non-French missionaries was more ambiguous, particularly in the years just after World War II.

The Stages of French-Administered Education

In French West Africa, just as in Equatorial Africa, Madagascar, Cameroon, and Togo, all children followed first the primary school, which in six years brought them up to the basic *certificat d'études.* From there, six more years led up to the *baccalauréat* (or matriculation), which entitled the holder to enter a university. For the most part, this basic system has been retained by each of the countries since independence. There were, as in France, various forms of *baccalauréat,* according to the relative emphasis given to humanistic studies, modern languages, or mathematics and sciences. Pupils who did not want or were unable to reach the matriculation degree could obtain, after three years in the secondary or technical schools, a *brevet d'études primaires superieures,* which is historically the most important degree. It was long the basis for recruiting junior civil servants, medical aides, accountants, and candidates for the teachers' schools. The most important teachers' school for West Africa was École William Ponty in the small village of Sebikotane near Dakar.

At the top of the West African educational system stood the central college in Dakar, which originally trained African physicians, then branched out into other faculties, and eventually became a full-fledged university in 1958. Its magnificent campus is still not quite finished, but the law, medical, science, and philological faculties are built and functioning normally.

School Attendance

The percentage of school-age children who actually attend school is a little over 16 per cent for the French-speaking West African states as a whole. This figure is not as low as it seems, especially if one takes into account that the area includes countries with vast desert sectors or small resources, where the maintenance of schools is difficult or even impossible, and that religious differences between the coastal and the inland states have made the response to education uneven. In most of the Moslem sectors, the local French schools have been viewed with diffidence. Chiefs compelled under administrative pressure to send their children to school often substituted children of poorer parents or clients, a practice that contributed to the breakdown of the traditional hierarchy by introducing a whole new power element into government and society. The status of women in Moslem countries also kept many girls away from school—or at least to a greater extent than in animist countries. Most Moslem children attend Koranic schools of the traditional type.

The lowest percentage of school attendance is to be found in the remote Niger Republic, where it has not reached 5 per cent; in Mauritania (7.3 per cent); in Upper Volta (8 per cent); and in Mali (10 per cent). Senegal, which is about 80 per cent Moslem, has 27 per cent of its school-age population under instruction. This seems to contradict the general pattern of lower rates in Moslem states, but Senegal holds quite a special position in the history of French colonization because it was the hub and showpiece of the old French West African Federation, educationally as well as economically. The oldest secondary school in West Africa (Lycée Faidherbe in St. Louis), the most famous teacher-training institute (William Ponty), and French Africa's only university were all on Senegalese soil. Although much of the Moslem resistance against European education in Senegal has been worn away during a century of close association with France, the percentage of school-age children enrolled in schools never reached as high a figure as in the Ivory Coast, Dahomey, and Togo, where French influence started far later than in Senegal but where the Moslem element was not predominant. In Dahomey and Togo, Christian mission schools have been a major factor in the higher literacy rate.

School-attendance figures have gathered increasing momentum since World War II, and especially since 1954, when the effects of the post-war investment programs of the French Fonds d'Investissements first became apparent. Between 1938 and 1946, for example, the over-all school-attendance rate climbed from 1 to 3.35 per cent. In the next five years, it jumped to 5.2 per cent. In 1954, 9.8 per cent of the school-age population in French West Africa was under instruction, and the tempo of the increase continued to accelerate in the next three years, reaching 13.5 per cent in 1957. Similarly, the percentage of girls among the school-going children (after remaining practically unchanged between 1946 and 1951, when it stood at around 20 per cent) rose in the next nine years to 24 per cent.

What Kind of an Elite?

There are and were many French as well as African critics of the highly centralized system established in these countries, with its emphasis on the sterile acquisition of facts, completely unrelated to the environment or to the individual needs of the pupils. The story is not apocryphal that at one time African boys and girls actually had to learn that "our ancestors, the Gauls, had blue eyes and red hair." These cruder mistakes were eliminated in the years after 1956; but the fact remains that the average French-educated African has lost contact with his own African milieu to a greater extent than his English-educated colleague. It was, for example, forbidden to speak any other language but French in the schools, whether public or private; similarly, one could not publish newspapers in any language except French without a special authorization, which was granted only when the colonial administration saw a direct interest in publishing texts in the vernacular languages.

The result is that even in 1961 it was very difficult, for example, for West African radio stations to find suitable editors for programs in vernacular languages. Those who speak them are either insufficiently educated to perform such skilled work satisfactorily or are assimilated to such a degree that they are unable to write and speak local tongues in a manner agreeable to the listeners. Moreover, local vernaculars have not been standardized, and it is therefore difficult to write a text that is easily understood by all.

An educational system based on assimilation assumes equal opportunities and an equal social standing for all those who partake of the same education. However, the stubborn social structure of the colonial society allowed for little social contact between the colonial administration and the educated African; it was not "fashionable" to meet educated Africans outside the office. On the other hand, the administration granted easy scholarships for the young people to be trained in France, where racial discrimination was minimal.

One may interpret the preference of many African students to remain in France as a success of assimilation, but it was also a result of the failure to build up cadres with the particular skills needed to develop their own countries. The recent independence of the French African states has reversed the previous trend, and African students are now streaming back to their homelands from Paris, hoping to get the jobs that were previously denied to them.

Leaving aside these deficiencies, however, France has a remarkable record in West Africa. What other colonial administration can boast of so impressive a roster of writers and poets? It is significant that only Guinea has set out deliberately to revamp its educational policies from the ground up, and even here there are compromises with the past: French is still the language of instruction, French teachers are widely used, and the respect for French intellectual traditions remains strong among the new political elite. In the Entente countries—Ivory Coast, Upper Volta, Niger, and Dahomey—there is increasing interest in developing two parallel systems of schooling, one to feed the elite and the other to raise the general level of education in the rural areas. Everywhere, ambitious plans for educational expansion remain heavily dependent on outside (largely French) financial and/or technical assistance. According to French sources, the governments of French-speaking West and Equatorial Africa requested a total of more than 3,000 teachers from France for the academic year 1961–62.

—Louis C. D. Joos

33. Senegal

Capital: Dakar
Population: 2,550,000 (est.)
Area: 76,084 sq. miles
Political status: Independent republic

DAKAR was the administrative capital and showpiece of the old French West African Federation, and thus Senegal fell heir to a magnificent port, the only fully operating university in the region, an international airport, a good transportation system, a highly developed radio network, an established press, and several important going industries. Senegal is the world's largest single exporter of peanuts—albeit to subsidized French markets—and has a developing phosphate industry, a profitable fishing business, considerable arable land not yet under cultivation, some promise of oil, the most elaborate economic-planning machinery in French West Africa, and a relatively high proportion of trained Africans. Its intellectual elite has a strong literary bent, and Senegal boasts more internationally recognized writers than any other single African country. Of these, the most notable is President Leopold Senghor, the country's poet-statesman.

Although the governing Union Progressiste Senegalaise won all seats in the Legislative Assembly in a hard-fought election in March, 1959, President Senghor and Prime Minister Mamadou Dia nonetheless have had their political problems. Internally, the younger Senegalese radicals are critical of the regime's close economic and emotional ties with Paris and the large number of French officials still employed in the bureaucracy. Moreover, the Senegalese Government found itself temporarily isolated politically after the breakup of its short-lived federation with neighboring Mali in late 1960, and only now is it beginning to reassert a role in African politics commensurate with its capabilities in such new groupings as the Union Africaine et Malgache (i.e., the Brazzaville Twelve) and the Monrovia Conference states. And while Dakar remains the principal industrial center of French-speaking West Africa, the pressure from competitive industries in the Ivory Coast is increasingly keen.

Educational Beginnings

Although the first French merchants settled near the mouth of the Senegal River in 1639, French culture and education did not spread throughout Senegal until the nineteenth century, and occupation of the territory was not complete until around 1900. The first French school—a small establishment for orphan girls—was founded in St. Louis by the congregation of the Sisters of St. Joseph de Cluny. Thirty years then passed before the government opened a second one—this time to teach French and the rudiments of civil administration to the sons of tribal chiefs. Graduates served as government or military interpreters until tribal thrones became vacant, or contented themselves with such minor posts as *chefs de canton*. A pervasive French educational system was finally introduced in Senegal under the Third Republic, after the four communes of St. Louis, Gorée, Dakar, and Rufisque were created.

The first teacher-training school was founded in Gorée, but later transferred to Sebikotane, a village near Dakar. Called École William Ponty, this school has special significance for the generation of educated West Africans between the ages of thirty-five and fifty: Almost all the ministers of West African governments attended it, and the personal bonds formed at Ponty have survived later political differences.*

Developments Since World War II

The main effort to produce a class of educated Senegalese came after World War II as a part of the French overseas development plan under FIDES and later FAC. In October, 1960, at the beginning of a new academic year, Education Minister François Dieng was able to announce that there were 140,000 students—or about 28.5 per cent of the school-age population—enrolled in primary, secondary, and technical schools, as compared with 100,000 the preceding year; and that there were 300 new classrooms at the primary level, bringing the total up to 2,233, and 272 more teachers for these classrooms. Encouraging progress has been made, too, in the training of Senegal-

* See Chapter 34 (the Ivory Coast) for a detailed analysis of Ponty's role in shaping the African elite.

ese teachers. For example, 75 per cent of the elementary-school teachers were African in 1958, and the number has since grown.

In 1959–60, 16 per cent of Senegal's operating budget—a total of about $8 million—was devoted to education, and 200 schools were under construction. In the same year, there were 3,500 teachers for 91,000 students on the elementary level; 285 teachers for 7,000 pupils in secondary schools; and 200 teachers for 2,000 students enrolled in technical schools.

An October, 1960, article in Senegal's *L'Unité Africaine* stated that a chief objective of the Ministry of Education is now decentralization of secondary schooling. There has been an alarming *déracinement* of thousands of young people who must study in Dakar or St. Louis. The expense involved for transportation and lodgings is high, and the loss of potential leaders on the regional level is even more costly to the nation. The new *lycée* at St. Louis will serve as a model for others to be built at Thies, Kaolack, and Ziguinchor; a *lycée* for girls will be constructed at Dakar. The St. Louis school, financed by 135 million CFA francs (over $500,000) from FAC, will offer, beginning in 1962, facilities for 1,500 students, of whom 500 will be boarders. Another innovation included in this program is the incorporation of the last two classes of the *lycée* into the Girls' College of Dakar and the colleges of Thies, Kaolack, and Ziguinchor.

The number of students in the nineteen technical schools, with some 200 teachers, rose from 2,320 in 1959–60 to 3,186 in 1960–61. Among these institutions are the High School of the Post, Telephone, and Telegraph Service at Rufisque; the Van Vollenhoven Lycée at Dakar; and the new Dakar school of mineral prospecting, which, under the direction of the Office of Mines, offers both formal instruction and on-the-job training. Dakar's Delafosse Lycée prepares students for the Certificate of Professional Qualification (*Certificat d'Aptitude Professionnelle*) and for the national schools of advanced engineering. Delafosse will include the proposed National Professional School of Public Works and the National School of Rural Cadres. The four-year course at the School of Public Works will lead to careers in civil engineering and surveying, the latter for private business as well as government projects. The School of Rural Cadres opened in 1960 for the first of three years of study in agriculture, cattle raising, water resources, forestry, and rural engineering. And in 1960, the Dakar Centre d'Apprentissage Féminin expanded to include technical and secretarial courses.

The relatively advanced state of Senegalese education is due in large measure to the sustained activities of the Catholic missions over more than a century. In 1958, the Catholics were operating 59 primary schools, with 281 classrooms. Catholic secondary schools include the normal schools of Thies (50 students), Ziguinchor (30 students), and Rufisque (50 students); the two colleges of St. Mary, one at Dakar (540 students), the other at Ziguinchor (80 students); the girls' school of Joan of Arc and the private boarding school of Notre Dame at Dakar (560 students); and two small seminaries, one a noviciate.

In January, 1960, three commissions were set up—for youth problems, mass education, and athletics. In February of the same year, a permanent Advisory Council on Mass Education, Youth, and Sports was created. Under Council auspices, a training course opened in April, 1960, at the National Center of Training and Action at Rufisque. Thirty-eight trainees, selected during regional preliminary courses, enrolled in the program. They will eventually organize and head youth centers, many of which the Ministry of Education hopes to open within secondary schools.

The University of Dakar

The first step in the development of Senegalese education at the university level was taken just before World War II, when a medical college (renamed the Medical and Pharmaceutical School in 1948) was established to train West Africans to be "African physicians"—a degree somewhat lower than that of fully trained French doctors. A veterinary college and law faculty followed. In 1950, the Medical School and the new faculties of Law, Science, and Liberal Arts were incorporated in the Institute of Higher Studies. The Institute became the University of Dakar in 1957.

Within the beautiful campus in the Fann Park area are now housed four faculties. The Faculty of Law and Economic Sciences offers the bachelor of law degree (*licence en droit*), the diploma of higher legal study, and the certificate of traditional and customary law. In this faculty are also the Institute of African Administrative Studies, which prepares students for the local civil-service exams, and the Tropical African Institute of Applied Economic and Commercial Sciences. The Faculty of Sciences is affiliated with the university's Institut Français d'Afrique Noire, which operates a first-class library on West African civilization and environment. The third faculty, that of Letters and Social Sciences, includes a preparatory institute for secondary-school teaching. This faculty cooperates with the Senegalese Institute of Applied Human Sciences, which in turn works closely with the universities of Bordeaux, Strasbourg, and Rheims. Finally,

University of Dakar.

the National School of Medicine and Pharmacology provides up to five years of training.

Among the departments recently added at the university are the Statistics and Documentation Centers; the Pedagogical Institute, created in 1959; and the African Cancer Research Center, the Institute of Social Pediatrics, and the School of Research, Study, and Documentation on African Institutions, all approved in 1960. The university also offers correspondence courses. It has helped to establish an Institut des Hautes Études at Abidjan and has sent specialists to several West African governments to work on such problems as migratory labor, customary land law, and resettlement of refugees from Mossi areas.

Student enrollment at the university was 1,040 in 1957–58, 1,316 in 1958–59, 1,285 in 1959–60, and 1,398 in 1960–61. However, it must be stressed that the University of Dakar is not restricted to Senegalese students. In 1960–61, 1 out of 7 students was non-African, and barely more than half the total enrollment was Senegalese. Aside from a temporary decrease in the number of students during 1959–60—due in part to the withdrawal of the entire Ivory Coast contingent because of political differences between the two countries—the progress of the university has been continuous.

The 434 Senegalese citizens out of the total enrollment of 1,398 at Dakar in 1960 were heavily concentrated in the Faculty of Law (239, as compared with 81 in Sciences, 65 in Letters, and 49 in Medicine). Law has long been the most popular profession in Senegal—partly because it is lucrative, partly because there were until recently barriers against Africans entering some other fields, and partly because law provides excellent preparation for politics. National Assembly Chairman Lamine Gueye, ex-Chairman Boissier-Palun and former Vice President A. Guillabert of the French West African Grand Council, Home and Defense Minister Valdiodio Ndiaye, former Minister of Justice Boubakar Gueye, Minister of Justice Gabriel d'Arboussier, and Foreign Minister Doudou Thiam are only a few of the prominent Senegalese lawyers.

What is true of the Senegalese is not necessarily true of other African contingents at the University of Dakar. The number of students in science exceeds those in law in the case of Niger (five law students, nine science students) and Upper Volta (eight law students, nine science students). A balance between law and science students is maintained in two other cases—those of Mali (thirty-two law students, thirty science students) and Mauritania (six law students, five science students). The countries that show a balance between law and science are those where underdevelopment is most pronounced, whereas Senegal, like other relatively more developed African states, shows a preference for law and, to a lesser degree, letters.

The government is attempting to augment the output from Dakar by sending selected personnel to French universities, specialized institutes, and various French administrative bureaus for accelerated training in particular areas of shortage. At the *enseignement superieur,* or university level, there were 220 Senegalese in France on government scholarships in 1961 and 168 *stagiaires* being trained under special conditions. In an effort to redress the balance between law and science, the emphasis in placing these students abroad is on science. Among the 220 students in France, 15 were studying engineering, 80 were preparing in the *grandes écoles* (Polytechnique, École des Mines, École Centrale, etc.) for science degrees, 16 were in agriculture, and 20 in law.

Among the Senegalese enrolled in accelerated courses, only eight at the French National Center of Legal Studies are studying law. Technical and administrative courses clearly predominate. In 1961, twelve students were training in agriculture and stock raising, three in printing, two in cartography; eight were studying at the atomic-research center at Saclay, and four were working at the Berliet automobile factory. Others were being trained at the French Foreign Ministry, the French meteorological institute, and the higher institute of the oil industry, or were taking courses in finance, customs, general administration, public health, journalism, and education.

Attitudes of the Elite

Although lawyers continue to predominate in the political life of Senegal, other professions are also represented. Of the fifteen ministers in the Senegalese cabinet in 1961, there were, besides the three lawyers already mentioned, two physicians, one veterinarian, and six primary-school teachers. In the administration, too, many posts have now been filled by teachers. In fact, the rush from the teaching profession into the civil service has reached such alarming proportions that the government decided, in November, 1960, to pay a special 20 per cent bonus to those teachers who remain in the classroom. As a result of the lure of politics and the civil service, only a small percentage of professionally trained Senegalese remain outside the orbit of government. There are practicing physicians, pharmacists, lawyers, and journalists, but they are few in relation to the nation's absorptive potential. Europeans are still dominant in Senegalese industry, and some 1,500 French are employed in the administration.

In view of the fact that most of the educated Senegalese will find jobs easily in the civil service during the next several years, it may seem surprising that opposition to the government is centered mainly in the younger generation of intellectuals. A poll of students at the University of Dakar would almost certainly record a widespread conviction that "traditional" and "French-oriented" elements in the government were stifling the development of Senegal's true African personality and the rise of younger politicians. Sékou Touré's Guinea is idealized as a model state by much of Senegal's educated youth.

Senegalese of all political viewpoints take justifiable pride in the country's literary tradition. Senegal boasts a nucleus of writers unequaled in French-speaking Africa—most of them graduates of École William Ponty. The most eminent is, of course, President Senghor, although he is a product of French and not West African schools. Other writers are Ousmane Soce Diop, whose novel *Karim,* in its fifth edition, is among the most circulated books of the French cultural center at Dakar; Abdoulaye Sadji, whose *Maimouna* has enjoyed a similar popularity; and Birago Diop, whose *Stories of Amadou Koumba* are well known to all literate Senegalese. Most of these authors deal with one major problem: the ways in which African traditions are to be united with modern civilization.

Sheikh Anta Diop's *Nations Nègres et Culture* has become the bible of the educated young Senegalese. It is a passionate plea for the dignity of "Negro civilization," from which, Diop argues, ancient Egyptian civilization and certain aspects of Judaism and Western civilization were derived. Diop accuses Western Egyptologists of fraud committed in the name of white racism for not recognizing the contribution of this ancient Negro culture. In a discussion of linguistic problems in Africa, he seeks Egyptian roots for Senegalese dialects. Finally, he attempts to demonstrate the flexibility of Negro languages by translating into his native Ouolof excerpts from scientific works on the theory of relativity.

The validity of Diop's argument is not relevant here. What is important is that he and the other Senegalese writers mentioned have profoundly influenced the thinking of many of their fellow countrymen, as well as that of Africans throughout French-speaking Africa. There are few countries in Africa where the educated elite has reached this stage in cultural development.

34. *The Ivory Coast**

Capital: Abidjan
Population: 3,200,000 (est.)
Area: 125,000 sq. miles
Political status: Independent republic

THE Ivory Coast's 3.2 million people, distributed over an area the size of New Mexico, constitute one of the more heterogeneous human mosaics in Africa. More than sixty variations of the spoken word have been noted in this country, formerly one of the eight territories of French West Africa. The many tribes can be classified into four major culture circles, none of which has its center of gravity within the country. The peoples of the eastern forest region—the Baoulé, Agni, and others—are Akans, related to Ghanaian groups; they are sharply differentiated from their western countrymen, who are related to the Liberian Kru. In the north, where the forest gives way to the savanna, are the two other major groups: the Senufo, a Voltaic people, and the Malinke, part of the Mende family, with their cultural center in Guinea and Mali. This pattern has been further complicated by recent immigration of Africans from other countries, attracted by the Ivory Coast's boom economy. Indeed, these foreign Africans constitute more than one-fifth of the total population. In recent years, increased communication among groups, internal migrations, and greater awareness of disparities in the economic and social status of diverse tribes have led to ethnic tensions. So far, national unity has been provided by an all-encompassing political movement, the Parti Démocratique de Côte d'Ivoire (PDCI). But occasional outbursts of violence have made the country's political

* Much of the material on which this study is based was gathered in interviews with Ivory Coast officials, teachers, and students, and through personal observations in 1959. Field study was made possible through a grant of the Ford Foundation.

leadership conscious of the need to promote national integration at the most basic level, that of the youth.

Until the middle of the nineteenth century, only the southeastern corner of the Ivory Coast had intermittent contacts with Europe; the western part of the coast, known as the Côte des Malgens, was thought to be inhospitable. Penetration into the hinterland began in earnest when Samory and the British threatened French dominion over the western Soudan in the last decades of the century. Resistance to European rule lasted in some regions until well into the twentieth century, and civilian administration was not instituted until after World War I. (Meanwhile, Senegal had already elected its first African representative to the French Parliament.) French assimilationist theories notwithstanding, few Ivory Coasters became French citizens; most of them were administered as subjects until 1946. The Ivory Coast made up for lost time, however, and by the end of World War II, it was the most highly developed French-speaking country of Africa south of the Sahara. Two valuable export commodities, coffee and cocoa, were largely responsible for the territory's rapid development. These resources are distributed among a large number of African farmers, who constitute an agricultural bourgeoisie of sorts.

Early Schools

Although at least one Ivory Coaster was educated during the eighteenth century by the famous Bishop Bossuet and Madame de Maintenon when brought as a hostage to the court of Louis XIV, the first European-style school in the country * was established by a planter in 1882, only to be abandoned soon afterward. The first government school was opened in 1887 and followed eight years later by a Catholic mission establishment. Since the main purpose of these early institutions was to train interpreters and copy clerks, emphasis was placed on the study of the French language and little else.

After 1903, an attempt was made to unify education for all of French West Africa.† Village schools, usually staffed by educated Africans from Senegal or Dahomey, taught basic skills; above them, regional schools manned by Frenchmen selected the best pupils for a three-year course leading to a certificate of agricultural or manual

* Koranic schools existed long before this in the Islamic north, of course, and the fame of those at Kong and Bondoukou reached as far as Djenne and Segou.

† See Georges Hardy, *Une Conquête Morale: L'Enseignement en A.O.F.* (Paris: Librairie Armand Colin, 1917). For information on the prewar educational system, see also F. J. Amon d'Aby, *La Côte d'Ivoire dans la Cité Africaine* (Paris: Larose, 1951).

proficiency. After 1908, some Africans were allowed to attend French-type schools, hitherto restricted to the children of colonial officials. A very few could then go on to a higher primary school at St. Louis (Senegal) or, from 1910 on, to the École Primaire Supérieure at Bingerville, then the capital of the Ivory Coast, where they received an additional two years of general education. This led to clerical jobs in the colonial administration or in private enterprise. Finally, the best EPS graduates were selected to attend the normal school in Senegal, from which they emerged as assistant teachers. Most of these schools were public rather than denominational and private. Catholic missions were restricted because of the struggle between church and state in France, although small subsidies were granted to mission schools that agreed to teach the prescribed government curriculum in French. These restrictions, basically political, effectively discouraged English-speaking Protestant missions and Germans. On the eve of World War I, an estimated 2,500 children were receiving some form of elementary education.

In 1915, educational personnel in the Ivory Coast consisted of the following: one educational inspector, two French male teachers, and three French female instructors, who directed the urban schools of Bingerville, Bassam, Abidjan, and Bouaké; seventeen African teachers, educated at the normal school of St. Louis, who were in charge of the regional schools; fifty African monitors, trained at Bingerville, who directed the village schools located near the administrative centers; and ten sub-officers, who were in charge of the village schools in the military area.

After 1920, in line with the over-all French objective of making the empire self-sufficient, the Ivory Coast was assigned the task of producing cocoa and coffee. French *colons* and some Africans were encouraged to develop plantations. Although this period is mainly remembered as the era of forced labor, it also witnessed the expansion of educational opportunities. Given the goal of intensive colonization, it was generally agreed that Africans had to be trained as auxiliaries of private enterprise and of the public services. In pleading for funds, officials of the education department of the Ministry of Colonies pointed out that Africans would require lower salaries than Frenchmen who had hitherto been imported to perform clerical jobs. There was much less agreement, however, on the goals of the system and on the form of its implementation. The partisans of an assimilationist policy advocated the training of a highly selected elite who would attain the status of Frenchmen through educational achievement; at the opposite extreme were the practical-minded, who advocated a colonial education designed to meet short-term needs of the system. The educational structure that prevailed until the end of World War II, and produced the contemporary elite, was a compromise between these two extremes. Its major concern was to avoid the creation of a class of discontented intellectuals.

Elementary education, conducted in French throughout, was more practical than its French equivalent, with emphasis on manual skills and on agricultural training. Children who attended the six-year public school paid no tuition; only one out of five were in mission schools. The total school population rose to 11,600 in 1940, when about 3 per cent of the children of school age attended. There were no secondary schools in the country, but about 200 children attended each of the two higher primary schools.

As in the past, a few were then selected to proceed to teacher training at the École William Ponty in Senegal or one of the other post-primary institutions in the Federation. In all of French West Africa, there was only one public secondary school, the Lycée Faidherbe, also in Senegal. Although it was theoretically open to African students from the eight colonies, only Senegalese and Europeans normally attended. In practice, Ivory Coasters did not have access to university education; only five are known to have acquired degrees before 1945. For the ambitious young man, École William Ponty was the apex.

Education and Politics

Although designated as a normal school, Ponty also produced, after World War I, junior civil servants and students eligible to attend a medical training course leading to the position of *médecin africain* or *pharmacien africain*. The first Ivory Coaster completed his training at Ponty in 1921; about 10 a year followed during the 1920's, and about 20 during the 1930's for the Ivory Coast and Upper Volta combined. The estimated 200 Ivory Coasters who had completed the course of study at Ponty at the end of World War II constituted the country's intellectual elite. Their education was decidedly limited on the intellectual side, however, for Ponty was in the hands of a staff trained in primary education exclusively. Scholarship, books, and laboratory work were less emphasized than agricultural and manual labor for the school's own maintenance.*

Nevertheless, Ponty served as the catalyst of political consciousness for a whole generation of Ivory Coasters. French political transformation under the Popular Front regime profoundly affected students

* See Hardy, *op cit.*, pp. 167, 172.

and recent graduates serving in the colonial administration. Many of those who later became leading political figures have vivid memories of their first contact with liberal-minded young Frenchmen with whom they celebrated Labor Day on May 1 and who introduced them to new currents of thought, including French Marxism.* This generation, most of them about thirty years old after World War II, supplied the entire political leadership of the Ivory Coast in the period of postwar nationalism. Furthermore, the contacts established at Ponty facilitated the creation of superterritorial movements such as the Rassemblement Démocratique Africain, of which the PDCI was a major component. The Popular Front also encouraged Africans to concern themselves with their own culture. Several of the outstanding Ponty students went on to become playwrights, poets, and novelists, as well as politicians. The theatrical tradition created there in the 1930's was still very lively in the Ivory Coast in 1961, when the Minister of Interior took time out from his official duties to supervise a new production of one of his plays (regretting, incidentally, that for the first time he could not also perform in it).

Given the liberalization of the colonial system under the Popular Front, the paternalistic and racist policies of the Vichy authorities were keenly resented by educated Africans deprived of some of their recently acquired privileges. They sought the support of the uneducated in order to organize protest movements. Political discontent was heightened in the Ivory Coast by the presence of white settlers who competed with African farmers. Félix Houphouet-Boigny, now President of the Republic, and other Ponty-educated plantation owners and members of the civil service organized the country's first political groups after 1945. They were more radical in tone than the prewar associations in Senegal, and the Ivory Coast soon became one of the trouble spots of French Africa.

The creation of the French Union in 1946 marked the beginning of a new era. Although self-government was not viewed as the final outcome, Africans participated in government through newly created territorial assemblies, a federal council, and representation in the two houses of the French Parliament and in the Assembly of the French Union. After a short period of intense agitation, Houphouet-Boigny's PDCI decided to cooperate with the French administration. In 1956, Houphouet-Boigny became the first African to hold the rank of cabinet minister in a French Government. By 1957, the PDCI had

*** For a vivid account of the reactions of a Ponty student during this period, see the partly autobiographical novel by the Ivory Coast poet Bernard Dadié, *Climbié* (Paris: Editions Seghers, 1956).**

achieved a political monopoly, and its Secretary-General, Auguste Denise (also a Ponty graduate), headed the first African government.

These political transformations were accompanied by corresponding changes in education. Africans demanded and eventually obtained an educational system similar to that of France in standards and in content. Many of the colonial features of the prewar system, such as agricultural training, were now considered degrading and were eliminated in response to these African pressures. The base of the educational pyramid was broadened; a full structure of secondary schools was built upon it; and it was crowned by offering the student ready access to a French university. France helped to defray the cost of this development through its Fonds d'Investissement Économique et Social (FIDES), which spent almost $5 million in the Ivory Coast between 1947 and 1957, mostly on the construction of secondary schools.* Since the Ivory Coast itself had a relatively sound economy, it was able to spend more than most other territories. African and European representatives in the territorial assembly demanded that a greater share of public funds be spent on education and other social or economic services than on overhead administration.

At the elementary level, the relative growth was greater than anywhere else in French West Africa, as is shown in Table 1.

Table 1
Postwar Growth of Primary Education in the Ivory Coast

	1947		1957	
Schools	Number of classes	Number of pupils	Number of classes	Number of pupils
Public	385	20,154	1,192	56,500
Private	172	8,239	817	34,500
Total	*557*	*28,393*	*2,009*	*91,000*

SOURCE: French West Africa, Direction Générale des Services Économiques et du Plan, *AOF 1957: Tableaux Économiques* (Dakar, 1957), p. 116.

During this period, the Ivory Coast rapidly bypassed most of the other territories. In 1947, only 3.79 per cent of its children of school age were in school, compared with the federal average of 5.3 per cent. In 1957, the equivalent figures were 25.5 per cent for the Ivory Coast and 13.4 per cent for the Federation. The development of post-primary and secondary education was even more striking: from three institutions with 192 students in 1947 to twenty institutions with nearly 5,000 students in 1957. Although there was no local university,

* Ivory Coast, Ministére du Plan, *Troisième Plan Quadriennal, 1958–62* (mimeographed; Abidjan, 1957), p. 57.

the Ivory Coast spent more than any other territory on scholarships for its students abroad.*

The School System in 1957

The Ivory Coast educational system on the eve of independence was closely patterned on that of France. The *enseignement du premier degré* consisted mainly of the six-year primary school, divided into two years each of the *cours préparatoire, cours élémentaire,* and *cours moyen*. Children normally started at age six and finished at twelve or fourteen, but many started and finished much later. Since they were not allowed to stay in school after fourteen, birth records were often falsified. Sixty per cent of the pupils were in public schools in 1957, where education was entirely free. As Table 1 indicates, however, the private schools had grown at an even higher rate than the public schools.

Not only did French remain the sole language of instruction throughout, but the curriculum was almost exactly the same as that of French schools, with comparable lessons in reading, writing, arithmetic, history, geography, and morals. A superficial effort had been made to add an African flavor to the schools by adapting textbooks, but this had not involved substantial revision of the system.

The approach of the teachers to their pupils was vastly different from the pupil-oriented education that has become almost standard in the United States. Large classes, with an average of forty-five pupils, limited the amount of individual attention that a teacher could give. The overcrowding also made for disciplinary problems. In a class of more than eighty pupils crowded into a room intended for forty, in Abidjan, the teacher despaired of being able to control her class and was forced to devote most of her time to meting out punishment. Yet, teachers were committed to mass education and believed that children should not be turned away for lack of space; many more were being admitted than there was room for, and it was expected that the worst ones would soon drop out. Since many teachers were inadequately trained, they felt too insecure to experiment with new methods, even when officially encouraged to do so. As in many schools in France, learning was often accomplished by rote: The visitor was frequently greeted at a school by the unmistakable sound of fifty children shouting irregular verb conjugations in unison. Competition was keen, and every pupil had a standing in his class based on regular examinations; failure to pass at the end of the year meant retention

* French West Africa, Direction Générale des Services Économiques et du Plan, *AOF 1957: Tableaux Économiques* (Dakar, 1957), p. 118.

in the same grade as many times as necessary. Teachers sympathized with their pupils' problems—often including the lack of home lighting and hence the near impossibility of doing homework, except by working outdoors under streetlamps, where they were available—but they did not hesitate to use public ridicule to drive their pupils to work harder.

The end of the sixth year of primary school was a crucial turning point in one's academic career. First, the pupil had to obtain the *Certificat d'Études Primaires Elémentaires* (school-completion certificate), given through country-wide examination. It was—and is—required for almost any salaried position. In 1957, of the 5,739 who reached the end of the sixth year—about one-third of those who began—only 2,114 obtained the CEPE. The others could try again the following year after spending another year in school if they were not too old. Secondly, if the pupil wanted to continue, he had to pass the *examen d'entrée en sixième,* the "sixth" being the first year of a six-year secondary course. Furthermore, he had to specify whether he wanted to pursue an academic course, leading potentially to the university, or a teacher-training course, which would limit his future to a career in the elementary-school system. Out of the 2,762 who took the examination in 1957, 750 were admitted. Thus, in that year, only 750 out of the 5,739 who completed primary school continued their education. Only a few of the 87 per cent of school leavers tried again later or entered vocational schools.*

The secondary level was organized as follows:

(1) A *premier cycle,* the lower four years, which included classical or modern academic courses at the *lycée,* the *collèges,* or the *cours secondaires;* technical courses at the *collège technique;* teacher-training courses in the *cours normaux.* At the end of their fourth year, students could obtain, through examination, the *Brevet d'Études du Premier Cycle,* somewhat similar to the prewar Ponty diploma; those who took teacher training could qualify as *moniteurs* after an additional year of professional training.

(2) Beyond the preceding, a *deuxième cycle,* the upper three years. Students at the *lycée* or the *collèges* prepared to take the first part of *baccalauréat* examination at the end of the sixth year of secondary school, and the second part the following year. In that last year, they could specialize in the liberal arts, mathematics, or science. This degree was required for entrance into universities. A similar pro-

* All figures for 1957 and 1958 were obtained from the Ivory Coast Government's own published report, *Rapport sur l'Activité Générale* (Abidjan: Imprimerie du Gouvernement, May, 1958), pp. 201–24 and 313–29. These figures sometimes conflict with others published by the same or later officials.

cedure was followed in the upper cycle of technical schools; the *baccalauréat technique* led to the engineering schools. The upper cycle of teacher training, given at the *école normale,* prepared students for the *baccalauréat de l'enseignement;* after an additional year of professional training, they could take the pedagogical examination and qualify for the rank of *instituteur ordinaire.*

The total enrollment at the secondary level was 4,350 in 1957: 3,209 in academic courses, 149 in technical courses, and 992 at teacher-training institutions. Several hundred more were studying abroad. There were also three trade schools, with a total student body of 384. As was the case in France, the rate of failure of candidates for the *baccalauréat* was very high: In 1957, 63 out of 143 passed the first half, and 45 out of 104 the second half. About one-third of those who obtained the degree were French residents. So few Ivory Coasters obtained the *baccalauréat* that anyone who did was almost certain to obtain a university scholarship. An estimated 500 students were then at French institutions of higher education, and 150 more attended the Institut des Hautes Études at Dakar, since then promoted to university status. Medicine was the first choice with most students, although many of them went on to other subjects after they failed; about one-fourth were registered as medical students. Law, sciences, and letters drew about 15 per cent each. The remainder were distributed among the technical fields, including agriculture and engineering. Since only a few students had obtained their degrees, the Ivory Coast did not then know the problem of the underemployed university educated.

Changes Since 1957

The French Union underwent major reforms in 1957. The Ivory Coast, along with other territories, obtained universal suffrage; separate representation for Africans and Europeans in the local assembly was abolished; the assembly's powers were widened to include almost complete control over internal affairs; and, finally, an African government shared executive responsibility with the governor. Two important political issues dominated the next three years. The Ivory Coast had always resented the burden of contributing to the maintenance of French West Africa as a whole and was active in bringing about the demise of that unit at the beginning of 1959. It promoted instead the creation of a loose alliance of four states, known since 1959 as the Conseil de l'Entente, in which policy in various spheres, including higher education, is coordinated on an *ad hoc* basis.

The most important issue, however, concerned the country's relationship to France. For several years, the PDCI leadership advocated the formation of some kind of Franco-African federation of states through which rapid economic development could be brought about. In 1958, when the Fifth Republic was instituted, overseas territories were given a choice between joining a French Community or cutting all ties that bound them to France. General de Gaulle warned that to vote "No" in the forthcoming referendum would entail loss of all French aid, immediate withdrawal of civil servants and expatriate teachers, and the end of technical assistance. It is therefore not surprising that only one of the thirteen territories, Guinea, voted "No." In December, 1958, the Ivory Coast became a self-governing republic within the Community, with control over all its affairs except foreign relations, defense, and higher education. But the Community was an ill-defined body, and political pressures in Africa to move toward complete independence mounted. On August 7, 1960, the Ivory Coast declared its independence from France and withdrew from the Community. Relations with France remained friendly, however, and in the spring of 1961 agreements of cooperation were negotiated that provide for continued French assistance in certain fields.

The development plan for 1958–62, formulated soon after the formation of the first African government, did not question the structure of the educational system described above. It emphasized quantitative achievements, especially in the sphere of school construction, and proposed to increase the percentage of school-age children in school by 15 per cent during the four-year period. The record, as of the fall of 1960, was even more spectacular than the plan had anticipated. This was due in part to autonomous community action: In some parts of the country, long-standing rivalries between villages, for example, were channeled into competition in school building. The Minister of Education proudly displayed telegrams he received at the beginning of the school year from many villages: "Have school, please send teacher." From 1959 on, PDCI officials were instructed to encourage further development of this wave of enthusiasm. A second factor that facilitated rapid expansion was the increase in government revenue that occurred when the Ivory Coast retained taxes formerly collected by the federal government and redistributed to the various territories according to need. Table 2 shows the increase in educational expenditures from 1958 to 1961.

The outcome of these efforts is visible in current data for plant and attendance, particularly at the primary level. The national plant grew from 653 schools with 2,009 classrooms in 1957 to 1,551 schools with

Table 2
Educational Expenditures, 1958–61

Fiscal year	Expenditure	Percentage of budget
1958	$ 4,650,000	16
1959	6,600,000	15
1960	8,580,000	10
1961	15,720,000	14

SOURCE: Computed from annual budget estimates for the years specified.

4,549 classrooms in 1959.* The slightly lower average number of classrooms per school reflects the mushrooming of numerous one- and two-room village schoolhouses throughout the country. They are strikingly similar in appearance, because blueprints have been standardized in order to cut costs and to facilitate self-help. Attendance at public and private schools has increased as follows: 91,000 in 1956–57, 145,650 in 1957–58, 198,858 in 1959–60, and 236,123 in 1960–61. The ratio of public to private (mostly Catholic) schools has remained approximately two to one, an indication that the Church has also increased its efforts.

It is extremely difficult to determine what proportion of children of school age are now attending school. Past censuses usually underestimated population figures and did not accurately reflect the population pyramid. The government reported a rate of 25.5 per cent as of January 1, 1957; 30 per cent as of January 1, 1958; and 43 per cent as of January, 1961. These figures are based on a school-age population estimated to be 15 per cent of the total population, but recent demographic studies suggest that an estimate of 20 per cent would be more realistic. On this revised basis, approximately 22 per cent of the school-age population was in school in 1957–58; now, based on an estimated 640,000 school-age children in 1960–61, the percentage is 37 per cent.

Table 3 reveals one of the most serious problems facing Ivory Coast development: the unevenness of the impact of development upon the various regions. Abidjan and Bassam districts, located in the southeast, include urbanized areas and the more prosperous cash-crop areas in the country; they also have the highest percentage of school-age children enrolled in schools. Adzopé and Gagnoa are farther inland, but still actively involved in coffee and cocoa produc-

* All information concerning education from 1959 on was obtained from issues of *Fraternité*, weekly organ of the ruling party and thus a quasi-official publication of the Ivory Coast Government. See especially the issues of September 30, 1960, and March 24, 1961, which contain reports by the Minister of Education.

Table 3
Primary-School Population in 1957–58

Educational district	School Population			Percentage of school-age children in school
	Public	Private	Total	
Abidjan	10,150	7,292	17,442	91
Adzope	15,950	4,225	20,175	45
Bassam	11,585	2,866	14,451	77
Bouaké	18,150	11,263	29,413	24
Daloa	16,900	7,352	24,252	21
Gagnoa	18,030	12,010	30,040	45
Korhogo	6,220	3,657	9,877	10
Total	*96,985*	*48,665*	*145,650*	*30*

SOURCE: Ivory Coast, Conseil de Gouvernement, *Rapport sur l'Activité Générale* (Abidjan: Imprimerie du Gouvernement, May, 1958), p. 201.

tion. Bouaké, in the center, and Daloa, in the west, include both forest and savanna sectors; on the average, they are poorer than the others already listed. The greatest educational lag is found in Korhogo, which includes all the northern *cercles,* where there has been relatively little economic change. Thus, by 1958, the north was distinct from the south not only in its traditional culture, but also because of its lesser involvement in modernizing developments. There has been much discussion of this danger of the north's alienation from the mainstream of national communication in recent years, and the north has been demanding a greater share of the national wealth. The government is now pledged to allocate future school construction in inverse proportion to existing plant. It has been announced that 180 classrooms will be built in Korhogo in 1961. The European Development Fund in May, 1960, agreed to finance two projects for the Ivory Coast—the construction of 60 primary schools at a cost of $1,216,000 and the construction of rural training centers at a cost of $912,000.

Unevenness also characterizes education for girls as compared with boys. In 1957, only 21 per cent of school children were girls. The ratio of girls to boys in school was lower than in any other territory of French West Africa, except Mauritania. Since the proportion of Moslems in the total population is smaller than in the other territories (except Dahomey), religion cannot be the cause of this phenomenon. In various interviews, Ivory Coast educators have suggested that parents feel that it is wasteful to educate girls as long as there is a shortage of schools, but so far there is no adequate explanation for the situation. Educated young men who must marry illiterate wives, as well as others, have become increasingly concerned, however, with the widening educational gap between men and women. This is seen as a major stumbling block in the path of the modernization of the Ivory Coast family and the source of great psychological tensions. Since most children are brought up by mothers who do not speak French, they are handicapped when entering school and must often repeat the first year two or three times. In order to overcome this, several centers have been created for women too old to attend public schools; they learn basic literacy, child care, homemaking, and sewing. Social workers are trying to convince families that they should send girls to school. These efforts have resulted in a slight improvement of the situation; in 1959–60, there were 27 girls out of every 100 children in school.

As noted earlier, only about 15 per cent of those who completed primary school continued their education in 1957. The remainder swelled the ranks of a large stratum of young people who refuse to work in agriculture but who are largely unskilled and not easily absorbed in the modern sector of the economy. This problem, noted in many other African countries, has been complicated in the Ivory Coast by tensions between natives and immigrants. In the past, territories such as Senegal and Dahomey, which had a higher percentage of school-age children in school, exported low-level white-collar workers to the Ivory Coast. Unemployed Ivory Coast school leavers attributed their difficulties to the entrenched position of these foreign Africans in private and in public bureaucracies. Latent antagonism erupted into open conflict in October, 1958, when school leavers were particularly active in xenophobic riots that occurred in Abidjan and elsewhere. Nearly 25,000 foreign Africans, including 150 qualified schoolteachers, were later evacuated. Discontent has continued to grow among the school leavers and the holders of the *brevet* who, although exposed to the promise of the modern world, remain unable to satisfy their newly acquired needs.

One of the solutions brought to bear upon this problem has been the creation of a number of *cours complémentaires,* four-year post-primary schools open to holders of the CEPE who did not do sufficiently well on the *examen d'entrée en sixième* to be admitted to secondary schools. These new institutions are distributed throughout the country, in an effort to ensure that their graduates contribute to their communities and do not flood the capital. The eleven schools opened in the autumn of 1957 have increased to thirty; current projects give high priority to the training of teachers for additional schools of this type. The curriculum will include manual and agricultural training. Thus, in one of its first initiatives, the Ivory Coast Government has borrowed from the experience of the prewar normal school.

A second approach has been the development of vocational education. Recognizing that many Ivory Coasters have come to consider literacy and work in industry or agriculture as being mutually exclusive, the government created a separate Ministry of Technical Education in 1957 in an attempt to raise the prestige of technical and vocational education. Two additional vocational schools, called *centres d'apprentissage,* were opened in 1959, bringing the total to five, including one for girls. Facilities have also been created for the training of railroad workers, mechanics, and others, with the help of private industry. Students who follow a short two-year course receive qualifying certificates; those who complete a long course (usually four years) obtain a *brevet industriel* or *commercial,* which qualifies them as foremen. The government intends to extend this program in the near future. In his first policy speech following his election as President of the Ivory Coast Republic in 1960, Houphouet-Boigny announced that children would no longer be allowed to leave school unless they had a job. Those who have none will be assigned to vocational centers, yet to be created, where they will be taught a trade that is considered useful for the country.*

Joachim Bony, the thirty-five-year old Minister of Education and the first Ivory Coast citizen to teach at the Abidjan *lycée,* has called the spectacular growth of secondary education "a tidal wave." In the fall of 1960, 3,403 students passed the *examen d'entrée en sixième,* more than four times as many as in 1957. Facilities have been rapidly expanding to accommodate them. There are now eleven *collèges,* including six public and five private ones, plus the Abidjan *lycée.* The *collège technique,* recently promoted to the rank of *lycée,* now has three sections: industrial, mathematical, and economics. The entire post-primary school population was as follows as of January 1, 1960:

Complementary and teacher training	3,630
Secondary (academic)	4,761
Secondary (technical) and vocational	1,730
Total	*10,121*

(By 1961, this total had risen to 11,444.)

Public schools accounted for a much larger share of the total than at the elementary level: 8,507 students, against 1,614 in private institutions. The proportion of girls is about 20 per cent in secondary aca-

* *Fraternité,* January 13, 1961.

demic schools, about the same in complementary and teacher training, but much lower in technical and vocational schools.

The Teacher Shortage

Notwithstanding the larger pool of educated Ivory Coasters, the educational system is far from being self-sustaining—that is, it does not produce a sufficiently large number of qualified teachers to maintain the desired rate of expansion without sacrificing quality at the primary level; at the secondary level, the problem is even more acute, since almost all teachers are still expatriates. Short cuts have been used. Because of the huge increase in primary-school enrollment Of the 1,073 individuals recruited, only 148 were qualified *instituteurs,* including 30 expatriates. The remainder were *moniteurs,* most in 1957, the government had to hire almost anyone willing to teach. of them holders of the CEPE only. Applicants were to be screened through a special examination; but since the rate of failure was high and the situation critical, many of those who fell just below the official passing mark were hired as *moniteurs suppléants* and assigned to classrooms after two months spent as student-teachers. Within one year, the level of teacher qualification went down drastically:

	Instituteurs	*Moniteurs*	*Total*
1957	923	427	1,350
1958	1,071	1,352	2,423

In 1960, once again, 400 new teachers had to be found to staff newly built classrooms. The teacher-training institutions graduated only 60 regular *moniteurs* and *instituteurs;* 340 unqualified substitutes were recruited.

The Minister of Education has recently acknowledged that quality has suffered from rapid expansion. An attempt is being made to remedy the situation by selecting school principals as counselors to groups of *moniteurs;* on-the-job training would be institutionalized on a permanent basis; intensive summer courses for substitutes are also being organized; a correspondence school has been created as well. But the core of the problem lies in current attitudes toward the teaching profession. Although the teaching corps was 96 per cent Africanized by 1957–58, educated Ivory Coasters refuse to become teachers because they do not want to live under poor conditions outside the major urban centers. The pay is low, and, in general, the profession lacks glamour. This is a recent phenomenon. In the previous generation, being a teacher represented one of the highest possible achievements for Africans. A large proportion of the political elite now in power is made up of Ponty-trained assistant teachers. The late Ouezzin Coulibaly, Ivory Coast deputy to the French National Assembly, and Philippe Yace, President of the Legislative Assembly and currently Secretary-General of the PDCI, are outstanding examples. They and many others owed their start in politics to their activities in the Syndicat des Instituteurs (Teachers' Union), one of the earliest and most powerful of the voluntary associations.

The Syndicat des Instituteurs, headed today by Lambert Amon Tanoh—also the leader of the all-inclusive national trade-union body, the Union Nationale des Travailleurs de Côte d'Ivoire—is very articulate, not only in regard to working conditions but also about educational policy in general. It has long fought against the granting of government subsidies to private (denominational) schools, in the best tradition of the French *instituteur laïque,* the major carrier of anticlerical traditions. To the public-school teachers' complaints that the private schools hire unqualified personnel and pay them low salaries, the Church hierarchy has answered that the government now does the same thing and that it has finally espoused the Church's position in favor of mass education. In justification of the subsidies, the Church points out that its schools educate children at less cost to the government per head than the public schools. At the end of 1958, the Syndicat demanded the nationalization of all parochial schools; shortly afterward, the Catholic hierarchy threatened to close its schools to demonstrate what would happen if they were put out of business. The former teachers who man the government put pressure upon their colleagues in the Syndicat to refrain from heightening the controversy, and the matter was quietly settled for the time being. In other respects, however, the teachers have been successful. At their annual congress in 1960, they demanded, among other things, improvement in the housing situation; faster promotions; better pay; and the unification of the separate ministries of Education, Technical Education, Youth, and Sports. They justified their demands by referring to the need to make the profession more attractive. Most of these demands were granted at the beginning of 1961; all teachers were also given a 20 per cent salary bonus for the year 1960, and teachers' homes will receive priority in future construction programs.

Special Training Facilities

An important consequence of the educational system the Ivory Coast inherited is the lack of Africans qualified to staff the middle and upper ranks of the civil service. As indicated earlier, the prewar educational structure produced low-level clerks and a few middle-rank financial and administrative clerks. Higher jobs, which in English-speaking Africa have long been held by Africans, were manned in the Ivory Coast by Frenchmen and their wives. The reforms of 1957 opened up the upper ranks of the civil service to Africans and allowed them to begin training at the French School for Overseas Administration (ENFOM) on the basis of preferential recruitment. Houphouet-Boigny stated that he would refuse to indulge in "cut-rate Africanization" until a sufficient number of trained personnel could be created, but African employees of the administration, who are highly organized, politically minded, and hopeful of rapid promotion, were very critical of this policy. Eventually succumbing to this pressure, the President approved the establishment of a temporary center for the rapid training of civil servants (Centre de Perfectionnement de la Fonction Publique) in 1959. Admission to the eight-month course was on a highly selective basis and open to civil servants only because of their objections against competing with recent school graduates who have a better formal education than themselves. Only 40 out of 254 recommended applicants were accepted; all but 2 graduated. Some were then sent to France for more advanced training. Plans are now being completed to create an *École Nationale d'Administration,* patterned after the French *grande école* of the same name. It will train high-ranking career civil servants, recruited at the level of the *baccalauréat.*

Higher Education

The number of university students in Paris and in Dakar has continued to increase. In 1959, there were 183 students—including 2 girls—at the University of Dakar, and nearly 1,000 in France. For the school year 1960–61, there were about 300 students at Dakar and 1,600 in France, 789 of whom (including 221 girls) had scholarships (receiving about $1,000 annually plus transportation home every two years). It is interesting to note that the Ivory Coast had more scholarship students in France in 1960–61 than any other former French West African territory and was the only one with four in a school of journalism. While the cost of this scholarship program to the Ivory Coast Government is high, the establishment of a university locally would be even more costly. Nevertheless, the government has become increasingly concerned with the creation of a university in Abidjan.

Ever since the reorientation of the PDCI and of its parent, the regional Rassemblement Démocratique Africain (RDA) in 1950, Ivory Coast students have been opposed to the general policies of their elders. They became increasingly vociferous in the late 1950's, when independence appeared as a possible alternative to the French Union or to the Community. The organized student bodies branded Houphouet-Boigny a traitor to the national cause and urged a "No" vote in the 1958 referendum. In 1959, many students lost their scholarships because of their political activities; their organizations were declared illegal in the Ivory Coast; several of their leaders were arrested, and others put under *résidence surveillée*. After the Ivory Coast became independent, many students remained in opposition to the regime and declared their preference for the Sékou Touré brand of African socialism. The students' major complaint, aside from ideological preferences, is that they have had no access to the highest ranks of the political elite. This was a justified complaint until 1957, but since that time the older generation of PDCI leaders have given at least token representation to the younger group, both in the assembly and in the government. In 1959, the PDCI allowed a parallel organization of youth, the Jeunesse RDA de Côte d'Ivoire, to be created. The JRDACI leadership, made up in large part of returning students, gained access to important political positions. Many students remain on the sidelines, however, and consider the others to have sold out to the "forces of reaction." While many Ghanaian students are in opposition because they view the government as anti-intellectual and overly radical, Ivory Coast students tend to take a similar position because they view their government as anti-intellectual and overly conservative.

Incumbent political leaders think that much of this is due to the students' remoteness from African realities and overexposure to Left Bank intellectual currents with little relevance to the problems of national construction. Furthermore, they maintain that French university education is not sufficiently adapted to African needs. The French, upon whom the burden of creating a university in Abidjan has rested, have urged instead the further expansion and use of the University of Dakar as a regional school. But relationships between the Ivory Coast and Senegal have not always been very cordial. Indeed, the traditional rivalry between Abidjan and Dakar was partly instrumental in bringing about the downfall of the Federation of French West Africa, and the Ivory Coast withdrew most of its students from Dakar at the height of the controversy.

A compromise was worked out in 1958 with the creation of an Institut des Hautes Études in Abidjan under the sponsorship of the University of Paris. Forty students began to take their first year of law; in 1959, a second year was created, together with a first year in science and letters. By 1961, 288 undergraduates, including a number of fourth-year law students, were enrolled. Under agreements of co-operation negotiated after independence, France will finance the transformation of this institute into a university, to begin operations in 1962. It will be independent of, but will maintain the same standards as, the French system and will grant *licenses* in law, the natural sciences, physics, and modern letters. Until the other Entente countries develop their own, this university will serve the needs of Upper Volta, Dahomey, and Niger. UNESCO has also undertaken to create in Abidjan an École Normale Supérieure to train secondary-school teachers for the Entente countries.

Research institutions are very limited. The local branch of the Institut Français d'Afrique Noire, set up in 1944, was transferred by the French to the local government in 1958; it was later split into two separate centers for the study of the social sciences (mostly ethnology), the arts, religions, and the natural sciences (mostly oceanography). The Institut d'Enseignement et de Recherches Tropicales has a local branch devoted largely to experimental agricultural research. It is still under French control, but Ivory Coast students who have studied the natural sciences in France can receive some research training there.

The Outlook

Although the Ivory Coast obtained control over education in 1957, its ambiguous position between colonial status and independence was reflected in continued adherence to the educational system created by the French. There was some awareness that the educational needs of a new nation might differ from those of a colonial country or of the metropole, but manifestations and initiatives that were inconsistent with the Ivory Coast's generally good relations with France were avoided. Although this was the official policy of the PDCI, to which little opposition was tolerated, there were already pressures in 1959 to approach the problem less conservatively. At the founding congress of the JRDACI, Amon Tanoh severely condemned colonial education on the ground that it neglected the masses, trained servants rather than masters, destroyed initiative, and prevented the development of national pride. Only if the last tinge of paternalism were removed from the educational system, he pointed out, would Africans lose their inferiority complex and youth acquire love for its fatherland. Furthermore, in order to build a modern nation, it would be absolutely necessary to instill civic spirit into Ivory Coast youth. In these three areas, the coming of independence has witnessed important departures from precedent.

None of the various forms of adult and mass education initiated by the French had ever gone much beyond the pilot stages. Now Africans are experimenting more boldly, combining pedagogy and political control. Centers for popular education are being created in the towns, where adults can learn to read and write during their lunch hour and at night. Teachers are encouraged to devote their spare time to adult education. *Moniteurs* are being trained to participate in mass-education teams. Helping the illiterates has been defined as one of the political duties of every literate member of the JRDACI. In 1959, a Service National d'Education Rurale began to train young people to launch community development projects and to disseminate modern agricultural techniques.

The goals of the educational system were redefined shortly after independence. The Minister of Education called upon all teachers to aid in the task of creating a national spirit in their students by following the example of ardent party workers who devote themselves to their tasks without let-up. He promised that an increasing number of subjects would be Africanized: that geography would stress Africa instead of France, and history would include African development. French will remain the sole language of instruction, because nationalism must not preclude international communication. But increased attention to Africa and its place in the world will permeate the curriculum at all levels, and textbooks and teachers' handbooks will be rewritten accordingly. Moreover, major emphasis is now placed on the introduction of English into more and more schools.

Beyond this, a serious effort will be made to use education in the struggle against local particularism and to create a truly national culture, hitherto barely existent. Institutional means to promote these objectives will include sending students to boarding schools in regions other than their own, in order to promote intimate contact with other children representing different regions and ethnic groups.

In his first message to the nation after his election as President of the Ivory Coast in 1960, Houphouet-Boigny stated that the youth would be asked not only to be ready to give its blood if necessary to preserve the country's sovereignty, but also to give its sweat to preserve true freedom—economic independence. It was announced shortly afterward that, beginning in 1961, twenty-year olds would be called upon to serve in the military and civic service, which would replace the French military service to which some had been subject in the past. The first group of 20,000 were to serve for fourteen months. They will receive, in addition to basic military training, a civic education in two parts: ideological and practical. The latter is the most important, and will consist of work on major public projects. In 1961, they were to search for diamonds and help the country become self-sufficient by planting rice in the northern regions. This is a significant manifestation of the Ivory Coast's break with colonial traditions of education and of the beginning of a new era of mobilization for national construction.

—VERA and ARISTIDE ZOLBERG

35. Dahomey

Capital: Porto Novo
Population: 1,713,000 (est.)
Area: 44,695 sq. miles
Political status: Independent republic

IN area, Dahomey is one of the smallest states in West Africa—44,695 square miles. It is bounded on the south by the Gulf of Guinea, on the north by Niger and Upper Volta, on the east by Nigeria, and on the west by Togo. These borders, like many in Africa, are a product of arbitrary nineteenth-century partition agreements reached by Britain and France, and largely ignore tribal affinities: The peoples of the north, for example, have considerably more in common with neighboring sections of southern Mali than with their own countrymen. The many migrations and invasions that characterized Dahomey's turbulent early history have left three major ethnic groups: the Fons, or Dahomans (about 700,000), who live in the south; the Adjas (220,000), who have settled along the Mono and Couffo rivers; and the Yorubas (160,000), who came from Nigeria and settled along the eastern border. Most of the population remain animist, though there are an estimated 250,000 Moslems and some 180,000 Christians. Agriculture is the principal occupation of the country, and the major exports (largely to France) are palm kernels, oil, peanuts, coffee, and cotton.

Early in the seventeenth century, the Portuguese established their first trading post along the Benin Gulf, naming it Porto Novo. Dahomey was at this time a composite of small and complex rival principalities, mostly tributary to the powerful kingdom of Abomey. British, French, Spanish, and Dutch traders followed. The French obtained rights to establish a trading post as early as 1669, but it was not until 1894 that the entire kingdom of Dahomey was annexed by France; then, by a decree of 1895, it was placed under the authority of the Governor-General of Senegal. Finding African society here well organized and hierarchized, French administrators adapted themselves to the situation by utilizing traditional rulers to administer justice and carry on the business of local government. With the reorganization of the French Empire into the French Union after World War II, Dahomey was joined with France's seven other colonies in West Africa to form the Federation of West Africa, centered at Dakar.

Dahomey became an autonomous state within the French Community in December, 1958; in May, 1959—after a brief flirtation with the embryonic Mali Federation—it joined with the Ivory Coast, Upper Volta, and Niger in organizing the antifederalist Conseil de l'Entente. Following Dahomey's accession to full independence in August, 1960, and its withdrawal from the French Community, a new constitution was adopted in November, 1960, calling for the establishment of a unitary state under a strong presidency. President Hubert Maga, once a northern Moslem schoolteacher, heads a conservative government that has gradually absorbed or eliminated a complex of competing parties since he came to power as head of a compromise coalition government in 1959.

Educational Development

Dahomey, in contrast to many wealthier nations of Africa, has no shortage of trained white-collar personnel for its civil service. Indeed, the country's leading export has long been white-collar workers and administrators recruited by neighboring African territories for posts in teaching, public health, and government. In the heightened emotional atmosphere of new-found independence, many of these Dahomeans have incurred the resentment of Africans in other French-speaking countries, with the result that neighboring governments are now under pressure to replace them with local personnel. The extent to which this returning elite finds a place for itself in the political, economic, and social structure of Dahomey may well affect the country's future stability.

Dahomey's favorable school picture is attributable, in part, to the work of missionaries and, in part, to the large percentage of the country's operating budget customarily devoted to education—24.6 per cent in 1957 and 20.54 per cent in 1960. During the 1960–61 school year, for example, a little over $4 million was designated for public education; in addition, $4,523,910 was spent on private education. The annual per capita cost of education in Dahomey is among the lowest of all the former French African countries: According to 1958 statistics, $19 provided public primary schooling for one student.

The over-all ratio of school children to the school-age population was 15.4 per cent in 1951, representing 35,700 school-going children; 24.3 per cent, or 57,200 children, in 1955; 29.1 per cent, or 71,100 children, in 1957. In 1958, the percentage remained about the same as in 1957, with 78,244 of the estimated 268,516 children of school age enrolled; in this same year, 25 per cent of the students were girls, and 50 per cent of all students attended private schools. These figures reveal that since 1951 the school-going population has more than doubled.

In 1958–59, 86 per cent of the primary-school teachers in the Dahomey school system were African, although a reported 54.4 per cent of these were insufficiently trained. In 1959–60, seventeen out of forty public secondary-school teachers were African, with training equal to that of their European counterparts; but the qualifications of the twenty-six Africans among the 74 private secondary-school teachers were said to be uneven.

In 1958–59, 782 public primary-school teachers taught 35,406 pupils in 230 schools; in 1960, there were 1,062 teachers for 88,189 students in 338 public primary schools. At the public secondary-school level, there were 34 teachers for 1,007 students in four schools in 1958; in 1960, there were 49 teachers for 1,613 pupils in eight schools. In 1958, there were 26 teachers for 387 students in two public technical schools; but in 1960, although enrollment was greatly increased and the number of technical schools rose to five, the number of teachers decreased to 25.

Private schools—which educate almost 50 per cent of all Dahomean students—are operated largely by Catholic missionaries from Lyon teaching in 183 institutions. Methodist teachers have approximately 3,500 pupils in continuation courses in Porto Novo and northern Dahomey, and American teachers of the Assembly of God operate several schools. There is also a Moslem school in Cotonou. These private organizations operated 204 elementary institutions for 40,000 pupils in 1958. In 1960, 220 private schools were open to 42,535 students. The complete picture of public and private education is shown in Table 1.

In all schools, French is the official language of instruction. However, certain vernacular languages—notably Fon, Yoruba, Nagot, Bariba, and Somba—are used in the adult-education programs recently introduced on radio.

Table 1
Dahomey School Enrollment, 1958–60

	First degree		Second degree		Technical education	
	1958	1960	1958	1960	1958	1960
Number of schools:						
Public	230	338	4	8	2	5
Private	203	220	7	7	2	2
Total	*433*	*558*	*11*	*15*	*4*	*7*
Number of classes:						
Public	743	n.a.	33	n.a.	13	n.a.
Private	817	n.a.	41	n.a.	6	n.a.
Total	*1,560*	n.a.	*74*	n.a.	*19*	n.a.
Number of teachers:						
Public	782	1,062	34	49	26	25
Pupils enrolled:						
Public						
Boys	26,487	n.a.	706	n.a.	359	n.a.
Girls	8,919	n.a.	301	n.a.	28	n.a.
Total	*35,406*	*45,654*	*1,007*	*1,613*	*387*	*732*
Private						
Boys	28,031	n.a.	905	n.a.	n.a.	n.a.
Girls	11,969	n.a.	345	n.a.	174	n.a.
Total	*40,000*	*42,535*	*1,250*	*1,562*	*174*	*162*
Grand Total	*75,406*	*88,189*	*2,257*	*3,175*	*561*	*894*

Higher Education

There is no university in Dahomey. The majority of students seeking post-secondary training go on scholarship to the University of Dakar or to French institutions. There were 138 Dahomeans at Dakar in 1959–60, and 211 in 1960–61, on government scholarships. Many more were there on private scholarships or at their own expense. Only one other African country had a larger contingent at Dakar in 1960.

Of the 195 bursary students from Dahomey in France in 1960–61, the largest number, 45, were enrolled in professional schools; engineering and medical schools also attracted a large percentage of Dahomeans—40 and 25 students, respectively. Table 2 presents a comparative picture of Dahomey students abroad from 1957 to 1961.

Plans for the expansion of education in Dahomey included the opening of a new *lycée* at Parkou sometime in 1961 and two *lycées* at Cotonou in 1962 (one for boys and the other for girls). The four new *cours complémentaires* schools opened in 1960 were to be followed by four per year in 1961, 1962, and 1963.

Table 2
Dahomey Students Abroad, 1957–61

	1957–58	1958–59	1959–60	1960–61
Scholarship students in France at all levels	49	55	218	195
Men in higher education	5	11	164	137
Women in higher education	—	—	9	8
Scholarship students at University of Dakar	n.a.	n.a.	138	211

UNESCO offered to send an officer to Dahomey in 1961 to help organize a national commission on education and volunteered to participate in the development of cadres for education and higher administration. UNESCO is also willing to aid Dahomey in the creation of a faculty of sciences, an institute of engineering, and a college of agriculture and to assist in developing cultural institutions for music, choreography, and the plastic arts.

36. Niger

Capital: Niamey
Population: 2,500,000 (est.)
Area: 495,000 sq. miles
Political status: Independent republic

IN 1958, when 1,489 students from various countries of French Africa were completing their education abroad, Niger was the only member of the French Union with no scholarship students in France for advanced studies. In 1961, only 29 out of a total of 2,208 French-speaking African students in Paris were from Niger. The country's rate of school enrollment is also the lowest by far in French Africa—4 per cent in 1957.

The country's geographical position and economic plight, more than its political history, explain Niger's slow entry into the modern world. For Niger is a vast plateau situated in the center of the continent at a great distance from the sea; it is bounded on the north, east, and west by the Sahara Desert, on the southeast by Lake Chad, and on the southwest by the Niger River. In an area of some 495,000 square miles (larger than Texas and California combined), a population of 2.5 million, one-third of them nomadic, eke out a meager existence. The name of the republic stems from the Niger River, which becomes increasingly sandy and muddy after leaving Mali and flows intermittently across the country before continuing its course into Nigeria. In Niger, unfortunately, the river is navigable only from Niamey to Gaya, and then not always twelve months of the year.

The population can be divided into two major categories. The Negro element, about three-fourths of the total, consists of settled Hausa farmers and fishermen along the river in the south, the Djerma, and the Songhai. The nomadic and seminomadic peoples of the north include the Tuareg, the Toubou, and the Peuls. Some 80 per cent of the population are Moslem, though animism is still strong in parts of the south. French is the official national language and the only common tongue for the diverse elements of the population; however, Hausa is the language of trade.

Niger's climate is exceptionally harsh. The northern desert seldom sees rain, and when it comes the heat is so intense that the moisture sometimes evaporates before reaching the ground. The only productive agricultural land is found in the southern savanna zone between Niamey and Lake Chad—a little less than one-fourth of Niger's entire area. Here wild life flourishes, and the sedentary farmers, mostly Hausa and Songhai, cultivate millet, sorghum, manioc, corn, beans, and fruit. In the last thirty years, the production of peanuts has been put on an industrial basis, but the problems of irrigation and export remain serious. The peanuts are sent through the Dahomey railroad and the port of Cotonou to subsidized French markets.

The rest of the country is barren desert, sprinkled periodically with oases. A mountainous area in the center, between the northern and the southern Sahara, where the famous town of Agades opens its gates onto the desert, rises to 5,900 feet. A few sedentary farmers cluster here to await the passing of the nomadic Peuls and Tuareg with their flocks. In the future, stock raising could become a source of considerable wealth for Niger. However, the Peul nomads arc interested not in the economic potential of their flock but in the prestige of their number; they do not sell the animals and only kill them for tribal or religious ceremonies.

The barrenness and isolation of Niger have held small appeal for European explorers and settlers, who were drawn to wealthier and more hospitable sectors of Africa. Apparently, the Romans traveled as far as Niger's central Air Massif, which later became a part of the Gao Empire after domination by Bornou and Mali successively. By the seventeenth century, the Tuareg and the Peuls had gained ascendance and introduced Islam. Ousman dan Fodio, a Peul conqueror, established the well-known Sokoto Empire at the close of the eighteenth century and consolidated the Islamic influence still predominant today.

The French did not come to Niger until 1890, after a Scot and several German explorers had already penetrated the country. And it was not until 1921, after thirty years of uncertain discussions between the English and the French as to the limits of penetration in these areas and a brief period of local military rule, that a French civil administration was established. From 1921 until independence on August 3, 1960, Niger's administration more or less conformed to the pattern of French colonial rule elsewhere in West Africa. President Hamani Diori came to power in 1958, campaigning on a platform of close cooperation with France, and has since consolidated his party's position by allying with the country's powerful Moslem chiefs and neutralizing the radical nationalist party that preceded him at the head of the government.

Niger became an autonomous member of the French Community in 1958 and joined with Ivory Coast, Upper Volta, and Dahomey to form the Conseil de l'Entente in 1959. All four Entente nations became independent in 1960 and withdrew from the Community, but have signed agreements of economic and political cooperation with France. Niger, especially, remains heavily dependent on French technical and administrative personnel to man its government.

Educational Progress, 1921–61

The educational system established in Niger when it was part of the Federation of French West Africa followed a typical pattern: Primary, secondary, and technical studies were provided locally, followed by higher education in France or in Dakar. However, the uneven distribution of the population, the nomads' perpetual migrations, and the absence of European settlers hampered development of a school system. Moreover, the role of the mission schools has been circumscribed in Niger because it is predominantly Moslem. In 1957, the proportion of students attending private schools compared to the total number in both public and private institutions was only 7.3 per cent, whereas it was 30.5 per cent for all of French Africa. These figures do not include the many local Moslem schools, which offered little more than oral religious education and made no attempt, as in Mauritania, to import a broader, cultural background.

The rate of school enrollment in 1945 was only 1 per cent, but France stepped up its educational efforts in Niger sharply after World War II, with the results noted in Tables 1 and 2.

Table 1
Growth of Niger School System, 1948–1957

Year	Students	Primary schools	Technical schools	Teachers	Percentage of school-age children in school
1948	3,400	32	n.a.	n.a.	n.a.
1951	6,200	63	53	n.a.	1.8
1955	8,700	69	39	203	2.6
1957	12,900	125	33	313	4

Table 2
Growth of Niger School System, 1958–60

	Primary education		Secondary education		Technical education	
	1958	1960	1958	1960	1958	1960
Total number of schools:	133	192	3	7	1	1
Public education	126	183	3		1	
Private education	7	9				
Total number of classes:	330	466	20		3	
Public education	302				3	
Private education	28					
Number of teachers:						
Public	376	485	11	34	3	6
Total number of students:	13,459	21,054	546	1,040	73	78
Public	12,904	18,940	546	1,040	73	78
Boys	9,424	13,652	483		58	
Girls	3,480	5,288	63		15	
Private	555	2,114				
Boys	227					
Girls	328					

SOURCES: 1958 figures from the Overseas Statistical Service, *Outre-Mer* 1958. 1960 figures from the services of the Republic of Niger for the Ministers' Conference on National Education for the French-Speaking African States, meeting in Paris, February 20–25, 1961.

By October, 1960, Minister of National Education Zodhi Ikhia announced that 27,000 students were enrolled in primary and secondary schools and that the rate of enrollment had risen to an estimated 6.7 per cent.

The Problem of Priorities

Secondary education has progressed particularly slowly, owing largely to the inadequacy of the teachers, 72.5 per cent of whom were insufficiently trained in 1958. In 1960, 300 students were admitted to the *Certificat d'Études,* about 50 to the BEPC, and some 20 to the *baccalauréat.* Indeed, the training of teachers is one of the vicious circles of educational expansion in an underdeveloped country such as Niger, for acceleration without adequate groundwork inevitably lowers the percentage of qualified teachers and thus lowers standards.

To offset these hazards, Niger continually pleads for more teachers from France. The Niger representative at the February, 1961, Ministers' Conference on National Education for the French-Speaking African States urged priority attention to his country's needs. Pointing to the lowest rate of school enrollment in French-speaking Africa, he asked for an accelerated recruitment and training program to provide staff for the 125 new classes per year needed to attain the goal of 15 per cent school enrollment (60,000 students) by 1964. Niger also endorsed the concept of specialized interstate universities and other cooperative educational institutions, which could broaden Niger's educational opportunities at nominal cost and thus speed up Africanization.

The government of President Hamani Diori, faced with underdevelopment in all areas, must measure the gains in educational development against those in economic investment. In 1958, it cost 18,395 CFA francs to maintain each student in a primary school, and per capita costs at other levels were even higher. In an article published in October, 1960, Niger's Finance Minister, Courmo Barcougné, indicated the government's thinking on this matter:

> The government is primarily concerned with improving the standard of living through social progress and educational development. But on this point the nation must be made aware of the facts.
>
> The country, in its present economic condition, cannot carry a burden of responsibilities heavier than those already assumed. The budget would not permit it. Therefore the time has come to revise our policy, which, noble though it may be, is not realistic economically.
>
> What would be the advantage of spending more for education if the very people who receive it are called upon to deprive themselves of minimal incomes in order to pay the heavy taxes needed to finance additional educational institutions, schools, and medical-care centers?
>
> We are confronted with a choice. We must concentrate our efforts on the economy, agriculture, and stock raising. This certainly does not imply abandoning our education or health programs, but for the time being at least we should maintain the present standard.
>
> Our role as free and universal human beings obliges us to create a policy within our means. Such are the demands of our new independence.

Niger's educational budget for 1960 was about $2 million, or 9.8 per cent of its total budget. This was the lowest percentage in all of French-speaking Africa.

Within the limits set by this policy, Niger has introduced a number of educational reforms aimed at some of the country's most serious problems. A crash campaign against illiteracy has been launched, for example, by sending monitors into the villages and providing courses on the Niger radio. Most of Niger's educational growth is being financed by France, however. With about $81,000 set aside by the OCRS (Community Organization for the Sahara Territories), schools for both the sedentary and nomadic population are being developed in the Fillingue region. In 1960, French sources provided subsidies amounting to more than $60,000 for private schools in Niger and more than $261,000 to the Niger Government for public education. Meanwhile, the European Fund has appropriated $2.78 million for school construction.

Higher Education

By 1961, Niger had more than seventy persons on academic scholarships in France or at the University of Dakar, as shown in Table 3.

Table 3
Niger's Scholarship Students Abroad

	1957–58	1958–59	1959–60	1960–61
In France [a]				
Higher education	0	2	25	29
Sciences		2	8	6
Advanced studies			9	8
Engineering			2	3
Medicine			1	3
Pharmacy			1	1
Veterinary medicine			2	4
Letters			1	3
Law			1	
Dentistry				1
Technical studies	5	7	8	7
Agriculture	5	7	6	6
Mechanics			2	
Domestic studies				1
First- and second-degree education	4	2	5	5
Secretarial				1
Midwifery	1	1	3	5
Nursing			2	
At University of Dakar			29	n.a.

[a] Of these, there was one woman in 1957–58 and 1958–59, eight women in 1959–60, and twelve in 1960–61.

This new elite, with its sometimes radical view of Niger's future, is not regarded as an unmixed blessing by the country's present conservative political leadership. Boubou Hama, President of the Niger Assembly, discussed this problem at the national conference of the Niger section of the governing Rassemblement Démocratique Africain in May, 1960:

> The elite who attend the institutions of advanced studies in Europe are generally assimilated into a Western concept of life, a way of understanding and acting which separates them from the Africa of the bush. . . . We feel that the differences that make these intellectuals take refuge in a special circle and that result in an uncompromising attitude may also lead them into an isolation which places them on the fringes of

society, delaying all true reconversion toward the meaning of Africa and preventing a return to global Africa. This global Africa is not merely a concept of color but also, above all, a state of being, a belief in life that is different from the non-African milieu of these elites.

To all, we say that Africa also has its imperatives and that people cannot always only support their own vision of things, or their own concept of a life they do not know and do not wish to know. . . . It is a question of training the primary schools to spread education throughout the land, to cut through the immense bush and, by becoming useful practitioners, living the life of the peasant to succeed in bringing a modern existence to all the African masses. . . . What an irony that immense Africa is the continent of community living, where to be isolated is to suffocate and die. There is perhaps a lesson in this that certain people should consider.

—FRANCETTE DRIN

37. Upper Volta

Capital: Ouagadougou
Population: 3,350,000 (est.)
Area: 105,900 sq. miles
Political status: Independent republic

UPPER Volta is a landlocked country with few natural resources and an inhospitable climate. Voltaic friendship is nonetheless much courted in West Africa in the 1960's because of the country's strategic geographical location at the crossroads of two major rival political groupings of African nations the Ghana-Guinea-Mali Union of African States and the French-speaking Conseil de l'Entente. In the Conseil de l'Entente, of which it has been a member since 1959, Upper Volta provides the essential land bridge between Ivory Coast and Niger and Dahomey. Meanwhile, Ghana's President Nkrumah has taken special pains to develop friendly economic and political relations with Voltaic President Maurice Yameogo, in part because Upper Volta provides the essential land bridge between Ghana and its Guinea and Mali partners.

With a population of some 3.35 million, increasing at the rate of nearly 2 per cent per year, Upper Volta is the most heavily populated country among the eight territories of former French West Africa. However, the density of population varies sharply from region to region—from three inhabitants per square kilometer in the *cercle* of Dori to eighty or more in the main cities of Ouagadougou and Bobo Dioulasso. The Mossi tribe is in the majority (about 1.7 million), and the other major groups are the Peuls (245,000), the Bobos (135,000), and the Gourounsis (102,000). Agricultural pursuits engage 95 per cent of the population.

According to oral traditions, the powerful empires that once included the Upper Volta region in their sway go back to the eleventh century. Certainly, the names of the Mossi, the main ethnic group in the country, and of Nassare, its warrior emperor, were known to fifteenth-century Europe. No Europeans ventured into its interior until the beginning of the nineteenth century, however, and French conquest of what is now Upper Volta was not completed until 1901. Upper Volta first appeared on modern maps as a separate political unit in 1919, when it was created from territory ceded from existing French colonies in the area. In 1932, however, Upper Volta disappeared again when France partitioned its land area among the three neighboring colonies of Niger, Soudan, and Ivory Coast in response to local political pressures. Its re-emergence as a separate territory in 1947 was again part of a larger tactical maneuver in the regional politics of the area.

Upper Volta's history during its last incarnation has followed closely that of sister states in French West Africa. Voltaic voters approved the constitution proposed by General de Gaulle in the referendum of September 28, 1958, and the country thereupon became a self-governing member of the French Community. On July 11, 1960, it became a fully independent state—although bound to Niger, Dahomey, and Ivory Coast through its membership in the Conseil de l'Entente, and to France through a number of economic- and technical-assistance agreements.

Education Prior to Independence

Because Upper Volta was not permanently established as a separate territory until 1947, the only statistics available are relatively recent ones, dating back to 1951. Nevertheless, these are sufficient to show the growth of school enrollment prior to Upper Volta's independence (see Table 1).

Table 1
School Enrollment Before Independence

Year	School enrollment			Percentage of school-age population in school
	Male	Female	Total	
1951	10,724	3,295	14,019	2.2
1954	16,690	5,525	22,215	4.7
1957	24,475	9,063	33,538	6.7
1958	28,901	10,995	39,896	7.8

By 1959, there were 51,500 children enrolled in 351 schools, representing about 9 per cent of the school-age population. There were 490 pupils in three public schools offering the complete primary course—at Koudougou and Ouahigouya for boys and at Ouagadougou for girls. The two public secondary schools offering the complete course of instruction leading to the *baccalauréat* (at Ouagadougou and Bobo Dioulasso) had a combined total of 800 pupils. Private schools (41 per cent of the primary schools and 36 per cent of the secondary and technical schools) have played a very important part in the development of education. Most of the schools in this category are operated by missionaries, chiefly Roman Catholic. Five private schools reported 550 students enrolled: the Catholic secondary school at Ouagadougou for boys, the Protestant secondary college at Ouagadougou for boys and girls, the Notre Dame Institute (secondary) at Ouagadougou for girls, and two Catholic primary schools (one at Toussinna for boys and one at Tounouna for girls). Private Catholic education is also given in two seminaries.

About 95.8 per cent of the children enrolled in school are at the primary level. Of the total enrollment, 0.4 per cent are in technical schools, and 3.8 per cent are pursuing studies at the secondary level. In 1957, twenty-nine out of forty-nine students sitting for the first part of the *baccalauréat* were successful, and eleven out of sixteen who sat for the second part passed.

Higher Education

There are no facilities for higher education in Upper Volta, so that those students who qualify for a university education or for specialized training customarily go either to the University of Dakar or to a French university. In 1958, 102 students from Upper Volta were enrolled at Dakar, and 59 were studying in France, though not all at university level. About 50 per cent of the students from Upper Volta who go to Paris to complete their studies go on French Government scholarships.

Table 2 gives information on recent French scholarship programs for both the secondary and university level.

Table 2
French Scholarship Programs

Year	Total scholarships awarded	Male	Female	Number of these in higher education
1957–58	18	18	0	1
1958–59	24	24	0	2
1959–60	68	61	7	50
1960–61	87	77	10	52

Major Problems in Education

In Upper Volta, as in the rest of former French West Africa, the chief obstacle to education has been inadequate funds and facilities; there is about one school for every 1,600 children of school age, and one teacher for every 650 possible pupils. Except in the cities, few schools have been able to teach the entire primary course (up to the *Certificat d'Études);* indeed, 80 per cent of the country's schools have provided only two years of elementary-level instruction. Almost 90 per cent of the teachers are Africans from Upper Volta, but only 21 per cent of the teachers in the system have been properly trained; most of the rest of them have had only a primary education or less.

The extension of education has met with various other barriers—including geographic, economic, religious, and social ones. The predominance of Islam has slowed the spread of education among girls, and educated young women continue to have difficulty finding suitable jobs within their own social groups. Teachers are reluctant to teach outside the major centers, and hard-pressed rural families have been inclined to resist giving up an extra pair of hands in the field for the luxury of schooling. Even the upper classes remained suspicious of modern education until recently, in part because the French requirement that a specific number of youths appear for class convinced many families that schools were a kind of punishment. To outwit the French, those with means often sent the children of their slaves to school—with the result that many of the higher administrative posts in government today are filled by persons of lowly ancestry.

Post-Independence Developments

In accordance with the French policy aim of assimilating its overseas populations, a French educational system was transplanted to Upper Volta. The newly independent government of President Yameogo has little quarrel with this system and no ideological reason to recast it abruptly. French will continue as the official language for instruction in the schools, since the several ethnic groups in the country have no common vernacular. (The vernacular is occasionally used in some primary schools so that the young children may understand the teacher better, but this practice is not encouraged.)

The government feels that the present system of classical education must be maintained to continue to mold a Voltaic elite, but that it is economically impossible—and practically undesirable in terms of job opportunities—to broaden its coverage too rapidly.* Only 1 per cent of the population are actually employed in industry or construction, and the administrative and service professions employ no more than 3 per cent of the population between them. As a matter of fact, there are not enough suitable jobs available at present for those who have been in school for more than five years.

It is the government's position that a new educational system should be developed, paralleling the existing system and keyed to the economic and social conditions of a largely rural nation such as Upper Volta. Urgent targets, the government believes, are adult literacy, improvement of sanitary conditions through a basic knowledge of hygiene, and the modernizing of traditional agricultural techniques. An expert from France's Société d'Études pour le Développement Économique et Social and another from the Institut Pédagogique National were sent to aid Upper Volta in drawing up a shortened first-cycle rural course of instruction.

The new system of education drafted by these planners and now approved by the Voltaic Government is to be developed in progressive stages over possibly a ten-year period, as the economy of the country develops and can support those costs not covered by outside assistance. The new approach is directed toward the twelve to fourteen year olds who are mature enough to take advantage of special training and apply it to their own daily agricultural or pastoral lives. The students will follow a special three-year primary course designed to teach them to read and write a simple, basic French and to count. In addition, they will receive practical instruction in agricultural skills and other training that will better equip them for rural community life and will help them to improve their standard of living.

These new schools will be administered under a Bureau of Rural Education, operated by an educator and by an agricultural technician versed in the ways of the rural African society. It will establish schools in villages that can serve the children within a three-mile radius, and will recruit teachers qualified to instruct the pupils at the simple and practical level described above. Curricula suited to different areas of the country will be developed in cooperation with the educational authorities, and the Bureau will distribute corresponding teaching materials as well as specialized agricultural and livestock information brochures. Classes and vacations will correspond to the planting and harvesting cycles of the various sectors in which the schools are established.

The European Development Fund approved credit in the amount

* The school-age population of Upper Volta, which was about 650,000 children in 1957, will reach nearly 850,000 by 1967.

of $2,025,000 for the Upper Volta plan on January 21, 1961. The Fund had already previously granted a sum of $1,115,000 to Upper Volta for the construction of fifty primary schools; and France, on its own, in 1960, made two grants through FAC for educational subsidies—$243,000 for public education, and $156,000 for private education. It should be noted also that for the same year, the expenditures for educational administration paid from the Upper Volta budget amounted to nearly $3.4 million, and its subsidy to private education amounted to almost $384,000. UNESCO assistance is also anticipated.

The Students and the Future of Upper Volta

From 1946 on, the French administration granted scholarships to French universities to increasing numbers of African students as part of a deliberate effort to mold an elite in the French image. Many of these young men became attracted to Marxism in Paris and have found it difficult to readapt to the African way of life upon their return, but there is no doubt that they have developed binding ties with French culture.

Although the present political leadership of Upper Volta does not always see eye-to-eye with the newly educated, it recognizes that the talents of the new elite are necessary to build a modern state. For the year 1960–61, seventy-seven boys and ten girls were granted scholarships to secondary and technical schools and universities in France, and about thirty other nonscholarship students were also studying in France. There are practically none in any other foreign country. Ten of the Upper Volta scholarship students at university level in France in 1960 were in medicine, three in pharmacy, two in dental school, six in veterinary school, twelve in sciences, ten in humanities, five in law, one in engineering, one in graduate school, and eight in classes preparing for graduate schools. There were also seventeen boys preparing to enter engineering and technical schools and seven preparing to become medical and social assistants. Of the ten girls on scholarship, four were studying to become midwives, one to become a nurse, and one a social assistant; the four others were attending varied classes.

According to the new conventions signed between France and the four states of the Entente in 1961, it is proposed that universities will be built in each of the four capitals, starting with Abidjan (Ivory Coast) and Ouagadougou (Upper Volta). This would automatically reduce the number of students going abroad, even those presently attending the University of Dakar.

President Yameogo, addressing the Assembly in April, 1960, summarized the country's hopes and plans:

> Our aim is easy to define. Until now, a victim of geography and history, of a poor land and of a temperamental sky, Upper Volta was not allowed to dream any grandiose dream. Nevertheless, our wishes are ambitious: to enrich and to educate our main potential power, our human resources. Our plans must be conceived with the most careful consideration of their beneficiaries—man, and above all, the peasant. His needs and aspirations must be met: to eat his fill every day, to have water fit to drink all the year round, to have enough money to buy better clothes and build better homes, to be cared for when sick, and to endow his children with an intellectual capital by sending them to school. Among these desires, two are essential—improvement of the standard of living and social advancement.

—Monique Dugue

38. Mali

Capital: Bamako
Population: 4,900,000 (est.)
Area: 465,000 sq. miles
Political status: Independent republic

VAST, landlocked Mali is bordered by the Algerian Sahara and Mauritania on the north and by black African countries to the south, east, and west. Islam, interest in Saharan development, and sympathy for the Algerian FLN bind Mali to the Maghreb. However, its ethnic and historical ties are with French-speaking West Africa, and there is a crucial dependence on the coastal states for trade outlets to the sea. A natural candidate for federation because of its inland geographic location and the strong pan-Africanist views of its leadership elite, Mali (then still known as Soudan) joined with Senegal in 1959 to form the abortive Federation of Mali. When this union foundered on ideological and personality differences, Mali went it alone temporarily, then announced adherence in April, 1961, to the year-old union between neighboring Guinea and Ghana.

While Senegal and Mali were almost ideal economic partners, the political differences between the regimes of President Leopold Senghor and Mali's President Modibo Keita were fundamental ones. Mali's governing elite, like that of Sékou Touré's Guinea, favors a strong unitary state based on a more radical form of socialism than that acceptable to the Senegalese. The governing Union Soudanaise won all seats in the Legislative Assembly in the 1959 elections and enjoys wide popular support for its socialist objectives. Although many Malians believe that their regal President, Modibo Keita, is a direct descendant of the Keita dynasty, which ruled over the old Mali Empire, there has been no attempt to develop a personality cult around this idea. Indeed, the present leadership of Mali is characterized by an emphasis, rare in Africa, on consensus rather than charisma.

Mass participation is sought in the wider echelons of government, and committee work, rather than one-man decisions, is the rule at the highest levels.

Externally, Mali is far more concerned than Senegal with the threat of European "neocolonialism" and more deeply committed to a position of positive neutralism in international affairs. At the Casablanca Conference of January, 1961, for example, Mali joined with Guinea, Ghana, the United Arab Republic, and Morocco in calling for an end to all forms of colonialism, the departure of all foreign troops and bases from African soil, and the creation of an African defense alliance.

Economically, Mali's underdeveloped agricultural economy invites drastic measures, and the government views the Israeli, Chinese, Yugoslav, and Guinean experiments as likely models for adaptation to the special needs of Mali. The French made no serious effort to organize a comprehensive economic development program for the former Soudan until the late 1950's, and even then emphasis was placed on the coordination of its economy with that of Senegal, not on making the Soudan self-sufficient. Cattle, groundnuts, cotton, and hides and skins are the principal products, but Mali's planners believe diversified agriculture would be possible with the introduction of large-scale irrigation projects and improved communications. The communications situation is particularly acute since Mali determined to boycott both the railway to Senegal and the harbor facilities at Dakar because of its political break with its coastal neighbor. Now, Mali's exports go to world markets—more slowly and at greater cost—through the Ivory Coast or occasionally Guinea.

Within Mali's 465,000 square miles live an estimated 4.9 million people, 92 per cent of whom are illiterate. The irregular distribution of the population over a sparse land has been a serious barrier to educational development, as is the principal religious faith of the country, Islam. Moslem leaders resisted the work of the Christian mission schools, which were for many years the chief vehicle of education in this part of Africa. The 7,000 Europeans are concentrated largely in Bamako, where they held most senior teaching and higher administrative posts until almost the end of French colonial rule. The number of Malians with technical, administrative, or professional skills remains small, and most of the educated elite are products of the postwar period. The Keita government, outspokenly critical of progress made under French rule, sees its educational role as a very broad one. The party, which is in a sense above the state, extends into every area of Malian life and controls all the institutions in the country. The Malian populace is enthusiastically loyal but only partially aware of the significance of self-government, and thus party leaders see political and educational goals as everywhere interrelated.

Major Educational Problems

There was no systematic approach to education in Mali until after World War II, and even then the effort was primarily directed toward the creation of an assimilated French-African elite. Schools in Mali tend to be found in the most easily accessible regions and in the larger towns; in many cases, they were built according to the preferences of favored tribal chiefs or territorial assemblies. The more inaccessible rural areas were largely ignored. The Mali Government believes that one of its major educational tasks is to decentralize the school system so that all sectors of the population may have the opportunity to participate. This is a difficult goal, for the cost of education in Mali is among the highest of all the former French African territories. For example, in 1958, the annual per capita cost for each primary-school student was estimated at $77; the annual cost of secondary education was $510 in the *cours complémentaires,* and $669 at the *lycée* level.

In addition, Mali faces an acute shortage of trained teachers and remains heavily dependent on expensive expatriate staff at the higher levels. In 1960, there were 85 expatriate teachers in public and private primary schools, 114 in secondary schools, and 40 in technical schools. Available training facilities for African staff, which turned out 75 teachers in 1948 and only about 90 in 1960, are far out of line with the 100 per cent jump in school population over the same period. Because of the necessity of employing monitors in a teaching capacity and the limited teaching material placed at their disposal, education given at Mali primary schools has often been little more than training in literacy. French teachers are not eager to teach outside of the larger towns, so that virtually all rural schoolteachers and monitors are Africans who may have studied at one of three normal schools in Sevare, Markala, and Banenkoro or at École William Ponty in Senegal and other teacher-training schools outside Mali—but, more often, have not.

During the 1960–61 school year, there were 58,080 boys and girls at the primary-school level in Mali and another 6,822 pupils in private primary schools. An additional 3,170 pupils were enrolled in public secondary schools (*lycées,* normal schools, colleges, and *cours complémentaires*), and 744 in private secondary schools. Technical colleges reported 484 students enrolled, and another 194 were

Table 1
Nationality and Distribution of School Personnel in Mali, 1960–61

	Malians	French	Other	Total
Public primary schools:				
Inspectors		3		3
Teachers	230	21	1	252
Assistants	805	9	4	818
Monitors	178	1	2	181
Miscellaneous	34			34
Total	*1,247*	*34*	*7*	*1,288*
Private primary schools:				
Administrative personnel	6	3		9
Teachers	101	48	8	157
Miscellaneous	2			2
Total	*109*	*51*	*8*	*168*
Public secondary schools:				
Principals	1	12		13
Administrative personnel	13	3		16
Letters	7	20		27
Philosophy		1		1
History-geography	2	7		9
English	1	7	1	9
Spanish		2	1	3
German		1		1
Arabic			2	2
Mathematics	3	14	1	18
Physics and chemistry	4	1		5
Natural science		2		2
Design		2		2
Music		1		1
Physical education	3	2		5
Miscellaneous	9			9
Instructors	2	4		6
Total	*45*	*79*	*5*	*129*
Private secondary schools:				
Administrative personnel	6	4	12	22
Teachers	5	31	1	37
Miscellaneous	5			5
Total	*16*	*35*	*13*	*64*

in the school of public works. Table 1 shows the over-all distribution and origin of teachers, administrative personnel, and teaching staff for both the public and private schools.

There are an estimated 570,000 children of school age, but only about 10 per cent of these are attending school. (As in other Moslem countries, the percentage of school-going girls continues to be low—about 25 per cent of total school attendance—primarily because of traditional religious customs.) Although the percentage of school-age children in school is among the lowest in Africa, the present 10 per cent marks a great improvement over the meager 2.6 per cent in school in 1943, when only 8,600 primary students were enrolled in 207 classrooms. Secondary education was not introduced until after World War II, when the primary school of Terrasson de Fougeres was transformed into a *lycée*. In 1948, the number of pupils had increased to 17,287, representing 3.8 per cent of the school-age population. In 1956, 31,000 children—or about 6 per cent of the educable population of 52,500—attended school. In 1957, the percentage of school-age children in school increased to 8 per cent, but population expansion brought the figure down to 7.9 per cent the following year. Then, in 1959, government action combined with the cooperation of the Mali people brought the ratio of school-age children in school up to 9 per cent, or 55,000 pupils in 1,017 classes.

Poor instruction, inadequate textbooks, and meager facilities contribute to the high attrition rate among those taking examinations at the primary and secondary levels. Of the 2,443 students taking the examination for entrance into the sixth form in 1960, fewer than half passed. A little more than one-third of those taking the CEPE examination passed. And at the local examination level, only 7 out of 72 passed. Results were more encouraging at the secondary level during 1960: 221 out of 384 taking the BEPC and BE exams passed; and 18 out of the 22 candidates for the *baccalauréat* were successful. Of the 159 who studied for examinations in the technical college of Bamako, 94 passed.

Paralleling the need for more and better teaching staff is the requirement for additional school construction at all levels. In 1946–47, there were 101 public primary schools, with 346 classes for 17,022 pupils, averaging 49 in each class. In 1951–52, there were 190 primary schools, with 595 classes for 24,850 students, averaging 42 in each class. By 1958, when Mali became an autonomous state, the French had built 247 schools, with 1,042 classes for 37,000 pupils, averaging 35 to a class.

In 1960, newly independent Mali had 383 public and 42 private primary schools; there was only one public *lycée,* one public normal school, one public and one private college, and eleven public and four private *cours complémentaires*. One technical college, with ten classes, existed; and one *centre d'apprentissage* with five classes.

Education and Politics

As in the other former French territories in Africa, the educational system inherited from the colonial era was closely patterned on that of the metropole. The break with this past has been far less sweeping in Mali than in Guinea, partly because there was no comparable withdrawal of French financial and technical assistance. The political function of education has been intensified, more attention is being given to basic education in rural areas, and curricula and texts are being revised to emphasize African history and geography, but French remains the official language of the republic and the language of school instruction. English, which is receiving more attention than in the past, is taught at the *lycée* and College of Bamako, at the Modern College for Boys in Dike, and in the *cours complémentaires* in Bamako, Ségou, Gao, Kayes, and Sikasso. *The New York Times* reported in January, 1961, that a USIS officer now gives English lessons three times a week to President Keita, his family, and cabinet members. Spanish and German are available at the *lycée* and College of Bamako, and Arabic is taught at the Modern College in Dike.

In 1936, appropriations for education represented 7.9 per cent of the total Malian budget. In 1946, the figure was 8.4 per cent; five years later, it had risen to 17.9 per cent; and in 1958, 20 per cent of funds available to the government were earmarked for education. Despite considerable political tension between Bamako and Paris in the wake of the break in the federal relationship with Senegal and Mali's withdrawal from the Community, French financial assistance to Mali between September, 1960, and January, 1961, totaled some $6 million, of which a considerable portion was used for education. The 500 French technicians in Mali during the same period under various aid agreements included 150 teachers.

Higher Education

There is no university in Mali, and the government believes that, given the country's limited resources, no attempt should be made to create one until the primary and secondary levels of Malian education are greatly strengthened.

After secondary school and the *baccalauréat* diploma, students deemed suitable for university education are most likely to go to the University of Dakar or Paris. In 1960, a total of 129 Malians were at Dakar on partial or full scholarship. There were 73 on government scholarships in French secondary and technical schools and universities in 1957–58, 82 in 1958–59, 86 in 1959–60, and 266 in 1960–61; of these, 13 were in higher education in 1957–58, 22 in 1958–59 and 1959–60, and 158 in 1960–61. Of the total number on scholarship, there were 21 women in 1959–60 and 51 in 1960–61. There were 60 Malians studying in Cairo in 1960–61. These figures do not give the whole picture, however, for almost twice as many other Malians were studying in France at their own expense. An appeal has been made to UNESCO for assistance in speeding the development of an educated elite for Mali, and cultural agreements are anticipated with a range of countries willing to receive Mali students in their universities.

Most of the Malian students now in French universities prefer law, medicine, or electrical engineering; many of the women are trained in midwifery. Members of these professions are needed in Mali, and virtually all graduates are given posts appropriate to their training by the central administration, but there are too few who return from France adept in anything else. The government has indicated that it will hold a tighter rein on students sent abroad in the future, and will specify the area of study in the light of national needs.

Adult Education

The governing Union Soudanaise Party is effectively convincing Malians of the necessity of education at all levels of society. It is the Union that is organizing adult-education classes to augment the few adult schools already in existence. Young people recently graduated from the first cycle of education with the *Certificat d'Études* are given a few weeks of teacher training, which is assumed to prepare them to head an adult school. Classes, separate for men and women, are held in the evening. Besides language, women also study hygiene and first aid.

Technical Education

The Ministry of Education is particularly interested in expanding vocational education. The Centre de Recherches Zootechniques in Sotuba specializes in animal husbandry and agriculture, as does the École d'Assistants d'Élevage, which was the first school of its kind in French West Africa. The École d'Apprentissage de L'Artisan Soudannais, with 68 students enrolled in a two-year course in 1960–61, trains jewelers and leather- and wood-craftsmen. The Technical College of Bamako has 284 students enrolled in a six-year course, and the Sections Manuelles trains 74 students.

Future Prospects

Although Mali clearly attaches very great importance to educational development, a fundamental decision has been made to give first priority in national planning to strengthening the country's economic base. In an article in the periodical *L'Essor Hebdomadaire* in June, 1960, Minister of Education Singare Aboulaye acknowledged the existence of a "sub-educated" population and expressed concern that financial resources were lacking to keep abreast of the educational needs of a country whose youth, "thanks to the progress made in modern medicine, increase without ceasing." He said that the government was convinced, however, that the evolution of the country could best be served by placing maximum effort at present in the field of economic development. "Until a solid economic structure has been created," he observed, "it would be vain to attempt to develop socially beyond the capacity of the country."

Within this context, the five-year school construction and expansion program put forward by the Consultative Council on Education in June, 1960, is ambitious. It calls for 10,000 new classrooms to accommodate as many as possible of the 500,000 children who are now unable to find places in school.

Two parallel systems of education are proposed as a temporary stopgap, following the pattern now being pioneered in Upper Volta and other West African states. Classical education of the normal six-year cycle leading to the sixth-form examination and certificate will be continued and extended to cover more students, with the objective of feeding a growing network of secondary schools. Meanwhile, at the rural village level, a self-contained four-year school system will be introduced in an effort to extend literacy to as large a sector of the population as possible. Since it is planned that these rural schools will eventually become regular six-year primary institutions, their programs will follow the general pattern of the first four years of the classical primary school. The gradual integration of these rural schools into the regular cycle will be conditioned by the availability of teachers, facilities, and, inevitably, money.

The willingness of local communities to construct schools and share in the costs of education will determine the number of four-year schools built. Initially, the schools will be run by monitors who will have completed one year of professional training in primary education on a regional basis. The young men admitted into this program will be between the ages of sixteen and twenty. During the training period, the monitors will receive a small sum from the government; when assigned, they will receive no fixed salary but will be temporary villagers paid for their services by the local councils.

This two-stream system is designed to further the goal of minimum universal education, ward off a rural exodus, enhance the sense of national mission, and spread limited resources as far as possible.

The introduction of the four-year system and the use of very young teachers indicate that Mali is convinced that minimal adult literacy is an essential national goal, even if it means a lower over-all standard temporarily.

Meanwhile, the political climate of Mali suggests that the products of the classical education system will be both inclined and able to employ their skills in the national effort. The intelligentsia is deeply committed to the Union Soudanaise and to the forging of a new Mali.

39. *Mauritania*

Capital: Nouakchott
Population: 725,000 (est.)
Area: 418,810 sq. miles
Political status: Independent republic

THE modernizing process that accompanied French colonial rule in other parts of Africa barely touched Mauritania, and the vast majority of its inhabitants still pursued a way of life that had endured for centuries when the country attained its independence in November, 1960. Bordered on the north by Rio de Oro and Morocco and on the west and south by Senegal and Mali, Mauritania forms a geographic and cultural bridge between black Africa and the Maghreb. This is reflected in the ethnic composition of the population, which numbers approximately 725,000. Of these, some 500,000 are Moors, a mixture of Arab and Berber stock, related to the Tuareg of the central Sahara. The Moors are divided into warrior and marabout tribes, around whom gravitate tributary tribes and groupings of ex-slaves (mostly Negroes).

French policy in Mauritania was largely based on the desire to maintain order with a minimum expenditure of funds and administrative personnel. Although traditional rulers were therefore granted much greater authority than in other parts of West Africa, their position has gradually weakened. The status of the warrior sheiks depended upon their ability to protect the other tribes from the threat of physical force. *Pax Gallica* removed their *raison d'être,* as well as an important source of income. The marabouts—more numerous than the warriors and the traditional repositories of Islamic culture and learning—were generally favored by the French, who drew from their ranks the majority of the indigenous civil servants. Although the rigid Islamic orthodoxy emanating from the marabouts still prevails in Mauritania, both the Koranic institutions and the position of this traditional elite group are being weakened as Mauritania's ties with the modern world expand. Indeed, the reaction of the marabouts to this derogation of their role constitutes a major social and political problem for the future, already reflected in a hostile attitude toward the introduction of a modern educational system.

The 150,000 darker-skinned people who constitute the remainder of the population live principally in the Senegal River valley and in the plains of Brakna and Gorgol. These are the Sarakolle, Wolof, Bembera, Fulani, and especially the Toucouleurs, all of whom have strong cultural and kinship ties with their brethren to the south. Antagonism between the two segments of the population dates back to the enslavement of the Africans by their Arab and Berber conquerors. More recently, the Moors viewed with misgiving the fact that the Africans' birth rate was almost four times as great as their own, and there was some jealousy of the Africans' relative prosperity. At the time of the 1958 referendum on the constitution of the French Community, an irredentist political party was formed in the south, with the active encouragement of Senegalese political leaders, advocating union with Senegal. Although this is no longer an effective threat, the Africans remain a restive minority, and educational policies are directed toward integrating the Negroes into Mauritanian society. State-sponsored schools are to be opened in the area for the first time, and the teaching of Arabic will be emphasized.

Islam is the principal unifying force in the country, as is indicated by the chosen name—the Islamic Republic of Mauritania. More than 95 per cent of the population are practicing Moslems, and the conservative Qadiriyya order is dominant throughout the area. While French is both the official and the national language in the other former French West African territories, Arabic is the national language in Mauritania, and French retains only official status. In contrast to the multiplicity of dialects spoken in most African countries, Mauritania has only one vernacular language—a form of Arabic known as Hassania, with an established literary and poetic tradition.

History and Politics

In the eleventh century, the Almoravides (Lemtuna Berbers) swept out of southern Mauritania to establish their power over Morocco and southern Spain. After the breakup of their empire, a series of Arab invasions pushed southward from Morocco, giving the Moorish population its present ethnic composition and much of its cultural heritage.

The first real contact with the West came in the fifteenth century —first with the Portuguese, followed by the Dutch, British, and French. The French established their hegemony in the late nineteenth century by a series of treaties concluded with local chiefs. Mauritania was declared a French protectorate in 1903 and a colony attached to French West Africa in 1920. In accordance with recent French policy, a gradual devolution of authority took place, culminating in full independence within the French Community on November 28, 1960.

For a number of years, Morocco has sought to win international support for its position that Mauritania is historically and ethnically Moroccan and should be brought under the Moroccan flag. Although all the Arab countries except Tunisia support the Moroccan position, Mauritanian independence has been strongly upheld by France and the twelve French-speaking "Brazzaville states" of sub-Saharan Africa. The U.S.S.R., for tactical reasons that had little to do with the Moroccan claim, effectively blocked Mauritania's admission to the United Nations for a year, but relented in October, 1961. Meanwhile, the pro-Moroccan political movement, Nahdat al-Watain, has been gradually neutralized by the government of President Mokhtar Ould Daddah; in December, 1961, all Mauritanian political parties merged to form a single national movement, Hisb Chaab (Party of the People).

Ould Daddah, who was the only candidate in the general elections of 1961, is a member of one of Mauritania's most respected marabout families and originally came to power with the support of traditionalist elements. He received his higher education at the Sorbonne and was the country's first lawyer; he is now taking constructive steps to broaden the base of his support and to modernize the Mauritanian economy and society.

Economics and Education

Mauritania's 418,810 square miles are mostly desert and semidesert, where the Moorish nomads drift seasonally from north to south in search of grass and water for their flocks. Settled agriculture is confined to scattered oases and to the northern banks of the Senegal River, where millet, dates, and numerous fruits and vegetables are grown. Salt, gum arabic, and fish are also produced in small quantities. Ninety per cent of the population live on this primitive and precarious agriculture. There were only 20,000 wage earners in the country at the time of independence, and 18,000 of these were civil servants or military personnel.

Intruding into this subsistence economy will be a program of economic development which—in proportion to the size of the population—may be unparalleled in Africa. Near Fort Gouraud, deposits of some 145 million tons of iron ore have been discovered. MIFERMA, an international consortium formed to develop these reserves, will spend a total of $190 million in the next few years, more than six times the present national income of the country. Related projects include the development of an electric power plant, the building of a 400-mile railroad, and the improvement of the port facilities at Port Etienne. Farther south, at Akjoujt, are known reserves of 500,000 tons of copper, with some sulphurous minerals and gold. Prospecting for oil is taking place in several locations. From 1960 to 1964, a net inflow of $236.7 million is expected from public and private sources—this in a country whose annual budget ($12 million in 1960) has been the smallest in the French Community. This rapid economic advance will profoundly influence Mauritania's educational development. Even with a steady increase in public expenditure, revenues from mineral exploitation should balance the annual budget by 1964 without further external aid. This places Mauritania in the rather unique position of eventually having adequate funds at its disposal for school construction and teachers' salaries.

The fact that the French have a controlling interest in the iron and copper mines reinforces their political stake in Mauritania. Thus, one may anticipate the continued extension of generous technical and financial assistance. The European Development Fund has recently awarded a credit of $1,496,000 to Mauritania for the construction of schools. France, in the course of 1960, granted an additional subvention of $320,000 for public education. In the same year, the Mauritanian budget (which is heavily subsidized by France) allocated over $1.6 million for the administration of public education. It must be noted, however, that the annual per-pupil cost is very high—$93 per child in primary schools for 1958.

The new economic activity is bound to have a significant impact on Mauritanian life. The towns to be constructed at Fort Gouraud, Port Etienne, and the new capital of Nouakchott—with anticipated populations of 35,000, 10,000, and 6,000 respectively—will be carefully planned. Vocational training centers, schools, hospitals, and other social services will be designed with the particular needs of Mauritania in mind. The mines and related industries will provide jobs and vocational training for several thousand Mauritanians. This will accelerate the decay of the existing social order, for members of the marabout and warrior tribes—who have traditionally left manual labor to tributaries and slaves—have already been drawn to the mines. The present negligible per capita income could become one of the highest in West Africa in a matter of years. The position of the small educated elite will be especially affected by these changes, for there will be a growing demand for its services by the administration and the new commercial enterprises.

The Educational System Today

Historically, Mauritania offered little in the way of commercial possibilities, and the colonial power made little effort to develop the country economically or to modernize its administration. Public education was not emphasized until recent years, partly because of limited funds and partly because of the desire to avoid impairing friendly relations with the traditional authorities. Christian missions provided some schooling for the Africans of the Senegal River valley, but missionaries could not function among the Moors because of the objections of Islamic leaders and the general conditions of nomadic life.

Traditional Islamic education has long flourished, however, especially among the marabout tribes. In accordance with Moslem tradition, the children of the upper classes studied simple arithmetic, Arabic, and the Koran within the family. At the age of eight, children of both sexes were sent to local Koranic schools, which generally maintained higher standards than the Koranic schools in Africa farther south. The girls remained for two years, while the boys continued their studies to age fifteen. Three principal marabout schools *(grandes Medersas)* are located at Boutilimit Kiffa, and Kerna. These schools offer instruction in grammar, logic, theory, methods, and mystique, as well as the traditional subjects. Mauritania boasts a number of eminent Arabic scholars, and more than 2,000 manuscripts have been left by former savants in medicine, history, and other disciplines.

Mauritania is the only country in West Africa that has an institute of higher Moslem learning of the traditional type—the Institute of Islamic Studies, founded at Boutilimit in 1955. This was attended by some 300 students from Senegal, Mali, Portuguese Guinea, and Nigeria in 1961. Plans have been made to enlarge the Institute to accommodate 1,000 students with the objective of serving the needs of Moslem youth throughout West Africa.

When government schools were eventually built by the French and staffed with French teachers, Moslem parents accepted the new form of education most reluctantly. This was especially true in the case of the girls, who were restricted by custom to the family tent as they approached a marriageable age. As a result, in 1957, only 7.8 per cent of the school population in Mauritania were girls, the lowest number in all former French African territories.

French authorities first sought to induce the chiefs to set an example by sending their sons to school. This effort encountered strong opposition, and some chiefs even secretly attempted to substitute slave boys. The French then established an École des Fils des Chefs in the hope of making attendance a matter of prestige. This school has since been closed, as diplomatic considerations necessitated the granting of diplomas regardless of the students' scholastic performance.

Gradual social change has encouraged the acceptance of European-type education by the Moors, however. Increasing numbers of parents have become dissatisfied with a type of religious instruction that stresses memory work rather than understanding and leaves the students ill prepared for productive life in twentieth-century Africa. Since World War II, there has been growing pressure from among Mauritania's less conservative elements for the reform of the Koranic schools, the introduction of religious instruction in the French primary schools, the teaching of Arabic in government secondary schools, and the establishment of a Franco-Arabic college. Initially, the colonial administration hesitated to make such changes, as it feared that these might violate the lay character of French instruction and that the teaching of Arabic might lead to political complications. At the request of the Territorial Assembly, the administration introduced a Franco-Arabic curriculum into the state primary schools in 1947; however, the demand for the introduction of compulsory education was resisted because of the shortage of qualified teachers and the difficulty of coercing many Moorish parents to send their children to school.

In 1952, the Territorial Assembly requested the Department of Education to set up a modern teacher-training program at Boutilimit, to raise teachers' salaries, and to appoint an Inspector of Arabic Education. Although most of these changes have been instituted, the staffing of Mauritania's schools remains a problem; in 1958, it was estimated that 79 per cent of the teachers were insufficiently trained. Because of the emphasis on Islamic learning and the suspicion of many Moors, expatriate teachers are often not suitable. Furthermore, as yet, it has proved impossible to utilize large numbers of the marabout teachers in public education. Many of them remain loyal to the educational aims of Koranic schools and resent the intrusion of a system that has destroyed their traditional monopoly on formal education.

The French system of education gradually introduced in Mauritania is based on a first cycle (primary school) and a second cycle (secondary school), leading to the *baccalauréat* (high-school diploma). Table 1 indicates the evolution of these schools from 1922 to 1959, and underlines the small percentage of the school-age population they have affected.

Table 1
Development of Primary Education, 1922–59

Year	Number of primary schools	Number of classes	Number of students
1922	6	8	160
1950	31	82	2,249
1956	71		5,500
1958–59	156	298	6,784

The first opportunity for education in the second cycle was provided by a first-course teacher-training school at Boutilimit in 1950. This was followed by a secondary school opened at Rosso in 1957 with 139 pupils and 10 professors, where 104 student-teachers were being trained.

More complete statistics are available for 1958—the last year of French administration, when the total population was 620,000, the estimated school-age population was 93,000, and the percentage of school-age children in school was 7.2 per cent. Table 2 shows the breakdown of the enrollment.

Table 2
School Enrollment, 1958

	Boys	Girls	Total	Percentage of girls
First cycle	5,974	519	6,493	7.9
Second cycle	276	15	291	5.2
Total	*6,250*	*534*	*6,784*	*7.3*

Since the Mauritanian Government has taken over with its own Ministry of National Education, slow progress has been made along similar lines. In 1960, the total school enrollment was reported to be 8,997 (501 in secondary schools), distributed among 152 schools (four of them secondary schools), taught by 496 teachers (20 in secondary schools). By 1960, approximately 600 students had received the *Certificat d'Études* and 50 the *Brevet d'Enseignement Industriel et Commercial.*

The first cycle was complete in primary schools in all of the *cercles.* Secondary schools were opened at Atar, Kaédi, and Aïoun al Atrous, all of which had one or more first forms. One *lycée* was opened in Nouakchott, beginning with the first two forms. The total second cycle has been taught there since October, 1961, including philosophy and elementary mathematics (subjects of the second part of the *baccalauréat*).

The Problem of Educating Nomads

A special type of school has been devised for the large numbers of nomad children who find it impossible to attend sedentary schools. The first such schools, begun in 1924, produced only a few students who went on to more advanced studies; however, since World War II, new methods of teaching have been introduced into the three main nomad territories. The school tent and its teacher move with the tribe to which they are permanently attached, and the hours of study and the curriculum are adapted to the nomad life.* The nomad school's mobility varies with the individual tribe. That of Adrar, for example, has traveled as much as 480 miles a year, while others migrate for short distances and move only two or three times a year. Under this system, children are not separated from their parents, and their monitor-teacher is generally a member of the tribe to which he is assigned.

These schools are not allowed to wander about the desert unsupervised, and their success in Mauritania has been due largely to one of the territory's inspectors of nomad schools, Marc Lenoble. He has been aptly described as a "peripatetic propagandist of nomad education [who] leads a hard and ascetic life that has won him the Moors' respect"†—a vitally important asset in his difficult task of persuading the chiefs to permit their children to attend a tent school. His efforts have been so successful that, as of 1954, there were twelve nomad schools giving instruction to 241 children.‡

Although this type of school is still necessary, President Daddah's government reportedly wishes to replace it wherever possible with boarding schools. The principal criticism of the nomad school is that

* *Le Monde,* Paris, July 24, 1952; cited by Virginia Thompson and Richard Adloff, *French West Africa* (Stanford, Calif.: Stanford University Press, 1957), p. 531.
† Thompson and Adloff, *op. cit.,* p. 531.
‡ *Ibid.*

the chiefs of the various tribes often predicate their acceptance of such a school upon the right to select the teacher. Too often, the teachers are chosen from among his personal family or friends, and it is said that an inspector from the Ministry of Education has at times found nomad teachers who could not even read or write properly themselves.

Technical Education

In 1958, an agronomical research station was established at Kaedi. Operating from it, there will be agricultural extension services in twelve locations, four of which have already begun to function. These will demonstrate improved farming methods directly to the rural population.

A technical training school to be established in Port Etienne will accelerate the training of adult mine workers. In the future, it will become a technical training school for pupils of age thirteen to eighteen. Additional vocational schools will be set up in connection with other commercial enterprises, and workers will have the opportunity for on-the-job training.

Higher Education

In 1961, it was estimated that Mauritania had thirty to forty university graduates, most of them educated in France. The distribution of scholarship students in French secondary schools, universities, and graduate schools from 1957 to 1961 is shown in Table 3. To

Table 3
Mauritanian Scholarship Students in French Schools, 1957–61

Type of school	1957–58	1958–59	1959–60	1960–61
Higher education:				
Engineering	1		1	2
Veterinary			2	5
Sciences			2	5
Letters			4	3
Law			2	3
Professional schools			1	4
Preparation for professional schools			8	4
Dentistry				1
Medicine				1
Advanced study	1		20	28
Technical schools	3	3	5	3
Agricultural schools	3	4	4	3
Women in secondary school				1
Total	*8*	*7*	*49*	*63*

these figures should be added twenty-five non-scholarship students, forty students at the University of Dakar, and an additional twenty students enrolled in schools in France offering post-secondary training in technical fields (such as telecommunications, journalism, and radio). An additional thirty-seven civil-service clerks and interpreters (age thirty to thirty-five) were sent by the government in 1961 for accelerated training courses lasting from a few months to two or three years. These scholarships were granted on the basis of administrative needs, and the recipients are expected to return to fill more responsible positions in the government. The thirty-seven students in France under this program in 1961 were in the following fields: twelve in administration and statistics, one in law, two in industry, nine in customs, two in agriculture, five teachers and physical monitors, two in aviation, two in diplomacy, and two miscellaneous. Twenty-five other trainees were studying law in Tunisia to prepare themselves to become Moslem judges.

The Outlook

To the young Mauritanian Government, an expanded educational system is seen as a principal means of overcoming ethnic and social differences, promoting national unity, and forming the necessary synthesis between Moorish and French traditions. As President Daddah has put it:

> It is necessary for the population as a whole to have a feeling of cultural unity. That is why the government has bent every effort to develop an educational system deeply impregnated with the original culture of the country, but nevertheless adapted to the needs of a modern state; a system that will be the crucible in which the soul of the nation is forged.*

The potentially strong financial position of the Mauritanian Government and the willingness of France to render extensive technical assistance make the outlook for Mauritania's educational development relatively more promising than in many other African territories. The major problem of the future will be to convince parents and traditional authorities of the value of public education. The quality of instruction given will greatly depend upon the ability to provide a more comprehensive program of teacher training and upon Moorish society's willingness to permit the full utilization of female talent in the schools.

* *The Islamic Republic of Mauritania* (Ambassade de France, Service de Presse et d'Information, 1960), p. 29.

Efforts at educational expansion and other programs of modernization could provoke an overt political conflict between the government and the traditional authorities. While the hold of traditionalism on the Mauritanian masses should not be underestimated, Daddah's position will be reinforced by his ability to offer tangible evidence of social and economic advancement. One of the crucial factors in such a struggle would be the attitude of the educated younger generation. The thin layer of university-trained Mauritanians now appear to be in intellectual accord with Daddah's goals of modernization and with the principle of Mauritanian separateness, and the educated should find ample outlet for their energies and ambitions in administrative careers for the foreseeable future. All these factors can strengthen the government's position as it faces the difficult task of reconciling traditional Islamic learning and social mores with the imperatives of nation-building.

40. Togo

Capital: Lomé
Population: 1,500,000 (est.)
Area: 22,000 sq. miles
Political status: Independent republic

THE Republic of Togo is the eastern portion of the former German colony of Togoland. From 1919 until it became fully independent in April, 1960, the territory was administered by France, first under a League of Nations Class B mandate, then under a United Nations trusteeship agreement. Its internal composition is similar to that of its two closest neighbors, Ghana (into which the western portion of the old German colony was incorporated in 1956 after thirty-seven years of British administration) and Dahomey. Like these countries, it has a relatively progressive southern region that has long been in contact with the outside world, and a less prosperous, more parochial northern region. The main tribes are the Ewes and Onatchis, in the south; the Akpossey and Anas, in the center; and the Cobocolis, Cabran, Tchokossis, and Mobas, in the north.

The obligations of the U.N. trusteeship resulted in an ambiguous French policy toward Togo. It was impossible for the French Government to treat the territory as an integral part of the French Republic, as was the pattern (if not the reality) of postwar policy in the surrounding French territories, because both United Nations supervision and the close relations of its inhabitants with fellow Togolese in the British trust territory to the west gave Togo a range of contact with the outside world not available to most French colonial territories.

French Educational Policy

The educational policy laid down by the French in Togo was little different in kind from French policy elsewhere in Africa, although it was necessarily more flexible. It provided for six years of primary and six or seven of secondary education leading to the *baccalauréat*. The curriculum was essentially French. It was designed to bring students into a French university and, more broadly, into the French way of life. Although only about half of the system was under direct governmental control, the Catholic and Protestant mission schools did not depart radically from this design. But the peculiar historical and geographical situation of Togo opened alternatives here that were not generally available to the French citizens of other African territories. The influence of French education was diluted by old men who remembered German from the pre-1919 educational system and by young men—especially from the vigorous Ewe people—who had easy access to jobs and education among fellow Ewe in British Togoland and later Ghana. The Prime Minister who came to power in 1958, Sylvanus Olympio, is a product of all these cultural influences and is equally at home in French, German, and English. As a result of his university training (at the London School of Economics) and long association with a British trading firm operating throughout West Africa, Olympio was beginning to envisage changes in Togo's French educational system well before the country achieved independence. Younger men, returning from universities in France under the influence of the French Left, were also inclined to question the existing educational order. Despite the pervasive French cultural influence and the powerful role of the French teachers who staffed Togo's central *lycée* at Lomé, it seems unlikely that the French educational system built up in Togo over four decades will remain intact.

The school system created under French stewardship was a very flat pyramid. Between 1948 and 1958, the number of public primary-school pupils increased from about 21,000 to about 41,000, but the number of public secondary-school students only increased from 436 to 807.

This approach produced large numbers of primary-school graduates, only small numbers of secondary-school graduates, and very few of the technicians and trained farmers so badly needed by the Togo economy. Furthermore, these graduates were produced at unit costs that rose more than almost any other costs in the economy.

In 1960, there were 87,461 primary pupils in public and mission schools, taught by 1,475 teachers; thus, about one-third of the school-age population was actually in school. At the end of the 1958–59 academic year, about 2,700 pupils successfully completed their primary education (6 to 7 per cent of those who theoretically should have done so). Only 535 were admitted to some kind of secondary school—

20 per cent of those having successfully completed primary school and only a little more than 1 per cent of those who theoretically should have been admitted. Only 90 of these were admitted to the *lycée* at Lomé, while the others went to other public and private secondary schools offering less chance of access to higher education. The total enrollment of the *lycée* in 1959 was only a little less than 500 (not all native Togolese), and the number who received the *baccalauréat* in that year was between 15 and 30, including candidates from mission schools. (More detailed statistics are presented in Tables 1 and 2.)

Table 1
School Enrollment and Examinations in Togo, January 1, 1960

	Primary	Secondary	Technical
Pupils:			
Public	45,349	1,212	182
Private	42,112	1,262	236
Total	*87,461*	*2,474*	*418*
Teachers:			
Public	784	96	16
Private	691	91	33
Total	*1,475*	*187*	*49*
		Attempted	Passed
Examination results:			
CEPE		3,982	2,215
Entreé en 6		2,074	535
BE		46	27
BEPC		220	96
Bac. 1		44	19
Bac. 2		42	28

Table 2
Budgetary Expenditures for Education, 1960
(in millions of CFA francs) [a]

	Overhead	Primary	Secondary	Technical	Unallocable and all other	Total
Personnel	15.8	268.2	44.9	8.3	2.4	339.6
Supplies	1.2	12.4	2.8	2.2	2.2	20.8
Subsidies	—	—	—	—	93.3	93.3
Scholarships	—	—	—	—	84.8	84.8
Other	—	—	—	—	8.0	8.0
Total	*17.0*	*280.6*	*47.7*	*10.5*	*190.7*	*546.5*

[a] One U.S. dollar is equivalent to 247 CFA francs.

The Problem of Drop-outs

Clearly a major weakness in this system was drop-outs. Since the curriculum in Togo was identical with that in metropolitan French schools, it is doubtful if pupils completing only six years—let alone the very large numbers who did not complete primary school—were in any way prepared for the life they were to lead in a predominantly rural society. Technical and vocational education was not sufficiently developed to staff even the more modern sectors of the economy and the public service.

The teaching staff at the primary level was inadequately trained in both public and mission schools. This was a defect that time and the Normal School at Atakpamè are only very gradually correcting. By the time of independence, this institute had about 130 students and was producing some 30 semitrained teachers per year. Since salary scales were keyed to qualifications, age, and seniority, improvements in the quality of the teaching staff automatically increased costs. This factor, combined with the steady rise in the number of students enrolled in schools, made it almost impossible to improve the material aids to primary education. Expenditure on equipment and supplies was less than a dollar per pupil per year by 1960.

The peak of the secondary system was the residential *lycée* at Lomé. Its curriculum and teaching methods were wholly French, and its courses were pointed toward preparing its graduates for further education—an opportunity that relatively few of them were likely to have. It was an extremely costly institution to operate because of the salary scales of expatriate teachers, the multiplicity of courses, the books and other aids to education required by its curriculum, and, of course, because it was almost wholly residential.

Secondary Education

In recent years, there has been a growing awareness of the vacuum to be filled at the post-primary level, which has led to the creation of some new educational institutions catering to specific Togolese needs. In an effort to decentralize secondary education, it was decided to establish a series of *cours complémentaires* throughout the country offering the first four years of secondary education to day pupils. Some few of their graduates were able to enter the *classe de seconde* (fifth year) at the *lycée,* but the level of instruction in the five *cours complémentaires* in existence by 1960 (with 360 students) was not really up to secondary-school standard because qualified staff was not available. Gradually, new subjects, designed for pupils who could not hope to go on to the *lycée,* are being added; but thorough reform of the curriculum needed to place the schools on a sound footing is yet to come.

Aside from the *lycée,* the *cours complémentaires,* and the normal school, the only other public secondary institution in Togo is a poorly equipped vocational school teaching mechanics and commercial subjects; it had 231 pupils in 1960.

Several private (mission) schools operate at the secondary level, including a normal school with 100 students. In addition, a considerable number of Togolese go to school in Ghana, mostly at the secondary level.

Higher Education

No accurate figures are available on the number of Togolese receiving post-secondary education abroad, although 150 were known to be in France and receiving assistance from the French or Togo governments in 1960. They were well distributed among the disciplines; nineteen were receiving agricultural instruction at various levels, the same number were in engineering schools, and twenty-one were in science.

A small civil-service school at Lomé has been created to train junior-level professionals for the administration and thus hasten Africanization. It had one full-time faculty member, a number of part-time lecturers drawn from the civil service, and some thirty pupils drawn from fourth-year secondary-school leavers in 1960.

The Nature of the Elite

The educated elite in Togo is remarkable for its diversity. Those in commercial and industrial employment who have studied or worked abroad, as well as "Ghanaian" Togolese returned to their native country, are a relatively sophisticated group. The government is controlled by the older and more conservative sector of this elite, and there are at least two fairly clearly defined groups of younger educated people. Many of those who have returned in recent years from a traumatic intellectual awakening in French universities are convinced that socialism (of one sort or another) is the answer to Africa's problems. When confronted with the realities of Togolese life, many of these rebels against the existing order integrate themselves into the establishment—but some do not. Those who have been trained elsewhere in Africa generally adapt themselves more easily to work in the public services, in commerce, or, more rarely, in industry than do those who have studied in France. Fortunately, there is no deep prejudice against commercial and industrial employment or the public services.

There are nonetheless some acute problems. Although the public services badly need more people, the salary scale is too high and the system too rigid to allow sufficient infusion of new recruits. In addition, Togo is a very small nation with limited economic prospects, governed by a President who is a businessman and is determined to achieve a balanced budget despite the odds. This makes it very difficult to create new jobs in a bureaucracy that has inherited an excess of underqualified personnel. Those with university training or good secondary education seeking employment are not being offered jobs commensurate with their aspirations or a chance at the positions of men already in the public service whose qualifications are lower. The government is attempting to solve the problem of employment among the primary-school leavers by expanding vocational education, but the models of vocational schools inherited from the French are not suited to Togo's specific needs, and present facilities are, in any case, grossly inadequate. On the university side, there is no problem that cannot be solved by an increase in scholarships.

41. Federal Republic of Cameroon

Capital: Yaoundé (Eastern Cameroun)
Total population: 4,051,000 (est.)
Eastern Cameroun: 3,225,000
Western Cameroon: 826,000
Total area: 183,381 sq. miles
Eastern Cameroun: 166,800 sq. miles
Western Cameroon: 16,581 sq. miles
Political status: Independent federal republic

On October 1, 1961, the former Southern Cameroons under British trusteeship and the Cameroun Republic merged to become the Federal Republic of Cameroon. The union was the direct result of a plebiscite conducted by the United Nations in both the southern and the northern sections of the British Cameroons on February 11 and 12, 1961. Asked to indicate whether they preferred union with Nigeria or with Cameroun, voters in the Northern Cameroons chose Nigeria, while those in the Southern Cameroons voted overwhelmingly to join the Cameroun Republic.* Following unification, the Southern Cameroons and the Cameroun Republic were renamed Eastern Cameroun and Western Cameroon.

The two members of the new federation, together with the former Northern (British) Cameroons, originally constituted undifferentiated portions of the German Protectorate of Kamerun. The Germans held the Kamerun from 1884 to 1916, when they were driven out by combined British-French military forces and the protectorate was partitioned between the victors. Britain obtained one-fifth of the old Kamerun, the French the other four-fifths. The Versailles Treaty ratified the division of the territory, and when the League of Nations

* The Northern Cameroons became a part of Nigeria on July 11, 1961. It had been hoped, in the event the Northern Cameroons opted for union with the Republic, to make it the third member of the federation.

was created, France and Britain retained their portions of the old Kamerun as mandates.

With the demise of the League and the creation of the United Nations (1946), the two mandates were converted into trust territories under the U.N.'s trusteeship system. In 1957, the French Cameroons became internally self-governing, and on January 1, 1960, it acquired full independence, taking the name of the Cameroun Republic.

The constitution of the Federal Republic provides for federal control over higher education and stipulates that jurisdiction over secondary and technical education will be assumed by the federal authorities after an undefined "transition period." Primary education, not mentioned in the document, remains—by implication and by application of certain reserve-powers clauses—within the aegis of the two states. Since there are as yet no institutions of higher learning in the federation, and inasmuch as the "transition period" is expected to last (at least) until 1963, education in the federation can only be meaningfully discussed as the separate educational systems of the two states—indeed, as the systems in operation *before* the federation was formed.

Eastern Cameroun

Located at the bend of the Guinea Gulf, Eastern Cameroun's 166,800 square miles (approximately the size of Oregon and Washington) embrace a varied topography, including fertile coastal lowlands in the south, the Adamawa Plateau rising to over 4,000 feet in the center, high mountains in the west, and savanna grasslands in the north. The coastal region, which includes the main commercial center of Douala, has a density of 230 persons per square mile, one of the highest in French-speaking West Africa. In 1958, an estimated 10 to 15 per cent of the Africans (and 70 per cent of the Europeans) lived in urban areas.

The territory's population of 3,225,000 (including 17,000 Europeans) comprises some 140 identifiable tribal groupings. This poses some serious problems of integration, aggravated by a pronounced split between the Moslem north and the Christian-animist south. The major dialects are Pahouin, Bamiléké, Hausa, and Fulfulde. Literacy (in the French language) has been estimated at 5 to 10 per cent, but this figure rises to 30 and 40 per cent in the southern sections of the country.

As in many neighboring territories, Eastern Cameroun's economic development has primarily affected the southern areas of the territory. In this region, 75 per cent of the primary-school graduates migrate to the towns, draining the countryside of necessary agricultural manpower. This condition accentuates the disparities between the south and the north, where 60 per cent of the rural working-age population have no productive occupations. The same contrast is found in basic economic development, which remains at a rudimentary level in much of the northern area. Federal economic planners believe that more equitable distribution of the country's communications, social services, and employment opportunities is required to reduce regional antagonisms.

Educational Development

The first Western schools in the Cameroons area were introduced by Baptist missionaries in 1843. For the next forty years, until the declaration of the German protectorate, missionaries from various denominations established themselves and set up schools. Even by 1913—after twenty-nine years of colonial administration—the public-school system consisted of only four schools, located at Victoria, Douala, Yaoundé, and Garoua; all the others were private mission schools.

A decree of July 25, 1921, provided the general framework for the educational system established by the French administration. It stipulated that the schools should bring the indigenous population into a closer association with the colonists by teaching the French language to the Africans and by familiarizing them with the methods and policies of the administering authority. A number of public schools were established, with French as the language of instruction. The cycles of study, the examinations, and the final certificates were patterned after those of metropolitan France.

Judged by the percentage of school-age children in school and the number of secondary and technical students, Eastern Cameroun ranks very high in French-speaking Africa. Enrollment trebled from 1946 to 1960, as the statistics in Table 1 indicate.

Table 1
School Enrollment in Eastern Cameroun, 1946–60

Year	Total enrollment	Girls (percentage)	Percentage of school-age population in school
1946	114,722	14.7	n.a.
1951	159,485	14.0	26
1954	180,006	24.4	39
1957	278,889	27.3	58.9
1958	303,966	28.6	64
1960	342,813	30.0	63

The rate of school attendance for boys reached nearly 100 per cent in 1960 in the south, but only 27 per cent of the girls of school age were actually in attendance. The figures for the Moslem north were 36 per cent for boys and 2 per cent for girls.

Eastern Cameroun's high attendance record continues to be due principally to the diligence of the missions, which account for two-thirds of the present school enrollments. A second factor promoting the growth of schools has been the relatively high proportion of the budget used for educational purposes (14 per cent in 1958 and about 16 per cent in 1960). The national budget for fiscal 1960 allocated more than $7 million for the administration of public education, plus subsidies of $700,000 for public education and nearly $187,000 for private schools.

Generous outside assistance has also been provided through FIDES. France contributed nearly $4 million from 1946 to 1953—and then over $11 million from 1953 to 1959. The Fund for Aid and Cooperation (FAC), which replaced FIDES in 1959, provided $1,632,000 in 1959–60 alone. The Cameroun Government also requested assistance from the European Development Fund for certain special projects.

The Franco-Cameroun treaty for economic and technical cooperation, signed in December, 1959, stipulated that French would remain the official language of Cameroun and that the rights of French educational institutions, public and private, would be guaranteed. It also affirmed the equality of rights of Camerounian and French students in French universities.

Educational System

The current Ten-Year Development Program (1960–70) places special emphasis on education, with a view to adapting the school system to national needs. Particular attention is to be given to the northern region, where it is hoped that 100 schools will be opened annually and that a 50 per cent rate of school attendance will be achieved by 1970. The plan also provides for the expansion of female education, vocational training, secondary schools, and adult literacy classes. (Some 400 adult classes were in operation in 1957–59, evenly distributed between the north and the south, but far more are needed.) Finally, it is anticipated that 200 to 250 new schools will be opened during the ten-year period to provide for a school population that should increase by 10,000 to 12,000 pupils per year.

Primary Education

Primary education accounts for 96.8 per cent of the total enrollment in Eastern Cameroun's schools. The average primary course, closely patterned on French models, consists of two years of preparatory courses, where the pupils learn to speak French; two years of elementary courses, where they are taught reading, writing, and arithmetic; and two years of intermediate courses, where they are taught grammar, history, geography, etc. Since January, 1960, there has been a more serious attempt to give the elementary history, geography, and civics courses an African and "national" orientation. Practical education designed to complement the territory's agrarian economy has been introduced by setting up gardens and school cooperatives for the boys and homemaking courses for the girls.

In June, 1961, primary education was offered in 2,741 schools—728 of them public, with 1,933 classes, and 2,013 of them private, with 5,220 classes. The enrollment was 330,983—229,673 boys and 101,310 girls. These schools were supervised by six inspectors (five French and one Camerounian) and staffed by Camerounian teachers.

Secondary Education

Eastern Camerounian secondary schools offer two alternative programs of study. The first is a short self-contained course (*cours complémentaire*) for ages twelve to sixteen, designed for those who do not plan to continue their studies. The curriculum includes French, civics, history, geography, mathematics, drawing, practical sciences, music, education, home economics, and manual training. At the end of the four years, specialized examinations are given in the various fields, with a general examination for the elementary certificate (BEPC).

A longer secondary course with a higher academic content is provided for pupils of ages twelve to nineteen, leading to the *baccalauréat*. In 1959, a total of 79 students received this degree, and 60 of these students were awarded scholarships for higher education in France. In 1961, there were 7,200 students enrolled in 104 classes in twenty-two secondary schools. The government has expressed its intention to expand secondary education progressively to keep pace with the graduates of primary schools, and official estimates forecast approximately 12,000 secondary students by 1970.

Technical Training

Eastern Cameroun has developed numerous and diversified facilities for technical training. In 1960, 4,359 pupils were enrolled in sixty-seven such schools. Training was provided in thirty-five tax-supported establishments, including one *lycée* and seven apprenticeship centers. Slightly more than half the students received instruction in twenty-four private institutions, including thirteen homemaking schools, three commercial schools, and six centers for handicraft workers and industrial technicians.

The present government plans to expand technical training and to relate it to the over-all program of economic development. High priority will be given to regional agricultural schools. In 1962, a vocational guidance and placement service will be established, which will utilize the most advanced techniques of aptitude determination and vocational counseling.

Teacher Training

As in most other African countries, a teacher shortage is the major bottleneck in plans for an accelerated educational program. In 1957, only 6,982 students of the 19,216 who took the various examinations passed. This is officially attributed primarily to the shortage of trained teachers, the attempt to enforce high standards, and the students' difficulties with the French language.

In 1960, there were 7,500 male teachers in Cameroun, of whom 5,250 were employed in private schools. As of June, 1961, schools in the first and second cycles, technical schools, and physical education and youth centers were all staffed by African personnel. However, the Ministry of Education has recognized the need for retaining expatriate teachers in order to maintain the standard of instruction.

Present development plans call for the training of some 500 teachers per year for the public schools alone. At least six new schools for training teachers at various levels are scheduled to open by 1962.

Higher Education

In 1961, more than 1,000 Camerounian students were in foreign secondary and technical schools and universities, 504 of them on scholarships in France. During 1957–58 and 1958–59, Cameroun had more scholarship students in France working for advanced degrees than any other African country. Although this is no longer true, the territory has the largest number of students studying scientific subjects. It was reported that in 1961 four Camerounian students were in Czechoslovakia, two in the U.S.S.R., one in Yugoslavia, two in Tunisia, and one in India.

The placement of scholarship students in France for the years 1957–61 is given in Table 2.

Table 2
Camerounian Scholarship Students in France

	1957–58	1958–59	1959–60	1960–61
Male students:				
Secondary education	267	198	234	186
Higher education				
Medicine	59	64	62	59
Pharmacy	18	21	19	16
Dentistry	3	3	3	2
Veterinary medicine	2	—	5	6
Sciences	24	45	59	70
Letters	25	36	36	44
Law	43	52	49	51
Fine arts	4	2	3	2
Higher professional education	9	15	9	28
Preparation for higher professional education	13	24	24	28
Engineers	1	16	20	5
Theology		4	9	7
Female students:			124	98
Secondary education			110	79
Higher education			14	19

A National Center for Advanced Study was opened in Yaounde in October, 1961. This Center, which will offer courses in law, science, and letters, is envisaged as the nucleus of a future Institute of Higher Education and possibly a University of the Cameroun. UNESCO is assisting with this project, and France has agreed to make available any teaching staff the government might request.

Western Cameroon

Western Cameroon—formerly the southern section of the trust territory of the British Cameroons—is a mountainous strip of land extending 230 miles northeast from the Gulf of Guinea. About the size of Denmark, with a total population of approximately 826,000, the territory lies wedged between Nigeria and Eastern Cameroun.

The constitution of the Federal Republic of Cameroon, as noted earlier, provides for state control of primary and—at least temporarily—technical and secondary education. At the very least, this implies retention of English as the language of instruction (although it is expected that classes in French will be offered soon at the principal secondary schools) and preservation of the present British-style grade and matriculation systems. How well this can be integrated with the French-derived system of the eastern state is not as yet clear. Neither the federal educational authorities nor the government of the western state had at this writing clarified the situation.

In any case, and whatever the changes that may occur in the future, the point of departure must inevitably be Western Cameroon's educational system as it existed prior to October 1, 1961. It is with conditions before that date that we shall be mainly concerned. Moreover, for certain purposes, an even earlier date is significant—October 1, 1960, when Nigeria became independent. Before that date, Nigeria administered the trust territory as an "integral part" of its domain, under British supervision, and most of the financial and some of the administrative responsibility for education centered in Lagos (for the Southern Cameroons) or in Kano (for the Northern Cameroons), rather than in Buea or Dikwa. In addition, Nigeria provided access to Nigerian secondary schools and the University College at Ibadan, as well as to the several technical schools scattered throughout the federation. The Nigerian accession to independence brought the trust territory under the direct administration of the trusteeship power, Great Britain, and meant that financial and administrative links with the federation were severed. Even though Nigeria intended to keep what Cameroonians there were in its schools, it was reluctant to pay their way or admit more of them. In discussing secondary and higher education, therefore, we shall mainly have reference to conditions existing before October 1, 1960.

Ever since the old Kamerun was split, two factors have dominated the growth and content of the educational system of the Southern Cameroons, and they will continue to shape whatever arises in the wake of unification. The first was the comparative isolation of the territory, and the second the dominant role played by voluntary agencies (the religious missions) in the educational system.

The geographical isolation of the former trust territory made it a sort of Nigerian "backwater." Communication with both the Republic and Lagos was always difficult at best; roads in either direction are few in number, impassable during much of the year, and generally little-traveled. The distance between Buea and Lagos, about 423 miles, is negotiated with difficulty by road, more frequently by sea and air. The area's general economic backwardness further served to isolate it from Nigeria and divert governmental interest to more advanced areas elsewhere. As a consequence of all this, the territory is poorly equipped, as far as government schools are concerned, and poorly endowed with operating funds. Only with the periodic infusion of British loans and grants and the massive effort of the voluntary agencies has the system managed to operate with any effectiveness. A measure of this state of affairs is the fact that only 75 of the entire trust territory's 543 schools were owned and operated by the government or the Native Authorities.

Western Cameroon, with a population of 826,000, now has a total of 478 schools, of which 468 are on the elementary level and the rest offer secondary or technical instruction. There are presently some 59,000 students enrolled in all types of schools.

The School System, 1960

From the very first days of the Kamerun Protectorate, the main burdens of education were borne by the mission societies. The English Baptists, the Basel Mission, the Catholic Pallotine Fathers, and the American Presbyterian Mission were among the earliest of the missionary groups operating in the Cameroons. The Germans, as did the British after them, encouraged the growth of missions, apparently happy to be relieved of the financial and staff responsibilities that a full-scale official system would entail. The pattern set in the earlier days has persisted until today. About 410 mission schools, owned by five main mission groups, operate in the territory. The largest number of schools is operated by the Roman Catholic Mill Hill Fathers—240 schools, with an enrollment of some 25,000. The next largest mission is that of the former Basel Mission (now the Presbyterian Church), followed by the Cameroons Baptist, and the smaller Sudan United and Church of the Brethren missions. In all, the mission schools enroll some 48,565 pupils and include in their teaching staffs about 100 full-time missionaries from abroad, as well as 1,600 teachers and teacher-trainees from the Cameroons and Nigeria.

The system is modeled along traditional British grade and matriculation patterns. Primary education is divided into two general levels, the junior primary and senior primary. The former division includes a beginners' section of two classes (Standards 1 and 2) and a junior primary section of two classes (Standards 1 and 2). The senior primary schools are of four classes (Standards 3 to 6). The aim of the junior primary course is to provide a basis for permanent literacy for those who complete the course and who make an effort to keep up in their reading after they have left school. Those who pass the eight-year course and pass the government Standard 6 examination receive a

First School Leaving Certificate, which is accepted as minimum qualification for most salaried jobs by employers such as the government, trading firms, and missions, as well as the stepping stone to secondary or technical education. The full elementary course is seven, rather than eight, years in the Northern Cameroons.

There is no compulsory education in Western Cameroon, and only in Adamawa and Dikwa Emirates in the Northern Cameroons did such compulsion exist. Many government and Native Authority schools provide free tuition in Western Cameroon; the missions charge nominal school fees varying between 18 shillings (beginners 1 and 2) and 60 shillings (Standards 5 and 6) per year. Most government schools charge similar fees.

In Western Cameroon, neither local law nor custom restricts girls' education, but parents usually prefer to spend their money educating boys. In the last few years, however, a noticeable increase in female enrollment has indicated a rising awareness of the values of education and a slow change in the status of women. Both the government and the voluntary agencies have devoted considerable effort to improving facilities for female students and encourage greater use of the existing facilities.

Secondary Education

Western Cameroon has three secondary schools, two for boys and one for girls. The boys' schools are St. Joseph's College, Sasse, near Buea, conducted by the Roman Catholic Mission, and the Southern Cameroons Protestant College, in the Bamenda area, run jointly by the Basel and Baptist Missions. The former offers a six-year course, the latter a five-year course, both leading to West African School Certificate examination. The girls' school, Queen of the Rosary College, opened its first classes in 1957; it also offers a five-year curriculum leading to the West African School Certificate.

The aim of secondary education in Western Cameroon has officially been described as intending to provide ". . . an education which, while complete in itself, will fit students to become responsible citizens and provide the groundwork for further training." * These purposes are served by a broad curriculum that emphasizes (for the West African School Certificate examination) English language and literature, mathematics, science, history, and geography. The medium of instruction is English, and no indigenous language is used. French

* *Report to the United Nations on the Cameroons under United Kingdom Administration, 1957* (London: Her Majesty's Stationery Office, 1957), p. 112.

and Latin are taught. Girls follow a similar curriculum, except that they study biology and domestic science instead of physical science. Provision has also been made for the study of commercial subjects in order to afford the girls wider opportunities of employment and to offer a greater selection of subjects to meet individual abilities and interests.

Higher Education

There are no higher educational establishments. Students from the Cameroons have had access to the University College at Ibadan (there were twelve there during 1959) and to courses provided at the Nigerian College of Arts, Science, and Technology at Ibadan, Enugu, and Zaria, on an equal footing with students from Nigeria. Government scholars have also been attending universities in England, several are to be found in American institutions, and two were at Kumasi College, Ghana. Most of these students have been financed through scholarships or grants provided by the Nigerian, British, or American governments.

Technical Education

Technical and vocational training is offered at three schools in the territory. Most of the courses lead to apprenticeship in mechanical trades such as bricklaying, carpentry, electricity, painting, sheet-metal working, machining, and automobile and motor mechanics. In addition, a class of ten prospective manual-arts teachers was trained at the Kumba Teacher Training College by an American ICA instructor.

Teacher Training

Teacher training is carried on in eleven voluntary-agency schools and two government institutions. An elaborate system of grading and certification, established by the Nigerian and Southern Cameroons governments, provides for a wide range of teachers placed and paid according to their educational attainments. This varies from the uncertificated, probationer, or ungraded teachers, who may receive as little as £48 a year (in the mission schools), all the way to those holding advanced secondary diplomas, paid up to £800. While this system has its disadvantages, such as relatively unskilled and unsophisticated teaching at the lower levels, it does provide an increasing supply of actual teachers, most of whom are continuing their own education.

Role of the Missions

Prior to 1961, ultimate responsibility and control over the trust territory's educational system lay outside the borders of the British Cameroons. For the Southern Cameroons, it was vested in the federal educational authorities in Lagos, and in the case of the Northern Cameroons it lay with the Ministry of Education of the Northern Region of Nigeria. From these centers of control, responsibility, devolved upon various local agencies and officers. The Chief Education Officer at Buea, for example, had control of the Southern Cameroons Education Department, which in turn had charge of the local education officers. Mission supervisors and managers maintain close liaison with government educational authorities and ensure the functioning and staffing of the mission schools according to official standards, requirements, and ordinances.

To a large extent, the mission schools operate independently of the government schools—that is, they continue to be administered, staffed, and largely financed by the voluntary agencies themselves. This quasi autonomy does not, however, permit them a completely free choice in the selection of teachers or curricula. Government-established subjects must be taught if the schools are to maintain their accreditation by the government. Moreover, it is this accreditation that makes the mission schools eligible for funds from the government. The official controls on the voluntary-agency schools have only rarely been challenged by the missions; usually, such challenges have centered about questions of finance rather than on issues involving subjects to be taught or standards to be maintained.

In summary, Western Cameroon's educational system is a hybrid of voluntary-agency and government schools, methods, and aims. Government and missions have evolved a nice balance of interests by which both official and mission aims may be served. This is a balance that permits standards and minimal curricula to be set by the government, while the missions have the latitude to further their own religious work. Thus far, the system has worked well, and its product—in terms of educational achievement—compares favorably with educated Africans from other, more developed African nations.

Table 3
Schools and Enrollments in and for the British Cameroons, 1925–58

Type of school and year	Total	Proprietorship: Government Enrolled	Government Schools	Voluntary agency Enrolled	Voluntary agency Schools
Primary					
1925	5,637	1,927	20	3,710	120
1935	7,777	2,047	22	5,730	210
1947	26,304	n.a.	51	n.a.	193
1953	37,302	6,282	60	31,020	340
1958	60,904	10,414	71	50,490	453
Secondary					
1925	12	12	1	0	0
1935	102	6	1	96	5
1947	263	0	0	263	1
1953	393	0	0	393	1
1958	513	0	0	513	3
Secondary, enrolled in Nigerian schools					
1935	18				
1947	259				
1953	30				
1958	63				
Normal (teacher training)					
1925	2	2	1	0	0
1935	n.a.	31	1	n.a.	n.a.
1947	n.a.	n.a.	1	n.a.	3
1953	134	79	1	55	3
1958	694	124	2	570	11
Vocational					
1947	n.a.	19	1	n.a.	n.a.
1953	n.a.	27	2	n.a.	n.a.
1958	228	192	2	36	1
Higher and other post-secondary, enrolled abroad					
1935	11				
1947	2				
1953	26				
1958	63				
1958 Totals	*62,465*	*10,730*	*75*	*51,609*	*468*

Southern Cameroons approx. 58,000 (78 per cent males, 22 per cent females)
Northern Cameroons approx. 4,500 (82 per cent males, 18 per cent females)

The Role of the Educated in Society

The Federation's foreign-trained university elite does not yet play a role in the public life of the country commensurate with its potential. Of the 100 deputies in the Assembly of Eastern Cameroun, for example, there are only 2 with university degrees; 46 hold primary-school certificates (certifying six years' schooling), and the rest have completed the eight-year *cours complémentaire*. A high percentage of important political and administrative positions are held by persons who have not completed secondary school.

Eventually, of course, as the number of opportunities for lucrative careers in government service decreases, and as more and more of the federation's educated youth enter politics, many young Cameroonians who now feel alienated from their society and complain of having been relegated to the sidelines will assume more active roles in the country's political and social life.

The creation of a local university and an increase in the number of Cameroonians with secondary education should also help to rectify this wasteful alienation of the country's youth—but it is only a partial answer. This cleavage is only one symptom of the country's continuing internal fragmentation. Despite many advantages lacking in other African states, it has yet to mold its disparate cultural, ethnic, and political segments into a stable national entity.

—VICTOR T. LE VINE and HENRI M'BALLAH *

* Originally, Dr. Le Vine and Mr. M'Ballah wrote separate chapters on the British Cameroons and the Cameroun Republic, respectively. The above chapter, prepared by Dr. Le Vine, incorporates both drafts.

42. Guinea

Capital: Conakry
Population: 2,727,000 (est.)
Area: 95,000 sq. miles
Political status: Independent republic

ONE of the first steps undertaken by newly independent Guinea in 1958 was a full re-examination of the premises on which the educational system of the country had been organized while the country was a constituent territory of the Federation of French West Africa. Shortly thereafter, it was decided to undertake extensive revision of the system to bring its objectives into closer harmony with the social and political goals of the new country as defined by the single national political party, the Parti Démocratique de Guinée (PDG).

In a country where more than fourteen distinct languages are spoken and that for centuries has been divided and ruled by three mutually antagonistic ethnic groups, the problem of creating a highly centralized modern nation-state based upon the acceptance of a common nationality is a staggering one. The efforts of the National Political Bureau, the Ministry of National Education, and the schools of Guinea toward this end have had impressive results.

A decade ago, almost any citizen of Guinea would have identified himself as a Soussou, a Foulah, or a Malinke. Today, he is more likely to say, "I am a Guinean." Building on the new sense of nationhood that marks the transition of a former colonial territory to independence and on the national emergency created by the abrupt withdrawal of French aid, civil administrators, and vital equipment, the Guinean Government has undertaken the delicate task of detribalizing Guinea without losing touch with the nation's tribal heritage.

Education has taken on a distinctively patriotic and nationalistic tone. Along with other institutions of national life, the national education system has been brought into the political arena and its programs and policies closely coordinated with other organs of the state concerned with the realization of national objectives.

Departing from the traditional educational policy followed by the French in West Africa—that of providing the opportunities of education to a relatively small minority of the population and forming from this minority a highly educated autochthonous elite fully assimilated into French culture—independent Guinea sets its sights on education of the masses. In August, 1961, President Sékou Touré announced that collective education would be improved by the forthcoming use of 123 loudspeakers in public listening centers and that this method would be extended throughout the country. He has emphasized that "individual differences in effort or intelligence" will still result in the creation of an elite at the apex of this broader base, however, and that there will be no sacrifice of quality at the higher levels.

Language and "Decolonialization"

Basic to the reforms introduced was the need to "decolonialize" Guinean education and give it more African content. African languages and history, as well as African geography, were introduced as important subjects in the curricula for the first time, and Guinean students are no longer required to study French history and geography in minute detail. A determined effort is being made to extend the knowledge of Foulah, Soussou, and Malinke, the three major vernacular languages spoken in the country. African languages are taught in all Guinean schools with the aim of ensuring that future generations of Guineans are competently conversant in the major languages of the country, and, except for subjects of a highly technical or scientific nature, all basic materials are henceforth to be drawn from primary (i.e., African) sources wherever possible. More and more students are sent to attend secondary schools in regions away from their own people, where they are obliged to learn the language and ways of another sector of Guinean society.

By the Franco-Guinean Accords of January 7, 1959, French is still the official language of the country and the principal vehicle of instruction in the schools. But the use of French is an expedient necessitated by historical circumstance, as indicated by President Touré's remarks at a PDG National Congress in September, 1959:

> It is well for us to have young people who speak English, German, or Spanish, but the Political Bureau makes obligatory only two foreign languages, French and English. . . . As to the use of French, we think that this language should be employed to make known to young people above all those things that are African. Thus, in the fields of history, geography, political economy, in a word everything that is not purely scientific and universal, the educational raw materials can only be drawn from Africa. . . . If we had gone to the trouble, we could have managed to teach all the lessons and principles of science or the liberal arts in Fulani, Soussou, or Malinke. . . .
>
> The Political Bureau has . . . prescribed the teaching of African languages in our schools with the thought that in the future the officials of the party and the state will be able, throughout Guinea, to speak directly to the people. We must not shrink from our obligation to train the young people who will be the adults of tomorrow. Knowing the language of a people, one feels a more direct human contact with them. In Guinea, what people think in the Fouta is, at bottom, what people think at the Coast, in the Forest Region, or in Upper Guinea. When all of them can communicate with each other and understand each other directly, their cooperation will become closer and more effective.

The retention of French as the official language of the nation and the schools has inevitably limited the "Africanization" of the educational system vigorously sought by the party as one of its major goals because it has implicitly required the recruitment of expatriate teachers capable of teaching French as a language as well as those equipped to use it as a medium of instruction for other subjects. Thus, even during the long period of hostile political relations with the French after the traumatic break with the metropole in 1958, Guinea continued to employ many French teachers in its school system, and the impact of French culture upon Guinea's youth remains considerable.

In an effort to mitigate this by-product of the use of French as a medium of instruction, the Ministry of National Education, at the behest of the party, has given increasing attention to the reorientation of the curriculum from its traditional Western framework to one that is more pointedly African. It is stepping up recruitment of French-speaking teachers and specialists from other nations, is sending more and more Guinean students to receive their advanced education in schools outside France, and is expanding its effort to make educated Guineans conversant in English as well as French. Even so, French sources report that Guinea's appeals for teachers from France outrun the available supply. In view of Guinea's political relationship with

France, many teachers have been fearful of compromising their careers and their position in their professional organizations by taking a contract in Conakry, with the result that a majority of those going to Guinea from Paris since 1958 have been young liberals, often holding Marxist views sympathetic to the Guinean political experiment.

The expansion of the English-teaching program has made considerable progress, particularly since 1960. Before 1958, few Guineans knew English, but it is now taught as a compulsory subject in the great majority of Guinean schools, including the Lycée Donka, the huge secondary school just outside the capital city of Conakry which is the largest teaching establishment in the country. American, British, and English-speaking Africans and nationals of other countries are employed by the Guinea Government to staff the growing English-language program.

The encouragement given the study of English in Guinea has been motivated by political as well as educational considerations. By encouraging and obliging Guinean youth to become bilingual, President Touré not only hopes to lessen his country's dependence on France, but also seeks to create a bilingual state as a means of adding substance to the Guinea-Ghana union consummated in May, 1959, and furthering the larger pan-African unity to which Guinea is committed.

While English and French are looked upon by most Guineans as temporary expedients to be used only until such time as an African language may be substituted in their place, the government is fully aware that the practical difficulties involved in using an African tongue as the official language are great. A hasty step in this direction could result in a grave deterioration in the whole educational process and might work against rather than toward the ultimate goals of unity espoused by the PDG.

Though rich in verbal expression reflecting regard for nuance and subtlety, the great majority of West Africa's local languages lack vocabulary for technical expression on subjects lying outside the perimeters of the traditional linguistic environment and experience. The task of providing any given language with a formal grammar and syntax, not to mention the herculean endeavor of writing text and reference books in its medium and assembling a teaching staff trained and capable of teaching in it, would be formidable. Finally, and for Guinea this has particular significance, the choice of one of the tongues native to Guinea (e.g., Foulah, Malinke, or Soussou) over the other two might revive the older ethnic and linguistic loyalties that both the party and the government have been seeking to bury in national consciousness.

Growth Since 1958

In recognition of the crucial role that education will play in the construction of the country, the Guinean Government has accorded it top priority in its long-range development plans. The National Conference of Economic Planning, held in Kankan on April 2–5, 1960, voted to devote 30 per cent of the budget of Guinea's first Three-Year Plan to social affairs, the greatest portion going to develop educational facilities in the country. In 1961, approximately 25 per cent of the national budget was set aside for this purpose.

The decision was also made to try to induce countries offering certain kinds of scholarships to Guinean students to contribute instead to the establishment of equipped basic training facilities (*centres d'apprentissages,* technical schools and *lycées*) in Guinea, thus eliminating students' human and financial problems abroad, assuring fuller development of the "African personality," and making sure that educational aid was "invested" in Guinea rather than "wasted" in international transportation and maintenance abroad. This approach, it was envisaged, would not exclude advanced training abroad at a riper age.

The vigorous drive to expand education has produced some staggering statistics. In 1958, on the eve of independence, there were 1,500 pupils in Guinea qualified to receive the CEP (Elementary School Certificate). By 1959, this number had increased to 4,000. In comparison to 900 students admitted to the first form in 1958, the following year saw the same group augmented by nearly 100 per cent to 1,750. In 1959, primary schools, both public and private, had a total enrollment of 52,000 pupils. By April, 1960, this figure had climbed to 84,000. In August, 1961, the President stated that there would be more than 100,000 pupils and a teaching profession of 2,380 for 1961–62.

In secondary education, gains were equally impressive. Enrollment in public secondary schools in Guinea in 1959 totaled 4,000, while private secondary schools had 480 students. Between 1960 and the early months of 1961, 2,050 more students were added, thus bringing the total to approximately 6,500. By projection, the Guinean Government estimated that 2,500 more students would be added during the period 1961–62.

In 1958, the number of pupils enrolled in denominational missionary schools represented a substantial proportion of the total school population. Acknowledging this fact, the government decided to continue state subsidies to such schools for a period of three years, beginning in 1959. It was made clear, however, that the objective was to diminish and eventually eliminate the influence of these private schools; thus, headmasters were forbidden to register any new pupils as of 1959. Pupils terminating their studies at the mission schools were judged eligible to take the competitive entrance examination (*concours de bourses*) for scholarships to public schools for continuation of their studies. In August, 1961, the National Conference of the Parti Démocratique de Guinée decided to nationalize the denominational schools. In his Report to the Nation, the President said the government deemed it essential for all private teaching establishments to close before the school year opened. Religious freedom would be respected. It was hoped that all religious organizations would have African clergy. The National Conference of the Parti Démocratique de Guinée in August, 1961, stated that basic education would comprise the primary and secondary grades completed by political instruction and that diplomas would be retained, but that the heads would pay greater heed to African conditions and requirements and technical courses would be granted higher priority.

Through its establishment and vigorous support of a national youth movement, the Jeunesse Rassemblement Démocratique Africain (JRDA), the party has effectively channeled the youth of disparate ethnic and linguistic backgrounds into cooperative activities beneficial to the state and thus enhanced a whole new generation's sense of public responsibility.

Guineans of all ages and occupations have been encouraged to pool their efforts in a volunteer labor program known as Investissement Humain (Human Investment), which has undertaken the construction of such worthy local projects as dispensaries, schools, or a stretch of road. This program has not only strengthened ties among diverse groups of the populace, but also helped to remove the distaste with which educated Africans have traditionally regarded manual labor.

Through these work programs, numerous new schools have been built, even in remote parts of the hinterland, in an all-out effort to attack the problem of illiteracy. Scores of new teachers, many of them possessing little more than an elementary education themselves, have been recruited into the educational system to meet the serious shortage of personnel. Indeed, the enthusiasm for building schools is so great that there are even new schools still without any teachers at all.

Developments in Higher Education

Owing to the absence of institutions of higher learning in Guinea, Guineans seeking advanced training must be sent abroad. For the period 1958–59, there was a total of 439 Guinean students in France, 50 per cent more than in 1955–56.* Of the 1958–59 total, 122 were studying at various French universities, 165 were attending secondary schools, and 152 were enrolled in the various technical schools of the metropole; 273 of them were there on scholarships provided directly by the French Government.

At the National Conference of Economic Planning in Kankan in 1960, the National Political Bureau of the PDG reported that, as of that time, 794 Guinean students were studying abroad on scholarships or fellowships,† distributed as follows: 356 in France, 186 in the U.S.S.R., 74 in Senegal, 56 in East Germany, 36 in Czechoslovakia, 23 in Mali, 14 in Poland, 8 in the U.S., 7 in Bulgaria, 7 in Hungary, 6 in Italy, 6 in Switzerland, 5 in the U.K., 4 in West Germany, 3 in Belgium, and 3 at the U.N. (in New York).

The distribution pattern has changed slightly since then. In September, 1959, under an ICA agreement signed between the United States and Guinea, the U.S. offered up to 150 scholarships over a three-year period to permit Guinean students to attend American schools and universities. A similar agreement was signed with AID in 1962, establishing 150 more scholarships. In August, 1961, President Touré stated that there would be 1,140 Guinean students abroad for 1961–62.

The New Elite

The type of educated elite that is emerging in Guinea in the 1960's is quite different from the typical product of the schools during the period of colonial rule. As a result of the deterioration in relations between Guinea and France, the reorganization of the nation's school system, the reorientation of the educational curricula, and the return of large numbers of Guinean students from schools in countries other than France, there is a conspicuous lessening of the orientation toward French civilization and culture. The projected establishment of an

* "Les étudiants guinéens en France 1958–59," *Marchés Tropicaux,* February 14, 1959, p. 330.

† *Rapport d'orientation du Bureau Politique National; Conférence nationale de planification économique,* (Conakry: Imprimerie Nationale, 1960), pp. 9–10.

institution of higher learning in Guinea itself—for which promised Soviet assistance seems to be lagging—would further this trend.

A second characteristic of the new elite is its intensive commitment to the political system under which it lives. For the great majority of Guinean intellectuals, the party represents not only the vehicle by which national independence was achieved, but, increasingly, the incarnation and guardian of the nation's sovereignty. Those who rule Guinea do so by virtue of political power and commitment to a common ideology; neither lineage, seniority, nor wealth are keys to authority.

The fact that the vast majority of the newly educated will most certainly be absorbed into the governmental apparatus itself as teachers, doctors, administrators, or technicians intensifies their commitment to the political system. The educated Guinean regards the PDG as the supreme authority in the nation, higher even than that of the government, and thus the primary source of favors, rewards, and hope for advancement within the total social system. So pervasive has its authority become, so immediate its presence in all phases of Guinean life, that existence outside its influence is virtually unthinkable.

A third characteristic of the emerging Guinean elite is that it is far more inclined to diversify its skills and professions than were earlier elite groups formed under the French. Of 794 Guinean students pursuing advanced work in various parts of the world in 1960, a significant majority, 560, were receiving technical training and instruction of one sort or another; 72 were studying to be teachers; 48, medicine and pharmacy; 47 were in economics or political science; 34 in liberal arts; and 33 in the natural sciences.

Thus, the traditional African proclivity toward a degree in law over one in science or engineering is clearly being altered. Part of this change, of course, has been due to the fact that the Ministry of National Education places students abroad on the basis of binding recommendations from a national committee on scholarship. This committee meets once a year to review and evaluate student dossiers prepared by the Ministry of Education in the light of the nation's personnel needs as indicated by manpower requests from various government agencies. It is this scholarship committee that is the final authority in deciding what and where Guinean students selected for overseas scholarships will study. As of 1960, moreover, all practicing lawyers were automatically declared to be functionaries of the state and absorbed into various ministries.

To understand Guinea's new elite, one must go back to the events of 1958. Guinea's decision to vote "No" in the constitutional referen-

dum of September 28, 1958, and to opt for independence rather than membership in General de Gaulle's newly conceived French Community brought swift retribution in the form of wholesale withdrawal of French functionaries, advisers, and equipment from the Guinean bureaucracy within the space of two months. The machinery of government was seriously handicapped by the sudden vacuum created in almost every department, but the apparatus did not grind to a halt, as some had feared and many had predicted. Despite an acute shortage of skilled and trained African personnel and the lack of a transition period, President Sékou Touré miraculously kept his government functioning, the country orderly, and his popular support unwavering while regrouping for the longer haul.

Rapid Africanization

Although some of the specific dislocations caused by the abrupt and definitive departure of the French are still not entirely erased, Guinea has been able to circumvent one of the most difficult problems confronting many other post-colonial governments in Africa—the useful employment of the newly educated. Except for the still considerable number of French and other expatriate teachers employed on a contractual basis by the Ministry of National Education, virtually all positions in the national government today are filled by Guineans.

The unique responsibility that has been thrust upon the young intellectual in Guinea has made of him something quite different from his counterpart in other countries. In contrast to many areas of Africa (and Europe), where the new university graduate feels underutilized and often assumes the unconstructive role of the nihilist in relation to society, the educated Guinean is actively caught up in a project he regards as historically momentous—the creation of a modern socialist but completely African state.

By structuring the national task in this manner, Sékou Touré has integrated the intellectual into the government and the nationalist movement more successfully than any other political leader in Africa, except perhaps Tunisia's President Habib Bourguiba. Unlike the intellectual in Nigeria, for example, who is obsessed with the frailties, faults, and contradictions of his own society, the Guinean tends to think of himself as a pioneering researcher, eager to rediscover a history and cultural tradition that he believes was ignored by a contemptuous colonial world. The Guinean's militancy finds articulate expression in the assertion of the "African personality" and the reversion to native dress, speech, and custom, as well as in a reappraisal of local folklore.

The Outlook

It is too soon to assess the social and political implications for the future of the politically oriented educational system that has been established in Guinea since independence or of the crash program of assigning large numbers of Guinean students to institutions of higher learning in both Communist-bloc and Western nations. There are some indications—including the signing of a new cultural agreement with France in 1961, which increased the number of French teachers to be sent to Guinea and called for French assistance in developing school examinations—that the Guinea Government was not entirely happy about examination results under the reformed system. Another question that President Touré's government is apparently asking itself in the wake of the December, 1961, "Marxist-Leninist plot against the nation" is whether the differences in training and association that its students abroad will be experiencing will affect the ability of Guinea's elite to maintain political consensus for the longer run. There is a new awareness that a pluralism could develop that the PDG's many provisions for the expression of dissent at all levels might not be able to contain.

—VICTOR DUBOIS